AF516365

Indian Diaspora and Transnationalism

Indian Diaspora and Transnationalism

Edited by

Ajaya Kumar Sahoo
Michiel Baas
Thomas Faist

RAWAT PUBLICATIONS

Jaipur • New Delhi • Bangalore • Hyderabad • Guwahati

ISBN 978-81-316-0515-8

Published by
Prem Rawat for **Rawat Publications**
Satyam Apts, Sector 3, Jawahar Nagar, Jaipur 302 004 (India)
Phone: 0141 265 1748 / 7006 Fax: 0141 265 1748
E-mail: info@rawatbooks.com
Website: www.rawatbooks.com

New Delhi Office
4858/24, Ansari Road, Daryaganj, New Delhi 110 002
Phone: 011 2326 3290

Also at *Bangalore, Hyderabad* and *Guwahati*

Typeset by Rawat Computers, Jaipur
Printed at Chaman Enterprises, New Delhi

Contents

Acknowledgements

For compiling a volume of this kind, we have received the support of many people who need to be acknowledged. We sincerely thank the authors who have contributed their papers specifically for this book. We thank Mr Pranit Rawat of Rawat Publications for his encouragement and useful suggestions at different stages in the preparation of this volume.

The editors wish to thank the following authors and publishers who have kindly given their permission to reproduce the copyright material:

1. Thomas Faist. 2010. 'Towards Transnational Studies: World Theories, Transnationalisation and Changing Institutions'. *Journal of Ethnic and Migration Studies,* Volume 36, No. 10: 1665–1687. Copyright © 2010 Taylor & Francis Ltd. Reprinted with permission from Taylor & Francis Ltd. (www.tandfonline.com).
2. Steven Vertovec. 2004. 'Trends and Impacts of Migrant Transnationalism'. *Centre on Migration, Policy and Society,* Working Paper No. 3, University of Oxford. Copyright © 2004 *Centre on Migration, Policy and Society (COMPAS)*. Reprinted with permission from the author.
3. Khachig Tölölyan. 2007. 'The Contemporary Discourse of Diaspora Studies'. *Comparative Studies of South Asia, Africa and the Middle East,* Volume 27, No. 3: 647–655. Copyright © 2007 The Duke University Press. Reprinted with permission from The Duke University Press.
4. Michel Bruneau. 2010. Diasporas, Transnational Spaces and Communities. *In:* Rainer Bauböck and Thomas Faist (eds.), *Diasporas and Transnationalism: Concepts, Theories and Methods,* pp. 35–50. Amsterdam: Amsterdam University Press. Copyright © 2010 The Editors [Rainer Bauböck and Thomas Faist] & The Amsterdam University Press. Reprinted with permission from the Editors & The Amsterdam University Press.
5. Selvaraj Velayutham and Amanda Wise. 2005. 'Moral Economies of a Translocal Village: Obligation and Shame among South Indian Transnational Migrants'. *Global Networks,* Volume 5, No. 1: 27–47. Copyright © 2005 John Wiley & Sons, Inc. Reprinted with permission from John Wiley & Sons, Inc.

6. Louise Meijering and Bettina van Hoven. 2003. 'Imagining Difference: The Experiences of 'Transnational' Indian IT Professionals in Germany'. *Area*, Volume 35, No. 2: 174–182. Copyright © 2003 John Wiley & Sons, Inc. Reprinted with permission from John Wiley & Sons, Inc.
7. Winifred R. Poster and Srirupa Prasad. 2005. 'Work-Family Relations in Transnational Perspective: A View from High-Tech Firms in India and the United States'. *Social Problems*, Volume 52, No. 1: 122–146. Copyright © 2005 University of California Press. Reprinted with permission from the University of California Press.
8. Heinz Scheifinger. 2009. 'Conceptualising Hinduism'. Working Paper Series No. 110, Asia Research Institute, National University of Singapore. Copyright © 2009 Author. Reprinted with permission from the author.
9. Irfan Ahmad. 2005. 'Between Moderation and Radicalization: Transnational Interactions of Jamaat-e-Islami of India'. *Global Networks*, Volume 5, No. 3: 279–299. Copyright © 2005 John Wiley & Sons, Inc. Reprinted with permission from John Wiley & Sons, Inc.
10. C.J. Fuller and John Harriss. 2005. Globalizing Hinduism: A 'Traditional' Guru and Modern Businessmen in Chennai. *In:* Christopher Fuller and Jackie Assayag (eds.), *Globalizing India: Perspectives from Below*. London: Anthem Press, pp. 211–236. Copyright © 2005 Anthem Press. Reprinted with permission from Anthem Press.
11. Vijay C. Mishra. 2005. 'The Diasporic Imaginary and the Indian Diaspora'. *Asian Studies Institute Occasional Lecture 2*, Victoria University of Wellington, New Zealand. Copyright © 2005 Asian Studies Institute. Reprinted with permission from the Asian Studies Institute (www.vuw.ac.nz/asianstudies).
12. Margaret Allen. 2005. 'Innocents Abroad' and 'Prohibited Immigrants': Australians in India and Indians in Australia 1890–1910. *In:* Ann Curthoys and Marilyn Lake (eds.), *Connected Worlds: History in Transnational Perspective*. Canberra: Australian National University Press, pp. 111–124. Copyright © 2005 Australian National University Press. Reprinted with permission from the Australian National University Press.
13. Caroline B. Brettell. 2005. 'The Spatial, Social, and Political Incorporation of Asian Indian Immigrants in Dallas, Texas'. *Urban Anthropology*, Volume 34, Nos. 2/3: 247–280. Copyright © 2005 The Institute, Inc. Reprinted with permission from The Institute, Inc.
14. Sangay Mishra. 2009. Transnationalism and Nationalistic Discourses: Indian Immigrants in the United States. *In:* Christian Collet and Pei-te Lien (eds.), *The Transnational Politics of Asian Americans*. Philadelphia: Temple University Press, pp. 107–118. Copyright © 2009 The Temple University Press. Reprinted with permission from The Temple University Press.

Contributors

Irfan Ahmad lectures in Politics at Monash University, Australia. He has taught at Utrecht University and University of Amsterdam from where he earned his Doctorate in Anthropology. He has published on political anthropology, cultural theories, social movements and culture, religion and politics of South Asia. He is the author of *Islamism and Democracy in India* (Princeton University Press, and Permanent Black) which was short-listed for the International Convention of Asian Scholars Book Prize, 2011, and was published in 2009. Irfan is on the Editorial Board of *South Asia: Journal of South Asian Studies*. He has held visiting fellowship at Max Planck Institute for the Study of Religious and Ethnic Diversity, Germany. Irfan's interviews have appeared in English, Dutch, Hindi, Malayalam, Turkish and Urdu media.

Margaret Allen is Professor Emerita in Gender Studies, University of Adelaide, Australia. She researches transnational, postcolonial and gendered histories. In particular she works on links between India and Australia from c 1880-1940. She has published on Indians living in Australia under the White Australia Policy and Australian women missionaries in India, among other topics.

Michiel Baas is a coordinator with the International Institute for Asian Studies in Amsterdam/Leiden. His dissertation, which he completed in 2009, dealt with the lives of Indian students in Australia and was recently published as a book by Anthem Press (2010) titled: *Imagined Mobility: Migration and Transnationalism among Indian Students in Australia*. Baas' other publications include those on the intersection of migration, class and gender; the entanglement of education and migration in the Australian education industry; and love and arranged marriages among Indian IT professionals. He is currently working on a number of different topics related to the Indian middle class in local/national/global/transnational settings.

Hurriyet Babacan is Professor and Director of The Cairns Institute at James Cook University, Australia. She has a distinguished career over the last 30 years as an academic, social worker, senior public servant, researcher, author, speaker and trainer. Hurriyet is recognized for her expertise in cultural diversity, multiculturalism, immigration, citizenship, identity, racism, health and well-being, public policy, social inclusion-exclusion, international development, human rights, and gender. She has published widely in national and international publications, including two publications for UNESCO. Her recent publications include: *Ethnic Minorities: Negotiating Identity in Australia* (VDM Verlag, Dr Muller Publications, 2009); *Situating Racism: the Local, National, and the Global*, co-authored with N. Gopalkrishnan & A. Babacan (Scholar's Publishing, 2009).

Pablo S. Bose teaches in the Department of Geography and contributes to the programmes in Environmental Studies and Asian Studies at the University of Vermont. His current research is on development and population displacement across the globe, refugee resettlement in the northeastern United States, climate change and forced migration, food practices and mobility, transportation equity and immigrant populations in North American cities, and transnational cultural and economic practices of diasporic communities, especially those from India. With Peter Penz and Jay Drydyk he is co-author of *Displacement by Development: Ethics, Rights and Responsibilities* (Cambridge University Press, 2011).

Caroline B. Brettell is a distinguished Professor of Cultural Anthropology at the Southern Methodist University, Texas. Her research interests include migration and immigration, the cross-cultural study of gender, the intersections of anthropology and history, and European ethnography, particularly Portugal. Some of her recent publications include: *Civic Engagements: The Citizenship Practices of Indian and Vietnamese Immigrants* (with Deborah Reed-Danahay), Stanford University Press, 2011; *Migration Theory: Talking Across Disciplines* (with James Hollifield), Routledge, 2008; *Crossing Borders/Constructing Boundaries: Race, Ethnicity and Immigration* (edited volume), Lexington Books, 2007; *Gender in Cross-Cultural Perspective* (co-edited with Carolyn Sargent), Prentice-Hall 2005; and numerous articles in peer-reviewed journals.

Michel Bruneau is Director of Research Emeritus in CNRS (French National Scientific Research Centre) and University of Bordeaux, France. His research focuses on migration, diasporas, transnationalization, memory in relation with places and territories. His field experience is mainly in Thailand, South-East Asia, Greece and Turkey. He published *Diasporas et Espaces Transnationaux* (Paris: Economica, 2004), and many articles or chapters in French, English and Greek in international journals and edited books.

Thomas Faist is Professor of Transnationalization and Development, Faculty of Sociology at the University of Bielefeld, Germany. His research focuses on migration, ethnic relations, social policy, comparative politics and transnationalization. His most recent publications include *Beyond a Border: The Causes and Consequences of Contemporary Immigration* (co-authored with Peter Kivisto, Pine Forge Press, 2010); *Diaspora and Transnationalism: Concepts, Theories and Methods* (co-edited with Rainer Bauböck, Amsterdam University Press, 2010); *Dual Citizenship in Global Perspective: From Unitary to Multiple Citizenship* (co-edited with Peter Kivisto, Palgrave Macmillan 2008); and *Citizenship: Discourse, Theory and Transnational Prospects* (co-authored with Peter Kivisto, Blackwell, 2007).

C.J. Fuller is Emeritus Professor of Anthropology at the London School of Economics. His current research in collaboration with Haripriya Narasimhan is about Tamil Brahmans and the professional middle class in Tamil Nadu; previously he did extensive research on the Minakshi temple in Madurai. His books include *The Renewal of the Priesthood: Modernity and Traditionalism in a South Indian Temple* (Princeton University Press, 2003), *The Camphor Flame: Popular Hinduism and Society in India* (Princeton University Press, 2004, revised edition), and *Globalizing India: Perspectives from Below*, co-edited with Jackie Assayag (Anthem Press, 2005).

Narayan Gopalkrishnan holds the position of Lecturer in Social Work and Community Welfare in the School of Social Sciences at James Cook University, Australia. Narayan's teaching and research interests relate to diversity, cross-cultural development, diaspora studies, racism, immigrant integration, multiculturalism, human rights, globalization, international aid and human development, policy and programme and service development, leadership and organizational change. Narayan has a number of publications in national and international scholarly publications. His recent publications include: *Situating Racism: the Local, National, and the Global*, co-authored with H. Babacan & A. Babacan (Scholar's Publishing, 2009); New Racisms and Asylum Seekers, in *Asylum Seekers: International Perspectives on Interdiction and Deterrence*, A. Babacan and L. Briskman, eds. (Cambridge Scholars Publishing, 2008).

John Harriss is Professor and Director of the School for International Studies at Simon Fraser University, Canada. Formerly he was Professor of Development Studies at the London School of Economics. His teaching and research interests include political economy of development, Indian politics, political participation and civil society, social policy in India, institutional theories, and agrarian change. Some of his recent publications are: *Globalization and Labour in China and India: Impacts and Responses* (edited with Paul Bowles; Palgrave MacMillan, 2010), *Power Matters: Essays on Institutions, Politics and Society in India* (Oxford University Press, 2006), and *Politicising Democracy: Local Politics and Democratisation in Developing Countries* (edited with Kristian Stokke and Olle Tornquist; Palgrave Macmillan, 2004).

Bettina van Hoven is Associate Professor of Cultural Geography at the University of Groningen. Her research focuses on gender issues, diaspora and migration, institutions, ethnicity, sexuality, disabilities, youth and nature. She is the author and editor of four books and contributed several articles and chapters to international peer reviewed journals and edited books. Her most recent publications have appeared in journals such as *Fennia, Social Geographies, Journal of Geography in Higher Education, European Spatial Research & Policy, Area, Environment and Planning D: Society and Space, Journal of Rural Studies, GeoJournal, Antipode,* and *Social Politics*.

Louise Meijering is Assistant Professor at the Department of Demography, University of Groningen. Her research interests include ageing, place identity, well-being, home, community, international migration, and urban-rural migration. She received her Ph.D. at the University of Groningen in 2006. Her recent publications have appeared in journals such as *Area* and *Rooilijn*.

Sangay Mishra is currently a USC Dornsife College Distinguished Post Doctoral Teaching Fellow at the University of Southern California, Los Angeles. He completed his Ph.D. from the University of Southern California in 2009. He has previously published in an edited volume titled *The Transnational Politics of Asian Americans* (Temple University Press, 2009) and has an article in a forthcoming volume titled *Faith and Race in American Political Life* (University of Virginia Press).

Vijay Mishra is Professor of English Literature and Australia Research Council Professorial Fellow at Murdoch University, Perth. He holds doctorates from the Australian National University and Oxford and is a Fellow of the Australian Humanities Academy. His recent publications include: *What was Multiculturalism?* (Melbourne University Press, 2012); *The Literature of the Indian Diaspora: Theorizing the Diasporic Imaginary* (Routledge, 2007); *Bollywood Cinema: Temples of Desire* (Routledge, 2002); *Devotional Poetics and the Indian Sublime* (SUNY Press, 1998); *The Gothic Sublime* (SUNY Press, 1994); and *Dark Side of the Dream: Australian Literature and the Postcolonial Mind,* with Bob Hodge (George Allen & Unwin, 1991).

Winifred R. Poster is a sociologist teaching at Washington University, St. Louis. She studies global inequalities, gender, race, ethnicity, and class, information and communication technology, transnational corporations and labour, work-family, and activism. She focuses on outsourcing from the US to India, and is currently researching transnational industries of computer manufacturing and call centres. Her research has appeared in *Gender & Society, Social Politics, Social Problems, American Sociological Review, American Behavioral Scientist, Industrial Relations, Research in the Sociology of Work, International Journal of Politics, Culture, and Society, Journal of Developing Societies,* and in books published from Stanford University, Routledge, and LEA Presses.

Srirupa Prasad is Assistant Professor in the University of Missouri-Columbia. She has a joint appointment in the departments of Women's and Gender Studies and Sociology. She is currently working on a manuscript *Sanitizing the Domestic: The Cultural Politics of Hygiene and Gender in Late Colonial Bengal*, which studies a particular genealogy of hygiene, one that was articulated through a vocabulary of domesticity, culture, and identity. She is also currently working on a project that looks at the rhetoric and practices of multiculturalism in the US academia. Her research interests also include globalization, feminist theory, South Asia, public health, and affect studies.

Ajaya Kumar Sahoo is Assistant Professor at the Centre for Study of Indian Diaspora, University of Hyderabad, India. His teaching and research interests include international migration, Indian diaspora, transnationalism, ageing, religion and social movements. His recent publications include *Sociology of Diaspora: A Reader* (co-edited with Brij Maharaj, Rawat Publications, 2007), *Tracing an Indian Diaspora: Contexts, Memories, and Representations* (co-edited with Parvati Raghuram, Brij Maharaj and Dave Sangha, Sage Publications, 2008), and *Transnational Migrations: The Indian Diaspora* (co-edited with William Safran and Brij V. Lal, Routledge Publications, 2009).

Heinz Scheifinger is Lecturer in Sociology-Anthropology at Universiti Brunei, Darussalam. His research interests are concerned with globalization and religion. His recent publications have appeared in *Australian Religion Studies Review*, *Asian Journal of Social Science*, and *Journal of Contemporary Religion*.

Khachig Tölölyan is Professor of Letters at the College of Letters at Wesleyan University in Middletown, Connecticut, USA. In 1991 he founded *Diaspora: A Journal of Transnational Studies* and continues to edit it. His publications concern the theoretical aspects of diaspora studies (e.g. 'Rethinking Diasporas: Stateless Power in the Transnational Moment', *Diaspora* 5: 1, 1996); the relationship of diasporas with nationalism (e.g. 'Beyond the Homeland: From exilic nationalism to diasporic transnationalism' in Allon Gal, A. Leoussi and Anthony D. Smith, eds., *The Call of the Homeland: Diaspora Nationalisms, Past and Present,* 2010) and the Armenian diaspora as a site of empirical study (e.g., 'Stateless Power and the Political Agency of Diasporas: An Armenian Case Study', Gloria Totoricaguena, ed., *Opportunity Structures in Diaspora Relations*, 2010). Prof. Tölölyan co-edited (with Waltraud Kokot and Carolin Alfonso) *Diaspora, Identity and Religion: New Directions in Theory and Research* (Routledge, 2004).

Selvaraj Velayutham is Senior Lecturer in Sociology at Macquarie University, Sydney. His research interests are in the areas of Indian/Tamil transnationalism, diasporic cultures, multiculturalism and the sociology of everyday life. He is the author of *Responding to Globalization: Nation, Culture and Identity in Singapore* (2007) and the editor of *Tamil Cinema: The Cultural Politics of India's Other Film Industry* (2008), *Dissent and Resistance in*

Asia's Cities (2009, with M. Butcher) and *Everyday Multiculturalism* (2009, with A. Wise) and has also published articles on South Indian migration and transnational practices and everyday life.

Steven Vertovec is Director of the Max-Planck Institute for the Study of Religious and Ethnic Diversity, Göttingen and Honorary Joint Professor of Sociology and Ethnology, University of Göttingen. His research interests surround globalization and transnational social formations, international migration, ethnic diasporas and multiculturalism. Professor Vertovec is co-editor of the journal *Global Networks* and editor of the Routledge book series 'Transnationalism'. He is author of *Hindu Trinidad* (Macmillan, 1992), *The Hindu Diaspora* (Routledge, 2000) and *Transnationalism* (Routledge, 2008) and editor or co-editor of twenty-eight volumes including *Migration, Diasporas and Transnationalism* (Edward Elgar, 1999), *Migration and Social Cohesion* (Edward Elgar, 1999), *Conceiving Cosmopolitanism* (Oxford University Press, 2003), *Anthropology of Migration and Multiculturalism* (Routledge 2009), *The Multicultural Backlash* (Routledge 2010) and *Migration: Major Works* (Routledge, 2010).

Amanda Wise is an interdisciplinary researcher working at the intersection of sociology, cultural studies and human geography. Her research into issues surrounding multiculturalism and migration draws primarily on ethnographic and qualitative methodologies. Amanda's research interests include multiculturalism (especially everyday multiculturalism); racism and interethnic relations; ethnicities; national and cultural identities; cultural attachments to and formations of place, hope and belonging in suburban Australia especially in relation to multicultural neighbourhoods; cities and diversity; diasporic, transnational and migrant communities; and experiences of low wage migrant labourers. In addition to numerous articles and chapters on these themes, she recently co-edited *Everyday Multiculturalism* published by Palgrave MacMillan. Presently, she is a Senior Research Fellow at Macquarie University, Australia.

1

Indian Transnationalism

Theoretical Developments and Practical Implications

Michiel Baas, Ajaya Kumar Sahoo and Thomas Faist

This book contains some of the most frequently cited papers written by leading commentators in the field of 'transnationalism' in general and 'Indian transnationalism' in particular. This volume on *Indian Transnationalism* has been put together, keeping in mind the growing recognition of the field that has evolved over the last two decades of research by international scholars. In doing so, our main objective is to provide students and the general readers a collection that introduces them to the theoretical and empirical perspectives on Indian transnationalism. The book, intended for the convenience of students of Indian diaspora, includes pioneering works by sociologists, anthropologists, historians, political scientists, cultural theorists, and literary authors from the United States, Great Britain, Canada, Australia, France, Germany, Portugal, Israel, and Brunei. This shows the diversity of theoretical and empirical work that has been evident in this field.

The book is divided into four sections: *Theories of Transnationalism*, *Transnational Family*, *Transnational Religion*, and *Transnational Politics*. While the first section focuses on the theoretical debates in transnationalism, the other three sections provide thematic debates on Indian transnationalism mainly the three areas where transnationalism research is most prevalent, i.e., family, religion and politics. The reason why 'Indian transnationalism' exists is because of the fact that the Indian diaspora is now one of the largest diasporas in the world, comprising more than 25 million people. Although that figure is small compared to more than a billion inhabitants in the homeland, the Indian diaspora has reached a critical mass in various host countries. It has developed institutions, orientations, and patterns of living specific to the institutional structures and sociopolitical contexts of different host lands. These patterns have been marked not only by the influences of the host land culture but also by relations with the homeland (Safran et al. 2009). Perhaps no other diaspora[1] in the world is characterized by such diversity in its population as the Indian diaspora in terms of culture, including languages, regions, religions, and other forms of social stratification. Interestingly, as we mentioned earlier, revolutionary developments in the spheres of transport and communications during the past three decades have introduced far-reaching changes in all societies, including the diasporic communities dispersed in different countries away from their countries of origin. In so far as the Indian diasporic communities are concerned, the ties with the motherland are not only reinforced and intensified but also extended to reach the members of Indian community settled in many other parts of the world.

In this introduction, we bring out major points of concurrence and contention about research on transnationalism and then sketch for a new research agenda. We pay considerable attention to how the study of transnationalism has developed itself, taking as a starting point the pioneering work by Basch et al. (1994), though also acknowledging that the use of the concept—in various forms—has a much longer history. The key is to understand with what questions the study has involved itself over time, and by doing so, provide the necessary tools to engage with the different studies presented in this book. However, this introduction comes with another ambition, which is to indicate what possible new fields the study of transnationalism might have to deal with in future, especially concerning India. In short: *from where we stand now, where do we go from here?*

Defining Transnationalism[2]

The study of transnationalism was born out of observations that migrants no longer simply cross borders to live elsewhere, but regularly turn this 'crossing borders' into a lifestyle of its own. This development is perhaps not all that surprising considering that current-day migration takes place in a world characterized by the compression of time and space (Harvey 1989; Mittelman 1996). Air travel has become cheaper than ever before and staying in touch, because of technological developments such as the Internet, has never been so easy. As Steven Vertovec (1999: 447) very aptly describes it:

> [D]espite great distances and notwithstanding the presence of international borders (and all the laws, regulations and national narratives they represent), certain kinds of relationships have been globally intensified and now take place paradoxically in a planet-spanning yet common—however virtual—arena of activity.

Although it can be argued that transnationalism as a concept has a much longer history, it was basically the work of Linda G. Basch et al. (1994) which set the tone for most future research on transnationalism for the years to come. According to them, transnationalism entails a process by which immigrants forge and sustain multi-stranded social relations that link together their societies of origin and settlement. Basch et al. (1994) emphasized that many migrants today build social fields that cross geographical, cultural, and political borders; however, crucial in this is that these migrants have involvements in both home and host country (see also Portes 1997).

According to Peter Kivisto (2001), reflecting on those early days of transnationalism studies, it was Basch et al.'s aim to introduce a new approach to understanding current-day migration. It would not take long for many others to follow, often making attempts to fine-tune the concept or to introduce whole new perspectives. What has remained at the core of almost all studies to follow, though, was the recognition of a new behaviour or state of being among migrant groups which could be observed everywhere and which *clearly* merited a different approach in terms of research. This became very explicit in studies conducted by Alejandro Portes, Steven Vertovec, Luis Guarnizo, Peggy Levitt, Alejandro Portes and others who collaborated and/or published with them.[3] Central to their approach was the need to identify, one could even argue 'label', that what was being observed in the field as something *truly* new.

What stands out in particular in early studies on transnationalism is that much of the discussion was about what, theoretically speaking, the concept of transnationalism was supposed to signify. Such questions were both informed and infused by other questions which were generally about newness and necessity. Was *this* transnationalism actually something new? Had migrants not always lived *such* lives? Was it actually necessary to invent a whole new study for *this*? Definitions, and elaborations on these definitions, quickly followed, either to tweak or to simply add new elements to the mix. Concepts such as transnational social spaces, fields and formations were introduced, the idea of the translocal was suggested (see also Velayutham and Wise, Chapter 6), and the rather intermittent 'transmigrant' besides the obvious 'transnational' made an entry.

Thomas Faist (1999), elaborating on the multiple ways of describing transnationalism and attempting to move beyond the social anthropological perspective which was introduced by Basch et al. (1994), introduced a more institutional perspective on transnationalism. According to Faist, transnationalism is about sustained ties of persons, networks, and organizations across the borders of multiple nation-states, ranging from weakly or strongly institutionalized forms. He stressed that transnationalism is not about fleeting contacts between migrants and relatively immobile people in the countries of origin and destination. In his work, he often refers to the concept of transnational social space which he defines as combinations of ties, positions in networks and organizations, and networks of organizations that reach across the borders of multiple states. These 'spaces' are dynamic social processes, definitely not static notions of ties and positions. 'Transnational social spaces and the other names we have given these phenomena are characterized by a high density of interstitial ties on informal or formal (institutional) levels' (1999: 4). Faist's remark on transnationalism not being about 'fleeting contacts' is clearly a response to the much heard critique that essentially transnationalism was often too broadly defined, encompassing a too wide range of migrant activities. It was indeed acknowledged that some of these could be labelled as transnational but others, it was argued, had always been part of migrants' lives and lifestyles.

The Question of Newness

Studies of migration, as Guarnizo et al. (2003) note, have focused on two central problems. The first problem was about finding out what determines migration and the second one how immigrants adapt in receiving societies. Usually this resulted in push-pull models which were used to explain a variety of characteristics of migrants lives and lifestyles, besides of course finding answers to the questions *why* migrants would (want to) leave their home countries in the first place. As Guarnizo and Díaz (1999) explain, political decision-makers, for instance, saw the international migration of Colombians mostly in economic terms. Underemployment, declining incomes and factors related to this, pushed highly skilled Colombians over the border. The economic situation of the United States, where the highly skilled were in 'high' demand, pulled them 'there'. In this sense, studies of transnationalism have been highly influenced by this. Roberts et al. (1999) and Popkin (1999) argued that transnational migration, at least at the community level, can be seen as a response to blocked opportunities in the home country and the country of destination. This is the reason why migrants mobilize the networks they have and start living the types of lives so commonly described in the studies of transnationalism.

It is clear that debates on transnationalism rely heavily on conclusions reached in other studies, particularly those on migration of course, but globalization itself also cannot be ignored here. For one the argument clearly is that it is globalization which is making transnationalism possible. Improvements in telecommunications (ranging from the mobile phone to the Internet) vastly reduced air travel tariffs, but a general sense of and desire for mobility as well (inspired by the earlier two) is what produces the transnational subject as such.

It is the overlap with other studies which has largely infused the debate on whether or not the study of transnationalism was presenting something truly new. And also in this book, this debate is ongoing, both Thomas Faist and Steven Vertovec are engaged in it. Much earlier, Alejandro Portes argued that transnationalism does not so much 'represent a novel perspective but a novel phenomenon' (1997: 2). Referring to the (monetary) remittances being sent home by migrants, he argued that capital always went abroad in search of valorization. He argued that the 'newness' of transnationalism is to be found in the modalities and intensity of the process, driven by technological improvements in communications and transportation (Portes 1997). Kastoryano (2000), putting this in a slightly different perspective, located the newness in its organizational aspect; the constructed networks and structured communities are what is truly new about this phenomenon, she argued.

Transnationalism in a Globalized World

Where migrants in the past almost made, what it seemed like, lifetime decisions to move to another country, migrants of today do not really seem confronted with such issues. As long as their countries of origin do not stop them at the border for leaving in the first place (as political refugees, for instance), it is basically relatively easy to travel regularly between a number of different locations/countries. And indeed, staying in touch has been easier today than in the past. With email, competitive phone deals, and the earlier mentioned cheaper-than-ever airline tickets, the migrants of today no longer have to worry about not seeing those they left behind ever again. And neither do they have to worry about losing touch with their culture or just the things that matter to them. Migrants, so to speak, often find themselves in a situation where they are in both places simultaneously (Portes 1997), or in neither places at all.

Globalization, it can be argued, is the great facilitator of transnational lifestyles. As Bailey argues, space and 'cost-shrinking technology has played an important facilitating role in the development of transnational communities' (2001: 418). However, this observation is also what informed 'the newness question'. Are these two in essence not about the same thing? Lionnet and Shih, for instance, argue that 'transnationalism shares with globalization the historical moment of late capitalism, characterized by the logics of finance capital, flexible accumulation, and post-Fordist international division of labor' (2005: 5).

It is thus clear that not only are the studies of globalization and transnationalism connected, they are also highly entangled. This adds an additional dimension to the preoccupation of scholars of transnationalism to provide a definition which truly captures what is being observed in the field. As a result, it has even been argued that there are actually two kinds of transnationalism: 'one from above' and 'one from below' (see also Vertovec, Chapter 3). 'Transnationalism from above' is almost considered synonymous with globalization: 'concerned mainly with macroeconomic processes that are not anchored in territories' (Al-Ali and Koser 2002: 2, referring to Guarnizo and Smith 1998). 'Transnationalism from below', on the other hand, is all about the relationships between everyday people in two or more nation-states. As Edmund Hamann argues, the term is mostly used to refer to 'active decision-making by members of economically vulnerable households to reduce their vulnerability by enacting strategies that take advantage of legal, economic, and cultural resources in more than one nation state' (2001: 37).

Others, further engaging in the globalization versus transnationalism discussion, argue for a less strict division between the two. To Sklair (1998), transnationalism overlaps with globalization but the former is more limited. Global processes are largely decentred from specific nation-state territories and take place in a world context above and below states. Transnational processes, on the other hand, are anchored in and span two or more nation-states. Glick-Schiller and Fouron (1999) find the term 'globalization' best employed for contemporary rapid and deregulated flows of capital that are restructuring patterns of investment, production, labour deployment, and consumption. In the course of this economic restructuring, ideas, technology, and goods and services of all sorts are moving rapidly across the globe. They term such flows 'global' in their scope and impact. Transnational processes, on the other hand, are more limited in scope. 'Transnational political, economic, social, and cultural processes (1) extend beyond borders of a particular state but are shaped by the policies and institutional practices of a particular and limited set of states; and (2) include actors that are not states' (Glick-Schiller and Fouron 1999: 343–44).

The Local, the Global, and the Transnational

A characterizing feature of the globalization debate has always been the question how the 'local' is affected by the 'global'. Kennedy and Roudometof (2001) argue that under globalized conditions, locality no longer is necessarily rooted in a particular place. The transnational experience, in this sense, can be classified as de-localized, de-territorialized. This transnational experience is largely about moving across international borders, settling and establishing ongoing social relations in a particular state, and then maintaining ongoing social connection with the country where the migrants came from (see Glick-Schiller and Fouron 1999). This leads to a (new sort of) global citizen, which could be labelled 'transmigrant' or 'transnational'. These transmigrants literally live their lives across international borders. They have in fact migrated and settled somewhere, but they still maintain familial, economic, religious, political, or social relations in the country of origin. What follows from this is that they live in the so-called 'transnational social fields', which include both country of origin and settlement. Transnational living, in this sense, refers to what Guarnizo called 'a wide panoply of social, cultural, political, and economic cross-border relations that emerge, both wittingly and unwittingly, from migrants' drive to maintain and reproduce their social milieu of origin from afar' (2003: 667).

How de-localized, disconnected, and in-between this alleged transnational existence might be, it did not take long for scholars to come up with the concept of transnational communities which are interpreted and understood as more or less part of the same 'shared' transnational social space. Portes (1997: 4) concluded about these communities that they are tied to the logic of capitalism itself: 'They are brought into play by the interests and needs of investors and employers in the advanced countries'. The idea of a transnational community can be connected to that of the so-called crisis of the nation-state. As Kastoryano (2000: 307) concludes, 'the emergence of transnational communities is a post-national phenomenon'. The transmigrants who fall under this heading do not refer to a 'mythical' territorial state but to their countries of origin as territorialized nations-states. 'In all cases, it is the chosen identity—linguistic, religious, regional—that constitutes a basis for transnational organisation' (Kastoryano 2000: 307). Transnationalism, in a way, offers the migrant a way out of national/local policies, and, in fact, creates a new space of socialization which results in networks across national borders (Kastoryano 2000).

An important question Kastoryano puts forward is whether transnational communities can be considered as the institutional expression of multiple belonging. The Mexican case presented by Roberts et al. (1999) certainly seems to concur with this suggestion. It is shown how Mexican transmigrants are subjected to considerable political pressure by the Mexican state to provide 'partisan' support. Mexican migrants/transnationals are, however, well aware of their importance for the Mexican economy for the remittances they send home. This is something that buys them, in return, considerable political power. From cases such as the one mentioned above, it also becomes clear that although transnationalism may have the aura of ungroundedness and in-betweenness, for it to function and be possible, at all, it depends on very specific legal constructs, which pave the way for a transnational existence and provide the way to enter a so-called transnational social field. Such a field does and, paradoxically, does *not* depend on international borders. On the one hand, it is highly dependent on international borders to come into existence in the first place; but on the other hand, they defy these exact borders by creating a field which overlaps these borders and, in a way, neutralizes them. This puts the nation-state in a difficult position as what happens in the field cannot be controlled. It happens outside the grasps of the nation-state. Yet governments have become very inventive, trying to (re-)incorporate transnationals into national economies and politics by offering them, for instance, tax reductions, the right to vote while being in another country, and even dual citizenships (see also Gamlen 2008).

The End of the Nation-State?

As increasing number of migrants live their lives across or in-between various international borders, such neatly drawn geographically borders that essentially define the nation-state seem to acquire a different meaning altogether. Portes (1997: 3–4) has argued that as a response to globalization, 'transmigrants' have created communities that 'sit astride political borders' and the economic activities that sustain their transnational existence are 'grounded precisely on the differentials of advantage created by state boundaries'.[4] Yet one wonders about such conclusions. For one, it relies very heavily on the assumption of a group of people who already lives such lives, but simultaneously ignores the reality that there are certain requirements to be met before such a life is actually 'legally' possible. Foreigners in other countries frequently are assigned the status of temporary residents, and thereby often limiting such a person in returning to the country of origin for longer periods of time. Becoming a transnational—a migrant who moves around in a so-called transnational social field—is therefore, in a way, dependent on the residency status itself. As transnational theorists will often argue that such a person is not 'grounded' anywhere—never being truly *here* or *there*—it is almost paradoxical that a permanent residence permit (or to hold a citizenship) is the way to become 'ungrounded' (see also Baas 2010).

Nation-states do not just give up but keep on finding new ways to form and sustain ties with people who initially 'left' them, reincorporating them back into the embrace of the nation-state. More than 10 years ago, Glick-Schiller and Fouron argued that Haiti was in the process of redefining itself so that both nation and state could be perceived as transnational, extending well beyond the territorial borders of the country itself (1999). Other countries, such as Colombia, Mexico, Brazil, the Dominican Republic, the Philippines, Portugal, and Greece, have all been known to engage themselves in finding new ways to redefine on the same line. Faist's (2010) more recent argument on the increasing number of countries that allow dual citizenship also fits in well here. Increasingly countries are thus defying the commonly held perception that citizens of a country actually live within the territorial borders of that particular country. As Glick-Schiller and Fouron (1999: 342) argue, in line with this: 'Instead, states are reformulating not only their institutional practices but also their national ideologies to adapt to the rapid movement of capital, people, and ideas that are accompanying the restructuring of global capitalist relationships'. Levitt and de la Dehesa (2003) have made this even more concrete. They found that nation-states adopt the following types of measures to 'compete' with transnationalism. First of all, certain nation-states have been known to reform their ministries and consular offices so that they can cater to their people living abroad. Investment policies which are designed to attract or channel migrant remittances can be understood as another attempt at reincorporating the transnational into the home economy. The extension of political rights in the form of dual citizenships or nationality, which usually comes down to the right to vote and to run for office, is often part and parcel of such policies. Other initiatives include the extension of state protection, even when living in another country, and the implementation of symbolic policies designed to reinforce emigrants' sense of enduring membership (Levitt and de la Dehesa 2003: 589–90). Also India has taken important steps in this regard. The Person of Indian Origin (PIO) Card and the Overseas Citizen of India (OCI) status are part of such policies.

Such attempts by local governments to make transnationals part of very specific economic, social, and political and most of all highly national agendas have also contributed to the feeling that migration itself is most definitely no longer simply understood as final, irrevocable, or irreversible decisions. In that sense, nothing is final or fixed. The 'local' may be expected to play a continuous role in giving shape and meaning to transnational existence. If we look at the cases produced by, for instance, Levitt (2001), Landolt et al. (1999), Popkin (1999), and many others it clearly shows two or more 'local situations', which colour the transnational experience. The de-localization which is often seen as an integral part of the transnational experience is thus in fact a multi-local experience. To put it differently, the transnational experience is actually a multiple local experience in a number of different nation-states.

This 'multiple local experience' that colours transnational life can be seen as communicating barrels with the exception that the various locations ('locals') will never really reach a state of equilibrium, in the sense that they will never truly be equals of each other. One of the reasons for this is the fact that the 'local' located in the receiving country is usually the one sending money home. According to Guarnizo, for instance, monetary remittances have been particularly effective in revealing migrants' commitment and support to their home countries: 'Analytically, monetary remittances represent long-distance social ties of solidarity, reciprocity, and obligation that bind migrants to their kind and friends across state-controlled national borders' (2003: 666, referring to Portes' 'bounded solidarity' 1998). Many sending countries all over the world, ranging from Colombia and El Salvador to India and Bangladesh, have become highly dependent on these monetary remittances. Migrants have become such major sources of hard currency that for some countries they now function as cornerstones of their 'macro-economic and social stability' (Guarnizo et al. 2003: 1214).

An Indian Transnationalism

India's tryst with transnationalism is both a short and long one. Short is in the sense of scholarly interest, something that is also confirmed by the fact that all the chapters that were selected for this book are from the last 10 years. And this is not simply for reasons of wanting to present the latest in research on 'Indian transnationalism'. Sure, Indian transnationalism has been a topic of research since the late 1970s, but the focus then was almost exclusively on transnational corporations. In 1977, for instance, one of the first of such papers came out. Its author was V. Gauri Shankar and the article titled 'The Growth of Transnational Corporations in India' appeared in the *India Quarterly*. The interest in transnational corporations, associated with economic, social, political, and environmental issues, continued well into the 1990s. In fact, it is only when we approach the millennium that papers started to appear dealing directly with the kind of transnationalism that is essentially a migration-related phenomenon.

However, if we let go of the requirement that transnationalism needs to be explicitly mentioned either in the title or at least in the text of the study, it turns out that India's history with transnationalism is a much longer one. As the chapters in this book also confirm, the experience of Indian transnationalism is highly infused by the 'diasporic experience'. In fact, it can be argued that the work that is currently being done on 'Indian transnationalism' often builds upon or is even the continuation of earlier work that concerned the Indian diaspora. Studies such as Margaret Allen's on Indians in Australia (and Australians in India), and even that of Vijay Mishra (writing on the diasporic imaginary) all underline that Indian transnationalism is highly entangled with the formation and development of Indian diasporas in various parts of the world.

Yet it is also interesting to note that these studies often appear to be fairly critical of what is actually labelled as 'transnational', especially where it concerns 'older' transnational connections. What this shows us, most of all, is that when it comes to (emerging) transnational lifestyles, this needs to be connected to and understood in light of the way the diaspora has dealt with its (in)mobility over time. And although such studies never quite show the kind of preoccupation that, for instance, studies focusing on the case of post-1945 Latin American migrants to the United States had with answering what is *truly* new about transnationalism, they do in fact demonstrate that transnationalism among diaspora communities should primarily be understood in terms of it being a continuation and intensification of something that was already inherently part of the diasporic experience.[5]

Family, Religion, and Politics

Research on Indian transnationalism has mostly focused on family, religion, and politics. Selvaraj Velayutham and Amanda Wise, looking into transnational connections between Tamil Nadu and Singapore, built a case for the concept of the translocal village which describes the highly circumscribed social relations that frequently emerge from small-scale translocalized rural villages. Louise Meijering and Bettina van Hoven's work on Indian IT professionals in Germany discusses the way differences between Indian and German family structures are experienced and how this permeates the transnational experience. Winifred R. Poster and Srirupa Prasad's paper focuses on the work and family relations of transnational Indians working in high-tech firms from a comparative perspective. Hurriyet Babacan and Narayan Gopalkrishnan in their work examine how Indian identity is being formed through partner choice and marriage among the members of Indian community in Australia. Family emerges as an important and central theme in all four chapters, highlighting the role the family and family ties play in the way transnationalism takes shape as well as is experienced.

The same can be argued for religion. Heinz Scheifinger's work on Hinduism alerts us to the variety of religious (Hindu, Muslim, Sufi, Sikh, etc.) practices among Indian diaspora and/or transnational communities. It clearly shows that there is no such thing as one Hinduism. On the other hand, however, C.J. Fuller and John Harriss built a case for 'globalizing Hinduism', which entails a transformation of Hinduism into universal, world religion that has a uniting capacity (especially concerning globalized, upper-middle-class Hindus living in India and overseas).

Irfan Ahmad makes an important appeal not only to limit ourselves in our understanding of religious movement to the context of the nation-state but also to study the transnational dimensions of such movements. By doing so, he argues for a more nuanced conceptualization of transnational movements, since existing theories are mostly based on the experience of Western democracies, thus 'insensitive to collective actions in undemocratic polities such as the Gulf States'. His work serves as an important bridge to the final section of the book which deals with transnational politics. Caroline B. Brettell's work deals specifically with this, bringing to our attention the case of Indians in Dallas, Texas. While Brettell's work is about incorporation, Margaret Allen's work deals with an explicit policy (the White Australia Policy), which was basically designed to keep Indians (and other Asians) out, especially in the period from 1901 till the mid-1960s. Sangay Mishra discusses the success of transnational political engagement of Indian community in the United States. Limitations in movement and otherwise are also a key ingredient in Vijay Mishra's work on the diasporic imaginary. Such 'imagination' can also take very concrete forms as Pablo S. Bose shows in his work on urban developments in Kolkata, about which he explains: 'These new housing projects are built and marketed with a self-consciously global aesthetic and are actively promoted to both overseas Indian communities and local elites as space in which one can embody a transnational, cosmopolitan, modern, and quintessentially urban lifestyle'.

Imagining (a) Future Research

The way Indian transnationalism has been studied so far differs considerably from other studies—most notably those on post-1945 immigration to the United States—which are much more migrant focused. The long history of Indian diaspora formation in many countries all over the world turns out to be an important starting point to explore transnational developments. However, transnationalism does not limit itself to groups of people who have already migrated a long time ago. Studies presented in this book such as the one by Meijering and van Hoven focus on a relatively new flow of migrants from India to Germany and do so by zooming in on the case of 'transnational' Indian IT professionals in Germany. These studies encourage us to go beyond the obvious and explore other terrains where transnationalism might be emergent or prevalent.

In his study on Indian (international) students in Australia—many who have become Australian permanent resident holders over the years—Michiel Baas (2010) engages in the question why Indian students are actually interested in migrating to Australia in the first place. One of his key arguments is that these students are not so much interested in Australia as much as they are in the flexibility the permanent residency (PR) status is believed to offer in terms of crossing borders. They imagine an Australian PR holder to facilitate transnational mobility. In this process of obtaining a PR, the locally established Indian community (which does not really refer to itself as a diaspora) plays only a rather marginal role. Although many migration agents assisting students in their PR application are members of this community, Indian students are not part of their networks, nor do they directly engage in each others lives. The underlying implication of these findings is that transnationalism has now become something that people (in this case Indians) actively aspire towards, even if they have no prior connections to or ties with Indian communities in other parts of the world. Almost none of these students had prior connections with

Indians already established in Australia. Many of these students hail from middle-class backgrounds, though, and as other literature also indicates, having a connection or even a more or less permanent residence status abroad remains highly sought after.

It is the Indian middle classes about whom it is argued that they are profiting the most from India's economic boom. The type of air travel common to Western middle classes for years has now also become an option for many middle-class families. As a result, crossing borders has become much more tied to certain expectations of desired lifestyles. However, while middle-class salaries may cover the price of an airplane ticket to 'the West', an Indian passport is still a rather limiting factor in actually entering 'Western' countries. It is clear that young Indians are acutely aware of this. With many middle-class Indian families at least having some connection abroad, it can only be assumed that most middle-class youngsters have grown up with some exposure to stories of life in Western countries. Castles, speaking about poor people in search of a better livelihood, has noted about such a situation that: 'even those who do not migrate are affected as relatives, friends or descendants of migrants; or through experiences of change in their community as a result of departure of neighbors or arrival of newcomers' (2000: 270). Middle-class Indians are certainly not poor; however, Castles' statement does guide us in the direction of a question which has received little attention so far: How do middle-class Indians actually reflect on 'others' having already made it abroad? How does this determine migration decisions? And how do they imagine a migration decision to work out in practical terms?

The combination of faster and more all-encompassing information flows with frequently returning transnationals can only be assumed to have a clear impact on the idea of the mobile/global person in the minds of young people who are still fixed (stuck, as the Indian students would have it) to a particular location. As research conducted by Baas (2010) also confirms, being part of and growing up in an Indian middle-class family most of the time means that 'abroad' is present in one form or the other—either because of direct links with family, friends, or acquaintances abroad, or because of other people belonging to the same circle (caste, community, social layer). The idea of a 'culture of migration' (Gardner 1993; Massey et al. 1994; Tsuda 1999; Deléchat 2001; Kandel and Massey 2002) also seems relevant here. Such a culture is about migration being or becoming so deeply rooted that migrating almost becomes a normative thing for young people to expect it to happen at some point (Kandel and Massey 2002). Studies by Katy

Gardner (1993; 1995) on Sylheti (Bangladeshi) migration and Tsuda (1999) on Japanese-Brazilian immigrant workers in Japan all hint in a similar direction. Connected to this is something what Peggy Levitt (2001) has conceptualized as 'social remittances'. Not only do migrants send money home, but they also send ideas. These 'ideas', which find their way from country of destination to country of origin, can have all sorts of shapes and forms: behaviours (newly acquired), identities (locally adapted) and social capital (accumulated), and so on.

In India, ideas on the quality of life outside the country often gain an extra dimension by the frequent romantization of it in the (Indian) media, most notably Bollywood movies. Paula Chakravartty (2006) has shown how this works in the case of highly skilled Indian migrants in the United States. One of her informants is Krishan who was the first person in his family to find a job in the United States. This did not mean that he did not already know people in the United States, though, or that he was not aware of what sort of life he could expect there: 'he had friends from college who were "already" in the U.S. and felt he had a clear sense of the "American lifestyle" from stories in college, his online research on the subject and from conversations with people who had worked abroad' (2006: 35). Networks of friends, family and colleagues who were already in the United States had certainly helped with the migration process and because of this: 'news and details of the American lifestyle were everywhere before the actual journey to the U.S. even began' (Chakravartty 2006: 35).

Migration is increasingly understood and referred to in terms of 'transmigration'. This clearly indicates that migrants are now almost expected to develop and maintain certain transnational ties or linkages. It is as if such lives are almost by definition expected to gain some kind of transnational dimension. What role diasporas or older established migrant communities will (continue to) play in this is still unclear though. What has emerged from recent studies (Baas 2010) is that there is not only considerable physical distance between Indian communities overseas and, for instance, young urban middle-class professionals with migration plans, but also mentally. While research has certainly not finished looking into the transnational dimensions of Indian diasporic life, we should be open for research that does not necessarily include Indians abroad who have migrated a long time ago. Nor should research limit itself to Indians who are *clearly* part of the kind of networks that have been so central to transnationalism research so far. With transnationalism—as a lifestyle—being aspired by an increasing number of middle-class Indians and influenced both by the notions of an ideal type life abroad and by the idea of Shining (and 'booming') India, research should also engage in the question, what strategies people employ to built a certain transnational existence for themselves. As Arjun Appadurai argued more than 15 years ago, 'more people than ever before are able to imagine that they or their children will live and work in places other than they were born' (1996: 6). And in line with this, he also argued that: '[m]ore persons in more parts of the world consider a wider set of possible lives than they ever did' (1996: 53). The studies in this volume will not only function as an important overview of the state of the study on Indian transnationalism, but also act as an important source of inspiration to think beyond the concept and the way it has been studied so far.

Notes

1. We use the word *diaspora* as a shorthand here, acknowledging that the use of the word is now very different from what it was initially referring to (the Jewish 'diaspora'). Diaspora may also be read as local or transnational community. For an extensive discussion on this topic, please see Chapters 4 and 5.
2. For a critical discussion of the 'ism' in 'transnationalism', please see Faist (2000).
3. Studies on Colombian transnational migration (Guarnizo and Díaz 1999), the Otavalo trade diaspora (Kyle 1999); Haitian transnational social fields (Glick-Schiller and Fouron 1999); Dominican transnationalism (Itzigsohn et al. 1999); Salvadoran transnationalism (Landolt et al. 1999); Guatemalan Mayan migration (Popkin 1999); and finally Mexican migration to the United States (Roberts et al. 1999) all show a relatively similar approach.
4. Portes concluded, consequently, that in this sense, they are no different from large global (transnational) corporations. The big difference of course is that transmigrants' activities are characterized by a certain level of informality. A couple of years later Portes (2003) concluded that transnationalism is basically a grassroots phenomenon. This way he limited transnationalism to that of 'below'. It could, in a way, produce a solution to the question where globalization ends and transnationalism begins. The only problem is that when discussing about globalization 'in practice', meaning the sort of effect it has on people's lives on a local level, one could argue that it is almost the same as 'transnationalism from below'.
5. For a discussion of the conceptual differences between the terms 'transnationalism' and 'diaspora' in social scientific literature, please see Faist (2010).

References

Al-Ali, N., and Koser, K. (2002) 'Transnationalism, international migration and home', in Al-Ali, N., and Koser, K. (eds.) *New Approaches to Migration? Transnational Communities and the Transformation of Home*. London: Routledge, 1–14.

Appadurai, A. (1996) *Modernity at Large*. Minneapolis: University of Minnesota Press.

Baas, M. (2010) *Imagined Mobility: Migration and Transnationalism among Indian Students in Australia*. London: Anthem Press.

Bailey, A.J. (2001) 'Turning transnational: notes on the theorisation of international migration', *International Journal of Population Geography*, 7, 413–28.

Basch, L.G., Glick Schiller, N., and Blanc-Szanton, C. (1994) *Nations Unbound: Transnational Projects, Post-Colonial Predicaments, and De-territorialized Nation-States*. Langhorne, PA: Gordon and Breach.

Castles, S. (2000) 'International migration at the beginning of the twenty-first century: global trends and issues', *International Social Science Journal*, 52(165), 269–81.

Chakravartty, P. (2006) 'Symbolic analysts or indentured servants? Indian high-tech migrants in America's information economy', *Knowledge, Technology, & Policy*, 19(3), 27–43.

Deléchat, C. (2001) 'International migration dynamics: the role of experience in social networks', *Labour*, 15(3), 457–86.

Faist, T. (1999) 'Transnationalization in international migration: implications for the study of citizenship and culture', *Transnational Communities Programme*, Oxford University, WPTC-99–08.

Faist, T. (2000) 'Transnationalization in international migration: implications for the study of citizenship and culture'. *Ethnic and Racial Studies*, 23(2), 189–222.

——. (2010) 'Diaspora and transnationalism: what kind of dance partners?', in Bauböck, R., and Faist, T. (eds.) *Diaspora and Transnationalism: Concepts, Theories and Methods*. Amsterdam: Amsterdam University Press, 9–34.

Gamlen, A. (2008) 'The emigration state and the modern geopolitical imagination', *Political Geography*, 27, 840–56.

Gardner, K. (1993) 'Desh-Bidesh: Sylheti images of home and away' [New Series], *Man*, 28(1), 1–15.

——. (1995) *Global Migrants, Local Lives: Travel and Transformation in Rural Bangladesh*. Oxford: Clarendon Press.

Glick Schiller, N., and Fouron, G.E. (1999) 'Terrains of blood and nation: Haitian transnational social fields', *Ethnic and Racial Studies*, 22(2), 340–66.

Guarnizo, L.E. (2003) 'The economics of transnational living', *International Migration Review*, 37(3), 666–99.

Guarnizo, L.E., and Díaz, L.M. (1999) 'Transnational migration: a view from Colombia', *Ethnic and Racial Studies*, 22(2), 397–421.

Guarnizo, L.E., and Smith, M.P. (1998) 'The locations of transnationalism', in Smith, M.P., and Guarnizo, L.E. (eds.) *Transnationalism From Below, Vol. 6: Comparative Urban and Community Research*. New Brunswick, NJ: Transaction, 3–34.

Guarnizo, L.E., Portes, A., and Haller, W. (2003) 'Assimilation and transnationalism: determinants of transnational political action among contemporary migrants', *American Journal of Sociology*, 108(6), 1211–48.

Hamann, E.T. (2001) 'Theorizing the sojourner student (with a sketch of appropriate school responsiveness)', in Hopkins, M.C., and Wellmeier, N. (eds.) *Negotiating Transnationalism: Selected Papers on Refugees and Immigrants* (Vol. IX). Arlington: American Anthropological Association, 32–71.

Harvey, D. (1989) *The Condition of Post-Modernity: An Inquiry into the Origins of Cultural Change*. Oxford: Basil Blackwell.

Itzigsohn, J., Cabral, C.D., Medina, E.H., and Vazquez, O. (1999) 'Mapping Dominican transnationalism: narrow and broad transnational practices', *Ethnic and Racial Studies*, 22, 316–39.

Kandel, W., and Massey, D.S. (2002) 'The culture of Mexican migration', *Social Forces*, 80(3), 981–1004.

Kastoryano, R. (2000) 'Settlement, transnational communities and citizenship', *International Social Science Journal*, 52, 307–12.

Kennedy, P., and Roudometof, V. (2001) 'Communities across borders under globalising conditions: new immigrants and transnational cultures', *Transnational Communities Programme*, Oxford University, WPTC-01–17.

Kivisto, P. (2001) 'Theorizing transnational immigration: a critical review of current efforts', *Ethnic and Racial Studies*, 24(4), 549–77.

Kyle, D. (1999) 'The Otavalo trade diaspora: social capital and transnational entrepreneurship', *Ethnic and Racial Studies*, 22(2), 422–46.

Landolt, P., Autler, L., and Baires, S. (1999) 'From Hermano Lejano to Hermano Mayor: the dialectics of Salvadoran transnationalism', *Ethnic and Racial Studies*, 22(2), 290–315.

Levitt, P. (2001) *The Transnational Villagers*. Berkeley: University of California Press.

Levitt, P., and de la Dehesa, R. (2003) 'Transnational migration and the redefinition of the state: variations and explanations', *Ethnic and Racial Studies*, 26(4), 587–611.

Lionnet, F., and Shih, S.M. (2005) *Minor Transnationalism*. Durham, NC: Duke University Press.

Massey, D.S., Goldring, L., and Durand, J. (1994) 'Continuities in transnational migration: an analysis of nineteen Mexican communities', *The American Journal of Sociology*, 99(6), 1492–533.

Mittelman, J.H. (ed.) (1996) *Globalization: Critical Reflections.* London: Lynne Rienner Publishers. International Political Economy Yearbook, Vol. 9.

Popkin, E. (1999) 'Guatemalan Mayan migration to Los Angeles: constructing transnational linkages in the context of the settlement process', *Ethnic and Racial Studies*, 22(2), 267–89.

Portes, A. (1997) 'Globalization from below: the rise of transnational communities', *Transnational Communities Programme*, Oxford University, WPTC-98–01.

Portes, A. (1998) 'Social capital: its origins and applications in modern sociology', *Annual Review of Sociology*, 24, 1–24.

——. (2003) 'Conclusion: theoretical convergencies and empirical evidence in the study of immigrant transnationalism', *International Migration Review*, 37(3), 874–92.

Roberts, B.R., Frank, R., and Lozano-Ascencio, F. (1999) 'Transnational migrant communities and Mexican migration to the US', *Ethnic and Racial Studies*, 22 (2), 238–66.

Safran, W., Sahoo, A.K., and Lal, B.V. (2009) *Transnational Migrations: The Indian Diaspora*. London: Routledge.

Sklair, L. (1998) *Transnational Practices and the Analysis of the Global System*. Seminar delivered for the Transnational Communities Programme Seminar Series, 22. London: London School of Economics and Political Science.

Tsuda, T. (1999) 'The permanence of "Temporary" migration: the "Structural Embeddedness" of Japanese-Brazilian immigrant workers in Japan', *The Journal of Asian Studies*, 58(3), 687–722.

Vertovec, S. (1999) 'Conceiving and researching transnationalism', *Ethnic and Racial Studies*, 22(2), 447–62.

——. (2003) 'Migration and other modes of transnationalism: towards conceptual cross fertilization', *International Migration Review*, 37(3), 641–65.

2

Towards Transnational Studies

World Theories, Transnationalization, and Changing Institutions

Thomas Faist

A transnational perspective should aim both to deal with the genesis and reproduction of new social formations *sui generis*, such as transnational social spaces, and to address how 'old' national, international, and local institutions acquire 'new' meanings and functions in the process of cross-border transactions. By now, there is a vast literature dealing with the emergence and above all the forms of transnational activities of migrants and the resulting consequences for the social integration of immigrants (for a succinct summary, see Levitt and Jaworksy 2007). In a nutshell, most studies have focused on cross-border migrant agency, usually including significant others, such as those left behind in regions of emigration—for example, relatively immobile persons (Hammar et al. 1997). Many studies have tried to come up with typologies of transnational life, such as diffusion, families, associations, networks, communities, and diasporas (see Bauböck and Faist 2010). Most transnational analyses have focused on migrant practices, but they have neglected the transformation of institutions in transnational spaces and how these changes interact with the transnational lifeworlds of migrants. A first step has been taken in pointing out that migrants contribute to 'broadening, enhancing, or intensifying transformation processes which are already ongoing' (Vertovec 2004: 972), such as migrant's financial and social remittances in the context of globalization. Now we need to take the next step and ask how institutions have been changing.

If transnational ties and formations are consequential for institutional transformation, we also need to find indications about changing institutions in the national, international, and local realms of transnational spaces. This should be self-evident from the very definition of transnational social spaces, which can be thought of as sustained and continuous ties and their concatenations in networks, groups, organizations, and communities across the borders of nation-states—and with institutions on all levels always being part of such social spaces. In order to be conceptually and politically significant, analyses of transnationalization as sets of sustained cross-border processes, and of transnationality as an awareness of such processes, need to go beyond building typologies and move towards explanations of how social formations in transnational spaces, on the one hand, and (inter-)national and regional institutions, on the other, interact.

Therefore, this chapter pursues a twofold agenda. First, it argues that both concepts of transnationalization—interchangeably called transnational social spaces/fields/formations—and world approaches—world polity and world systems theories—could be useful lenses through which to describe different aspects of transnational processes, boundaries, and identities, and thus changing institutions, practices, and cognitions. While these two sets of approaches indeed pursue different agendas, they give us valuable insights into transnationalization and transnationality. Both world theories and transnational perspectives are elements of a field we could call transnational studies (Khagram and Levitt 2008).[1]

Second, transnational studies need to engage concepts such as social mechanisms to advance our understanding of sustained cross-border (ex-)change (Bunge 1997; Elster 1989; Hedström and Swedberg 1998). These analyses can be carried out on a systemic or macro level (e.g., path dependency), a collective or meso level (e.g., social closure, opportunity hoarding, and brokerage), and a cognitive or micro level (e.g., symbolic recognition). Social mechanismic explanations (which are usually not necessarily mechanistic) are not law-like statements but offer context-dependent and process-oriented explanations, which open the black box of variable-oriented social sciences. In this way, disparate theoretical and conceptual approaches such as transnational social spaces and world theories may complement each other, without implying the need for one big, overarching theory dealing with transnational processes.

To give examples of social mechanisms to be identified when using transnational and world approaches, I use growing legal tolerance towards dual citizenship. Citizenship is a particularly useful case because it signals social closure towards outsiders and newcomers and raises questions of boundaries to overcome for inclusion into membership. Citizenship concerns various aspects: first, equal political freedom, democracy, and thus political participation; second, rights and legal status; and third, affiliation to one or several political communities. As to the first aspect, dual citizenship as full membership overlapping two or more states raises the question of who is included in democratic processes, among those resident in the territory inside or outside of a state. As to immigrants, the question is whether those who reside in a state can be excluded from political participation; as to emigrants, whether and to what extent they have a stake in the affairs of the country of origin. Regarding the second aspect, questions arise as to which rights can be legitimately claimed by those absent and present. The third aspect, at least over much of the nineteenth and twentieth centuries, was tied to heated discussions on the loyalty of citizens with ties to more than one state.

At this point, a clarification of how the key term *transnationalization* differs from *internationalization* and *globalization* is in order. These remarks also apply to the terms *transnationality*, *internationality*, and *globality*. *Transnationalization* refers to sustained cross-border ties, events, and processes across the borders of several national states. Both non-state agents and states participate. Examples include transnational social spaces or the UN Global Compact. A lot of emphasis is on social formations overlapping national states. This is different from *internationalization*, which deals with ties, events, and processes involving almost exclusively states and their agents. An example would be the (partial) international regime protecting refugees, based on the Geneva Convention (1951) and subsequent protocols. *Globalization* differs from both transnationalization and internationalization in that it takes a bird's eye view. It takes world-spanning structures as a point of departure and asks how such structures and associated processes impact and shape lower-level structures and processes—for example, on the level of national states and below. In a way, it moves from the 'outside' towards the 'inside'. In certain regional contexts, globalization is reflected in more delimited developments, such as 'EU-ization' in Europe. World systems theory and world polity theory also share this aspect of the globalization view. However, these two theories are different from globalization studies in that they claim to go beyond the empiricist thrust of the latter and offer causal explanations.

The first section of this chapter outlines two types of world theories mentioned, looking at world systems theory and world polity theory as examples of macrostructural theories. My argument is that macrostructural theories emphasizing the diffusion of rational norms in the world polity open a panoramic view for transnational settings but cannot account for power, conflict, and issues of legitimation. The second section then outlines transnational approaches. Such an optic is helpful to start thinking about the reorganization of social practices. Nonetheless, there are also considerable lacunae, in particular the underplayed focus in connecting transnationalization to institutional change on various scales. Transnational approaches need to be extended to specify the social mechanisms by which boundaries are redrawn in the context of sustained cross-border interactions. The utility of this extension is shown in the discussion of the term 'diaspora'. The very fuzziness of the term is a result of constantly changing socio-political boundaries and transactions across and within such boundaries, which constitute (situational) identities. The third section of the chapter uses growing legal tolerance of dual citizenship to suggest the utility of both world polity theory and a transnational approach when looking at boundaries and identities. It specifies the social mechanisms on the macro, meso, and micro levels, which have operated to bring about increasing tolerance, and may also account for reversals in the future. The conclusion considers whether and under what circumstances 'old' concepts, such as citizenship, are adequate in capturing the impact of transnationalization and transnationality, and thus how 'old' institutions may acquire 'new' meanings.

The World Explained: World Systems and World Polity Approaches

Sociology as a discipline lagged behind political science in empirical globalization studies, which document an increasing flow of resources across the borders of national states (cf. Held et al. 1999). Yet sociology has to offer two sets of approaches, which go beyond empirical observations of globalization studies. First, there is a rich mine of various theories conceptualizing global exchange and communication processes. Marxist world systems theory and neo-institutionalist world polity theory are the most prominent exemplars. Moreover, there are transnational approaches. All are heavily interdisciplinary.

'World' approaches posit a coherent, self-sustaining entity such as an economic world system or a world polity. They focus on processes of constant differentiation between systems and environment or, in older versions, identify structures within that entity by their location within the entity as a whole. While such approaches give answers to the question of how to connect small-scale and large-scale social processes, they face enormous difficulty of identifying and bounding relevant systems. By contrast, transnational approaches take bounded transactions among social sites as points of departure. In general, transnational analysis is oriented towards analysing enduring and continuous features of transactions between specific social locations across the borders of states.

In the following subsections, two prominent world theories—world systems and world polity theories—are outlined and contrasted with transnational approaches. The main argument is that world theories are helpful in conceiving social structures beyond the national state as part of larger processes. However, if we want to understand the drawing of boundaries between groups, changing collective identities and altered boundaries of political institutions such as citizenship, it is also important to bring in another perspective, one which looks at transnational boundary-making (Wimmer 2007), the cross-border processes of 'drawing boundaries'.

World Systems Theory: Power Asymmetries in the Capitalist World Economy

Building upon dependency theory (e.g., Amin 1973; Cardoso and Faletto 1979), world systems theory seeks to delineate the genesis and reproduction of the modern capitalist world economy in successive periods from a macro-perspective. The world systems theory can be conceived as a set of mechanisms which redistribute resources from the periphery to the core. In this view, the core is the economically developed and democratic world, and the periphery is the underdeveloped part of the world. There is a fundamental and institutionally stabilized 'division of labour' between core and periphery: while the core has a high level of technological development and manufactures complex products, the role of the periphery is to supply raw materials, agricultural products, and cheap migrant labour for the expanding agents of the core. The economic exchange between core and periphery takes place on unequal terms, based on a fundamental power asymmetry: the periphery is forced to sell its products at low prices, but has to buy the core's products at comparatively high prices (Wallerstein 1983). The statuses of core and periphery are not, however, mutually exclusive and fixed to certain geographic areas; instead, they are relative to each other and shifting. There is also a zone called 'semi-periphery', which acts as a periphery to the core, and a core to the periphery. At the end of the twentieth century, this zone would include, *inter alia*, Eastern

Europe, China, and Mexico. A crucial insight to be derived from world systems theory for the analysis of transnational processes is that transnational flows in the context of migration strongly coincide with the economic and derivative political power asymmetries of the world economy. Dense and continuous transnational flows build upon migration systems (Kritz et al. 1992), which in turn are structured by core-periphery relations. Yet such asymmetries are not sufficient to account for transnational formations.

World Polity Theory: Rational Organizations

In the world polity theory of John W. Meyer and the Stanford School, the starting point is the existence of a world culture, which is culture exogenous to local contexts, worldwide, and based on the premises of modern rationalization in Max Weber's sense (Meyer et al. 1997). This world culture is rationalistic in that it does not primarily consist of values and norms which are debated and towards which actors orient their behaviour; rather it consists of 'cognitive models'. Actors accept such cognitive models, even though they may not be ready to act according to the standards prescribed; for example, in taking over English-language curricula without a suitable overall curriculum. In essence, world polity theory prioritizes the rational orientation of organizations.

Problems with the World Optic

There are various problems with world systems theory and world polity theory. First, while there are examples for the fruitful use of world systems theory for transnationalization (e.g., Basch et al. 1994; cf. Smith and Guarnizo 1998), its economistic bias reduces its potential for the analysis of political (see, e.g., Zolberg 1983) or cultural processes. For example, it is quite evident that national states are the main regulators of international migration flows and also structure transnational ties through policies, determining external voting rights or dual citizenship. Moreover, world systems theory cannot pay enough attention to how the exact ties between core and periphery are negotiated on the level below macro-economic relations.

Second, world polity theory postulates a priori and without further systematic empirical consideration that a world polity actually exists. We can certainly observe the emergence of global institutions, for example, in the realm of political governance, such as the United Nations and its sub-organizations or the World Trade Organization (WTO). Other prominent examples are the national state as a universal principle of political organization; the use of money as a medium of economic exchange; and global standards in travel, time, and communication. Yet such global structures or globally diffused institutions only exist in selected policy domains. While some policy fields such as trade have been regulated by complex and evolving international regimes which may amount to elements of global governance, cross-cutting issue areas such as geographical mobility are a long way from being regulated by such mechanisms. Social protection and social insurance in many parts of the world are just one crucial example (Faist 2009a). Also, there is no international or even global migration regime. In the realm of the United Nations, various UN agencies compete for competence in these fields. Even if we turn to the universal semantics of human rights, rule of law, democracy, or gender equity, we observe that they do not rule universally, although most states have adapted their discourses to these meta-norms.

Third, the two world theories offer top-down views, which define the properties of lower-order subsystems. There is little room for thinking about local autonomy. Moreover, according to such views, it is modern organizations and networks which rule the societal world, while social formations such as families, tribes, and communities play a negligible role. World polity theory maintains that cognitive models shape the actors, although it is plausible that it is not only the world polity that shapes actors but it is also agents who shape world polity. For example, the very fact that the World Bank has championed the diaspora model of development has very real consequences for conceptualizing development (for a critical assessment, see Glick Schiller and Faist 2009). Different agents hold divergent notions of development. The notions of the World Bank, changing over time, are different from those of grassroots organizations. In essence, it is not clear why some patterns are more or less universal, while others are not. We can list many local or national patterns, which do not necessarily go back to global models. For example, states in the OECD countries have employed very different models of incorporating migrants at the national level, ranging from assimilationist to multicultural paradigms. Moreover, states have viewed very differently the desirability of migrants' transnational ties. While former colonial powers with a long experience in penetrating developing countries have seized quickly upon the idea of co-development, that is, employing migrants as development agents, others, often characterized by less intense transnational and international ties, have only recently started to think about such models. Examples of the former category are France, the United Kingdom, Spain, and the Netherlands, and for the latter, Germany, Austria, and Sweden.

Fourth, the world polity approach predicts that actors reap benefits from adapting to cognitive models such as the mainstreaming of tertiary education frameworks, for example, the 'Bologna Process' in the European Union. Political conflict over the very definition of such processes is merely semantic. However, to reduce the analysis of social and societal formations to instrumental concerns, and to occlude normative and ethical or expressive dimensions is to truncate the rich variety of the orientation of agency. Conflicts over whether social orders or systems are legitimate are a driving force of social change and transformation (Finnemore 1996). For example, political agents active in pushing for gender equity criticize existing political arrangements and justify their strategies by reference to overall meta-norms such as human rights. In a similar way, those diasporists trying to establish a national state from abroad through secession may refer to norms such as national self-determination. In these two very different cases, it is the legitimacy of existing orders which is at stake, both on the level of empirically observable acceptance of authority and power and on the level of normative criteria used to evaluate institutions.

Despite these common shortcomings, there are differences in how useful the two theories are for transnational analysis. World polity theory offers concepts such as the diffusion of organizational models and norms (e.g., human rights) which can be empirically operationalized. World systems theory is useful in outlining the asymmetric power relationships between emigration and immigration regions. Ultimately, the litmus test for the applicability of such theories for transnational processes is their ability to suggest social mechanisms which help to understand the changes in 'old' institutions and possibly the emergence of 'new' ones. Before doing so, a contending conceptual approach needs to be discussed: the transnational optic.

The Transnational Perspective

To start with a general observation, the term 'trans-national' first suggests that something is to be overcome, namely, the national, as in moving beyond methodological nationalism. Yet, in the same breadth, it draws attention to the implication that what it aims to overcome from a methodological perspective—the 'nation(al)'—is in productive tension with the global (cf. Ong 1999). To assert that transnational scholars have proclaimed the withering away or the decreasing significance of the national state (Waldinger and Fitzgerald 2004) is simply incorrect. Obviously, these authors confuse transnationalization with post-nationalism. And even concepts such as post-national membership (e.g., Soysal 1994) depend on the continued vitality of nation-states as sites of contention and enforcement of rights. Equally important, world polity theory is not concerned with the demise of the nation-state model but with its universal spread. At any rate, the transnational perspective is able to look both at new social formations *sui generis*, such as transnational social spaces (e.g., Faist 2000), and at how old national institutions acquire new meanings and functions in the process of cross-border transformation.

In this latter respect, which is the focus of this analysis, it has more affinity with world polity theory. Transnational views thus argue against a simplistic top-down world polity version of global or 'glocal' conditions, which suffers from an exogenous rational-actor model. Transnational approaches certainly do not form a coherent theory or set of theories. They can be more adequately described as a perspective, which has found entry into the study of manifold cross-border phenomena. These are usually not connected to each other. An incomplete list would figure, for example, transnational terrorist and criminal networks, transnational organized crime (Shelley 1995) and 'new wars' (Kaldor 1999), transnational religions and communities (Levitt 2007), transnational financial flows (Held et al. 1999), transnational (viz., global) commodity chains (Gereffi 1994), transnational non-governmental organizations (Boli and Thomas 1997) and transnational social movements and counter-hegemonic globalization (Evans 2000), transnational networks and advocacy groups (Keck and Sikkink 1998), transnational feminist praxis (Naples 2002), transgovernmental relations (Slaughter 1997), and transnational (cultural) diffusion (Appadurai 1996). Closer to migration, there is also a variety of often fuzzy terms, which nonetheless share a focus on migrant agency: transnational social spaces (Faist 2000), transnational social fields (Basch et al. 1994), transnational social formations (Smith and Guarnizo 1998), and transnational communities (Portes et al. 1999); the last term is sometimes used interchangeably with diaspora(s).

The Oxford Dictionary of English dates the emergence of the term 'transnational' to around 1920, documented with a quotation from an economic text that saw Europe after World War I characterized by its 'international or more correctly transnational economy' (Soanes 2003: 1762). The term re-emerged only in the late 1960s to denote increasing economic and political interdependence between industrialized countries (Keohane and Nye 1977; for an updated extension, Risse-Kappen 1995). Transnational relations in political science pointed beyond the state-centrism and the billiard ball models of international relations. In short, it held that the non-state relations crossing the borders of states would lead to an ever-growing interdependence between states. Preferred fields of analysis were large-scale and powerful actors such as multinational companies and, to a lesser extent, political parties such as the Socialist International. It found its extension in neo-Gramscian analyses of what is sometimes labelled as neo-liberal ideology, and social groups putting forward such ideas, for example, the 'transnational capitalist class' (Sklair 2001). The latest round of the term transnational, which started in the late 1980s and early 1990s, asked about migrants as agents in constellations of increased cross-border flows (Basch et al. 1994). It is within this most recent context that transnational approaches in migration and immobility studies have flourished.

Transnational social formations—also, fields and spaces—consist of combinations of social and symbolic ties and their contents, positions in networks and organizations, and networks of organizations that cut across the borders of at least two national states. In other words, the term refers to sustained and continuous pluri-local transactions crossing state borders. Most of these formations are located in between the lifeworld of personal interactions, on the one hand, and the functional systems of differentiated spheres, such as the economy, polity, law, science, and religion, on the other. The smallest element of transnational social formations is transactions, that is, bounded communications between social agents such as individual persons. More aggregated levels encompass groups, organizations, and firms. It is an empirical question whether such transnational transactions are global or regional.

Transnational perspectives on cross-border societal formations mostly relate to the concepts of fields and spaces. The notion of fields refers to the inner logic of social action of functionally differentiated realms. Although Pierre Bourdieu's notion of fields points towards the internal logic of systems, such as the economy, polity, science, or law, his understanding does not presume an evolutionary and linear logic of a trend towards a functionally differentiated world polity or world society. In this view, the boundaries of a field are fluid, and the field itself is created by the participants, such as persons or organizations, who struggle for social position (Bourdieu and Wacquant 1992). The notion of transnational social fields is thus concerned with issues of agency: 'We define social field as a set of multiple interlocking networks of social relationships through which ideas, practices, and resources are unequally exchanged, organized, and transformed' (Levitt and Glick

Schiller 2004: 1009). Moreover, the concept of social field in general, and transnational social fields in particular, calls attention to the ways in which social relationships are structured by power. The notion of transnational social space is built on this notion and adds the spatial dimension of social life. Nonetheless, the changing boundaries of transnational fields are usually not systematically explored.

The notion of social space in particular is useful to show the significance of a transnational approach. Social space has been neglected for several decades in the social sciences (Faist 2004). In world theories, time definitively trumps place. The now-often-used description of the world as a 'space of flows' is a creative reformulation of Marx and Engels' famous dictum on capitalism: 'All that is solid melts into air'. The latter statement is still the clearest expression of the claim that there is an annihilation of space by time (Marx and Engels 1972). Neo-functionalist world society theory argues that migration can be substituted by routines (Stichweh 2005). The core argument is that functional differentiation leads to the disappearance of social space and the diminishing relevance of face-to-face communication in social systems. In a way, it would be the end of geography. The counter-argument is equally simple but based on empirical evidence: social geographers, for example, have firmly established that face-to-face contact is the main functional reason for the spatial clustering of knowledge and skills. This is exactly why nowadays there is great fanfare about clusters of excellence in academia, such as Oxbridge in the United Kingdom, or clusters of growth in industry, such as the Rhine valley or Shanghai. Other examples are international financial centres in places such as New York, London, Tokyo, or Frankfurt (see, for example, Thrift 1996). We observe a spatial clustering of practical knowledge, tacit knowledge, and scientific knowledge. This trend is tied to production processes, which require simultaneous inputs and feedbacks (Sassen 2006: 72). Social spaces expand and direct contacts grow as technological possibilities grow, and the short-term and even long-term mobility of persons certainly does not decline but has steadily increased. This insight also applies to the lifeworlds of migrants, new telecommunications that are a complement to, rather than a substitute for, face-to-face contact. It appears that information is still an 'experience good' and that face-to-face contact still helps to build the trust needed to close deals (Rauch 2001), or to build reciprocity and solidarity in kinship groups. This example indicates that spaces of flows—not only those of persons but also of goods—are embedded in spaces of places. In other words, intensive and continuous cross-border flows of persons, ideas, and goods do not necessarily result in a de-bordered world. Instead, boundaries and borders are constantly redrawn.

Lacunae in the Transnational Perspective

Innovative social anthropologists around Nina Glick Schiller placed migrants and their ties and collectives firmly at the centre of an agency-oriented approach (Basch et al. 1994). Yet Glick Schiller's equally important macrostructural positioning of transnationalization in world systems theory got lost very soon when picked up by subsequent analysts. One important strand of this thinking has become the social-relational approach, linking up with migration and migrant network analysis (see Portes et al. 1999) and, partly, with social constructivist ideas—called 'constructivist transnationalism' (Khagram 2004). However, this perspective has not been systematically presented as a perspective involving boundaries (including borders) and associated identities of the agents involved. Moreover, it has not engaged in activities presenting the mechanisms of how ties, networks, and organizations change the institutions involved.

A Modest Proposal: Focus on Changing Boundaries and Their Transformation

It is therefore helpful to think about how boundaries change and by which mechanisms such transformations occur (Tilly 2005). Social boundaries interrupt, divide, circumscribe, or segregate distributions of persons and groups within social spaces which cross the borders of national states. Shifting boundaries are indications of the changing of institutions, practices, and cognitions. The dynamics of changing boundaries can be nicely captured in the debate on the 'newness' of transnational social spaces. Some transnational scholars early on claimed the newness of such phenomena. It did not take long until historically-minded social scientists showed convincingly that not only have return migration and occasional visits to home regions existed for quite some time (Foner 2001), but also that 'transnational communities', with dense internal ties both within states of immigration and towards regions of emigration, have likewise existed for a long time. Max Weber, for example, spoke of the *Auslandsgemeinschaften* of German immigrants in South and North America, which introduced the concept of 'leisure' (*Freizeit*) through choirs and gymnastics clubs (Weber 1980: 234). To take an example from the political realm, participants in diasporas, such as Russian Jews or Armenians, have been active in homeland politics since the idea of a national state has taken hold.

Certainly, these cases were not as widespread as they are today and were not further encouraged by means of instant long-distance communication. Yet these technological changes would not have translated into social change if it had not been for the right towards collective self-determination, and boundary shifts in thinking and acting upon cultural diversity which have produced the new trends. The premature semantic death of multiculturalism in the public debates of Europe and parts of North America—and the alleged return of assimilation—are claims against all the empirical evidence (Faist 2009b). Take only the official policy of the EU. It espouses an understanding of immigrant integration in the European Union (EU) as a 'dynamic two-way process of mutual accommodation by all immigrants and residents of Member States'.[2] The term 'multiculturalism', being gradually replaced by 'diversity' in EU documents, in transnational platforms, and in nationally-bounded policy discussions, is not an indication of the decline of the tolerance towards pluri-local identities. Actually, the reverse could be the case. There is indeed a stark contrast between the rabid nationalism faced by immigrants at the turn of the nineteenth to the twentieth century when compared to a hundred years later, despite widespread xenophobia in the contemporary period. Only in this semantic field, could technological opportunities make for increased 'community without propinquity'. We now need to see what can be explained by various theoretical approaches dealing with transnational phenomena. This task necessitates an analysis on macro, meso, and micro levels. Most importantly, we have to identify social mechanisms operative in changing boundaries, such as path dependency, social closure, opportunity hoarding, and symbolic recognition.

Social Mechanisms in the Case of Dual Citizenship

In the past, including the recent past, policymakers considered dual citizenship a problem. Leading politicians of previous centuries saw it as an abhorrence of the natural order, the equivalent of bigamy. Citizenship and political loyalty to the state were considered inseparable. Policymakers worried that dual citizens would not integrate in the host country and would keep exclusive loyalty to the country of original citizenship. And in times of war in the nineteenth and early twentieth centuries, they feared 'foreign' interference by citizens belonging to the enemy. Moreover, democratic legitimacy was at stake. Policymakers feared that dual citizenship would violate the principle 'one person, one vote'. Also, diplomats pointed out that they could not protect their new citizen in the country whose citizenship the newly naturalized citizen also held. Yet over the last few decades, an astonishing change has taken place: an increasing number of governments regard dual citizenship not as an insurmountable problem for integration, legitimation, foreign policy, and diplomatic protection, but instead as a challenge that needs to be negotiated from standpoints ranging from (mostly) pragmatic tolerance to active encouragement. Certainly, dual citizenship is not a completely new phenomenon, but it is only recently that we have witnessed its rapid spread. More than half of all the states in the world, countries of immigration as well as emigration, now tolerate some form or element of dual citizenship (Figure 1). Even in countries which do not accept dual citizenship as a rule, such as Germany, Denmark, or Iceland, the number and percentage of dual citizens have been steadily growing.

The question is not simply what causes dual citizenship to change towards a higher degree of tolerance over recent decades. Instead, it is more a case of how political boundaries form and change, in this instance becoming more permeable. The world polity perspective is useful to outline the broad contours of how dual citizenship changes as a result of the path-dependent diffusion of human and gender rights through international law. Yet this analysis would remain incomplete if it did not include perspectives on the meso- and micro-level aspects of states and migrants dealing with dual citizenship.

Macro Level: Path Dependency

Much of the literature on transnationalization is concerned with the social integration of migrants. Oddly enough, much less attention is paid to whether and how the organizations or institutions of 'main-stream' or 'majority' categories of society adapt and change in the face of pluralizing society (Faist 2009b). To use a metaphor by Max Weber, we observe the 'iron cage' of integration opening up and new boundaries being drawn, as national states increasingly tolerate (not necessarily accept) multiple memberships, such as dual citizenship, or rejuvenate local or urban citizenship. The spread of such norms of membership is induced by international migration and, above all, changes in family and gender law. In general, the changes are slow and sometimes path-dependent developments in international law which have filtered down, and are resisted or embraced by national states.

World polity theory suggests that human rights norms spread from international to national law. Indeed, we observe a first type of path dependency to this effect. Legal norms on statelessness and gender equity have acted as a lock-in mechanism, tying liberal-democratic

Figure 1

Restriction and Tolerance Towards Dual Citizenship Around the World

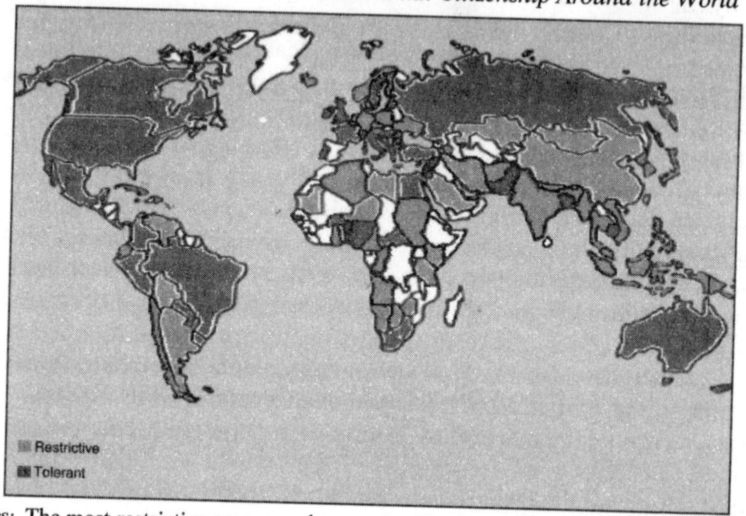

Notes: The most restrictive cases are characterized by the following criteria:

(1) *Assignment by birth* only one citizenship possible (Afghanistan, Iran, North Korea, Vietnam);

(2) *Obligation to choose* one citizenship on reaching maturity (Finland, Germany, Chile, Dominican Republic, Venezuela, Angola, Botswana, Kenya, Namibia, Tanzania, Brunei, Fiji, Japan, Papua New Guinea, Philippines, Singapore, Solomon Islands, and Thailand);

(3) *Renunciation requirement* (in some cases, proof also required) upon naturalization in another country (Andorra, Czech Republic, Denmark, Finland, Germany, the Netherlands, Norway, Poland, Brazil—though tolerant, Columbia—though tolerant, Chile, Cuba, Dominican Republic, Ecuador—except for Spanish citizens, Venezuela, Botswana, Burundi, Cameroon, Congo, Djibouti, Kenya, Namibia, Tanzania, Afghanistan, Armenia, Brunei, China, Fiji, India, Indonesia, Japan, Kiribati, Malaysia, Nepal, Papua New Guinea, Philippines, Singapore, Solomon Islands, Thailand, and Vietnam); and

(4) *Forced expatriation* upon naturalization in another country (Austria, Belgium, Denmark, Finland, Germany, the Netherlands, Norway, Argentina—except for Spanish citizens, Chile, Dominican Republic, Ecuador—except for Spanish citizens, Venezuela, Algeria, Angola, Botswana, Burundi, Cameroon, Congo, Djibouti, Kenya, Namibia, Tanzania, Afghanistan, Armenia, Brunei, Fiji, India, Indonesia, Japan, Malaysia, Nepal, Papua New Guinea, Philippines, Singapore, Solomon Islands, and Thailand).

The more strictly the acquisition of a citizenship is governed by principles (1) to (4), the more restrictive the regime; conversely, the more lenient the procedure, or the more exemptions there are from these requirements, the more tolerant the regime in question is to dual citizenship.

Source: United States Office of Personnel Management, Investigations Service: '*Citizenship Laws of the World*': http://opm.gov/extra/investigate/IS-01.pdf

national states to universal norms. Regarding statelessness, the Convention on the Reduction of Statelessness in 1961 is now adhered to by all liberal democracies. With respect to gender equity, the Convention on the Nationality of Married Women in 1957, the UN Convention against the Discrimination of Women in 1985, and the European Convention on Nationality in 1997 have been incorporated into national law. On the national level, lobby groups have worked hard to implement international conventions. In Germany, for example, the 'Association of Women Married to Foreign Men' (*Verein der mit den ausländischen Männern verheirateten Frauen*) engaged in effective pressure politics in the 1970s and 1980s. Ultimately, the two main consequences of the conventions, pressure-group politics from below and national laws, have been that women do not lose their citizenship upon marriage with a man of another nationality, and that children from bi-national marriages are entitled to dual citizenship.

There has also been a second type of path-dependent mechanism, at least in the EU's liberal democracies, namely a disincentive effect. On the national level, the concept of democratic legitimation provides two options to achieve the congruence of the demos and the resident population: extend political rights to non-citizens or ease naturalization. Dual citizenship has been a prime case for the latter. In main European countries, national courts have strengthened the rights of non-citizen residents since the 1960s. Also, on the supranational level within the EU, the principle and thus mechanism of reciprocity among member states has led many states to strike out the renunciation clause when citizens of other member states naturalize. Emigration countries have followed the lead of immigration countries and have increasingly used dual citizenship as a means to relate to their diaspora.

World polity theory analysis cannot account for the fact, however, that the increased toleration of dual citizenship has been a bumpy road. Although there has been a seminal trend of liberalization in this case, many countries still do not recognize dual citizenship as a rule. Moreover, some countries have experienced protracted struggles over dual citizenship—for example, Germany and the Netherlands (Faist 2007). In short, world polity thinking cannot capture the evolution of human and citizen rights as contentious political processes. To simply overlook the salience of political contention and claims making and the meta-norms of political and other forms of equality is to lose sight of the agentic mechanisms driving conflicts around membership.

Citizenship has been a fundamental process of boundary-drawing, inclusion, and exclusion across much of the world over the last two centuries. The struggles over and within political institutions such as citizenship regularly involve conflicting claims over which political identities have public standing (e.g., full member of a polity), who has rights or obligations to assert those identities, and what rights or obligations attach to any particular identity. In the case of dual citizenship, the identities and thus memberships involved also concern transnationality, the identification with collectives cutting across the borders of national states. A transnational perspective asks the following questions: first, by what mechanisms are the boundaries of full membership in states (re)drawn, so that overlapping membership is tolerated? Second, what are the consequences of boundary (re)drawings for plural identities? Such a perspective places the practices of agents at the forefront of analysis—involving governments, migrants and migrant associations, and international organizations.

Meso Level: Social Closure and Opportunity Hoarding

Governments in general have used citizenship as a mechanism of social closure to distinguish between members and non-members. In the age of national states, this meant the congruence of state authority, state territory, and a state people (demos). The emergence of aliens with partial membership rights, the so-called denizens, has provided dual citizenship with a new challenge, since their accession to full membership could go through either increasing rights without full legal membership or easing their access to full membership. Tolerance towards dual citizenship is obviously an example for the latter case, in which immigration countries make it easier to retain original citizenship, naturalizing without renunciation. One prominent argument to rationalize this kind of liberalization by way of dual citizenship has been to promote the social integration of immigrants through ensuring the congruence of the demos and resident population. All along, this main argument has been sitting uneasily with the rights of emigrant citizens where the 'genuine link' between citizen and state is more tenuous. In the so-called immigration countries, the two sides—immigrants 'inside' and emigrant citizens 'outside'—were even weighed against each other, as in the Netherlands and Sweden. Usually, states stipulate rules for emigrants and their children to retain citizenship. The categorical distinction of the mechanism of social closure has thus acquired the elements of a more gradual distinction.

For emigration countries, instrumental concerns are squarely at the centre of these considerations. Countries with significant shares of emigrants, that is, emigration countries, have also subsequently adapted their citizenship laws, verging towards more tolerance of dual citizenship among their citizens abroad. The case of dual citizens in diasporas is an interesting case. Migration usually only implies geographical exit and not a permanent loss of membership in formations such as kinship systems or states. Thus, the transition from regarding emigrants as 'traitors' to 'heroes' has been possible. Subsequently, emigration countries have changed their policies. A prominent example is the discursive and institutional changes the People's Republic of China has implemented since the late 1970s. Discursively, the slogan to 'serve the country' replaced the motto 'return to serve' (Nyíri 2001: 637). A caveat is in order: in general, the relationship between state governments and emigrants outside the state territory is still ambiguous and has not simply changed towards embracing the 'diaspora'. Much of the ambivalence can be traced to the fact that emigrants with transnational ties constitute agents who are much less subject to political control than those persons and associations mainly residing in the respective state.

Two social mechanisms are important here. Both have reinforced the spread of toleration towards dual citizenship on the part of emigration countries. First, the mechanism of adaptation eases day-to-day interactions between governments and emigrants abroad. Although governments may still be distrusting the loyalty of (some of) their emigrants abroad, toleration has the advantage of adhering semantically to the ever-increasing international credo of mobility as a resource for development—as evidenced by the (former) Global Commission on International Migration (GCIM) and the policies of the World Bank since 2002. Migration and thus also emigration have supposedly mutated from a problem signalling underdevelopment to a solution of the so-called development question. The second mechanism is emulation. It consists of taking over patterns and routines practised by other governments of emigration states. Nonetheless, one needs to be careful in jumping to conclusions and falsely imputing emulation. For example, in their study of five emigration countries (India, Philippines, Mexico, Turkey, and Morocco), Castles and Delgado Wise (2008) found that they had all changed their rules on dual citizenship and overseas voting about the same time. Yet they found no evidence of contact between the governments, or even knowledge of each other's action.

Micro Level: Symbolic Recognition

The cognitive mechanism of symbolic recognition is a prime example of a changing boundary. First, many migrants commonly have attachments and involvements in two or more places across national state borders, and consequently they have plural identifications and loyalties. When dual citizens regard their citizenship(s) as an essential part of their identity, they often express emotional difficulties deciding which citizenship they would keep if they had to give up one of them. The acceptance of dual citizenship may recognize the specific symbolic and emotional ties immigrants have. Sociocultural transnational activities of immigrants can reinforce their self-images and collective solidarities. In these cases, they regard the respective state's acceptance of dual citizenship as a kind of official legitimation of their pluri-cultural identity (Pitkänen and Kalekin-Fishman 2007). Second, the attachment or even loyalty of children with dual citizenship is facilitated if the respective state accepts or, better, embraces dual citizenship. This is mainly because the self-confidence in developing specific competencies related to a transnational background, such as bilingualism and inter-cultural role-taking, are encouraged. In Germany, for example, those who have been dual citizens since birth—children of binational marriages—regard dual citizenship as important for their process of integration. Moreover, it is exactly this category of dual citizens who identify themselves most often as European citizens (Schröter and Jäger 2007).

Dual citizenship has been discussed here as an example of a national institution, partly changing its character in that the boundaries of political membership have partially become more permeable. The key is the multiplying of loyalties and cross-cutting identities. By increasing tolerance towards dual citizenship, national citizenship has implicitly transnationalized by way of increasing toleration. It is distinct from novel forms of citizenship such as EU citizenship. While citizenship as a mechanism of social closure has not changed its character in principle, its boundaries have become slightly more permeable—which is not to claim that such liberalization would not be irreversible in times of war and intense conflict. At the very least, these processes strengthen cross-border mechanisms of opportunity hoarding in the economic and political realms. Also, these social mechanisms are reflected in cognitive mechanisms and awareness, such as symbolic recognition.

The mechanisms on the various levels—macro, meso, and micro—interface with and co-constitute each other. One particularly interesting phenomenon is tension between the levels. For example, it could be that citizenship laws and regulations, on the one hand, and the practices of migrants, on the other hand, are at odds with each other. To take an example from the meso and micro levels: in 2000, the German government decided to enforce the rule that the renunciation clause is to be observed. This means that those who naturalize had to give up their former citizenship before acquiring German citizenship (not regarding exceptions which amount to about 40 per cent of those who naturalize!), and that these new citizens are not allowed to reacquire their former citizenship. Yet the latter is exactly what thousands of new German citizens of Turkish descent had been doing for years. In this case, this practice did not entail significant material benefits for the migrants and their significant others, which they could also have acquired through the Turkish 'Pink Card', but mostly symbolic rewards. Nonetheless, in order to enforce the mechanism of social closure in the wake of a significant liberalization of German citizenship law in 2000, the German government—against the opposition of the Turkish government—decided to uphold the restrictive renunciation clause. This occurred not in spite of, but perhaps because of, other citizenship rules that were liberalized at the very same time.

Outlook: The Danger of Conceptual Stretching

One of the central contentions has been that transnational approaches should be able not only to account for the emergence of transnational structures *sui generis* and new institutions, but also to gauge the changes of national, international, and local institutions and practices. In order to study transnational relations in all their facets of transnationalization and transnationality systematically, one needs conceptual tools, such as the notion of boundary. Changes in boundaries between groups and in organizations are hints towards changing institutions and practices. The goal then is to look at changing boundaries in national, local, and global institutions.

In order to grasp the architecture of transnational politics, which—as suggested by the examples discussed in this article—involves more agents and institutions than national states, we need sophisticated models to understand *de facto* multi-level and transnational governance. Usually, multi-level governance is used in obvious cases such as EU governance. However, there are many issues discussed in transnational studies, such as migration or ecology, which can only be captured by an expanded notion of governance. Regarding dual citizenship, for example, not only international and national courts and the executives of national states but also local, national, and transnational migrant associations have been key players. To give another example, development cooperation relates to interlocking webs of international and national development organizations, international organizations, national states with ministries, and migrant associations.

In order to analyse the impact of transnational processes for institutions and organizations from the vantage point of political sociology, world polity theory—on the one hand—and meso-level transnational perspectives—on the other hand—seem to be most promising. Taken together, these two sets of approaches are central elements of the field of transnational studies, to be complemented by world systems theory from an economic sociological viewpoint. Transnational studies needs to become an ecumenical field, which leaves conceptual and methodological space for both top-down/outside-inside views and the constructivist perspectives of boundary-making and change. My analysis in this chapter has illustrated this very general idea by using the case of dual citizenship, which exemplifies the changing boundaries and thus also identities of the political. Cases such as dual citizenship are of great importance in addressing the question of whether national institutions can 'jump track' to support new, perhaps even transnational orders. More specific questions would be, for example, whether pluri-local integration and thus the various paths of incorporation of immigrants results in a devaluation and/or revaluation of national citizenship. One may also go beyond this more traditional concern and ask whether dual citizenship is serving a transnational logic, in which the elements of citizenship as a political concept are not only disaggregated but also assembled in new ways. For example, citizenship is not only a multidimensional concept, which relates to democracy, rights and obligations, and collective identity, but also a multi-tiered concept. Max Weber argued in his social and economic history that citizenship was first conceived and practised at the municipal level in Ancient Greece and Medieval Europe, before it moved up one level and became *de jure* and *de facto* congruous with membership of a territorial national state (Weber 1981: 315–37). The disaggregation of citizenship should lead to a renewed emphasis on citizenship above and below the national state (cf. Benhabib 2007). This process is important for understanding genuinely not only new forms of membership, such as EU citizenship, but also old forms transformed. Moreover, there is also a large scope for analysing the transactions of migrants and relatively immobile persons on the municipal level, such as indigenous self-governance across Central and North America (e.g. Besserer 1999), or chieftaincy across Europe/USA and Sub-Saharan Africa (Sieveking et al. 2008).

The general question raised by such an extension is whether we overstretch the notion of citizenship when going beyond national states. Several critics have argued that citizenship only makes sense when tied

Table 1

Restriction and Tolerance Towards Dual Citizenship Around the World

Europe		*America*		*Africa*		*Asia and Oceania*	
Tolerant	*Restrictive*	*Tolerant*	*Restrictive*	*Tolerant*	*Restrictive*	*Tolerant*	*Restrictive*
Bulgaria	Andorra (3)	Antigua/ Barbuda	Argentina*** (4)	Benin	Algeria (4)	Australia	Afghanistan (1, 3, 4)
Fed. Rep. Yugoslavia	Austria (4)	Barbados	Bahamas	Burkina Faso	Angola (2, 4)	Bangladesh**	Armenia (3, 4)
Sweden	Belgium (4)	Belize	Bolivia	Cape Verde	Botswana (2, 3, 4)	Cambodia	Azerbaijan
Cyprus	Croatia	Brazil (3)	Chile (2, 3, 4)	Central African Rep.	Burundi (3, 4)	Israel	Bahrain
France	Czech Republic (3)	Canada	Cuba (3)	Egypt	Cameron (3, 4)	Jordan	Belarus
Greece	Denmark (3, 4)	Chile**	Dominican Rep. (2, 3, 4)	Nigeria	Congo (3, 4)	Lebanon	Bhutan
Switzerland	Finland (2, 3, 4)	Colombia (3)	Ecuador *** (3, 4)	Mauritius	Djibouti (3, 4)	New Zealand	Brunei (2, 3, 4)
Serbia/ Montenegro	Germany (2, 3, 4)	Costa Rica	Venezuela (2, 3, 4)	South Africa	Ghana	Pakistan*	Burma
Hungary	Iceland (2, 3, 4)	El Salvador			Kenya (2, 3, 4)	Russia	China (3)
Ireland	Netherlands (3, 4)	Mexico			Namibia (2, 3, 4)	Syria	Fiji (2, 3, 4)
Italy	Norway (3, 4)	Peru			Tanzania (2, 3, 4)	Tonga**	India (3, 4)
Latvia	Poland (3)	USA			Zimbabwe	West Samoa	Indonesia (3, 4)
Portugal	Romania						Iran (1)

Cont'd...

...Cont'd

Lithuania	Ukraine	Japan (2, 3, 4)
Macedonia		Kiribati (3)
Malta		Korea North (1)
Spain**		Malaysia (3, 4)
Turkey		Nepal (3, 4)
United Kingdom		Pap. N. Guinea (2, 3, 4)
		Philippines (2, 3, 4)
		Singapore (2, 3, 4)
		Solomon Is. (2, 3, 4)
		Thailand (2, 3, 4)
		Vietnam (1, 3)

Note: ** only in certain cases, *** except for Spanish citizens. The most restrictive cases are characterised by the following criteria: (1) assignment by *birth:* only one citizenship possible; (2) obligation to *choose* one citizenship on reaching maturity; (3) *renunciation requirement* (in some cases proof also required) upon naturalisation in another country; and (4) *forced expatriation* upon naturalisation in another country.

The more strictly the acquisition of a citizenship is governed by principles (1) to (4), the more restrictive the regime; conversely, the more lenient the procedure, or the more exemptions there are from these requirements, the more tolerant the regime in question is to dual citizenship.

Source: United States Office of Personnel Management, Investigations Service: *'Citizenship Laws of the World'*: http://opm.gov/extra/investigate/IS-01.pdf

to national states (e.g., Turner 2001). While one may not share the scepticism when it comes to European Union citizenship, the problem of 'conceptual stretching' is evident. In his review of 'transnational citizenship' beyond the borders of national states, Jonathan Fox (2005) concluded that only dual citizenship as discussed earlier in the text lives up to fulfilling criteria such as codified rights and obligations and full membership. Nonetheless, we should not get embroiled in definitional exercises but analyse closely in what ways and with which consequences agents reconstruct notions such as citizenship to transform boundaries and, in doing so, contribute to institutional change and perhaps even social transformation.

Acknowledgements

The author thanks Stephen Castles for constructive comments on an earlier version of this paper. The author also gratefully acknowledges the research assistance of Julia Aßhorn and Christiane Meyer in the construction of the map in Figure 1.

Notes

1. Here I use the term 'transnationalization' to connote cross-border processes. I do not refer to the term 'transnationalism', as '-ism' always suggests an ideology.
2. See COM (2005) 389 final.

References

Amin, S. (1973) *Le Développement inégal. Essai sur les formations sociales du capitalisme périphérique*. Paris: Editions de Minuit.

Appadurai, A. (1996) *The Social Life of Things: Commodities in Cultural Perspective*. Cambridge: Cambridge University Press.

Basch, L., Glick Schiller, N., and Szanton Blanc, C. (1994) *Nations Unbound: Transnational Projects, Postcolonial Predicaments, and Deterritorialized Nation-States*. Langhorne, PA: Gordon and Breach.

Bauböck, R., and Faist, T. (eds.) (2010) *Diaspora and Transnationalism: Concepts, Theories and Methods*. Amsterdam: Amsterdam University Press.

Benhabib, S. (2007) 'Twilight of sovereignty or the emergence of cosmopolitan norms? Rethinking citizenship in volatile times', in Faist, T., and Kivisto, P. (eds.) *Dual Citizenship in Global Perspective: From Unitary to Multiple Citizenship*. Basingstoke: Palgrave Macmillan, 247–71.

Besserer, F. (1999) 'Estudios transnacionales y ciudadaný´a transnacional', in Mummert, G. (ed.) *Fronteras Fragmentadas*. Zamora: El Colegio de Michoacán, 215–38.

Boli, J., and Thomas, G.W. (1997) 'World culture in the world polity: a century of international nongovernmental organisation', *American Sociological Review*, 62(2), 171–90.

Bourdieu, P., and Wacquant, L. (1992) *An Invitation to Reflexive Sociology*. Chicago: University of Chicago Press.

Bunge, M. (1997) 'Mechanism and explanation', *Philosophy of the Social Sciences*, 27(4), 410–65.

Cardoso, F.H., and Faletto, E. (1979) *Dependency and Development in Latin America*. Berkeley: University of California Press.

Castles, S., and Delgado Wise, R. (2008) *Migration and Development: Perspectives from the South*. Geneva: International Organization for Migration.

COM (2005) 389 final. Communication from the Commission to the Council. Brussels: The European Parliament, The European Economic and Social Committee and The Committee of the Regions.

Elster, J. (1989) *Nuts and Bolts for the Social Sciences*. New York: Cambridge University Press.

Evans, P. (2000) 'Fighting marginalisation with transnational networks: counter-hegemonic globalisation', *Contemporary Sociology*, 29(1), 230–41.

Faist, T. (2000) *The Volume and Dynamics of International Migration and Transnational Social Spaces*. Oxford: Oxford University Press.

——. (2004) 'Social space', in Ritzer, G. (ed.) *Encyclopedia of Social Theory*. Beverly Hills, CA: Sage, 760–63.

——. (2007) *Dual Citizenship in Europe: From Nationhood to Societal Integration*. Aldershot: Ashgate.

——. (2009a) 'The transnational social question: social rights and citizenship in a global context', *International Sociology*, 24(1), 7–35.

——. (2009b) 'Diversity: a new mode of incorporation?', *Ethnic and Racial Studies*, 32(1), 179–90.

Finnemore, M. (1996) 'Norms, culture, and world politics: insights from sociology's institutionalism', *International Organisation*, 50(2), 325–48.

Foner, N. (2001) 'Transnationalism then and now: New York immigrants today and at the turn of the twentieth century', in Cordero-Guzma´n, H.R., Smith, R.C., and Grosfoguel, R. (eds.) *Migration, Transnationalisation, and Race in a Changing New York*. Philadelphia: Temple University Press, 35–57.

Fox, J. (2005) 'Unpacking transnational citizenship', *Annual Review of Political Science*, 8, 171–201.

Gereffi, G. (1994) 'The organisation of buyer-driven global commodity chains: how US retailers shape overseas production networks', in Gereffi, G., and Korzeniewicz, M. (eds.) *Commodity Chains and Global Capitalism*. Westport, CT: Greenwood Press, 95–122.

Glick Schiller, N., and Faist, T. (eds.) (2009) 'Migration, development, and transnationalisation: a critical stance' [special issue], *Social Analysis*, 53(3): 1–122.

Hammar, T., Brochmann, G., Tamas, K., and Faist, T. (1997) *International Migration, Immobility and Development: Multidisciplinary Perspectives*. Oxford: Berg.

Hedström, P., and Swedberg, R. (1998) 'Social mechanisms: theoretical status and use in sociology', in Hedström, P., and Swedberg, R. (eds.) *Social Mechanisms*. Cambridge: Cambridge University Press, 1–30.

Held, D., McGrew, A., Goldblatt, D., and Perraton, J. (1999) *Global Transformations: Politics, Economics and Culture*. Cambridge: Polity Press.

Kaldor, M. (1999) *New and Old Wars: Organized Violence in a Global Era*. Stanford, CA: Stanford University Press.

Keck, M.E., and Sikkink, K. (1998) *Activists Beyond Borders: Advocacy Networks in International Politics*. Ithaca, NY: Cornell University Press.

Keohane, R.O., and Nye, J.S. (1977) *Power and Interdependence: World Politics in Transition*. Boston, MA: Little, Brown.

Khagram, S. (2004) *Dams and Development: The Transnational Struggles for Water and Power*. Ithaca, NY: Cornell University Press.

Khagram, S., and Levitt, P. (eds.) (2008) *The Transnational Studies Reader: Intersections and Innovations*. London: Routledge.

Kritz, M., Lim, L.L., and Zlotnik, H. (eds.) (1992) *International Migration Systems: A Global Approach*. Oxford: Clarendon.

Levitt, P. (2007) *God Needs No Passport: Immigrants and the Changing American Religious Landscape*. Boston, MA: New Press.

Levitt, P., and Glick Schiller, N. (2004) 'Conceptualizing simultaneity: a transnational social field perspective on society', *International Migration Review*, 38(4), 1002–39.

Levitt, P., and Jaworsky, B.N. (2007) 'Transnational migration studies: past development and future trends', *Annual Review of Sociology*, 33, 129–56.

Marx, K., and Engels, F. (1972) 'Manifest der kommunistischen Partei 1848', in Marx, K., and Engels, F. (eds.) *Werke*. Berlin: Dietz Verlag, 461–74.

Meyer, J.W., Boli, J., Thomas, G.W., and Ramirez, F.O. (1997) 'World society and the nation-state', *American Journal of Sociology*, 103(1), 144–81.

Naples, N.A. (2002) 'The challenges and possibilities of transnational feminist praxis', in Naples, N.A., and Desai, M. (eds.) *Women's Activism and*

Globalisation: Linking Local Struggles and Transnational Politics. Ithaca, NY: Cornell University Press, 267–82.

Nyíri, P. (2001) 'Expatriating is patriotic? The discourse on "new migrants" in the People's Republic of China and identity construction among recent migrants from the PRC', *Journal of Ethnic and Migration Studies*, 27(4), 635–54.

Ong, A. (1999) *Flexible Citizenship: The Cultural Logics of Transnationality*. Durham, NC: Duke University Press.

Pitkänen, P., and Kalekin-Fishman, D. (2007) *Multiple State Membership and Citizenship in an Era of Transnational Migration*. Rotterdam: Sense Publishers.

Portes, A., Guarnizo, L., and Landolt, P. (1999) 'The study of transnationalism: pitfalls and promise of an emergent research field', *Ethnic and Racial Studies*, 22(2), 217–37.

Rauch, J. (2001) 'Business and social networks in international trade', *Journal of Economic Literature*, 34, 1177–204.

Risse-Kappen, T. (1995) 'Bringing transnational relations back in: introduction', in Risse-Kappen, T. (ed.) *Bringing Transnational Relations Back In: Non-State Actors, Domestic Structures, and International Institutions*. Cambridge: Cambridge University Press, 3–33.

Sassen, S. (2006) *Territory, Authority, Rights: From Medieval to Global Assemblages*. Princeton, NJ: Princeton University Press.

Schröter, Y., and Jäger, R. (2007) 'We are children of Europe. Multiple citizenship in Germany', in Pitkänen, P., and Kalekin-Fishman, D. (eds.) *Multiple State Membership and Citizenship in an Era of Transnational Migration*. Rotterdam: Sense Publishers, 67–90.

Shelley, L. (1995) 'Transnational organized crime: an imminent threat to the nation-state? (transcending national boundaries)', *Journal of International Affairs*, 48(2), 463–89.

Sieveking, N., Fause, M., and Faist, T. (2008) *Gutachten zum entwicklungspolitischen Engagement der in NRW lebenden MigrantInnen afrikanischer Herkunft*. Bielefeld: COMCAD, Working Paper 38/2008. http://www.uni-bielefeld.de/tdrc/ag_comcad/downloads/workingpaper_38_Sieveking,Fauser+Faist.pdf

Sklair, L. (2001) *The Transnational Capitalist Class*. Oxford: Blackwell.

Slaughter, A.M. (1997) 'The real new world order', *Foreign Affairs*, 76(5), 183–97.

Smith, M.P., and Guarnizo, L.E. (1998) *Transnationalism From Below*. New Brunswick: Transaction.

Soanes, C. (ed.) (2003) *Oxford Dictionary of English* (2nd ed.). Oxford: Oxford University Press.

Soysal, Y.N. (1994) *The Limits of Citizenship*. Chicago: University of Chicago Press.

Stichweh, R. (2005) *Migration und Weltgesellschaft*. Bielefeld: Institute for World Society Studies. No. 3/2005. Http://www.uni-bielefeld.de/soz/iw/pdf/stw.migration.PDF.

Thrift, N. (1996) *Spatial Formations*. Thousand Oaks, CA: Sage.

Tilly, C. (2005) *Identities, Boundaries and Social Ties*. Boulder, CO: Paradigm.

Turner, B.S. (2001) 'The erosion of citizenship', *British Journal of Sociology*, 52(2), 189–210.

Vertovec, S. (2004) 'Migrant transnationalism and modes of transformation', *International Migration Review*, 38(3), 970–1001.

Waldinger, R., and Fitzgerald, D. (2004) 'Transnationalism in question', *American Journal of Sociology*, 109(4), 1177–95.

Wallerstein, I. (1983) *Historical Capitalism*. London: Verso.

Weber, M. (1980) *Wirtschaft und Gesellschaft* (5th ed.). Tübingen, Germany: J.C.B. Mohr.

Weber, M. (1981) *General Economic History*. New Brunswick, NJ: Transaction.

Wimmer, A. (2007) *How (Not) to Think About Ethnicity in Immigrant Societies: A Boundary-Making Perspective*. Oxford: University of Oxford, COMPAS Working Paper WP-07-44.

Zolberg, A. (1983) '"World" and "system": a misalliance', in Thompson, W.R. (ed.) *Contending Approaches to World System Analysis*. Beverly Hills: Sage, 269–90.

3

Trends and Impacts of Migrant Transnationalism

Steven Vertovec

Migrant Transnationalism and Modes of Transformation

The transnational lens on migrant activities shows that some significant things are changing. Notwithstanding certain criticisms of how this lens or research perspective should be fashioned, it is clear that many migrants today conduct activities and orientations that link them with significant others—for example, family, co-villagers, political comrades, and fellow members of religious congregations—who dwell in nation-states other than those in which the migrants themselves reside. What kind of changes are stimulated by these connections? In what spheres of life? How deep are the changes and how long-lasting? These are high among the analytical questions begged by transnational takes on migrant dynamics.

In this chapter, I suggest that current migrant practices can be seen to involve modes of transformation on different levels of abstraction in three basic domains of activity. These include the following: (a) perceptual transformation (affecting what can be described as migrants' *habitus*) in the sociocultural domain, (b) conceptual transformation (affecting meanings within the analytical triad 'identities–borders–orders') in the political domain, and (c) institutional transformation (affecting forms of financial transfer and local development) in the economic domain. Each set of transformations involves multiple causes, linked processes, and observable outcomes.

This chapter commences with a view of the transnational approach to migrant practices, including a look at the most common criticisms levelled at the perspective. Thereafter, a brief discussion of the concept of transformation is provided in order to set the scene for three subsequent sections on migrant transnational practices and modes of transformation in, respectively, sociocultural, political, and economic spheres of activity.

The Transnational Lens and Its Critics

Transnationalism—a set of sustained long-distance, border-crossing connections—is not of course representative of migrant populations alone. Such kinds of connection are to be found within global corporations, media and communications networks, social movements, and criminal and terrorist groups. Structural comparisons between these and migrant forms of social organization have rarely been explored (see Vertovec 1999a, 2003).

Specifically with regard to migrants, over the past 10–15 years, the study of transnationalism has rapidly ascended within social scientific research on migration. The general perspective is summarized by Ayse Caglar (2001: 607):

> Current scholarship on transnationalism provides a new analytic optic which makes visible the increasing intensity and scope of circular flows of persons, goods, information and symbols triggered by international labour migration. It allows an analysis of how migrants construct and reconstitute their lives as simultaneously embedded in more than one society.

Just as in the broader study of migration, the study of transnational connections among migrants also carries sub-themes focusing on important areas such as ethnicity and identity, gender, family, religion, remittances, entrepreneurship, and political participation.

Since transnationalism hit the migration studies scene in the late 1980s, however, one of the central questions asked by scholars of the subject is: how is the so-called transnationalism different from other aspects of, or takes on, migration?

Gathered from a variety of published articles, conference sessions, and workshop debates concerning the transnational lens on migrant communities, a recurrent set of criticisms—'the usual suspects'—are evident. I call these 'the usual suspects' by way of two meanings: (a) the same criticisms are persistently repeated (often without taking account of how they have actually been addressed by a variety of scholars) and (b) although purporting to critique 'the transnationalism literature', critics (such as Kivisto 2001; Fitzgerald 2002; Nagel 2002) most often focus on specific works by a small set of authors (especially Glick Schiller, Basch, and Szanton-Blanc, the contributors to Smith and Guarnizo 1998, and Portes 2001/2003). This latter characteristic is particularly remarkable, since in the last decade ideas around transnationalism and the transnational approach to migration research have expanded extraordinarily across academic disciplines, spawning a rapid proliferation of publications, PhD theses, seminars, conferences, and research projects. It would be difficult for any one bibliography, to say nothing of a single critical review, to account for the current extent and variety of intellectual debate surrounding the topic of transnationalism.

The usual suspect criticisms entail one or more of the following issues:

- *Conceptual conflation and overuse*: 'Transnationalism' is often used interchangeably with 'international', 'multinational', 'global', and 'diasporic'. There is also the problem of suggesting that all migrants engage in transnationalism;
- *Oldness/newness*: Questions abound as to whether transnational activities among migrants are new, and to how, or to what extent, they are new;
- *Sampling on the dependent variable*: Researchers have looked for transnational patterns and found them. What about the cases in which transnationalism does not develop, or what conditions give rise to particular forms of transnationalism?
- *Trans-what?*: Research and theory have not adequately problematized the difference between trans-*national*, trans-*state*, and trans-*local* processes and phenomena;
- *Transnationalism versus assimilation (vs. multiculturalism)*: False dichotomies between these terms have been posited, rather than a robust account of their interrelationship;
- *Technological determinism*: are contemporary forms of migrant transnationalism, merely a function of today's modes of real-time communication and cheap transportation?
- *Not all migrants are transnational*: Even within specific groups or local communities, there is great variation in migrants' border-crossing practices;
- *Generational limitation*: are current patterns of transnational participation among migrants going to dwindle or die with the second and subsequent generations?

Of all these critiques, the oldness/newness one is probably raised most often. Questions as to what's old and what's new about transnational migrant practices have been ably handled by scholars such as Ewa Morawska (1999), Nina Glick Schiller (1999), Nancy Foner (2000), and Rob Smith (2003). Alejandro Portes (2001) has notably dealt with this issue, too, by recalling Robert Merton's notion of 'the fallacy of adumbration': that is, once a social scientific idea has been formulated, it is easy to find historical anticipations of it. This does not dismiss the idea. As Smith (2003: 725) says, 'if transnational life existed in the past but was not seen as such, then the transnational lens does the new analytical work of providing a way of seeing what was there that could not be seen before'. Still, it might be true to say that long-distance connections maintained by migrants 100 years ago were not truly 'transnational'—in terms of one contemporary sense of regular and sustained social contact (Portes et al. 1999); rather, such earlier links were just border-crossing migrant networks that were maintained in piecemeal fashion as best as migrants at that time could manage. Theoretically, it is in fleshing out just such differences between the meaning of transnational practices and migrant networks that research, data, analysis, and criticism can importantly contribute to migration studies.

To call the above-mentioned criticisms 'the usual suspects' is not to underestimate their importance. It is indeed true that much criticism of transnationalism often comes by way of tiresome conceptual nitpicking. And none of these critiques, contrary to some critics' own beliefs, deliver a knock-out blow. The critical assessments outlined earlier in the text do represent important caveats, problematics, and grounds for theoretical correction. Not least since they have been made so recurrently over the past decade, in publications, seminars, and conferences, they are all points that have been or are currently being engaged by a wide variety of social scientists, including the usual suspect authors.

It is clear that much more conceptual and empirical work remains to be done with regard to sharpening the transnational approach to migration research and analysis. One way to do this is by better disaggregating and characterizing types and levels of transnational activity (cf. Smith 2001; Levitt 2001a; Riccio 2001; Fitzgerald 2002). There is need for this despite the fact that, as Alejandro Portes (2003: 888) points out, 'it has been recognized from the start that transnational activities are quite heterogeneous and vary across immigrant communities, both in their popularity and in their character'. And, if it still needs saying, most scholars recognize that not all migrants develop transnational practices, and many do so only in one sphere of their lives (Faist 2000).

Recently, we have seen considerable conceptual tuning concerning modes, levels, extents, and impacts of transnationalism. For example, theorists have formulated typologies such as:

- transnationalism 'from above'—global capital, media, and political institutions; and 'from below'—local, grassroots activity (Smith and Guarnizo 1998);
- 'narrow'—institutionalized and continuous activities; and 'broad' transnationalism—occasional linkages (Itzigsohn et al. 1999);
- 'great'—of state and economy; and 'little' transnationalism—of family and household (Gardner 2002);
- 'linear'—including plans to return to place of origin; 'resource-based'—linked with labour market position and mobility; and 'reactive' transnationalism—especially based on discrimination (Itzigsohn and Giorguli Saucedo 2002);
- 'broad'—including both regular and occasional activities; and 'strict' transnationalism—regular participation only (Portes 2003);
- 'core'—patterned and predictable around one area of social life; and 'expanded' transnational activity—occasional practices in a wider array of spheres (Levitt 2001a, 2001b).

Such types of transnationalism are variably manifested among different categories of people whose quests for work or 'mobile livelihoods' (Sørensen and Olwig 2001) involve them in transnational migration circuits (Rouse 1991) or patterns of circular migration (Duany 2002). These categories include undocumented migrants (Hagan 1994), refugees and asylum seekers (Koser 2002), religious figures (Riccio 1999), highly skilled workers generally (Vertovec 2002), and information technology workers employed through 'body shopping' (Xiang 2001) along with programmes to encourage the so-called 'brain circulation' of trained occupational specialists between diasporas and homelands (Meyer and Brown 1999).

Arguably, too, each kind or degree of transnationalism differentially affects people: (a) who travel regularly between specific sites, (b) who mainly stay in one place of immigration but engage people and resources in a place of origin, and (c) who have never moved, but whose locality is significantly affected by the activities of others abroad (Mahler 1998; Levitt 2001b).

The examples of types, specificities, and differences surrounding migrant transnationalism are perhaps conceptually burdensome, but are arguably necessary refinements in order to counter the kinds of criticism that the notion of transnationalism has attracted. The refinements provide clearer ways of mapping the infrastructures of transnational relations (cf. Held et al. 1999). Transnational patterns and their impacts naturally vary with regard to a host of factors, including family and kinship structures, conditions in places of migrant origin and reception, transportation or smuggling routes, communication and media networks, financial structures and remittance facilities, legislative frameworks regarding movement and status, and the economic interlinkage of local economies. Such infrastructures have at least two effects on transnational linkages.

> Infrastructures may facilitate or constrain the extensity and intensity of global connectedness in any single domain. This is because they mediate flows and connectivity: infrastructures influence the overall level of interaction capacity in every sector and thus the potential magnitude of global interconnectedness. (Held et al. 1999: 19)

Given that migrant transnationalism and its consequences take many forms, how can we begin to think about possible broader social transformations that arise in their wake?

What is Transformation?

Most studies of migrant transnationalism describe facets of social morphology (Vertovec 1999a). That is, social scientists in this field tend to research the nature and function of border-crossing social networks, families and households, ethnic communities and identities, power relations surrounding gender and status, patterns of economic exchange, and systems of political organization. Social change, in migrant transnationalism studies, tends to be gauged with reference to the ways in which conditions in more than one location impact upon such social structures and the values, practices, and institutions that sustain them. By referring to 'transformation', some theorists seek to paint on a wider canvas, depicting widespread—indeed, global—shifts in social, political, and economic organization.

For instance, in contrast to social change affecting specific institutions, Kenneth Wiltshire (2001: 8) suggests that 'transformation ... describes a more radical change, a particularly deep and far-reaching one which within a relatively limited time span modifies the configuration of societies'. Neil Smelser (1998) stresses, moreover, that such profound social transformations develop out of both individual and collective short-term actions within immediate environments, accumulating in often unexpected ways to constitute changes in societies. And Stephen Castles (2001: 14) explicitly links the contemporary study of social transformation to the analysis of transnational connections affecting national societies, local communities, and individuals:

> The point is that global change and the increasing importance of transnational processes require new approaches from the social sciences. These will not automatically develop out of existing paradigms, because the latter are often based on institutional and conceptual frameworks that may be resistant to change, and whose protagonists may have strong interests in the preservation of the intellectual status quo. If classical social theory was premised on the emerging national-industrial society of the nineteenth and early twentieth centuries, then a renewal of social theory should take as its starting point the global transformation occurring at the dawn of the twenty-first century.

Such an approach to cumulative societal transformation is exemplified by the work of Manuel Castells (especially 1996; 1997) as he describes the impacts of various kinds of enhanced computer-mediated communication on work patterns, collective identities, family life and structure, social movements, and the state.

Held et al. (1999: 15–17) also seek to understand how a constellation of conditions and parallel processes combine to bring about large-scale patterns of transformation. They especially concentrate on the following dimensions that can be analysed both quantitatively and qualitatively: (1) 'the extensiveness of networks of relations and connections', or the stretching of social relationships 'such that events, decisions and activities in one region of the world can come to have significance for individuals and communities in distant regions of the globe'; (2) 'the intensity of flows and levels of activity within these networks' that are not occasional or random, but somehow regular or patterned; and (3) 'the velocity or speed of interchanges' of resources and information that provide immediate feedback, often in real time. These are all dimensions of transformation to be found in modes of migrant transnationalism.

What is not transformative in migrant transnationalism? The widening of networks, more activities across distances, and speeded-up communications might be important forms of transnationalism in themselves. But they do not necessarily lead to long-lasting, structural changes in global or local societies. We are back to the oldness/newness critique: migrants have historically maintained long-distance social networks, and the fact that messages or visits take shorter time does not always lead to significant alterations in structure, purpose, or practice within the network.

But sometimes the matter of degree really counts. The extensiveness, intensity, and velocity of networked flows of information and resources may indeed combine to fundamentally alter the way people do things. As Patricia Landolt (2001: 220) suggests with regard to migrant transnational activities, there are times when 'a quantitative change results in a qualitative difference in the order of things'. In this field of study, we can sometimes observe—following Smelser—how transformation is brought about by numerous individual and collective short-term actions within social environments that span distance locales. As portrayed by Portes (2003):

> Despite its limited numerical character, the combination of a cadre of regular transnational activists with the occasional activities of other migrants adds up to a social process of significant economic and social impact for communities and even nations. While from an individual perspective, the act of sending a remittance, buying a house in the migrant's hometown, or travelling there on occasion have purely personal consequences, in the aggregate they can modify the fortunes and the culture of these towns and even of the countries of which they are part.

In this cumulative way, migrant transnational practices can modify the value systems and everyday social life of people across entire regions (see, for instance, Shain 1999; Kyle 2000; Levitt 2001b).

Processes and practices of migrant transnationalism that can lead to broader transformations take place on different scales in at least three domains of human activity. Of course, as Luis Guarnizo (2003) reminds us, 'Everyday transnational practices are not neatly compartmentalized, and nor are their consequences'. Dividing up the discussion in this way is simply for heuristic purposes. That said, in this chapter it is suggested that such scales and domains of transformation fostered by migrant transnationalism include basic structures of individual *habitus*, fundamental political frameworks, and integral modes of economic development.

Sociocultural Transformation: Re-orienting *Habitus*

As mentioned earlier, most work on migrant transnationalism has examined social morphology or the configuration of social groups as they adapt to long-distance, cross-border contexts. There has been a considerable amount of research that has detailed 'the emergence of transnational social practices and institutions that create a field of sociability and identification among immigrants and people in the country of origin' (Itzigsohn and Giorguli Saucedo 2002: 788). While this approach has certainly been significant and instructive—and there is still much to do, perhaps there has been an overemphasis on the social institutions of transnationalism. To balance the picture, we also need to observe transnationalism as it occurs within, and has impact upon, the daily lives of individuals (Voigt-Graf 2002). While actor-centred approaches carry the danger of overlooking larger structural conditions, they have the advantage of emphasizing motivations, meanings, and the place of people as their own agents in processes of change.

The following subsections suggest just a few ways through which transnationalism has transformed the everyday social worlds of individuals in both migrant-sending and migrant-receiving contexts.

Telephone Calls

One of the most significant (yet under-researched) modes of transnational practice affecting migrants' lives is the ability to telephone family members. This has become a particularly salient feature in recent years through the dramatic fall in the cost of international telephone calls. In many cases, calls abroad that used to cost several dollars per minute now cost a few cents per minute. Connected with this fact, throughout the world there was a doubling of the number of international phone calls between 1985 and 1995 (Guillén 2001), and the trend has continued sharply upward. The number of calls made from the United States to other countries increased from 200 million in 1980 to 6.6 billion in 2000 (FCC 2002).

The telecommunications consultancy TeleGeography, Inc., surveys statistical research on global telephone traffic. A comparison of the company's 1995 and 2001 data, looking at the number of minutes of tele-traffic between specific countries with strong migration connections, suggests a remarkable growth in traffic. In practically all countries examined, the total volume of all international calls originating from that country roughly doubled (i.e., rose 100 per cent) during this period. International calls from Germany to Turkey increased 54 per cent, while calls from Turkey to Germany increased 35 per cent, Turkey to the Netherlands rose 58 per cent, and Turkey to Belgium 80 per cent. Calls from Pakistan to the United Kingdom increased 123 per cent, 141 per cent to Saudi Arabia, and 556 per cent to Canada. Calls from the United Kingdom to India swelled by 439 per cent, to Pakistan 390 per cent, and to Hong Kong 292 per cent. Calls from Mexico to the United States—the destination that comprises over 80 per cent of all Mexican calls abroad—grew by 107 per cent. In turn, calls from the United States to Mexico now account for the largest destination of all outgoing American telecommunications, having increased 171 per cent between 1995 and 2001. In this same period, calls from the United States to the Philippines increased 452 per cent, to India 408 per cent, to Brazil 206 per cent, to the Dominican Republic 189 per cent, to Jamaica 127 per cent, to China 93 per cent, and to Colombia 95 per cent. The TeleGeography figures are highly indicative of the massive expansion marking patterns of transnational communication between specific countries. Of course, we cannot account for the proportion of calls actually made by transnational migrant families; a considerable number of the international calls will be for the business market. Yet it is highly likely that the number of telephone calls between members of migrant families comprises a significant share, and reflects the same extraordinary scale of increase, in each case.

An important factor contributing to the expansion of international telephoning has been the development and spread of pre-paid telephone cards. Use of these cards—which are easily available at gas stations, newsagents, and convenience stores in most urban areas—has doubled between the years 2000 and 2002 alone (Wolfe 2002). Over half of all traffic carried via phone cards is international (Brown 2003). Moreover, industry analysts state that:

> It is well known that the main users of prepaid calling cards are first generation immigrants. Their desire to stay connected with family at home, strong networks within their US-based community, and the ability to pass the news of a well-priced product help drive the competition among providers. These ethnic markets, also known as 'bodega' markets, require different marketing strategies for different cultural groups. Although producers of prepaid cards have responded to this by creating various pricing patterns in their cards that attract certain ethnic users, success still lies in their placement. Proper distribution is the main factor in their sale. (Mensah and Reed Smith 2002)

One phone card distributor interviewed for a corporate study claimed to sell almost exclusively to 'the ethnic markets', saying most of his prepaid cards are currently being sold to Brazilians, then Chinese, Dominicans, various ethnicities from Africa (especially Ugandans, Ghanaians, and Nigerians) and the Middle East (mainly from Lebanon, Syria, and Egypt) (Mensah and Reed Smith 2002). Other distributors now target specific immigrant communities, such as Chinese in the Pacific Northwest, Israelis in New York, Indians in Silicon Valley, and Cubans in Florida (de la Cruz 2002).

The 'ethnic market' for long-distance calls is substantial elsewhere, too. In Germany, for instance, Deutsche Telekom lost 190,000 Turkish customers—whose telephone bills are twice as high as the average German household due to calls abroad—to the telephone company

Otelo; this has prompted a fierce competition in Turkish-speaking marketing between the two companies (Caglar 2002).

New technologies around telephoning are having impact in less developed contexts where migrants' families remain. One example is a recently unveiled product that will allow Mexican-Americans to pay for communications services or facilities for family and friends in Mexico. Another product is a 1–800 service that allows friends and family in Mexico to call the United States at rates significantly cheaper than collect calls. Telecommunications infrastructure is developing in poor areas, too, largely on the back of transnational migration practices. In many places, one can witness the increasing use of public telephones in village centres, reduced-rate telephone cards, and cellular phones, even in fairly remote villages. The Dominican Republic represents one case of recent advances in communications infrastructure: now, the 'teledensity' (lines per capita) of cellular phones on that country is actually higher than that of main line phones (Intelecard 2003). In Bangladesh, the innovative microfinance institution (MFI) Grameen Bank has created a telecommunications branch and 'village phone' programme, providing infrastructure and 950 cellular phones in village and urban areas that give telephone access for 65,000 people (Richardson et al. 2000). By far, most of the uses of the village phones are to talk with migrant relatives overseas—and particularly to discuss remittances (Richardson et al. 2000).

The personal, real-time contact provided by international telephone calls is transforming the everyday lives of innumerable migrants. Among transnational Salvadorans, for example, new telecommunications infrastructures mean that 'times have changed; they are still physically distanced, but they can now feel and function like a family' (Mahler 2001: 584). Non-migrant families commonly have discussions across a kitchen table (e.g., can we buy a refrigerator? what do we do about the teenager's behaviour? when, where, and for how long does someone or all of the family next travel?); now many migrant families conduct the same discussions across oceans. Cheap telephone calls have largely facilitated this. For a single family to be stretched across vast distances and between nation-states, yet still somehow functioning for collective gain, is now a commonality.

There is still a grossly uneven distribution of telecommunications infrastructure in the developing world. Telephone calls can only provide a kind of punctuated sociality that can heighten emotional strain as well as alleviate it. This mode of intermittent communication may add to the stress of marital and family relationships, since it cannot bridge all the gaps of information and expression endemic to long-distance separation (cf. Mahler 2001). Nevertheless, telephone calls are increasingly used transnationally to link migrants and homelands in ways that are deeply meaningful to people on both ends of the line.

Families

The everyday provenance of most migrant transnationalism is within families. In many cases, family life has been extensively modified in light of transnational practices (see, for instance, Fouron and Glick Schiller 2001; Gardner and Grillo 2002; Bryceson and Vuorela 2002). Guarnizo (1997) proposes that changes in family and household organization can be approached by way of residential arrangements, budget management, and intergenerational cultural reproduction. Yet there are other dimensions of transnational family life that need attention too, such as the nature of parenting, gender relations, and the situation of children. As suggested with regard to telephone communication within families, the impacts of transnational practices within many of these dimensions have not been without emotional costs.

'Long-distance parenthood' linking 'fractured families and geographically dispersed homes' is a common feature characterizing much contemporary migrant experience (Lobel 2003). Within dispersed family structures, practically regardless of cultural origins of migrants, it is 'transnational motherhood' among female migrants which 'radically rearranges mother-child interactions and requires a concomitant radical reshaping of the meanings and definitions of appropriate mothering' (Hondagneu-Sotelo and Avila 1997: 557). Such rearrangements are known to cause considerable emotional distress, anxieties, sacrifices, financial pressures, and difficult negotiations with caregivers who must often fill-in for distant parents.

Indeed, shifting work and travel arrangements mean that today more than ever, circularly migrating parents often rotate periods of migration to ensure that one of them remains with the children while the other works abroad. The difficulties of juggling the responsibilities of parenting is also related to phenomena surrounding the so-called 'global care chains' (Hochschild 2000) in which women from developing countries migrate to take care of other people's children while financially supporting, and needing to find caregivers for, their own children. These and other patterns of transnational family life have necessitated new forms of managing and coping with mixed motivations, strategies, and emotional tribulations among parents with regard to their children 'left behind' (Orellana et al. 2001). Such patterns entangle parents' anxieties over their children's welfare with the desire to improve the possibilities for their future.

Emotional entanglements do not just relate to children 'left behind'; they pertain as well to children who accompany their migrant parents and to 'parachute kids'—such as Chinese or Korean children sent to the United States or Canada to attend school with the hope of eventually gaining admission to North American universities (Zhou 1997). In each case, there is often a feeling of being 'caught between two nations, educational systems, and ways of growing up, [that] conveys one of the risks of transnational childhoods—feeling marginal in both places' (Orellana et al. 2001: 583). Similarly, Cecilia Menjívar (2002) found that Guatemalan '1.5 generation' (born abroad, migrated young) children in the United States only partially inculcated the transnational orientations of their parents. This was compounded by the inability to travel to Guatemala (given the undocumented status of their parents), poor linguistic competence, and a dearth of community institutions to foster and sustain transnational links.

> This does not imply that the children's lives are played out independent of their communities of origin, because important decisions in their lives often involve families in both places. The children's ties with the parental homeland, however, depend on the parents' activities and interests, and the children themselves cannot always make sense of the parents' efforts to keep them oriented to home. (Menjívar 2002: 547)

The disjuncture between parents' transnational orientations and children's local ones may lead to exasperation. Marjorie Faulstich Orellana and her colleagues (2001: 581), researching among Mexicans, Koreans, and Yemenis, found that 'Parents expressed frustration that their children [in the USA] didn't appreciate the things their children back home would never have, and they thought about "sending kids back" to give them another perspective on life'. Using 'back there' as a reference point for values and behaviour, 'transnational disciplining' serves as an important strategy for some parents to control children's behaviour. But as Guarnizo (1997: 301) points out, when followed through this strategy often backfires because of the wearing down of kin support—a migrant's 'most valuable asset in the country of origin'—and the occasional unwilling return of mothers to take care of forcibly repatriated children.

However, these developments do not always entail a clash of social worlds. Drawing upon a detailed ethnography of Mexicans living between Mexico and New York City, Fernando Herrera Lima (2001: 91) suggests that 'the transnational family is buffered by its extensive social networks, allowing the transnational experiences to form a fluid continuum, rather than a radical divide compartmentalizing life into two separated worlds'. Such networks surrounding transnational families allow for the circulation of people, goods, jobs, and information as well as for the re-creation and modification of cultural values and practices.

The 'everyday routinized activities and practices' within transnational families have obvious significance for gender relations (Al-Ali 2002: 250). Transnational families demonstrate how culturally constructed concepts of gender operate within and between diverse settings. In various related ways, the position of women in households—and thereby daily gender relations—may be fundamentally altered and liberating, especially when it is the wives and daughters who have migrated to become the breadwinners for the families who have stayed (Hondagneu-Sotelo 1994). In other cases, a patriarchal grip on women within families may be reinforced due to the perceived threats, posed by transnational existence, to cultural notions of feminine virtue. It should be stressed that the significance of gender manifests in numerous spheres outside of family and household as well, of course, especially in transnational community associations, religious congregations, and places of work (see among others Goldring 2001; Mahler and Pessar 2001; Salih 2003).

Norms

For many individuals, families, and communities in both migrant-sending and migrant-receiving contexts, transnational patterns of everyday activity, communication, and exchange have become normative (Portes et al. 1999). The norms that develop involve what Patricia Landolt (2001: 217) calls 'circuits of transnational obligations and interests'. Migrants' social patterns that span borders variously condition people's everyday expectations (about potentials for migration, work, household development, and individual life course), moral duties (for disseminating information to friends and kin, engaging in reciprocal exchange of resources, and enlisting in mutual support), institutional structures (including how best to organize or participate in religious communities and hometown associations), and relations to the state (fashioning practices to manipulate it, contest it, or avoid it altogether).

Such norms become embedded in a kind of transnational moral economy of kin. This is underlined in Carmen Voigt-Graf's (2002) study of Punjabis, Kannadigas, and Indo-Fijians in Australia. 'Given that kinship is the organising principle of Indian transnationalism', she observes, 'the type and regularity of transnational flows depends primarily on what happens within the extended family rather than on the economic or political situation in the home or host country' (Voigt-Graf 2002: 286). Migration and transnational communication within extended families involve tactics for collective upward mobility, while marriages are arranged to strategically extend a family's kinship networks. In this way, the social capital of families can be transformed into economic possibility if the need arises (also see Ballard 2003).

The norms that manage and sustain migrant transnationalism do not determine individual behaviour nor ensure social cohesion within the migrant group and its extended network in the place of origin. Such norms may in fact stimulate new social tensions, fragmentation, and disarticulation within families and local communities. Alison Mountz and Richard Wright (1996) describe how, within a Mexican transnational community, both cultural traditionalists in the home village and a variety of 'dissenters' abroad oppose a number of emergent norms within a transnational community (the latter set includes *los irresponsables*—the irresponsible ones—who fail to communicate or send money, and 'practical questioners' who wish to pursue their own goals independently of family and community).

On the whole, one of the strongest set of sustained—and indeed embellished—norms surrounding migrant transnationalism is that concerning migration itself. It is now a rather well-known dictum that, at least for a period, migration leads to more migration: migrants find jobs and send money back, encouraging and facilitating others to migrate. Now, many nation-states expect—indeed encourage—migrants to stay abroad permanently and to send money home (see the following text). Rapid and real-time communication fuels anticipation among would-be migrants. Information about living conditions, job opportunities, and people's experiences circulate widely throughout immediate and expanded social networks. These usually underscore local perceptions in migrant-sending areas that 'in order to move up you need to move elsewhere' (Sørensen 2000: 3). Hence, in an increasing number of local communities in developing countries, it is almost taken for granted that certain members of the family will emigrate using pre-existing transnational social networks. Norms around migration and transnational life naturally overlap with, or mutually reinforce, the kinds of social practices already described by way of telephone calls and family concerns. Together, for migrants all of these shape what we might call such kind of transnational as *habitus*.

Habitus

Pierre Bourdieu's (1977; 1990) concept of *habitus* refers to a socially and culturally conditioned set of dispositions or propensities, acquired by individuals in the course of their life experiences, which generates everyday social practices in the context of immediate circumstances. This repertoire of neither wholly conscious nor wholly non-conscious perceptions, outlooks, values, and points of reference guides personal goals and social interactions.

> The power of the *habitus* derives from the thoughtlessness of habit and habituation, rather than consciously learned rules and principles. Socially competent performances are produced as a matter of routine, without explicit reference to a body of codified knowledge, and without the actors necessarily 'knowing what they are doing' (in the sense of being able adequately to explain what they are doing). (Jenkins 1992: 76)

Most practices, Bourdieu (1990: 56) posited, can only be accounted for by relating them between 'the social conditions in which the *habitus* that generated them was constituted, to the social conditions in which it is implemented'. This relation between partially or non-conscious dispositions and contextualized action makes *habitus* a more useful concept than the older, related anthropological concept of 'worldview'—described as a kind of cognitive map or complex of motivations, perceptions, and beliefs (see, for instance, Jones 1972). While abstract concepts, both *habitus* and worldview, manifest themselves in individual narratives and directly observable, daily practices and social institutions.

How does the concept of *habitus* relate to migrant transnationalism? A number of scholars bring into play similar notions to describe the nature and impact of transnational outlooks and experiences of migrants. Smith (2001), for example, invokes such a meaning when he describes the practices and relationships linking home and abroad as a 'lifeworld' among immigrants and their descendents. Guarnizo (1997) draws directly upon Bourdieu's ideas of *habitus*. He suggests we might think of a transnational *habitus* as entailing:

> ... a particular set of dualistic dispositions that inclines migrants to act and react to specific situations in a manner that can be, but is not always, calculated, and that is not simply a question of conscious acceptance of specific behavioural or sociocultural rules. ... The transnational *habitus* incorporates the social position of the migrant and the context in which transmigration occurs. This accounts for

> the similarity in the transnational *habitus* of migrants from the same social grouping (class, gender, generation) and the generation of transnational practices adjusted to specific situations. (Guarnizo 1997: 311)

Guarnizo (1997) further writes of how Dominicans retain 'a dual frame of reference' through which they constantly compare their situation in their 'home' society to their situation in the 'host' society abroad. Roger Rouse (1992), too, described the 'bifocality' of people's daily rhythms and routines of life joining localities in Michoacán and California. 'Their bifocalism', thought Rouse (1992: 46), 'stemmed not from transitional adjustments to a new locale, but from a chronic, contradictory transnationalism'. Sarah Mahler (1998) takes up Rouse's notion, which emphasized the ways in which researchers need to look at the nature of transnational migrants' 'lived reality' to determine whether or how they might be 'bifocal' with regard to their social ties and personal outlooks.

The complex *habitus* of migrant transnationalism has been described in other related ways. In a transnational community, spanning 'OP'—Oaxaca and Poughkeepsie, New York—Mountz and Wright (1996: 404) describe how members 'act daily in pursuit of shared objectives and with an acute awareness of events occurring in other parts of (OP)'. Aspects of life 'here' and life 'there'—whether perceived from the migrant's starting or destination point—are perceived as complementary (cf. Salih 2002). This relation is clearly conveyed in Katy Gardner's (1993; 1995) accounts of the interplay between notions of *desh* (home) and *bidesh* (foreign contexts) among Sylhetis in Britain and Bangladesh. While in everyday discourse, *desh* is associated with the locus of personal and social identity and religiosity, *bidesh* conveys material bounty and economic opportunity. Gardner (1993: 1–2) describes a kind of cognitive tension among Sylhetis that likely characterizes the predicament of a great many migrants around the world:

> The economic dominance of families with migrant members has meant that *bidesh* is associated with success and power, which *desh* is unable to provide. Statements concerning *bidesh* are therefore part of a discourse about the insecurity of life in Bangladesh and the continual economic struggle which villagers face. ... Individual opportunism and enterprise are therefore channelled towards attempting to go abroad, leading to dependency on something which for many is no more that a fantasy, a dream-land, which few villagers will ever see.

> Co-existing, sometimes uneasily, with this set of images and ideals is the centrality of *desh* to group identity, and the spiritual powers with which it is linked. There is therefore a constant balancing of the two views, between the economic and political power of *bidesh*, and the fertility and spirituality of *desh*. This continual ambivalence, and negotiation of what might appear to be oppositional presentations of the world, is an integral part of migration and the contradictions which it involves.

Ambivalence and negotiation around *desh-bidesh* are expressed and reproduced in a variety of ways, including the exchange of goods, images, and ideas between the two settings. Gardner (1993: 5) further describes *desh-bidesh* not as polar opposites, but as sites in 'local mental maps [that] involve a geography of power, in which locations are points along a continuum, with different types of empowerment to be found at each'.

The effects of transnationalism for changing meanings, attitudes, and experiences both 'here' and 'there' are relevant to recent studies concerning migrants and transformations of the meaning of 'home' (Rapport and Dawson 1998; Al-Ali and Koser 2002). An illustration of this is provided by Ruba Salih (2002; 2003), who details how Moroccan women in Italy engage in material practices representing the two countries. Whether in Italy or Morocco, the women buy, consume, display, and exchange commodities from their 'other home' in order to symbolize their ongoing sense of double belonging.

Once such kind of *habitus* of dual orientation is constructed and reproduced by migrants, it might have further impacts. For one, it is hard to dismantle. David Kyle (2000: 2) discusses at least one informant who foresees 'no clear exit strategy from the binational life he had built over eleven years of shuttling back and forth' between New York City and his village in Ecuador. Another consequence concerns the transformation of outlook and practice among those closely associated with the transnational migrant. Here, through the experiences of his informants, Kyle came to think of the links between these distinct places 'as more of an emergent transnational social reality, involving migrants and non-migrants alike, than simply an international movement of labor' (2000: 9). The point about non-migrants is significant: such a transnational social reality incorporates and infuses what we can call the *habitus* of many people 'left behind' but whose lives are still transformed by the transnational activities and ideologies among those who actually move (cf. Kyle 2000: 202).

Relatedly, Rebecca Golbert (2001) documents the case of young Ukrainian Jews who have developed 'transnational orientations from home' towards the Ukraine, Israel, and other Jewish communities in the United States, Germany, and elsewhere. She describes how young Ukrainian Jews undertake the evaluation of everyday experiences, the past, and the future with 'a double consciousness' garnered from transnational links and a transnational conception of self. 'Their daily reality', Golbert (2001: 725) observes, 'is embedded in a transnational frontier of intersecting ideas, relationships, histories and identities; at the same time, transnational practices are localised through intimate and shared experiences'. Recounting narratives and the sharing of experiences—particularly regarding Israel—Golbert shows how returnees have had a powerful impact even on the transnational orientations of those who have never left Ukraine. They, too, have a *habitus* reoriented to more than one locality.

By way of conceptualizing transnational experience through *habitus*, social scientists might better appreciate how dual orientations arise and are acted upon. Values, perceptions, and aspirations that may be grounded in a pre-migration setting get situated in relation to structural opportunities and constraints (including laws, bureaucracies, labour markets, patterns of racism, and sexism) in post-migration settings.

This perspective also has bearing for questions as to how members of second and subsequent generations following the migrant generation are affected by transnationalism. This is an understudied area and one that appears on the list of usual suspect criticisms. There is one common view that transnational practices among second-generation youth are currently minimal and likely to dwindle further in the course of time. However, another view—and one in line with an understanding on how a transnational *habitus* is shaped and acted upon—suggests that there exist 'strong influences in the transnational social fields in which the second generation is embedded. This view stresses the importance of the sending-country individuals, resources, and ideas that are a constant presence in the lives of the second generation and holds that even selective, periodic transnational practices can add up' (Levitt and Waters 2002: 4). Recent research suggests patterns of intensive transnational activism at a particular life-stages among the second generation (Levitt 2002; Smith 2002), as well as a considerable variety of patterns and kinds of transnationalism among different groups of second-generation youth (Kasinitz et al. 2002). In each case, the interplay is apparent of parents' transnational *habitus*, which is a host of local conditioning factors, and second-generation youths' own hybrid or multicultural *habitus*. Thus, among young Indian-Americans, Sunaina Marr Maira (2002: 23) observes that 'second-generation youth culture becomes a site of struggles to define notions of authenticity that, while drawing on transnational imaginings of "India," also work to position these youth in relation to hierarchies of race, class, gender, and nationalism that mark them as "local"'. Such studies suggest that even though specific transnational orientations and practices of communication and exchange may not be sustained in strong forms by second and subsequent generations, the process of being socialized within a milieu of such transnational orientations and practices will often have a substantial influence on long-term configurations of outlook, activity, and identity.

Summary

As Castles (2002: 1158) submits, 'It is possible that transnational affiliations and consciousness will become the predominant form of migrant belonging in their future. This would have far-reaching consequences'. One possible approach to trying to understand such a process and its consequences is to analyse how patterns of immigrant transnationalism are reorienting individual *habitus* towards 'bifocality' or senses of dual orientation in light of shifting conditions. The structure and workings of *habitus* are certainly hard to 'measure', but they are arguably discernable in social practices and conveyed in narratives. The dispositions and practices generated by a transnational *habitus* are not, moreover, evenly spread within a group or family. Yet these are nonetheless not to be underestimated because such dispositions and practices have substantial impact on individual and family life course and strategies, individuals' senses of self and collective belonging, the ordering of personal and group memories, patterns of consumption, collective sociocultural practices, approaches to child-rearing, and other modes of cultural reproduction. These latter functions particularly concern ways in which the reorienting of first-generation *habitus* conditions that of second and subsequent generations.

Political Transformation: Reconfiguring Identities–Borders–Orders

There is now a very large literature spanning the social sciences in which scholars debate whether or how processes of globalization have affected political structures, particularly the nation-state system (see Guillén 2001). For instance, Martin Albrow (1997) sees the nation-state as an outdated form of social and political organization;

Susan Strange (1996) describes the 'declining authority of states', while Saskia Sassen (1996) asserts that economic globalization is leading to a fundamental redefinition of nation-state sovereignty and territoriality; Martin Carnoy and Manuel Castells (2001) depict a dramatic decline in nation-state autonomy and nation-states' rising dependence on globalized processes of production and trade, other states, and lower levels of the state. In probing the concept of 'cosmopolitanism', a range of authors—including Craig Calhoun, David Held, Ulrich Beck, Rainer Bauböck, and Mary Kaldor (all cited in Vertovec and Cohen 2002)—describe how diverse sets of inter-state, intra-state, and ultra-state practices test the viability of a conventional model of the nation-state and the international system based around it.

The conventional model of the nation-state involves borders presumed to 'contain' people characterized by some linguistic, social, and presumed cultural/ethnic identity, who are themselves organized by an ideational, legal, and democratic or authoritarian framework. 'States are institutions, nations are cross-class collectivities which share a sense of identity and collective political fate on the basis of real, imagined and constructed cultural, linguistic and historical commonalities' (Held et al. 1999: 48).

In some quarters, the arguments around globalization and political change have gone to extremes, suggesting we are witnessing the 'death of the nation-state'. Others point to the continuation, if not strengthening, of the legitimacy and capacity of states to enforce their laws and policies. Whether they are sceptics, hyper-globalists, or transformationists (Held et al. 1999), most observers agree that the nation-state has been radically challenged, at least, by processes and phenomena surrounding such things as the emergence of complex global economic patterns, massive and instantaneous international financial flows, an array of regional pacts and multi-lateral agreements (on trade, the environment, crime and terrorism, etc.), and 'humanitarian' military interventions—all things which seem to upset long-standing notions of cultural and political sovereignty. While not necessarily dying, the nation-state is transforming into a type of political organization or apparatus involving more multiple and overlapping jurisdictions, sets of identities, and social orders that borders no longer really contain (cf. Beck 2002).

The juxtaposition between immigration and the nation-state has long been focus of considerable discussion by sociologists, political scientists, and political philosophers (e.g., Bauböck 1994; Soysal 1994; Joppke 1998; 1999). While debates over globalization and political change, immigration, and the nation-state continuing to rage, we can see that migrant transnationalism itself does not itself bring about transformations of the nation-state. Such transformations are happening anyway, due to a confluence of processes within global political economy. But debatably, migrant transnationalism importantly contributes to such significant shifts. In what ways, is this happening?

Identities–Borders–Orders

Currently within the field of International Relations, one way of attempting to understand broad contemporary political challenges is through the 'analytical triad' or 'dynamic nexus' between the concepts of 'identities–borders–orders' (Albert et al. 2001). The idea here is that, in order to appreciate changes happening in any one of these three conceptual domains, it must be assessed in relation to the other two. Yosef Lapid (2001: 7) writes:

> Processes of collective identity formation invariably involve complex bordering issues. Likewise, acts of bordering (i.e., the inscription, crossing, removal, transformation, multiplication and/or diversification of borders) invariably carry momentous ramifications for political ordering at all levels of analysis. Processes of identity, border and order construction are therefore mutually self-constituting. Borders, for instance, are in many ways inseparable from the identities they help demarcate or individuate. Likewise, they are also inseparable from orders constituted to a large extent via such acts of individuation and segmentation. Thus, in any specific case, if we want to study problems associated with any one of our three concepts, we can richly benefit from also considering the other two.

In other words, as with the conventional model of the nation-state, some sense of identity is presumed to characterize a people; this identity of people is believed to be contiguous with a territory, demarcated by a border, and within the border, laws underpin a specific social and political order or system; this social order—which is conceived to be different from orders outside the border—both draws upon and reinforces the sense of collective identity. 'Identities–borders–orders' are legitimated and reproduced through a system of narratives, public rituals and institutions, formal state bureaucracies and informal social relationships, written and unwritten regulations, and sets of assumptions and expectations of civility and public behaviour (Schiffauer et al. 2003).

Various processes of globalization and the rise of regional, global, or 'cosmopolitan' structures of governance assail essential components of national 'identities–borders–orders' by compounding identities, ignoring borders, and overruling orders. Migration itself confronts 'identities–borders–orders'. 'One reason migration enters political agendas with greater frequency and salience now', suggests Martin Heisler (2001: 229), 'is that, 'at least in some host societies, it *disturbs the sense of boundedness*' (emphasis in original).

> The ability to change countries of residence with relative ease and the possibility of reversing the move can vitiate the need to make lasting identitive commitments. Identities can thus be partial, intermittent, and reversible in the modern Western democratic state. Order no longer depends on unalloyed loyalty stemming from immutable national identity—identity for which there is no plausible or legitimate alternative. Countries' borders are not seen as coextensive with a comprehensive political community. (Heisler 2001: 236)

Nowadays, Heisler (2001: 237) concludes, 'migration tends to attenuate territorial sovereignty, monolithic order, and identitive solidarity'. In various ways, some of which are described in the following text, the political dimensions of migrant transnationalism inherently involve questions of identity (Vertovec 2001) and often raise contentious issues concerning civic order and the cohesiveness of 'host' societies (Vertovec 1999b).

With regard to the '*identities*' being part of the analytical triad, politicians contribute to senses of 'peoplehood' by enacting laws of membership, determining who is included, who is excluded, and determining what are their respective rights and duties (Pickus 1998). This need not be monolithic, of course; recent trends in broadening such a national sense of identity can be seen in contemporary citizenship tests for immigrants and policies crafting multiculturalism. However, what such 'peoplehood' means is also affected by concurrent policies in many states extending and withholding rights, voice, and welfare access to immigrants. These effectively create a multiple-tiered sense of membership (Motomura 1998).

With regard specifically to migrant transnational practices, David Fitzgerald (2000: 10) observes that transnational migrants challenge nation-state ideals of belonging in both sending and receiving countries. They do this not least by moving back and forth between states, sometimes circumventing state controls over borders and taxes. 'Transnational migrants often live in a country in which they do not claim citizenship and claim citizenship in a country in which they do not live', Fitzgerald (2000: 10) points out; 'Alternatively, they may claim membership in multiple polities in which they may be residents, part-time residents, or absentees'. This phenomenon is witnessed in examples of immigrants—even naturalized ones—going 'home' from Germany or the United States to vote in Turkey or Dominican Republic.

Such trends run counter to orthodox assimilation theories that assumed immigrants would be less likely to continue involving themselves in the political concerns of their nation-state of origin. Instead, for many migrants with transnational networks and lifestyles, 'the country of origin becomes a source of identity and the country of residence a source of right ... The result is a confusion between rights and identity, culture and politics, states and nations' (Kastoryano 2002: 160). Once more the question of durability enters: are such border-crossing political identities merely an issue for first-generation migrants? Bauböck (2003) addresses this by suggesting that 'even if transnationalism remains a *transient* phenomenon for each migration cohort, the emergence of new legal and political conceptions of membership signifies an important *structural* change for the polities involved' (emphasis in original).

With regard to the *'borders'* being part of 'identities–borders–orders', Sassen (1996) suggests that states are 're-nationalizing' themselves in this area more than others. 'There is a growing consensus in the community of states to lift border controls for the flow of capital, information, and services and, more broadly, to further globalization', Sassen (1996: 59) notes; 'But when it comes to immigrants and refugees, whether in North America, Western Europe, or Japan, the national state claims all its old splendor in asserting its sovereign right to control its borders'. Almost regardless of global economic flows, interstate pacts, and other sides of globalization, nation-states firmly retain the right to admit or expel aliens, to maintain jurisdiction over what happens within their own territories, and through their border policies to control migration and membership. 'Territoriality', Fitzgerald (2000: 29) contends, 'continues to define the state even as its citizens cross state borders'.

Although challenging 'identities' and 'orders', migrant transnational practices do little to challenge state border controls (other than practices which sometimes seek to circumvent such controls). Indeed, it is usually the other way around: border policies often considerably impact on migrant transnational practices. Jacqueline Hagan (1994) shows how state policies are central to the formation of migrant communities, their survival strategies, and transnational practices. She demonstrates how legal status—a powerful facet of border control—facilitates regular back and forth movement and exchanges, while lack of legal status seriously hinders such transnational practice. This is evident, too, following the recent beefing-up of border control measures in the United States (including, over the past decade, a tripling of its budget and a doubling of the size of the border patrol): these measures have meant that many undocumented Mexicans stay put in the United States rather than move back and forth through transnational circuits (Cornelius 2001).

With regard to the '*orders*' being part of the triad, a broad range of policies surrounding migration and migrants is concerned with reproducing certain legal, social, and political systems. In the realm of economic and cultural policy, for instance, 'migration has transformed the domestic political milieu ... the collective strength and pattern of alliances of political actors has changed; and migration has reshaped political interests and perceptions of these interests' (Held et al. 1999: 322). Perhaps foremost in this field, however, political sociologists and political scientists have been interested in the relationship between migration and citizenship. In much literature, nationality and citizenship are treated as co-equivalent (although some scholars such as Michael Jones-Correa [2001] argue that we should differentiate nationality as formal status of state membership, and citizenship as rights and duties within the nation-state). Notions of order, particularly within the identities–borders–orders framework, are severely put to the test by emerging migrant transnational practices around dual citizenship/nationality and 'homeland' political allegiances.

Dual Citizenship/Nationality

It has been suggested that dual citizenship/nationality represents one of 'the most fundamental questions about the relation between immigration and citizenship in the next century' (Pickus 1998: xxvii). Dual citizenship/nationality has a long history that is not always tied to the subject of immigration (see Koslowski 2001). Dual citizenship or dual nationality can be claimed through birth, marriage, claiming ancestral lineage, or through naturalization.

Until recently, there was a 'prevalent distaste' for dual nationality in states around the world; now, particularly post-Cold War, that distaste is dissipating and we may be witnessing a long-term shift towards a more universal acceptance of dual nationality (Spiro 2002: 19–20). Long ago, the League of Nations emphasized 'one nationality only', a platform reiterated in the early 1960s by the Council of Europe Convention on the Reduction of Multiple Nationality (see

Aleinikoff and Klusmeyer 2001). By 1997, the Council of Europe set forth its European Convention on Nationality emphasizing that both parents may transfer their respective nationalities to their children (see Faist 2001).

There is now an upward trend in claims for dual citizenship/nationality, produced especially through migration. The loosening of rules concerning dual citizenship represents a global trend, particularly among migrant-sending countries (Hansen and Weil 2002). It is reported that at present some 89 countries—about half the world's countries—have some form of dual citizenship (Fritz 1998; Rogers 2001e). 'International and regional instruments', a United Nations report (UNPD 1998) points out, 'also seem to be reconciling principles of nationality with the trends towards multiple identities. This is evident by the reorientation of instruments regarding dual or multiple nationality'.

From an American perspective, Peter Schuck (1998: 153) writes that 'with current legal and illegal immigration approaching record levels, naturalization petitions quintupling in the last five years to almost two million annually, and legal changes in some of our largest source countries that encourage (and are often designed to encourage) naturalization in the United States, dual citizenship is bound to proliferate'. It is estimated that more than a half million children born in the United States each year have at least one additional nationality (Aleinikoff and Klusmeyer 2001). Among the one million people that naturalized in the United States in 1996, nine out of ten main countries of origin allow some form of dual nationality or citizenship (Fritz 1998). Similarly in 1996, seven of the ten largest immigrant groups in New York City had the right to be dual nationals (Foner 2000).

In other Western states, official attitudes on dual citizenship or dual nationality vary considerably. The United Kingdom 'is perfectly indifferent', while France is tolerant and increasingly liberalizing (Hansen and Weil 2002: 6–7). Even in countries such as Germany that traditionally do not tolerate dual citizenship, Thomas Faist (2001) points out, about one-fourth to one-third of all naturalizations from the 1970s to the 1990s resulted in multiple citizenship. Additionally, every seventh German marriage is with a foreigner, leading to two nationalities of the offspring under German law, and the millions of *Aussiedler* (ethnic German repatriates) were not obliged to give up their Russian or Kazakh citizenship (Thränhardt 2002).

The transnational identities, border-crossings, and mixed political orders suggested by dual citizenship/nationality can be posed either as contributing to or as hindering the integration of newcomers (Faist 2001). Such arguments are taken up by Randall Hansen and Patrick Weil (2002), who discuss five arguments against dual citizenship/nationality: (1) it can produce competing loyalties, (2) it creates a security threat, (3) it impedes immigrant integration, (4) it increases international instability, and (5) it violates equality by giving dual nationals a wider range of rights and opportunities. Hansen and Weil engage these arguments by pointing out, among other things, that: (1) loyalty can indeed be multiple (e.g., the project of the European Union is based on this), (2) the security threat exists independently of dual citizenship/nationality, (3) far from impeding immigrant integration, dual citizenship/nationality furthers it (policies tolerant of dual citizenship/nationality are shown to increase naturalization rates), (4) the instability problem—exemplified in matters of military service, taxation, and inheritance rules—is lessening through bilateral negotiations, and (5) equality issues are a concern, but the additional rights and opportunities offered by dual citizenship/nationality are often not much greater than those already extended by permanent resident status.

A kind of watering down of the meaning of citizenship and nationality is another concern for many as well. 'A second or even a third passport', writes Mark Fritz (1998: 1), 'has become not just a link to a homeland but also a glorified travel visa, a license to do business, a stake in a second economy, and escape hatch, even a status symbol'. This is seen by some as promoting a kind of 'citizenship of convenience' (Fritz 1998: 1).

On the migrant-sending countryside, dual citizenship has been difficult to push through many parliaments since domestic politicians see more disadvantage than advantage in allowing this (Østergaard-Nielsen 2003b). They often feel that emigrant or diaspora participation in domestic politics is distinctly not welcome—particularly absentee voting which might give too much domestic oppositional influence to people actually living outside the country.

In any case, as noted earlier in the text, the incidence and impacts of dual citizenship/nationality are on the rise around the world, and migrant transnationalism plays a key role in this growth. In addition to shaping actual practices of migrants, such a trend is having important outcomes in government policy. As T. Alexander Aleinikoff and Douglas Klusmeyer (2001: 87) understand it, there is 'an emerging international consensus that the goal [of state policies] is no longer to reduce plural nationality as an end in itself, but to manage it as an inevitable feature of an increasingly interconnected and mobile world'.

'Homeland' Political Allegiances

Once more harking back to the what's old/what's new question around transnationalism, it is well documented that over 100 years ago many migrants maintained acute interest in the political plight of their place of origin (see, e.g., Foner 2000). Now such interests—and particularly the ability to act upon them—have been heightened due to advances in communication, cheapness of transport, and policy shifts such as the extension of dual citizenship/nationality.

Within and around transnational migrant communities, the politics of homeland can take a variety of forms (see Koopmans and Statham 2001; Guarnizo et al. 2003; Østergaard-Nielsen 2003a). Such forms include exile groups organizing themselves for return; groups lobbying on behalf of a homeland, external offices of political parties, and migrant hometown associations, and opposition groups campaigning or planning actions to effect political change in the homeland. Some migrant associations also manage to carry out dual programmes of action aimed at both sending and receiving countries (Østergaard-Nielsen 2001). Guarnizo et al. (2003: 1227) outline two major modes of transnational political participation:

> Transnational electoral participation includes membership in a political party in the country of origin, monetary contributions to these parties, and active involvement in political campaigns in the polity of origin. Transnational non-electoral politics includes membership in a hometown civic association, monetary contributions to civic projects in the community of origin, and regular membership in charity organizations sponsoring projects in the home country. Non-electoral activities are political because they influence local and regional governments by determining which public projects receive migrants' financial support. By so doing, they compel authorities to take immigrant wishes and priorities into account.

'Homeland' political allegiances may involve additional dimensions, as well, in such highly diverse forms as:

- *Diasporic politics*: These include the interests of long-established, subsequent generations stemming from migration (e.g., Irish Americans concerned with the situation in Northern Ireland) or religious/ethnic communities that may have never even lived in a 'homeland' (e.g., relationships between some diasporic Jews and the state of Israel).
- *Provisions for absentee voting*: Examples can be found among overseas nationals returning home en masse to vote in elections in Israel—sometimes with political parties paying for flights,

high-profile unofficial polls among expatriate South Africans, and large-scale voting at overseas embassies as in recent Indonesian and Algerian elections (Rogers 1999b).

- *Buying-in to dubious regimes*: A prime illustration occurred in 1990 when Croatians abroad paid $4 million towards the election campaign of Franjo Tudjman and were rewarded with representation in parliament: 12 of 120 seats were allotted to diaspora Croats, more than to Croatia's own ethnic minorities (*The Economist* 2003).
- *Key roles in war and peace*: For years, the financial backing of Tamil and Eritrean migrants sustained the wars in Sri Lanka and along the border with Ethiopia, but now these migrant diasporas are having a role in shaping the peace and facilitating post-conflict reconstruction (Koser 2002; *The Economist* 2003).
- *Mass protest and consciousness-raising*: A successful model of this followed the 1999 capture of Kurdish leader Abdullah Ocalan, when within a day organized mass demonstrations among Kurds took place around the world, bringing Kurdish issues to global attention (Rogers 1999a).
- *Overseas support for insurgency and terrorism*: The potential role of migrant communities appears in backing guerrilla movements such as among Tamils or Kurds (Byman et al. 2001) and terrorist actions as among Palestinian or Irish political movements (Hoffman 1998).

The kind and degree of participation in 'homeland' politics differs with reference to a series of contextual factors, including the history of specific migration and settlement processes and political conditions in the country of origin. Through a substantial survey a various migrant groups in the United States, Guarnizo et al. (2003) demonstrate that Colombian immigrants are the least likely to take part in homeland politics, while Salvadorans and Dominicans are equally likely to do so. The broadest patterns of political transnationalism, as Guarnizo et al. (2003: 1233) find, are 'a product of greater human capital, greater stability and experience in the receiving society, plus strong social connections and enduring moral ties with sending communities'.

At a deeper level, homeland political allegiance and engagement rests on the reconfiguration of identities–borders–orders, such that people from a particular place regard themselves as legitimate members of the collective identity and social order of a place even though they are outside of its borders. According to Fitzgerald (2000: 106), such a reconfiguration posits 'a model of citizenship that emphasizes rights over obligations, passive entitlements, and the assertion of an interest in the public space without a daily presence'. There is a tension, he goes on to say, between 'a reconceptualization of the polis as the transnational public space of the imagined community and the assertion that the polis should still be defined as a geographic space where citizens live together'. Hence, governments of countries of emigration increasingly invoking national solidarity across state borders. This was exemplified by Vicente Fox's campaigning among Mexicans in California during 2000, in which he played upon the broader boundaries of an imagined nation and declared he would be the first President 'to govern for 118 million Mexicans', including 100 million in Mexico and 18 million living outside the country (Fitzgerald 2000; Rogers 2000). Similarly, following the Los Angeles riots of 1992, South Korean politicians evoked images of Korean-Americans as a 'colony' of the homeland (Shain 1999: 5), while in her 1990 inaugural address as Irish President, Mary Robinson proclaimed herself leader of the extended Irish family abroad. During recent election campaigns in Turkey and the Dominican Republic, candidates went abroad to encourage support through overseas 'nationals'. These visions of nationals abroad are akin to the notion of 'deterritorialized nation-state', in which the boundaries of the nation-state are defined socially rather than geographically (Basch et al. 1994; Glick Schiller and Fouron 1998).

Common rhetoric about extended nations abroad help explain the fact that overseas communities are increasingly engaging themselves in the economic, social, and political life of their country of origin, while sending states and other political actors 'are trying to channel this engagement to their own advantage' (Østergaard-Nielsen 2003b). But although they use the same rhetoric, migrants and their sending states often have different expectations. Eva Østergaard-Nielsen (2003b) explains that:

> While sending countries are quick to call for their expatriate population's economic and political contribution to development in the country of origin it is clear that most expatriates and their representative organizations expect this to be a two way deal. Emigrants want their country of origin to support their struggle for equal rights and against discrimination on the labour market. More established migrant and diaspora groups demand more transparency and good governance in order to feel that their remittances and foreign direct investment is spent in the best possible way. And if migrants are expected to be good representatives and do some lobbying for their

country of origin abroad, then they would often like some influence on the policies that they are expected to represent.

Ideas, activities, and rhetoric find their way into government policies. There are a variety of reasons why specific countries develop certain kinds of policies towards expatriates (Levitt and de la Dehesa 2003). Policies regarding overseas nationals are usually to encourage a sense of membership (but not return) among sending states towards their perceived national communities abroad (Østergaard-Nielsen 2003b). These include special ministries or government offices devoted to overseas nationals, special investment opportunities, special voting rights and, as we have seen, dual nationality/citizenship. Their effects, however, are broadly similar. 'Such policies', Levitt and de la Dehesa (2003) believes, are reinventing the role of states outside of territorial boundaries and in this way reconfiguring traditional understandings of sovereignty, nation, and citizenship.

Migrant transnational practices play a direct part in reconfiguring identities–borders–orders. However, it is clear that at the same time many basic structures of the nation-state are intact as it continues to exercise sovereignty over populations present on its territory. Ruud Koopmans and Paul Statham (2001) stress that the different ways migrants are enabled, or constrained, to make their homeland (and local) political claims in different countries demonstrate that the nation-state is alive and well and shaping transnational practices. The transnational allegiances and political practices of migrants appear anomalous juxtaposed with the persistent principles of territorially based sovereign rule.

Summary

The discussion in this section has endorsed the view, expressed by Held et al. (1999: 9), that 'the power of national governments is not necessarily diminished by globalization but on the contrary is being reconstituted and restructured in response to the growing complexity of processes of governance in a more interconnected world'. Political features of migrant transnationalism—particularly surrounding dual citizenship/nationality and 'homeland' allegiances—are contributing to a fundamental reconfiguration of the conceptual nexus 'identities–borders–orders'.

Though conceptual, such reconfiguration has real impacts in policies, legal structures, and national imaginaries. This is apparent when we recall what each part of the analytical triad entails. Here, among other things, 'identities' concern matters of membership, belonging, loyalty, and moral and political values; 'borders' involve territoriality, admission, legal status, and deportation; 'orders' relate to sovereignty, implications of legal status, civil, social and political rights, obligations, and access to public resources. Migrant's transnational practices have bearing on each one of these topics—and on more than one at a time, in keeping with the 'identities–borders–orders' insistence on mutual consideration of issues.

The challenges that political forms of migrant transnationalism pose to 'identities–borders–orders' seem to counter the continuing salience of the nation-state, at least in terms of border control and immigration. A possible way through this seeming contradiction is offered by Bauböck (2003), who proposes that:

> A political theory of transnational migration must therefore carefully distinguish two different phenomena: an increasing *permeability* of international borders for geographic mobility, which does not challenge territorial jurisdictions, and an increasing *overlap* of political identities and legal statuses between the sending and the receiving polity. (emphasis in original)

Economic Transformation: Re-institutionalizing Development

Guarnizo (2003) emphasizes that economic aspects of migrant transnationalism involve multiple economic activities and myriad multiplier effects generated by migrants' relations with their homelands. Such variety may often be seen within a single group, as shown by Patricia Landolt (2001) when she describes the range of variation of individual and household-level transnational economic activity among Salvadorans, despite common origins and post-migration contexts. Some activities directly involving migrants, such as transnational ethnic entrepreneurship (Portes et al. 2002) or the facilitation of international trade (Light et al. 2002). Others only indirectly involve migrants, especially spin-off industries catering for migrant transnational practices. Indeed, Guarnizo (2003) discerns, 'some of the fastest segments of the telephone, air transportation, and financial industries are international long-distance calling, ethnic tourism, and the private remittance of money'. Some industries or enterprises (such as supermarkets or breweries) are based in migrant-sending countries but reach out to customers in diaspora. In Ecuador, for instance, hundreds of new business services have been established catering to emigrants, including travel agencies, cyber cafes, and companies specializing in shipping abroad traditional Ecuadorian foods and medicinal herbs (Rogers 2001c). Yet other economic facets of migrant transnationalism involve government schemes to attract migrants' foreign currency, such as expatriate bonds, high-interest foreign currency accounts, and tax exemptions for saving and investment.

Economically, by far the most transformative processes and phenomena of migrant transnationalism have concerned remittances, the money migrants send to their families and communities of origin. The following sections consider several significant dimensions of remittances and their transformative effects and potentials.

Remittances

'Remittances have become the most visible evidence and measuring stick for the ties connecting migrants with their societies of origin', writes Guarnizo (2003). There are a great many studies probing the volume of remittances, their determinants and impacts (especially their 'productive' uses) in migrant sending contexts, and their channels of transference. Remittances are sent by all types of migrant workers: male and female, legal and undocumented, long-term and temporary, and manual and high skilled. Money is transferred through banks, agencies of various kinds, directly online, through professional couriers, or through social networks.

Drawing upon research in El Salvador, Landolt (2001: 234) richly describes some of the ways remittances transform families and communities:

> Households that receive remittances demonstrate tangible improvement in their standard of living. Remittance dollars grant access to education and health, and may permit a family to buy agricultural land or make improvements on an existing property. Remittances, combined with knowledge of wages and conditions in Salvadoran settlement cities, may also alter the labourer's relationship to the local economy. Weighing the value of their labour in transnational terms, workers have more leverage to reject the miserably low wages offered by Salvadoran employers. Entire communities are transformed, as enterprises, land holdings, and basic survival increasingly revolve around the remittance transfer. In turn, locals inserted in the circuits of Salvadoran economic transnationalism prosper relative to marginal, non-transnational locations, which remain mired in poverty. As they subsidize households and alleviate the worst forms of poverty, remittances finally have the unintended consequence of perpetuating a bankrupt economic system.

As Landolt suggests, remittances have broad effects, including the stimulation of change within a variety of sociocultural institutions (such as local status hierarchies, gender relations, marriage patterns, and consumer habits; see Vertovec 2000). However, it is the economic impacts of remittances that receive most attention.

In numerous settings around the world, remittances have been shown to be directly invested in small businesses such as manufacturing and crafts companies, market halls, bakeries, and transport agencies (Taylor 1999; van Doorn 2001). However, various studies show differing proportions of remittances spent on consumer goods versus 'productive' investments. Among the reported negative impacts of migrant remittances are the following (Vertovec 2000). Remittances tend to: displace local jobs and incomes; induce consumption spending (often on foreign imports); inflate local prices of land, housing, and food; create disparity, envy between recipients and non-recipients; and create a culture of economic dependency.

However, J. Edward Taylor (1999), among others, has criticized much conventional research on remittances. He points out that common surveys assume a naïve model of remittance expenditure; instead, there is a need to consider whole-household and community economy. Taylor (1999: 64) emphasizes that 'remittances may reshape migrant-sending economies through indirect channels that are missed by traditional research approaches'. This view corroborates the often-cited research by Durand et al. (1996) demonstrating the multiplier effect of 'migradollars'. Durand and his associates (1996: 425) argue that work focusing solely on the productive uses of remittances 'have ignored the indirect effects that consumer spending has on economic production and income'. Their research on multiplier effects suggests that, at that time, the $2 billion in remittances that entered the Mexican economy were responsible for $6.5 billion increase in production in agriculture, manufacturing, services and commerce. 'In short', says Taylor (1999: 72), 'an important channel through which remittances stimulate productive investments may, paradoxically, be though migrant-households' consumption spending'. Supporting this view and confirming the data of Durand et al., one study in Bangladesh estimated that remittances of $610 million created demand for $351 million in Bangladeshi goods and services and generated at least 577,000 jobs (Arnold 1992).

It must be stressed that a large proportion of migrants send money to families for mere subsistence (Suro et al. 2002). Also, schooling and other costs of education are often not factored into studies on the 'productive' use of remittances. 'In any case', argues Peter Stalker (2000: 81), 'it can be argued that many forms of consumption, particularly on housing, better food, education, and health care, are a good form of investment that will lead to higher productivity'.

In order not to paint a misleading picture, it needs underlining that migrants do indeed often channel remittances directly into investment, and that in this field we are not just talking about countries of the South. Throughout Central and Eastern Europe, for instance, thriving remittance systems are in place among migrants. Polish workers in Germany, for instance, send home as much as 80 per cent of their earnings (Vickerman 2002). Recent research suggests that throughout Central and Eastern Europe, moreover, migrants' money goes more towards investment—especially for establishing small businesses—than it does towards consumption (Piracha and Vickerman 2002).

The sheer scale of contemporary global remittances itself represents a type of transformation. Figures from the annual International Monetary Fund's (IMF) report show a massive increase in the amount of formal remittances worldwide, from less than $2 billion in 1970 to at least $105 billion in 1999 (van Doorn 2001). Over 60 per cent of this amount goes to developing countries, and over the last decade remittances have become a much larger source of income for developing countries than official development assistance (Gammeltoft 2002). Such figures, it is often pointed out, must be taken as merely suggestive, since the categories used to estimate them are contestable. Moreover, these figures rely on official transfers reported by central banks of receiving countries, who in turn rely on reports filed by remittance intermediaries. Therefore, the IMF estimates are likely to be considerably short of real remittance values—indeed, it has been suggested that officially recorded remittances represent 'only the tip of the iceberg' (Puri and Ritzema 1999: 3).

Beyond official figures, unofficial remittance transfers may amount to another $15 billion (*The Economist* 2003). As much as 46 per cent of Mexican remittances may be hand-carried to recipients (Lowell and de la Garza 2000). In many African countries, it is estimated that perhaps only about 50 per cent of remittances go through official channels (Mohan 2002: 134). One survey in Japan found that 70 per cent of Thai and Filipino workers sent money home by illegal means, while in 1998 Japanese police found underground banks sending up to 176 billion yen ($1.48 billion) in illegal transfers to China, Thailand, South Korea, Iran, Taiwan, Myanmar, and Nepal (Rogers 1999c). In Pakistan formal remittances (currently over $1 billion) are thought to represent only a fifth or sixth of all remittances (Rogers 2001d).

Whether through official or unofficial means, remittances mean a lot to the countries—to say nothing of the families and communities—that receive them. In 2000, remittances from abroad comprised more than 10 per cent of the gross domestic product (GDP) of countries such as El Salvador, Jamaica, Haiti, Ecuador, Eritrea, Jordan, and Yemen (UNPD 2002). They account for as much as one-quarter of national income of Nicaragua. Remittances have exceeded the total value of exports in El Salvador and constitute more than half the value of exports in the Dominican Republic and Nicaragua (Orozco 2001). The Inter-American Development Bank calculates that across Latin America the annual growth of remittances is 7–10 per cent: the 2001 figure of more than £23 billion in remittances for this region may be worth more than $70 billion by 2012 (Rogers 2002). Remittances are so important to the current and future economy of many nations that they are now used as a valuation instrument to upgrade the credit-worthiness of impoverished countries to secure large-scale international loans (Guarnizo 2003).

Still, most experts on remittances argue that recipient groups and countries are not getting their worth. Most formal financial transfer institutions charge a fee from 6 to 15 per cent and additional costs can make the total deduction over 20 per cent (Lowell and de la Garza 2000). Of Latin America's $23 billion in remittances in 2001, it is reckoned approximately $3 billion was lost in transfer fees (Rogers 2002). Government investigations, campaigns by non-governmental organizations (NGOs) and class action law suits have all focused on the often exorbitant fees charged by international transfer agencies such as Western Union and MoneyGram. The high and uncertain costs of transfers are known to be the most serious concern voiced by remitters (Suro et al. 2002).

It is widely believed that the value of remittances would be much higher if the cost of transferring money was lower. A study of over 70 remittance companies demonstrates that improved and increased competition in the financial transfer sector will drive down the level of fees (Orozco 2002). Within Latin America, it is estimated that reducing the transfer costs to 5 per cent would free up more than $1 billion a year for some of the poorest, migrant background households in the United States (Suro et al. 2002). Some agencies are considering moves towards a flat fee rather than percentage. There are currently a number of moves within government (such as the Wire Transfer Fairness and Disclosure Act of 1999), among NGOs and in financial institutions themselves, to create more transparency in pricing and greater consumer awareness.

More money, effectively transferred, should have considerable consequences for those who get it. Given that recipients of remittances are largely in underdeveloped contexts, how can remittances contribute to development?

Remittances and Development

It is widely recognized that remittances by themselves are not a panacea for impoverishment. Indeed, 'remittances flowing to emigration areas often wind up producing what John Kenneth Galbraith called "private affluence and public squalor," or new homes reachable only over dirt roads. What is clearly needed is some way of harnessing some fraction of the remittances in order to develop the infrastructure that can help a region develop economically' (Widgren and Martin 2002: 223). Some advisers have suggested that migrant-sending countries could earmark, perhaps through an import tariff, a portion of remittances for a specific development fund. Only North Korean has successfully implemented such a scheme, while there have been failed attempts to create such funds in the Philippines, Pakistan, Thailand, and Bangladesh (Puri and Ritzema 1999). It is likely that most migrants themselves are or would be sceptical to such schemes: this is due not only to anxieties over possible corruption, but also to past experiences and frustrations with the ineffective, preferential, or non-existent development programmes of national governments and international agencies.

Susan Martin (2001: 5) asks, 'to what effect can the multiplier effect of remittances be increased by initiatives to encourage local purchase of locally-produced goods'? Perhaps a more laissez-faire policy climate will suffice, such that migrants and their families can find themselves the right ways to develop their communities themselves, albeit perhaps with some NGO advice, appropriate banking schemes, and government support (but not control). Schemes and initiatives of these kinds are described later in the text.

The multiplier effect involves a tricky equation, however. It is never so clear as to what counts as costs, and what as benefits, and what as ultimately productive spending of remittances. For instance, remittance investment in housing is said to generate more multiplier effects than any other industry (Taylor 1999). But in Ecuador, for example, where approximately 95 per cent of remittances are spent on new housing, this expenditure fuelled substantial inflation in land prices and construction costs that impacted negatively on most of the local population (Rogers 2001c). In Egypt, remittances are often used to purchase gold, which has a high cultural status value. This would appear to be a fairly non-productive use without multiplier effects. Yet in Egypt and many other settings, gold is locally regarded as a kind of insurance—something that will retain financial value in times of uncertainly and high inflation, which can be advantageously cashed in at a later date (Fouad Ibrahim, personal communication).

It should be born in mind that 'development' should include not only matters of economic growth, but also social (including gender, health, and civil and democratic), environmental, and technological issues. In many places, one of the most common and extensive uses of remittance money is towards health care expenses (DeSipio 2000). Some NGOs are developing schemes to creatively use remittances to provide regular transnational health care coverage. A different kind of multiplier or 'protective effect' concerns the general development of health profiles among remittance-receiving families. Research by Reanne Frank and Robert Hummer (2002) point to a direct correlation indicating that infants in migrant-sending families are less likely to suffer infant death or to be of low-birth weight—a key determinant in health outcomes later in life. Remittances offset the effects of poverty by raising standards of living, improving nutrition, and facilitating access to medical care. It is conjectured that financial remittances are also likely to flow alongside what Levitt (2001b) calls social remittances (values and behaviours)—in this case health information and practices. Frank and Hummer (2001b: 761) conclude that more attention should be given to 'how transnational activity affects the relationship between health and migration and in what ways'.

To more fully appreciate the impact of remittances on development, it must also be recognized that the implications of migration and remittances for development vary according to level of analysis, from individual to community, nation, or state (Skeldon 1997). A kind of level or institutional structure linking these other levels can be found by way of migrant associations.

Remittances and Hometown Associations

There is a long history of migrant associations sending money for collective benefit in the home town or village. Nancy Foner (2000: 171–172) illustrates this by pointing to how, between 1914 and 1924, New York's Jewish *landsmanshaftn* or hometown associations (HTAs) sent millions of dollars to their war-ravaged home communities. Yet now 'we are seeing a very specific type of home-town association, one directly concerned with socio-economic development in its communities of origin and increasingly engaging both governmental and civic entities in sending and receiving countries in these projects' (Sassen 2002: 226).

There has been a marked growth in the number and function of migrant HTAs throughout the 1990s (see, for instance, Lowell and de la Garza 2000; Orozco 2000a, 2001; Alarcón 2001). A concomitant change in HTA structures and roles has been observed as well (Goldring 1998; Mahler 1998; Alarcón 2001; Levitt 2001a; Martin 2001). Their significance should not be underestimated. One study in Los Angeles found that 'HTAs are clearly the most numerous and ubiquitous form of voluntary organization among first generation immigrants' (Zabin and Rabadan 1998: 1). Furthermore, HTAs represent the clearest form of institutionalization of transnational ties (Orozco 2001).

Manuel Orozco (2000a) contends that HTAs exhibit at least four features. They conduct a range of activities, from charitable aid to investment; their structures vary; their decisions depend on factors such as resource base, organizational structure, and relationship with hometown; and they tend to have a small economic base. HTA activities embrace charitable work such as donating clothes, goods for religious festivals, and construction materials for repairing the town church. They raise money for improving infrastructure such as sewage treatment plants and health care facilities. They support educational institutions, such as providing scholarships and library books. Yet another kind of HTA activity involves managing collective capital investment for income-generating projects in sending contexts that are often co-managed by locals and migrants (Orozco 2000b; World Bank 2001). HTAs also play a significant role in organizing disaster relief following catastrophes such as Hurricane Mitch in Central America in 1998 and the earthquakes in Turkey in 1999 and in Gujarat in 2001 (Rogers 2001b).

HTAs are not of a single kind, nor are they the only mode of migrant transnationalism involved in collective remittance sending. Caroline Ndofor-Tah identifies a range of diasporic organizations involved in African development, including hometown associations, ethnic associations, alumni associations, religious associations, professional associations, investment groups, political groups, and supplementary schools (cited in Mohan and Zack-Williams 2002). Their activities include community-to-community transfers, identity-building, lobbying in current home on issues relation to homeland, trade and investment with homeland, and payment of taxes in the homeland. Whatever the form of collective remitting, Alejandro

Portes and Patricia Landolt (2000: 543) conclude, 'Life conditions in municipalities that receive grassroots transnational aid confirm the relevance of this collective remittance strategy. Towns with a hometown association have paved roads, electricity, and fresher painted public buildings. The quality of life in transnational towns is simply better'.

'Consider the Salvadoran "United Community of Chinameca": their first largesse was $5,000 to build a school, and then they built a septic tank worth $10,000. Later they constructed a Red Cross clinic at a cost of $43,000, and bought an ambulance worth $32,000' (Lowell and de la Garza 2000: 2). Hagan (1994) likewise describes how a hometown group in Houston, calling themselves *Amigos de San Pedro*, organized and paid for medical supplies and a health clinic in San Pedro, Guatemala. They also established organization linkages and exchange programmes with American health workers. Another noteworthy case is the University of Hargeisa, which was established in 1998 in Somaliland (Mohan 2002). This was made possible by transnational networking of Somalis in Australia, Italy, Sweden, Kuwait, Canada, the United States, and Britain. While local businesses in Somaliland took responsibility for rehabilitating a dilapidated, government-owned school building, Somalis in Sweden provided 750 chairs and tables and Somalis in Kuwait provided computers. The Somaliland Forum, which is an Internet-based diasporic network, raises money, maintains email groups, and forms taskforces to support the university.

Such forms of migrant transnational organization are so importantly engaged in local development that, Smith (1998: 227–8) believes, they are generating 'parallel power structures' and 'forcing the state to engage them in new ways, either in kind or degree, but engage the state they must'. Some state and local governments match the funds raised by HTAs in order to magnify their impact (Martin 2001). Since 1993, one of the most noted programmes of this type has been the 'two for one' initiative of the *Programa para las Comunidades Mexicanas en el Extranjero* (PCME, Program for Mexican Communities Abroad; see Goldring 1998, 2001; Smith 1998; Mahler 2000). The programme operates through a network of 42 consulates and 23 institutes or Mexican cultural centres in the United States (Orozco 2001). The idea of 'two for one' is that for every dollar raised by a hometown association abroad, the state (e.g., of Zacatecas) and the federal government each put in a dollar for a community project. In 1995, in Zacatecas alone the 'two for one' programme added to the HTAs' $600,000 to provide $1.8 million towards 56 projects in 34 Mexican towns (Mahler 1998).

'Two for one' was subsequently extended to a 'three for one' programme, in which each migradollar is matched with one dollar from the federal government, one from the state government, and one from the municipal government. Between 1999 and 2001, migrants invested $2.7 million into such programmes (World Bank 2001). Despite some limitations, these initiatives in Mexico 'have produced a deep impact in the local communities and have been recognized as new and effective forms of public-private collaboration' (World Bank 2001: 6). The ultimate objective, according to World Bank analysts, would be 'to develop a self-sustainable private system for the development of projects and local programs financed totally or partially with remittances and savings from the Mexican community abroad. Available funds of international cooperation could be used for supporting some of the initiatives' (World Bank 2001: 7).

HTAs are not the only players in these kinds of schemes. Financial services firms such as Raza Express have joined in, contributing $0.75 to the collective funds for each $300 sent through their company. In this way, Raza Express has contributed more than $50,000, alongside $500,000 from the government of Jalisco, in schemes creating 15,000 jobs (Orozco 2001).

The collective remittance work of HTAs for development is not entirely rosy, however. Disagreements on how to use the funds raised by HTAs are endemic. For example, the association from Jalpa, a town of 13,500 in the state of Zacatecas, raised $2 million, but got into a serious dispute over how to spend the money in Jalpa (*Migration News*, December 2002: http://www.queensu.ca/samp/migrationnews/2002/dec.htm). Sarah Mahler (1998) and Luin Goldring (2001) both emphasize that while HTAs enjoy a veneer of altruism and democratic structure, they often significantly exclude women, reinforce existing power relations within a community, sometimes promote projects which are not the most needed but which generate the most symbolic power, and may be open to co-optation and exploitation by government.

The relationship between HTAs and the state of origin is not unproblematic, either. HTAs might be 'left doing the lion's share of the government's work' in development while the government itself steps back from this responsibility (Levitt 2001a: 209). Mahler (2000) predicts that in Central America, the region will see an ever-increasing amount of government activity concerning emigrants abroad, particularly regarding their remittances. 'While such efforts are comprehensible', she (Mahler 2000: 32) says, 'they are drawing increasing criticism because they place responsibility for Central

America's economic stability disproportionately on the shoulders of migrants'. Moreover, the more governments attempt to control and channel remittances, the more migrants are pushed towards remitting via unofficial means (Meyers 1998).

In proportion to total remittances sent through families, collective remittances channelled through HTAs and other migrant transnational frameworks are small, although likely to increase (Orozco 2001). Despite this fact, and that of the sometimes problematic nature of such organizations and their relationship to the state, the forms of institutionalization they represent have much valuable potential for effectively directing remittances to highly needed and effective forms of local development. Other, newer forms of institutionalization in the shape of microfinance present important possibilities as well.

Remittances and Microfinance

Taylor (1999: 74) usefully proposes that 'Migration is likely to have a larger effect on development where local institutions exist to gather savings by migrant households and make them available to local producers—that is, where migrants do not have to play the simultaneous roles of workers, savers, investors, and producers'. National governments have sought to establish economic schemes, such as special investment funds or savings accounts, to channel remittances and encourage business development. These have met with very mixed results (Puri and Ritzema 1999).

MFIs offer prospects for channelling migrant remittances in ways similar to those suggested by Taylor. The idea of MFIs began in the 1970s but took off among development agencies and researchers throughout the 1990s. More recently, there has occurred what Marguerite Robinson (2001) describes as 'a paradigm shift' in microfinance development strategies, from government- or donor-subsidized credit delivery systems to self-sufficient institutions providing finance on very local levels. MFIs have the potential to meet a massive global demand for local banking services that many governments and donor agencies increasingly recognize as a priority (Robinson 2001; also see www.microfinancegateway.org).

A core function of MFIs is to provide small, low-interest loans (microcredit, e.g., from $10 to $3,000) and savings services to poor families—and often specifically to women, who ordinarily do not have access to formal financial institutions. Such loans are to help people engage in productive activities (involving, for instance, small farms, petty trading, craft enterprises, or local business). MFIs offer credit, savings, and insurance in often remote rural areas. They may also give financial and business advice and training. Many MFIs are non-profit NGOs, credit unions, or cooperatives, while there are also new commercial MFIs. Currently augmented by new information technologies, MFIs are growing in number, extent, and function throughout the developing world.

One critical problem facing 'the microfinance revolution' is scarcity of capital (M. Robinson 2001). Therefore, channelled remittances—especially pooled funds represented by HTAs—can go a long way towards supporting the establishment and work of MFIs. In contrast to rural credit programmes, which earlier absorbed large sums of money over several decades, many relevant agencies—such as the International Labour Organization, the World Bank, and the Inter-American Development Bank—are increasingly interested in the potential interface between remittances and MFIs. The Multilateral Investment Fund of the Inter-American Development Bank promotes and funds initiatives that will allow emigrants to invest their money in development projects in places of origin. In 2001, the fund extended a grant of $1.1 million to support projects in Mexico, facilitating the linkage of remittance transfers, local financial services, and productive investments by migrants and their families. A further six such projects have been developed in 2002.

At one workshop on these issues convened by the International Labour Organization (ILO 2000: 15), it was agreed that MFIs 'appear particularly well suited to capture and transform remittances for several reasons: (i) they deal with small-scale transactions where personal relations were important, (ii) they extensively involve groups and associations of intermediaries and (iii) they integrate the formal and the informal sector practices'. The ILO workshop group also advocated a number of additional factors that should contribute to the successful linkage of MFIs and remittances, including the provision of a large number of local contact points, a wide range of financial services products at the local level, and the widening of partnerships between MFIs and other organizations. The ILO group also believed that governments should at best mainly observe, but also act to create a positive regulatory framework and ideally provide matching funds to stimulate the use of MFIs for routing remittances for local community development.

Shivani Puri and Tineke Ritzema (1999: 25) suggest in a report to the ILO that:

rather than focussing on 'migrant-specific' investment programmes, labour exporting countries might wish to induce micro-finance institutions to capture remittances. The basic idea would be to design policies to transfer funds of the migrant workers through to entrepreneurs. Savings and credit schemes and investment instruments specifically designed to suit migrant workers' risk profiles could be important vehicles.

Puri and Ritzema emphasize that labour-exporting countries would benefit from policies and programmes that enable micro-finance institutions that are trusted at the village level to play a key role in directing remittances, thus ensuring that families have access to safe and secure savings and credit schemes as well as business skill development programmes.

One of the best ways to achieve remittance-MFI benefits may be through credit unions, which would use any transfer fees to reinvest in community development (Martin 2001). Especially in comparison to banks and financial transfer agencies, credit unions are shown to offer some of the best practices in remitting opportunities to migrants (Orozco 2002). In fact, the World Council of Credit Unions has recently established the International Remittance Network, or IRNet (Grace 2001). Set up originally in cooperation with the Mexican government, this should enable credit union members to use IRNet's money-transfer services to 41 countries at one-third to one-half the commercial cost (Rogers 2001a). Indeed, IRNet charges less than $7 for most transactions. The use of credit unions can also provide needed access to savings, loans and insurance services, as well as broadly to 'increase the culture of banking' in both migrant sending and receiving countries (Grace 2001: 4). This may represent a particularly significant transformation, as research shows that many if not 'most remittance senders and receivers do not currently have bank accounts of any sort and probably never have' (Suro et al. 2002: 17).

Another set of proposals seeks largely to cut out the financial middleman altogether. In 2002, the Bank of America began a low-cost service that allows people to use tellers, phone calls, or the Internet to send money to relatives in Mexico, who in turn can get cash from any of the 20,000 automated teller machines throughout the country (Wessel 2002). Naturally, this idea is only good for those with realistic access to such machines. A further idea is that of creating 'telecenters-cum-microbanks' in an array of village localities (Robinson 2001). In this way, it is proposed that a collectively managed and secure system of digital remittance pooling through Internet satellite facilities could considerably lower the transfer cost (from currently sometimes 20 per cent down to perhaps 5 per cent) while providing rural areas with microcredit and banking services. These centres might be appendices to established credit unions or local savings and loan institutions. 'On the back side of each village microbank is a telecenter—a public, low-cost access point for Internet and IP services, including telephony' (Robinson 2001: 4). These could have a role in local institutions and training programmes, especially as auxiliaries to schools, continuous education colleges, and health clinics.

Bangladesh's Grameen Bank is often regarded as an exemplary MFI (cf. Robinson 2001; Jain and Moore 2003). Grameen services 2.4 million borrowers—95 per cent of whom are women—through 1176 outlets. In recent years, the bank has branched into a variety of enterprises, including telecommunications (and the 'village phone' programme mentioned earlier). The combined facilities for microbanking, overseas transfers, and international telephony have great development potential, as concluded by one report for the Canadian International Development Agency:

> The Grameen Bank's long-term focus on providing electronic communication facilities between its head office, zonal offices and branch offices, together with the telecommunication infrastructure of GrameenPhone, are important steps in enabling it to provide safe electronic banking services that could assist with channelling remittances from overseas workers to their relatives in villages (Richardson et al. 2000: 28).

MFIs are certainly not a solution to all economic problems in developing countries, and they are not without their problems and failures (cf. Jain and Moore 2003). Nevertheless, MFIs and the innovations in technology surrounding them have much transformative potential steering remittances—perhaps particularly collective ones—towards optimal development outcomes.

Summary

Drawing on a variety of studies for the Inter-American Development Bank, Orozco (2001: 36) observes that 'The links established through remittances suggest radical changes are remaking the look of countries' economies'. Migrant-sending countries themselves certainly recognize this. Consequently, many have introduced policies to maximize their benefits; in this way, 'Cooperation to increase remittances, reduce the cost of transferring money, and matching that share of remittances that are invested could open a new era in cooperative economic development' (Widgren and Martin 2002: 223).

This section has focused on means through which patterns of immigrant transnationalism are re-institutionalizing (or have the potential to introduce) new local and national structures of development. Throughout many periods of migration, hometown associations have sent money back to villages for the repair of schools and churches. Now the sheer scale, kind, and degree of institutionalization (increasingly involving the sending state) and use of advanced telecommunications and cheap travel have meant that remittances can transform the nature and pace of local development in migrant-sending areas.

Several significant questions continue to concern the place of remittances, including how long remittances will continue to flow, and whether high levels of international migration are needed to sustain remittance levels. Most remittances worldwide continue to be sent by individuals, and these may indeed tail-off over time. Although this source of remittances will diminish, HTA or other forms of institutionalized collective remittance sending—particularly utilizing MFIs—may be better poised to persist and provide the broadest benefits.

Conclusion

The ties between the kinds of migrant transnational practices and modes of transformation suggested in this chapter reflect the progression of changes considered by Portes (2001: 191):

> Once migrant colonies become well established abroad, a flow of *transnational* economic and informational resources starts, ranging from occasional remittances to the emergence of a class of full-time transnational entrepreneurs. The cumulative effects of these dynamics come to the attention of national governments who reorient their *international* activities through embassies, consulates, and missions to recapture the loyalty of their expatriates and guide their investments and political mobilizations. The increased volume of demand created by migrant remittances and investments in their home countries support, in turn, the further expansion of the market for multinationals and encourage local firms to go abroad themselves, establishing branches in areas of immigrant concentration. (emphasis in original)

These and other processes described in this chapter will carry through into the near future. Many patterns of migrant transnationalism and their associated modes of transformation are likely to widen, intensify, and accelerate. The governments of migrant-sending and -receiving states will continue to address a range of migrant transnational practices with greater attention and policy intervention. Technological changes (especially the building and extension of infrastructures in developing countries) will make it ever easier and cheaper to communicate and exchange resources, including remittances, across borders, and at long distance. Hometown associations and other such diasporic organizations have become institutionalized to a degree that they will likely be sustained, and probably enhanced, over the next several years. Individuals within post-migration second and subsequent generations will probably not maintain the everyday orientations and practices of their migrant forebears, but such orientations and practices will continue to have an enduring impression on their identities, interests, and activities.

Each set of processes, it has been suggested, entails small-scale and everyday practices of individuals and groups. Incrementally and cumulatively, these practices may produce far-reaching modes of transformation affecting migrants, their families and communities in places of origin, and wider populations surrounding transnational networks.

Acknowledgements

The author wish to especially thank members of the Wissenschaftskolleg zu Berlin/Institute for Advanced Study, Berlin, for providing the superb conditions under which this paper was written. The author is also grateful to Heather Tinsley of TeleGeography, Inc., for her kind provision of data.

References

Al-Ali, N. (2002) 'Gender relations, transnational ties and rituals among Bosnian refugees', *Global Networks*, 2(3), 242–62.

Al-Ali, N., and Koser, K. (eds.) (2002) *New Approaches to Migration? Transnational Communities and the Transformation of Home*. London: Routledge.

Alarcón, R. (2001) *The Development of Home Town Associations in the United States and the Use of Social Remittances in Mexico* [Final Report]. Washington, DC: Inter-American Dialogue.

Albert, M., Jacobson, D., and Lapid, Y. (eds.) (2001) *Identities, Borders, Orders: Rethinking International Relations Theory*. Minneapolis: University of Minnesota Press.

Albrow, M. (1997) *The Global Age: State and Science beyond Modernity*. Cambridge: Polity Press.

Aleinikoff, T.A., and Klusmeyer, D. (2001) 'Plural nationality: facing the future in a migratory world', in Aleinikoff, T.A. and Klusmeyer, D. (eds.) *Citizenship Today*. Washington, DC: Carnegie Endowment for International Peace.

Arnold, F. (1992) 'The contribution of remittances to economic and social development', in Kritz, M.M., Lim, L.L., and Zlotnik, H. (eds.) *International Migration Systems*. Oxford: Clarendon, 205–20.

Ballard, R. (2003) 'The South Asian presence in Britain and its transnational connections', in Singh, G., Parekh, B., and Vertovec, S. (eds.) *Culture and Economy in the Indian Diaspora*. London: Routledge, 197–222.

Basch, L., Glick Schiller, N., and Szanton Blanc, C. (1994) *Nations Unbound: Transnational Projects, Postcolonial Predicaments and Deterritorialized Nation-States*. Amsterdam: Gordon and Breach.

Bauböck, R. (1994) *Transnational Citizenship: Membership and Rights in International Migration*. Aldershot: Edward Elgar.

——. (2003) 'Towards a political theory of migrant transnationalism', *International Migration Review*, 37, 700–23.

Beck, U. (2002) 'The cosmopolitan perspective: sociology in the Second Age of modernity', in Vertovec, S., and Cohen, R. (eds.) *Conceiving Cosmopolitanism*. Oxford: Oxford University Press, 61–85.

Bourdieu, P. (1977) *Outline of a Theory of Practice*. Cambridge: Cambridge University Press.

——. (1990) *The Logic of Practice*. Stanford: Stanford University Press.

Brown, L. (2003) 'Ethnic power', *Intele-CardNews*, January. www.intelecard.com.

Bryceson, D., and Vuorela, U. (eds.) (2002) *The Transnational Family: New European Frontiers and Global Networks*. Oxford: Berg.

Byman, D.L., Chalk, P., Hoffman, B., Rosenau, W., and Brannan, D. (2001) *Trends in Outside Support for Insurgent Movements*. Santa Monica, CA: Rand.

Caglar, A. (2001) 'Constraining metaphors and the transnationalisation of spaces in Berlin', *Journal of Ethnic and Migration Studies*, 27(4), 601–13.

——. (2002) 'Media corporatism and cosmopolitanism', in Vertovec, S., and Cohen, R. (eds.) *Conceiving Cosmopolitanism*, Oxford: Oxford University Press, 180–90.

Carnoy, M., and Castells, M. (2001) 'Globalization, the knowledge society, and the network state: Poulantzas at the millennium', *Global Networks*, 1(1), 1–18.

Castells, M. (1996) *The Rise of the Network Society*. Oxford: Blackwell.

——. (1997) *The Power of Identity*. Oxford: Blackwell.

Castles, S. (2001) 'Studying social transformation', *International Political Science Review*, 22(1), 13–32.

——. (2002) 'Migration and community formation under conditions of globalization', *International Migration Review*, 36(4), 1143–68.

Cornelius, W.A. (2001) 'Death at the border: efficacy and unintended consequences of US immigration control policy', *Population and Development Review*, 27(4), 661–85.

de la Cruz, V. (2002) 'Selling southward', *Intele-CardNews*, August. www.intelecard.com.

DeSipio, L. (2000) *Sending Money Home ... For Now: Remittances and Immigrant Adaptation in the United States*. Washington, DC: Inter-American Dialogue and the Tomás Rivera Policy Institute, Working Paper.

Duany, J. (2002) 'Mobile livelihoods: the sociocultural practices of circular migrants between Puerto Rico and the United States', *International Migration Review*, 36(2), 355–88.

Durand, J., Parrado, E.A., and Massey, D.S. (1996) 'Migradollars and development: a reconsideration of the Mexican case', *International Migration Review*, 30(2), 423–44.

Faist, T. (2000) *The Volume and Dynamics of International Migration and Transnational Social Spaces*. Oxford: Oxford University Press.

——. (2001) *Dual Citizenship as Overlapping Membership*. Malmö, Sweden: School of International Migration and Ethnic Relations, Willy Brandt Series of Working Papers 3/01.

FCC/Federal Communications Commission (2002) *Trends in Telephone Service* [Report]. Washington, DC: Federal Communications Commission.

Fitzgerald (2002) 'Locating the national and local in "transnationalism"', Paper presented at the UCLA Second Annual Interdisciplinary Conference on Race, Ethnicity and Immigration, Los Angeles.

Fitzgerald, D. (2000) *Negotiating Extra-Territorial Citizenship: Mexican Migration and the Transnational Politics of Community* [Monograph Series No. 2]. La Jolla, CA: Center for Comparative Immigration Studies.

Foner, N. (2000) *From Ellis Island to JFK: New York's Two Great Waves of Immigration*. New Haven, CT: Yale University Press.

Fouron, G., and Glick Schiller, N. (2001) 'All in the family: gender, transnational migration, and the nation state', *Identities*, 7(4), 539–82.

Frank, R., and Hummer, R.A. (2002) 'The other side of the paradox: the risk of low birth weight among infants of migrant and nonmigrant households within Mexico', *International Migration Review*, 36(3), 746–65.

Fritz, M. (1998) 'Pledging multiple allegiances', *Los Angeles Times*, 6 April.

Gammeltoft, P. (2002) 'Remittances and other financial flows to developing countries', *International Migration*, 40(5), 181–211.

Gardner, K. (1993) 'Desh-Bidesh: Sylheti images of home and away', *Man*, 28(1), 1–15.

——. (1995) *Global Migrants, Local Lives: Travel and Transformation in Rural Bangladesh*. Oxford: Clarendon Press.

——. (2002) 'Death of a migrant: transnational death rituals and gender among British Sylhetis', *Global Networks*, 2(3), 191–204.

Gardner, K., and Grillo, R. (2002) 'Transnational households and ritual: an overview', *Global Networks*, 2(3), 179–90.

Glick Schiller, N. (1999) 'Transmigrants and nation-states: something old and something new in the U.S. immigrant experience', in Hirschman, C., Kasinitz, P., and DeWind, J. (eds.) *The Handbook of International Migration*. New York: Russell Sage Foundation, 94–119.

Glick Schiller, N., and Fouron, G. (1998) 'Transnational lives and national identities: the identity politics of Haitian immigrants', in Smith, M.P., and Guarnizo, L.E. (eds.) *Transnationalism From Below*. New Brunswick, NJ: Transaction, 130–61.

Golbert, R. (2001) 'Transnational orientations from home: constructions of Israel and transnational space among Ukrainian Jewish youth', *Journal of Ethnic and Migration Studies*, 27(4), 713–31.

Goldring, L. (1998) 'The power of status in transnational social fields', in Smith, M.P., and Guarnizo, L.E. (eds.) *Transnationalism From Below*. New Brunswick, NJ: Transaction, 165–95.

——. (2001) 'The gender and geography of citizenship in Mexico-U.S. transnational spaces', *Identities*, 7(4), 501–37.

Grace, D. (2001) 'The development potential of remittances and the credit union difference', Paper presented at the Regional Conference Remittances as a Development Tool, Washington, DC: Multilateral Investment Fund, Inter-American Development Bank.

Guarnizo, L.E. (1997) 'The emergence of a transnational social formation and the mirage of return migration among Dominican transmigrants', *Identities*, 4(2), 281–322.

——. (2003) 'The economics of transnational living', *International Migration Review*, 37, 666–99.

Guarnizo, L.E., Portes, A., and Haller, W. (2003) 'Assimilation and transnationalism: determinants of transnational political action among contemporary migrants', *American Journal of Sociology*, 108, 1211–48.

Guillén, M.F. (2001) 'Is globalization civilizing, destructive or feeble? A critique of five key debates in the Social Science literature', *Annual Review of Sociology*, 27, 235–60.

Hagan, J.M. (1994) *Deciding to be Legal: A Maya Community in Houston*. Philadelphia, PA: Temple University Press.

Hansen, R., and Weil, P. (2002) 'Introduction: dual citizenship in a changed world: immigration, gender and social rights', in Hansen, R., and Weil, P. (eds.) *Dual Nationality, Social Rights and Federal Citizenship in the U.S. and Europe*. Oxford: Berghahn, 1–15.

Heisler, M.O. (2001) 'Now and then, here and there: migration and the transformation of identities, borders, and orders', in Albert, M., Jacobson, D., and Lapid, Y. (eds.) *Identities, Borders, Orders*. Minneapolis: University of Minnesota Press, 225–47.

Held, D., Mcgrew, A., Goldblatt, D., and Perraton, J. (1999) *Global Transformations: Politics, Economics and Culture*. Cambridge: Polity Press.

Hochschild, A.R. (2000) 'Global care chains and emotional surplus value', in Giddens, A., and Hutton, W. (eds.) *On the Edge: Globalization and the New Millennium*. London: Sage, 130–46.

Hoffman, B. (1998) *Inside Terrorism*. New York: Columbia University Press.

Hondagneu-Sotelo, P. (1994) *Gendered Transitions: Mexican Experiences of Immigration*. Berkeley: University of California Press.

Hondagneu-Sotelo, P., and Avila, E. (1997) '"I'm here, but I'm there": the meanings of Latina transnational motherhood', *Gender and Society*, 11(5), 548–71.

ILO/International Labour Organization (2000) *Making the Best of Globalization: Migrant Worker Remittances and Micro-finance* [Workshop Report]. Geneva: International Labour Organization, Social Finance Unit.

Intelecard (2003) 'One hot country' [Staff Report], *Intele-CardNews*, January. www.intelecard.com.

Itzigsohn, J., and Giorguli Saucedo, S. (2002) 'Immigrant incorporation and sociocultural transnationalism', *International Migration Review*, 36(3), 766–98.

Itzigsohn, J., Dore Cabral, C., Hernández Medina, E., and Vázquez, O. (1999) 'Mapping Dominican transnationalism: narrow and broad transnational practices', *Ethnic and Racial Studies*, 22(2), 316–39.

Jain, P., and Moore, M. (2003) *What Makes Microcredit Programmes Effective? Fashionable Fallacies and Workable Realities*. Brighton: Institute of Development Studies Working Paper 177.

Jenkins, R. (1992) *Pierre Bourdieu*. London: Routledge.

Jones, W.T. (1972) 'World views: their nature and their function', *Current Anthropology*, 13(1), 79–109.

Jones-Correa, M. (2001) 'Under two flags: dual nationality in Latin America and its consequences for naturalization in the United States', *International Migration Review*, 35(4), 997–1029.

Joppke, C. (1999) *Immigration and the Nation-State: The United States, Germany and Great Britain*. Oxford: Oxford University Press.

——. (ed.) (1998) *Challenge to the Nation-State: Immigration in Western Europe and the United States*. Oxford: Oxford University Press.

Kasinitz, P., Waters, M.C., Mollenkopf, J.H., and Anil, M. (2002) 'Transnationalism and the children of immigrants in contemporary New York', in Levitt, P., and Waters, M.C. (eds.) *The Changing Face of Home*. New York: Russell Sage Foundation, 96–122.

Kastoryano, R. (2002) 'Türken mit deutschem Pass: Sociological and political aspects of dual nationality in Germany', in Hansen, R., and Weil, P. (eds.) *Dual Nationality, Social Rights and Federal Citizenship in the U.S. and Europe*. Oxford: Berghahn, 158–75.

Kivisto, P. (2001) 'Theorizing transnational migration: a critical review of current efforts', *Ethnic and Racial Studies*, 24(4), 549–77.

Koopmans, R., and Statham, P. (2001) *How National Citizenship Shapes Transnationalism: A Comparative Analysis of Migrant Claims-Making in Germany, Great Britain and the Netherlands*'. Oxford: ESRC Transnational Communities Programme Working Paper WPTC-01-10. www.transcomm.ox.ac.uk.

Koser, K. (2002) 'From refugees to transnational communities?', in Al-Ali, N., and Koser, K. (eds.) *New Approaches to Migration?* London: Routledge, 138–52.

Koslowski, R. (2001) 'Demographic boundary maintenance in world politics: of international norms on dual nationality', in Albert, M., Jacobson, D., and Lapid, Y. (eds.) *Identities, Borders, Orders*. Minneapolis: University of Minnesota Press, 203–23.

Kyle, D. (2000) *Transnational Peasants: Migrations, Networks, and Ethnicity in Andean Ecuador*. Baltimore, MD: Johns Hopkins University Press.

Landolt, P. (2001) 'Salvadoran economic transnationalism: embedded strategies for household maintenance, immigrant incorporation, and entrepreneurial expansion', *Global Networks*, 1(3), 217–41.

Lapid, Y. (2001) 'Identities, borders, orders: nudging international relations theory in a new direction', in Albert, M., Jacobson, D., and Lapid, Y. (eds.) *Identities, Borders, Orders*. Minneapolis: University of Minnesota Press, 1–20.

Levitt, P. (2001a) 'Transnational migration: taking stock and future directions', *Global Networks*, 1(3), 195–216.

——. (2001b) *The Transnational Villagers*. Berkeley: University of California Press.

——. (2002) 'The ties that change: relations to the ancestral home over the life cycle', in Levitt, P., and Waters, M.C. (eds.) *The Changing Face of Home*. New York: Russell Sage Foundation, 123–44.

Levitt, P., and de la Dehesa, R (2003) 'Transnational migration and the redifinition of the state: variations and explanations', *Ethnic and Racial Studies*, 26, 587–611.

Levitt, P., and Waters, M.C. (2002) 'Introduction', in Levitt, P., and Waters, M.C. (eds.) *The Changing Face of Home*. New York: Russell Sage Foundation, 1–30.

Light, I., Zhou, M., and Kim, R. (2002) 'Transnationalism and American exports in an English-speaking world', *International Migration Review*, 36(3), 702–25.

Lima, F.H. (2001) 'Transnational families: institutions of transnational social space', in Pries, L. (ed.) *New Transnational Social Spaces*. London: Routledge, 77–93.

Lobel, O. (2003) 'Family geographies: global care chains, transnational parenthood and new legal challenges in an era of labour globalization', in Holder, J., and Harrison, J. (eds.) *Law and Geography*. Oxford: Oxford University Press, 156–78.

Lowell, B.L., and de la Garza, R.O. (2000) *The Developmental Role of Remittances in U.S. Latino Communities and in Latin American Countries* [Final Project Report]. Washington, DC: Inter-American Dialogue.

Mahler, S.J. (1998) 'Theoretical and empirical contributions toward a research agenda for transnationalism', in Smith, M.P., and Guarnizo, L.E. (eds.) *Transnationalism From Below*. New Brunswick, NJ: Transaction, 64–100.

——. (2000) 'Migration and transnational issues: recent trends and prospects for 2020', Hamburg: Institut für Iberoamerika-Kunde, CA 2020 Working Paper No. 4.

——. (2001) 'Transnational relationships: the struggle to communicate across borders', *Identities*, 7(4), 583–619.

Mahler, S.J., and Pessar, P.R. (2001) 'Gendered geographies of power: analyzing gender across transnational spaces', *Identities*, 7(4), 441–59.

Maira, S.M. (2002) *Desis in the House: Indian American Youth Culture in New York City*. Philadelphia, PA: Temple University Press.

Martin, S.F. (2001) 'Remittance flows and impact', paper presented at the Regional Conference on Remittances as a Development Tool, Multilateral Investment Fund, Inter-American Development Bank, Washington, DC.

Menjívar, C. (2002) 'Living in two worlds? Guatemalan-origin children in the United States and emerging transnationalism', *Journal of Ethnic and Migration Studies*, 28(3), 531–52.

Mensah, I.L., and Reed Smith, J. (2002) 'Distributors rule … or do they? Finding success in the volatile prepaid market', *Intele-CardNews*, April. www.intelecard.com.

Meyer, J.B., and Brown, M. (1999) *Scientific Diasporas: A New Approach to the Brain Drain*. Paris: UNESCO-MOST Discussion Paper No. 41.

Meyers, D.W. (1998) *Migrant Remittances to Latin America: Reviewing the Literature*. Washington, DC: Inter-American Dialogue and the Tomás Rivera Policy Institute, Working Paper.

Mohan, G. (2002) 'Diaspora and development', in Robinson, J. (ed.) *Development and Displacement*. Milton Keynes: Open University Press, 77–139.

Mohan, G., and Zack-Williams, A.B. (2002) 'Globalisation from below: conceptualising the role of the African diasporas in Africa's development', *Review of African Political Economy*, 92, 211–36.

Morawska, E. (1999) *The New-Old Transmigrants, Their Transnational Lives, and Ethnicization: A Comparison of 19th/20th and 20th/21st C Situations*. Florence: European University Institute Working Papers EUF No. 99/2.

Motomura, H. (1998) 'Alienage classifications in a nation of immigrants: three models of "permanent" residence', in Pickus, N.M.J. (ed.) *Immigration and Citizenship in the Twenty-First Century*. Lanham, MA: Rowman & Littlefield, 199–222.

Mountz, A., and Wright, R.A. (1996) 'Daily life in the transnational migrant community of San Agustín, Oaxaca, and Poughkeepsie, New York', *Diaspora*, 5(3), 403–28.

Nagel, C.R. (2002) 'Geopolitics by another name: immigration and the politics of assimilation', *Political Geography*, 21(8), 971–87.

Orellana, M.F., Thorne, B., Chee, A., and Lam, W.S.E. (2001) 'Transnational childhoods: The participation of children in processes of family migration', *Social Problems*, 48(4), 572–91.

Orozco, M. (2000a) *Latino Hometown Associations as Agents of Development in Latin America* [Final Report]. Washington, DC: Inter-American Dialogue.

——. (2000b) *Remittances and Markets: New Players and Practices*. Washington, DC: Inter-American Dialogue and the Tomás Rivera Policy Institute, Working Paper.

——. (2001) 'Globalization and migration: the impact of family remittances in Latin America', paper presented at the Inter-American Foundation/UN ECLAC/World Bank conference on Approaches to Increasing the Productive Value of Remittances, Washington, DC.

——. (2002) *Attracting Remittances: Market, Money and Reduced Costs* [Report]. Washington, DC: Multilateral Investment Fund of the Inter-American Development Bank.

Østergaard-Nielsen, E. (2001) 'Turkish and Kurdish transnational political mobilisation in Germany and the Netherlands', *Global Networks*, 1(3), 261–82.

——. (2003a) *Transnational Politics: Turks and Kurds in Germany*. London: Routledge.

——. (2003b) 'International migration and sending countries: key issues and themes', in Østergaard-Nielsen, E. (ed.) *Sending Countries and International Migration*. Basingstoke: Palgrave, 3–30.

Pickus, N.M.J. (1998) 'Introduction', in Pickus, N.M.J. (ed.) *Immigration and Citizenship in the Twenty-First Century*. Lanham, MA: Rowman & Littlefield, xvii–xxxiii.

Piracha, M., and Vickerman, R. (2002) *Borders, Migration and Labour Market Dynamics in a Changing Europe* [Final Project Report]. Economic and Social Research Council (UK).

Portes, A. (2001) 'The debates and significance of immigrant transnationalism', *Global Networks*, 1(3), 181–93.

——. (2003) 'Theoretical convergencies and empirical evidence in the study of immigrant transnationalism', *International Migration Review*, 37, 874–92.

Portes, A., and Landolt, P. (2000) 'Social capital: promise and pitfalls of its role in development', *Journal of Latin American Studies*, 32(2), 529–47.

Portes, A., Guarnizo, L.E., and Landolt, P. (1999) 'The study of transnationalism: pitfalls and promises of an emergent research field', *Ethnic and Racial Studies*, 22(2), 217–37.

Portes, A., Haller, W., and Guarnizo, L.E. (2002) 'Transnational entrepreneurs: the emergence and determinants of an alternative form of immigrant economic adaptation', *American Sociological Review*, 67, 278–98.

Puri, S., and Ritzema, T. (1999) *Migrant Worker Remittances, Micro-finance and the Informal Economy: Prospects and Issues*. Geneva: International Labour Organization, Social Finance Unit, Working Paper 21.

Rapport, N., and Dawson, A. (eds.) (1998) *Migrants of Identity: Perceptions of Home in a World of Movement*. Oxford: Berg.

Riccio (2001) 'From "ethnic group" to "transnational community"? Senegalese migrants' ambivalent experiences and multiple trajectories', *Journal of Ethnic and Migration Studies*, 27(4), 583–99.

Riccio, B. (1999) *Senegalese Transmigrants and the Construction of Immigration in Emilia-Romagna (Italy)*, DPhil. Thesis, Social Anthropology, University of Sussex.

Richardson, D., Ramirez, R. , and Haq, M. (2000) *Grameen Telecom's Village Phone Programme: A Multi-media Case Study* [Final Report]. Hull: Canadian International Development Agency.

Robinson, M.S. (2001) *The Microfinance Revolution: Sustainable Finance for the Poor*. Washington, DC: The World Bank and the Open Society Institute.

Robinson, S.S. (2001) 'Rethinking telecenters: knowledge demands, marginal markets, microbanks, and remittance flows', *On the Internet*, March/April. www.isoc.org/oti.

Rogers, A. (1999a) 'Capture of PKK leader causes worldwide Kurdish protest', *Traces*, 5. www.transcomm.ox.ac.uk/traces/issue5.htm.

——. (1999b) 'Voting from abroad: airlifts and Internet', *Traces*, 6. www.transcomm.ox.ac.uk/traces/issue6.htm.

——. (1999c) 'Remittances and underground banking in Asian economies', *Traces*, 6. www.transcomm.ox.ac.uk/traces/issue6.htm.

——. (2000) 'Mexico's historic elections spill over into the USA', *Traces*, 10. www.transcomm.ox.ac.uk/traces/issue10.htm.

——. (2001a) 'Competition over wire transfer business in N. America and Asia', *Traces*, 13. www.transcomm.ox.ac.uk/traces/issue13.htm.

——. (2001b) 'Gujaratis overseas respond to earthquake disaster', *Traces*, 13. www.transcomm.ox.ac.uk/traces/issue13.htm.

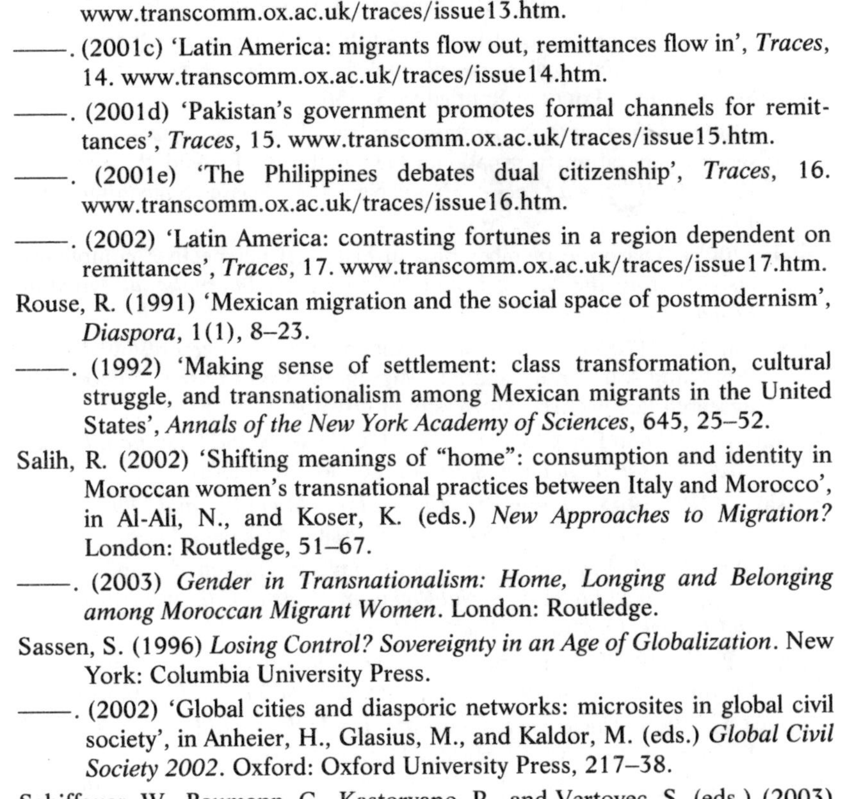

——. (2001c) 'Latin America: migrants flow out, remittances flow in', *Traces*, 14. www.transcomm.ox.ac.uk/traces/issue14.htm.

——. (2001d) 'Pakistan's government promotes formal channels for remittances', *Traces*, 15. www.transcomm.ox.ac.uk/traces/issue15.htm.

——. (2001e) 'The Philippines debates dual citizenship', *Traces*, 16. www.transcomm.ox.ac.uk/traces/issue16.htm.

——. (2002) 'Latin America: contrasting fortunes in a region dependent on remittances', *Traces*, 17. www.transcomm.ox.ac.uk/traces/issue17.htm.

Rouse, R. (1991) 'Mexican migration and the social space of postmodernism', *Diaspora*, 1(1), 8–23.

——. (1992) 'Making sense of settlement: class transformation, cultural struggle, and transnationalism among Mexican migrants in the United States', *Annals of the New York Academy of Sciences*, 645, 25–52.

Salih, R. (2002) 'Shifting meanings of "home": consumption and identity in Moroccan women's transnational practices between Italy and Morocco', in Al-Ali, N., and Koser, K. (eds.) *New Approaches to Migration?* London: Routledge, 51–67.

——. (2003) *Gender in Transnationalism: Home, Longing and Belonging among Moroccan Migrant Women*. London: Routledge.

Sassen, S. (1996) *Losing Control? Sovereignty in an Age of Globalization*. New York: Columbia University Press.

——. (2002) 'Global cities and diasporic networks: microsites in global civil society', in Anheier, H., Glasius, M., and Kaldor, M. (eds.) *Global Civil Society 2002*. Oxford: Oxford University Press, 217–38.

Schiffauer, W., Baumann, G., Kastoryano, R., and Vertovec, S. (eds.) (2003) *Civil Enculturation: State, School and Ethnic Difference in Four European Countries*. Oxford: Berghahn.

Schuck, P.H. (1998) 'Plural citizenships', in Pickus, N.M.J. (ed.) *Immigration and Citizenship in the Twenty-First Century*. Lanham, MA: Rowman & Littlefield, 149–91.

Shain, Y. (1999) *Marketing the American Creed Abroad: Diasporas in the U.S. and Their Homelands*. Cambridge: Cambridge University Press.

Skeldon, R. (1997) *Migration and Development: A Global Perspective*. Harlow: Longman.

Smelser, N.J. (1998) 'Social transformations and social change', *International Social Science Journal*, 156, 173–8.

Smith, M.P., and Guarnizo, L.E. (eds.) (1998) *Transnationalism From Below*. New Brunswick, NJ: Transaction.

Smith, R. (1998) 'Transnational localities: community, technology and the politics of membership within the context of Mexico and U.S. migration', in Smith, M.P., and Guarnizo, L.E. (eds.) *Transnationalism From Below*. New Brunswick, NJ: Transaction, 196–238.

——. (2001) 'Comparing local-level Swedish and Mexican transnational life: an essay in historical retrieval', in Pries, L. (ed.) *New Transnational Social Spaces*. London: Routledge, 37–58.

——. (2002) 'Life course, generation, and social location as factors shaping second-generation transnational life', in Levitt, P., and Waters, M.C. (eds.) *The Changing Face of Home*. New York: Russell Sage Foundation, 145–67.

——. (2003) 'Diasporic memberships in historical perspective: comparative insights from the Mexican and Italian cases', *International Migration Review*, 37, 724–59.

Sørensen, N.N. (2000) 'Notes on transnationalism', paper presented at the Workshop on Transnational Migration: Comparative Theory and Research Perspectives, University of Oxford.

Sørensen, N.N., and Fog Olwig, K. (eds.) (2001) *Work and Migration: Life and Livelihoods in a Globalizing World*. London: Routledge.

Soysal, Y.N. (1994) *Limits of Citizenship: Migrants and Postnational Membership in Europe*. Chicago: University of Chicago Press.

Spiro, P.J. (2002) 'Embracing dual nationality', in Hansen, R., and Weil, P. (eds.) *Dual Nationality, Social Rights and Federal Citizenship in the U.S. and Europe*. Oxford: Berghahn, 19–33.

Stalker, P. (2000) *Workers without Frontiers: The Impact of Globalization on International Migration*. Geneva: International Labour Organization.

Strange, S. (1996) *The Retreat of the State: The Diffusion of Power in the World Economy*. New York: Cambridge University Press.

Suro, R., Bendixen, S., Lowell, B.L., and Benavides, D.C. (2002) *Billions in Motion: Latino Immigrants, Remittances and Banking* [Report]. Washington, DC: Pew Hispanic Centre and Multilateral Investment Fund.

Taylor, J.E. (1999) 'The new economics of labour migration and the role of remittances in the migration process', *International Migration*, 37(1), 63–88.

The Economist (2003) 'Special report: diasporas. A world of exiles', 4 January, 25–7.

Thränhardt, D. (2002) 'Prophecies, *Ius Soli* and dual citizenship: interpreting the changes in the German citizenship system', paper presented at the Workshop on Transnational Ties and Identities Past and Present, Netherlands Institute for Advanced Study, Wassenaar.

UNPD (2002) *International Migration 2002*. New York: Population Division, Department of Economic and Social Affairs, United Nations.

UNPD/United Nations Population Division (1998) *International Migration Policies*. New York: Population Division, Department of Economic and Social Affairs, United Nations.

van Doorn, J. (2001) *Migration, Remittances and Small Enterprise Development*. Geneva: International Labour Organization.

Vertovec, S. (1999a) 'Conceiving and researching transnationalism', *Ethnic and Racial Studies*, 22(2), 447–62.

——. (1999b) 'Introduction', in Vertovec, S. (ed.) *Migration and Social Cohesion*. Cheltenham: Edward Elgar, xi–xxxvii.

——. (2000) *Rethinking Remittances*. Oxford: ESRC Transnational Communities Programme Working Paper WPTC-2K-15. www.transcomm.ox.ac.uk.

——. (2001) 'Transnationalism and identity', *Journal of Ethnic and Migration Studies*, 27(4), 573–82.

——. (2002) *Transnational Networks and Skilled Labour Migration*. Oxford: ESRC Transnational Communities Programme Working Paper WPTC-02-02. www.transcomm.ox.ac.uk.

——. (2003) 'Migration and other forms of transnationalism: towards conceptual cross-fertilization', *International Migration Review*, 37, 641–65.

Vertovec, S., and Cohen, R. (eds.) (2002) *Conceiving Cosmopolitanism: Theory, Context and Practice*. Oxford: Oxford University Press.

Vickerman, R. (2002) 'Migration myths', *The Guardian*, 10 December.

Voigt-Graf, C. (2002) *The Construction of Transnational Spaces: Travelling between India, Fiji and Australia*, PhD Thesis, Geography, University of Sydney.

Wessel, D. (2002) 'Banking on technology for the poor', *Wall Street Journal*, 2 May.

Widgren, J., and Martin, P. (2002) 'Managing migration: the role of economic instruments', *International Migration*, 40(5), 213–29.

Wiltshire, K. (2001) 'Management of social transformations: introduction', *International Political Science Review*, 22(1), 5–11.

Wolfe, D. (2002) 'Card usage climbs', *Intele-CardNews*, January. www.intelecard.com.

World Bank, The (2001) *Migrants' Capital for Small-Scale Infrastructure and Small Enterprise Development in Mexico*. Washington, DC: The World Bank.

Xiang, B. (2001) 'Structuration of Indian information technology professionals' migration to Australia: an ethnographic study', *International Migration*, 39, 73–88.

Zabin, C., and Rabadan, L.E. (1998) *Mexican Hometown Associations and Mexican Immigrant Political Empowerment in Los Angeles*. Washington, DC: The Aspen Institute, Nonprofit Sector Research Fund Working Paper 98–042.

Zhou, M. (1997) '"Parachute kids" in Southern California: the educational experience of Chinese children in transnational families', *Educational Policy*, 12, 682–704.

4

The Contemporary Discourse of Diaspora Studies

Khachig Tölölyan

My discussion of the current state of diaspora studies must note, without the luxury of further elaboration, that multidisciplinary[1] area studies have proliferated for several reasons: the internal dynamics and theoretical urgencies generated by scholarly inquiry; the needs and demands of academic administrators; external sponsors such as the US federal government and other institutions driven by policy; and political and identitarian constituencies both in the university and in American and other societies. As a result, area studies are frequently nagged by the possibility that it lacks intellectual coherence, both because of its many patrons and clients and because its methods have been created by the disaggregation of disciplinary enterprises and the (occasionally contingent) reaggregation of some portions thereof in entities labelled 'studies'.

Despite these factors, and although they tend to be characterized by a seemingly unwieldy diversity of personnel and research agendas, there are several reasons why the multidisciplinary area studies programmes produced by bricolage are held together. First, the sponsors, consumers, and users of these new constellations of knowledge, ranging from governments to students motivated by issues gathered under the umbrella of 'identity', have imposed a certain direction and 'discipline' on these programmes. Second, the emerging multidisciplinary studies programmes have always been able to count on some scholars to remain uneasily aware of the makeshift emergence of their new fields and so to remain self-critical at a theoretical level. The debates they have repeatedly initiated by asking what are the discourse and object of knowledge proper to their fields have created a certain cohesion: areas of inquiry can be united not just by agreement but also by persistent disagreements and debates that produce intellectual community without the illusion of false unity.

Diaspora studies share many of these characteristics. It emerged in fragmentary fashion, without fanfare or theoretical self-consciousness, as earlier disciplines dealing with nation, ethnicity, race, migration, and postcolonialism felt the need to adjust their methods and categories to the pressures of new transnational and global phenomena; ironically, they found a twenty-three-hundred-year-old concept, 'diaspora', to be suitable to their needs. The publication of the first issue of *Diaspora: A Journal of Transnational Studies*, in May 1991, provides a convenient marker for the consolidation of the field, whose conceptual vocabulary has been productively beset by several tensions, which have been mentioned in this chapter. The most important, and with which this chapter is concerned, are those between dispersion and diaspora; the *emic* 'study of diasporas' and the *etic* field of diaspora studies; disciplinary appropriations and inflections of diaspora; and the emergence of a supradisciplinary discourse of diaspora. An analysis of these is best situated in a brief narrative of the field's emergence.

At a late stage of the field's emergence, in 1993, Luigi Luca Cavalli-Sforza and Francesco Cavalli-Sforza published *The Great Human Diasporas: The History of Dispersion and Evolution*.[2] Their title takes the Greek word *diaspora* that Jews of Alexandria first used around 250 BCE to signify their own scattering away from the homeland into *galut*, or collective exile, and makes it very nearly indistinguishable from the 'dispersion' of their subtitle. By identifying the waves of protohuman and human migrations out of Africa by these two terms in this way, the authors claim either and both as signifiers for any combination of mobility, scattering beyond a territory of origin, and resettlement elsewhere. Though conceptually untidy, this is one of the ways *diaspora* is commonly used today. For example, the dispersion of poor and often black people from New Orleans, Louisiana, after Hurricane Katrina is now routinely called 'the Katrina diaspora'.[3]

This is problematic. Until recently, 'dispersion' was a very large category of which diaspora was a specific subset, a part not identical with the whole. Its paradigmatic example was the Jewish diaspora; the other two 'classical' or traditional diasporas were the Armenian and the Greek.[4] In this discursive field, a diaspora was understood as a social formation engendered by catastrophic violence or, at the very least, by coerced expulsion from a homeland, followed by settlement in other countries and among alien host societies, and, crucially, capped by generations of survival as a distinct community that worked hard to maintain its old identity or to create new ones that sustained its difference from the host society. Finally, diasporas were identified by their efforts to retain contact with kin communities elsewhere and with the homeland.[5]

This definition was constraining. It excluded the Indian and Chinese overseas communities, communities of African origin, and many more. It began to enlarge in 1965, when the historian George Shepperson gave a paper at a conference in Dar-es-Salaam, Tanzania, in which he pointed out that people of African origin did in fact constitute a diaspora—their departure from their homeland was coerced, their suffering indisputable and massive, and their continuing distinctness as a community was perpetuated by racism.[6]

I cannot recapitulate here the details of how the extension of the term *diaspora* to old and new dispersions gathered momentum from then on. Today, some four decades later, there are around three dozen transnational communities in which either their own intellectuals, artists, and political elites use the term *diaspora* to describe themselves or scholars studying them do so, or both. This extension is due to a change in the prestige of the term, which once connoted deracination, sorrow, and powerlessness, and it blurs several distinctions that should continue to matter, whatever terminology is employed.[7] In my own work as a scholar and as an editor of *Diaspora*, I have come to accept, with many misgivings, the increasing collapse of the distinction between diaspora and dispersion. When ethnics, exiles, expatriates, refugees, asylum seekers, labour migrants, queer communities, domestic service workers, executives of transnational corporations, and transnational sex workers are all labelled diasporas, the struggle to maintain distinctions is lost, only to resume in another guise. It becomes displaced into a new effort to recall how very different the communities gathered under the label diaspora remain. Several of the most persistent distinctions and the issues they continue to raise must be briefly considered.

First, a diaspora that is born of catastrophe inflicted on the collective suffers trauma and usually becomes a community to which the work of memory, commemoration, and mourning is central, shaping much of its cultural production and political commitment. It is helpful to distinguish it from a dispersion that is the consequence of individual and chain migration, motivated by economic reasons; in such communities, nostalgia can be strong, but commemoration and collective mourning are less prominent.[8]

Second, an ethnic community produced by migration should be distinguished from one that is diasporic (be it Jewish or Tamil, Armenian or Haitian). All diasporic communities are also ethnic communities, but not all ethnic communities are diasporic; to put it another way, when strictly defined, diasporas are a specific subset of ethnic minorities. The defining characteristics of diasporas are, first, a culture and a collective identity that preserves elements of the homeland's language, or religious, social, and cultural practice, either intact or, as time passes, in mixed, bicultural forms; the best known subset of biculturalism is denoted by the term *hybridity*. By contrast, ethnic groups at best exhibit a diluted form of biculturalism (which is further discussed in this chapter).

A third salient characteristic of diasporas, especially those dispersed by catastrophic destruction in the homeland, is a rhetoric of restoration and return that, in practice, takes the form of a sustained and organized commitment to maintaining relations with kin communities elsewhere, and with the homeland, to which diasporans either return literally or, more commonly, 're-turn' without actual repatriation: that is, they turn again and again towards the homeland through travel, remittances, cultural exchange, and political lobbying and by various contingent efforts to maintain other links with the homeland. When later generations of diasporans cease to feel that they are guests in a host society because they feel entirely at home in it as citizens, they still maintain links with the 'homeland' of their ancestors.[9] In some instances, as in many communities of the Black Atlantic, consciously organized ties with homeland territories become impossible to sustain for some generations, but they can be revived, at least among a minority, under certain circumstances. Ethnic communities are not characterized by such sustained contact with the homeland.

Fourth, the accommodating redefinition of diaspora as dispersion raises conceptual problems. When Walter Connor defines *diaspora* simply as 'that segment of a people living outside the homeland', he typifies a problem characteristic of much contemporary diaspora discourse.[10] He neglects the possibility that at a certain point, after several generations, the descendants of the first generation of emigrants cease to be a 'segment' of the homeland's population in any meaningful sense; to claim that they continue to be such a segment only because they share (an increasingly mixed) gene pool incurs a certain danger of biologism, which lingers in most easy-going definitions of diaspora.

I concede that there is an element of terminological fussiness here, but I would argue that it pays good dividends. It allows one to track the defining elements of an uncertain, indeterminate process of diasporization, that is, a process of becoming a part of diaspora, rather than assuming its existence in any form of dispersion. It may be best to think of diaspora not as the name of a fixed concept and social formation but as a process of collective identification and form of identity, marked by ever-changing differences that chart the shifting boundaries of certain communities hierarchically embedded as enclaves with porous boundaries within other larger communities. To make this abstraction more concrete, I must first define some other premises.

Diasporicity manifests itself in relations of differences. The diasporic community sees itself as linked to, but different from, those among whom it has settled; eventually, it also comes to see itself as powerfully linked to, but in some ways different from, the people in the homeland as well. In the countries of settlement, either such difference is sustained by persecution and the rejection of assimilation by the majority among whom the diasporic community settles or, when assimilation is permitted, even encouraged, the diasporic community chooses to do cultural and political work in order to sustain crucial kinds of differences.[11] The precise nature and intensity of these efforts depend on the policies of the empires or nation-states hosting a particular diaspora. When possible, diasporic communities seek integration and citizenship without assimilation. They do this by policing their own communal boundaries and encouraging endogamy and bilingualism, strict adherence to tradition, and displays of loyalty to old and new identities, however hybridized. In long-lasting mobilized diasporas, to use John Armstrong's term, their cultural and political reproduction is organized, institutionalized, funded, and also carried out by the work of artists, performers, political entrepreneurs, clerics, and other elites working with a more or less cooperative population.[12]

The complex constellation of practices and relations that mark difference from the surrounding society and underscore a sometimes fictional 'sameness' shared within the community change over time and space. We are different, the first immigrants say, from the people of this place where we have settled. We care about, remain connected to, and behave with the values of the population of the homeland; in this case, it is our first generation of immigration. In subsequent generations, this feeling of sameness and easy kinship becomes impossible to maintain. Both the dispersed and the people in the homeland change. Among the dispersed, ethnicization and assimilation set in. The alternative to these, successful diasporization, happens when effect is no longer enough or natural and when the dispersed can no longer strongly miss third cousins whom they barely know or feel nostalgia for a homeland they have visited rarely and whose language they can no longer speak. Dispersions that successfully transform themselves into diasporas do so during these transitional periods, which come no earlier than the second and third generations, when it becomes obvious to the diaspora that it can no longer presume an automatically shared 'sameness' with the people in the homeland (though some continue to claim an essentialist identity, or 'blood' and the like). When a significant number of individuals, especially among the cultural elite, acknowledge how much everyone has changed, and in what different directions they have gone, then the tenor and volume of the discourse of identification changes and a specifically diasporic set of discursive practices emerges: either old national tropes are refurbished or new fictions of shared identity are invented. The community endures as a distinct diaspora, not because its members individually remember grandmother or the village, but thanks to the collective work of memory and commemoration, the performance of difference, the cultivation of ideologies of identity, and the institutionalization of practices of connection to the homeland. In later stages and among the most sophisticated diasporans, a variant of identification, of a form of special caring that can be called political solidarity, can supplement or even replace the need for claiming a shared identity. As mentioned earlier, most members of such achieved diasporas do not generally aspire to permanently return, but rather they turn insistently towards the homeland and kin communities elsewhere in multiple forms of connection, such as travel and communication, in political solidarity, in tension and debate, and do so long after the intimate ties with and experiential memories of the original migrant generations have faded. Diasporas are resolutely multi-local and polycentric, in that what happens to kin communities in other areas of dispersion as well as in the homeland insistently matters to them.[13]

I make a final qualification. What I have described applies to dispersions as they have been known. It may well be that it will no longer apply to some new ones, such as the Latin American, Caribbean, or East and South Asian communities in Canada and the United States. If sizable migration continues uninterrupted, then even as ethnicization and assimilation claim some members, new ones will replace them, and the social formation will persist without needing to develop all the features that ensure diasporization. If a true transnational social field can persist after several generations, whether between Hong Kong and Vancouver or Port-au-Prince, Haiti, and Miami, Florida, thanks to continued ease of communication, travel, investment, endogamy, and life on a circuit between home and homeland, new and different outcomes will probably ensue.[14]

However, even in the era of highly mobile transnationalism and globalization, sedentariness and location continue to matter more than the most ardent diasporists are willing to acknowledge. The great diasporic metropolises—say, New York for Jews, San Francisco for Chinese, and Paris for Maghrebis—are locations whose people may change but whose institutions endure, and they enable forms of religious, cultural, and economic production that contribute a great deal to the continuity of the more mobile diasporic populations. Nor does mobility by itself guarantee the persistence of diaspora. Robert Smith's work on the weakening of diasporic commitment already apparent among some second-generation Mexicans in New York and Richard Alba and Victor Knee's argument that assimilation remains a powerful force in contemporary America must qualify transnational enthusiasms concerning mobility as a guarantor of diasporicity.[15]

Finally, even when differences persist in certain diasporas, they do so in wholly new forms. In France, for example, globalization has not necessarily enabled second- and third-generation Moroccan, Algerian, or Tunisian diasporas to persist in unproblematic ways. Knowledge of Arabic has weakened rapidly, as have bilocal ties. However, France's unwillingness to integrate the immigrants, now aggravated by the difficulty of overcoming concerns about Islamic terrorism, appears to be leading to the emergence of a new kind of Franco-Muslim enclave society that is neither a diaspora of any one North African country nor a diasporic fragment of a traditional Muslim society.[16]

This discussion of contemporary diasporicity would be incomplete without reflection on transnationalism and its associated border crossing that is characteristic of diasporas, which have existed since ancient times by virtue of movement and exchange across the borders of societies and empires. As Gabriel Sheffer and William Miles have argued, there were trans-state diasporas before there could be transnational ones, because there were states and empires long before there were nation-states.[17] I use the term *transnational* differently from many colleagues, in part because the history of the word obliges me to do so. Its first use comes in an essay of 1918 by the American intellectual Randolph Bourne, but its recent origin is in the practice of 1960s corporations, principally the now defunct ITT (International Telephone and Telegraph), then headed by Harold Geneen.[18] In such corporations, *transnational* was used intramurally to distinguish certain corporate practices and entities from the international and the multinational.

Political scientists picked it up in 1969, when James Rosenau of the University of Southern California (USC) first used it. By 1973, he headed the small Center for Transnational Studies at USC, while two very famous political scientists, Joseph Nye and Robert Keohane, used the word differently yet again, to mean 'interdependence'. The first example of interdependence they offered was the relationship that then prevailed between Canada and the United States.[19] Subsequently, the term was picked up by other political scientists, who applied it to phenomena such as transnational terrorism; Palestinian airline hijackings, which had begun in 1968, and Armenian terrorism, which had begun in 1975, were both referred to as transnational by the late 1970s. When the journal *Transnational Corporations* was founded with support of United Nations in the late 1980s, the term became a permanent fixture of economic and political, and later also sociological, discourse.[20] Though it is often used carelessly as a synonym for 'globalization', *transnational* properly designates an action or a relation that involves the crossing of a national border by a non-state entity. Transnational phenomena involve the crossing of one or more state boundaries by actors of whom at least one is not a state organization but rather an individual, a family, a corporation, a non-governmental organization, or indeed any other non-state organization, be it a terrorist group or a social movement.

Trans did not and does not mean *supra*. The European Union is a supranational construct, not a transnational entity. I teach a course titled DTG: Diaspora, Transnationalism, and Globalization, and I always begin by insisting that the first term is nested in the next, larger term, and the second in the third, like Russian dolls. Fortunately, there is uncommon consensus about the key elements of globalization. It refers to the techniques of rapid and inexpensive transport and communication that make the transfer of information, ideas, capital, goods, and people ever cheaper and faster, if not always instantaneous. The beginning of contemporary globalization is marked by the invention of the shipping container in 1956 and capped by the invention of the Web in 1989. Like Nancy Foner, Gregory Jusdanis, Niall Ferguson, and others, I am quite willing to consider pre-1914 globalization a fact, but one that was decisively interrupted and resumed half a century later in a different form.

Bernard Shaw's witticism, to the effect that the British and Americans are divided by the illusion that they share a common language, applies to the discursive languages that divide diaspora studies today; what I have been trying to do is provide a guide to those elements of its conceptual vocabulary that I find indispensable. To finish doing so, I must also speak of the slightly different ways 'diasporists' use the notions of ethnicity and mobility.

All diasporics are ethnic, but all ethnics are not diasporic. Currently, Italian-Americans, for example, are ethnics. They may mark symbolic boundaries that preserve a collective identity other than the hegemonic one that dominates the larger society in which they live and which is, in fact, their home. Yet an ethnic community differs from a diaspora because the former lacks the latter's twin commitment to maintain connections with its homeland and its kin communities in other states and to sustain self-representation and the perpetuation of significant differences. At best, such commitment is manifested weakly, intermittently, and by individuals rather than the community as a whole. Italian-Americans' self-identification as 'Italian' manifests itself in fragmentary culinary, musical, religio-festive, and linguistic practices and rituals, many observed only on very special occasions, such as when parades are organized, flags are flown, and decals displayed. Individual Italian-Americans manifest concern for the well-being of relatives in other countries or in the homeland, and fraternal, *paisan*, or landsman-type organizations occasionally raise funds for the ancestral hometown or village. But they are highly unlikely to act in consistently organized ways to develop an agenda for *self-representation* in the political or cultural realm, either in the host land or across national boundaries. Organized protest against stereotypic representations of the Mafia in films is one of the few real but very intermittent efforts that Italian-American ethnics have undertaken on behalf of their cultural and political representation. The consciousness that underpins such action is absent, and the need for it not felt. When Benito Mussolini ruled Italy and sought to attack exiles in the Italian-American ethnic community who criticized him, the struggle between the two temporarily animated but did not durably alter the community's movement towards ethnicization.[21]

The lines separating ethnic behaviour from diasporic are not always clear-cut, and they shift in response to a complex dynamic. For example, the Cuban-American 'community' contains a few assimilated members, a larger number of ethnics, and an even larger group, whose size is fervently debated, that forms an 'exile community' committed to the overthrow of Cuban communism and to a physical return to the island; some of the exiles display the full range of diasporic behaviour, engage actively in political and cultural self-representation, and care about maintaining contact with Cuba and Cuban communities in other countries, such as Puerto Rico, Mexico, and Spain. I emphasize that the boundaries between these groups are not fixed but porous and fluid. They will continue to change as the change emerges in Cuba and in the United States' attitude towards Cuba. The size and commitment of exiles, ethnics, and diasporics waxes and wanes in response to both the internal dynamics of the community and in reaction to the policies, economy, and changing social and cultural allure of the host land and homeland.

Finally, in this survey of the conceptual vocabulary that characterizes the discourse of diaspora studies, I turn to 'mobility', fully agreeing with Shalini Puri's comment (at the Toronto conference where the first draft of this paper was presented) that it must always be remembered that a only small percentage of the people of the world are actually mobile migrants—she offered the figure 2.5 per cent. I can imagine reasons for disputing the exact figure, but the scale is on target. Yet some of the finest minds in the field, such as Arjun Appadurai and James Clifford, have inadvertently contributed to privileging a logic of mobility that has become oddly attached to denunciations of nationalism. Between 1990 and today, as the current discourse of diaspora studies was emerging, the Soviet Union and Yugoslavia collapsed and images of beastly behaviour by nationalists were everywhere; consequently, the language of nationalism was identified as the language of those who would commit ethnocide to achieve settled and rigid borders and of those who fancied themselves guardians of homogeneity and purity; meanwhile, diasporas came to be celebrated as exemplars or advocates of penetrated and porous borders, heterogeneity, hybridity, and, importantly, mobility. A disdain of the sedentary and the immobile diaspora (and their link to vile forms of nationalism) was barely restrained in the work of some students of diaspora who, paradoxically, thought of themselves as advocates of the local and the indigenous people.

In my recent work, I have found myself arguing against the logic of privileged mobility with a countering logic of the sedentary.[22] Specifically, I have been arguing that while certain diasporic elites celebrate their mobility and certainly know how to take socio-economic advantage of it, the advantages and costs of mobility need to be examined more carefully; those who pay the costs are often not the ones who enjoy its advantages. Global cultural flows translate too easily into other assumptions about easy mobility for all, especially when diasporas are being discussed in the context of globalization. Bill Maurer points out that 'discussions about globalization are founded on assumptions about movement', and these attach themselves inappropriately to discussions of diaspora.[23] As I have argued, just as electricity does not simply flow across a space but rather flows between relatively fixed nodes or poles whose differences enable the flow, so also transnational diasporic life requires nodes in its networks, nodes marked by a relative sedentariness and the differences produced in them; such nodes continue to enable the production of the cultural work that sustains diasporas, and that occurs only in situations that are more sedentary than the new rhetoric celebrates.[24] Both Pnina Werbner and I have argued that contemporary transnational diasporas require settled diasporic nodes in which a public sphere and civil society peculiar to them develop.[25] As several colleagues variously argued at the Toronto conference, some of the privilege that the new logic of spatialization and mobility has taken away must be restored to locality and place. Enthusiasms concerning mobility have delayed recognition of the immense tasks diasporas face and carry out locally.

The current discourse of diaspora studies is characterized, then, by some disagreement and divergent uses of its key concepts, such as diaspora and dispersion, ethnic and diasporic, transnational and global, mobility and sedentariness, network and node, and local and global. *Eppur si muove*; and yet diaspora studies flourishes even as these internal discontinuities persist. However, in that flourishing at least one 'external' discontinuity remains significant, yet insufficiently noted. It is the difference between the emic discourse that diasporas used to talk about themselves to themselves, in what I call the *study of diasporas*, and the more recent etic scholarly activity called diaspora studies.[26] The self-study of diasporas produced representations and various forms of self-knowledge, some embodied in quotidian practices, some in public performances, and others in oral and written archives and the thriving native-language press of groups such as the Armenians and the Chinese.[27] Such emic self-representation also flourishes on the Internet, the site of diasporic self-study that, being often conducted in English, is the one form of it that is explored by scholars studied nowadays, in particular with reference to the South Asian community.

Who represents diasporas—the community itself or scholars—matters. As the works of Louis Althusser and Pierre Macherey imply, the diasporic social domain that exists only when emic study and self-representation is going on takes a different shape when it is constituted as the object of knowledge of diasporic studies. At that point, theoretical conceptions, specialized terminologies, acknowledged and unacknowledged disciplinary interests and intentions, a will to knowledge, and a variety of methodologies combine to reformulate diasporas. Living diasporas are objects of knowledge that can, however, react: they talk back, not only to the way they are represented in media and the administrative-juridical languages of administration, but also to disciplinary, scholarly discourses. They become simultaneously objects of knowledge and cosubjects. Depending on the questions one asks, one must hope for more of one or the other.

A corollary of this point is that the object of knowledge in area studies is also always, in some sense, given and always, in another sense, created. For example, the territory and populations of the Middle East existed as sociopolitical domains before orientalism, and then Middle Eastern studies represented and transformed them into disciplinary objects. They continue to exist, but in subtle ways how they think of themselves, how they act, and what they are, is altered by the dialectic between self-study and the disciplinary and area studies emanating from powerful quarters.

Given these interactions, there is nothing preordained about the kind of diaspora studies that may emerge in the near future at centres like the new one whose founding at the University of Toronto occasioned this essay or in journals such as the one I edit. The outcome will depend on a configuration of factors too complex to catalogue, because they will include elements ranging from the unpredictable effects of post-9/11 security and immigration concerns to the simplifications that the all-too-powerful media will deploy to explain diasporas to their audience. However, despite such uncertainty emanating from potent non-academic settings, one can be sure that a particular set of elements within scholarship will also have an important role.

Of these, one will be the discipline-specific construction and valuation of diaspora, which differs widely in, for example, postcolonial literary studies and American sociology or in European historiography as contrasted with American anthropology. Another element will be the rapidly evolving conceptual vocabulary that disciplines exchange directly with one another or, more commonly, that they contribute through theorization to the common pool of tropes and ideas that is the core of the supradisciplinary discourse of diaspora studies. The final element from within the institutions of scholarship that will decide the shape and future of diaspora studies is the collection of multidisciplinary practices that include American studies or Canadian studies or Jewish studies, each of which turns to the study of diasporas from a perspective that often tries to finesse the distinction between ethnicity and diasporicity. It remains very difficult to generalize about the rapidly increasing number of fields that now define themselves with the suffix 'studies'. On my bookshelves, they range from the august ancestor of all area studies, classical studies, to post-Soviet studies, and in my university they include but are not limited to American studies, classical studies, ethnic studies, queer studies, women's studies (now renamed feminist, gender, and sexuality studies), German studies, Russian studies, and so forth. Each of these, for example, German studies as it deals with what began as a Turkish labour migration and is now a potent diaspora, has its own specific approach to diaspora studies, shaped by both local exigencies and the ideas and methods it draws from and contributes to the shared supradisciplinary procedures of diaspora studies, which thrives because of that exchange.[28]

Acknowledgement

The author thanks Ellen Rooney for her detailed comments and Ato Quayson for creating the occasion where an earlier version of this paper was delivered and for his patience as it was revised.

Notes

1. The more frequently used 'interdisciplinary' is almost always unjustified. In area studies, existing disciplines such as history and literature are brought to bear one after another, providing a binocular perspective on the topics studied, but without producing a truly new, hybrid method and object of knowledge.
2. Luigi Luca Cavalli-Sforza and Francesco Cavalli-Sforza, *The Great Human Diasporas: The History of Dispersion and Evolution* (Reading, MA: Addison-Wesley, 1993).
3. 'Hundreds of thousands of evacuees from the New Orleans area stranded in overcrowded hotels, motels and makeshift shelters and on highways across much of the South underscored a new reality on Tuesday: an extended *diaspora* of a city's worth of people, one rarely seen in the annals of urban disaster'. Kate Zenike and Judy Wolgren, 'In Search of a Place to Sleep, and News of Home', *New York Times*, 31 August 2005. The *New York Times* has repeatedly used the term since.
4. See Simon Dubnow's entry on 'Diaspora' in *Encyclopaedia of the Social Sciences*, ed. Edwin R. Seligman and Alvin Johnson (New York: Macmillan, 1931–1935), 3:126–30, for a formulation of the earlier consensus.
5. The classical paradigm also stipulated a desire by diasporans to return eventually to the homeland, but this was a desire ritually and rhetorically proclaimed, realized occasionally by individuals but very rarely on a

communal scale until the emergence of nationalism precipitated group movements to the homeland in the later nineteenth century.

6. Shepperson's paper was first published in *African Forum: A Quarterly Journal of Contemporary Affairs* 2 (1966): 76–93, which is not easily accessible. It is commonly known from a later version, 'The African Abroad or the African Diaspora', *Emerging Themes of African History*, ed. T.O. Ranger (London: Heinemann, 1968), 152–76.
7. That change in prestige is due to a dozen factors discussed in Khachig Tölölyan, 'Rethinking Diaspora(s)', *Diaspora: A Journal of Transnational Studies* 5 (1996): 3–37.
8. Of course, poverty functions as a form of coercion and initiates migrations that can lead to dispersion. But such dispersions, unless accompanied by catastrophes like the Irish famine in 1845, or the dire conditions of travel like those experienced by Indians shipped to the Caribbean after 1834, do not usually lead to cultures constructed around traumatic memory.
9. A terminological problem dogs diaspora studies when 'home' is at issue. The actual home of many diasporic peoples may be the United States or Canada, yet scholars continue to speak of such countries as the host land. For the first generation, this is true. But in the case of those born in these and similar receiving countries, where the extension of citizenship to the native-born is very nearly automatic (as it is not, say, for Kurds born in Germany), to speak of the United States or Canada as a host land after the first generation of migration is odd. To address this oddity, in my own work I now refer to the United States as my home and the home of its Armenian diaspora and to Armenia as the homeland (of my ancestors).
10. Walter Connor, 'The Impact of Homelands upon Diasporas', *Modern Diasporas in International Politics*, ed. Gabriel Sheffer (New York: St. Martin's, 1986), 16–46.
11. The former is most commonly the case when visible racial differences or major religious differences invite prejudicial exclusion—people of colour, Muslims, Jews, and others experience this regularly. In cases such as that of African slaves in America, even when homeland languages and kin ties are lost and religious and social practices survive in fragments, the discriminatory treatment suffices to sustain an ethnoracial community that can be reimbued with notions of diasporicity.
12. John Armstrong, 'Mobilized and Proletarian Diasporas', *American Political Science Review* 70 (1976): 393–408.
13. For a fine study of diasporic polycentrism among Armenians, see Sebouh Aslanian, *Dispersion History and the Polycentric Nation: The Role of Simeon Yerevantsi's Girk or Kochi Partavjar in the Armenian National Revival of the Eighteenth Century* (Venice: Bibliothèque d'Arménologie Bazmavep, 2004).

14. Exemplary in their demonstrations of the ways in which the transnational circuit sustains the transnational social field, altering both the receiving and the sending societies, are Roger Rouse's early study of the diaspora of the Mexican municipality of Aguililla in California, 'Mexican Migration and the Social Space of Postmodernism', *Diaspora* 1 (1991): 8–23; and Peggy Levitt's study of Dominicans in New England, *The Transnational Villagers* (Berkeley: University of California Press, 2000).
15. Richard Alba and Victor Knee, *Remaking the American Mainstream: Assimilation and Contemporary Immigration* (Cambridge, MA: Harvard University Press, 2003).
16. The debates about this new social formation, engendered in the French media by the scholarship of Olivier Roy, continues to rage, aggravated by *banlieue* riots and fears of terrorism. The language, musical culture, social structure, and political organization of this new social formation are unstable, under pressure by French state intervention, and impossible to characterize adequately at this time.
17. Gabriel Sheffer and William Miles, 'Francophonie and Zionism: A Comparative Study of Transnationalism and Trans-statism', *Diaspora* 7 (1998): 119–48.
18. Randolph Bourne, 'Trans-national America', *Atlantic Monthly* 118 (1916): 86–97.
19. Robert O. Keohane and Joseph Nye, 'The Complex Politics of Canadian-American Interdependence', in *Canada and the United States: Transnational and Transgovernmental Relations*, ed. Annette Baker Fox, Alfred O. Hero Jr., and Joseph S. Nye (New York: Columbia University Press, 1976).
20. Within sociology proper, the key texts that established the term were Nina Glick Schiller, Linda Basch, and Cristina Szanton Blanc, eds., *Towards a Transnational Perspective on Migration: Race, Class, Ethnicity, and Nationalism Reconsidered* (New York: New York Academy of Sciences, 1992); and Linda Basch, Nina Glick Schiller, and Cristina Szanton Blanc, *Nations Unbound: Transnational Projects, Postcolonial Predicaments and De-territorialized Nation-States* (Amsterdam: Gordon and Breach, 1994).
21. These comments on Italian-American ethnics paraphrase some passages in my 'Rethinking Diaspora(s): Stateless Power in the Transnational Moment', *Diaspora* 5 (1996): 3–37.
22. Khachig Tölölyan, 'Restoring the Logic of the Sedentary to Diaspora Studies', in *Les diasporas: 2000 ans d'histoire*, ed. Lisa Anteby-Yemeni, William Berthomiere, and Gabriel Sheffer (Rennes, France: Presses Universitaires de Rennes, 2005), 137–48.
23. Bill Maurer, 'A Fish Story: Rethinking Globalization in Virgin Gorda, British Virgin Islands', in *The Anthropology of Globalization: A Reader*, ed. Jonathan Xavier Inda and Renato Rosaldo (Oxford: Blackwell, 2002), 101.

24. Tölölyan, 'Restoring the Logic of the Sedentary'.
25. Pnina Werbner, 'The Place Which Is Diaspora: Chaordic Leapfrogging, Replicating, and Transnational Networking' (paper presented at the International Workshop on Transnationalism, University of Manchester, 16–18 May 1998).
26. I use the terms in their original sense, pioneered by the linguistic anthropologist Kenneth Pike in the 1950s and widely used until the 1970s. *Emic*, modelled on phonemic, refers to the perspective of the insider, the native user of a language, or, by extension, the discourse by which members of a diaspora talk about themselves to themselves as they study their own social formations. *Etic*, modelled on phonetic, refers to the discourse by which linguists discuss a language not their own, which they characterize by a professional terminology not known to native speakers; by extension, this refers to the discourse of diaspora studies, which the ordinary members and even elites of specific diasporas often fail to understand and, when they do, adopt selectively while disputing many of its assertions. The reluctance to acknowledge such disputes—which would reveal the racism and nationalism found in some diaspora populations—mars the discourse of several utopianist scholars of diaspora.
27. See, e.g., Sheng-mei Ma, *Immigrant Subjectivities in Asian American and Asian Diasporic Literatures* (Albany: State University of New York Press, 2003); and Khachig Tölölyan, 'Armenian-American Literature', in *Immigrant Literatures in the United States*, ed. Alpana Sharma Kniplling (Westport, CT: Greenwood, 1996).
28. The exchange between the supradisciplinary discourse of diaspora studies and the studies of diaspora conducted within specific disciplines may have as much in common with disciplines such as Marxism or psychoanalysis as with area studies. There are no departments of Marxism and very few of psychoanalysis; both are supradisciplinary discourses with no disciplinary home. But scholars of, say, the English novel, or French feminism, or racial stereotyping freely draw on both and contribute to their continuing vitality and relevance.

5

Diasporas, Transnational Spaces, and Communities

Michel Bruneau

The term 'diaspora', long used only to describe the dispersion of Jewish people throughout the world, has in the last 30 years elicited unprecedented interest, attracting the attention not only of the academic world but also of the media. In everyday language, the term is now applied to all forms of migration and dispersion of a people, even where no migration is involved; this corresponds not only to the development and generalization of international migrations throughout the world, but also to a weakening, or at least a limitation, of the role played by nation-states at a time when globalization has become a dominant process. I have chosen here to address the concept of diaspora from a geographical standpoint, taking into account its materiality in terms of space, place, and territory.

In this chapter, I shall try first to differentiate the concept of diaspora from that of others such as migration, minority, transnational community, and territory of movement, and then complement the resulting definition with a typology of diasporas. My hypothesis is that the related concepts of diaspora and transnational community could be applied to different types of trans-border or transnational societies and thus help improve our understanding of the different spatial and temporal processes involved.

The Concept of Diaspora

A community diaspora first comes into being and then lives on owing to whatsoever in a given place forges a bond between those who want to group together and maintain, from afar, relations and other groups which, although settled elsewhere, invoke a common identity. This bond can come in different forms, such as family, community, religious, sociopolitical, and economic ties or the shared memory of a catastrophe or trauma suffered by the members of the diaspora or their forebears. A diaspora has a symbolic and 'iconographic' capital that enables it to reproduce and overcome the—often considerable—obstacle of distance separating its communities (Bruneau 2004: 7–43). Members of a diaspora coalesce the whole set of micro-places (e.g., city neighbourhoods or villages) occupied or crossed by those whom they recognize as their own in their present place of settlement. Each of these places acts as a centre in a territory where social proximities suppress spatial and temporal distances (Prévélakis 1996). All diasporas are socio-spatial networks necessarily undergoing territorial expansion because they aggregate both places of memory and places of presence (Offner and Pumain 1996: 163).

Diaspora areas and territories must be assessed in steps: first in the host country, where the community bond plays the essential role; then in the country or territory of origin—a pole of attraction—via memory; and, finally, through the system of relations within the networked space that connects these different poles. It should, however, be borne in mind that the term 'diaspora' often plays more of a metaphorical than an instrumental role. The different criteria suggested by most authors (Cohen 1997; Sheffer 2003) can be narrowed down to six essential ones, which are focused around dispersion under pressure, choice of destination, identity awareness, networked space, duration of transnational ties, and relative autonomy from host and origin societies as indicated in the following text:

1. The population considered has been dispersed under pressure (e.g., disaster, catastrophe, famine, abject poverty) to several places and territories beyond the immediate neighbourhood of the territory of origin.
2. 'The choice of countries and cities of destination is carried out in accordance with the structure of migratory chains which, beyond the oceans, link migrants with those already installed in the host countries, the latter thought of as conveyors towards the host society and the labour market, and guardians of the ethnic or national culture' (Dufoix 2000: 325). Such a choice may, however, also be determined by the conditions of traumatic dispersal, in which case, even though there may be far less choice, previous migratory routes can be used.

3. The population, integrated without being assimilated into the host countries, retains a rather strong identity awareness—which is linked to the memory of its territory and the society of origin—with its history. This implies the existence of a strong sense of community and community life. As in the case of a nation, it is an 'imagined community', relying on a collective narrative that links it to a territory and to a memory (Anderson 1983). Intergenerational transmission of identities is also at work.
4. These dispersed groups of migrants (or groups stemming from migration) preserve and develop among themselves and with the society of origin, if one still exists, multiple exchange relations (people, goods of various natures, information, etc.) organized through networks. In this networked space, which connects essentially non-hierarchical poles—even if some are more important than others—relations among groups dispersed over several destinations tend to be horizontal rather than vertical.
5. These diasporic migrants have an experience of dispersion, including several generations after the first migration. They have transmitted their identity from one generation to the other in the *longue durée*.
6. A diaspora tends to be an autonomous social formation from the host and the origin societies, thanks to its numerous cultural, political, religious, and professional associations. Lobbying in favour of their origin society is not uncommon among diasporas, but neither is resistance against instrumentalization by the homeland.

Against this concept of a 'community' diaspora (e.g., Jewish, Greek, Armenian, or Chinese diasporas), Chivallon (2004) posits a 'hybrid' diaspora, distinguished very clearly from any 'centred model'. This 'hybrid' model has been defined by Anglo-American authors on the basis of the black diaspora of the Americas, using the approaches of postmodernist cultural studies. These authors, Hall and Gilroy especially, refer to the philosophy of Deleuze and Guattari and to the image of the rhizome as opposed to that of the root—i.e., to a world of dissemination and hybridization, as opposed to a world of filiation and heritage. There is no hard core of identity—no continuity or tradition—as in the community model, but a variety of formations. This hybrid diaspora rejects all reference to the nation and to nationalist ideologies. However, albeit for a relatively limited period of time (1919–1945), a minority of intellectuals gravitating around Garvey and Du Bois did promote a pan-African nationalist ideology.

For a diaspora to be able to live on by transmitting its identity from one generation to the next, it must as much as possible have places for periodic gatherings of a religious, cultural, or political nature, in which it can concentrate on the main elements of its 'iconography'. The concept of iconography, introduced in the 1950s by Gottmann (1952: 219–21), shows the importance of visible and palpable symbols, such as the monasteries that the Greeks of Pontos (the Black Sea region in Turkey) reconstructed in Northern Greece. Such symbols contribute to consolidating social networks and to preserving them during the hard times of exile. The symbols that make up an iconography are akin to three main fields, religion, political past (memory), and social organization: 'Religion, great historical recollections, the flag, social taboos, invested and well grounded/anchored interests are all part of what is called iconography' (Gottmann 1952: 136). Those symbols are the object of a virtual faith that singularizes a people as different from its neighbours, who are attached to other symbols. The rooting of national iconography in the minds of citizens is all the deeper as it is transmitted to children very early by the family and the school. It unquestionably constitutes the main factor of sociopolitical partitioning in space. It is also what allows a diaspora not to become diluted into the host society and to keep its distinct identity. This concept particularly applies to 'nations' or, more exactly, to nationalities within great multi-ethnic empires, such as the Ottoman or the Russian. Their territorial inscription is neither continuous nor homogeneous, unlike what is implied by the ideal territory of a contemporary European nation-state. The case appears very close to that of the diasporas, to which it can apply with equal relevance.

These 'places', where we can find the main components of the iconography, include sanctuaries (churches, synagogues, mosques), community premises (conference rooms, theatres, libraries, sports clubs) and monuments that perpetuate memory. They also include restaurants and grocery shops, and newsagents and the media (newspapers, community magazines, local radio and television stations, websites). These various places may be concentrated in the same 'ethnic' neighbourhood, the same locality, or be dispersed throughout a city or some bigger territory.

Since 'iconography'—in the Gottmannian sense—is the material and symbolic condensation of the intricate web of linkages between the members of a community and their territory, a perfect reproduction of its elements (e.g., reconstructing the Pontiac monasteries in mainland Greece) is simply not possible: territory cannot be moved from one location to another. The material aspects of social networks depending on locations, territories, landscapes, or monuments that are usually associated with rootedness, immobility, and autochthoneity have, in the course of time, become mobile. The fact that members of a diaspora create 'places of memory' in the host country is made possible by gathering of the icons.

By introducing the spatial and temporal dimensions of territoriality into the concept of diaspora, it can be shown how the reproduction of memory goes hand in hand with the construction of monuments and other symbolic and sometimes also functional places that constitute the instruments for a re-rooting in the host country.

Four Major Types of Diasporas

Different diasporas are distributed unequally throughout the world at the beginning of the twenty-first century, with a generally confirmed tendency for them to be found on one or several continents. In every diaspora, culture in the widest sense—folklore, cuisine, language, literature, cinema, music, the press as well as community life and family bonds—plays a fundamental role. Family bonds, in fact, constitute the very fabric of the diaspora, particularly in the case of diasporas stemming from Asia and the eastern Mediterranean, with their well-known extended family nature; similarly, the community link is always present in, and constitutive of, all types of diasporas. What distinguishes diasporas, however, is the unequal density of their organizational structure, and the greater or lesser influence exerted by, if it still exists, their nation of origin. Religion, enterprise, politics, and a combination of race and culture are the four major domains in which these two discriminating features manifest themselves. The combination of these criteria allows a typology of diasporas to be sketched out here, as four types, and illustrated with a few examples:

1. A first set of diasporas is structured around an entrepreneurial pole; everything else is subordinated to it or plays only a secondary role: the Chinese, Indian, and Lebanese diasporas are the best examples of this. Religion here does not play a structuring role, essentially because of its very diversity: Christians, Muslims, Hindus, or Buddhists. Nor does the nation-state of origin exercise any decisive influence, for a variety of reasons: there may be several such states instead of one homeland clearly defined (Hong Kong, Taiwan, mainland China, South East Asia for the Chinese); it may be deliberately disengaged and intervened only in case of extreme difficulties (India); it may be too weak and divided

(Lebanon). Entrepreneurship constitutes the central element of the reproduction strategy of these diasporas, most of them emerging from a colonial context in which the ruler assigned their various commercial and enterprise activities (Indians and the Lebanese in Africa, the Chinese in South East Asia).

2. Another set of diasporas is that in which religion, often associated with a particular language, is the main structuring element: this is the case of the Jewish, Greek, Armenian, and Assyro-Chaldean diasporas. In these cases, the religion is monotheistic, and the language of a holy script or a liturgy may itself be regarded as essential. Greek and Armenian are taught alongside religion in diaspora schools. Synagogue and church, each with their pronounced ethnic hue, are constitutive places for these diaspora communities. Where nation-states have been formed, they have exercised an increasingly stronger influence on these diasporas. Nevertheless, even where this influence is greatest, as is the case for the Greek diaspora whose cohesion is secured by the Orthodox Church, the diaspora has managed to preserve relative independence. When the Holy Synod of the Athens Church (1908–1922) tried to take over control of the Greek Orthodox Church in the United States, strong resistance led to restoring the jurisdiction of the Ecumenical Patriarchate.
3. A third set of more recent diasporas is organized chiefly around a political pole. This is particularly so when the territory of origin is dominated by a foreign power, and the main aspiration of the diaspora population is the creation of a nation-state. An example of this is the Palestinian diaspora: having succeeded in setting up a real state-in-exile, the Palestinian Liberation Organization (PLO), whose objective of establishing a nation-state next to the state of Israel has already been partially achieved by the creation of the Palestinian Authority, which has been endowed with territories that it has administered since 1994. The Palestinian diaspora's collective memory is rooted in the historical events that mark the trauma of dispersal and occupation, especially the catastrophe (*nakba*) of 1948. This is 'the core event of their imagined community, the criterion of its alterity and the main founder of the diaspora' (Kodmani-Darwish 1997: 194).
4. A fourth set is organized around a racial and cultural pole. This is the case, for example, of the black diaspora, which has been shaped by several attempts at defining a shared identity. Centred on the 'negro race', what separates it from the other types is, first, the fact

that this diaspora has no direct reference to definite societies or territories of origin. The black diaspora is defined first and foremost by socially constructed 'race', and only subsequently by culture. Whereas the definition of race is, of course, contested and subjected to various debates and interpretations, as is the very conception of African Americans as a diaspora, collective memories refer to the traumatic experiences under which this diaspora formed the slave trade and the slave economy of the plantations. Few contemporary African Americans define their identity in relation to ancestral African homelands. We can also include the European Roma in this category, as they share many of the same characteristics. One commonality with the black diaspora is a decentred community structure, not unified by the transmission of a codified tradition or by political organization, but characterized by the non-hierarchical proliferation of community segments, that is, small groups not organized as a structured society. The logic of cultural hybridization, which implies borrowing from the host society, comes into full play in both cases amidst highly diverse host societies, even if Roma society is characterized by high degrees of endogamy and very low rates of mixed marriages. Racial discrimination and a strong tendency towards ghettoization are also common features, as is the great difficulty of upward social mobility to escape poverty (Cortiade et al. 1993).

The concept of diaspora cannot be used to describe all types of scattered populations issued from a migration process: other types of social formations were to emerge in the post-colonial period and societies within migration fields. Concepts other than that of diaspora—like those of transnational communities and territories of movement—can be invoked; although they do share some characteristics with diasporas, they also have their own specific features.

From Migration Field to Transnational Space: The Turkish Example

An international migration field results from the 'structured coupling of the places produced by the flows between the different points of the migration system' (Faret 2003: 283). Such a field comprises places of departure, route, settlement, resettlement, and even places of return. This concept applies particularly well to Turkish migration in Central and Western Europe.

In the second half of the twentieth century (1957–2000), more than three million Turks migrated to Western Europe, with two-thirds going to Germany (De Tapia 1995: 187). This was essentially an international labour migration, often the subject of agreements between states. Nevertheless, further analysis reveals this field to be relatively complex, because the subsequent migration of shopkeepers, carriers, and various investors—not to mention social migrations such as family reunifications, second- and third-generation marriages as well as collective solidarities—all superimpose themselves on labour migrations. In a subsequent phase, political migrations by asylum seekers—for example, Kurds, Assyro-Chaldeans, Armenians, and Alevis as well as refugees of leftist parties—have acquired ever increasing importance. There is, consequently, great diversity in the reasons for, and causes of, Turkish migration. The migration movement inside this field is intense, owing to the road, sea-going, and air network forms of transport that Turks themselves use and run, largely based within their own travel agencies, transport companies, and communication satellites.

In the case of Turks, the diaspora does not precede the emergence of the nation-state, but comes after it. Is it therefore a diaspora or, rather, a transnational migration field that favours the emergence of a transnational community? The Turkish nation-state is recent (1923); it has not completely succeeded in unifying the national identity of the different segments of society around a Sunni and Kemalist hard core. The high segmentation and internal disparities of Turkish society appear more in dispersion and migration than they do in the national territory where the minorities are not fully recognized and are hidden by an apparent national homogeneity. This society is a community composed of different sociocultural milieux that, though they do interact, have also acquired their own organizational and social networks. The divisions are not only ethnocultural but also religious or ideological. The Kurds, whose migrations—owing to the repression directed against them since the 1980s—are increasingly political in the current period, find themselves increasingly distinguished from other Turks and it is they, more than other Turkish-speaking Muslims, who come under the heading of diaspora (Wahlbeck 2002).

It is therefore difficult to differentiate a diaspora from the economic and political migration of a people stemming from a socially segmented society and comprising notable differences of identity. The recent character of migration (since 1957) and the segmented type of society constitute obstacles to the recognition of a real diaspora. To take better account of these phenomena, researchers such as Vertovec (1999) and Kastoryano (2000) have suggested the concept of transnational community.

Transnational Communities

In the 1990s, a new concept emerged in academic discourse: 'transnational community'. Countries at the edge of the industrialized and tertiarized world of the North's major powers (the United States, Canada, Western Europe, Japan), often former colonies or old countries of the Third World, send more and more migrants in search of employment and remittances to their families in the 'place of origin'. These rural, mostly unskilled economic migrants set off from a village, a basic rural community to which the migrants remain strongly attached and to which they return periodically. The family structure, more than the village community of origin, is essential in explaining the cohesion of these networks. Those from a rural community in a Latin American country or the Philippines, for instance, increasingly migrate to urban centres of various sizes in the United States, with a migration movement being established between the place of origin and the places of settlement and work. The migration territory also comprises relay places, most often a large city, which serve as hubs for a migratory route network: for example, Dallas and Chicago for Mexicans from Ocampo (Faret 2003) and Buenos Aires for Bolivians from the Cochabamba region (Cortes 1998). The strong association with these different places, based upon the movement of the population of one village, where the dominant activity is migration in a variety of forms, constitutes a transnational migration territory.

A transnational community is based on specific mobility know-how, 'migration expertise'; the inhabitants of these places, so strongly marked by migration, have made it their essential activity. Some mobility may be based on the experience of mountain husbandry, which has always had to adapt to the seasons—whether for transhumance in certain cases or in the case of Andean peasants, because several distinct ecological mountain levels are concerned. Peoples with a long nomadic tradition, such as the Turks or Mongols, can also be moulded more easily in these transnational spaces (De Tapia 1995). A transnational community links the global to the whole range of greatly different local networking places, without hierarchy between these different hubs. The role of the border is very much curtailed by a migrant population whose essential element of identity is knowing how to first cross the border itself, pass through the border area, and then live outside the border area, while avoiding expulsion.

These migrants come from a nation-state, where they have lived for a relatively long time, returning periodically, and then investing part of their income in their village of origin, which they, or at least part of their family, do not plan to quit for good. The members of a transnational community seek to acquire the citizenship of their host country, while retaining that of their country of origin. This double affiliation is not only a question of facility but also a chosen way of life. However, there is no uprooting from the territory and society of origin, nor trauma, as in the case of diasporas. There is no strong desire to return, because transmigrants never actually leave their place of origin, with which they retain family and community ties that are greatly simplified thanks to the growth, regularity, and safety of communications.

As Foner (1997) has shown for immigrants in New York, both today and at the turn of the twentieth century, modern-day transnationalism is not altogether new but instead has a long history. Russian Jews and Italians maintained family, economic, political, and cultural links to their home societies at the same time as they developed ties within their host land. Expecting to return home one day, they sent their savings and remittances homeward and kept up their ethnic allegiances. A transnational social space already existed, but it may have been harder than it is now to maintain contacts across the ocean. Today technological changes have made it possible for immigrants to maintain closer and more frequent contact with their home societies. International business operations in the new global economy are much more common. Telephones, emails, and internet-based telecom allow immigrants to keep in close touch with the family members, friends, and business partners they had left behind in their home country. With greater US tolerance for ethnic pluralism and multiculturalism, maintaining multiple identities and loyalties is now seen as a normal feature of immigrant life. Nowadays, too, a much higher proportion of these immigrants (e.g., Indians and Chinese) arrive with advanced education, professional skills, and sometimes substantial amounts of financial capital that facilitate these transnational connections (Foner 1997: 362–9).

The concept of transnational community is also used by researchers who have studied transnational nationalism. According to Kastoryano (2006), for example, Turkish transnational communities live in a four-dimensional space: that of the immigration country, the country of origin, the immigrant communities themselves, and the transnational space of the European Union. The concept of 'long-distance nationalism' (Anderson 1998) refers to the nation-state of departure, for example, Turkey, which acts on its exiled population by way of language, religion, and dual nationality. This nation-state tries to reinforce as much as possible the loyalty of its nationals residing outside its frontiers. But the transnational networks of migrant associations can bypass the states by acting directly on transnational European institutions. We can observe the emergence of a transnational space, characterized by the dense interaction of actors belonging to different traditions (e.g., Islamist and secular Turks, Alevis, Kurds, Lazes). It is a new space of political socialization, one of identification beyond that of national societies. The EU has created a transnational civilian society in which national, provincial, religious, and professional networks compete and interact among themselves, thereby promoting the logic of supranationality.

For Kastoryano (2006: 90), the concept of diaspora is more aptly applied to populations scattered prior to the making of their nation-state, such as Jews and Armenians, for whom nationalism refers to a mythical place, a territory to be recovered, or a future state-building project. This more restricted meaning takes into account the extended history of diasporas who may have built their own nation-state after a lengthy period without a state, which is exactly the case of the Jews, Greeks, and Armenians. Nation-states emerged only in nineteenth- and twentieth-century Europe, and these diasporas were already in existence a long time before that. Migrations occurred often after this state building within the former reticular space of their diaspora. But diasporas may also have emerged from the forced exile of religious or national minorities of a nation-state after its creation (e.g., the Tutsis of Rwanda, Assyro-Chaldeans or Kurds of Turkey, Tamil of Sri Lanka, Tibetans of China). Such diasporas are organized around an unsettled nation-state problem; this is not the case of transnational communities that do not contest the home or host nation-state. A transnational community is economically oriented, and its political interest is restricted to the migration policies of both its home and host country. There is, equally, another form of transnational community in which cross-border migrants, using a network of acquaintances, are continually circulating between their home place and a variety of host places to sell goods; this kind of quasi-nomadism requires the use of another concept, as discussed in the following text.

Territories of Movement

In the name of an anthropology of movement, Tarrius works in the tradition of analysing the emergence and development of new migratory forms in Europe, which have been studied by researchers since the 1980s. Marseille is the observation site for the construction of these underground international economies dealing with licit or illicit products. A world of 'small migrants'—i.e., 'merchandize/goods conveyers'—is devoted to the transportation and trade of goods imported outside official EU quotas of forgeries and smuggled goods, between the North African countries and France via Spain. They take advantage of the spatial, economic, and social closeness that exists between the south and the north of these Mediterranean countries due to the colonial and migratory past of those spaces. Localist analysis must be overcome to study those migrant societies that generate 'new cosomopolitisms', which are now invisible or hidden or displayed in mixity. They result in encounters between mobile, more or less steady and enduring groups. New forms of identities then occur, which are founded on the capacity of multiple belonging.

'Territories of movement' (Tarrius 2001) link the place where goods for consumption are shipped out (for instance, in the Maghreb) to the places they are delivered in Western Europe, within which there are further underground economy networks. They may seem to resemble transnational communities, in so far as they link the formerly colonized country where the migrants' community of origin is situated with the migrants' current residence. They are, however, actually very different. The transnational community essentially moves people who are going to 'sell' their labour and send part of their wages back to their community of origin in the form of remittances. Conversely, in the territory of movement, the cross-border entrepreneurs and nomads move with goods they loaded up in their place of origin to sell in different cities of the host country that they are familiar with. Having in some cases lived in the latter for a lengthy period, they have been able to establish a helping network of acquaintances and support—the 'informal notaries' of Tarrius (2001: 52–56).

These intermediaries take commercial advantage of the wealth differential between their place of origin and their host place, circulating goods between poor and rich countries. Their expertise in moving goods especially—by crossing borders and circumventing taxation mechanisms of the states is as important for them as the expertise of a Mexican or Bolivian is within the migration field of a transnational community. Their host places are only points of passage or way stations, not places of settlement and integration. The only essential place for them is the one of their origin, whence they leave with their goods; they return regularly and invest their earnings there. They never actually leave: it is their only base. Their identity is not a diasporic one: it is a 'nomadic identity' based on 'partial and short-lived hybridization [*métissage*]' acquired in the course of the selling activity through which they socialize. In their place of origin, the link is based on family and community ties, whereas in the host and transit places, well-established local intermediaries—informal notaries with diaspora experience—are needed.

Those informal notaries are interlocutors who are very much valorised by regional and local, political and police authorities who actively take part in the life in emerging mosques in large Southern cities. They contribute to institutionalising uncontrolled areas, of land's ends within Schengen space, such as those identified by Italian researchers around Trieste, or Bari, Sicily, in Naples and in Milan's suburbs (Tarrius 2001: 55).

Without their intermediation nothing is possible and the smuggler cannot maintain his activity and presence on the selling places. These brokers maintain relationships with local, political, and police powers, with official representatives of the migrants' home states as well as with their religious representatives, open trading and various underground networks. They sit astride numerous borders of norms and interests.

The territories of movement and transnational communities are produced by globalization and result from socio-economic inequalities, which tend to increase, such as differences in the price of goods and wages between countries of the North and South. They lock nation-states into an asymmetrical situation, one of dominating and being dominated. The base in the host country, although weak for territories of movement (in the transit place), can, on the contrary, be strong for transnational communities (in the host place); in both cases, however, the rooting in the community of origin remains very significant and may prevail over that in the country of settlement or transit.

Originality and Value of the Concepts of Diaspora and Transnational Community

The value of the diaspora concept is that it shows sedimentation over time, often a long period of time, of communities dispersed throughout the world, which vary considerably from one diaspora to another. These diasporas are characterized by the search for a certain cultural or religious—at times even political—unity. They have been formed, over the course of time, by several waves of migration, each of which could have different or several causes at once. It is this long-term sedimentation that makes a diaspora. This is not the case either for transnational communities, which have been formed recently in response to a call for labour, or for smugglers depending on an underground economy. Each diaspora member, wherever he or she may be, adjusts his or her own cultural and social unity to the local and national features, with integration characterizing intergenerational trajectories: he or she produces *métissages*. For instance, Greek-Americans are different from those living in Canada or Australia because their various migration trajectories combine with the integration policies of these different states. The first, second, or third generations, in turn, produce their own different types of 'mixities' within each of these host countries. There are several ways to keep one's identity in exile and dispersion, as diasporas firmly rooted in their various places of settlement have taught us. They have an exceptional symbolic and 'iconographic' capital that enables them to reproduce and then overcome the obstacle of the—often considerable—distance that separates their communities. This symbolic capital lives on, particularly in shared memory.

So the relationships between diasporas and space or territories have their own specificities. Belonging to a diaspora implies being able to live simultaneously on the transnational world scale, the local scale of the community, and the scale of the host or home country, thereby combining the three scales while privileging one or two of these. This combination differs from one individual to another, according to their position in the genealogy of generations. For instance, the first generation, those who were born and have lived in the society of origin, tend to privilege the local scale of the host country and the national scale of the home country where they lived before their migration. The second generation takes into account more often the local and national scales of the host country, where they were born and have lived and, sometimes, the transnational scale; the third generation, in search of its origins, moves on two or three of these scales.

A diaspora is a patchwork of families, communities, and religious networks integrated in a territory by a nation-state, within its borders. These patchworks of families, clans, villages, cities, etc., are contained inside the borders of this nation-state where circulation and exchanges are easier inside than with the outside. The nation-state creates an arbitrary limit between the networks inside it and those that are outside. Diasporas, however, cannot benefit from this extraordinary tool of integration. They function, as previously mentioned, as a hinge between different spaces and different geographical scales. Their networks belong to each of the host countries as well as to a trans-state diasporic network. Their global network, with its economic, cultural, social, and political functions, can play the stabilizing role that nation-states cover less and less.

Through migration, diaspora members have lost their material relationship to the territory of origin, but they can still preserve their cultural or spiritual relationship through memory. Territory or, more precisely, territoriality—in the sense of adapting oneself to a place in the host country—continues to play an essential role. Memory preserves part of territoriality, while the trauma of uprooting creates conditions of mobilization that can play a substantial role in integrating and unifying various family, religious, or community sub-networks into a real diaspora. The construction of commemorative monuments, sanctuaries, monasteries, and other symbolic (and sometimes functional) places is an essential means, for the members of a diaspora, of a re-rooting in the host country.

Unlike people of the diaspora, transmigrants and cross-border entrepreneurs or smugglers do not seek to establish a social network destined to last or a transnational social group based on the richness of a symbolic capital and a memory transmitted from one generation to the next. They seek first and foremost to build a house in their home village and climb the social ladder there, and then to do so in their place of settlement if such a place exists. Transmigrants are far too dependent on their community of origin and on their host country to become as independent as people of the diaspora are. The social group to which they belong often does not exceed the community of origin and the network of its migrants, whereas the people of the diaspora have the feeling of belonging to a nation-in-exile, dispersed throughout the world, bearing an ideal. But transnational communities, like the Turkish one, are sometimes the bearers of a transnational nationalism, which appears with the interactions of their different actors and tries to influence the nation-state of their origin and that of their settlement. Dual nationality and migratory circulation within the framework of a transnational region like the EU favour the emergence of new trans-border communities differing from the long-term diasporas.

It is, in my view, this relationship to places and territories that enables us to distinguish between diasporism and transnationalism. Diaspora implies a very strong anchoring in the host country and, sometimes, when the home country is lost or is not accessible (as with the Greeks of Asia Minor, Armenians, or Tibetans), a clear-cut break with it. This is compensated, in the host country, by the creation of territorial markers, places of memory, favoured by an 'iconography' fixing the link with the home country. That gives some kind of autonomy from host and origin societies to the diasporic social formation compared to the transnational community. In transnational spaces and territories of mobility, this break does not take place, nor is there the need to be re-rooted elsewhere on the host territory. Any particular family has two parallel lives in two or more nation-states: the home country is dominated and the host countries, where the family has migrated, are dominant. In the autochthonous model, the fact of having 'always been there', on which the nation-state is based, means that identity is constructed in close connection with place over a greater or lesser period of time. On the contrary, in a diaspora, identity pre-exists place and tries to re-create it, to remodel it, in order to reproduce itself. Individuals or communities in diasporas live in places that they have not themselves laid out and that are suffused with other identities. As such, they will try to set up their very own place, one that is redolent of their home place within the bosom of which their identity, that of their kinfolk, of their ancestors, has been formed. De-territorialization goes with, or is followed by, re-territorialization.

References

Anderson, B. (1983) *Imagined Communities: Reflections on the Origins and Spread of Nationalism*. London: Verso.

——. (1998) *The Spectre of Comparisons: Nationalism, Southeast Asia and the World*. London: Verso.

Bruneau, M. (2004) *Diasporas et espaces transnationaux*. Paris: Anthropos-Economica.

Chivallon, C. (2004) *La diaspora noire des Amériques: Expériences et théories à partir de la Caraïbe*. Paris: CNRS-Éditions.

Cohen, R. (1997) *Global Diasporas: An Introduction*. London: UCL Press.

Cortes, G. (1998) 'Migrations, systèmes de mobilité, espaces de vie: À la recherche de modèles', *L'Espace géographique*, 3, 265–75.

Cortiade, M., Djuric, R., and Williams, P. (1993) 'Terres d'asile, terre d'exil: l'Europe tsigane [Special Issue]', *Ethnies*, 8(15).

De Tapia, S. (1995) 'L'émigration turque: Circulation migratoire et diaspora', in M. Bruneau (ed.) *Diasporas*. Paris: RECLUS-La Documentation Française, 174–88.

Dufoix, S. (2000) 'Note de lecture: La structuration de l'expérience collective à l'étranger', *Cahiers d'Études sur la Méditerranée Orientale et le Monde Turco-Iranien*, 30, 319–32.

Faret, L. (2003) *Les territoires de la mobilité. Migration et communautés transnationales entre le Mexique et les États-Unis*. Paris: CNRS-Éditions.

Foner, N. (1997) 'What's new about transnationalism? New York immigrants today and at the turn of the century', *Diaspora*, 6(3), 355–75.

Gottmann, J. (1952) *La politique des États et leur géographie*. Paris: Armand Colin.

Kastoryano, R. (2000) 'Immigration, communautés transnationales et citoyenneté', *Revue internationale des sciences sociales*, 165, 353–59.

——. (2006) 'Le nationalisme transnational turc ou la redéfinition du nationalisme par les Turcs de l'extérieur', in Berthomière, W., and Chivallon, C. (eds.) *Les diasporas dans le monde contemporain*. Paris: Karthala-MSHA, 87–105.

Kodmani-Darwish, B. (1997) *La diaspora palestinienne*. Paris: PUF.

Offner J.M., and Pumain, D. (eds.) (1996) *Réseaux et territoires*. Montpellier: Éditions de l'aube.

Prévélakis, G. (ed.) (1996) *Les réseaux des diasporas*. Paris/Nicosie: L'Harmattan-KYKEM.

Sheffer, G. (2003) *Diaspora Politics: At Home Abroad*. Cambridge: Cambridge University Press.

Tarrius, A. (2001) 'Au-delà des États-nations: des sociétés de migrants', *Revue européenne des migrations internationales*, 17(2), 37–61.

Vertovec, S. (1999) 'Conceiving and researching transnationalism', *Ethnic and Racial Studies*, 22(2), 447–62.

Wahlbeck, O. (2002) 'The concept of diaspora as an analytical tool in the study of refugee communities', *Journal of Ethnic and Migration Studies*, 28(2), 221–238.

6

Moral Economies of a Translocal Village

Obligation and Shame among South Indian Transnational Migrants

Selvaraj Velayutham and Amanda Wise

In this chapter, we advance the notion of 'translocal village', which, we argue, represents a distinct theoretical subset of the broad category 'transnationalism'. We develop the translocal village thesis by way of an in-depth case study of the transnational dimensions of a South Indian village in Tamil Nadu. We demonstrate how place or village-level social relations are extended yet circumscribed by an affective moral economy within which ritual, caste, and kin relations are reproduced. This village-defined moral economy extended across borders is what we describe as the translocal village.

The contemporary Indian diaspora is, perhaps, a transnational community *par excellence*. A plethora of academic research has explored the reproduction of diasporic relations, with a particular focus on identity and cultural reproduction. Very often the focus of such studies has been on the circulation and consumption of cultural traffic such as food, Bollywood films (cf. Tambiah 2000; Vertovec 2000; Shukla 2001; Mishra 2002; Falzon 2003), and scholarly accounts of long-distance nationalist practices (Van der Veer 1995; Fuglerud 1999). Moreover, while there has been much work done on North Indians, to our knowledge, research delving into the intricate differences and patterns of transnational Indians from various parts of rural South India is still relatively rare (cf. Osella and Osella 2000), as is work that explores the transnational extension of traditional moral economies of kinship, caste, and village alliances. In this chapter, we investigate how traditional modes of obligation, responsibility, and kinship are being reworked in creative and entrepreneurial ways by villagers in India and by their transnational kin in Singapore to ensure the maintenance and continued success of the village. Through an auto-ethnographic study[1] of co-author Selvaraj's home village and his transnational family responsibilities to it, we demonstrate how social structures and cultural practices among translocal villagers in Singapore mirror those in the village in India. Second, we show how his home village functions as a powerful moral economy reproduced through codes of responsibility and obligation, which in turn is policed translocally through affective structures of shame, guilt, and the panopticon-like gaze of fellow caste members abroad.

Indians arrived in Singapore at the time of its foundation as a British trading post in 1819.[2] Since then there has been a steady stream of Indian migrants to the colony in search of employment and commercial and trading opportunities. The separation of Singapore from Malaysia in 1965 resulted in a gradual slowing of Indian migration due to increasingly stringent immigration controls with Singapore's formal nation-state status (Sandhu and Mani 1993: 777). However, Indians now make up the third largest ethnic community, constituting 8 per cent of the total population in Singapore after the Malays and Chinese. The Indians who came to Singapore were predominantly from villages in Tamil Nadu, with smaller numbers originating from Kerala, Sri Lanka, Punjab, Bengal, and Gujarat. Those residing in Singapore today are mostly Tamil speaking and are a mixture of newer migrants from India and second-, third-, and fourth-generation Singapore born. In the section that follows, we explore the translocal relations of one particular group in Singapore—the caste members of Selvaraj's home village of Soorapallam.

Soorapallam Writ Large

Soorapallam is a small village in the Thanjavur district in the state of Tamil Nadu, southern India. Close to the town of Pattukkottai, the village lies about eight hours south of Chennai and about half an hour from the Coromandel Coast. Soorapallam and its neighbouring villages in the region form part of the rice bowl of Tamil Nadu. With the river Kaveri flowing through the region, agriculture has been the main source of livelihood. Soorapallam has a population of around 5000 people, of whom more than 50 per cent belong to the Musuguntha Vellalar caste, who are the primary landowners and cultivators.[3] Only the main road from Pattukkottai is tarred and on the small dirt roads stemming from it lie little hamlets of homes, some built from mud and thatch, others from brick and cement with tiled roofs, most of which draw their water from communal taps because there is no internal plumbing in these dwellings. The village also has several temples and schools. Within the village are pockets of coconut and mango trees and small plantations of tamarind and bananas, while the village itself is almost entirely surrounded by paddy fields. Most of the Musuguntha Vellalars own land in and around the village where, among other things, they cultivate rice, groundnuts, pulses, and vegetables.

The Musuguntha Vellalar community also extends to 31 neighbouring villages in the Pattukkottai region where related caste members reside. Musuguntha Vellalars were originally part of the Karkatha Vellalar caste found in the Tirunelveli region of Tamil Nadu. They gradually migrated down to the Thanjavur district settling around the town of Pattukkottai (Annamalai 1984). Through endogamous marriage practices, inhabitants of the 32 villages around Pattukkottai eventually evolved into their own sub-caste and are now known as Musuguntha Vellalars, after the name of the region in which they settled.[4] As Banks (cited in Fuglerud 1999: 187) explains, the expanded kin networks emanating from the practice of cross-cousin marriage are conceived of as castes in their own right. Tamil villagers such as Soorapallamers will make a distinction between kin and non-kin, *sondakara* and *sondakara illai*. In this way, the boundaries of the Musuguntha Vellalar caste group are regulated through marriage. As Fuglerud points out, 'Rather than the establishment of "alliances" between patrilineages, marriage is seen as reproducing the already existing kindred. That is the explicit reason why cross-cousin marriage is valued, as expressed in the saying *sondam viddup pokhamal* (the *sondam* [kin] should not be lost)' (1999: 147).

As a closed community, marriage partners are sought only from within these villages and, as Annamalai (1984) points out, this is a strictly policed rule; marriage beyond these villages is rare due to the very real threat of ostracism. The practice of endogamy and cross-cousin marriage (mother's brother's daughter is the preferred ideal) has meant that the Musuguntha Vellalar community in Soorapallam and its 31 neighbouring villages is a tightly knit social unit bounded at once by place and extended family-caste relations. Similarly, ceremonies, rites of passage, and so forth are conducted within the social bounds of these Musuguntha Vellalar villages. This wider village caste network is embodied in the term *sonda jati*, which translates roughly as 'fellow caste members'.[5]

Since the late 1950s, many Musuguntha Vellalars have ventured overseas in search of better economic opportunities. A large number of them migrated to Singapore, and there are a few families in Australia and the United States. Others still travel to the Gulf States to take up short-term contract work. The endogamous nature of the Musuguntha Vellalar's kinship network has meant that the small community of around 80 families living in Singapore are related to one another by descent, translocally expanding the boundaries of the *Musuguntha jati* to Singapore, making it the 33rd village. Of these, roughly 30 families originate from the Soorapallam village, the balance from the surrounding villages. Most of these families came to Singapore during the late 1960s and after. More recently, there has been an influx of single young men from the *Musuguntha villages*, often IT workers, who have come to Singapore on professional employment visas and have subsequently taken up permanent residence.

Selvaraj's[6] home village in Tamil Nadu, Soorapallam, began its process of translocalization in the late 1950s. Just teenagers at the time, Selvaraj's father and his brother obtained passage to work in Singapore in 1958. To circumvent strict immigration laws, they presented the immigration authorities with falsified identity documents bearing the surname of their uncle who was already residing in Singapore.[7] They were eventually granted citizenship, but all their citizenship documents still carry their uncle's name rather than that of their own father who remained in the village in Tamil Nadu. Their uncle's willingness to assist their immigration to Singapore remains an important memory among his extended family in India and is one of the defining links in the moral economy of his now translocalized village. As we discuss in more detail in the following text, such acts of filial obligation set in train reciprocal obligations and responsibilities that carry through till the present day.

In 1963, five years after their arrival in Singapore, Selvaraj's father returned to Soorapallam to marry. The marriage to his cousin (mother's brother's daughter) was prearranged, fulfilling the family's obligation to his bride's branch of the family. Following the wedding, he immediately returned to Singapore for his work, leaving his new wife, but returned each year to visit. In 1975, he arranged for his wife, and by now three children, to immigrate to Singapore: after settling permanently in Singapore, the family would return to Soorapallam during school holidays once every two years or so. On these visits, Selvaraj's family was expected to present gifts to its extended family, and in some instances assist with cash to help needy relatives, offer disaster relief, contribute funds to village projects, and assist with finance to build new houses in the village for extended family.

Selvaraj's family was also obliged over the years to facilitate the social mobility of relatives who were struggling to make ends meet. This often included finding job opportunities for their sons in Singapore, contributing to their children's education, making financial contributions towards their dowry, and so forth. They were often called upon to sponsor migration applications, post security bonds, and arrange marriages that would assist villagers to attain permanent residency in Singapore. Like other village families in Singapore, Selvaraj's family often hosted relatives on visitors' visas in their home, helping them to find employment, sometimes in the informal economy. Such assistance is seen as a means of facilitating the social mobility of other caste members, fulfilling an obligation to offer the same opportunities made available to Selvaraj's parents when they migrated. This assistance is based on an unwritten law that, given Selvaraj's family's privileged position as successful migrants, they have an obligation and social responsibility to take care of the needs of their *sonda jati* back in the village. All Musuguntha Vellalar families in Singapore feel a similar sense of duty towards their co-villagers at home.

This transnational moral economy of the village also extends to younger Tamils abroad, especially when it comes to marriage. Most second-generation Indians in Singapore, whose parents emigrated from villages in Tamil Nadu and who have reached an eligible age for marriage, are expected to return to marry a person of the same caste group in the home village. Through the continued migration of individuals from the village, there is now a network of Musuguntha Vellalar residents in Singapore. Selvaraj has observed, without exception so far, that the second-generation offspring of Singapore-based Soorapallamers and fellow Musuguntha Vellalar villagers have returned to the village for marriage partners and subsequent weddings, despite the presence of co-caste members in Singapore. There appear to be two main reasons for this. First, there are not enough potential marriage partners of the right age or availability within the caste group resident in Singapore. Second, the rules around endogamous cross-cousin marriage further limit the pool of compatible marriage partners, and consequently arranged marriages from the village are more likely. However, unlike popular representations of the Indian diaspora, Soorapallam's translocal marriages are not arranged through a marriage broker or matrimonials. Rather, because the villagers are intimately acquainted with one another, they are generally aware of when the children of their co-villagers, in India or abroad, are of marriageable age and thus are able to put forward marriage proposals. For example, when a young woman in Singapore finishes her studies, she is sure to be approached by a number of families from the village, through phone calls and letters, to canvass the possibility of marriage.

The story of Selvaraj's cousin Murugan is a good example of typical translocal marriage practice among Soorapallam villagers. At 26 and in secure work in Singapore, his parents felt that it was time he married. Prior to this, there had been several expressions of interest in his marriageable status back in the village. Based on the subsequent correspondence from families of potential marriage partners, the field was narrowed to a young woman, a second cousin on his mother's side. After astrological consultation, an engagement was made. Marriage preparations were set in train and relatives based in Soorapallam on both the groom's and bride's sides took charge of the arrangements for the ceremony to be held there. Two months before the wedding Murugan's entire family travelled to the village where the marriage took place. With new bride in tow, they travelled back to Singapore soon after the ceremonies, and the couple moved into Murugan's family home. As is the standard practice, Murugan's family held a second reception on their return to Singapore to which other Musuguntha Vellalars were invited so that they too could celebrate the marriage. While the most obvious role of arranged marriage is to reproduce and maintain the *sondakara* network, marriage arrangements are also made as a way of returning favours or facilitating the social mobility of a particular member of the family. For example, after Murugan's wedding, he was obliged to assist his new brother-in-law by sponsoring his visa application to work in Singapore.

In addition to marriages, translocal villagers in Singapore also commonly return to Soorapallam to conduct other important rites of passage. For example, when Murugan's two young daughters were aged two and four, the family returned to the village so that they could partake in the traditional Hindu tonsuring ritual of *Mottai Addithal*. The ritual forms an offering to the *grama theyvam* (village deity) in return for the child's protection and good health. Similarly, death too entails rituals in the home village. In a number of instances, the body of the deceased has been flown from Singapore back to the village for the cremation and funeral ceremonies. Sometimes ashes are taken back to the village, while in other instances the ashes are scattered to sea in Singapore but the family will return to the village for prayers and rituals.

The level of awareness of one another's life events emanates from a sophisticated communication network between the village and those in

Singapore. When a marriage is announced or a death occurs, a flurry of phone calls are made. Within no time, the village is mobilized in preparation for an imminent 'ritual return' from Singapore, and preparations are made for the village activities centred on it. These ritual returns highlight the maintenance of a physical presence in the village by those living abroad.

Among those Soorapallamers in Singapore, the maintenance of a physical presence almost without exception extends to having a functioning house in the village. For example, Selvaraj's parents not only maintain a home in the village, but they, like many others who have gone abroad, also have made a significant investment in rebuilding their house in a larger and more modern style than their previous two-room mud and thatch home. Their new house in Soorapallam is divided into two: three paternal uncles, their wives, and children occupy one side, and Selvaraj's maternal grandmother, and his parents on their frequent and lengthy trips back to India, occupy the other. This is the case with most of the Singapore-based Musuguntha Vellalar families.

Relations of trust in times of life crises are another important translocal boundary marker. For example, trust networks were an important aspect in Selvaraj's father's decisions about his care when he fell seriously ill with a heart condition in Singapore, requiring a triple bypass. Despite the exceptionally high standards of hospital care and specialists in Singapore, Selvaraj's father, on the advice of fellow villagers, returned to Tamil Nadu for his operation. At times of serious health crisis, many such as his father feel that Singaporean doctors are not to be trusted to care for them in the way a Tamil doctor in India would. There are anxieties around communication with the predominantly non-Tamil-speaking Chinese doctors in Singapore and a distrust of their bedside manner. Despite being gravely ill, Selvaraj's father checked himself out of the hospital in Singapore and flew to Tamil Nadu, ensuring that a Tamil doctor would be treating him at a hospital and, most importantly, a Tamil doctor his fellow villagers had recommended. After his operation, he spent some months recuperating in Soorapallam, with the support of Selvaraj's mother and extended family, before returning to Singapore.

The literature on transnationalism has a tendency to focus on flows *between* home and host places. However, we argue that an equally important dimension is the replication, or mirroring, of village activities in the place of settlement. While translocal ritual returns, physical involvement in Soorapallam, and obligations to assist with the social mobility and migration of fellow villagers are important dimensions of the translocal village, there are also significant activities that take place in Singapore that mirror or extend the village relations there. For example, political representation and financial organization are replicated to some extent in Singapore. Traditionally, village-scale projects in Soorapallam such as building schools, providing irrigation, installing plumbing in the village, and upgrading or maintaining temples are administered by a group of village elders (the *ooru panchayat*—the village council) headed by the village thalaivar[8] (headman). It is to the *panchayat* that financial contributions are made, and they are also charged with resolving village disputes, often around matters of land, marriage, or crime. Importantly with respect to our arguments about translocality, there is also a second nominal *thalaivar* in Singapore, normally an elder in the community. Those in Singapore are able to contribute to village projects through him. The Singapore *thalaivar* frequently travels back to Soorapallam to dispense the collected funds and oversee activities in the village, and he is also often called upon to assist in dispute resolution in Singapore. His presence signals the extension of village administration across borders.

Similarly, rites of passage are celebrated among fellow Musuguntha Vellalars in Singapore. If a Musuguntha Vellalar family faces a major life event such as a birth, major illness, or house-warming, fellow caste members in Singapore are sure to be present and if a family makes a ritual return to Soorapallam, invariably a second celebration is held on their return to Singapore. For example, when Selvaraj's grandfather in India died, large numbers of fellow villagers came to their Singapore home to attend the wake. Similarly, when Selvaraj's cousin, Murugan and his wife moved from the family home to their own home in Singapore, fellow Musuguntha Vellalars all came to their *griha pravesham* (house-warming).[9] Importantly, significant occasions such as funerals, childbirth, coming of age ceremonies, or housewarmings are almost invariably attended *only* by fellow caste members and not by other Singaporean friends, Indians, or otherwise, however close. This has the effect of creating a translocal sense of village and *jati* identity, belonging, and boundary. Similarly, important religious festivals such as *Pongal* (the harvest festival), *Thaipusam* (a day of consecration of the Hindu deity Subramaniam), *Varusa Pirappu* (Tamil New Year), *Deepavali* (the festival of lights), and *Thimithi* (firewalking) are celebrated in Singapore specifically with other Musuguntha Vellalars, which, depending on the festival, involve visiting one another's homes for feasts and attending prayers and ceremonies together at the temple.

The kin practices of Soorapallamers also play an extremely important part in maintaining and reproducing the boundaries of their translocal social field and determine the relations that take place within it. Most significant is the fact that the endogamous nature of Tamil kinship is distinctly different to marriage practices among North Indians. First, Tamils practise cross-cousin marriage, while higher caste North Indians have an exogamous marriage system prohibiting marriage with all paternal and maternal kin. North Indian girls are married into a strange family, ideally one with whom her family have no previous association, whereas Tamil girls marry into families that are already known. For this reason, rural North Indian women are often married to men who live at greater distances than would traditionally have been the case for their Tamil counterparts (Wadley 1980). These differences in marriage practices mean that the translocal social relations among Tamils are much more closely bounded and regulated than those of Indians from the north. Most importantly, Tamils will know co-members of their translocal social field and have a responsibility to maintain close relations and links with fellow Musuguntha Vellalars in the village and abroad.

The returns, remittances, flow of obligations, and the replication of village practices and boundaries in Singapore demonstrate that Soorapallam and its moral community has become thoroughly translocalized and, as we have shown in this section, the translocal relationship between Singapore and Soorapallam has multiple dimensions. This includes the continued migration and cementing of *sondam* through marriage in the home village; the sense of obligation to assist villagers from Soorapallam to migrate and find secure employment and to facilitate their social and economic mobility; the obligation to make financial contributions to village infrastructure and disaster relief; the maintenance of a physical home back in the village; the reproduction of affective and spiritual ties through ritual returns; the continued involvement in village social activities; and the maintenance of relationships with family in the village and visits to home whenever possible. The community is further cemented through the participation of fellow Musuguntha Vellalars in collective activities taking place in Singapore, often mirroring the social and ritual practices that would have occurred in the village. In the next section, we explore some of the more coercive means through which these obligations are reproduced.

Policing the Translocal Village

As with all social relations, the above practices are not entirely voluntary. They are regulated and perpetuated through various means of social control. This theme is often overlooked in transnational studies. The focus on flows and how social ties are maintained through them emphasizes the agency of the transnational migrant and their community's resourcefulness in maintaining their social viability across borders. However, many studies neglect the *affective* means of gate-keeping that perpetuate the transnational social field (or translocal in our case) and, as with all forms of society, the translocal traffic in sentiments (Werbner 1999: 26) entails a degree of social coercion. Appadurai calls this a 'community of sentiment' (1996: 8). What we are arguing is that the Singapore arm of the village perpetuates its existence, not only through relations with the homeland and the various social activities and gatherings in Singapore, but also through policing and reporting on the activities of co-members in Singapore, through guilt, shame, and fear of ostracism, and through the obligations of moral community. Importantly, these dynamics of social control are an almost exact replication of those that exist in the village itself.

Perhaps the most important means of policing these relations is through the panopticon-like gaze of the *ooru*, a Tamil word invoking at once the notion of home village, home country, or place of origin. The *ooru* is not just a village. For Tamils, the word evokes a sense of origin, ancestral roots, or a place whose soil nourished one's ancestors, the 'real' home, however far away one might live (Wood 1995: 80). It is a term used within a family and among fellow villagers in specific reference to the village. It is used in expressions such as 'the whole *ooru* is talking about you', invoking both place and a specific moral community made up of close family (*pangali*), fellow villagers, and the Musuguntha Vellalar *jati* at large. In this way, the *ooru* signifies the collective moral gaze of the village whose members maintain a watchful eye on one another. This self-governing/regulating and self-generative network gaze is imagined as ever present and inescapable, embodying and policing the boundaries of the translocal village and its moral community.

The power of the gaze lies in the fact that one's reputation, status, and so forth emanates from the village, and failing to fulfil certain social obligations, such as marrying your son to a villager, threatens serious loss of face in the village and among fellow caste members. Translocal Soorapallamers usually feel deeply compelled, for example, to present gifts and financial assistance on visits to the village. Gifts are also sometimes given to prevent attracting the 'evil eye' through feelings of envy aroused among villagers by the migrant's alleged prosperity (Osella and Osella 2000), a constant risk and something that is best avoided. Similarly, members are usually quizzed about their adult children's marriage plans on each return to Soorapallam, and the status and situation of these children is quickly reported throughout the village. Or, for example, if a translocal villager is perceived to have been a bit wayward, perhaps by not sending money back regularly, they will be pulled into line by co-villagers. The gaze functions equally well in Singapore. Selvaraj's younger brother was recently confronted by his parents, who had heard through his sister-in-law, who in turn had heard through a distant relative, that he had been seen 'in the CBD in unsuitable attire' (wearing an old t-shirt and jeans). Another time, the translocal village network sprang into action when another Musuguntha Vellalar saw him 'hanging out' with some 'undesirable' teenage boys. Phone calls were made to his parents to report on this perceived misdemeanour. Similarly, young Musuguntha Vellalar women in Singapore are regularly subjected to a round of phone calls to parents should they be seen dressed 'inappropriately' or in the company of boys. While the callers in such instances are unlikely to say directly 'your child is wayward', the clear subtext communicated is that the parents are not disciplining their child and are failing in their duties. Parents on the receiving end of such calls are keenly aware they are being watched and judged and that the behaviour of their children reflects on them. The transnational village gaze often also extends beyond Singapore to third countries, as Selvaraj discovered recently. Speaking on the telephone from Sydney to an aunt in Singapore, he was amazed to hear that she had somehow heard through various networks that Selvaraj had been seen in a South Indian restaurant in Sydney with an Anglo-Australian girl. He was regaled with accusations that he had secretly married. This news made its way back to his family in Singapore through a fellow villager who was acquainted with one of the waiters at this Sydney restaurant.

The power of gossip and the gaze lies in the influence of affective structures of guilt, shame, and fear of ostracism. Fears of ostracism from the translocal village are not ungrounded. Selvaraj's uncle, the brother with whom his father came to Singapore in the 1950s, was cast out of the community in the early 1980s when he married an Indian woman from Singapore of a different caste. All communication between him and Selvaraj's family was severed despite the fact that they had lived in neighbouring apartment blocks for many years and that he was the only immediate relative, apart from his wife and children, that Selvaraj's father had in Singapore. He was no longer welcome to return to Soorapallam and co-villagers in Singapore no longer invited him to occasions or events, and there has been no softening of this stance to this day. Although such deviations from the duties of the moral community are rare within the translocal village in Singapore, the story has achieved fabled status and functions as a constant reminder to others of the fearful consequences of such behaviour. His 'wayward' actions also brought great shame upon Selvaraj's family, and in response his parents were even more vigilant with regard to the behaviour of their own children. In this way, reproach, guilt, and shame transfers from the individual who has 'deviated' to his or her immediate kin. Failure to conform to expectations can result in ostracism, enduring and shameful stigma, and loss of status for the individual and their family. In the case of marriage outside the group, such impurity-causing transgressions can affect the marriage prospects of unmarried family members. In these situations, guilt and shame are often used to manipulate a potentially 'deviant' member into conforming lest it be construed that they do not care for their unmarried siblings. Such emotional blackmail is a regular occurrence.

The story of Elangovan, another young Musuguntha Vellalar man, is a good example of the emotional pressure brought to bear on young translocal villagers in Singapore. Because he was deeply and romantically involved with a young Indian woman of a different caste background, Elangovan refused to accept his parent's insistence on an arranged marriage with a young woman from the village. He was subjected to a verbal onslaught by his parents and extended family who regularly accused him of 'irresponsibility', 'disregarding his parents' wishes', and 'failing in his duties as a son'. There is an expectation upon all young Musuguntha Vellalar people in Singapore that they marry on completion of their studies or at least once they are stably employed. The fact that Elangovan broke with this expectation incurred extra wrath because he was also involved with a woman of another caste. Constant telephone calls from 'concerned' extended family and co-caste members in Singapore and the village were made, each accusing him of abandoning his duties to his family and reminding him that he would bring great shame upon those for whom he cared for if he continued to ignore his obligations. His parents constantly reminded him that if he wanted to marry someone else he must not, therefore, love his parents or his sisters because his actions would bring shame on them all. They genuinely seemed to fear ostracism. They expressed their fear that if Elangovan married outside the caste, his whole family would be considered impure, for which his younger sisters would suffer because this stigma would affect their marriage prospects. Despite his desperate feelings of guilt, however, Elangovan remained firm in his stance because he loved the young woman with whom he had formed a relationship.

His parents decided to change tack and appeared to let up in their demands. Not long after they asked him to fly to India and visit his 'dying' grandmother in Soorapallam one last time. On arriving in the village alone, Elangovan discovered that his grandmother was not in fact ill. He was immediately swamped by a large number of caste members residing in the village, each demanding he fulfil his obligations to his parents. His visit to Soorapallam was filled with a constant stream of Musuguntha Vellalars coming to visit to suggest potential marriage partners. Indeed, so concerned were they at his obstinacy, some threatened to wed Elangovan right there. It appeared Elangovan's parents had clandestinely planned his visit to his grandmother in order to present him to potential in-laws in the hope that he would succumb to the inevitable pressure in the village. Elangovan was only able to leave the village on the promise that he would finally agree to an arranged marriage once he returned to his parents in Singapore. Although he initially tried to hold out on his return, his parents were so emotionally distraught at the prospect of his out-marriage that they threatened suicide. Because he genuinely cared for his family, Elangovan felt that the burden of his parents' death because of his 'selfish' act would be one he could not bear and he thus felt no option but to give in to their demands.

We would like to argue that these examples demonstrate that translocal affective structures are a fundamentally important aspect of social control and translocal boundary maintenance in the case at hand. In other words, the regulation of behaviour through regimes of affect such as stigma, embarrassment, shame, and guilt functions to delimit the boundaries of the translocal village. Gossip, as Gluckman (1963: 313) has pointed out, is 'generally enjoyed by people about others with whom they are in a close social relationship'. It functions as a means of social control because 'when you gossip about your friends to other mutual friends you are demonstrating that you all belong to one set which has the duty to be interested in one another's vices as well as virtues' (Gluckman 1963: 313–14). Gossip and surveillance have important affective consequences, among them guilt and shame, are powerful means of social control in all societies, as many scholars have shown. Scheff (1990) calls pride and shame the 'primary social emotions' that communicate the state of a social bond. In Scheff's view, 'pride is the sign of an intact bond; shame a severed or threatened bond' (Scheff 1990: 95). Finding its power through constant self-monitoring, 'conformity to exterior norms is rewarded by others' deference and a feeling of pride, while non-conformity is punished by non-deference and feelings of shame' (cited in Lupton 1998: 19). In this way, shame and guilt operate as powerful affective sanctions among the translocal *ooru* in Singapore.

Although diffuse, this policing takes place within the bounds of the moral community of Soorapallam and, collectively, affect, obligation and responsibility are absolutely fundamental dimensions of its perpetuation. In her work on Manchester Pakistani Muslims, Pnina Werbner (2002) points out, following Bauman (1993), that moral communities are the product of a sense of responsibility for others. While many studies have focused on the communicative and aesthetic dimensions of diaspora, she argues that there is a need to acknowledge that diasporas are equally communities of co-responsibility characterized by gestures of 'reaching out' beyond localism (Werbner 2002: 61). It is through such performative gestures of giving within recognized limits of trust that transnational moral communities become actualized (Elias 1978). Of course, members of a diaspora can be part of many overlapping and differently scaled moral communities, from the village, to the local community in the host society, to the homeland nation to a broader Hindu identity. However, in some instances, and we argue that this is the case with many rural transnational villagers from South India, the primary sense of membership is to the moral community of the village. That is, in the case at hand, there is an acute and specific orientation to the moral community of the Soorapallam *ooru*, and translocal practices and relations are delimited by its ordering principles. In this case, as we have shown, those ordering principles and boundaries imposed by village, kinship, and caste relations largely determine the moral community. Collectively, the responsibilities outlined so far, especially those pertaining to marriage and to financial and migration assistance, are embodied in the Tamil notion of *nandri-kaadan*. *Nandri-Kaadan* roughly translates as 'thankful indebtedness'. It implies a deep moral duty to return favours present and past and to feel and show thankfulness and obligation to fellow Musuguntha Vellalars. Although somewhat similar to the Punjabi notion of *kidhmat* (Werbner 2002: 61), *nandri-kaadan* has a greater emphasis on indebtedness and the obligation to return. Perhaps most importantly for the continued reproduction of the translocal *ooru*, the exchange relations implied in *nandri-kaadan* form a never-ending set of relations continually cycling through notions of receipt and repayment, whereby the 'debt' incurred through the 'gift of social life' (Hage 2002) is never repaid. Hage describes this as a moral economy of social belonging, whereby members of a community are indebted to that community in a reciprocal gift-exchange relationship. This debt is incurred by the individual in receipt of the gift of community belonging and social life. In this reciprocal relationship, according to Hage, one repays the gift of communality through life-long participation in the communal group (Hage 2002). Indeed, he argues that for this reason migration is a particularly guilt-inducing process, and many migrants experience a strong desire to be seen as actively repaying this debt. Importantly, it is those to whom Soorapallamers at home and in Singapore feel a sense of *nandri-kaadan* that determines the limits of the translocal village.

There are several means through which the boundaries of the translocal village and the relations of *nandri-kaadan* are reproduced. First, as in Soorapallam, only kin and fellow caste members are invited to collective events in Singapore. Second, membership and participation in the gossip network is confined to the Musuguntha Vellalars; third, the social violence of shame is circumscribed by and experienced only within and before the *jati* members, demonstrated, for example, by the fact that an out-marriage brings no loss of face with Singaporean Indians of other castes; and finally, the boundaries of trust are limited to the Musuguntha Vellalar *jati*, as are the flows and returns we have described. Together with the emphasis on caste purity (cf. Dumont 1980) and its importance for identity status, these things form the social field of the translocal village, creating a sense of place, sociality, and belonging within its boundaries and rendering others, even other Tamils in Singapore, largely irrelevant.

What function does this translocal moral community of Soorapallam serve? The main role of the translocal dispersal of its members is that it ensures the social and economic viability of the village. That is, while migration is obviously about social and economic mobility for individuals and their immediate families, it is also supported and encouraged by co-villagers because of the broader benefits it has for Soorapallam and Musuguntha Vellalars as viable entities. The networks formed through co-villagers' migration increase the possibilities for other Soorapallam Musuguntha Vellalars to achieve similar mobility through marriage and employment prospects in Singapore. Funds from those abroad flow back into the village to be spent within families to build houses, to educate or marry their children, and to enhance important village infrastructure such as schools, temples, roads, and sewerage. What we can say about the translocal *ooru* in this case is that while it is translocal, the orientation is distinctly towards the viability of Soorapallam. How then might we characterize the example of Soorapallam in theoretical terms?

Theorizing the Translocal Village

In much of the literature on diasporas, the terms 'transnational' and 'translocal' are used interchangeably. It is our view that there is significant merit in working out the phenomenological differences between these two terms as they each signal related but different forms of imagined community. We wish to expand this a step further to explore what we have termed, throughout this chapter, the 'translocal village' to describe a particular form of moral community based around village-scale, place-oriented familial and neighbourly ties that have subsequently expanded across extended space.

In the early literature, transnationalism is conceived rather broadly by scholars such as Basch et al. (1994: 7) as the building of multi-stranded social relations encompassing a disparate range of processes that include familial, economic, social, organizational, religious, and political relationships, which give shape to transmigrant identities connecting their societies of origin and settlement. Moreover, it is generally agreed in the literature that these relations function to connect one or more localities. As Pnina Werbner (1999: 26) argues, the 'traffic in objects, persons, places and sentiments ... is one of the most significant bridges of distance spanning global diasporic communities and transnational families'.

We support Vertovec's critical observation, however, that there is now a need to develop a more complex typology of transnationalism. As he has argued, 'transnationalism is a notion that has become over-used to describe too wide a range of phenomena' (Vertovec 1999, 2001). There are studies on the transnational that refer to vastly different forms and scales of relations. Some use it to refer to transnational formations that are not necessarily about relationships of locality or linked to a physical place (see, for example, Ong 1999). Other studies use the idea of transnational community to refer to long-distance nationalist projects centred on homeland fantasies (Appadurai 1995). However, those involved in such projects are not necessarily involved with those in the homeland at the level of the everyday, at the level of the local, of 'neighbourhood'. Still other studies refer to transnational organizations, NGOs, and political movements, or refer broadly to migration circuits or flows of capital (Vertovec 1999).

While scholars such as Faist (2000) and Vertovec (1999) have made significant contributions to the critical development of a more detailed typology of transnationalism, one important category we wish to propose is that of the *translocal village*. While the terms 'transnational villagers' (Levitt 2001) and 'translocal village' (Peleikis 2000) have appeared occasionally in recent literature, they have been employed fairly to refer to transnational relations of villagers and are not really worked out in any categorical specificity. Both Levitt and Peleikis use the terms generally and neither of them develops the idea of 'translocal' or 'translocal village' beyond using them broadly to refer to transnational relations among villagers. The concept of 'translocal village' we wish to advance here not only embodies these relations but also more importantly flags the affective moral economies that emerge from small-scale, village-level social relations. We are not seeking to claim that the translocal dimensions of the Soorapallam village and the Musuguntha Vellalar community are exceptional or contrary to the norm. Rather, these specific relationships and practices provide a much deeper insight into the production of locality in an increasingly globalized world.

Relationships stemming from Soorapallam village, and this is our first key point, are of a very localized village and caste nature rather than signalling a broader scale such as trans- 'national' or even the idea of an 'Indian diaspora'. What we want to argue is that many 'Indians' abroad do not especially identify first and foremost with India or Indianness as deriving from the Indian nation. In Selvaraj's case, for example, he and his family, and fellow caste members, do not speak Hindi and have little sense of identification with India as nation; neither do they primarily identify themselves as Tamils. While the reproduction of the Tamil language and culture is important to them, it is part of ensuring the reproduction of a sense of identity that is primarily connected to their *ooru*. They feel very little affinity with North Indians, more affinity with South Indians, yet more with Indians from Tamil Nadu but primarily their sense of identity and connection is to those caste members belonging to Soorapallam first and then the 32 villages from which the Musuguntha Vellalars come. It is their *ooru*, *sondam*, and *jati* then that defines to a large extent the boundaries of their transnational or translocal relations, orientations, imaginations, and relations. Moreover, the translocal *ooru* is not merely an imagined place but one that emanates from concrete social relations. Its members have met face to face, and they are linked through endogamous marriage practices.

As we have shown, the expanded village relationships and the practices that go into reproducing them are able to create an extended space of belonging for members of Soorapallam. It is this space that we call *translocality*. Arjun Appadurai (1996: 178–99) has articulated a theory of the production of *locality*, wherein locality is an essentially relational and contextual knot of relationships, rather than something necessarily in space or place. Appadurai's conceptualization of the *translocal* (1996: 192)—while able to encompass many of the broader relations outlined in the general literature on transnationalism (Basch et al. 1994; Smith and Guarnizo 1998; Vertovec 2001)—places an additional emphasis on those processes of actual everyday relations, and in our view forms a distinctive subset of the broader notion of transnationalism. As a subset of transnationalism, the translocal allows us to envisage the everydayness of material, family, social, and symbolic networks and exchanges that connect, in this case, Soorapallam to Singapore. Locality encompasses the emotional and social character of neighbourliness in a way the notion of transnational does not. Locality, as Appadurai argues, has an inherently 'phenomenological quality, constituted by a series of links between the sense of social immediacy, the technologies of interactivity, and the relativity of contexts', which is expressed through particular modes of agency, sociality, and reproducibility (Appadurai 1996: 178). Translocality stretches these relations across borders.

Extending this concept one step further, the translocal village encompasses the notion of sociality linked to a small-scale place from which the translocal community originates. While members of Soorapallam are situated in a transnational relationship, as it is popularly understood, their practices are not about nationalism or connection to nation, or simply cultural flows. Their practices are very clearly tied to a physical place and the maintenance of the community; the caste and kin-based relations that emanate from such practices are determined and reproduced by that place. As we have shown, the translocal village is reproduced through multiple strands of translocal relations that mirror, to a large extent, the social relations in the village itself. Hence, the reproduction of the translocal village occurs through the extension of affective regimes of guilt, shame, obligation, and *nandri-kaadan*, through a sense of membership to the caste and through ritual returns. It is reproduced politically through the presence of a Singapore *thalaivar*, its economic viability is perpetuated through migration, employment, financial repatriation, and contributions to village infrastructure. The translocal village's orientation is to the physical village, in this case Soorapallam.

Furthermore, in Appadurai's view, the phenomenological quality is the main predicate of locality. He argues that rites of passage rituals such as naming, tonsuring, scarification, segregation, and deprivation are techniques for the 'inscription of locality onto bodies', and they are means to 'embody locality as well as to locate bodies in socially and spatially defined communities' (Appadurai 1996: 179). This bodily inscription of locality plays a significant part in creating an affective boundary around the translocal village and the Musuguntha Vellalars. As in the case of all rituals and rites conducted both in Singapore and Soorapallam, they function as a way of inscribing in bodily and affective ways one's origin and caste identity. This realm of affect has been much neglected in the literature. We also argue that, especially with small-scale village communities, affect and the obligations surrounding *nandri-kaadan* are extraordinarily important elements in the reproduction of the village's social relations, despite the fact that the village now extends across borders. In other words, the traffic in structures of affect, which emanate from the original small-scale community, is one of the most important defining characteristics of the idea of the translocal village. Policed through the surveillance techniques described earlier in the text, these things together function as gate-keeping mechanisms for the village. As Appadurai argues, locality has to be *worked at*. It is an inherently fragile social achievement and requires local subjects possessed of the knowledge to reproduce it.

In sum, the translocal village has the following features. It is about local fields, not about the nation or transnation, as in 'the Indian Diaspora'. It is not just about family ties across extended space. As Appadurai has argued, the translocal represents a relational and contextual knot of relationships and implies an emphasis on processes of everyday relationships, the everydayness of family, social, and symbolic networks and exchanges. It encompasses the social character of neighbourliness and has, importantly, a phenomenological quality, of social immediacy and the relativity of contexts (Appadurai 1995). The translocal village has certain additional features. It features forms of sociality emerging from and reproducing relations of a small-scale place. That is, the social relations emanate from and are determined by the relations stemming from the village. Although inevitably modified in the new context, these relations, such as kinship, financial, political or ritual practices, often mirror those that take place in the village. Moreover, the social field of the translocal village is reproduced as much through the translocalizing of affective regimes emerging from the village, while rituals, sentiment, and affect are means of inscribing locality onto bodies, creating a sense of boundary across extended space. And, finally, the key orientation among translocal villagers is towards the village proper, despite long-term migration elsewhere.

The Importance of Host Country Citizenship in Reproducing the Translocal Village

It should be pointed out, however, that while the translocal villagers of Soorapallam in Singapore have a primary sense of identification and engagement with the moral community of their home *ooru*, this is made possible, or is cushioned, by the cultural production of the broader Tamil community in Singapore and the institutional support from the state through official multiracialism, which takes on the responsibilities of reproducing Tamil language, culture, and religious practices.

The multiracial policy introduced in Singapore recognizes four racial categories as the foundational makeup of its society. Indians are recognized as one of the four official 'racial' groups (along with Chinese, Malays, and Eurasians/Europeans),[10] and with this recognition comes a series of government-sponsored rights and services directed specifically at the Tamil Indians. Because Tamils form the majority of Indians in Singapore, and Tamil is one of the four official languages. It is taught in schools and there are state-sponsored Tamil media (Chua 1998; Clammer 1998). Within this context, members of the Soorapallam translocal village are able to draw on these resources, thus ameliorating their concerns about the survival of their language and culture and, at the same time, through the practices of moral community, enabling them to delimit and reproduce themselves as distinct from other Singaporean Tamils.[11]

The security achieved through citizenship rights in a multiracial or multicultural society such as Singapore provides the resources needed to maintain translocal relations. Rights accorded through citizenship such as the ability to travel freely, to sponsor a marriage partner or close kin to migrate to Singapore, the security afforded by public housing in Singapore, all these provide a solid foundation to support the translocal *ooru*. The contrast with Soorapallamers who have gone to work in the Gulf States emphasizes this point. In the last 10 or 15 years, a large number of young men from Soorapallam have followed one another to take up contract-based work in the Middle East. Working as unskilled or semi-skilled foreign labourers in the oil industries of the Gulf States, there are no possibilities for migration or permanent settlement.[12] These men simply go to work and send home money. It is a masculine network; only men travel to these places for work, and they do not bring wives or children. Many are unmarried young men who delay marriage until their return or are newlyweds who leave their new brides at home. Consequently, there is little in the way of 'community' established in these host nations, and it is a form of temporary migration where young men go for up to five years and return more or less permanently to the village after the end of their employment tenure. In Singapore, however, the migration is generally permanent, despite the continual return visits to India.[13] In contrast to workers in the Gulf States, the cycle of migration and return visits creates a translocal social field of neighbourly and family relations, stretching the *ooru* across borders. This process is supported by the firm foundation offered by the rights accorded under Singapore's multiracial policy.

The citizenship rights and cultural context of Singapore also has a bearing in terms of the identification with the *ooru* rather than a more amorphous notion of 'Indianness' or even 'Tamilness'. As Mishra has argued, diasporic imaginaries often grow out of a sense of being marginalized, 'of being rejected outright by nation-states' (Mishra 2002: 237). As scholars such as Werbner (1997) have shown, the schismogenetic nature of identity is such that marginalization can create a sense of solidarity and identification with the co-marginalized, as is the case with the new sense of Islamic 'Umma' where an increasing identification has occurred between Pakistani and Arabic Muslims in the United Kingdom under a broad banner of Islam. Similarly, the increasing 'Desi' pan-Indian identity popular among many young Indians in the United Kingdom may be read as a response to the forces of marginalization experienced there. So, instead of the more regionally based identifications of their parent's generation, these young Indians have a less specific sense of cultural Indianness supported in part through the vast cultural resources produced through the Bollywood cinema phenomenon. A similar example is the sense of pan-Tamilness that has emerged from the Sri Lankan Tamil struggle, which extends to the Sri Lankan Tamil refugee diaspora (see Fuglerud 1999).[14]

Conclusion

Although we can expect to see changes in the translocal village over the ensuing generations, there is an argument to be made that those rural Indian migrants who arrived in Singapore in and after the 1950s may continue to maintain their translocal village relations for more generations than was previously the case. As has been well documented in the literature on globalization and transnationalism (Mahler 1998; Fuglerud 1999; Ong 1999), the technologies of travel and communication make possible the maintenance of ties and social relations across extended space. The fact that the members of Soorapallam in Singapore are returning to their village to marry their second-generation children suggests that connections may continue through subsequent generations.

The continual sourcing and emigration of marriage partners from the village and the ability through technology and travel to do that means that in each family there is always a first-generation migrant from the village with first-hand connections to, and memories of, the village and who has kin relations there. Technology and travel have meant that the viability of the village has not been challenged, so far at least, by the translocalization of its social relations.

Through our account of Soorapallam and its translocal village, we explored the ways in which the home village is maintained as a viable social unit despite its dispersal. We have advanced the theoretical notion of the translocal village to further typologize the notion of transnationalism. As we have argued, the notion of the translocal village recognizes the small-scale place orientation of such translocal communities.

Through a case study of the translocal village of Soorapallam, we have explored the means through which the Musuguntha Vellalars reproduce themselves as a community in and between the village and Singapore. As with all transnational communities, Soorapallamers and fellow Musuguntha Vellalars participate in a wide range of economic and sociocultural activities. However, we have argued that the ordering principles of what we have termed the translocal village are equally circumscribed through its moral economy and its affective regimes. We concluded the chapter by arguing in favour of the idea of the translocal village as a subset category of transnationalism as it is able to embody the phenomenological affective, ritual, neighbourly, kin, and caste relations that stem from small-scale communities, such as the rural South Indian village we have discussed here.

Notes

1. Auto-ethnography is increasingly seen as a legitimate research methodology. We use it here to refer to Selvaraj Velayutham's status as 'insider anthropologist' (see Reed-Danahay 1997).
2. See Arasaratnam 1970, Sandhu 1969, Sandhu and Mani 1993, and Siddique and PuruShotam 1982 for well-documented historical and sociological accounts of Indians in South East Asia, Malaya, and Singapore.
3. Indian society is divided into four main caste groups, known as *varnas*. The four *varnas* are the Brahmins (priests), Kshatriyas (the king and warriors), the Vaishyas (who, with the rise of trade and agriculture, became the farmers and merchants), and the Shudras (servants), and

finally the outcaste or untouchables (Chandalas, otherwise known as Dalits). A system of subcastes, or *jatis*, evolved, related to each occupation. Individuals of a particular *jati* are constrained in various social aspects, especially marriage, to remain within their *jati*. The Vellalars, members of the Vaishyas, were primarily cultivators. According to Pandian (1987: 23), *jati* groups, whose identity was linked with specialized and/or specific occupations, were usually named by the occupations they performed. The term Vellalar refers to 'cultivator', and Musuguntha Vellalar are a subset of this caste. See also Dumont (1980).

4. Musuguntha country consists of the following 32 villages: Aaladikkumaulai, Alampallam, Alathur, Athikkottai, Enadhi, Natuchchalai, Patikadu, Palamuththi, Pudhukkottai, Ulloor, Sempaalur, Soorapallam, Thittakudi, Vendakkottai, Pulavanji, Karuppur, Musiri, Vattakudi, Madukkur, Andami, Pallathur, Palaya Madukkur, Thamarankottai, Mannankadu, Kasangadu, Moothakurichi, Suthanpatti, Sevanthanpatti, Mathangal, Kirathur, Silambavelangadu, and Sengapaduthangadu.
5. The reproduction of caste and kinship in this way is not new, as demonstrated in the case of South Indian Tamil labourers in British Ceylon in the 1920s. Jayaraman (1975) points out that large-scale family migration and the Kangani system of recruitment (recruiters recruiting from their own caste and kinship groups) prevented labourers from changing their castes as individuals either before departure or after reaching Ceylon.
6. The research presented in this chapter is based on the auto-ethnographic reflections of the co-author, Selvaraj, and information gathered from members of his family and his community in Singapore and India. We have changed names and some relationships to maintain the privacy of his family and other members of the community.
7. The Immigration (Prohibition of Entry) Ordinance of 1953 restricted the entry of non-British-born and naturalized subjects into Malaya. Only returning residents, wives, and children and a small number of professionals were allowed to come to Singapore thereafter (Sandhu 1969: 151).
8. For an explanation of many of these Tamil terms and caste relations, see Pandian (1987).
9. House-warming is an exceptionally important ritual for Hindus generally.
10. See Siddique (1989) for further discussion on the CMIO model and the construction of a Singaporean identity.
11. Conversely, Virginia Dominguez (1998) has also argued that racialized societies such as the United States allow some groups to assimilate and not others, forcing those who are not assimilable within the national space to find alternative spaces of belonging, very often transnationally.
12. For a discussion of South Indian men from Kerala and their transnational work practices in the Gulf States, see Osella and Osella (2000).

13. The exception is the return of elderly migrants to the village after retirement.
14. Of course, it is not marginalization alone in these cases, but a combination of generational differences in the case of *desi* youth or the urban sending context of Jaffna Tamils that also impact the Sri Lankan Tamil diaspora.

References

Annamalai, M. (1984) *Culture in Rural Practice* [in Tamil, Namathu Panpatil Nadapura Illakium]. Chennai: Maruthemalaiyan Publisher.

Appadurai, A. (1995) 'The production of locality', in Fardon, R. (ed.) *Counterworks: Managing the Diversity of Knowledge*. London: Routledge, 204–25.

——. (1996) *Modernity at Large: Cultural Dimensions of Globalisation*. Minneapolis: University of Minnesota Press.

Arasaratnam, S. (1970) *Indians in Malaysia and Singapore*. Kuala Lumpur: Oxford University Press.

Basch, L., Glick Schiller, N., and Szanton Blanc, C. (1994) *Nations Unbound: Transnational Projects, Postcolonial Predicaments and Deterritorialized Nation-States*. Langhorne, PA: Gordon and Breach.

Bauman, Z. (1993) *Postmodern Ethics*. Oxford: Blackwell.

Chua, B.H. (1998) 'Culture, multiracialism and national identity in Singapore', in Chen, K.H. (ed.) *Trajectories: Inter-Asia Cultural Studies*. London: Routledge, 186–205.

Clammer, J. (1998) *Race and State in Independent Singapore, 1965–1990: The Cultural Politics of Pluralism in a Multiethnic Society*. Brookfield, VT: Ashgate.

Dominguez, V. (1998) 'Asserting (trans)nationalism and the social conditions of its possibility', *Communal/Plural: Journal of Transnational and Crosscultural Studies*, 6, 139–56.

Dumont, L. (1980) *Homo Hierarchicus: The Caste System and Its Implications* [translated by Sainsbury, M., Dumont, L., and Gulati, B.]. Chicago: University of Chicago Press.

Elias, N. (1978) *The Civilising Process*. Oxford: Blackwell.

Faist, T. (2000) 'Transnationalization in international migration: implications for the study of citizenship and culture', *Ethnic and Racial Studies*, 23, 189–222.

Falzon, M.A. (2003) '"Bombay, our cultural heart": rethinking the relation between homeland and diaspora', *Ethnic and Racial Studies*, 26, 662–83.

Fuglerud, O. (1999) *Life on the Outside: The Tamil Diaspora and Long Distance Nationalism*. London: Pluto.

Gluckman, M. (1963) 'Gossip and scandal', *Current Anthropology*, 4, 307–16.

Hage, G. (2002) 'The differential intensities of social reality: migration, participation and guilt', in Hage, G. (ed.) *Arab Australians Today: Citizenship and Belonging*. Melbourne: Melbourne University Press, 192–205.

Jayaraman, R. (1975) *Caste Continuities in Ceylon: A Study of the Social Structure of Three Tea Plantations*. Bombay: Popular Prakashan.

Levitt, P. (2001) *The Transnational Villagers*. Berkeley/Los Angeles: University of California Press.

Lupton, D. (1998) *The Emotional Self*. London: Sage.

Mahler, S. (1998) 'Theoretical and empirical contributions toward a research agenda for transnationalism', in Smith, M.P., and Guarnizo, L.E. (eds.) *Transnationalism from Below*. New Brunswick, NJ: Transaction Publishers, 64–102.

Mishra, V. (2002) *Bollywood Cinema*, London: Routledge.

Ong, A. (1999) *Flexible Citizenship: The Cultural Logics of Transnationality*. Durham, NC/London: Duke University Press.

Osella, F., and Osella, C. (2000) 'Migration, money and masculinity in Kerala (South India)', *Journal of the Royal Anthropological Institute*, 6, 117–31.

Pandian, J. (1987) *Caste, Nationalism and Ethnicity: An Interpretation of Tamil Cultural History and Social Order*. Bombay: Popular Prakashan.

Peleikis, A. (2000) 'The emergence of a translocal community: the case of a South Lebanese village and its migrant connections to Ivory Coast', *Cahiers d'études sur la Mediterranée orientale et le monde Turco-Iranien*, 30, 297–317.

Reed-Danahay, D. (ed.) (1997) *Auto/ethnography: Rewriting the Self and the Social*. Oxford: Berg.

Sandhu, K. (1969) *Indians in Malaya*. London: Cambridge University Press.

Sandhu, K., and Mani, A. (1993) *Indian Communities in Southeast Asia*. Singapore: Institute of Southeast Asian Studies.

Scheff, T. (1990) *Microsociology: Discourse, Emotion and Social Structure*. Chicago: University of Chicago Press.

Shukla, S. (2001) 'Locations for South Asian diasporas', *Annual Review of Anthropology*, 30, 551–73.

Siddique, S. (1989) 'Singaporean identity', in Sandhu, K., and Wheatley, P. (eds.) *Management of Success: The Moulding of Modern Singapore*. Singapore: Institute of Southeast Asian Studies, 563–77.

Siddique, S., and PuruShotam, N. (1982) *Singapore's Little India: Past, Present and Future*. Singapore: Institute of Southeast Asian Studies.

Smith, M.P., and Guarnizo, L.E. (eds.) (1998) *Transnationalism from Below*. New Brunswick, NJ/London: Transaction Publishers.

Tambiah, S.J. (2000) 'Transnational movements, diaspora and multiple modernities', *Daedalus*, 129, 163–94.

van der Veer, P. (1995) *Nation and Migration: The Politics of Space in the South Asian Diaspora*. Philadelphia: University of Pennsylvania Press.

Vertovec, S. (1999) 'Conceiving and researching transnationalism', *Ethnic and Racial Studies*, 22, 447–62.

——. (2000) *The Hindu Diaspora: Comparative Patterns*. London: Routledge.

——. (2001) 'Transnationalism and identity', *Ethnic and Migration Studies*, 27, 573–83.

Wadley, S.S. (1980) 'The paradoxical powers of Tamil women', in Wadley, S.S. (ed.) *The Powers of Tamil Women*. Syracuse: Maxwell School of Citizenship and Public Affairs, Syracuse University, 153–70.

Werbner, P. (1997) 'Essentialising essentialism, essentialising silence: ambivalence and multiplicity in the constructions of racism and ethnicity', in Webner, P., and Moddod, T. (eds.) *Debating Cultural Hybridity: Multicultural Identities and the Politics of Anti-racism*. London: Zed Books, 226–54.

Werbner, P. (1999) 'Global pathways: working class cosmopolitans and the creation of transnational worlds', *Social Anthropology*, 7, 17–35.

Werbner, P. (2002) *Imagined Diasporas among Manchester Muslims*. Oxford: SAR Press and James Currey.

Wood, M. (1995) *The Smile of Murugan*. London: John Murray Publishers.

7

Imagining Difference

The Experiences of 'Transnational' Indian IT Professionals in Germany

Louise Meijering and Bettina van Hoven

In spite of the admission of five million guest workers since the 1960s (Vertovec 1996), Germany has refused to be called an 'immigration state' (Bude 1996; Akashe-Böhme 2000). Recently, however, political parties have begun to rethink their attitudes towards immigration, as well as their immigration policies based on an emerging economic need (DPA 2001a; Gaserow 2001).[1] Since 1999, Germany's IT industry has struggled with the lack of sufficiently skilled and specialized workers and an estimated 75,000 job vacancies (Welsch 2001). The new migration policies have recognized pressures to fill such labour market niches by widening the possibilities to admit skilled labour, based on the green card model[2] (DPA 2001b).

From 1 August 2000, when the green card scheme was implemented, 20,000 IT-specialists from outside the EU were permitted to live and work there for a restricted period of five years. This measure was devised to prevent their permanent settlement in Germany, as had happened with 25 per cent of the guest workers (Vertovec 1996). But in spite of the expectation that 10,000 green cards would have been given out by the end of 2000 (UNI 2000), the actual number of immigrants has been lower than the government expected. Only on 27 October 2001 was the 10,000th green card issued (Leven 2001).

Indian IT professionals are in many ways privileged as migrants in Germany as a result of company benefits packages. However, their experiences are coloured by their imaginations of Germany, such as those created by the (Indian) media (most notably the perceived threat of right-wing extremist groups) and the migrants' family, and by their own expectations of Germany. Such imaginations and the *de facto* culture clash lead to a contentious role for Indian migrants in their host society. Many migrants 'live their lives simultaneously across different nation-states, being both "here" and "there", crossing geographical and political boundaries' (Riccio 2001: 583). Both economic resources and symbolic resources (such as goods or food from 'home') play an important part in establishing the migrants 'transnational livelihood' (Salih 2001).

This chapter explores the motivations to migrate and migration experiences, with a focus on cultural clashes, of 22 Indian IT specialists in Germany. A central question in this chapter is how Indian IT professionals' images of Germany shape their experiences in the country and vice versa. Before turning to data collection and the respondents in this study, we provide a brief discussion of the concepts behind transnationalism and skilled international migration. The next sections focus on the respondents' personal experiences after they migrated to Germany for their work. We conclude that the migrants face personal struggles, such as leaving their (extended) families for the purpose of career advancement, while feeling estranged from the cultural context of their host culture. These struggles appear to encourage them to unite in transnational communities. In addition, the migrants' accounts help shed light on the low level of interest in the green card scheme.

Transnationalism

Transnationalism is a widely used but ambiguous term (Vertovec 2001), generally referring to the combination of attachment to 'host' and 'home' country or society that migrants tend to develop, which is facilitated by increased communication and transportation systems (Faist 2000; Bailey 2001; Vertovec 2001; Menjívar 2002; Remennick 2002; Willis and Yeoh 2002). Essential in transnationalism is that it transcends the level of the nation-state (Bailey 2001), whereby transmigrants 'develop and maintain multiple relations—familial, economic, social, organisational, religious, and political that span borders' (Glick Schiller et al. 1992, cited in Bürkner 2000: 106). Much of the literature on transnationalism in skilled migration focuses on 'transnationalism from above', which refers to processes at the supra-national level (Willis and Yeoh 2002). This research aims to look at transnationalism on a smaller scale, i.e., on the individual or group level, which is called 'transnationalism from below'.

The social networks that transmigrants develop can be referred to as transnational social spaces, which is defined by Faist as 'combinations of ties, positions in networks and organisations, and networks of organisations that reach across the borders of multiple states' (2000: 191). He distinguishes three types of transnational social spaces: transnational kinship groups, transnational circuits, and transnational communities. In the first group, remittances that are sent home to family members and characterized by reciprocity are important. Trading networks are a typical example of transnational circuits. Transnationalist social space is always a negotiation between attachments to different places, based on perceptions of the host society by the transmigrants (Bürkner 2000). Although transnational communities have perhaps been associated more with 'permanent' migrant groups, such as the Jewish or Mexicans, more recently similar developments have been observed among mobile and changing groups of migrants. For example, British expatriates in Singapore developed a mixed network in the work place, which they saw as useful for their careers. Their social network, however, excluded Singaporeans, due to the strong ties with other expatriates and cultural differences in socializing (Beaverstock 2002).

Skilled Migration

The increase of international labour migration can be related to globalization of the world economy (Sassen 1988). Within international labour migration, a distinction between skilled and unskilled migration should be made, which Sassen refers to as 'a new geography of centrality and marginality' (1998: xxv). This materializes in a network of global cities specializing in finance and services and in a less successful and integrated periphery (Sassen 1998). Flows of skilled migrants have been neither extensive in numbers nor long in duration (Hardill 1998). However, their influence on the world economy has been considerable (Massey and Jess 1995). Although the majority of skilled international migrants currently move from 'developing' to 'developed' countries (Iredale 1999), earlier studies have concentrated on the movement of managers of transnational corporations (TNCs)[3] from the headquarters in developed countries to subsidiaries in less developed countries (Beaverstock 1990, 1991, 2002; Findlay 1990; Cheng and Yang 1998). This study contributes to the existing literature on international skilled migration by focusing on migration of professionals from a developing to a developed country.

Willis and Yeoh (2000, 2002) suggested that most literature on skilled international migration focuses on the workplace and the male individual, and is linked to intra-company labour markets. The result has been a failure to recognize the gendered aspects and the household context of skilled migration. Notable exceptions are, for example, studies by Hardill on British expatriates (1998) and by Willis and Yeoh themselves on Singaporean migration to China (Yeoh and Willis 1999; Willis and Yeoh 2000, 2002). Nonetheless, as the greater part of skilled migrants has consisted of single men, a research focusing on individual males instead of households is justifiable (see also Beaverstock 1996). In the context of this research, the reason for the dominance of male interviewees lies in the cultural context from which the respondents originate. In general, it is not socially acceptable for women to have paid jobs, particularly abroad.[4]

Most international migrants depend on intermediaries who make arrangements for the work and accommodation of migrants in their host country. Intermediaries can, for example, be personnel offices of TNCs that facilitate international movements of their staff, recruitment agencies, educational institutions, or informal international networks of family and friends. Intermediaries function as 'migration channels' by channelling information and resources (Findlay and Garrick 1990). Recruitment agents (inter-firm migration; Tyner 2000) and personnel managers (intra-firm migration; Beaverstock 2002) are of particular importance, since they can contribute to a biased (for example, gendered) selection that fits the prejudices of the employers (Tyner 2000).

Aside from company policies, other important factors are shortages and saturation in domestic and international labour markets for certain occupations (Beaverstock 1991). Furthermore, individual motivations, aspirations, and decisions by migrants themselves influence the nature of skilled migration as well. Among others, Beaverstock (1991) argued that there are three key individual motivations that influence the decision to work abroad: career-path improvement, personal development, and financial gain. More recently, Stalker (2000) emphasized financial gain as the key motivation for migration, while other motivations are the desire to escape from limited promotion opportunities and the wish to travel and live abroad (Amit-Talai 1998). In particular, where migration from 'developing' to 'developed' countries is concerned, unfavourable living conditions at home can also be a stimulus (Tzeng 1995). Cheng and Yang (1998) stated that confrontation with a Western lifestyle by migrants from less developed countries increases awareness of and dissatisfaction with material inequality and eventually leads to permanent emigration.

Data Collection

To collect data for this study, 22 in-depth interviews were conducted. Data were transcribed and analysed with the help of the computer package QSR N4. Initially, one interview per respondent was held, but the respondents agreed to be contacted again by email or telephone in case of uncertainties or the need for feedback. All interviews were held with Indian IT professionals, working for TNCs in the Frankfurt am Main metropolitan area in Germany. The respondents were recruited using a snowball approach. Three further respondents were contacted with the help of the *Industrie- und Handelskammer* (Chamber of Commerce) in Darmstadt. This was the only official channel through which respondents were found. Official institutions were very reluctant to give information for reasons of privacy (*Datenschutzgesetz*). It was impossible to establish contact with Indian employees who were the only foreigner working for a small company in non-metropolitan areas.

This approach led to a sample of predominantly male respondents (18 male and four female respondents) between 23 and 30 years old, single, Hindu, (upper) middle class and educated either in computer science or in engineering. The respondents were all employees of TNCs and had come to Germany through the Indian counterparts of their companies. Only six respondents held green cards, while the others had a long-term visa. At the time of the interviews, the respondents had spent time periods roughly varying between six months and two years in Germany. Most planned to stay about one and a half years in Germany altogether.

Key Motivations for Migration

The analysis of interview data revealed a range of motivations for respondents to come to Germany (Table 1). The three key motivations mentioned by the Indian IT specialists correspond with the findings by Beaverstock (1991), Amit-Talai (1998), and Stalker (2000) outlined earlier in the text: career, money, and personal experience. Nineteen respondents stated they had come to Germany as a career move, 18 for the experience, and 13 for the additional income. One respondent explained the career move accordingly: 'I'm willing to sacrifice it if I thrust up my career. If I thrust up money in life, a few years doesn't matter' (14).[5]

Table 1

Motivations for Coming to Germany by Respondent and by Motivation

Respondents	*Career*	*Travel and Personal Growth*	*Money*	*German Culture*	*Europe Over US*	*Company Placement*	*Help India*	*Quality of Life*
1	•					•		
2	•		•	•			•	
3		•			•	•		
4	•	•			•		•	
5	•	•	•	•				
6	•		•					
7	•	•		•				
8	•				•			
9	•	•	•		•			•
10	•	•	•	•	•			
11	•	•	•	•		•	•	
12	•	•	•	•				
13	•	•						
14	•	•	•			•		•
15	•	•	•			•		
16	•	•	•	•				
17	•	•	•	•				
18	•	•		•				
19	•					•		
20		•		•	•			
21	•	•	•	•	•			
22		•	•	•	•	•		
Total	19	17	13	12	8	7	3	2

This quote illustrates an aspect that has been neglected in earlier studies. Although other authors have also mentioned career improvement as a motivation for working abroad, they do not stress the sacrifices made in family life while pursuing career improvement. In contrast to the findings of earlier studies (see Hardill 1998; Yeoh and Willis 1999; Willis and Yeoh 2000), the move by female respondents was not motivated by their husbands. Instead, the key motivation was, equally to the male respondents, a career move.

As the respondents moved from a 'developing' to a 'developed' country, it could be expected that a better quality of life was a key motivation for working abroad (Tzeng 1995). This could not, however, be substantiated in the context of this study. A possible explanation is that all respondents come from at least middle-class families in India. The standard of living that they are used to may be comparable to what they found in Germany. Relatively, however, they were more prosperous in India. Various respondents commented on the value of money in India and on the prestige attached to it. One respondent illustrated:

We have more value [...] for money, than here. I [can] buy a DVD-player over here, and no one cares about it. But in India if I buy a DVD player, it's something (21).

The findings of this research suggest that the relative quality of life is more important than an absolute improvement achieved by moving to a more developed country, as was suggested by Cheng and Yang (1998). It is notable that 18 respondents emphasized motivations less oriented towards materialistic improvement such as personal growth, travel, and German culture. Many respondents emphasized both the educational and the 'fun' sides of their stay. They felt that they were expanding their horizons, being confronted with the lifestyles and habits of another country, thus showing an eagerness to stimulate their cultural imagination. For example:

I thought it's good, one thing is to learn a different culture, learn a different language, meet more people [...] My personal opinion is, the more you travel, your outlook on life [...] changes, you become more tolerant of different cultures, you learn a lot more. [...] I want to open my horizons (17).

Experiences in Germany

In the following paragraphs, we explore five themes that were significant to the respondents: language, family structures, social structures, working culture, and racial discrimination. The respondents observe that Germans are distant towards them, which they relate to a perceived inward orientation of German families, differences in socializing, and intentions of racial discrimination. A combination of these factors discourages them from understanding German culture and integrating, for example, by learning German. Social contacts remain largely restricted to English-speaking (Indian) colleagues. Instead of taking part more actively in German society, they unite in a transnational community. Outside the 'safe' environment of the transnational community, the respondents feel insecure and 'out of place'. The negative images that the respondents have of Germans and German society tend to be reinforced by reciprocal sceptical and expectant attitudes. A lack of mutual understanding reproduces barriers between the groups.

Language

Language proficiency is regarded as an important means by which culture can be transmitted (Hofstede 1991). Without knowing the language, the communication of feelings is impaired and a barrier between cultures remains (Benmayor and Skotnes 1994). Although various respondents stated their wish to learn about the culture, remarkably few expressed their aim to learn the German language.

Most respondents have little knowledge of the German language. People who have been in Germany longer tend to speak the language better, but never exceed the basic level.[6] Therefore, most people communicated in English. However, many respondents also believed that outside the working environment, Germans 'don't speak English at all' (3), and 'it's not easy to survive here if you don't know German' (22). Communication with Germans remained problematic and a number of interviewees 'overcame' this problem by establishing contact almost exclusively with Indians or a handful of English-speaking people. In so doing, cross-cultural adjustment became problematic and many interviewees were prevented from fully participating in or adjusting to the host culture. In addition, the proximity to Indian-speaking peers and the restricted period of residence in Germany contributed to the perception of most respondents that learning the language was not essential.

As long as you can understand some little words, I think that's okay. (12)

There's no necessity for me to learn German. (15)

The respondents acknowledged the resulting lack of opportunity to establish contact with 'average' Germans who do not speak English. They justified this, however, by arguing that German society itself is too different and difficult to access. Key differences that the respondents commented upon were the family structure, social structure, working culture, and racial discrimination. These aspects are discussed in turn in the following text.

Family Structures

During the interviews, most respondents described significant differences between German and Indian family structures. Due to the specific cultural context in India, the structure of Indian families was often spoken of as being important. Indians are closely in touch with their families:

I call my parents every once or twice a week or something like that. [...] family bonds are very very tightly knit in India, so [I] really can't help it. (8)

In contrast, the respondents felt that German people live their lives independently from each other and that little time is reserved for people outside the nuclear family. Even in social life, the respondents perceived that friends make appointments in order to meet each other rather than visiting spontaneously. As a result, home has become a very private part of life to which only close friends are invited. The following quote illustrates the respondents' perceptions:

> I feel they are always wanting privacy […]. And the house is their palace. I mean palace is a very good thing, but you should welcome people to your palace. They're very restrictive. You don't know whether you would be welcome in their house or not. In India, you don't phone before you go to somebody's house […] And […] if I see the Germans, [they live separated from] their parents […], the children after eighteen they [live] separate, the brother and sister [live] separate, sometimes the husband and wife are separate[d] […] Everybody is living his own life. (14)

In India, the respondents function as parts of the extended family, which determines their identity to an important extent. The group provides safety and protection beyond adulthood. In contrast, Germans live in the context of the nuclear family. Rather than being dominated by their social context, personal preferences form the most important part of their identities. In Indian culture, the extended family strongly influences individual decisions. The effect of individual actions on the extended family is always considered before making a decision. The individual move abroad does not necessarily contradict this as careers and status are valued highly, and personal achievement reflects positively on the family as a whole. Together with sending home remittances, improving the status of the family indicates that the respondents exist as part of a closely knit transnational kinship group. Simultaneously, the respondents develop a transnational community in their host country.

Social Structures

It was noted earlier that most respondents have only Indian friends and do not interact much with Germans in their personal lives. Half of the respondents have a social circle that consists of Indian colleagues, which indicates that the respondents have few contacts originating outside the workplace and their own peer group. If they have German friends, which was the case for seven respondents, it is essential for most of them to speak English. It is easy to meet other Indians at work, since many are working in the same company. They are all in the same situation and can support each other. Respondents indicated that they highly valued the convenience of having people around who understand their problems but, more importantly, their way of life and their culture. An important part of socializing is the preparation and sharing of Indian meals. Like the women in Salih's (2001) study, the (male) migrants use symbolic resources from India to construct their personal homes in the foreign culture.

The sharing of a common way of life and consequent development of a shared identity indicates that the respondents form transnational communities that are sometimes organized at an inter-regional scale (Green card Indians 2001; Munichmela 2001). Although the data from this research suggest that, as time elapses, more contacts with Germans develop, many people were satisfied with a (almost) completely Indian circle of friends. In addition to mutual prejudices or differences between Indians and Germans, the respondents also perceived racist attitudes and the lack of initiative by Germans to approach them as reasons for the restricted intercultural friendships. A respondent remarked:

Nobody [of the Germans] has asked me [to go out with them], first of all. That's one thing. Here I don't think people generally come and ask you, do you wanna do this? (17)

The respondents related this largely to the German close nuclear families and individualism discussed earlier in the text.

Working Culture

A key cultural difference relates to people's attitude to the work process and, in particular, the working hours. The respondents perceived that in Germany most people work eight hours a day and then go home. At work, their main objective is to work, thus keeping the time for breaks to a minimum. The respondents concluded that Germans may thus be unable to make many friends in the context of the workplace. In contrast, in India, it is common to take more breaks during work and to socialize with colleagues.

Furthermore, many interviewees noted that Germans work for 40 hours a week, even in busy periods such as when several projects need to be completed. In India, the respondents were used to working more hours when there was much work and fewer hours when there was little work. When necessary, they also worked on weekends. Although some respondents stayed behind at work in the evenings, or worked on weekends in Germany as well, they explain that they do so predominantly when they feel lonely. It must be noted that the interviewees also described a number of other features of German work culture that they valued highly, such as discipline, methodological approach, professionalism, and more equal work relations.

Several other cultural differences were encountered by the respondents, among which were food, German directness, planning, and aloofness. In the context of this chapter, however, we will close the discussion with a view to the issue of racial discrimination.

Racial Discrimination

When the green card system was announced, this resulted in a wave of political protests. In North Rhine-Westphalia, the CDU-candidate for premier, Jürgen Rüttgers, ran a campaign under the slogan: 'Kinder statt Inder' (Children instead of Indians). Indian applicants for green cards were described as new guest workers, who would take away potential jobs for unemployed Germans (Leithäuser 2000), in particular those in the former GDR.

In the attitude towards immigrants, the notion of citizenship as 'an institutionalised form of solidarity' (Faist 2000: 202) is important, since this is lacking in Germany. For example, until 2000 immigrants could not obtain German nationality if they did not have 'German blood' (Faist 2000; Kastoryano 2000), and they were denied political rights (see discussions in Rex 1994; Aspeslagh and Raven 1997; Guiberneau and Rex 1997; Doomernik 1998; Schuck and Münz 1998; Joppke 1999). The prevalence of racism and intolerance towards different cultural habits by some Germans further prevented integration. In the Indian media, too, Germany was portrayed as a racist country:

Racism rears its ugly head yet again (Mehta 2000).

German politicians [...] using foreigners as scapegoats (Mehta 2000).

The general impression [is] that Germans do not welcome foreigners, especially coloured ones (Guha 2000).

Activities of a small group of right-wing extremists in (particularly East) Germany are extensively reported abroad. They perceive foreigners as a threat to economic prospects for themselves and as opposing German culture, rather than viewing foreign workers as a trigger for economic development (Kim 2001). Although the respondents' personal confrontations with racial discrimination were few and restricted to being ignored or ill-treated, their accounts suggested that they were careful and tried to avoid places they believed were dangerous. It is important to note that the respondents' fear of racial discrimination plays a limited role in their attempts to develop social ties with Germans. It is notable that the interviewees generally perceived

West Germany as safe and (North) East Germany as unsafe. Three respondents did not want to travel to East Germany because they were scared:

I don't go to East Germany. [I] even [don't go to] North Germany, or Berlin. I'm afraid. I'm scared to go to Berlin. I don't want anything to happen with me. (14)

Although other respondents had travelled to those parts, they also stated that they were scared and therefore careful, for example:

When I went to Berlin, I was really scared, because people had told me that it's not a very safe place to [visit]. So nothing happened, but it was always on the back of my mind, that anything could happen anytime. (1)

People who had not been to the North or the East based their opinion mostly on the Indian media and stories from acquaintances. However, they also noted that since they did not go there themselves, they found it hard to pass judgement.

Conclusion

Germany has recently begun to revise its migration policies. In spite of its historical denial of being an immigration state, several measures were implemented to facilitate skilled migration into market niches such as the IT industry. Against this background, we studied the experiences of Indian IT professionals who migrated to Germany through migration channels within TNCs. In many ways, these migrants are privileged, as they are provided with generous reallocation packages, hence economic security and quasi-guaranteed career advancement. During their stay, they aimed to advance their careers, gain money, and gain personal experience. It appears that the relationship between the skilled migrant and the host culture is largely one of economic functionality that serves the needs of both.

Nevertheless, the personal narratives of the respondents to this research indicate that their migration experiences must be seen as more than simply functional. Their experiences are marked by daily struggles when trying to establish a sense of home. One of the first, but major, problems is the inability of the migrants to speak German fluently, while German people in their immediate environment are equally lacking English language proficiency. This problem is particular for Germany, since other major destination countries for Indian IT professionals such as the United States and the United Kingdom are English speaking. Inhibited by language problems, the respondents were reluctant to establish contacts with Germans, particularly as they perceived additional differences in family structures, social structures, and working culture. Furthermore, and largely based on an image created through the media, they feared racial discrimination. They felt not welcomed but threatened by representations of them as guest workers taking over 'German' jobs. Simultaneously, we observe the development of transnational kinship groups either by phone or by mail to the family 'at home', as well as the development of transnational communities in Germany through the establishment of Indian circles of friends. Symbolic resources, in particular the preparation and sharing of (Indian) meals, remain important mechanisms that emphasize the dislocation of the migrant from her/his host culture. Binding factors based on a shared culture and on common rejection of parts of the host culture result in a closely knit transnational community. The experiences outlined in this chapter explain, at least in part, why interest in the German green card scheme has been lacking. In addition, it can be suggested that legal measures to limit the migrants' stay are rather superfluous and concerns about permanent settlement premature, since migrants show little dedication to their host culture.

Acknowledgement

The authors would like to thank the Faculty of Spatial Sciences at the University of Groningen (The Netherlands) for their financial support through the 'Challenge Program'.

Notes

1. See also Klusmeyer (2001) for a discussion on proposals of migrant integration by political parties such as the CDU.
2. An alternative to the green card is a long-term visa. This is a work and residence permit for up to one and a half years with a possibility of extension. Even after the introduction of the green card, the German government has continued to give out long-term visas.
3. International transfer of human capital, such as managers and professionals, is essential in TNCs (Beaverstock and Boardwell 2000). For a more elaborate discussion on TNCs, we refer to analyses of Bartlett and Ghoshal's (1989) organizational typology by Leong and Tan (1993) and Harzing (2000).
4. See also discussion in Chant and Radcliffe (1992) on a household strategy approach in the understanding of gender selectivity in migration patterns.
5. The number following the quote refers to the number of the respondent allocated in this research for reasons of confidentiality.
6. Except for three respondents who had either studied in Germany or studied German in India.

References

Akashe-Böhme, F. (2000) *In geteilten welten: fremdheitserfahrungen zwischen migration und partizipation* [In divided worlds: experiences of otherness between migration and participation]. Frankfurt am Main: Brandes & Apsel.

Amit-Talai, V. (1998) 'Risky hiatuses and the limits of social imagination: expatriacy in the Cayman Islands', in Rapport, N., and Dawson, A. (eds.) *Migrants of Identity: Perceptions of Home in a World of Movement*. Berg: Oxford, 41–59.

Aspeslagh, R., and Raven, S. (eds.) (1997) *De multiculturele samenleving—een wensdroom? De integratie van migranten in de samenlevingen van Nederland en Duitsland* [Multicultural society—wishful thinking? The integration of migrants in Dutch and German societies]. Den Haag: Nederlands Instituut voor Internationale Betrekkingen Clingendael.

Bailey, A.J. (2001) 'Turning transnational: notes on the theorisation of international migration', *International Journal of Population Geography*, 7, 413–28.

Bartlett, C.A., and Ghoshal, S. (1989) *Managing Across Borders: The Transnational Solution*. Boston, MA: Harvard Business School Press.

Beaverstock, J.V. (1990) 'New international labour markets: the case of professional and managerial labour migration within large chartered accountancy firms', *Area*, 22, 151–8.

——. (1991) 'Skilled international migration: an analysis of the geography of international secondments within large accountancy firms', *Environment and Planning A*, 23, 1133–46.

——. (1996) 'Migration, knowledge and social interaction: expatriate labour within investment banks', *Area*, 28, 459–70.

——. (2002) 'Transnational elites in global cities: British expatriates in Singapore's financial district', *Geoforum*, 33, 525–38.

Beaverstock, J.V., and Boardwell, J.T. (2000) 'Negotiating globalization, transnational corporations and global city financial centres in transient migration studies', *Applied Geography*, 20, 277–304.

Benmayor, R., and Skotnes, A. (eds.) (1994) *Migration and Identity*. Oxford: Oxford University Press.

Bude, K.F. (ed.) (1996) *Migration—ethnizität—konflikt: systemfragen und fallstudien* [Migration—ethnicity—conflict: conceptual issues and case studies]. Osnabrück: Universitätsverlag Rasch.

Bürkner, H.J. (2000) 'Western migrants in central Europe: isolated individuals or members of transnational communities?', *GeoJournal*, 50, 105–8.

Chant, S., and Radcliffe, S.A. (1992) 'Migration and development: the importance of gender', in Chant, S. (ed.) *Gender and Migration in Developing Countries*. London: Belhaven Press, 1–29.

Cheng, L., and Yang, P.Q. (1998) 'Global interaction, global inequality, and migration of the highly trained to the United States', *International Migration Review*, 32, 626–53.

Doomernik, J. (1998) *The Effectiveness of Integration Policies towards Immigrants and Their Descendants in France, Germany and the Netherlands*. Geneva: International Labour Organization.

DPA (2001a) 'Union übt scharfe Kritik an Süssmuth-Kommission [Union strongly criticises Süssmuth-Committee]', *Bramscher Nachrichten*, 5 July.

——. (2001b) 'Bewerbung um die besten Köpfe [Application for the best brains]', *Süddeutsche Zeitung*, 4 July.

Faist, T. (2000) 'Transnationalization in international migration: implications for the study of citizenship and culture', *Ethnic and Racial Studies*, 23, 189–222.

Findlay, A. (1990) 'A migration channels approach to the study of high level manpower movements: a theoretical perspective', *International Migration*, 28, 15–22.

Findlay, A., and Garrick, L. (1990) 'Scottish emigration in the 1980's, *Transactions of the Institute of British Geographers*, 15, 177–92.

Gaserow, V. (2001) 'Klarer Ruf nach Zuwanderung [Clear call for immigration]', *Frankfurter Rundschau*, 4 July.

Glick Schiller, N., Basch, L., and Blanc-Szanton, C. (1992) 'Towards a definition of transnationalism: introductory remarks and research questions', in Glick Schiller, N., Basch, L., and Blanc-Szanton, C. (eds.) *Transnationalism: A New Analytic Framework for Understanding Migration*. New York: Annals of the New York Academy of Sciences, ix-xiv.

Green Card Indians (2001) *GINDS—Indians in Deutschland*. http://groups.yahoo.com/groups/GINDS (accessed on 4 July 2001).

Guha, S. (2000) 'German green cards go abegging', *Times of India*, November.

Guiberneau, M., and Rex, J. (eds.) (1997) *The Ethnicity Reader: Nationalism, Multiculturalism and Migration*. Cambridge: Polity Press.

Hardill, I. (1998) 'Gender perspectives on British expatriate work', *Geoforum*, 29, 257–68.

Harzing, A. (2000) 'An empirical analysis and extension of the Bartlett and Ghoshal typology of multinational companies', *Journal of International Business Studies*, 31, 101–19.

Hofstede, G. (1991) *Cultures and Organisations: Software of the Mind*. London: McGraw-Hill.

Iredale, R. (1999) 'The need to import skilled personnel: factors favouring and hindering its international mobility', *International Migration*, 37, 89–123.

Joppke, C. (1999) *Immigration and the Nation-State: The United States, Germany and Great Britain*. New York: Oxford University Press.

Kastoryano, R. (2000) 'Settlement, transnational communities and citizenship International', *Social Science Journal*, 52, 307–12.

Kim, L. (2001) 'Grading Germany's "green card"', *Christian Science Monitor*, 12 February.

Klusmeyer, D. (2001) 'A "guiding culture" for immigrants? Integration and diversity in Germany', *Journal of Ethnic and Migration Studies*, 27, 519–32.

Leithäuser, J. (2000) 'Immigration issue heats up once again', *Frankfurter Allgemeine Zeitung*, 19, June.

Leong, S.M., and Tan, C.T. (1993) 'Managing across borders: an empirical test of the Bartlett and Ghoshal (1989) organizational typology', *Journal of International Business Studies*, 24, 449–64.

Leven, B. (2001) *Statistical Data on Green Card Immigrants*. http://www.Bonn-ZAV.IT-Experts@arbeitsamt.de (accessed on 1 December 2001).

Massey, D., and Jess, P. (1995) *A Place in the World? Places, Cultures and Globalization*. Oxford: The Open University Press.

Mehta, M. (2000) 'Racism rears its ugly head in Germany yet again', *India Abroad*, 30 June.

Menjívar, C. (2002) 'Living in two worlds? Guatemalan-origin children in the United States and emerging transnationalism', *Journal of Ethnic and Migration Studies*, 28, 531–52.

Munichmela (2001) *A guide for Indians in Germany*. http://www.munichmela.de (accessed on 4 July).

Remennick, L. (2002) 'Transnational community in the making: Russian-Jewish immigrants of the 1990s in Israel', *Journal of Ethnic and Migration Studies*, 28, 515–30.

Rex, J. (1994) 'The second project of ethnicity: transnational migrant communities and ethnic minorities in modern multicultural societies', *Innovation: The European Journal of Social Sciences*, 7, 207–17.

Riccio, B. (2001) 'From "ethnic group" to "transnational community"? Senegalese migrants' ambivalent experiences and multiple trajectories', *Journal of Ethnic and Migration Studies*, 27, 583–99.

Salih, R. (2001) 'Moroccan migrant women: transnationalism, nation-states and gender', *Journal of Ethnic and Migration Studies*, 27, 655–71.

Sassen, S. (1988) *The Mobility of Labor and Capital*. Cambridge: Cambridge University Press.

——. (1998) *Globalization and Its Discontents*. New York: The New Press.

Schuck, P.H., and Münz, R. (1998) *Paths to Inclusion: The Integration of Migrants in the United States and Germany*. New York: Berghahn Books.

Stalker, P. (2000) *Workers without Frontiers: The Impact of Globalisation on International Migration*. Boulder, CO: Lynne Rienner.

Tyner, J.A. (2000) 'Global cities and circuits of global labor: the case of Manila, Philippines', *The Professional Geographer*, 52, 61–74.

Tzeng, R. (1995) 'International labor migration through multinational enterprises', *International Migration Review*, 29, 139–54.

UNI (2000) 'German green cards off to good start', *India Abroad*, 24 August.

Vertovec, S. (1996) 'Berlin multikulti: Germany, "foreigners" and "world-openness"', *New Community*, 22, 381–99.

——. (2001) 'Transnationalism and identity', *Journal of Ethnic and Migration Studies*, 27, 573–82.

Welsch, J. (2001) *Wachstums- und beschäftigungsmotor ITbranche: fachkräftemangel, green card und beschäftigungspotenziale* [Monitor for growth and employment in the IT-sector: need for experts, green card and employment opportunities]. Bonn: Friedrich-Ebert-Stiftung.

Willis, K.D., and Yeoh, B.S.A. (2000) 'Gender and transnational household strategies: Singaporean migration to China', *Regional Studies*, 34, 253–64.

——. (2002) 'Gendering transnational communities: a comparison of Singaporean and British migrants in China', *Geoforum*, 33, 553–65.

Yeoh, B.S.A., and Willis, K. (1999) '"Heart" and "wing", nation and diaspora: gendered discourses in Singapore's regionalisation process', *Gender, Place and Culture*, 6, 355–72.

8

Transnational Love and Marriage in the Australian-Indian Diaspora

Hurriyet Babacan and Narayan Gopalkrishnan

The globalized world is one of migration and transnational location. There are different explanations of why people move: to seek better economic opportunities and lifestyles; to find employment; natural disasters, human atrocities including persecution, war, torture, and violence; family-kinship-marriage; and a vision to create a better society (Bretell and Hollifield 2000). Whatever the reason for migration, the nature of global migration allows people to occupy transnational spaces, that is, to go back and forth between their 'homelands' and forge new links within the setting to which they have migrated (Babacan 2009).

The term *transnational* is used to refer to varied transactions and processes that migrants maintain between home in the place of birth and home in the place of settlement (Westwood and Phizacklea 2000). Friesen et al. (2005) remind us of the different dimensions of transnationalism as a social morphology spanning borders. The authors point to different dimensions of transnationalism: ethnic diaspora and emphasizes of networks; as a type of consciousness marked by dual or multiple identities which may result in both a physical and perceptual multi-locality as a mode of cultural reproduction which is often associated with a fluidity of constructed styles, social institutions, and everyday practices; as an avenue for capital, both at the scale of large transnational corporations and at smaller scales such as migrant remittances; and as a site of political engagement (Friesen et al. 2005).

Transnational migration reflects the realities of individuals, families, and groups whose lives are rooted in more than one nation-state and where people's lives are characterized by simultaneous connections and identities as they negotiate multiple host societies and transnational relationships (Smith 2006). The increased tendency of migrants to lead transnational lives is inextricably linked to the changing conditions of global capitalism (Portes 2001). These arenas in which this takes place are multilayered and multi-sited, including not only the home and the host countries but also other sites around the world that connect migrants and non-migrants.

Studies of transnational migration often focus on economic and political frameworks of migration. Until recently there has been little attention paid to everyday lived experiences of transnational immigrants. In the context of writing about South Asians in the United Kingdom, Ballard (2001: 46) points to the importance kinship relationships and concludes that 'it is above all through the principles and practice of kinship reciprocity that translocal networks of trust and solidarity have been constructed and maintained'. It is also pointed out that a transnational moral economy often involves putting family first (Schmalzbauer 2004). For the children of immigrants, marriage options, occupational choices, and the amount of resources available to pursue life plans are dependent on the weave of this moral economic fabric (Levitt 2009).

People, who migrate, move with their cultural and social histories and experience these processes subjectively. Our identities are intricately bound up with the places we move from and to. The articulation of 'identity' highlights unpredictability and notices the immigrant's role as both product and producer, as construct and constructor of what they are and what they become. By stressing the ambiguity of cultural identity, an appreciation of ambiguity of the notion of place leads Sarup (1994) to link its social constructedness to issues of power and hierarchy. Unlike the places of origin where family home, hearth, village, city, or street are the focus of a person's feelings or belonging, such relations do not necessarily exist in the place of arrival of new migrants and are reconstructed through negotiation. Information and knowledge brought by the migrant results in cultural capital and values, which enable negotiation of belonging and identity. As Das Gupta (1997) points out, people crossing borders hold at least two frames of reference: their homeland and the country to which they have migrated. Moreover gendered differences in power and status characterize family networks that cross borders (Pessar and Mahler 2003; Gopalkrishnan 2006; Smith 2006).

This chapter aims to provide insights into the journey of partner choice and marriage among the members of the Indian community in Australia. Based on interviews with young people and parents, elders, and community leaders in three states, we demonstrate that these intimate processes are complex, contradictory, and selective processes impacted upon by the context of the diaspora and the movements to and from multiple locales in the world (including their country of origin). The analysis in this chapter does not include those of Indian descent who have migrated to Australia from other places such as Fiji, Malaysia, South Africa, Uganda, and Singapore as there are significant differences in history, identity, and cultural practice introduced by abode in different localities.

Our study indicates that patterns of marriage and choice of partner are not constant phenomena but are negotiated within the context of past history and current considerations of being migrants in a new homeland. Central to negotiations about partner choice and relationships is the construction of self in the context of migration: an 'Indian' identity, and imagination of home which are used as anchors for identity formation, memories of parents and community, connections with kin, perceptions, and the psyche of loss of culture in the 'new country'.

Indian Diaspora in Australia

Australia has often been referred to as 'the land of immigrants' and is the product of British colonialism (Collins 1991; Hage 2003). Contemporary Australia is a multicultural country with approximately 23 per cent of its citizens being born overseas (2001 Census, ABS). Race, ethnicity, and immigration have been at the heart of nation-building in Australia.

The term 'Indian' represents a complex process covering a myriad of identities, languages, cultural practices, histories, religions, and locations (Faria 2001). While individuals of the diaspora identify as 'Indian', their sense of self, in relation to other Indians, is undergoing change markedly. Distinctions of region, class, caste, community, and education (including whether English speaking or not) serve as boundaries for identification and mark out self from others. Furthermore, those from the vast Indian diaspora, such as people of Indian descent in Fiji, in many parts of Africa and Asia, are often not considered 'true' Indians by others moving directly from the subcontinent, even though the Indian Government officially recognizes them (Ministry of External Affairs 2005).

The history of migration of people from India to Australia dates back to the 1850s. In the last four decades of the nineteenth century, people of Indian origin migrated to Australia as agricultural labourers, traders, and hawkers and the arrival of Punjabis to rural areas such as Woolgoolga dates back 150 years (Martin 1978). Migration from India was curtailed after the Australian Government introduced the Immigration Restriction Act 1901. India's Independence from Britain in 1947 was significant in terms of migration as the number of Anglo-Indians and India-born British citizens immigrating to Australia increased. In the decade leading up to August 2006, 78,165 India-born settlers arrived, with 82.0 per cent for the Skill stream, 17.8 per cent for the Family stream, and 0.2 per cent in the Humanitarian Program. India continues to be a major source country to Australia's net migration with almost 10 per cent of migrants coming from India in 2006 (ABS 2008).

At the time of the 2006 Census, the Indian diaspora was the sixth largest ethnic group in Australia, and there were 234,720 persons who identified as being of 'Indian' ancestry, comprising 1.18 per cent of the total Australian population. Of these, 147,111 identified as being born in India. Of the India born, approximately 55 per cent were male and 45 per cent were female. The sex ratio was 123.2 males per 100 females. The median age of the India born in 2006 was 35.8 years compared with 46.8 years for all overseas born and 37.1 years for the total Australian population. The age distribution showed 7.3 per cent were aged 0–14 years, 14.8 per cent were 15–24 years, 45.0 per cent were 25–44 years, 22.8 per cent were 45–64 years, and 10.2 per cent were 65 and older. The main languages spoken at home by India-born people in Australia were English (34.4 per cent), Hindi (19.9 per cent), and Punjabi (10.3 per cent). The major religious affiliations among India born were Hinduism (64,970 persons), Catholic (34,510 persons), and Sikhism (16,470 persons). Ninety-four per cent identified as speaking English very well or well and only 5 per cent identified as speaking English not well or not at all (DIAC 2006). The high level of skilled Indian-born immigrants is reflected in their income levels, both individual and household income. The median individual income of people born in India was $539 per week as compared to $484 for Australian-born people. Similarly, the median household income for people born in India was $721 per week, significantly higher than the $639 for Australian born (ABS 2008).

Indian Family in the Global Context

In the context of transnational migration, the focus on the family is important and the notion of examining the family across nations is not new (Foner 2000). The process of migration has an important impact on the family and the kinship relationships. It is a process where the past exerts a continuing influence on the present. The responses to transnational movement or displacement caused by migration triggers a range of feelings such as fear, nostalgia, anguish, exile, trauma, sense of loss, and longing for the homeland on the one hand, and the need to adjust, assimilate or integrate, and connect globally on the other hand. Strict migration laws break up traditional family structures, reduce family support structures, and limit the connection between generations. It is possible to have ethnic communities whose children have no first-hand experience of the traditional family life in the country of origin. While the younger generations may grow up with cultural references to tradition, they may be unaware of the impact of the migration experience on the older members of their family (Hartley 1995; Babacan 2006). There is an increase in the level of interconnectedness in contemporary family relationships as compared to earlier histories of relationships, facilitated by information and communication technology and transportation.

The Indian family needs to be considered through an understanding of the phenomenon of the internationalization of the middle-class family and the consequent problem of the cultural reproduction of Indian identity in transnational locations (Uberoi 2003). Jayaram (2004: 26) argues that the evolution of the Indian diaspora lies in their ability to adapt their ancestral social institutions to the lands they have migrated to, particularly relating to family, rites (marriage), and relationships (kinship). Elements of pre-migration culture are recreated in their new environment, albeit selectively. What is included and what is left out and reshaped are determined not only by factors in the present (multicultural policies, racism, integration factors) but also by factors in the past that are triggered by memories, kinship ties, and family histories.

Some scholars place transnational family at the centre of diaspora studies (Uberoi 2003; Voigt-Graf 2005; Singh 2006). Drawing attention to the connection between diasporic identity and transnational relations, Uberoi argues:

> the challenge of being (and, more importantly *remaining*) Indian in a globalised world is one that must be met equally by those who stay at home and those who live abroad ... Secondly, whether at home or abroad, it is the *Indian family system* that is recognised as the social institution that quintessentially defines being 'Indian'. (Uberoi 1998: 308).

The Indian family system is here recognized as the social institution that quintessentially defines being 'Indian' and an institution that is now projected as portable and stable. Uberoi argues that Indian 'family values' are the crucial markers of Indianness and 'happily, and enviably, they are also believed to correlate positively with the achievement of worldly success in competitive foreign settings' (Uberoi 1998: 309).

Authors point to the transnational family networks, indicating an increasing acknowledgement of the importance of kin in the construction of transnational spaces (Ballard 2001; Voigt-Graf 2005). Kinship solidarity is at the heart of migratory processes (Portes 2001; Voigt-Graf 2005). Marriages are particularly important in perpetuating migration and strategically extending kin networks (Ballard 2001, 2003).

The focus on family relationships needs to account for the dynamics of social change. Singh (2006) reminds us that the reference points for the family are not only changing outside India, but also within India. She notes that the tussle between consumer values and individualism on the one hand, and traditional family norms on the other hand, is as much a part of the family in India as it is overseas. Appadurai (1996: 45) points to the tension on the family in the context of globalization:

> Because both work and leisure have lost none of their gendered qualities in this new global order but have acquired ever subtler fetishized representations, the honor of women becomes increasingly a surrogate for the embattled communities of males, while their women in reality have to negotiate increasingly harsh conditions of work ... deterritorialized communities ... may enjoy the fruits of ... capital and technology, [but] have to play out the desires and fantasies of these new ethnoscapes, while striving to reproduce the family as microcosm of culture.

What this also points to is the role of women in diaspora. Clifford (1994) reminds us that diasporic experiences are always gendered. The family is a key site where the intersections of gender, power, race, class, and nation are manifest and reproduced (Yuval-Davis 2006; Holvino 2010). The projection of the anxieties of modernization and identity loss, typically focused on women's sexuality, has been a fairly consistent theme in Indian popular culture such as films for the last 50 years. Pointing to patriarchal nature of family relationships in the Indian diaspora in the United Kingdom, Uberoi (2003) asserts that the dissident minority within the expatriate community which questions the family values from a feminist standpoint is branded as 'shamelessly anti-national'. Sathian (2010: 26) identifies that there is a constant tension between ideals of femininity and the reality of a constantly modernizing woman in the Indian diaspora. She points out that there are two extremes in Hindu notions of femininity, one of which is docile, such as Sita, and the other powerful, such as Kali or Shakti. This is an uncomfortable dichotomy for women, since they are perceived as either passive or excessively powerful, meaning they have to either be worshiped or be tamed. Roles and responsibilities within the household, particularly for women, are rooted in the ideology of patriarchy and the sexual division of labour, both of which have been historically and culturally situated in Indian society (Mazumdar and Sharma 1990). Sathian (2010: 27) states that 'Such repressions of sexuality mirror real-life suppressions of aspects of many women's experiences in the diaspora'. She posits that we see two diasporic women: one who travels independently and is therefore fiercely nonconformist, and the other who travels to follow and is subordinate to her husband. These views are perpetuated through popular culture such as films. Examining portrayals of women in Bollywood, Sathian argues that Bollywood traditionally prefers to represent the latter (i.e., the subordinate) as the desirable diasporic woman, but in more recent films it has allowed the first type to play the protagonist, perhaps indicating a slow acceptance of female autonomy in the diaspora. Joshi (2000), writing from the context of Australia, differentiates between first- and second-generation Indian women. She argues that the first-generation Indian women is seen as culturally static and represent unadulterated traditional values of the old country. The behaviour of the second-generation women is seen as a representation of how assimilated they are, sometimes equated with modernity. An immense burden is placed on second-generation women for cultural allegiance, family loyalty, and racial purity.

The question of how children of immigrants identify has also been the area of considerable debate. Families stay connected over time through inter-generational transmission of legacies. Legacies help family members articulate family identity, learn more about family history, and provide succeeding generations with information about the family culture and ethnicity. Transmission of legacies leads to cultural continuity. But these are selective processes and depend upon favourable conditions. This can only take place through experience and interaction in a culture that is enjoyed over time (Babacan 2006). The subsequent generations tend not to have the first-generation Indian immigrants' emotional investment in the idea of India, although family legacies are passed on. The children of immigrants are not likely to engage in their ancestral homes with the same intensity and frequency as their parents, nor will they be as influenced by homeland values and practices (Levitt 2009). In the context of globalization, there are challenges to generational stability. Appadurai (2003: 42) notes:

> the sort of transgenerational stability of knowledge which was presupposed in most theories of enculturation (or, in slightly broader terms, of socialization) can no longer be assumed. As families move to new locations, or as children move before older generations, or as grown sons and daughters return from time spent in strange parts of the world, family relationships can become volatile … . Generations easily divide, as ideas about property, propriety, and collective obligation wither under the siege of distance and time.

Levitt argues that when children grow up in households and participate in organizations in which people, goods, money, ideas, and practices from their parents' countries of origin circulate in and out on a regular basis, they are socialized not only into the rules and institutions of the countries where they live, but also into those of the countries from whence their families come. They acquire social contacts and skills that are useful in both settings. They master several cultural repertoires that they can selectively deploy in response to the opportunities and challenges they face (Levitt 2009)

Methodology

This chapter draws on our work with people born in mainland India who have migrated to Australia. The analysis in this chapter does not include those of Indian descent who have migrated to Australia from other places such as Fiji, Malaysia, South Africa, Uganda, and Singapore as there are significant differences in history, identity, and cultural practice introduced by abode in different localities. This work covers a group of young people aged 17–24 years old who live in Australia. The data for this analysis come from a number of projects with young people conducted by the Centre for Multicultural and Community Development, University of the Sunshine Coast across Victoria, New South Wales, and Queensland in 2003–2004 involving 60 people. This was supplemented by informal semi-directed discussions with parents, elders, and community leaders. These projects were focused on leadership capabilities for young people of culturally diverse backgrounds.

The projects identified, through a mixed methodology, factors that acted as facilitating or hindering factors for developing leadership.

Many personal elements of the lives of young people were explored including issues of belonging, friendships, family relationships, and marriage. Domains of exploration ranged from the day-to-day lived practice to much more complex topics such as marriage, love, identity, and belonging. In relation to mate selection, love, and marriage, the context of the family emerged as important. The rest of this chapter takes a journey through the issues confronted by Indian transnational families and uncovers the difficult issues and how they are negotiated.

Indian Family Identity in Australia

The discussion on marriage, intimacy, mate selection, and love takes place within accoutrements of a 'modern' and 'western' lifestyle placed against a backdrop of expression for continuity, tradition, and ritual to determine Indian identity in the Australia. Some of the factors that influence transmission of values in this context include personal characteristics of the first generation (such as education, age, gender), family interaction variables (such as parenting styles, approaches to discipline and nature of marital relationships) and social environment (such as assimilationist pressures, oppression, loss of economic status, presence of other community members) (Bertelli 1985; Babacan 2006). Conflict, negotiation, and accommodation characterize transnational relationship formations (Guarnaccia and Lopez 1998). These processes revolve around the tensions of difference and continuity, managing hybridity, and the reconciliation of 'being in-between'.

In this study, a number of areas were identified as problematic by both young people and elders in the process of settlement and legacy transmission. Some of the issues raised included diminishing parental authority, increasing influence of peers, rejection of traditional values, eroding of ethnic cultural heritage including loss of language, difficulties with family communication patterns, conflicts over perceived roles and behaviours, selection of spouses or partners or dating, caring responsibilities, especially of elders and conflicting role demands from society, lack of achievement values, rejection of parental aspirations, and collectivist values being influenced by individualism and consumerism. Although immigrant acculturation and the development of young people are highly public debates, these issues were largely confined to the private sphere of the home and considered the private business of the family.

In reality, the young people and their parents were acting from the *positionality* of being immigrants and belonging to a minority culture in the context of a predominantly white, Anglo Saxon society

(Hage 2003). The youth were negotiating their identity between familial expectations (the Indian tradition) and the expectations of 'being Australian'. What was clear was that there is a being in-between culture for young Indians reflected in contradictory ways, such as wanting to completely fit in with mainstream Australia, constructing their difference in some way, or rejecting the West. These were complex processes and largely determined by factors such as origin of family in India, level of education, peer pressures, extent of connection with mainstream Australia in the settlement process, and linkages with relatives in the homeland. A picture emerged of young people negotiating tensions between obligation and independence, East and West, belonging or exclusion, and constraints and new opportunities of being.

Similar dilemmas were equally faced by their families about loss of culture, needing to fit in, success of their children, and re-evaluation of their identity strategy in such a way that enables reconciliation of the discomfort felt by the tensions of migration. This is an emotional process that involves reflection, pain, confusion, and ambiguity. It also requires a choice about what cultural practices and resources are appropriate for the multiple points of reference in Australia, back home, and other locations in which family is found. Some areas were easier to negotiate than others—marriage, love, and mate selection proved to be among the more difficult and controversial—and can be examined as the 'cultural strategies of identity' (Freidman 1999), which describes the way in global and small and more personal action takes place. These strategies are hybrid and carry distinct public-private demarcation and separation of lived practices. However, at all points, they involve an intermingling with mainstream society and a blend of Indian and Australian. This has been referred to as *chutneyfication* (Rushdie 1997), and the metaphor of the chutney often comes in the discourses on cultural practice in the diaspora. While the implication of a term such as cultural strategy is a rational and conscious decision-making, many of the practices come out of struggles, negotiations, and conflict at the personal and societal levels, with outcomes not always deliberate, intended, or calculated.

The family dynamics of the participants varied. However, there was an overwhelming sense of 'correct family' relationships and expectations. These revolved, to more or lesser extent, around power dynamics within the household (head of household), obligations for respect, financial matters, gender roles, and duties within the household. For some, placing the 'traditional Indian family' at the centre was the key way of defining themselves. This included preserving traditions, speaking their mother language at home, stricter gender roles, and attitudes to dating. Generational differences in attitudes towards these relationships and expectations were a major source of conflict for many respondents in this study. As one Punjabi female respondent stated:

> When we first got to Australia my mother wanted me to wear the salwar kameez to school. I was determined not to. It caused a lot of fights in the house and in the end they gave up hassling me. Then I was not allowed to go out with my friends in school. Our visiting is my family's social circle. Now the next battle is around dating. I am not allowed to have a boyfriend or go out alone with a man.

Other families did not place emphasis on tradition but were concerned with how they fitted into Australian society. They emphasized speaking English at home and mixed with a broad range of people. They encouraged interaction of their children with 'Australians'. As a Maharashtrian male respondent said:

> My father says we live in Australia now and we should behave like Australians. We speak English at home and my parents are OK with me having an Australian girlfriend.

While drawing from the past and cultural practices of their family, many saw new opportunities within the new environment that they were living in and had changed their expectations in some areas while still maintaining others. As an Australian-born female respondent from a Kerala family stated:

> My mother got married when she was 19 and had four children. She did not follow her career even though she's got a good education. They do not want me to go in the same way. They want me to get married but not so young. They understand that I will have a career.

While the expectations regarding work had changed for this young person, she also reported that she was expected to marry a boy from her own caste. Similarly several others reported varying degrees of openness to negotiation within the family, based on the level of importance given to that aspect of 'Indianness' for their family.

Transnational Family Connections

Many of the Indian families had transnational family connections and responsibilities to family and kinship networks in India and other parts of the world, although the nature of these linkages showed extensive variability. Many of the respondents reported that information and communication technology greatly facilitated their communication through the Internet, email, letters, telephones, webcams, video, and other means. Travel to connect with kin was also much easier, although this depended partially on the economic status in Australia. Some families could afford to travel to India or other parts of the world to be with their family at least once a year, while others could not. Thus, the ease with which families maintained linkages was partially countered by the economic marginalization that transnational migrants confront. For many Indians arriving in Australia, despite a high level of education, fluency in English, and international work experience, human capital loss and loss of status were a reality. Many found work in low-wage jobs with limited mobility and career advancement prospects. This changed over time for many but took significant number of years. Even then, many pointed to the racialized nature of the workforce where employers held negative attitudes towards people who were visibly different or held overseas qualifications.

Transnational Indian migrants' family connections were closely linked to their perception of migration. For many Anglo-Indians, the link with Australian and Anglo-society was important and they saw their future linked with incorporation into the mainstream. There were respondents who stated that the mainstream 'did not see them as any different from other Indians' and perceived this as a major problem for their integration. Thus, the two-pronged approach to identity—a sense of self-identification and how others identify you—determined the psyche of belonging and integration, which in turn affected how they linked with family members abroad. The practices reported demonstrated different nature of relationships as illustrated by the following comments:

> My parents ring India at least once a week and they send money to them from time to time. At least mum or dad visits once a year even if we cannot all afford to go. (female respondent)

> My mother wants me to learn Indian classical dancing since when we go for visits our family will expect this. It also improves my chances in the Indian marriage market. (female respondent)

> We visit once every two years, I cannot get used to the food there. It is a bit of a holiday for me but it is a very emotional time for my parents. (male respondent)

> We went to Mumbai to see our family; they are more Western than we are. (male respondent)

> Although we live in Australia my mum worries about what her family will think in India. (male respondent)

A small proportion had cut themselves off almost completely, having very little to do with their kin in their country of origin. The reasons for this included a desire to assimilate, the gravity of expectations of family members, and other family conflicts.

Transnational family is full of tensions and problems. Some of these problems included resentment of the family for migrating, seen to be rejecting Indian ways or becoming too Western, expectations of greater sacrifices from family members (e.g., demands to send more money back home), false images that their families have of lives in Australia, criticism of the behaviour of children, and changed gender roles. These tensions, involving pain, grief, and emotion, were resolved in complex ways.

Marriage as a Means of Retaining Cultural Identity

There is a strong relationship between marriage and cultural identity in the context of migration. Individuals and families struggle not only between integration and cultural maintenance but also creating hybrid ways of belonging transnationally (Ballard 2003; Levitt 2009). On this issue, Uberoi makes a pertinent point:

> newspapers at home and abroad bear ample witness to this dilemma of continuity as parents seek to channel and discipline the romantic aspirations of their children and to ensure the perpetuation of Indian 'culture', 'tradition' and 'values' into the next generation even as they continue to enjoy the material and professional advantages of expatriate living. (Uberoi 2003: 308)

As outlined earlier in the text, identity formation and settlement patterns determine behaviours of family. The findings from the studies indicated that identity built around communities of religion, caste, race, or geographical location was a constant factor in the decision-making processes of marriage. By marrying within the community, the children continued to maintain a sense of communal identity, however dynamic and changing that may be (Nagar 1998). This caused tension in families, if children chose to marry outside the community or the faith. A female respondent from Uttar Pradesh stated:

> We are Muslims and I am expected to marry within the faith if not within the community.

Similarly, another female respondent from Kerla said:

> My parents will never allow me to marry a boy who is not a Nair.

Maintaining a tightly knit network within the community with plenty of opportunities for the younger generation to interact is one way of preventing intermarriage and promoting marriage within the community (Hooghiemstra 2001). A number of social, religious, and other occasions are used as ways of young people meeting socially acceptable partners in informal yet safe environments. Some of these include the Garbha nights organized by the Gujarati community, Dussehra celebrations organized by the Bengali community, and youth conventions organized by several different communities.

Intermarriage

Intermarriage relates to the smaller proportion of marriages that take place outside the strict boundaries of tradition, religion, caste, and geographical origins. Nativity, gender, and socio-economic status all play a part in levels of intermarriage. This also has consequences on linkages with the community and changing friendship networks. The cooking of food in the Indian household is also a ritual that has very strong implications of purity and sacredness around who does the cooking and how it is done. This has implications in terms of 'pollution' of the family if inter-community or, more glaringly, inter-religious marriages take place. Further, intermarriage has consequences on the identity of the offspring, both in terms of how they identify themselves and how society identifies them.

Intermarriage in the Indian community occurs in two ways: intermarriage with Indians from outside their community, religion, or caste, and intermarriage with non-Indians. Despite negative stances on intermarriage, mixed background marriages within the Indian community were quite visible among older couples and in the newer marriages. It was seen as being better than being married to a non-Indian. There was also the attitude among many young people that orthodox religious observances, caste systems, and adherence to diet and to forced arranged marriages were outdated in Australia. Some the comments from young people indicate the expectations placed upon them:

> My parents want me to marry an Indian girl. (male respondent, Bengal)

> My father has told me that he wants an Indian son-in-law. (female respondent, Orissa)

Some of the young people identified that intermarriage within the Indian community was a compromise reached within the family about whom they can and cannot marry. In many instances, this was seen as a compromise in the face of what parents perceived as loss of cultural heritage. Significant importance was placed upon education for both boys and girls. It aided in the meeting of family responsibilities and attainment of social status. Thus, education was a key factor in unlocking the rigid norms and rules for marriage across different elements of caste, class, religion, and community.

Many young people wanted to blend with their peers and move beyond fixed rigid criteria, although this had to be negotiated within a complex family, extended kinship, and community relationships. In very few instances, parents with more contemporary approaches encouraged broader partner choice including intermarriage with non-Indians, that is out-marriage. However, this was not a simple process. Penny and Khoo (1996) present a typology of intermarriage that runs along a continuum from the 'exotic orientation' where the Australian partner immerses themselves in the other's culture, religion, language, and community, to the 'assimilationist' where all things Anglo-Australian are adopted.

Respondents identified the ways in which relationships were forged with people who were non-Indians. One female respondent stated:

> Some of the men I go out with think that I wear saris and exotic costumes, can do Bollywood dancing and cook exotic curries. I do wear the saris sometimes but I do not regard them as costumes, I cannot dance or hold a beat and my curries are not that good.

One of the measures used in sociological studies of immigrant integration is intermarriage to others outside their own culture (i.e., non-Indians). This kind of intermarriage provides a basis for interaction across two different communities that may otherwise not forge relationships. The degree of out-marriage depends on the strength of family and social networks, the level of westernization, the ability to speak English, levels of education, cultural practice of out-marriage in community of origin, and approaches to migration and settlement. The kinship relationships with the country of origin were an important element. If strong transnational connections were maintained, then there were greater pressures by families on young people not to marry outside either their own community or the Indian community. Birrell and Healy (2000) examine sponsorship of spouses from overseas countries across a number of ethnic communities in Australia. The study indicates higher proportions of sponsorship of brides and grooms by the Indian community in Australia as related to many of the larger ethnic communities. The data further indicate that the number of women being sponsored as brides is triple the number of men (Birrell and Healy 2000: 40–42). This is closely related to the gendered processes of migration that we will discuss later in the text.

Ways of Meeting

One of the main problems of diasporic communities is the loss of the traditional matchmaking services and opportunities that exist within the extended family in the homeland. These included the informal arrangements of uncles and aunts acting as matchmakers and the more formal priests and astrologers providing the appropriate service. Many respondents talked about the difficulty of meeting and dating within their community in Australia. One female respondent stated:

> We are a small community and everyone knows each other. Even though you can meet a person you cannot go out with them because it will get around the community quickly and you and your family's reputation is ruined.

Many families take their children back to the homeland to find partners for them. The wedding season in India, mainly in the winter months, is seen as a wonderful time to visit India for several reasons. First, it fits in well with the holiday season in Australia. Second, it is a good time to attend the weddings of the extended family and friends and thereby fulfil social obligations. Third, it provides a wonderful social networking opportunity and enables those parents, with children of marriageable age, to link up with other parents with the intention of organizing matches. It also provides an opportunity for unmarried boys and girls to meet in informal settings while maintaining the basic criteria of class, caste, or religion.

Ethnic matchmaker services are a popular way of helping parents to secure an appropriate spouse for their children. Personal ads in the ethnic newspapers and websites are another way to meet potential partners. The two major newspapers in New York, *India Abroad* and *The India Post*, carry several pages of marriage classifieds every day. Community newspapers such as *Bharat Times* in Australia continue to play a role in connecting people through the matrimonials. The criteria stated in most of the advertisements are quite exact as to the boundaries within which the search is being conducted, incorporating astrology, class, caste, geographical origins, and religion. For example:

> brilliant engineer (B.Tech. Hons, doing M.E), Australian citizen … seeks girl from (State in India and Caste) high status family, pretty, slim, tall, homely, very fair, within 22 years, with Indian values.

> Suitable match required for beautiful … innocent divorced girl, convent educated, (caste) (Birth date/time/city in India) (height) residing in (city in Australia).

Younger men and women are increasingly turning to new methods of contact such as dating portals, speed dating, SMS dating, and singles nights (Doshi et al. 2005). Correspondence relationships that are built using technology as a medium continue to exist around some basic guidelines of what will and will not be acceptable to parents. Among the better-known Internet matrimonial sites are Shaadi.com and SikhMatrimonials.com. The profiles posted by users are often built around the standard arranged marriage guidelines. Interestingly enough, speed-dating events have also been organized, maintaining the basic parameters of separation based on religion. The Internet-based matrimonial advertisements are well utilized by young Indian people and their families. There are increasing numbers of people from Australia posting matrimonial advertisements in these sites.

Dating

Dating practices varied based on attitudes—by young people, their family, and community. This was a controversial element of the relationship between young people and one of the key causes of conflict within the household. More traditional approaches still prevailed among some young people and their families. Young men did not date Indian girls and viewed Indian girls dating others (both Indian and non-Indian) as bad practice. Young women placed more emphasis on serious relationships in dating, while some of the young men practiced casual dating. In several communities, the boys were allowed to date non-Indians, and the girls were not allowed to date since it would bring dishonour to the family. Those young people who were born in Australia or arrived very young in Australia had more liberal approaches to dating, although this caused family tension in the family. Some dated without letting their family know, as this would avoid conflict. In those instances, the young people did not know if they would want to marry their boy/girlfriend.

Arranged Marriage/Assisted Marriage/Decision-Making

The attitudes towards arranged marriages varied across the participants in this study. One consistent factor was that parental input was important even for those who wanted self-selection. Arranged marriages are where family or kin determine the marriage. In arranged marriages, more thought is given to the desired characteristics of a potential mate with individuals marrying according to their family's wishes, and the focus on accepting and adjusting to partners after marriage. Some young people held the view that, contrary to Western belief, it is possible for men and women in arranged marriages to be happy and satisfied. Many had their own parents' example. Thus, love is viewed in a variety of ways, and romantic attraction was not seen as a necessary precursor to marriage. Instead, love is expected to grow as the spouses learn more about each other as the years go by. For many parents, arranged marriages represented an opportunity to strengthen connections with their communities and the kin that they have been separated through migration. Furthermore, it offered a trusted and safe source of partners for their children. A female respondent stated:

> It is not realistic to expect to fall in love with someone who you don't get to spend time with. Instead, I look for their family values, how they treat women, in particular daughters in law, their attitude to women working and what kind of family relationships they have. I do not want to marry into a very traditional family, which is my only criterion. My parents will take into consideration all the other factors.

Likewise, another female respondent said:

> I must at least like the man I am to marry.

Some negative stereotypes of arranged marriages were prevalent. These included the overbearing mother-in-law, jealous sister-in-law, vulnerable bride, the ghar jamai (son-in-law who goes to live in the wife's parents' house) as well as the oppressed daughter-in-law. This is presented in great detail in many Bollywood films but is also supported in writings on arranged marriages (Jeffery and Jeffery 1996). The converse of this argument was also presented. Some respondents believed that if there were problems with the marriage, they could turn to their family for support if their marriage was arranged. This was seen as more of a protection for women than men.

Other young people thought that marriage is a matter between two individuals and interference by the family made it difficult. Some, where there was parental opposition, acted in defiance of the authority. Despite a general acceptance of arranged marriages, many young people did not want their marriage to be arranged and wanted some say in the matter of their mate selection. The practice of arranged marriages has been amended in the transnational process to accommodate the demands of Westernization. 'Love-cum-arranged marriage' is the new way of bringing the custom of arranged marriage in line with the demands of the younger generation. A modified arranged marriage system, called *assisted marriage*, was a common form of arranging marriage in the Australian context. The parents identify a set of prospective spouses based on criteria around religion, caste, and geography, among others. They find socially acceptable ways in which they can introduce their children. Not only are the criteria subject to negotiation with the children but also the children hold the veto power on the choice of groom/bride, a far cry from the traditional system where the parents took the decisions. Assisted marriage is increasingly popular as it enables the preservation of not just Indian cultural identity, but also the sense of identity that derives from religion, class, lineage, and regional ethnicity. A female respondent stated:

> I think the modern arranged marriage is a much better process. It enables me a lot more choices of proposed partners but also I can have a say on who I marry.

Similarly, a male respondent stated:

> Arranged marriages can work, one has to be reasonable with parents. It is good to have the best of both worlds.

Even when the decision-making is finally left to the concerned son or daughter, there is clearly a process of weighing up the pros and cons, one in which the wishes of the parents play a significant role. Many of the younger participants expressed the wish to marry someone they choose themselves but do not wish to go flagrantly against their parents' wishes. This leads to what we call 'practical love marriages' where a relationship is built within the eligible group only.

The choice of marriage partner is one based on the optimum economic and emotional returns to the household that will be formed after the marriage (Hooghiemstra 2001). In the case of most Indian families, these returns are calculated in terms of the extended family as the household, not just the nuclear family. Other criteria included the status of the family, education of proposed partner, place of abode beyond marriage, and values around gender. Further, decision-making is impacted on by friendship networks, memberships to community organizations, and institutions such as the temples and the church, as well as the community in general.

Dowry or Bridewealth

These are payments made from the bride's or groom's family to the other family. In most parts of India, it is the groom's family that receives the payment, while in a very small minority it is the bride's family. The purpose of dowry is manifold: it legitimates the new reproductive and socio-economic unit to be created through marriage, it establishes the legality of marriage, especially entitling the husband to domestic, economic, sexual, and reproductive capacities of his wife, it establishes obligations to stabilize marriage, and it leads to wealth transfer from one family to another, from one generation to another, and can be used to secure the position of women in the household of their husbands (Burn 2005).

Dowry in the Indian context is often negotiated at the time of proposals for marriage and arranged by the elders. This was seen as an outdated practice by majority of the respondents including the parents. Although dowry was paid in their parents' marriage, all respondents in this study indicated that this was not a major issue for marriages in Australia. It is still an issue that is raised for discussion in marriage, particularly when the spouse is based in India. Examples were cited of circumstances in which the prospective bride's family (in India) made offers of dowry to the boy's family in Australia.

Gender Attitudes

Ng (1986) has argued that migration places women in a secondary position—even when the female is the main applicant in the migration process. The Migration Institute information indicates that most migration statistics and research have suffered from gender blindness. The experience of migrant women has often been subsumed under that of migrant men: the migrant experience becomes that of the principal applicant, usually male, and women are viewed primarily as part of the family unit. In a study of settlement and adjustment in Australia, Wooden et al. (1994) have concluded that compared with men, women are more likely to have limited economic means and be subjected to traditional family constraints on behaviour. Separation from family and kin-based social support systems is a particularly important factor for women. Unfavourable employment and housing circumstances, prejudice, and discrimination in the labour market and in the community also have disproportionate impacts on women. Pettman (1992) has pointed to the role that migrant women play in keeping families together and the new impositions that have been placed on ethnic women including the double jeopardy of caring and domestic responsibilities as well as employment outside the home while struggling with settlement and adjustment.

All societies have cultural constructions of gender and gender roles and distinguish patterns of behaviour appropriate to different sexes (Kimmel 2004; Burn 2005). In the Indian community, gender emerged as a key area in which there were differences in the expectations and experiences of men and women (Derne 2003). Traditional approaches to gender roles and the social constructions of femininity and masculinity prevailed. Because of the social value placed on marriage and the family within Indian society, many Indian girls felt the pressure to fulfil familial expectations around mate selection and marriage. There were clearly gender role differentiation and expectations that were adopted by the younger generation. For example, roles assigned to women were nurturing, caring, and involved being feminine. Men were stronger, had breadwinner roles, and did not have caring responsibilities. The construction of gender roles was perpetuated by images of sacred figures such as Sita (in the Hindu religion) or through myths, stories, and history. These were reflected in approaches to marriage. The image of the 'mother' as pure, sacred, and nurturing prevailed. Women's role as 'reproducers' in bearing and rearing children were reinforced. This provided a source of identity for many women.There continued to be the celebration of the 'good woman' as against the sexualized 'other', where the good woman is the compromising girl from one's own community, while the 'other' is often a woman of Anglo-Australian background with whom one can have a 'fling' but not marry.

Different approaches towards women were identified in the men. One group wanted to marry girls from 'back home' with an emphasis on virginity of women. Several of these young men had engaged in relationships with non-Indian girls for sexual purposes without consequences in the community, while Indian girls were just friends. A variation in this way of thinking was men who formed relationships with Indian and Western women but wanted to marry only 'virgins'. A second group of men were more liberal and westernized and open to the possibilities of marrying women who are not 'virgins'. Virginity and sexual relationships prior to marriage did not make a big difference for this second group, but they were more interested in compatibility, similarity of values, and factors that would make for a 'good life partner'.

For young women there emerged a different picture. From the point of view of parents, there were two main drivers to the pressure for early marriage of their daughters. The first was the fear of sexual impropriety by the girls and its possible consequences in terms of unwanted pregnancies and/or loss of standing in the community. It was not so much the protection of 'virginity' that is the issue as much as providing for the daughter's social future in a potentially dangerous environment. These sexual mores do not apply to male children. The second was the fear that the older a daughter gets, the less would be the chances of getting a 'suitable' match, as the pool of eligible bachelors begin to diminish. Some parents set age limits by which their daughters must be married, which tended to be around the early 20s. Some of the young women were concerned with the double standards for gender and often looked for gender values and practices in the proposals they received for marriage.

Processes of Negotiation

Transnational family relationships are altered in many ways and can place considerable tension on family cohesion. Some the dimensions which are affected include *structure*—who lives *with whom*; *association—communication and activities shared with* relatives; financial functions—transfers and exchanges of money and goods; socio-economic status (or loss of); *feelings*—of affection, closeness, and satisfaction with relationships; and *value systems*—beliefs about family culture, obligations, and role definition. This is coupled with rapid social change where the younger and older generations are subject to different historical milieu. There can be differences in generational approaches within age cohorts (e.g., differences between older and younger siblings) (Babacan 2004). Also relevant are the factors of ability to connect with family networks. Sometimes transnational dislocation occurs where strict migration processes breakdown family structures and kinship connections. In the context of the diaspora, this can be compensated for by other members of the community becoming symbolic uncles, aunties, and grandparents. This depends on the size of the community, social cohesion within the community, and resources available to them (Sedikides and Brewer 2001).

Families had complex patterns of relating to each other. Patterns of family formation, activities shared, and feelings of closeness and obligations showed considerable variation. Communication on issues of marriage and mate selection varied from open and frank communication in a small number of families to mainly indirect methods of conveying messages. The respondents identified some areas which were taboo topics to talk to elders about. These included sex before marriage, homosexuality, and to a lesser extent cohabitation. Respondents stated that these subjects were never canvassed with their parents, and for many the practices of cohabitation or sex before marriage were not possible. Generational gaps across siblings were also identified. Older siblings were identified as having 'more traditional approaches', while those of similar age cohorts were more able to communicate about the taboo subjects. Some young people identified that they would not talk to some of their friends about such topics either due to negative perceptions. Also difficult were conversations between friends of opposite genders around topics such as sex and homosexuality, although boyfriends and dating were discussed among close friends.

Some key factors emerged in the maze of relationships: respect for family, reverence for the wisdom of elders, transmission of 'Indian values', family honour and social and community standing, 'what others will think', expectations of family in India (where the links were strong), and gender roles. Many pointed to the emotional elements of the processes of negotiation and where parents used 'emotional blackmail' to pressure their children. This elicited a number of responses, including rejection of parental values and norms, submission to wishes of parents, or compromises by young people and parents. In situations of conflict with parents over marriage and dating, many young people turned to their siblings (of similar age groups) for support or to friends. Very few identified as turning to other relatives such as aunts or uncles.

Conclusion

Partner choice, marriage, and love are complex processes for any individual and their families. This chapter drew attention to the complexities regarding marriage choice within the Indian diaspora in Australia. Indian families orient and evaluate their sense of identity and belonging in a transnational context, within the confines of macro processes and totalizing definitions of what it means to be Indian, ethnic or Australian. While the 'traditional Indian family' was central to the ways in which the respondents in this study defined themselves, it was also the source of much conflict because of changing attitudes and expectations. The young people in this study were acting from within a being-in between culture, negotiating tensions between family expectations and those of the larger society around them.

The cultural spaces of marriage and partner choice in this context were being defined, redefined, and reconfigured through mixed and hybrid practices, drawing selectively from the remembered past, family legacy, and current situational influence. The construction of self in the context of migration was central to marriage and partner choice. As demonstrated in this study, there were numerous culturally rooted pressures that young people face when choosing life partners in Australia. These pressures arose from the societal context, cultural norms and values, demographic composition on selection options, immediate social environment, transnational family connections and expectations, and personal characteristics of individuals. It was clear that young people in the Indian diaspora in Australia were negotiating their identities through multidirectional forces of gendered, racialized, and generational positioning.

References

ABS (2001) *Census of Australia 2001*. Canberra: Australian Bureau of Statistics: http://www.abs.gov.au/.

——. (2008) *Census 2006: People Born in China and India*. Canberra: Australian Bureau of Statistics, Commonwealth of Australia.

http://www.abs.gov.au/AUSSTATS/abs@.nsf/Previousproducts/3416.0Main%20Features22008?opendocument&tabname=Summary&prodno=3416.0&issue=2008&num=&view= (accessed on 10 June 2011).

Anthias, F. and Lazaridis, G. (2000) *Gender and Migration in Southern Europe: Women on the Move*. Oxford: Berg.

Appadurai, A. (1996) *Modernity at Large: Cultural Dimensions of Globalization*. Minneapolis/London: University of Minnesota Press.

——. (2003) 'Disjuncture and Differences in Global Economy', in Braziel, J.E. and Mannur, A. (eds.) *Theorizing Diaspora: A Reader*. Oxford: Blackwell, 25–48.

Babacan, H. (2006) 'Families in a multicultural society: policy and program responses', Keynote address given at the *Multicultural Families: Investing in the Nations Future Conference*, University of the Sunshine Coast, Caloundra.

——. (2009) *Ethnic Minorities: Negotiating Identity in Australia*. Saarbrücken, Germany: VDM Verlag Dr Muller Publications.

Ballard, R. (2001) 'The impact of kinship on the economic dynamics of transnational networks: reflections on some South Asian Developments', paper presented at the workshop on *Transnational Migration*, Princeton University, Princeton, 29 June–1 July. http://www.transcomm.ox.ac.uk/working%20papers/Ballard.pdf (accessed on 24 May 2011).

——. (2003) 'The South Asian presence in Britain and its transnational connections', in Parekh, B., Singh, G., and Vertovec, S. (eds.) *Culture and Economy in the Indian Diaspora*. London: Routledge, 197–222.

Birrell, B. and Healy, E. (2000) 'Out-marriage and the survival of ethnic communities in Australia', *People and Place,* 8 (3): 37–46.

Bretell, C.B., and Hollifield, J.F. (2000) *Migration Theory: Talking Across Disciplines*. New York: Routledge.

Burn, M.S. (2005) *Women Across Cultures: A Global Perspective*. New York: McGraw Hill.

Clifford, J. (1994) 'Diasporas', *Cultural Anthropology*, 9(3), 302–38.

Collins, J. (1991) *Migrant Hands in a Distant Land* (2nd ed.). Leichhardt: Pluto Press.

Das Gupta, M. (1997) 'What is Indian About You? A Gendered Transnational Approach to Ethnicity'. *Gender & Society*, 11 (5): 572-96.

Derne, S. (2003) 'Arnold Schwarzenegger, Ally McBeal and arranged marriages: Globalization on the ground in India', *Context,* 2 (3): 12–18.

DIAC (2006) *Community Information Summary–India Born*. Canberra: Department of Immigration and Citizenship, Commonwealth of Australia. http://www.immi.gov.au/media/publications/statistics/comm-summ/_pdf/india.pdf (accessed on 10 June 2011).

Doshi, A., Drvaid, S., Giri, R., and David, S. (2005) 'Sweepstake: Technology, television and the fast pace of modern life have drastically altered the rules of the dating game'. *India Today*, 20 June 2005.

Faria, A.I. (2001) 'The future of Indian ethnicity in Australia: an educational and cultural perspective', *International Education Journal*, 2(4), 134–43.

Foner, N. (2000) *From Ellis Island to JFK: New York's Two Great Waves of Immigration*. New Haven: Yale University Press.

Friedman, J. (1999) 'Class Formation, Hybridity and Ethnification in Declining Global Hegemonies', in K. Olds, P. Dicken, P. Kelly, L. Kong and H. Wai-Chung Yeung (eds.), *Globalisation and the Asia-Pacific*. London: Routledge, 183–201.

Friesen, W., Murphy, L., and Kearns, R. (2005) 'Spiced-up Sandringham: Indian transnationalism and new suburban spaces in Auckland, New Zealand', *Journal of Ethnic and Migration Studies*, 31(2), 385–401.

Gamburd, M.R. (2000) *The Kitchen Spoon's Handle: Transnationalism and Sri Lanka's Migrant Housemaids*. Ithaca, NY: Cornell University Press.

Gopalkrishnan, N. (2006) 'Infeartainment: the convergence of fear, diversity and governance', *International Journal of Diversity in Organisations, Communities and Nations*, 5(2), 85–90.

Guarnaccia, P.J. and Lopez, S. (1998). 'The mental health and adjustment of immigrant and refugee children', *Child and Adolescent Clinics of North America,* 7(3): 537–53.

Hage, G. (2003) *Against Paranoid Nationalism: Searching for Hope in a Shrinking Society*. Annandale, VA: Polity Press.

Hartley, R. (1995) *Families and Cultural Diversity in Australia*. Sydney: Allen and Unwin.

Holvino, E. (2010) 'Intersections: the simultaneity of race, gender and class in organization studies', *Gender, Work & Organization*, 17(3), 248–77.

Hooghiemstra, E. (2001) 'Migrants, partner selection and integration: Crossing borders', *Journal of Comparative Family Studies,* 32(4): 609–26.

Jayaram, N. (2004) *The Indian Diaspora: Dynamics of Migration*. New Delhi: Sage.

Jeffery, P. and Jeffery, R. (1996) *Don't Marry Me to a Plowman!* Boulder, CO: Westview Press.

Joshi, V. (2000) *Indian Daughters Abroad: Growing Up in Australia*. New Delhi: Sterling.

Kimmel, M.S. (2004) *The Gendered Society*. Oxford: Oxford University Press.

Levitt, P. (2009) 'Roots and routes: understanding the lives of the second generation transnationally', *Journal of Ethnic and Migration Studies*, 35(7), 1225–42.

Martin, J.I. (1978) *The Migrant Presence: Australian Responses 1947–1977*. Sydney: Allen & Unwin.

Mazumdar, V., and Sharma, K. (1990) 'Sexual division of labour and the subordination of women: a reappraisal from India', in Tinker, I. (ed.) *Persistent Inequalities: Women and World Development*. New York: Oxford University Press, 185–97.

Ministry of External Affairs (2005) *Indian Diaspora*. http://indiandiaspora.nic.in/ (accessed on 10 Sepetember 2010]. Nagar, R. (1998) 'Communal discourses, marriage, and the politics of gendered social boundaries among South Asian immigrants in Tanzania', *Gender, Place and Culture,* 5(2): 117–139.

Ng, R. (1986) 'The Social Construction of Immigrant Women in Canada', in Hamilton, R. and Barrett, M. (eds.), *The Politics of Diversity*. London: Verso, 269–86.

Penny, J. and S. Khoo 1996. *Intermarriage: A Study of Migration and Integration*. Canberra, Australia: Government Publishing Service.

Pessar, P.R., and Mahler, S.J. (2003) 'Transnational migration: bringing gender in', *International Migration Review*, 37(3), 812–46.

Pettman, J. (1992) *Living in the Margins: Racism, Sexism and Feminism in Australia*. St Leonards, Australia: Allen and Unwin.

Portes, A. (2001) 'Introduction: the debates and significance of immigrant transnationalism', *Global Networks*, 1(3), 181–93.

Rushdie, S. (1997) Interview. *India Today,* 14 July 1997: 88–90.

Sarup, M. (1994) 'Home and identity', in Robertson, G. (ed.) *Travellers Tales: Narratives of Home and Displacement*. London: Routledge, 93–104.

Sathian, S. (2010) 'Gender and nation in the South Asian diaspora: transnational cultural spaces in Bollywood cinema', *The Columbia Undergraduate Journal of South Asian Studies*, 2(1), 22–41.

Schmalzbauer, L. (2004) 'Searching wages and mothering from afar: the case of Honduran transnational families', *Journal of Marriage and Family*, 66(5), 1317–31.

Sedikides, C. and Brewer, M.B. (2001) *Individual Self, Relational Self and Collective Self: Partners, Opponents and Strangers*. Philadelphia: Psychology Press.

Singh, S. (2006) 'Towards a sociology of money and family in the Indian Diaspora', *Indian Sociology*, 40(3), 375–98.

Smith, R.C. (2006) *Mexican New York: Transnational Lives of New Immigrants*. Berkeley: University of California Press.

Uberoi, H. (2003) 'Imagining Indian diasporas in Canada', in Parekh, B., Singh, G., and Vertovec, S. (eds.) *Culture and Economy in the Indian Diaspora*. London: Routledge, 183–96.

Uberoi, P. (1998) 'The Diaspora Comes Home: Disciplining Desire in DDLJ', *Contribution to Indian Sociology,* 32(2): 305-36.

Voigt-Graf, C. (2005) 'The construction of transnational spaces by Indian migrants in Australia', *Journal of Ethnic and Migration Studies*, 31(2), 365–84.

Westwood, S., and Phizacklea, A. (2000) *Trans-Nationalism and the Politics of Belonging*. London: Routledge.

Wooden, M., Holton, R., and Sloan, J. (1994) *Australian Immigration: A Survey of the Issues*. Canberra: Australian Government Publishing Service.

Yuval-Davis, N. (2006) 'Intersectionality and feminist politics', *European Journal of Women's Studies*, 13(3), 193–209.

9

Work-Family Relations in Transnational Perspective

*A View from High-Tech Firms in India and the United States**

Winifred R. Poster and Srirupa Prasad

To many observers, the realms of work and family in the United States appear to be converging (Nippert-Eng 1996; Hochschild 1997; Darrah et al. 2001). As demands of family life and the workplace increasingly compete, activities within these historically distinct institutions often overlap and have the effect of blurring, if not obliterating, customary boundaries and distinctions. Trends towards globalization suggest that this process may be transnational. These developments prompt several compelling questions. If labour patterns are converging globally (Lincoln and Kalleberg 1990), will this merging of work and family happen in other countries as well? If large corporations are becoming increasingly global, will (or should) their international branches establish work-family arrangements and policies that reflect current developments from their home countries, in our case those of the

*Earlier versions of this paper were presented at meetings of the American Sociological Association, and the Sloan Foundation's *Work and Family Conference* (2000). Data collection was conducted with support from the National Science Foundation, the University of California at Berkeley Professional Studies Abroad in India Program, and a Stanford University McCoy Fellowship. Analysis was supported by the University of Illinois at Urbana-Champaign Research Board and the Center for International Business Education and Research. We are grateful to study participants for their time and stories, and we are grateful for the excellent comments of our colleagues Elizabeth and Joseph Pleck, Maud Schaafsma, and Nicole Ranganath, and of *Social Problems* editors James Holstein and David Smith and nine anonymous reviewers. The opinions expressed herein are the authors' alone.

United States (see also Florida and Keeney 1991 on Japanese firms)? In short, are US work-family patterns the inevitable model for the rest of the world?

This chapter addresses these questions through a transnational analysis of work-family relations. While the growing literature in this field provides an increasingly nuanced understanding of work-family dynamics, we remain dissatisfied with the theoretical and empirical orientations in the field for three reasons. First, work-family research tends to focus on Western and Northern societies, virtually ignoring Southern countries. Most transnational studies focus on the United States, Europe, and highly industrialized Asian societies such as Japan. While these studies note that work-family relations may differ among Western countries (Bailyn 1993), they neglect the wide range of global variation (Ishii-Kuntz 1994). Excluding Asia, Africa, and Latin America from the analysis impedes the development of broad-based theoretical insights into the possible globalization of domesticity, labour, power, and inequality.

Second, we find the understandings of the socio-historical *context* in the work-family literature to be insufficiently developed (Bowen and Pittman 1995; Barnett 1998; Rudd 2000). Many studies reduce complex relations to a list of variables, reifying and freezing them for quantification rather than treating them as situated, emergent, socially diffused practices. Other studies—understandably daunted by the task of narrowing the list of possible explanatory factors—focus on internal organizational features and ignore broad questions of context altogether (e.g., Perlow 2001).

Third, explanations of transnational work-family patterns are often unidimensional and/or oversimplified. Relying upon constructs such as 'culture' or 'technological development', research often focuses too narrowly on particular values and norms (e.g., Hofstede 1991) or very restricted technological concerns (e.g., Bell 1973) to explain work-family dynamics. While we agree that shared norms and technological development have an impact on relations between work and family, these explanations are insufficient by themselves. Such accounts overlook socio-historically located trends and institutions in which ideologies and technologies are embedded, as well as the systems of power and inequality that shape their enactment and implementation. In addition, these explanations neglect the dynamics of hierarchical relations between countries, which may shape work-family relations in their own right. To address these shortcomings in the literature, this chapter analyses data from the United States and India to elucidate work-family relations transnationally.

Towards a Contextual Approach to Work-Family Relations

The realms of home and family are often conceptually distinguished from the worlds of paid labour and the workplace (see Gubrium and Holstein 1990, 1997; Holstein and Gubrium 1995). As separate spheres of activities and interests, work and family can be conceptualized territorially and functionally. This chapter focuses on the physical spaces of the household and workplace—the tasks, objects, and symbols associated with maintaining the separate domains of work and family (i.e., caring for the family versus profit-seeking activities for an outside employer).[1] We presume that workplaces and households pose different demands for individual members. As individuals manage competing demands, they, in turn, actively construct boundaries that separate work and family life. Thus, work and family are managed as separate realms defined by boundary-making and maintaining processes (see Epstein 1989; Bailyn 1993; Nippert-Eng 1996; Perlow 1998; Clark 2000).

Our analysis of work-family relations is based on an ethnographic study of employees at one of three 'high-tech' firms—a US company in Silicon Valley, California (AmCo), a subsidiary of that company in New Delhi, India (TransCo), and a local company in New Delhi, India (IndCo). Even though these employees work for similar companies with similar demands for long work hours, they manage relations between work life and home life in different ways. The US high-tech employees often merge work life and family life to satisfy simultaneously competing demands, while the Indian employees tend to separate work and family.

Christena Nippert-Eng (1996) has argued that work-family relations can be viewed as positions on a continuum. As ideal types, the realms of work and family comprise completely *separate* or segmented worlds.[2] They represent two mutually exclusive categories with no conceptual, physical, or temporal overlap between realms. At the other end of the continuum, work and family are completely *integrated*. There are no distinctions between what belongs to 'home' or to 'work'; work and family blend seamlessly. In practice, however, real-life situations seldom approach the extremes of the continuum. Instead, work and family are neither totally separate nor completely integrated. In dealing with these amorphous realms as practical concerns, persons are constantly engaging and constructing boundaries that designate the parameters of work and family within the context of everyday life.

Work-Family Boundaries

Boundaries, of course, can be more or less rigid. They can be constructed and maintained as solid barriers, elastic borders, or permeable dividers between spheres of activity (Clark 2000). Nippert-Eng (1996) argues that highly permeable boundaries are associated with an *integration* of spheres, while solid boundaries are associated with *separate* spheres. The traditional 'nine-to-five' office job, where one works exclusively in a designated workplace during business hours and reserves nights and weekends for family life at home, represents the prototypic separation of work and family. Alternatively, a home-based business (such as catering, group childcare, or webpage design), where one works and lives in the same place, exemplifies the integration of work and family; such boundaries are hardly distinct.

Constituent elements of work and family may 'cross over' between realms, penetrating boundaries and integrating spheres. For instance, a person may attend a lunch meeting at work and afterward bring the catering leftovers home to recycle as meals for children's lunchboxes. Or, tracing movement in the opposite direction, an employee may bring family photos, microwave ovens, and other personal effects to the office to make it more 'homelike' (Darrah et al. 2001). Such permeability may operate in both directions or may be restricted to one direction (e.g., work may be taken home at night and on weekends, but personal effects are not allowed in the workplace). In either case, the permeability of boundaries, like the separation or integration of spheres, is a practical feature of everyday work-family relations.

Work-family literature currently fails to describe where and when particular kinds of boundaries might arise, especially in transnational context. In response, this chapter offers a detailed view of the separation and/or merger of work and family *transnationally*. Many studies find evidence of considerable work-family integration in the United States, especially in 'high-tech' and 'high-commitment' firms (Nippert-Eng 1996; Hochschild 1997; Perlow 1998; Darrah et al. 2001; Meiksins and Whalley 2001; English-Lueck 2002).[3] This study addresses the question of whether this tendency to erase work-family distinctions is expanding transnationally, to Indian high-tech firms.

Socio-Historical Context

An assessment of the erosion of work-family distinctions is connected in part to the broader socio-historical context in which these firms operate. Socio-historical context comprises more than culture or politics alone. It may be composed of many interrelated components, including (but not limited to) social and historical trends, economic conditions, ideological commitments, and pervasive or local social institutions. Our analysis identifies two features of socio-historical context that influence work-family relations among AmCo, IndCo, and TransCo workers: social contracts and historically shifting relations between work-family spheres. Because the relation between individuals, institutions, and their contexts is mutually constitutive, it is impossible to separate one from the other. Our approach, then, is to treat work-family boundaries as both embedded in, and constitutive of, the wider institutional environment.

- *A social contract favouring work over family*. Work-related 'social contracts' extract concessions from employees in exchange for provisions or benefits from corporations and governments (Rubin 1996). In the United States, this social contract commonly invokes greater access to jobs, but weaker family-related benefits, relative to Southern nations such as India. Although provisions for family support have expanded over the last century, culminating in the Family and Medical Leave Act of 1993 (Wiatrowski 1990), current state benefits in the United States are meagre—especially material ones. Globally, many national governments provide better support and subsidies for childcare, health care, and parental leave (Lewis et al. 1992; Lewis and Lewis 1996; Haas et al. 2000). In contrast, the US state, through its indifference to these issues, has shifted responsibility for family benefits to employers (Gonyea and Googins 1996). The result is a set of US family-related policies that ensure that workers continue to 'give priority to work over family' (Lambert 1993: 252). Furthermore, the social contract in the United States erodes worker power. Only about 14 per cent of the labour force is unionized, and federal restrictions on union tactics have undermined workers' abilities to organize effectively for family support policy.
- The trade-off, of course, is that US workers benefit from comparatively large labour markets, as well as more stable, better paying jobs. Global economic and political power helps Northern nations insulate their labour markets and protect jobs in ways that Southern nations cannot. Indeed, even with the vagaries of downsizing and layoffs (Schor 1992), unemployment rates in the United States are far lower than those of India (5 per cent versus 20 per cent) and per capita incomes are far greater (at $21,500 versus $465 respectively) (UNDP 1999).
- In sum, the social contract in the United States promotes the merging of work and family. Conversely, the social contract in India—which provides greater institutional support for

families—helps to maintain separate work and domestic spheres and facilitate solid boundaries for IndCo and TransCo employees.

- *Historically shifting work-family relations*. Patterns of work-family relations are also influenced by broader historical and social trends in the separation/integration of work and family. Throughout the pre-industrial era, households were sites of both production and reproduction and thus were highly integrated (Cowan 1983). However, as production moved to the public realm with the rise of industrial capitalism, separate spheres of work and family emerged, along with the taken-for-granted boundary between the workplace and the household (Zaretsky 1976). Within the last few decades, this boundary has begun to erode for urban middle-class families in the United States (especially compared to those in India). This erosion is evident in several recent developments.

First, new forms of work organization have permeated the US landscape. 'High commitment' firms now compose more than one-third of US organizations (Osterman 1995). De-industrialization and the transfer of factory labour to the global South have led to the expansion of professional, managerial, and other types of white-collar work where high commitment is requisite. Some argue that the high-commitment trend is characterized by organizational strategies for extracting more time and labour from workers. Organizations use systems of normative control to create emotional bonds that elicit loyalty to the firm (Kunda 1992). Structural inducements such as flat hierarchies, job teams, and family-friendly, work-based programmes also serve to increase employee participation and feelings of commitment and 'empowerment' (Smith 1997). In return, however, the high-commitment firm expects 'voluntary' long hours and a willingness to subordinate other aspects of one's life to the demands of work. Merging work and family spheres accommodates such demands.

Second, households have become increasingly flexible regarding the demands of work. US families have become smaller and less stable over the past century (Wiatrowski 1990). The extended family which shares a single household is on the wane. Even among Northern countries, US households are especially fluid and shifting. Only one-quarter to one-third of US families are composed of a married couple and children, almost half of new marriages end in divorce, and the odds of remarriage are about 80 per cent (Coltrane 1996). Some scholars argue that these trends generate a sense of insecurity about the household, especially relative to one's job. For this reason, employees commit more energy and attention to the workplace, which they see as more viable and stable (Hochschild 1997).

Another important change in US households is the accelerated pace of family life. The corporatization of the household—prompted by marketing and consumer industries—encourages routines to become faster and more time-efficient (Hochschild 1997). These changes have been accompanied by a rapid growth of service industries, which specialize in the outsourcing of domestic chores such as 'internet grocery delivery, taxi services [for] the timely delivery of children at activities, and personal assistants who purchase gifts and entertain visiting relatives' (Darrah et al. 2001: 44). Whether intentional or not, these consumer industries provide a support structure for individuals to economize time in the household. In turn, this makes households more amenable to work pressure.

Although many of these broader trends are also found in India (especially since the turn of the millennium), they have occurred neither at the same pace nor to the same extent. This leaves the socio-historical context of work-family relations somewhat different for US employees of AmCo when compared to their Indian counterparts at TransCo and IndCo. Employees of the two Indian companies demonstrate visible resistance to the integration of work and family, even though the companies for which they work are similar in many ways to the US firm. As our study shows, Indian workers occupy larger, more interdependent households than do US workers and work for employers who make fewer demands to work at home. Together, these circumstances mitigate pressures for work-family integration. They represent features of the socio-historical context of urban middle-class India that affect work-family relations for the employees of this study differently than for those in the US context.

The social contract and the reversal of the historical work-family divide, then combine with other contextual features in India such as trends of globalization, legacies of colonialism, and the politics of the Hindu Right to shape spheres of work and family and the boundaries between them. As we show, Indian employees more often construct solid boundaries around separate spheres, while US workers tend to draw flexible, permeable boundaries which integrate work with family life. This difference persists even though the Indian companies we studied are quite similar to their US counterpart in many important ways.

The Cases and Methodology

The high-tech industry provides rich grounds for transnational comparison. India and the United States are both leaders in computer and software development, ranked among the top three in the world for technological and scientific expertise (Sekaran 1992). Accordingly, our analysis is based on case studies of three computer companies chosen for their differing locations and positions in the global economy, but similar size, industry, and market characteristics. First, *AmCo,* a US company located in Silicon Valley, California, is a member of the Fortune 500. One of the founders of the high-tech industry in Silicon Valley, it has subsidiaries around the world. Next, *TransCo* is one of the AmCo subsidiaries with offices in New Delhi and a factory in Bangalore. TransCo has US ownership, management, and employment policies, but is staffed entirely by Indians (with a few US expatriates). Finally, *IndCo,* the Indian counterpart to AmCo, is owned by Indians and is located in New Delhi. IndCo is a leading high-tech company in India, with subsidiaries worldwide (including in California). All three companies deal in software development and hardware production, and all three represented (at the time of the study) the top tier of their markets. Each employs more than 500 employees and maintains similar employee gender ratios (at roughly 25 to 30 per cent female).

Data were collected from fall 1995 through spring 1996. TransCo was approached first, as a leading computer firm in both India and the United States. Contacts made at this site during fieldwork facilitated access to both of the other firms. The study employs naturalistic ethnographic methods (Gubrium and Holstein 1997), including observational fieldwork at each location by the first author of this chapter. At each site, the first author studied two-work units—the corporate office and a factory. Jobs in the corporate offices involve management, marketing, engineering, accounting, and administration. Jobs in the factories primarily involve circuit board manufacturing and computer assembly. Ultimately, the first author conducted 34 interviews at AmCo, 60 at TransCo, and 51 at IndCo.[4] In addition, the first author also examined company documents such as organizational charts and corporate philosophies for discussions of work-family issues. Finally, semi-structured interviews were conducted with both workers and managers to assess demographic and educational backgrounds, work experiences, and household characteristics.

Interviewees were told that this was a study about employment in transnational firms. They were not told of the project aims regarding work-family issues, in order to avoid biased responses. Interviews were conducted on site, either in English or in Hindi with the assistance of an interpreter, and lasted about an hour. Sample selection was based on employee lists provided by the human resource department of each firm.

Respondents were chosen randomly, although samples were balanced by gender and occupational level.

There are many demographic parallels among the employees in our samples. Most are relatively young, ages 30–40. They are also well-educated. Even at the factories, the majority have high school diplomas (75 per cent), and many of them hold technical or graduate degrees as well (37–50 per cent). Finally, they also share similar domestic situations. More than half are married and have one or two children (Table 1).

Given these similarities, what then accounts for the differences in work-family boundaries? The following sections answer this question by comparing the three organizations. Due to space limitations, we provide greater detail on the cases of IndCo and TransCo than AmCo and refer readers to the surfeit of research on US firms for further background (e.g., Hochschild 1997). First, our comparison focuses on the internal dynamics of households and workplaces, tracing the factors that influence and sometimes pressure employees at IndCo and TransCo to solidify work-family boundaries. We then explore how workers manage these pressures in their boundary strategies. Finally, we outline features of the Indian context that promote the separation of the household and workplace. Our conclusion addresses implications of these findings for a transnational approach to work and family.

Household Pressures for Work-Family Separation

Workers at IndCo and TransCo describe their family lives as less integrated with work than do workers at AmCo. Indian employees portray aspects of their urban environments and large extended families as sources of pressure to separate work life from domestic life. For example, the vagaries of the Indian infrastructure render many problematic aspects of middle-class family life that are taken for granted in the United States, such as the lack of access to even the most basic services such as electricity and plumbing. These conditions increase household chores in many ways: the lack of refrigeration results in more frequent shopping trips to the market and the lack of running water leads to more time and energy carrying heavy barrels from outdoor spigots to the house (Desai 1996; Blair 1997). Managing a middle-class household for the Indian workers in our study entails a more extensive range of routine tasks than for our workers in the United States.

For instance, even workers who have refrigerators have difficulty using them because of the poor management of state utilities. Spontaneous power outages are frequent in big cities, and water and electricity

Table 1

Family and Household Characteristics

	AmCo[a]			*TransCo*			*IndCo*		
	Total *n*=34	*Women* *n*=17	*Men* *n*=17	*Total* *n*=60	*Women* *n*=29	*Men* *n*=31	*Total* *n*=51	*Women* *n*=26	*Men* *n*=25
Currently married (%)	58	50	65	67	62	71	80	73	88
Spouse works (%)	82	100	67	74	100	59	63	100	32
Average number of children	2	2	2	1	1	1	1.5	1	2
Household structure (%)									
Single family	66	56	81	58	59	58	49	50	48
Joint family	34	44	19	42	41	42	51	50	52

[a]Excludes two respondents at AmCo. See text (Note 4) for discussion.

are often shut off for hours, if not days. In addition, household tasks are made more difficult by a cumbersome state bureaucracy that pervades public service institutions. At the time of the study, for example, respondents often had to pay their bills in person rather than by mail, and routine activities such as reserving train or plane tickets could take hours of standing on line at the depot. A female engineer at IndCo explains, 'Air travel is such a pain. You can't book a ticket on the phone. You don't get reservations so easily. It is bad'. Therefore, household-related chores require frequent trips and take longer for Indian workers than they would in the United States.

The relative impact these factors have on household strain for workers at IndCo and TransCo is apparent in Tables 1 and 2. First, the Indian employees spend more time on housework (Table 1). While AmCo workers report an average of 10 hours a week on domestic labour, those at TransCo and IndCo report 13 and 18 hours, respectively.[5] Second, Indian workers list additional activities not mentioned at AmCo (Table 2). While cooking, cleaning, and childcare may be common at all three companies, other chores (such as the 'outside' tasks of water collection and bill paying) are mentioned mostly by IndCo and TransCo employees.

Large family networks also promote a separation of work and family. TransCo and IndCo workers live in bigger households than those at AmCo (Table 1). They are more likely to be married: 80 per cent of IndCo employees have spouses compared to 58 per cent at AmCo. They are also more likely to live in joint households, that is, with relatives other than spouses and children. While 51 per cent of workers at IndCo and 42 per cent at TransCo live in such households, only 34 per cent at AmCo live in joint households.[6] Furthermore, joint families in the US sample are much smaller than those in India; AmCo workers live with a maximum of five other people, whereas IndCo workers report as many as sixteen.

Joint family living for IndCo and TransCo workers leads to more housework. Even with more hands to help out, large families require more chores. For instance, women at IndCo and TransCo more frequently list cooking and childcare than those at AmCo (Table 2), even though they report similar numbers of their own children (Table 1). Indian workers in the sample may also have children who are younger. Although we lack comprehensive data on children's ages, we know that at least 30 per cent of TransCo workers have children under the age of three or on the way, while AmCo workers describe adult or school-age children.

Table 2

Housework: Hours and Types

	AmCo			*TransCo*[a]			*IndCo*		
	Total $n=34$	*Women* $n=17$	*Men* $n=17$	*Total* $n=60$	*Women* $n=29$	*Men* $n=31$	*Total* $n=51$	*Women* $n=26$	*Men* $n=25$
Time spent on housework (Mean hours per week)	10	12	8	13	17	9	18	24	10
Most common types of housework[b] (per cent of total household chores)									
Cooking	26	31	21	28	33	22	23	40	5
Cleaning	50	47	52	30	39	22	21	37	7
Childcare	7	6	7	12	11	12	20	17	23
Gardening	8	10	7	2	0	3	4	0	7
Socializing	0	0	0	2	3	0	5	2	7
Miscellaneous: pets, repairs	5	0	10	5	3	7	5	2	7
Outside chores: shopping, bank, bills, water retrieval	5	6	3	22	11	34	23	2	44
Total number of household chores listed	n=61	32	29	77	36	41	91	48	43

[a]Excludes seventeen respondents at TransCo. See text (Note 4) for discussion.

[b]Based on an open-ended question asking respondents to list their regular housework activities, the columns here represent the per cent of all chores listed by all employees in each organization.

In addition to having large families *within* the household, IndCo and TransCo workers have larger extended family networks as well (Sekaran 1992). In turn, 'socializing'—attending family functions such as weddings, birth celebrations, and funerals, and hosting relatives at home—is a chore listed mostly by Indian workers in the sample (Table 2). While *business* socializing (like having bosses over for dinner) is typical of AmCo family routines (Di Leonardo 1987), *extended family* socializing is more often a significant dimension of household life at IndCo and TransCo. A male business manager at IndCo explains how these family functions outrank other household chores: 'Small things I have time to ignore: like going to a parent's meeting at school, shopping, and a small party. [But] we have a commitment to major social appointments. I definitely attend some weddings in the family or for relatives, and those particularly relating to children. That I don't ignore'. Finally, IndCo and TransCo workers assume substantial financial obligations for their extended family networks as well. A manager at the TransCo factory explains that many of her employees 'cannot afford things or cannot live like others because they live with parents or have to take care of the schooling of their sisters'.

Of course, large families also benefit IndCo and TransCo employees. They help in practical ways, such as with childcare. While most AmCo workers use daycare centres for small children, 60 per cent of IndCo workers rely on their families, if not on nannies (see Note 5). Large households also help ease emotional burdens. A male clerk at the IndCo factory declares, 'No, I do not have any problems. I have a joint family. Our problems are shared'. In contrast, AmCo families report problems because their families are small, isolated, and sometimes headed by one parent (Sharma 1986). Furthermore, AmCo workers more often live in dual-earner households (67 per cent, versus 59 per cent at TransCo and 32 per cent at IndCo; see Table 1), where neither partner is at home full-time. Thus, both types of households have benefits and drawbacks in relation to family members' work lives.

Still, Indian households in our sample are less receptive to workplace demands than are those of AmCo. For the most part, AmCo households compress family functions and/or inter-weave them with work activities. As a female scientist describes,

> Sometimes it feels like I am running all day to try to get done what I have here [at the office], and what I have to do at home. Last week I needed to go home early to wait for an appliance repair person. But I have a computer at home, I have a modem and dial in to work. As soon as I got home I dialed in, because if I don't catch up with my e-mail I

can have 300 hundred messages in a day. I absolutely have to keep up. So when I went home, I worked on that.

Yet, instead of 'running all day' to integrate work and family, IndCo and TransCo workers are much more likely to reserve and extend time for family. Thus, they express a different type of pressure: 'When I go back home, I can't work' (TransCo male branch manager). This means that there are significant limitations for the Indian employees to place a high priority on work. For instance, a female TransCo executive discontinued night time MBA courses that would help towards a promotion at work because of an ailing mother-in-law. Another woman executive at IndCo declined an overseas assignment due to obligations to her extended family.

Cumulatively, then, Indian family life exerts a number of pressures on employed family members to separate their work lives from their family lives. Employees tend to bow to the greater demands of domestic life and treat the workplace and the household as distinct spheres of activity and interest, even if there are workplace costs for the employees. At the same time, features of the workplace also pressure employees to keep work-related matters separate from family, as we shall describe in the next section.

Workplace Pressures for Work-Family Separation

Factors in the workplace also contribute to work-family separation at IndCo and TransCo. Whereas AmCo workers experience strong pressure from their firm to prioritize work over family and to take work home, Indian employees receive a different signal: to leave work at the office door. This pattern is especially noteworthy since workers in our Indian samples are asked to work long hours, just like their US counterparts. In fact, the Indian-based employees report working more hours per week in the office than do AmCo employees. Yet unlike the 'high-commitment' scenario common at AmCo, Indian employees report less interest in working long hours. This section describes how 'bureaucratic' controls at IndCo and TransCo are central to this outcome. First, we examine how they contribute to a containment of work within the office, thereby preventing the movement of work across workplace-household boundaries. Second, we consider how bureaucratic controls facilitate a reward system that discourages workers from prioritizing work over family. These workplace factors combine to exert pressure on Indian workers to maintain separate and distinct spheres of work and family life.

Restrictions on Work Time and Place

Bureaucratic control systems often demand long work hours through rules and regulations (Edwards 1979; Baron et al. 1988). This system contrasts with normative control, which uses loyalty to the firm and feelings of job fulfilment (i.e., 'norms') to compel employees to work long hours. Managers at TransCo and, especially, IndCo rely primarily on bureaucratic control. They keep work inside the workplace so it can be easily monitored, and so productivity can be measured by units of time spent 'on the job' or at a desk. A TransCo employee notes, 'In Indian companies, how management works, the way they view the employee, is absolutely different [than U.S. companies]. They would say you have to sign the attendance register every day. There is obviously no flexibility. You are expected to work at least ten hours a day in the office'. Rules about work time are strict; daily attendance and morning arrival times are carefully monitored. An IndCo executive observes:

> I have to be here at 9:00 a.m. I have to. Supposing I go home at 8:00 p.m. one night. I don't have the flexibility to come in the morning at 10:00 a.m. or 11:00 a.m. If I have to come late, then I have to tell my boss. Otherwise, they will put a cross on the register that the person is not there.

Bureaucratic systems enforce such rules through material penalties. IndCo workers are only allowed two late arrivals a month, after which a half day's pay is deducted from their wages. Workers are also required to work in the office two Saturdays a month.

This work arrangement contrasts sharply with AmCo, where one employee says, 'We don't punch a time clock, and if you're done, they don't expect you to work eight hours exactly. Some days I work ten hours, sometimes I work seven'. A female marketing manager concurs, 'They are more aware over here [at AmCo] regarding flexibility, especially in timing. If you say you need to do some work at home—office work at home—and ask, "Can I come late in the morning?" That is flexible. You have all the various options to do that'. While all three firms give somewhat less latitude to their factory employees than to corporate personnel (because production work is organized by shifts), the Indian firms are more rigid in their scheduling. AmCo managers have alternate day and night shifts during periods of speed-up, whereas IndCo and TransCo managers combine them so that operators are working around the clock.

The end result of bureaucratic control and its strict rules about scheduling is a longer day in the office for the Indian employees (Table 3). While AmCo workers report an average of 9.4 hours per day, TransCo workers report 10.1 hours, and IndCo workers report 10.6 hours. Indeed, despite recent reports of long work schedules in the United States, it is not the US workers in our study who spend the most hours in the office.

In addition to strict scheduling rules, the Indian firms have more rules about workplaces. As a point of contrast, AmCo employees have many field assignments: they travel regularly to meet vendors, suppliers, customers, and to visit other AmCo divisions. Managers also schedule company meetings off-site, as regular long-distance 'retreats'. Yet extensive travel is rare at IndCo and TransCo. As shown in Table 3, IndCo employees report fieldwork almost 20 per cent less often than do those at AmCo. Not only do AmCo employees travel more frequently, but also greater distances, the majority being 'inside the country' or 'abroad' (84 per cent). At IndCo, most of those who travel stay close to home, either 'within the city' or 'within the country' (90 per cent). TransCo has not only a large number of workers who travel, but also the greatest share of those who move within the smallest geographic range, 'inside the city' (53 per cent).

Similarly, AmCo employees do more work at home.[7] Thirty-nine per cent of the non-production employees at AmCo report working at home on nights or weekends (Table 3), where they typically spend several hours catching up on phone calls and email, or reading and writing reports.[8] This parallels other studies of US workplaces (e.g., Hochschild 1997; Women of Silicon Valley 2001). However, at IndCo and TransCo, rules about when and where employees may work are strict. Only 22 per cent of non-production employees at TransCo and 17 per cent at IndCo report working at home, making this trend almost two times less likely than at AmCo. A female secretary explains:

> In this organization, if you have been given a job, you have to finish the job in the office. It doesn't matter what time you come, but the job will have to be done. That means more than eight hours. Also, because I am not able to finish the job on Fridays, I have to come on Saturdays.

In fact, workers sometimes find themselves sitting idle just to fill the time, as a female senior executive explains: 'I have to stay after 5:30 p.m. irrespective of whether my work finishes by 2:00, 4:00, or 5:00 p.m. I would have to sit here and do nothing. And I wish I could have gone home because there are times we are staying here till 8:00 p.m.'.

Table 3

Office Work: Time and Place

	AmCo (n=34)			*TransCo (n=60)*			*IndCo (n=51)*		
	Total	*Women*	*Men*	*Total*	*Women*	*Men*	*Total*	*Women*	*Men*
Work time Mean hours in the office per day	9.4	9.6	9.2	10.1	9.9	10.2	10.6	11.6	9.6
Work location In the field:									
Have field assignments (%)	62	50	73	70	59	81	43	27	60
Farthest distance traveled for field assignments (%):									
Within the city	16	20	12	53	67	38	28	29	27
Nationally	51	40	63	35	27	43	62	71	53
Abroad	33	40	25	13	7	19	10	0	20
Total[a]	100	100	100	101	101	100	100	100	100
At home:[b]									
Nights and weekends (%)	39	53	24	22	21	22	17	11	24

[a]Some percentages exceed 100 due to rounding.

[b]Excludes factory operators, who are not allowed to take work home.

In these ways, bureaucratic policies at IndCo and TransCo keep tasks inside the office. With rules against working in non-traditional locations (including the household) and at non-traditional times, Indian employees in our sample have fewer opportunities to merge work and family spheres. Work-family boundaries are strictly maintained.

Fewer Normative Rewards and Benefits

Rewards systems are the second organizational factor contributing to solid boundaries at IndCo and TransCo. To begin with, there is less material pay-off at IndCo and TransCo for employees to assume extra workloads. Monthly wages at the Indian-based firms are one-sixth to one-tenth of those at AmCo: on average, \$352 at IndCo and \$547 at TransCo, versus \$3,766 at AmCo (Table 4). These Indian wages are higher than other local industries and government jobs, yet still substantially lower than those of AmCo, where the jobs are almost exactly the same. In addition, while AmCo managers often use normative incentives to motivate long hours and loyalty to the firm, IndCo and TransCo managers use seniority-based career ladders, which reduce performance pressures, and a pragmatic corporate philosophy, which finds less need to make job satisfaction part of the reward structure.

Other organizational features, such as promotion policies, deter extra workloads as well. While career ladders at AmCo are based on performance, those at IndCo and TransCo are based on seniority. This policy eliminates the need for workers to display 'extra effort' as proof of commitment to the firm. Two features of bureaucratic control ensure this system: decoupling productivity from pay raises and removing the lag time between promotions and raises. A TransCo manager explains how this policy orientation differs from that of his own US parent company:

> If we promote somebody in the States, you don't necessarily get a raise at all for a year. People have to see that when they put in the extra effort, their contribution pays off—and not that it just does not make any difference [whereas at TransCo] years of experience determines what level you get brought in at. If we promote somebody, they go a big jump.

The fact that job security is a perk of seniority-based raises, and promotions helps explain why Indian-based employees put up with strict bureaucratic controls.

Finally, another organizational difference between the firms is the use of symbolic and nonmaterial rewards to motivate extra work. IndCo, for instance, lacks the 'empowerment' strategies of corporate governance that AmCo uses as a compensation for overtime and extra work. Instead of having flat hierarchies, decentralization, open communication, and team work arrangements (Smith 1997), IndCo is described by a female product manager in this way: 'My observation here is that it's more like autocracy. People at the senior level, they give instructions and you are supposed to follow. It's not a participative relationship'. With features such as top-down, decision-making, hierarchical relationships and close monitoring of workers (Edwards 1979), managerial power at IndCo is readily apparent and unapologetic. The organizational philosophy has little pretence of creating a 'supportive environment' for employees.

Moreover, IndCo and TransCo lack the social and entertainment activities that encourage workers to treat 'work as home' (Hochschild 1997). AmCo goes to great lengths to make the office environment less like work and more like fun. The company provides ping-pong tables, basketball courts, and sports matches, even at the factory. 'Play' is an integral part of the work experience: a factory supervisor explains that 'you hear a lot of talk and laughter' on the production line. At the corporate office, there is a similar atmosphere: 'When we are learning together and playing together, and our communications open up, it makes a work/business relationship as well as a friendship'.

Alternatively, bureaucratic policies at IndCo discourage an 'outlook of the company [towards] employee welfare and internal satisfaction', as a male custcmer support manager explains. 'Employee welfare means having some recreation so that you can let off the steam somewhere, or other curricular activities—these are typically missing in the Indian companies'. Without such rewards, workers at the Indian-based firms have a more pragmatic view of their jobs. An export production manager in the TransCo factory put it this way: 'I visited the U.S. once, and my feeling is that the culture in the U.S. is like this—you don't have to work hard for something. You don't have to work that hard to live. But here in India, you have to work hard to live'. In general, employees of the Indian firms understand work in a less romantic way and are less likely to view work as a source of personal fulfilment, than are AmCo employees. In sum, bureaucratic control undermines the work-as-priority ethic at IndCo and TransCo, and encourages employees to separate work from family.

Managing Work and Family Pressures

Taken together, the previous sections reveal how institutions of the workplace and household operate collectively and interactively to

Table 4

Average Monthly Salary by Job Level and Gender

Job Level	*AmCo*			*TransCo*[a]			*IndCo*[a]		
	Total *n*=31	*Women* *n*=15	*Men* *n*=16	*Total* *n*=56	*Women* *n*=29	*Men* *n*=27	*Total* *n*=48	*Women* *n*=24	*Men* *n*=24
All Levels	$3,766	$3,500	$4,017	$547	$372	$729	$352	$253	$455
Manager	$4,720	$3,867	$6,000	$1,076	$625	$1,230	$731	$557	$811
Executive, Sales, Engineer	$5,449	$5,338	$5,523	$513	$431	$612	$316	$333	$296
Admin., Secretary[b]	$4,583	$4,583	—	$349	$349	—	$164	$199	$136
Operator, Technician	$2,273	$2,137	$2,391	$90	$60	$107	$90	$90	$91

[a]Wages at IndCo and TransCo have been converted from rupees, at a rate of 34.5 rupees per dollar (applicable to the year of the interview).

[b]Blank entries indicate a lack of respondents in the sample for this category.

generate boundary pressure for workers. At AmCo, elements of both the workplace and household promote work-family integration. In contrast, employees at TransCo and IndCo experience pressures to separate work and family, both at work and at home. At AmCo, the pressure is somewhat more likely to emanate from the workplace bureaucracy; the firm literally exports work beyond standard business hours and locations. Employees' households generally absorb the overflow. Conversely, IndCo and TransCo workers experience greater pressure from their household demands, given the context of larger Indian families and less predictable urban environments. The workplace indirectly accommodates pressures from the family sphere by limiting work to fixed hours within the office.

Ironically, the sources of boundary pressure come from, and move in, opposite directions in each case. Yet, because households and workplaces largely act as a system, the implications for work-family boundaries are unambiguous in each context. Elements of both the workplace and household promote work-family *integration* at AmCo, while the same institutions promote work-family *separation* at TransCo and IndCo.

Feeling the Pressures

At this point we ask, How do workers react to the pressures emanating from work-family relations? Although there is considerable variation in how employees respond in all the cases, workers at AmCo tend to manage tensions around work-family boundaries in ways that merge the two spheres, while their Indian counterparts maintain stronger, more rigid boundaries that circumscribe the household and separate it from the workplace.

Our interviews asked employees, 'What is the most common way you feel tension managing work and family?' Three general themes emerged in each of the firms (Table 5): (1) work tends to interfere with *family life*, (2) work tends to interfere with *personal life*, or (3) family life interferes with *work*. Given these common concerns, the difference between the firms lies in which theme is most prominent. AmCo workers are more concerned with the latter two themes, as 42 per cent of their responses highlight intrusions on personal and work lives. In direct contrast, IndCo and TransCo workers rarely mention family intrusions into work life as a problem or source of tension and, in fact, are much more likely to mention the first theme of work interfering with family.

At AmCo, institutional priorities appear to place work ahead of family. Sometimes employees attribute pressures directly to bosses. As expressed by a female executive at the corporate office, 'Lately I have had some urgent projects come up, and I have been requested not to take vacations, and to arrange my plans for the weekends, and to come and get work done. This is the third time in the last three months'. Other employees describe a personal motivation to put in 'extra' time at work. As a male executive in the corporate office explains:

> I am trying to find out what is a good balance between work and home—but I am also trying to prove myself. Although I like to get home on time, I usually spend an extra hour when everyone else has gone home, just to try and get some stuff done. When I go home, it is just to get ready to work for the next day.

Even operators at the factory discuss the demands of family on work: 'I always try to balance it, but you never get it 100 per cent. Sometimes it is hard. You have to balance [chores] at your home *without interfering with your work*' (emphasis added).

In contrast, tensions at the Indian firms focus on households to a greater degree. Indian employees at TransCo and IndCo frequently mention 'insufficient time for family, children, and housework' as a source of tension (up to 93 per cent of their responses). Although AmCo workers also note these sources of tension, the Indian workers mention them almost twice as often, in some cases. A TransCo general manager explains why:

> There are always sporadic work-life issues. What is very important in my job, and for quite a few colleagues in my department, is that our schedules are not really dictated or decided by us. I wish I could control that, frankly speaking, because sometimes you may miss your daughter's birthday. I have missed it a couple of times in the last five years. I wish I had more control over these kind of things.

Extended family socializing is another part of home life that the Indian employees in our sample sometimes compromise because of work obligations. 'I can't go to social functions and marriages because of work', says a male wiring operator at the IndCo factory. They also mention missing time for housework and daily family activities. A female manger at the IndCo factory reflects:

> We never thought that it would be that difficult to work both at home and at the office, but only after working I do find that there is not enough time to do justice to your family. We reach home by 7:00 p.m., and sleep by 11:00 p.m. In that time, you have to do cooking, you have to eat, and you have to manage for the next day also.

These insights into managing work and family reflect the countervailing institutional pressures in the work sites we studied. While AmCo

Table 5

Work-Family Tensions: Per cent of Employees Feeling Main Impact on Family, Individual, and Work

	AmCo			*TransCo*			*IndCo*		
	Total	*Women*	*Men*	*Total*	*Women*	*Men*	*Total*	*Women*	*Men*
Work interferes with family:									
Insufficient time with family and children	34	29	40	63	62	64	62	46	77
Insufficient time for household work	24	29	20	30	38	22	4	7	0
Work interferes with personal life:									
Insufficient time for personal chores	0	0	0	0	0	0	17	20	15
Drains energy	17	13	20	0	0	0	17	27	8
Family life interferes with work:									
Family takes time from office work	25	29	20	7	0	14	0	0	0
Total	100	100	100	100	100	100	100	100	100

employees are more likely to prioritize work, those at IndCo and TransCo are more likely to express family-centred concerns about the interference of work with family.

Boundary Strategies

The experience of tensions leads to well-formulated strategies for managing work-family boundaries. At AmCo, workers frequently integrate work and family activities. Sometimes this means blending *work into home life*, as a female facilities specialist states:

> I work later in the evenings about three days a week, for a three-week duration; then I might have a normal week, and then it starts up again. I bring work home too, for about three hours: I might be here [in the office] for two hours, and then take an additional hour to go home and have some dinner, and then work an extra hour at home. So, it'd be a kind of combination. Then on the weekends, I come in too.

Similarly, a female product manager describes, 'I work at night since I don't like to work real early in the morning. So if I work late, I work from home. [My coworkers] do understand so nobody has said anything to me'. Workers also use their flexible schedules to enhance their personal comfort during work or to increase efficiency. A female manufacturing development engineer explains, '[I go in on] either Saturday or Sunday when I have to catch up on stuff. It is quiet here and I know that I can get it done'.

AmCo employees also blend *home into work* by making the office a pseudo family zone. Many AmCo employees integrate leisure activities into the office environment instead of keeping them at home. A male corporate employee explains, 'I am usually here on weekends whether it is for [athletic] workouts or if it is for catching up with work. I have a bike here and I come here to work out. Sometimes I spend all weekend here'. Employees sometimes bring their families to the office, and although the company does not currently provide daycare, a woman in the corporate office wishes they did so she could spend more time with her infants at work: 'With childcare on site, you can go pick up your kids on time, and bring them over to your office'.

Moreover, the types of family activities brought to the office are not just the enjoyable ones. A female scientist describes how she uses corporate programmes to help manage conflicts in her household: 'They have brown bag lunches that are specifically about things that are important to women who are working and have children. You [can] listen to someone speak about behavior problems with children in the ages of 5 to 10. And I've gone to those because of my grandchildren'.

To a degree, then, AmCo workers practice a 'reversal' of work and home spheres (Hochschild 1997). AmCo workers are thus more likely to integrate the two spheres and create permeable boundaries: 'work' can be done anywhere, including the home, and some 'home' activities can be done at work.

In contrast, many of the Indian workers manage tensions by actively separating the workplace from family life. They establish clearly distinct functions for the household and workplace: 'work' is what happens inside the office, and 'family' is what happens inside the household. A male personnel executive at TransCo declares:

> I hardly carry home my work. I have definitely a personal life to manage. I have my kids, I have my granny, and that is as important as my job. I need to balance my work life. When I am in the office, I am in the office. Period. If I am at home, I am at home.

In another contrast to AmCo, family space is reserved not just for obligations or chores, but also for leisure. A junior engineer at the IndCo factory says, 'We should not need to work late hours or on Saturday and Sunday, because we find it odd. All my friends working in other places definitely have off on Sunday, and we could meet them and relax'. A female administrator at the TransCo factory concurs, '[We should have] a longer weekend, more leisure hours, and more time to do other work. Weekdays I just spend a lot of time commuting and have long hours. So, why not … take Friday off?' These IndCo and TransCo employees reject the acceleration of family life, and as part of this process, they construct work-family boundaries that are firmer and more impermeable than those of AmCo workers.

Bending to Institutional Boundary Pressures

Wouldn't we expect workers to resist the institutional pressures of their respective scenarios, at least to some degree? We do find that workers in all our samples balk at working long hours. Still, we are surprised to find that in all three firms, few workers challenge the pressures (exerted by their respective companies and social contexts) regarding *boundaries*. Instead, most workers generally yield to those boundary pressures in their work-family management strategies.

For instance, even while AmCo employees might ideally like to insulate their home lives from the intrusions of work, their practices are in fact very accommodating. An indication of this is in Table 5, which shows how many AmCo employees describe a lack of time with family; yet at the same time, few request policies that might separate work from family. Instead, AmCo workers tend to ask for *more control* over the work-family integration process. A male quality engineer at AmCo explains:

> The biggest problem I have with balancing my work and home is … when I work at home and have a *deadline*. If I have something due tomorrow, I will sit up [until early] in the morning and do it. Like yesterday I put in four hours even though I was sick. And I have to meet another deadline tomorrow.

Given the sporadic demands of the work, the main point of contention is *who* generates work schedules, rather than where or when the work is to be done. Furthermore, control over scheduling is sometimes more important than reducing their overall hours worked. An AmCo female corporate office employee says, 'I try to get out by 8:30 p.m. because by that time it is getting too late. When it starts getting to be eleven hours or twelve hours, then my happiness goes down tremendously. But ideally, I would like to work 10-hour days. That would just be ideal for me'. In sum, while these AmCo employees sometimes challenge long hours, they do not challenge the basic premise that work may intrude into the household.

In contrast, one might expect IndCo and TransCo employees to be more interested in flexibility, given the rigidity of their schedules and the length of time they spend in the office. While some of these workers do ask for flexible scheduling, most would rather repackage work within fixed 'business hours'. In fact, they would prefer both a significant reduction in, and standardization of, their work hours. A corporate office executive at IndCo articulates, 'I would come to the office at 9:00 a.m., and leave exactly at 5:30 p.m. These are the office timings'. A TransCo secretary concurs, 'The timing should be strict: 9 to 5. Eight hours means eight hours. That is one thing which I would like to change—time with family and children. We should also devote some time to family'. In this way, Indian workers support work-family separation.

Employees often approach work-family boundaries in ways that secure practical, everyday benefits. For example, many AmCo employees actively integrate work and family activities because they enjoy flexible schedules and the opportunity to participate in both work and family events as they arise, rather than according to tightly restricted protocols or timetables. Yet while these strategies may reflect personal preferences, they also embody institutional demands beyond employees' control. Even though employees may *like* the opportunity to work at home from time to time, they have little opportunity to do otherwise because their employers also *demand* it. In addition, the broader socio-historical context continuously affects workers' 'preferences' for how work-family relations are managed.

The Context for Work-Family Separation

Employees at IndCo and TransCo tend to keep work and family separate in part because they inhabit significantly different socio-historical contexts than AmCo workers. In contrast to that of the United States (as outlined in the introductory section), the socio-historical context for the Indian workers of our study varies in terms of the orientation of the social contract, and the direction of historically shifting relations between work-family spheres.

An Indian Social Contract Favouring Work-Family Separation

In India, the family has an institutionalized foundation of support within the state, unlike in the United States. This dates back to India's independence, when the activism of both Gandhian nationalist movements and women's movements helped to secure substantial rights for families in the constitution (Kumar 1993). For instance, the Factory Act of 1948 requires daycare centres in organizations with more than 30 workers.[9] Similarly, the Maternity Benefit Act of 1961 requires employers to provide female employees with 3 months of leave *at full pay* and to guarantee jobs at the same level when employees return. These legal mandates are largely responsible for IndCo's and TransCo's paid maternity leave policy.[10]

Even without state laws, many Indian organizations offer additional material family benefits, such as bonuses and time off for family emergencies (Weiss 1984; Desai 1996). The IndCo president offers this explanation: 'The Indian philosophy is like a family. The boss is the head of the family and, therefore, looks after their problems: he attends their weddings; if somebody is sick, he gives them money; he gives loans; he helps with housing. It is more as a social obligation'. This corporate philosophy (albeit paternalistic) reveals how the social contract at IndCo and TransCo favours material assistance for families.

The Indian social contract also empowers labour unions to a greater extent than in the United States. There are, for example, more than a hundred types of labour legislation in India (Budhwar and Khatri 2001). These laws not only give workers more secure collective bargaining rights, but also provide the means to ensure that family policies are enforced (Gothoskar 1992). For example, many of the past gains at IndCo, like on-site daycare at the factory, were the result of union activism by women workers. In contrast, AmCo has neither a union nor daycare benefits. This is typical of Silicon Valley high-tech firms (Louie 2001).

The cost of this social contract for IndCo and TransCo workers is fewer job opportunities and lower wages than in the United States (Table 4). Globally, the Indian economy has been undermined by colonial control of local industries, and more recently (since 1991) by IMF loans and their mandatory structural adjustment programmes, which require dismantling socialist protections for workers (Shah 1998). At the local level, political and business elites have supported these agendas and pushed extensive liberalization policies, as part of their quest for global capital. In turn, unemployment levels and labour market competition have increased. Thus, Indian workers and managers in our sample view employment prospects and conditions differently from their US counterparts. On one hand, workers are more likely to hold onto jobs even if they are bad and are less likely to regard them as a source of fulfilment (Sekaran 1992). On the other hand, managers are not inclined to make jobs more fulfilling. Indian employers may feel less pressure to offer normative rewards to attract, motivate, and retain workers, but they also operate under a different social contract regarding employee policies. The IndCo president reveals this as he critiques US firms for their elaborate work environments and social activities:

> An American company comes in [to India], and they are more worried about how the office looks in terms of carpets on the floor, jacuzzis on every alternative floor (I'm just joking), all that kind of stuff. Whereas an Indian company is not that fussy about the job and the working environment, but they give challenging jobs.

Job conditions and work environments are clearly less important under the Indian social contract.

The Persistence of the Socio-Historical Work-Family Divide

The other buttress for solid boundaries among Indian workers in our study is the persistence of socio-historical divisions between workplaces and households in the wider society. Whereas workers at AmCo find these divisions to be eroding rapidly, Indian workers find them to be more enduring. To begin with, the organizational environment in India contributes to this split through strict bureaucratic control systems which, deliberately or not, separate work from family (Khare 1999). The prevalence of bureaucratic control in India is, in part, a vestige of British colonialism. As a TransCo employee explains, 'The working environment in India, it is all this British system. There is all this hierarchy—you call your boss "Sir", and to do certain things, you have to go through many different levels'. Because the British influence was strongest in governmental organizations, these settings tend to be the most bureaucratic even today. Private industries are comparatively less bureaucratic, and multinational corporations are even less so. Even so, while bureaucracy in the United States is described as fading (Edwards 1979; Baron et al. 1988; Saxenian 1994), such bureaucracy is comparably more enduring in India (Gupta 1999; Budhwar and Khatri 2001). The extent of bureaucratic control in IndCo and, especially, TransCo is a testament to this.

Contextual factors in households also deter the blurring of boundaries common at AmCo. In general, Indian families are much larger and more interdependent than those in the United States. Nearly half of all Indians live in some type of extended family, almost double the percentage in the United States (Census of India 1991). There is also less variation in family size and form. Divorce rates are very low (Sureender et al. 1992) and even if marriages dissolve, extended families often remain intact to buffer the transition. These factors, however, are not necessarily associated with better family relationships; they generate their own tensions and problems, not the least of which is domestic abuse. Yet if, as Arlie Hochschild argues (1997), the *instability* of family life is one reason why US workers are turning their attention towards work, then the relative *stability* of Indian households may explain why Indian employees in our study are less likely to do so. In turn, the relative stability may reduce Indians' motivation to merge family with the workplace.

Consumerism and the mass media also encourage the work-family split in India. Unlike in the United States, where such institutions promote an acceleration of family life, Indians receive different, and sometimes contradictory, messages (Chakravarti 2000). Consumer products are geared less towards accelerating household routines or replacing household chores. At the time of our study, for example, stores offered few frozen or prepared foods, and restaurants were unlikely to package meals for takeout. A TransCo manager observed, 'You don't get "ready-made" anything here'. Furthermore, marketing campaigns are less likely to exploit or fuel tensions of working parents. Indian TV commercials for 'two-minute noodles' show a housewife preparing a fast snack for her children's party, in contrast to US ads showing tired parents coming home from the office to make the family dinner. Supplanting the 'super-mom' image with one of female domesticity in India is similarly problematic for women. Even so, one advantage is fewer messages urging women to merge work into the home than are found in the United States.

Finally, the Indian political context tends to support the ongoing separation of spheres. If the home has historically symbolized a 'haven' against the turbulence of the economy in the United States (Lasch 1977), in India it has represented a shelter against imperialism (Chatterjee 1989). Under colonialism, and especially later during the rise of the nationalist independence movement, the home represented one of the few social settings where Indians could escape the brutality of the British and exert autonomy as citizens and control over their daily affairs. More recently, this vision has been reinvigorated by the Hindu Right. In part due to globalization, fundamentalist political groups in India have been re-empowered in the last decade. In fact, during the year of our study, they achieved control of the state with the election of the Bharatiya Janata Party. One of their main platforms was to promote the family as a source of Indian authenticity, especially in opposition to a morally corrupt West (Kapur and Cossman 1996; Oza 2001).[11] This ideology places a heavy burden on Indian citizens, making them responsible for protecting family life from *global* as well as local threats. In sum, the socio-historical trajectory and contemporary political environment of IndCo and TransCo have put pressure on workers to insulate their families in ways not common at AmCo.

Betwixt and Between: The Multinational Case

TransCo deserves a brief note because, contrary to common assumptions about transnational firms, its employees manage work-family relations in ways that are more similar to their counterparts at IndCo than to those at the parent company AmCo. Indeed, the US ownership and corporate policies of TransCo might lead us to expect more workplace intrusions on the family among its employees. Yet because of the strong influence of the socio-historical context in India, TransCo's human resource policies often promote a separation of spheres.

For instance, we see this pressure for a separation of spheres in TransCo's job structures and rewards. Managers explain that they have a long-term plan to emulate the parent company, but in the meantime job arrangements remain in limbo between the hierarchical structures like those of IndCo and the flat structures of AmCo: 'We have fewer titles than most [Indian] companies here, and at the same time we have more titles than we have in the States'. Further, TransCo managers are influenced by locally pervasive rewards systems like those at IndCo as they make the transition to the wage and promotion structures of AmCo:

> We are on seniority-based salary systems here but we really focus on performance and not how long you continue to breathe. We do it because of the way this economy is in this time. Here, so much of things are based on years of experience rather than performance. Because even in the software industry [in India], you see the kind of the mentality where people are more on an hourly basis—this much an hour, that much an hour, etc.

Thus, when it comes to career ladders and wages, Indian bureaucratic environments are an important source of policy for TransCo, as with IndCo.

The socio-historical context shapes TransCo's work-family programme as well. TransCo managers have a unique vision to combine policy features of both AmCo and IndCo by integrating job restructuring benefits like flexitime, flexplace, and job sharing with material family benefits such as paid maternity leave. However, features of the context allow for more effective implementation of the latter. For instance, bureaucratic organizational practices render job-restructuring benefits such as flexplace difficult to enforce (Poster 2000). At the same time, the local social contract provides many incentives for employees to favour material family benefits. Given the comparatively lower wages at TransCo versus AmCo, policies such as paid maternity leave have greater appeal to local Indian workers than do those like flexitime.

Work and Family in an Era of Globalization

At the outset, we asked three guiding questions: If labour patterns are 'converging' globally, are US work-family patterns inevitable worldwide? Will international branches of US corporations promote work-family arrangements that reflect current developments of their head offices based in the United States? Will separate rather than integrated work-family spheres become the international norm? Our analysis of two Indian-based firms and one US firm suggests qualified negative responses to all three queries: employees of the Indian firms have not duplicated patterns of integrating work and family typical of employees at the US firm.

At AmCo, we find that more than one-third of the workers take work home at night, many bring their family and leisure activities to the office, and some even resolve family conflicts in the workplace. Furthermore, 42 per cent of AmCo employees claim that family interference with 'work' or 'personal life' is a significant source of work-family tension (unlike the Indian firms, where it is mentioned rarely or not at all). AmCo workers' strategies for handling this interference combine activities from both domains. In this way, boundaries for AmCo workers tend to be permeable; work and family tend to merge. IndCo and TransCo employees work longer days in the office, but are much less likely to take work home with them than employees at AmCo (among non-production workers). Few Indian employees conceive of the workplace as home-like or satisfying, and few employees describe households that would be amenable to more work-family integration. Instead, 60–90 per cent of the Indians in our sample list 'insufficient time for family, children, or housework' as the major source of work-family tensions (compared to 34 per cent at AmCo), and their boundary management strategies tend to separate work from family as much as possible. The result is separate work and family spheres with relatively solid boundaries.

Our findings confirm other work-family studies like that of Nippert-Eng (1996) in showing there is, in fact, a range of boundary types and management patterns. While none of the firms represent the extremes of Nippert-Eng's continuum, they do reflect the polar differences. Our findings also corroborate other international studies (e.g., Wharton and Blair-Loy 2002), showing that US workers are more prone to 'overtime cultures' than are workers in other nations—in our case, India.

However, our study also challenges the work-family literature on transnational grounds. First, it provides a clearer conceptualization of 'context', helping to explain differences across national sites. The influence of socio-historical context in our study is apparent in that the work-family patterns at TransCo end up looking more like patterns at IndCo than at its own parent company, AmCo. By more adequately specifying context, we hope to address some of the unanswered questions in transnational studies (e.g., Perlow 2001) by identifying *external* as well as internal factors that affect work and family arrangements.

Second, we show that a transnational perspective can improve upon the oversimplified explanations of work-family patterns emerging from standard theoretical models. In particular, this approach recasts the common explanations of 'culture' and 'development' for our cases by acknowledging the multiple factors within sites that shape work-family relations.

For instance, a typical 'cultural' argument regarding pressures on Indian households suggests that cultural preferences for hot meals create greater time demands on family members for cooking. Yet our informants, like of those of other studies (Shah 1998; Rout et al. 1999), report that this 'cultural trait', in fact, depends upon household size, networks, and power relations. Elaborate cooking is more common at extended family events, rather than at daily meals, and in joint families where senior males are more likely to make such requests and have the power to enforce them. Workers at IndCo and TransCo from smaller families (which represent a minority group in our sample) report more modest meals and egalitarian cooking arrangements.

The 'development' argument about greater family pressure in India is that limitations of infrastructure and technology reduce household access to electricity and running water. Yet, again, we see other intervening factors as equally relevant, including the context of Indian governance and bureaucracy. An industry journal survey has rated India as 'worst among Asian countries for the integrity and efficiency of its bureaucracy' (Saxenian 2000), and Nobel Prize-winning poverty scholar Amartya Sen has called the Indian state 'completely counter-productive' in managing some of its development programmes (Economic Bureau 2003). Because the Indian state has been inept in managing its 'underdeveloped' status, household technologies may function differently in India than in other Southern countries.

A contextual approach also recasts conventional explanations about the low priority of work among Indians in samples like ours. The cultural account suggests that 'cultural programming' among Indians makes employees 'hard-working only when needed' (Hofstede 1991: 37). At IndCo and TransCo, however, we find that these 'cultural values' are structurally embedded in organizational systems of bureaucratic control. These systems discourage 'cultures of overtime' through formal rules about finishing work inside the office and reduce performance pressure through seniority-based, rather than performance-based reward systems.

Development models, on the other hand, would attribute Indian work patterns to a lack of technology, which prevents employees from working outside the office. It is true that India has a weaker technological infrastructure than does the United States, particularly in terms of resources for high-tech workplaces with personal computers and Internet connections (UNDP 1999); however, organizational policies in the firms in our study also limit the way workers use them. In fact, IndCo has a peculiar 'anti-technology' work environment, despite the fact that it is a computer firm. The president refuses to use a computer in his own work: 'I don't have a PC on my table. If I need information, I call up'. Many employees follow his lead, and the few IndCo and TransCo workers who take work home do so without laptops or

Internet connections (e.g., printing out email messages at the office to be read at home). In these examples, the complexity of the context plays a role in shaping work-family boundaries in ways ignored by more simplistic accounts of development and culture alone.

Third, our study challenges the work-family literature to become truly international. We argue that this field can be theoretically and empirically enhanced by expanding its scope, especially towards the global South. Most comparative work-family research misses the crucial role of North-South asymmetries, due to its narrow focus on the United States and Europe. Focusing on Southern nations such as India allows a critical view of the role of global inequality in work-family dynamics. For instance, in our study, separation strategies at IndCo and TransCo are partly the product of *global marginalization* in India from colonialism, structural adjustment, and liberalization. Similarly, work-centred integration strategies at AmCo are partly related to the *global economic privilege* of the United States, which endows its firms with greater resources to provide employees with material incentives to prioritize work.

In addition, a transnational view can improve our conceptualization of the mechanisms of work-family dynamics. Conventional approaches tend to see these patterns as *internally* generated by or within the nation-state. Yet, we see them emerging from global sources as well. In fact, this view is a key to our definition of 'context'; it involves an interactive process *across* different national sites that shape work-family boundaries. The implication is that factors like high unemployment and low-economic development are not merely self-generating problems for countries like India, but are perpetuated by countries like the United States through their support of unfair trade policies and international debt. Similarly, a preference for work-family separation is not necessarily inherent in Indian 'cultures'. This preference is sometimes linked to the activities of foreign groups, like the immigrant 'Non-Resident Indian' groups in the United States who financially and ideologically support the Hindu Right movement in India. In short, Northern countries often contribute to India's putative 'underdevelopment'. Moreover, they may also affect Indian 'cultural values' that, by the other accounts, are the ultimate source or result of work-family dynamics. Instead, our transnational approach views global and local politics as intertwined and emphasizes the way global power in the North contributes to and magnifies inequality in the South.

With respect to social policy, we do not see either integrated or separate work-family spheres as ideal, given that both come with costs.

In the case of AmCo, permeable boundaries of overlapping spheres give employees more leeway in scheduling, but are accompanied by an acceleration of family life which compromises the quality of time with family. Many scholars also suggest that the benefits of flexibility are greater for firms than for workers (Osterman 1995; Smith 1997). Indeed, some AmCo employees use their work flexibility in ways that enhance productivity for the firm, but lengthen work hours and reduce family time. Taking advantage of such flexibility can also make work less visible to managers and therefore more difficult to assess and reward (Clark 2000). This is a particular dilemma within AmCo's context, which is inclined towards performance-based rewards.

Alternatively, solid boundaries between separate work-family spheres at IndCo and TransCo come with many costs as well. In the office, these costs include hierarchy, centralization, and strict enforcement of the rules, as well as a lack of satisfying working conditions (which many scholars argue can lead to improved family lives). In addition, because their households tend to resist workplace demands, some Indian employees are unable to pursue extracurricular activities that would advance their careers, such as international travel and night-time MBA classes. For these reasons, we conclude that neither integration nor separation of the workplace from the family is inherently superior, since there is 'no one desirable state' for work-family relations (Clark 2000).

This observation may recast some assumptions about work-family policy in the literature. Contrary to the expectations of convergence or modernization theories, our study indicates that there may be a downside to exporting US work-family policy to India. If maintaining work-family boundaries is the preferred strategy of IndCo and TransCo workers, then policies such as flexitime and flexplace, which undermine boundaries, may not be appreciated (Poster 2000).

Similarly, contrary to the expectations of cultural theories, there may be a downside to exporting India's policy to other Southern countries, and vice versa (even among those countries displaying similar 'collectivist' values). The president of IndCo shares this sentiment:

> I used to work in a British multinational corporation in India, and I had a boss. He used to keep saying, 'In Zimbabwe we do this ... In Zimbabwe we did that ... Why can't you do it here?' You need to design systems which are native, home-grown, and useful for the local conditions, and not say, 'I just bring this system. What's good for Zimbabwe is good for India'.

Such cases discourage the development of cookie-cutter models of work-family policy, which would inappropriately lump together different nations and sites (especially Southern ones). Rather, work-family policy, such as work-family theory, will need to account for such intersections of global and local contexts.

Finally, there are several limitations of this analysis, which might be addressed in future research. As a case study, our study reflects only one snapshot of work-family relations. It also considers only one kind of organizational environment: large firms in the high-tech industry. The literature would benefit from a view of other firms, other industries, and other sizes of organizations to assess the broader applicability of our findings.

We especially regret neglecting issues of race, class, gender, life course, and region in this analysis. This gap is purely a function of limited space, as we do indeed find variations in work-family patterns in relation to such factors. While issues of class, gender, and life course frequently have been addressed in the literature, transnational analyses are rare and deserve greater attention. Both the United States and India are highly diverse societies requiring careful analyses of inequality and stratification. We hope future studies will explore the implications of these cleavages for work-family relations.

Notes

1. We use the term 'work' to refer to wage-earning jobs outside the household. However, this is not intended to diminish the importance of other sorts of labour, such as unpaid labour in the household.
2. This analysis is indebted to the work of Nippert-Eng (1996) for its conceptual models. Nippert-Eng (1996) uses the terms *segmented* and *separate* more-or-less interchangeably, while, in this chapter, I employ the term *separate* to avoid confusion that might be induced by the multiple meanings of the word *segmented*, especially connotations that suggest the breaking of a whole into parts.
3. Debate over the pervasiveness of work-family integration in the United States centres on whether *all* kinds of workers and families face the same pressure to integrate spheres, and whether these individuals are doing so 'voluntarily' versus 'coercively'. While we do not have the space to engage in this debate, our claims about the high degree of integration at AmCo are based on our copious fieldwork data (which we are not able to present here), and numerous ethnographies of similar high-tech firms and families living in Silicon Valley that have yielded similar conclusions (cited in the text).

4. Our data collection procedures have several imperfections. The AmCo human resource department for world-wide operations felt some of our questions were overly sensitive and asked us to make them optional. Most workers at AmCo and TransCo were comfortable with these questions and chose to answer anyway. Nonetheless, some missing data are evident in Tables 1 and 2. Two AmCo workers declined to answer questions regarding marital status and family structure, and 17 TransCo workers declined to answer questions regarding housework time and activities. While this compromises the findings for these particular questions, we believe the smaller sample size does not dramatically undermine our analysis. Because the TransCo sample is larger to begin with, the reduction in cases actually means that TransCo's sample size more directly resembles that of AmCo. Furthermore, the missing cases arise randomly and do not suggest a bias based on gender, occupation, age, etc. Finally, we were able to supplement missing data from those particular questions with information gleaned from other parts of the interview schedule. For example, respondents often volunteered information about household experiences when answering other open-ended questions. Still, this gap in our data poses a constraint on our analysis.
5. Reports of housework time for employees of these companies tend to be conservative for both countries: larger scale studies report an average of 33 hours per week among workers in the United States (Blair 1997) and 37 hours per week among workers in India (Ramu 1989). It is also noteworthy that, although Indians in our sample report spending more time on housework than the Americans, upper-middle-class workers also have an edge when it comes to domestic service. Managers and other upper-middle-class employees at IndCo and TransCo very often have live-in servants, such as cooks, gardeners, nannies, and chauffeurs; even some factory workers in our sample reported hiring a daily dishwasher. In contrast, AmCo employees hire housekeepers much less frequently. Even with all this help, housework time among Indian employees is still greater, indicating their extra burden.
6. One group represents an exception to this pattern: AmCo women. They have a high number of joint families, falling between those of TransCo and IndCo. These employees are largely older women who provide care for grandchildren during the day or full-time.
7. This does not refer to 'tele-commuting' or 'flexplace' policies which apply to regular business hours, but rather taking work home after office hours, whether at night or on weekends.
8. Although none of the production workers in our samples were given work to take home, this is a fairly common occurrence in Silicon Valley. For instance, electronics workers assemble computer components in their households at night as piece-rate work, which Hossfeld (1990) refers to as a 'triple shift' for working-class women.

9. A notable contradiction here is that the Indian state requirement for on-site daycare promotes a *merging* rather than separation of spheres (i.e., bringing children and families to the workplace). While this case reminds us that greater state 'support' for family may not always lead to a separation of the household from work, it still indicates how the Indian social contract provides more legislative interest in providing childcare by the state than does the US social contract.
10. There are downsides to these laws as well, such as poor implementation and enforcement. In addition, while the state may be incorporating 'family' in many positive ways, it also tends to justify women's subordination in the home and unequal access to rights in the public sphere. These dualisms highlight the contradictory role of state legal systems regarding women (Kapur and Cossman 1996).
11. There are also certain cases in which the Hindu Right advocates public- and career-oriented roles for women (Sarkar 1996). An example is the 'Anti-Mandal agitations' of the early 1990s, when women were recruited to stand with their male allies in defence of upper-caste Hindu privileges in employment, against the challenges by marginalized groups such as the Scheduled Castes.

References

Bailyn, L. (1993) *Breaking the Mold: Women, Men, and Time in the New Corporate World*. New York: The Free Press.

Barnett, R.C. (1998) 'Toward a review and reconceptualization of the work/family literature', *Genetic, Social and General Psychological Monographs*, 124, 125–82.

Baron, J., Jennings, P.D., and Dobbin, F. (1988) 'Mission control? The development of personnel systems in U.S. industry', *American Sociological Review*, 53, 497–514.

Bell, D. (1973) *The Coming of the Post-Industrial Society*. New York: Basic Books.

Blair, S.L. (1997) 'The division of household labor in cross-cultural perspective', in Dubeck, P.J., and Borman, K. (eds.) *Women and Work: A Reader*. New Brunswick, NJ: Rutgers University Press, 440–43.

Bowen, G.L., and Pittman, J.F. (eds.) (1995) *The Work and Family Interface: Toward a Contextual Effects Perspective*. Minneapolis, MN: National Council on Family Relations.

Budhwar, P.S., and Khatri, N. (2001) 'HRM in context: applicability of HRM models in India', *International Journal of Cross-Cultural Management*, 1, 333–56.

Census of India (1991) *India at a Glance: Number of Households and Household Types*. Retrieved on 31 July 2000 from http://www.censusindia.net.

Chakravarti, U. (2000) 'State, market and freedom of expression: women and electronic media', *Economic and Political Weekly*, 35(18), 12–17.

Chatterjee, P. (1989) 'The nationalist resolution of the women's question', in Sangari, K., and Vaid, S. (eds.) *Recasting Women: Essays in Indian Colonial History*. New Brunswick, NJ: Rutgers University Press, 233–54.

Clark, S.C. (2000) 'Work/family border theory: a new theory of work/family balance', *Human Relations*, 53, 747–70.

Coltrane, S. (1996) *Family Man: Fatherhood, Housework, and Gender Equity*. New York: Oxford University Press.

Cowan, R.S. (1983) *More Work for Mother: The Ironies of Household Technology from the Open Hearth to the Microwave*. New York: Basic Books.

Darrah, C., English-Lueck, J.A., and Freeman, J. (2001) *Families and Work: An Ethnography of Dual Career Families* [Unpublished manuscript]. San Jose, CA: Department of Anthropology, San Jose State University.

Desai, N. (1996) 'Women's employment and their familial role in India', in Shah, A.M., Baviskar, B.S., and Ramaswamy, E.A. (eds.) *Social Structure and Change, Vol. 2: Women in Indian Society*. Thousand Oaks, CA: Sage, 98–112.

Di Leonardo, M. (1987) 'The female world of cards and holidays: women, families, and the work of kinship', *Signs*, 12, 440–53.

Economic Bureau (2003) 'Subsidise food buyers and not producers, says Amartya Sen', *The Financial Express*, January 11, 9.

Edwards, R.C. (1979) *Contested Terrain*. New York: Basic Books.

English-Lueck, J.A. (2002) *Cultures@SiliconValley*. Stanford, CA: Stanford University Press.

Epstein, C.F. (1989) 'Workplace boundaries: conceptions and creations', *Social Research*, 56, 571–90.

Florida, R., and Keeney, M. (1991) 'Transplanted organizations: the transfer of Japanese industrial organization to the U.S.', *American Sociological Review*, 56, 381–98.

Gonyea, J.G., and Googins, B.K. (1996) 'The restructuring of work and family in the United States: a new challenge for American Corporations', in Lewis, S., and Lewis, J. (eds.) *The Work-Family Challenge: Re-thinking Employment*. London: Sage, 63–78.

Gothoskar, S. (1992) 'Struggles of women workers in the pharmaceutical industry in Bombay', in Gothoskar, S. (ed.) *Struggles of Women at Work*. New Delhi: Vikas Publishing House, 132–43.

Gubrium, J.F., and Holstein, J.A. (1990) *What Is Family?* Mountain View, CA: Mayfield.

——. (1997) *New Language of Qualitative Method*. New York: Oxford University Press.

——. (2000) 'Analyzing interpretive practice', in Denzin, N.K., and Lincoln, Y.S. (eds.) *Handbook of Qualitative Research* (2nd ed.). Thousand Oaks, CA: Sage, 487–508.

Gupta, R.K. (1999) 'The truly familial work organization: extending the organizational boundary to include employees' families in the Indian context' in Rao, H.S.R., Sinha, D., and Wilpert, B. (eds.) *Management and Cultural Values: The Indigenization of Organizations in Asia*. New Delhi: Sage, 102–20.

Haas, L., Hwang, P., and Russell, G. (eds.) (2000) *Organizational Change and Gender Equity: Inter-national Perspectives on Fathers and Mothers at the Workplace*. Thousand Oaks, CA: Sage.

Hochschild, A.R. (1997) *The Time Bind: When Work Becomes Home and Home Becomes Work*. New York: Metropolitan Books.

Hofstede, G. (1991) *Cultures and Organizations: Software of the Mind*. London: McGraw-Hill.

Holstein, J.A., and Gubrium, J.F. (1995) 'Deprivatization and the construction of domestic life', *Journal of Marriage and the Family*, 57, 894–908.

Hossfeld, K.J. (1990) 'Their logic against them: contradictions in sex, race, and class in Silicon Valley', in Ward, K. (ed.) *Women Workers and Global Restructuring*. Ithaca, NY: ILR Press, 149–78.

Ishii-Kuntz, M. (1994) 'Work and family life: findings from international research and suggestions for future study', *Journal of Family Issues*, 15, 490–506.

Kapur, R., and Cossman, B. (1996) *Subversive Sites: Feminist Engagements with Law in India*. New Delhi: Sage.

Khare, A. (1999) 'Japanese and Indian work patterns: a study of contrasts', in Rao, H.S.R., Sinha, D., and Wilpert, B. (eds.) *Management and Cultural Values: The Indigenization of Organizations in Asia*. New Delhi: Sage, 121–38.

Kumar, R. (1993) *A History of Doing: An Illustrated Account of Movements for Women's Rights and Feminism in India, 1800–1990*. New Delhi: Kali for Women.

Kunda, G. (1992) *Engineering Culture: Control and Commitment in a High-Tech Corporation*. Philadelphia, PA: Temple University Press.

Lambert, S. (1993) 'Workplace policies as social policy', *Social Service Review*, 67, 237–60.

Lasch, C. (1977) *Haven in a Heartless World*. New York: Basic Books.

Lewis, S., and Lewis, J. (eds.) (1996) *The Work-Family Challenge: Rethinking Employment*. London: Sage.

Lewis, S., Izraeli, D.N., and Hootsmans, H. (eds.) (1992) *Dual-Earner Families: International Perspectives*. London: Sage.

Lincoln, J.R., and Kalleberg, A.L. (1990) *Culture, Control, and Commitment*. Cambridge: Cambridge University Press.

Louie, M.C.Y. (2001) *Sweatshop Warriors: Immigrant Women Workers Take on the Global Factory*. Cambridge, MA: South End Press.

Meiksins, P., and Whalley, P. (2001) 'Controlling technical workers in alternative work arrangements: rethinking the work contract', in Baldoz, R., Koeber, C., and Kraft, P. (eds.) *The Critical Study of Work: Labor, Technology, and Global Production*. Philadelphia, PA: Temple University Press, 236–57.

Nippert-Eng, C.E. (1996) *Home and Work: Negotiating Boundaries through Everyday Life*. Chicago: University of Chicago Press.

Osterman, P. (1995) 'Work/family programs and the employment relationship', *Administrative Science Quarterly*, 40, 681–700.

Oza, R. (2001) 'Showcasing India: gender, geography, and globalization', *Signs*, 26, 1067–95.

Perlow, L.A. (1998) 'Boundary control: the social ordering of work and family time in a high-tech corporation', *Administrative Science Quarterly*, 43, 328–57.

Perlow, L.A. (2001) 'Time to coordinate: toward an understanding of work-time standards and norms in a multi-country study of software engineers', *Work and Occupations*, 28, 91–111.

Poster, W.R. (2000) 'Challenges for work-family policy in global corporations: lessons from high-tech companies in India and the United States', paper presented at the Alfred P. Sloan, Business and Professional Women Foundation, and Center for Working Families *Work and Family: Expanding the Horizons Conference*, the University of California, Berkeley, March 3, San Francisco, CA.

Ramu, G.N. (1989) *Women, Work and Marriage in Urban India: A Study of Dual- and Single-Earner Couples*. New Delhi: Sage.

Rout, U.R., Lewis, S., and Kagan, C. (1999) 'Work and family roles: Indian career women in India and the West', *Indian Journal of Gender Studies*, 6, 91–108.

Rubin, B.A. (1996) *Shifts in the Social Contract: Understanding Change in American Society*. Thousand Oaks, CA: Pine Forge Press.

Rudd, E.C. (2000) 'Work against family: work-family conflict and the context of rising in-equality', paper presented at the annual meeting of the American Sociological Association, August, Washington, DC.

Sarkar, T. (1996) 'Woman, community, and nation: a historical trajectory for Hindu identity and politics', in Jeffery, P., and Basu, A. (eds.) *Appropriating Gender*. New York: Routledge, 89–104.

Saxenian, A. (1994) *Regional Advantage: Culture and Competition in Silicon Valley and Route 128*. Cambridge, MA: Harvard University Press.

Saxenian, A. (2000) 'Bangalore: Silicon Valley of Asia?', paper presented at the Center for Research on Economic Development and Policy Reform Conference on *Indian Economic Prospects: Advancing Policy Reform*, Stanford University, May, Stanford, CA.

Schor, J.B. (1992) *The Overworked American: The Unexpected Decline of Leisure*. New York: Basic Books.

Sekaran, U. (1992) 'Middle-class dual-earner families and their support systems in India', in Lewis, S., Izraeli, D.N., and Hootsmans, H. (eds.) *Dual-Earner Families: International Perspectives*. London: Sage, 46–61.

Shah, S. (1998) 'Three hot meals and full day at work: South Asian Women's Labor in the United States', in Dasgupta, D.D. (eds.) *A Patchwork Shawl: Chronicles of South Asian Women in America*. New Brunswick, NJ: Rutgers University Press, 206–22.

Sharma, U. (1986) *Women's Work, Class, and the Urban Household: A Study of Shimla, North India*. London: Tavistock Publications.

Smith, V. (1997) 'New forms of work organization', *Annual Review of Sociology*, 23, 315–39.

Sureender, S., Reddy, G.C., and Baburajan, P.K. (1992) 'Divorce in India: a macro level analysis', *Social Change*, 22, 3–8.

United Nations Development Program (UNDP) (1999) *Human Development Report*. New York: Oxford University Press.

Weiss, A.M. (1984) 'Tradition and modernity at the workplace: a field study of women in the pharmaceutical industry of Lahore', *Women's Studies International Forum*, 7, 259–64.

Wharton, A.S., and Blair-Loy, M. (2002) 'The "Overtime Culture" in a global corporation: a cross-national study of finance professionals' interest in working part-time', *Work and Occupations*, 29, 32–63.

Wiatrowski, W.J. (1990) 'Family-related benefits in the workplace', *Monthly Labor Review*, 113(3), 28–33.

Women of Silicon Valley (2001) 'Unfinished business: women in the Silicon Valley economy', Retrieved on 14 August 2002 from http://www.womenofsv.org/.

Zaretsky, E. (1976) *Capitalism, the Family, and Personal Life*. New York: Harper & Row.

10

Conceptualizing Hinduism

Heinz Scheifinger

There is not a homogenous religion that can be referred to as Hinduism. Instead, 'Hinduism' encompasses a diverse range of practices, beliefs, and groups that can be subsumed under the term 'Hindu' (see, e.g., Burghart 1987; Flood 1995; Jackson 1996; Vertovec 1997: 265).[1] Despite this, Hinduism is often used in both popular and academic works to refer to a religion that is comparable to, for example, Christianity or Islam. This is clearly highly problematic. In this chapter, I show that although there is certainly not a homogenous religion that can be referred to as Hinduism, the use of the term is still acceptable. However, use of the term demands that it is adequately conceptualized. With such a conceptualization, the term can be used with confidence.

After I have shown that the term 'Hinduism' should be retained, I want to briefly consider aspects of Hinduism in the light of key ideas in the work of Jean Baudrillard. The reason for this is that Baudrillard has interesting things to say regarding the nature of images, and the image is of extreme importance within Hinduism. Furthermore, it is worthwhile considering Baudrillard's ideas in the light of Hindu images because in his work 'Simulacra and Simulations' (l983a) he makes specific reference to religious images. I will argue that his conclusions regarding religious images are not universal and are highly questionable when applied to Hinduism. Finally, despite my reservations concerning the applicability of Baudrillardian ideas to Hinduism, I consider online images of Hindu deities in the light of the theory of simulacra. This is because there does appear to be a strong link between the medium of the Internet and Baudrillard's notion of hyper-real simulacra. However, I conclude that replicated images of Hindu deities on the WWW are no more hyper-real than their original counterparts.

Religion

Any attempt to conceptualize Hinduism is a difficult undertaking from the outset because the term 'religion' itself is contested. For example, I have claimed that Hinduism is not a homogenous religion but 'religion' itself does not have a universally accepted definition. As Bryan Turner points out, 'although the question of the nature of religion has been endlessly discussed by philosophers, sociologists and theologians, the conceptual cows have yet to come home' (1991: 242). *The Concise Oxford Dictionary* defines 'religion' as: 'the belief in a superhuman controlling power, especially a personal God or gods entitled to obedience and worship' (Allen 1990: 1015). While this is far from perfect, such a commonsense dictionary definition is sufficient because in my discussion of Hinduism, the term does not necessitate or invite further definition or explanation. There is, therefore, no need to debate the merits of the various definitions of and approaches to religion offered by, for example, Tylor, Engels, Pareto, Freud, Durkheim, Horton, Spiro, Goode, Otto, Wach, Berger, Weber, Geertz, Bell, Turner, Robertson, Goody, Babb, and Yinger (see, e.g., Turner 1991; Hamilton 1993; Beckerlegge 2001a).

It is worth noting, though, that both the category of religion and various religious traditions are (regardless of whether or not religious experiences are supernatural) social phenomena which are socially constructed (Beckford 2003: 2–8). That is, the meanings attributed to both the category of religion and to various religions are not fixed and instead are constantly negotiated. For example, a group that was previously not considered to be religious could, after a long complex process of argument and counterargument, achieve recognition as being a bona fide religion. Within traditions, opposing groups may denounce the philosophy and practices of other groups as not being valid expressions of the religion or even religious at all. It is particularly worth mentioning this here because the constant renegotiation of meanings is especially the case within Hinduism because of its diversity that has been briefly mentioned earlier and will be discussed in detail later in this chapter.

While it is not necessary to consider in detail what exactly 'religion' is in an attempt to conceptualize Hinduism, it is worthwhile briefly mentioning some specific difficulties surrounding the term 'religion' in relation to Hinduism. This provides some details as to the nature of Hinduism prior to my discussion later in the following text, which addresses Hinduism directly.

The Indian law courts have faced difficulties regarding the nature of religion (which provides a clear example that religion is socially constructed). It was reported in May 2004 that it was necessary for the Supreme Court to examine 'what constitutes an essential part of a religion with reference to a particular doctrine or religious practice followed by a particular community' (*IANS* 8 May 2004, online). Because of the problems regarding the terms 'religion' and 'religious', such a question would be difficult for any law court. However, regarding Hinduism this problem is exacerbated. This is for two main reasons.

First, as David Pocock points out in his anthropological account of an Indian village, in the West the word 'religion' refers to 'an area of the *special*, a mode of reasoning about the universe governed by rules which are not those of day-to-day thought' and that therefore '*the* religious remains ... a separate area of life in the West' (1973: xiii). However, in Hinduism there is not this separation between the secular and the religious, and the religious should not be seen as constituting a separate sphere from that of daily life. James Preston alludes to this when he points out that 'Hinduism is one of the world's most complex religions ... [and] ... is compose of tightly-knit myths, rites and customs' (1980: 1). James Beckford makes the same point as Pocock and argues that 'only in modern times and predominantly western societies has religion been categorically separated from the rest of culture' (2000: 167). Although the argument that religion only constituted a category when it became separated from the secular in the course of Western modernity is valid, I am not convinced that a lack of a distinction between the sacred and everyday life in Hinduism is as a result of non-exposure to modernity. For example, Indians were subject to modernizing tendencies during the colonial era, and in modern India even among highly educated individuals who embrace modernity, it is still common for their lives to be inextricably bound up with religion. This is the case even in the diaspora (see, e.g., Carey 1983; Carman 1996; Williams 1996; Sekhar 1999). Therefore, when Hinduism is referred to as a religion, there must at least be the understanding that, as Hinduism is inextricably bound up with everyday life, the term 'religion' as used here is somewhat different from how the term is conventionally understood in the West.

The second reason why Hinduism is problematic in relation to the term 'religion' is more serious. I have asserted that the term is sufficient for the purpose of this discussion as there is some commonsense understanding of what is being referred to when it is used. I have argued that religion is not a separate category in the life of a Hindu. I have also argued that when this is explicitly recognized and appreciated, the term 'religion' can remain in use and it is thus acceptable to refer to Hinduism as a religion. However, this argument is dependent upon an understanding of what Hinduism is, and this in itself is far from straightforward. I will explain fully why this is the case and then proceed, drawing upon the work of Gabriella Eichinger Ferro-Luzzi (1997), to back up my initial claim in this chapter. That is, that an understanding of what constitutes Hinduism *can* be achieved, and this results in a conceptualization of Hinduism which makes clear what is being referred to when this term is used. Therefore, the term 'Hinduism' can certainly be used without any threat to academic rigour, and this does not imply a lack of awareness of diversity within Hinduism.

Hinduism

I opened this paper with the claim that Hinduism is incredibly diverse. Importantly, it lacks a central 'church-like institution' (Srinivas 1962: 60; Kanitkar and Cole 1995: 206; Smith 2003: 6). It is true that the eighth Century AD Saint Adi Shankara, the founder of the philosophy of *Advaita Vedanta* (see later in this chapter), created four monastic Orders which still have their *maths* (monastic institutions) today (see Gupta 2002; Bhatt 2001). However, while Adi Shankara contributed to the revival of Hinduism, these *maths* have certainly not given rise to a central authority within Hinduism. It is important to emphasize though that the heterogeneity inherent within Hinduism is far more extreme than the lack of a central church-like authority alone indicates. For example, some traditions that are referred to as being Hindu are actually vehemently opposed to one another in terms of beliefs and practices. Indeed, it has been said that to put all the groups that are generally thought to belong to Hinduism in this all-encompassing category is comparable to lumping together religions such as Judaism, Islam, and Christianity and calling them something like 'The Semitic religion' (see Svarûpa-dasâ 1996: 101).

Robert Jackson (1996) argues convincingly that the reason for the confusion over what Hinduism actually is largely stems from the British in Bengal during the second half of the eighteenth century. The plethora of diverse beliefs and practices of the Indian subcontinent could not be seen as constituting a religion as such. However, because of their Western cultural paradigm, the British assumed that there was 'a coherent system of beliefs and practices that could be compared with other religious systems' (Jackson 1996: 88) such as Christianity, which did constitute a coherent system. The diverse beliefs and practices were lumped together, and by the early nineteenth century these were collectively referred to as 'Hinduism'. Within a short period of time, Hindus themselves started to use the term (Jackson 1996: 88–89). Hinduism subsequently came to be known as a 'world religion' along with other religions such as Islam which, unlike Hinduism, *did* have a single holy book upon which authority was based. For example, Hinduism was one of the 'world religions' at the 'World's Parliament of Religions' held in Chicago in 1893. Hinduism is still commonly referred to as a 'world religion' today (e.g., Hamilton 1998) and is placed alongside religions such as Christianity, Islam, Judaism, and Buddhism in, for example, *The Usborne Internet-Linked Encyclopedia of World Religions* (Meredith et al. 2005) and in academic books such as Coward's *Pluralism: Challenge to World Religions* (1985). In his research which covered England and Wales, Jackson (1996: 95–97) also concluded that it is 'extremely common for Hinduism to be taught as a discrete religion in schools'.

Even though the term 'Hinduism' is extremely problematic, it seems intuitively clear that there *is* such a thing as Hinduism (although there is disagreement among scholars as to what this might be). For example, even though academics may struggle with the term, many people would comfortably assert that they are a Hindu. Flood notes that 'Most Hindus will be certain that their identity contrasts with that of Christian, Muslim or Buddhist' (1995: 5). To a large degree, this reflexive thought arises only as a result of questions posed through living in an environment (such as in the diaspora) where 'Hindus practise self-consciously'—unlike in India where this is not the case for the majority of the population (see Knott 1986: 233; Michaelson 1987: 46; Thomas 1993: 187). However, some reflexive thought *is* also occurring in India, largely as a result of an increase in Hindu nationalism which makes the question 'What is Hinduism?' a political one (see Bhatt 1997: 157).

Others reject the term 'Hinduism' altogether, instead referring to their beliefs and practices as the *Sanatana dharma*. This is not easily translatable but can be roughly translated as the 'eternal way of life' (see, e.g., Weller 1997: 290). It is often translated as 'the eternal religion', but this is inadequate because those who advocate the use of the term are usually attempting to reject the Western term 'religion' which is seen as being unsuitable.

I will now briefly consider the views of four scholars (Madeleine Biardeau, Brian K. Smith, Günther-Dietz Sontheimer, and Heinrich von Stietencron) on the validity of the construct of 'Hinduism'. These approaches are summarized and commented upon by Aditya Malik (1997) in his aptly named chapter, *Hinduism: Three-Thousand-Three-Hundred-and-Six Ways to Invoke a Construct* which I will draw upon. I will then go on to look in more detail at the approach of Gabriella Eichinger Ferro-Luzzi (1997).

There is a similarity between the first four scholars in that they attempt to construct a 'unity within Hinduism' and define it. However, they do this differently, even though they 'make reference to similar terms and materials'. The first three attempt to 'develop a holistic version of Hinduism', while von Stietencron 'asserts the coherent nature of individual traditions' (Malik 1997: 13). Eichinger Ferro-Luzzi, on the other hand, argues that Hinduism displays unity within diversity.

Madeleine Biardeau presents a structuralist approach. She believes that a whole society desires 'to present itself as a well-ordered whole … [and that] … Unity is sought at a deeper level … on the basis of the explicit or implicit norms which every Hindu carries in his head' (Biardeau 1981/1994: 2/16, cited in Malik 1997: 13). Therefore, the *Veda*[2] is seen '… not as a corpus of very ancient texts, but above all as a universal reference' (Biardeau 1981/1994: 14/16, cited in Malik 1997: 14).

As Malik notes, this does not allow for the possibility of individual agency. Furthermore, there is an absence of any intention whatsoever to engage in dialogue with Hindus themselves and, in Malik's opinion, dialogue could undermine the theory's claim of unity. Nevertheless, I do not think it wise to completely reject Biardeau's theory. After all, as mentioned, many Hindus do seem to know intuitively that they belong to a unified group.

Brian K. Smith's view is quite similar. Smith asserts that in Hinduism, tradition is transformed with 'legitimizing reference to the authority of the *Veda*' (Smith 1989: 13f., cited in Malik 1997: 14). The *Veda* is referenced in a number of ways. For example, people may claim that something *is* the *Veda*, that it is *based* on the *Veda*, is a *simplified version* of the *Veda*, or that it is an enlargement of the *Veda* (see Smith 1989: 29, cited in Malik 1997: 14). There are some groups that actually *reject* the *Veda* (Flood 1995: 9). Therefore, it may be prudent to add such groups to Smith's list. Even if they reject it, such groups are still technically referring to the *Veda*.

Malik points out that the approach is top-heavy as it does not take into account those groups which make no reference whatsoever to the *Veda* (Malik 1997: 14). Such groups predominantly engage in rituals and make no reference to the scriptures. Malik argues that although the rituals practised by such groups are certain to have antecedents in the *Veda*, the practitioners themselves do not consciously attempt to legitimize them through reference to the *Veda*—it is only the scholar that does this (Malik 1997: 15). Furthermore, this 'popular' or 'folk' Hinduism is the most common manifestation of Hinduism in India (see Fuller 1992), and this emphasizes that Smith's approach is insufficient.

Günther-Dietz Sontheimer argues that Hinduism is made up of five components that together make up Hinduism (Malik 1997: 16). These components are as follows: 'The work and teachings of *Brahmans* (members of the priestly caste), Asceticism and Renunciation, Tribal religion, Folk religion, and *Bhakti* (devotional worship)' (Malik 1997: 28). The components have a 'dynamic and fluid' interrelationship, and Folk religion is the most important of these (Malik 1997: 16).

Malik notes that there are a number of problems with this. First, the approach is, like Biardeau's, ahistorical because it advocates that the 'five components have existed since Hinduism began' (Malik 1997: 17). It is clear that this is highly unlikely. Although some Hindus refer to their tradition as eternal, it is continually evolving. Furthermore, even if the tradition is not eternal, although the historical date of the inception of Hinduism cannot be ascertained, it seems impossible that all of the components would have arisen simultaneously. Furthermore, argues Malik, Sontheimer's approach is flawed because it is highly unlikely that the different groups engage in discourse at the same level (see Malik 1997). This seems like a valid criticism. For example, urban *Brahmans* who study the scriptures are likely to be far removed from illiterate villagers who worship local deities at village shrines.

Heinrich von Stietencron argues that it is wrong to see Hinduism as one religion. Therefore, he departs from the previous approaches outlined. However, he does regard Hinduism as a single sociocultural unit. In his opinion, this unit contains many distinct religions which are coherent and can thus be compared with other 'world religions'. These religions cannot be placed together under the term 'Hinduism' (here 'Hindu religion') because there are so many contradictions between them. Malik identifies two major problems with this approach. First, it attempts to judge others using the Western system of reference as it uses Christian concepts such as 'religion [and] culture'. Furthermore, because of this, different groups within Hinduism are compartmentalized, even though (as will be demonstrated) it is clear that there are overlaps (see Malik 1997).

Gabriella Eichinger Ferro-Luzzi

In her chapter, *The Polythetic-prototype Approach to Hinduism*, Gabriella Eichinger Ferro-Luzzi (1997) puts forward an approach to understanding Hinduism, which appears to overcome the problems inherent within the previous approaches to Hinduism. She maintains that we should not get rid of the term 'Hinduism' or deny Hinduism the status of a religion. She argues that it is not Hinduism per se which causes problems but the false belief that all concepts can be defined because they must possess common attributes and clear-cut boundaries (see Eichinger Ferro-Luzzi 1997: 294). This can be rectified if we utilize 'Wittgenstein's discovery that concepts need not have common attributes and clear-cut boundaries but may be held together by a complicated network of similarities overlapping and criss-crossing' (Eichinger Ferro-Luzzi 1997: 295). In other words, there may be a 'family resemblance'. Eichinger Ferro-Luzzi emphasizes that such (polythetic) concepts should not be defined but exemplified, and Srinivas's claim that 'While it is not possible to define a Hindu, it is not difficult to identify a person as a Hindu' (Srinivas 1960: 575, cited in Eichinger Ferro-Luzzi 1997: 295) backs up this assertion. It would be difficult to disagree with Srinivas. Indeed, any study concerning Hinduism rests on the supposition that there are individuals and groups that can be clearly identified as being Hindu.

Before going on to show how her approach can be applied to Hinduism, Eichinger FerroLuzzi mentions some of the previously inadequate approaches such as those by, for example, Weber, and Radhakrishnan, who both look for a 'core' within Hinduism. Weber saw this as the belief in *karma* (the theory that every action has a consequence), while Radhakrishnan saw it as Adi Shankara's philosophy of *Advaita Vedanta* (see Eichinger Ferro-Luzzi 1997: 295–96). However, any such approach is flawed because there will always be some concepts that do not apply to all groups. For example, Cohn (1959) points out that some Hindus are unaware of the notion of *karma* (cited in Hamilton 1998: 68), while some concepts are shared by followers of Buddhism and Jainism (Eichinger Ferro-Luzzi 1997: 296).

Eichinger Ferro-Luzzi goes on to give examples of how different traditions in Hinduism can be held together by overlapping similarities. I present here the best of her examples which clearly shows the application of the approach:

> Village Hinduism with its worship of mostly bloodthirsty goddesses who have to be placated and Sanskritic rites addressed to gentle Gods like Krishna have nothing in common as long as we remain on this

> general level of description … [However,] … the fact that one deity is female and the other male creates no problem because a village goddess often has male servants who participate in her offerings and Krishna may be worshipped together with … [his female consort] Rādhā. Another overlapping similarity consists in the fact that non-Brahmin *pūjāris* [performers of devotional rituals] just like Brahman temple priests approach their respective deities in a state of ritual purity … Furthermore, the blood demanded by the goddess and the milk pudding relished by Krishna may either be subsumed under the heading of food or it may be pointed out that, while Krishna never accepts any blood offering, village goddesses enjoy both blood and sweet dishes.
>
> (Eichinger Ferro-Luzzi 1997: 298)

It would at first appear that there could be the objection that if this approach is used then it automatically means that Buddhists, Jains, and Sikhs are Hindu because they are linked to groups which would conventionally be regarded as being Hindu by virtue of their overlapping similarities. However, Eichinger Ferro-Luzzi points out that it is exactly her purpose to show that polythetic concepts have no clear boundaries and that such groups remain separate from Hindus only 'because of their members' wish to be separate and not because of an intrinsic criteria justifying their separate status' (Eichinger Ferro-Luzzi 1997: 300). A problematic aspect of this is that Eichinger Ferro-Luzzi does not take into account the fact that the desire for certain groups to remain distinct from Hindus could be ignored and the approach could be used for political ends. For example, it is common for 'Hindu nationalists' to assert that Buddhists, Jains, and Sikhs are Hindus (see McKean 1996: 118; Williams 1996: 236; Mannur 2003: 287; Smith 2003: 5) and the approach could be used to back up this assertion.

A completely polythetic approach to Hinduism would be very vague. However, Eichinger Ferro-Luzzi also stresses the importance of a number of features within Hinduism which she refers to as 'prototypes'. All of the criteria that previously 'have been pointed out by scholars as characteristic of Hinduism and useful to identify a Hindu remain valid as prototypical features' (Eichinger Ferro-Luzzi 1997: 301). However, the key features that make up the prototypes are, according to Eichinger Ferro-Luzzi, those features that are frequent and highly prestigious. Such features include the worship of the gods *Shiva*, *Krishna*, and *Ganesh*, the visiting of temples and going on pilgrimage, and belief in the concepts of *dharma* (religious duty, law, and custom), *karma, moksha* (liberation from the cycle of rebirth), and *Brahman* (the supreme Reality [see later in this chapter]) (Eichinger Ferro-Luzzi 1997: 301). Because these prototypical practices and concepts are not essential though, what results is an aid to help scholars employ the overall polythetic–prototype approach which accepts both that 'Hinduism' exists and that there is real unity in extreme diversity.

This amounts to a kind of common sense approach. As mentioned earlier, it is usually possible to tell who is a Hindu; and there is usually the intuitive realization that there are common links between what might appear to be very diverse groups. In the quote presented earlier concerning goddesses and *Krishna*, Eichinger Ferro-Luzzi gives quite an extreme example, but there are more extreme ones. For instance, even before learning of the polythetic–prototype approach, it appeared intuitively clear to me that there was a common thread of overlapping similarities inherent within Hinduism. For example, I could see a near naked ascetic who lived in a cremation ground and who practised various austerities, and a businessman with a family who conducted a daily *puja* (devotional ritual) in his home—and have no qualms about regarding them both as being Hindu. It thus appears necessary that when considering Hinduism we 'accept vagueness and disorder' (Eichinger Ferro-Luzzi 1997: 303) instead of insisting on boundaries where, it appears, they do not exist.

Darshan

One of the most important prototypes of Hinduism is the practice of *darshan. Darshan* involves a devotee gazing into the eyes of an image of a deity. Through this process, a devotee is able to receive the divine glance of the deity (Eck 1985; Beckerlegge 2001b). Beckerlegge emphasizes that the practice of *darshan* is so persuasive that it manages to cut across sectarian boundaries and that even Hindus who tend to think in abstract philosophical terms usually still regard the image as being of some use and an acceptable focus of devotion for those Hindus who are not philosophically minded. He further concludes that in Hinduism 'what unites worshippers from the most ardent to the most pragmatic is the belief in the need to stand in the presence of the deity or deities [and] to have the *darshan* of the deity' (Beckerlegge 2001b: 60–2). Therefore, it is clear that the religious image is of paramount importance within Hinduism.

As indicated in the introduction to this chapter, Jean Baudrillard considers the nature of images in general and then further discusses religious images (see Baudrillard 1983a). Because the use of images of

Hindu deities is an essential prototypical feature of Hinduism, it is worthwhile investigating the extent to which Baudrillard's important theoretical observations can inform our understanding of the nature of such images.

Jean Baudrillard and Hinduism

Mark Poster claims that, according to Baudrillard, 'Culture is now dominated by simulations [and that] objects and discourse ... have no firm origin, no referent, no ground or foundation' (1988: 1). By a simulation, Baudrillard means that there is no distinction between the object and its representation. He calls these simulations 'simulacra', and he asserts that the world is made up of these simulacra which 'have no referent or ground in any "reality" except their own' (Poster 1988: 5).

Baudrillard's comments concerning religious images appear in his 'Simulacra and Simulations' (1983a). In this work, Baudrillard applies his idea of the simulacrum to religious images, and this leads him to interesting conclusions which invite theoretical analysis in the light of Hinduism. Baudrillard's opinion is that the simulacrum does not represent the real; it becomes the real. Because of this, Baudrillard concludes that this is why iconoclasts wanted to destroy images of God. He asserts that iconoclasts sensed the 'omnipotence of simulacra' as they have the facility of 'erasing God from the consciousnesses of people'. This suggests that 'ultimately there has never been any God; that only simulacra exist; indeed that God himself has only been his own simulacrum' (Baudrillard 1983a: 169).

As for the iconolaters, Baudrillard claims that they were 'content to venerate God at one remove' (Baudrillard 1983a: 169). He also adds, however, that perhaps they were aware of the nature of simulacra but did not want to unmask images as this would reveal the fact that there was nothing behind them (Baudrillard 1983a). Despite the fact that the scholar of Hinduism David Smith agrees with Baudrillard and asserts that images of 'Hindu gods are simulacra' (Smith 1993: 162), this view is very problematic indeed when applied to Hinduism. First, Baudrillard only makes a distinction between iconolaters and iconoclasts. He does not appreciate the diverse range of meanings that are placed upon the image in Hinduism by devotees. For example, an image (usually in the form of a *murti*—or religious statue for want of a better term) may be regarded as being the embodied deity, the location of a deity's power or merely representative of the deity (see Beckerlegge 2001b: 108). Use of the image should certainly not indicate iconolatry in the sense that it is the actual image that is being worshipped.

Furthermore, it appears that Baudrillard's view of religion is anchored in a Western understanding. For example, he is of the opinion that those who used images were content to venerate God 'at one remove'. However, the aforementioned philosophy of *Advaita Vedanta* puts forward the notion of *Brahman* which challenges this idea. *Vedantic* philosophy holds that an individual must realize[3] that everything that is impermanent is unreal and that the only thing that is changeless and hence real is their pure consciousness (known as the *atman*). Before this is realized, this consciousness is known as the *jiva* and is present in successive physical incarnations. However, realization results in the merging[4] of the *atman* with the *formless Brahman.* By its very nature, *Brahman* cannot be sufficiently defined but it can be tentatively referred to as being 'undifferentiated existence, consciousness and bliss' (Krishnananda 1994: 102). In many cases, the image is used as an aid in the quest to gain appreciation of this formless *Brahman*, which 'though it is everywhere, it *cannot be seen'* (Krishnananda 1994: 102 [my emphasis]). In the case of Hinduism then, it appears that Baudrillard's view that those who use images are afraid to unmask them because this would reveal the fact that there was nothing behind them is inappropriate. It is more apt to suggest that it would be a desirable goal for many Hindus to be able to unmask the image because behind the image is the 'opposite' of 'nothing'. It is thus fair to say that it is necessary to be careful when considering Baudrillard's idea of simulacra in the light of Hindu religious images. Baudrillard does not entertain the notion that owing to the unique way in which individuals may perceive Hindu religious images as distinct from other simulacra, it is possible that other variables might come into play.

Aside from his remarks regarding images, Baudrillard makes a further claim which calls into question the applicability of his ideas to Hinduism. In *Fatal Strategies* (1983b), Baudrillard asserts that 'gods can only live and hide in the inhuman … and not in the human realm … [and that] … a human-god is an absurdity' (Baudrillard 1983b: 200). In contrast to this claim, Hinduism has a long history of belief in the presence of *avatars*—manifestations of God on earth in physical form—and this belief is still very popular today (Smith 2003). Ramakrishna (1836–1886) was a famous *avatar* (see Smith 2003), and a good example of a contemporary *avatar* is the recently deceased Sathya Sai Baba who enjoys a huge worldwide following (see Sharma 1986; Fuller 1992; Smith 2003). There are also countless others who enjoy lower levels of popularity. For example, Pocock writes that it is common that men are elevated to the 'status of godhead' (1973:

98–99). Furthermore, in addition to *avatars*, gurus in Hinduism are also seen as 'being God' (see Hutchinson 1996: 110; Juergensmeyer 1996; Smith 2003) (there is thus an overlap between an *avatar* and a guru). It is also important to note that during the Hindu wedding ritual the bride and groom *assume a divine form* and are worshipped by their family and friends 'in much the same way as deities are worshipped before their images in temples' (Fuller 1992: 30–31 [my emphasis]). In addition to these examples which show that a 'human-god' is certainly not an absurdity in Hinduism, there is the example of priests in some South Indian temples who, on one level at least, actually become the god *Shiva* during worship (Fuller 1992: 61; see also Smith 1993: 163). It is clear, then, that a consideration of certain Baudrillardian ideas in the light of Hinduism suggests that these ideas are not universal.

Online Images of Hindu Deities

Baudrillard's ideas regarding images have undergone renewed interest since the commercial introduction of the Internet. This is because with each successive communications technology, it seems reasonable to suggest that the notion of the simulacrum becomes stronger as images drift further away from their original reference points. This would seem to be especially the case with the Internet because of the WWW which gives primacy to images (Wertheim 1999; Brasher 2004; Cowan 2005).

This idea has been put forward by the theorist Manuel Castells who draws directly upon the work of Baudrillard. Castells asserts that 'there is no separation between "reality" and symbolic representation' (Castells 2000: 403) but wishes to make it clear that this has always been the case and has not just arisen as a result of electronic communication. He claims that 'all realities are communicated through symbols [and] in human, interactive communication, regardless of the medium, all symbols are somewhat displaced in relation to their assigned semantic meaning'. Therefore, in Castells's view: 'In a sense, all reality is virtually perceived' (Castells 2000: 404). However, Castells believes that the difference with the Internet is that it not only 'induces virtual reality' but actually 'constructs real virtuality' (Castells 2000: 403). This is because:

> It is a system in which reality itself (that is, people's material/symbolic existence) is entirely captured, fully immersed in a virtual image setting, in the world of make believe, in which appearances are not just on the screen through which experience is communicated, but they become the experience. All messages of all kinds become enclosed in the medium because the medium has become so comprehensive, so

> diversified, so malleable that it absorbs in the same multimedia text the whole of human experience, past, present, and future. (Castells 2000: 404 [emphasis in original])

It is worth noting here that these assertions are hyperbolic—a charge also often levelled against the work of Baudrillard, who, in the opinion of Poster (1988: 7) tends to talk about media images 'as if nothing else in society mattered' (Poster 1988: 7). However, despite this and the other points that I have made which call into question the applicability of Baudrillardian ideas when Hinduism is taken into account, it is worthwhile looking at whether or not the Internet can exacerbate the extent to which Hindu images can be considered to be simulacra. This is because there are a large number of images of Hindu deities associated with physical sites that have been replicated on the WWW[5] and increasingly large numbers of people are spending time online. I say *exacerbate* because both Castells and Baudrillard would assert that an original image in a Hindu temple is already a simulacrum. However, it is possible that whereas the original image is securely bounded in a referential context, the image replicated on the WWW is far removed from this context and thus becomes more of a simulacrum. Thus, if the initial theory of simulacra is accepted, as a result of the Internet it might now be apt to speak of there being different degrees of simulacra.

In an investigation as to whether this is the case in the context of images of Hindu deities online, it is productive to take into account the meanings that devotees give to original images and then to compare the perceived status of these images with those on the WWW. In this way, any differences in the status of the images can indicate whether or not the online Hindu image has become more of a hyper-real simulacrum than the original image. Ultimately, this can suggest possible consequences for Hinduism and the experiences of its practitioners as a result of images of Hindu deities being placed online.

As I have emphasized, the practice of *darshan* which necessitates images of deities is a prototypical feature of Hinduism. Therefore, when considering the nature of such images online it is prudent to assess the extent to which online images can allow for the practice of *darshan. Darshan can* be received from online images of Hindu deities (Scheifinger 2008, 2009). However, the fact that devotees have different views as to the nature of original images directly affects the perceived level of efficacy of online *darshan.* For example, for those to whom the original image is considered to be sacred in itself, the replicated online image cannot have an equal status and consequently the *darshan* that it can provide is not as powerful as that from the original image. Therefore, for such devotees, it is still necessary to gaze upon the original image in order to receive full *darshan* and so therefore the online image has not become more real than, or even as real as, the original image.

Some Hindu devotees do not assign any intrinsic sacredness to the physical image of a deity in a temple and instead may regard it as being a symbolic aid to their contemplation of the divine. For such individuals, a replicated online image can have the same status as the original image and can provide a *darshan* experience equal to that at the physical site (although visiting a sacred site can still be preferable for a number of other reasons [see Scheifinger 2009]). This might initially suggest that such an image does become hyper-real to a greater extent. This is because the online image appears to have become completely freed from its original referential context yet it is still providing a function for devotees. However, closer examination reveals that such an image is still related to the original image. It is the particular deity which gives meaning to the online image. For example, those who seek to receive online *darshan* from an image of the goddess *Kali* from the temple at Kalighat, Kolkata, are entering into a relationship with this particular *Kali*—not a generic *Kali* disembedded from any referential locality. Therefore, even for those who believe that an online image has a status identical to that of the original image, replicated images on the WWW have not become more hyper-real. In this sense, the placing of images of Hindu deities online is unlikely to constitute a major development within Hinduism.

Notes

1. The word 'Hindu' can be traced back into 'ancient antiquity' where it is 'referred to the natives of northern India' (Frykenberg 1997: 83–84).
2. The *Veda* literally means 'knowledge' and is seen by many to be an essential component in any definition of Hinduism. The *Veda* comprises four texts (often collectively known as the *Vedas*) that were written down around 5000 years ago. Previously, the knowledge was transmitted orally. They are the most sacred ancient texts in Hinduism and are believed to be eternal (see Weller 1997: 291). The *Vedas* are often seen as 'the "canon" of Hindu Scripture' (see Zaehner 1966: v–vi), although such a description is perhaps evidence of the problematic aforementioned attempt to understand Hinduism through a Western frame of reference.
3. This type of realization differs from ordinary realization and refers to perfect understanding on an experiential level.

4. The use of the word 'merging' should not give the impression that there is actually a duality at any stage between the *atman* and *Brahman*.
5. There is no prohibition against the replication of deities in Hinduism (see Eck 1993).

References

Allen, R.E. (ed.) (1990) *The Concise Oxford Dictionary of Current English*. Oxford: Oxford University Press.

Baudrillard, J. (1983a) 'Simulacra and simulations', in Poster, M. (ed.) (1988) *Jean Baudrillard: Selected Writings*. Cambridge: Polity Press, 166–84.

Baudrillard, J. (1983b) 'Fatal strategies', in Poster, M. (ed.) (1988) *Jean Baudrillard: Selected Writings*. Cambridge: Polity Press, 185–206.

Beckerlegge, G. (2001a) 'Introduction', in Beckerlegge, G. (ed.) *From Sacred Text to Internet*. Milton Keynes: The Open University, 1–7.

Beckerlegge, G. (2001b) 'Hindu sacred images for the mass market', in Beckerlegge, G. (ed.) *From Sacred Text to Internet*. Milton Keynes: The Open University, 57–116.

Beckford, J.A. (2000) 'Religious movements and globalization', in Cohen, R., and Rai, S.M. (eds.) *Global Social Movements*. London: The Athlone Press, 165–83.

Beckford, J.A. (2003) *Social Theory of Religion*. Cambridge: Cambridge University Press.

Bhatt, C. (1997) *Liberation and Purity: Race, New Religious Movements and the Ethics of Postmodernity*. London: UCL Press.

Bhatt, C. (2001) *Hindu Nationalism: Origins, Ideologies, and Modern Myths*. Oxford: Berg.

Brasher, B. (2004) *Give Me That Online Religion*. New Brunswick, NJ: Rutgers University Press.

Burghart, R. (ed.) (1987) *Hinduism in Great Britain*. London: Tavistock Publishing.

Carey, S. (1983) 'The Hare Krishna Movement and Hindus in Britain', *New Community*, 10(3), 477–86.

Carman, J.B. (1996) 'Handing down and reaching across: stability and movement in Indian religious traditions', in Williams, R.B. (ed.) *A Sacred Thread: Modern Transmission of Hindu Traditions in India and Abroad*. New York: Columbia University Press, 7–20.

Castells, M. (2000) *The Information Age: Economy, Society and Culture* (2nd edn. Vol. I). Oxford: Blackwell.

Cowan, D.E. (2005) 'Online U-Topia: cyberspace and the mythology of placelessness', *Journal for the Scientific Study of Religion*, 44(3), 257–63.

Coward, H.G. (1985) *Pluralism: Challenge to World Religions*. Maryknoll, NY: Orbis.

Eck, D. (1985) *Darsan: Seeing the Divine Image in India*. Chambersburg, PA: Anima Books.

Eck, D.L. (1993) *Banaras: City of Light*. New Delhi: Penguin Books.

Eichinger Ferro-Luzzi, G. (1997) 'The polythetic-prototype approach to Hinduism', in Sontheimer, G.D., and Kulke, H. (eds.) *Hinduism Reconsidered*. New Delhi: Manohar, 294–304.

Flood, G. (1995) 'Hinduism, Vaisnavism, and ISKCON: authentic traditions or scholarly constructions', *ISKCON Communications Journal*, 3(2), 5–15.

Frykenberg, R. (1997) 'The emergence of modern "Hinduism" as a concept and as an institution: a reappraisal with special reference to South India', in Sontheimer, G.D. and Kulke, H. (eds.) *Hinduism Reconsidered*. New Delhi: Manohar, 82–107.

Fuller, C.J. (1992) *The Camphor Flame: Popular Hinduism and Society in India*. Princeton: Princeton University Press.

Gupta, S.S. (2002) *Puri: Lord Jagannath's Dhaam*. New Delhi: Rupa & Co.

Hamilton, M. (1993) *The Sociology of Religion: Theoretical and Comparative Perspectives*. Oxford: Blackwell.

Hamilton, M. (1998) *Sociology and the World's Religions*. Basingstoke/London: MacMillan Press.

Hutchinson, B. (1996) 'The divine-human figure in the transmission of religious tradition', in Williams, R.B. (ed.) *A Sacred Thread: Modern Transmission of Hindu Traditions in India and Abroad*. New York: Columbia University Press, 92–124.

IANS (2004, May 8) *Supreme Court to Define 'Essential' Part of Religion*. http://wwrn.org/articles/13742/?&place=india§ion=church-state (accessed on 1 February 2005).

Jackson, R. (1996) 'The construction of 'Hinduism' and its impact on religious education in England and Wales', *Panorama: International Journal of Comparative Religious Education and Values*, 8(1), 86–104.

Juergensmeyer (1996) 'A new international religion: Radhasoami', in Williams, R.B. (ed.) *A Sacred Thread: Modern Transmission of Hindu Traditions in India and Abroad*. New York: Columbia University Press, 278–99.

Kanitkar, V.P., and Cole, O. (1995) *Hinduism*. London: Hodder & Stoughton.

Knott, K. (1986) *Hinduism in Leeds: A Study of Religious Practice in the Indian Hindu Community and in Hindu-Related Groups*. Leeds: University of Leeds, Department of Theology and Religious Studies.

Krishnananda, S. (1994) *A Short History of Religious and Philosophic Thought in India*. Shivanandanagar, India: The Divine Life Society.

Malik, A. (1997) 'Hinduism or three-thousand-three-hundred-and-six ways to invoke a construct', in Sontheimer, G.D., and Kulke, H. (eds.) *Hinduism Reconsidered*. New Delhi: Manohar, 10–31.

Mannur, A. (2003) 'Postscript: cyberspaces and the interfacing of diasporas', in Braziel, J.E., and Mannur, A. (eds.) *Theorizing Diaspora*. Oxford: Blackwell, 283–90.

McKean, L. (1996) *Divine Enterprise*. Chicago: Chicago University Press.

Meredith, S., Hickman, C., and Le Rolland, L. (2005) *The Usborne Internet-Linked Encyclopedia of World Religions*. London: Usborne.

Michaelson, M. (1987) 'Domestic Hinduism in a Gujarati trading caste', in Burghart, R. (ed.) *Hinduism in Great Britain*. London: Tavistock Publishing, 32–49.

Pocock, D.F. (1973) *Mind, Body and Wealth: A Study of Belief and Practice in an Indian Village*. Oxford: Basil Blackwell.

Poster, M. (1988) 'Introduction', in Poster, M. (ed.) *Jean Baudrillard: Selected Writings*. Cambridge: Polity Press, 1–9.

Preston, J.J. (1980) *Cult of the Goddess: Social and Religious Change in a Hindu Temple*. Ghaziabad: Vikas.

Scheifinger, H. (2008) 'Hinduism and cyberspace', *Religion*, 38, 233–49.

Scheifinger, H. (2009) 'The *Jagannath* Temple and online *Darshan*', *Journal of Contemporary Religion*, 24(3), 277–90.

Sekhar, R. (1999) 'Authenticity by accident: organizing, decision making and the construction of a diasporic Hindu Temple in the nation's capital', in Rukmani, T.S. (ed.) *Hindu Diaspora: Global Perspectives*. Montreal: Chair in Hindu Studies, Concordia University, 307–28.

Sharma, A. (1986) 'New Hindu religious movements in India', in Beckford, J.A. (ed.) *New Religious Movements and Rapid Social Change*. London: Sage, 220–39.

Smith, D. (1993) 'The premodern and the postmodern: some parallels, with special reference to Hinduism', *Religion*, 23, 157–65.

Smith, D. (2003) *Hinduism and Modernity*. Oxford: Blackwell.

Srinivas, M.N. (1962) 'A note on Sanskritization and Westernization', in Srinivas, M.N. (ed.) *Caste in Modern India and Other Essays*. London: J.K. Publishers, 42–62.

Svarûpa-dasâ, R. (1996) 'A response to Daniel Acharuparambil, "Hinduism in interreligious dialogue"', *ISKCON Communications Journal*, 4(2), 100–5.

Thomas, T. (1993) 'Hindu dharma in dispersion', in Parsons, G. (ed.) *The Growth of Religious Diversity—Volume 1: Traditions*. London: Routledge in association with the Open University, 173–204.

Turner, B.S. (1991) *Religion and Social Theory*. London: Sage.

Vertovec, S. (1997) 'Hinduism in diaspora: the transformation of tradition in Trinidad', in Sontheimer, G.D., and Kulke, H. (eds.) *Hinduism Reconsidered*. New Delhi: Manohar, 265–93.

Weller, P. (ed.) (1997) *Religions in the UK: A Multi-Faith Directory*. Derby: University of Derby and The Inter Faith Network for the United Kingdom.

Wertheim, M. (1999) *The Pearly Gates of Cyberspace: A History of Space from Dante to the Internet*. London: Virago Press.

Williams, R.B. (1996) 'Sacred threads of several textures: strategies of adaptation in the United States', in Williams, R.B. (ed.) *A Sacred Thread: Modern Transmission of Hindu Traditions in India and Abroad*. New York: Columbia University Press, 228–57.

Zaehner, R.C. (1966) *Hindu Scriptures*. London: Everyman's Library.

11

Between Moderation and Radicalization

Transnational Interactions of Jamaat-e-Islami of India

Irfan Ahmad

Soon after the 11 September attack on the twin towers in New York, Daniel Pipes wrote an article explaining the danger Islamic militancy posed to the United States. Sharply critical of President George W. Bush's post-September 11 remark that 'there are millions of good Americans who practise the Muslim faith ... who salute the flag as strongly as I salute the flag', he warned him not to be complacent (Pipes 2001: 19). He then went on to name and discuss Muslim individuals and organizations that, in his view, sought to transform America into an Islamic theocracy. He suggested several steps to counter the so-called Islamic threat. One such remedy he proposed was making the existing American immigration laws more stringent so as to 'prevent a further influx of visitors and residents with any hint of Islamist ideology' (Pipes 2001: 24). The implication of Pipes's argument is clear: the transnational links between Muslims in the United States and those with 'any hint of Islamic ideology' abroad is extremely dangerous to the country's safety and that transnational links between activists of Islamic movements always lead to extremism and violence.

More recently, Bernard Lewis (2003) has argued along similar lines. He seems to imply that Islamic activists from non-Western countries develop an absolute contempt for Western ways of life once they go there and forge links with like-minded individuals and organizations. Several years before Pipes and Lewis, it was Huntington who had made this argument. In the fault-line wars between faith-based civilizations, for example, between Islam and Christianity, he argued, the diaspora played a key role in so far as it supported heart and soul the primary level participants—be they state-aided organized groups or states themselves. In Huntington's formulation too, transnational connections between Islamic activists thus always and necessarily lead to a sharpening of the conflict between Islam and the West (Huntington 1997).

In this chapter, I call into question the alarmist thesis advocated, though differently, by Pipes, Lewis, and Huntington. I argue that the transnational connections forged by Jamaat-e-Islami Hind (JIH), a contemporary Indian Islamist[1] movement, with Gulf countries, the West, and Iran did not lead simply to its militancy or radicalization. In complex and apparently contradictory ways, it also substantially led to moderation of its ideology and practices and created conflicts within JIH. Further, I argue that JIH's transnational links should be conceived as a transnational social movement. Such an argument entails a broadening of social movement theories to include the forms of collective action in undemocratic regimes. This chapter is in five parts. In first part, I discuss the research question, fieldwork experience, and quickly move to lay out the theoretical outline pertinent to my argument. Here I show how the existing social movement theories, often based on the specific experiences of the Western democracies, fail to account for the dynamics of Islamist movements in the non-Western societies presided over by monarchy, dictatorship, or autocracy. This calls for a more nuanced conceptualization of social movement theories which are able to address the experiences of societies that do not allow open political mobilization. I also question the structuralist biases of such theories and argue for attention to the biographies of the movement leaders. In the second part, I briefly introduce JIH and its student organization, the Student Islamic Movement of India (SIMI) and their interactions with ideologically similar movements and networks in the Gulf countries. In the third part, I describe in detail how the interactions of JIH activists with Gulf countries (Saudi Arabia and Kuwait in particular) and the United States thickened from the mid-1970s onwards. Here I also describe how JIH activists found innovative ways to enact political mobilization there, especially in Saudi Arabia. In the fourth part, I dwell on the ways in which the Iranian revolution impacted on JIH and SIMI, the network that evolved between Islamists in India and those in Iran. Here I also examine the conflict within SIMI. In the final part, I discuss the outcome of the transnational connections in terms of simultaneous processes of JIH's radicalization and moderation.

Research Question, Fieldwork, and Theory

As part of my ongoing doctorate, provisionally titled, 'From Islamism to post-Islamism: the Transformation of Jamaat-e-Islami in North India' at the University of Amsterdam, I conducted the first phase of my fieldwork between October 2001 and October 2002, mainly in Aligarh, India. I made another short fieldwork trip between January and May 2003. However, since my research was based on a multi-sited ethnographic approach (Marcus 1995), I also spent a considerable amount of time in four other Indian cities—Azamgarh, Delhi, Patna, and Rampur—that were crucial points of the JIH network. The aim of my research was to find out if and how, in postcolonial India, JIH accepted secularism and democracy, which it had condemned as *haram* (religiously forbidden) in the colonial era. Put differently, I was interested in JIH's ideological transformation. I chose its student activism as one arena to examine the transformation. I selected Aligarh Muslim University (AMU), Aligarh, as my main fieldwork location for many reasons. First, as the only Muslim university in post-colonial India, AMU has a symbolic significance for the Muslim community, which proudly considers it as its unofficial leader. In fact, AMU's contentious status as a minority institution became the symbol of a struggle for Muslim identity in postcolonial India (Graff 1990). Given this, JIH has always tried hard to establish its hegemony over AMU. Second, soon after its formation, Jamaat's student activism began at AMU. SIMI was formed there in 1977 and remained headquartered there for several years. Third, Aligarh is one of the few towns in North India with a sizeable Muslim population, officially 38 per cent, though Muslims believe that they are 50 per cent (Brass 2003). My purpose was to see how JIH and SIMI function in a setting like Aligarh.

Only two weeks before I arrived in Aligarh, the Government of India led by the right-wing Bharatiya Janata Party (BJP) had, following 9/11, banned SIMI on the charges of 'sedition' and fomenting 'communal disharmony' (*Hindustan Times* 2001). Following the ban, SIMI's offices throughout India, including Aligarh, were sealed and its leaders arrested. SIMI activists were initially extremely fearful to talk to me. They thought that I was part of the Western conspiracy to harm Islam and thus an agent of the West deputed to collect information about them.[2] The conspiracy theory was based, *inter alia*, on the fact that I was affiliated to a Western university.[3] Both SIMI and JIH activists believed that the West would allow me to research JIH in its university only if it served 'the anti-Islam interest of the West'. Further, they wondered how my adviser, a Christian by birth and unfamiliar with the Quran, could supervise research on Islam. Why did I not instead, they suggested, do my research with an Islamic scholar based in India?

Initially, I thus felt lost and frustrated. One of the crucial ways I could overcome the conspiracy net and demonstrate my academic autonomy was through personal interactions based primarily on questions relating to my biography. My informants always asked me from which state in India I had come, where I studied, what my father and brother (never my mother or sisters) did, or whether I had ever associated with JIH. Because of the near distrust by JIH–SIMI of Western academe, my 6 years of initial education in an Islamic seminary and bachelor's degree from Jamia Millia Islamia, New Delhi, proved a valuable vehicle of trust with them. A significant breakthrough in the rapport, however, came when a close relative of one of my distant friends, who was then a top JIH leader, assured them of my credentials. Another influential JIH leader, based in Aligarh and with a degree from Harvard University, appreciated my research and favourably introduced me to the JIH circle. Both of them wanted me to highlight JIH's positive contribution. Once introduced to the JIH circle, I approached the former SIMI members first. Compared with the current members, they were much less afraid, for they did not fear government action against them. Through them I approached the current members who gradually began to trust me.

As an anthropologist interested in social movements, I had planned participant observation as the main tool of my fieldwork (Lichterman 1998). However, since SIMI ceased to function openly after the ban, participant observation of its activities was unfeasible. My source of data on SIMI thus consists of informal, unstructured conversations with its former as well as current members. They also provided me with important documents and literary sources. In contrast to SIMI, JIH functioned openly and, therefore, I conducted participant observation with the latter.

Theoretical and Methodological Issues

Jamaat-e-Islami Hind and its transnational interactions can be regarded as a transnational social movement. This approach, however, goes against the dominant theories of transnational social movements. In what follows, I question the pitfalls of such theories based on the experiences of Western democracies and argue for the inclusion of the dynamics of collective mobilization in non-Western polities. Tarrow (1999: 184) defines a transnational social movement as 'sustained contentious interactions with opponents—national or non-national—by connected networks of challengers organized across national borders'. Going by this definition, JIH's transnational interactions fail to qualify as a transnational social movement on three counts. First, the ties between its activists and their counterparts outside India are not sustained over time. Second, they are not integrated or organizationally institutionalized. Third, challenges bringing together the two sets of actors across the national border against a common opponent are insufficiently contentious.

This definition is clearly too restrictive. More importantly, it is narrowly premised on experiences of Western democracies and their distinct social formations to the neglect of others (Aminzade and Perry 2001). Benítez-Rojo (1996), Oommen (1995), and Palmié (2002) have alerted us to the danger of applying Western concepts to explain the realities of the non-Western world.[4] Following their lead, I contend that Tarrow's conceptualization is also based on Western specificities and does not address, even remotely, the realities of Muslim societies. It presupposes democracy and hence citizens' rights to mobilize collectively or form organizational networks. As such, it excludes the majority of Muslim nation-states and their governments presided over by monarchs, dictators, and military regimes hostile to collective mobilization, particularly the religious-political ones. The absence of sustained or organizational connections between, for example, JIH members in India and their counterparts in Iran, Saudi Arabia, and other Gulf countries is not through lack of desire but through a denial of freedom by the undemocratic states to religious actors to forge collective action there.

The major reason for excluding Muslim societies in conceptualizing social movements, however, stems from a much larger assumption. Social movements, to quote Tarrow again, are 'an invention of the modern age and an accompaniment to the rise of the modern state' (Tarrow 1999: 2). Tilly (2002) shares Tarrow's view and adds that electoral politics and civil associations are preconditions for the emergence of a national social movement (Tilly 1984). Since most Muslim societies, unlike their Western counterparts, presumably have yet to experience 'modernity', lack fully developed modern states, and barely have electoral politics, much less civil associations, as the argument so loudly implies, they can at best have only mutiny or rebellion as it existed in the pre-modern age but no social movement that is the gift of modernity. This is one possible explanation for why mainstream social movement theorists have long neglected the study of Islamic movements (Kurzman 2004). Moreover, based as they are on an ill-founded premise of an already accomplished fact of secularization in the West, most social movement theories have historically addressed the so-called good and progressive, rather than the supposedly backward, religious movements (Smith 1996; see also Guidry et al. 2000). With a few exceptions, they are based on the empirical cases of non-Muslim societies. As such, there is a crying need to update, revise, and recast them in the light of the realities of Muslim societies.

From the above-mentioned critique of Tarrow, it thus follows that an absence of sustained and institutionalized interactions across national borders is not a problem of the movement *per se* but of its conceptualization and the political set-up under which it operates. In contrast to Tarrow, I consider the linkage between JIH/SIMI members and Islamists in Saudi Arabia, the United States, and Iran or elsewhere not as an example of what he prefers to call diffusion or political exchange (Tarrow 1999: 184–6) but as a robust case of transnational social movement. I use transnational in the sense that Vertovec (1999: 448) defines it, which presumes neither democracy nor untested secularization and is analytically broad.

To clear further ground for my argument, I find Tarrow's structuralist bias disabling in explaining the moderation of JIH. As a self-designated 'recovering structuralist', Tarrow (2003: 134) is barely, if at all, enthusiastic about giving any agency to actors outside his straightjacket structuralism. Posing a misleading dichotomy between the individual and the social, he says that 'The collective action problem is social, not individual' (Tarrow 1994: 23). As Jasper (1997: 57) rightly points out, Tarrow's is a false dichotomy and calls for bestowing agency upon actors by focusing, among others, on biography. I strongly agree with Jasper's call in that it makes a case for recognizing the role individuals, particularly movement leaders, play in changing the directions of a movement (Jasper 1997: 319). To overcome the structuralism that has long dominated social movement theorization (Kurzman 2003) and has ignored the role of leadership (Barker et al. 2001), I will focus on the biographies of key leaders who thickened the transnational interactions of JIH and moved it away from its old path to a new one. But first, a word about JIH.

Differentia Specifica of JIH

By the 1930s and early 1940s, the Indian freedom struggle against British rule had entered a critical phase. Muslims were broadly divided into two streams. Led by the traditional clergy of the Deoband seminary, Darul Uloom, a majority of them supported the Indian National Congress and its goal of a composite, secular, and united India (Hasan 1979; Sisson and Wolpert 1988; Madni n.d.). Opposed to the Congress, the Muslim League advocated a separate homeland for Muslims (Hasan 1979; Jalal 1994). In 1941, Syed Abul Ala Maududi

(1903–1979) formed Jamaat-e-Islami as an alternative to both the Congress and the League. His opposition to the League was not about whether or not a Muslim homeland should be created but about its ideological content. Should it be based on Western-style democracy and ruled by Westernized Muslims, or should it be based on divine laws, *sharia*—caliphate[5]—and be ruled by ulema (plural of *alim*, cleric)? Maududi unambiguously favoured the latter (for details see Ahmad 1998; Nasr 1994a). The constitution of Jamaat thus characterized its goal as the establishment of *hukumat-e-ilahiya*, 'Allah's government' (Maududi 1942: 173). Since, in Maududi's view, both the Congress and the League stood for an anti-Islamic system based on human laws as opposed to *sharia*, he warned Muslims not to participate in them because it meant rebellion against their belief in monotheism. Participation in a secular system, such as becoming a member of parliament or of the assembly, he decreed, was *haram* (Maududi 1999: 304).

Following the creation of Pakistan in 1947, Jamaat-e-Islami was divided into Jamaat-e-Islami Pakistan and Jamaat-e-Islami Hind (India), or JIH. Muslims were reduced to less than 12 per cent of India's total population and were territorially dispersed. Notwithstanding the political convulsion of 1947, JIH constitutionally persisted with its goal of establishing 'Allah's government' in India. The phrase expressing its goal, *hukumat-e-ilahiya*, however, was replaced by *iqamat-e-deen*, 'establishment of religion'. But it noted that the replacement was more terminological than substantive ideological (*Dastoor-e-Jamaat-e-Islami* n.d., p. 12).

In the wake of the partition, Maududi chose to settle in Pakistan where, after a lull for some years, he launched a fervent campaign to enshrine the Islamic state in its constitution (Binder 1963; Bahadur 1977; Nasr 1994a). An interesting puzzle remains today: how did JIH envisage establishing 'Allah's government' in a religiously plural and Muslim-minority India? Maududi left a blueprint for the JIH to follow towards the success of what he called 'Islamic revolution'. It had two major directions. First, Indian Muslims must not, as the League did before, call for any representation in assemblies or government services. 'They should rather develop', he advised, 'indifference towards the new government and political system' (Maududi 1996: 32). Second, Muslims should radically transform themselves into true Muslims and start preaching Islam to non-Muslims. If they harnessed all their intellectual resources and zeal in the ceaseless propagation of Islam (*dawat*), predicted Maududi, in the future (he did not specify the time frame) JIH will succeed in inaugurating an Islamic revolution in India as well. JIH has broadly followed Maududi's blueprint, with one notoriously controversial difference. During the mid-1980s, it allowed its members to vote in elections for a secular system, as opposed to the one based on *sharia*.

Student Activism and Transnational Links

Without going into further details of how JIH coped with the new situation of post-partition India (for details, see Ahmad 1998, 1999), I now turn to the formation of its student wing and how it was implicated with transnational Islamist actors. Throughout the 1950s and 1960s, JIH did not have an all-India student wing. In several towns with significant Muslim populations in the state of Uttar Pradesh (UP), students associated with JIH were working without a formal organization, or coordination among them. AMU, Aligarh, was the only town with a formal organization, called Student Islamic Organization (SIO), formed in 1956 (Salfi n.d.). It was essentially local. But given the significance of AMU for Muslims, the best and most active minds were concentrated there. AMU was thus the nerve centre of Islamist students. Students under JIH's influence in Uttar Pradesh, especially SIO, were persuading the leadership to form an all-India organization and to allow them to play a far more independent and interventionist role (Salfi n.d.).

This demand arose because of the increasing power and role of students in Indian universities during the 1960s and 1970s (Altbach 1966, 1968; Jayaram 1989; Oommen 1974, 1995; Rudolph et al. 1971; Vishwa 1973; see also Shah 1991), which the 1960s' student movement in Europe and North America had obviously influenced. In particular, student organizations associated with communist parties were quite influential throughout India, including at AMU, Aligarh (Bari 2001: 289–94). In addition, Islami Jamiat Talaba (IJT), the student wing of Jamaat-e-Islami Pakistan, was already very active on university campuses in Pakistan (Nasr 1992, 1994a), which obviously provided a role model for its counterparts in India. Students under JIH's influence wanted to have an independent organization of their own. Initially, the JIH leadership rejected such a demand on the grounds that conditions were still unfavourable. Later, when agreed under pressure, it laid down the proviso that the would-be organization must function under the leadership's constitutional tutelage. This condition was introduced because of a fear that once formed the organization might take a violent turn and get out of control, as IJT had indeed done in Pakistan (Nasr 1992). Students did not agree to this. A fierce disagreement on an independent role of the would-be organization continued between students and the JIH leadership.

Meanwhile, JIH had developed close links with the Gulf countries following the oil boom of the 1970s. Thousands of Indian Muslims (as well as Kerala Christians and to a limited extent Hindus) went to Saudi Arabia and other Gulf countries as temporary contracted semi-skilled and skilled workers, mostly in the field of construction (Weiner 1982; Madhavan 1985; Jain 1993; Nayyar 1994; see also Halliday 1984). A small but highly influential section of JIH members also went to Saudi Arabia, often to universities and educational cum religious organizations.

One man credited with introducing JIH to Muslim countries, especially Saudi Arabia, was its president (*amir*) Mohammad Yusuf. As *amir* (1972–1981), he frequently travelled to Saudi Arabia and other Gulf countries. A university graduate, he had earlier resigned his judicial job to join JIH. He considered it *haram* to be part of an anti-*sharia* judicial system. Later he learnt Arabic and became so proficient in it that he could deliver speeches in Arabic in Muslim countries and would stay abroad for several weeks on end. During his decade-long presidency, Yusuf visited Gulf countries so frequently that cynics in JIH would joke about whether he was president of JIH or of an Arab country. The new and increased transnational ties were most visible in JIH's sixth all-India session (at Hyderabad) in 1981 and celebrated as the beginning of the new fourteenth Islamic century. At this conference, activists of Islamist movements from Gulf countries such as Saudi Arabia, Kuwait, the United Arab Emirates, and Iran, as well as from the United States, the United Kingdom, and Sri Lanka, actively participated. The vice chancellors of Muhammad Bin Saud University, Riyadh, and Medina University, Islamic University of al-Madinah al-Munawarah also participated.

The oil boom in the Gulf coincided with the formation of a number of international Islamic organizations to promote a distinctive type of puritan, anti-Sufism Islam—Wahabism. As a matter of fact, the oil wealth propelled a fusion of Wahabism and state power (Lewis 2003). The aim of these Islamic organizations was to export Wahabism worldwide to Muslims, including diaspora Muslims in the West, and to counter, at the behest and with the support of the United States, any communist influences among Muslims, such as Jamal Abdul Nasir's support for socialism in Egypt (Mejcher 2004). The Muslim World League, with headquarters at Mecca, was formed in 1962 'to advance Islamic unity and solidarity' (*Islamic Voice* 1998) and to counter communism (Masud 2000). The Islamic Development Bank (at Jeddah) was established in 1973 to boost economic development in consonance with *sharia* in its 55 member Muslim countries as well as in Muslim communities elsewhere. With headquarters in Riyadh, Saudi

Arabia, the World Assembly of Muslim Youth (WAMY) was founded in 1972 'To preserve the identity of Muslim youth and overcome the problems they face in modern society ... [and] to introduce Islam to non-Muslims in its purest form as a comprehensive system and a way of life' (World Assembly of Muslim Youth 2004).

By the early 1970s, as noted before, JIH had already established links with Saudi Arabia and with Islamic organizations based there. WAMY was one of them. Amjad Panji,[6] a key WAMY leader and science professor, was given the responsibility to consolidate the newly formed assembly on a world scale. An experienced student activist, he was one of the key leaders to form the Muslim Student Association of the United States and Canada in 1963. In 1974, he visited India to participate in JIH's fifth all-India session held in Delhi. He was pleased to know that students were planning to form an independent organization of their own. Despite JIH's reservations, he supported its formation. Panji came in close contact with core student leaders based in Aligarh—Imran Khan, Ramiz Raja, Ijaz Akbar, and Rahmat Bedar—and he encouraged them to go ahead with their plan.[7] Emboldened by Panji's support and inspiration, they finally formed SIMI in Aligarh on 25 April 1977. Raja was elected as its interim president. Officially, the JIH leadership seemed unhappy about the formation of SIMI. As a matter of fact, the latter had defied the authority of the former by establishing an organization without waiting for its consent (for an account of this conflict, see Student Islamic Organization of India 1998; Salfi n.d.). In the end, it gave its cautious approval and also welcomed it. However, unofficially, many prominent JIH leaders not only supported it but were also at the forefront of its formation right from the beginning. Maulana Syed Hamid Ali, a central leader from UP, was one among several other leaders to play a crucial role in SIMI's formation.

Transnational Interactions Thicken

Let me now come back to the role Amjad Panji from the WAMY played in the formation of the SIMI. With his guidance and support, all four of SIMI's core leaders went abroad. Indeed, he arranged their trips in all respects. Khan and Bedar had been JIH members since before 1974. Raja became a member before his migration. Only Akbar was not a formal member, even though he grew up in a JIH family. His father had been one of the first to become a member and had also served as an *amir* of Aligarh town. Imran, Raja, and Akbar went to the United States, and Bedar, the eldest of them all, went to Saudi Arabia. In 1981, Raja, with a Masters degree in physics from AMU, went to the United States where he acquired both a Masters and a Ph.D., and where he has been teaching since 1987. Akbar too went to the United States to do a Ph.D. but, unlike

Raja, he did not complete it and returned to India to become a lecturer at AMU. Imran, the most active of the four and in more ways than one their leader, went to the United States to teach philosophy and Islam.[8]

Unlike his fellows, in 1978 Bedar went to Saudi Arabia and joined King Abdulaziz University where he taught until 2000. In 2001, he moved to the United States and joined a research centre. Considered as an influential leader-ideologue, he has been a member of the *markazi majlis-e-shoora* or Central Advisory Council (CAC), the highest decision-making body of JIH, since the mid-1960s. As one of the pioneers of Islamic economics (originally Maududi's idea), in the early 1980s the Saudi Arabian government awarded him the King Faisal Award. At present, he divides his time between Aligarh and the United States where his children and extended family are settled, Raja being his real nephew.

Three more JIH members from Aligarh followed Bedar to Saudi Arabia: Saqlain, Obaid Anwar, and Azhar Kamal. Born in a village of Jaunpaur (UP), Saqlain came into contact with JIH while he was a student at Allahabad University. In the early 1950s, he went to study Islam and Arabic at JIH's institute in Rampur, which had been set up for university students, *sanawi darsgah*. There he became its formal member. Later, he joined AMU as an economics lecturer. In 1977, he moved to King Abdulaziz University. Then, having taught there for 11 years, he returned to Aligarh where he is presently based. Regarded as one of the ideologues, he has been a member of JIH's CAC for over three decades.

A few years later Anwar followed Saqlain to Saudi Arabia and worked there for eight years. A native of Gorakhpur (UP), he was a supporter of the League and, recalling his school days, told me that a Hindu student had once proudly said 'Victory to India' (*jai hind*) to which he had replied by shouting 'Division of India' (*taqseem-e-hind*). Like Saqlain, he too went to Rampur's *sanawi darsgah* where he became a member. In Saudi Arabia, Anwar was also in charge—*zimmedar*—of JIH activities. Since a considerable number of its members were already there by the end of the 1970s, a loose organizational network had developed. Being a *zimmedar*, Anwar was responsible for arranging the visit to Saudi Arabia of JIH's then *amir*, Maulana Abul Lais Nadwi. Under WAMY's auspices, he booked him into a five-star hotel, but Anwar's employer, an Arab, remarked: 'I am afraid Nadwi will go mad in the five-star hotel'. Humiliated by this comment, Anwar proudly told me that he almost had a fight with his employer as a result of which he lost his job. This blatantly demeaning behaviour by an Arab was a total shock to him. It went against his almost mythical-sacred image of Saudi Arabia as the land of Islamic culture and of the Prophet Muhammad.[9]

Kamal was the last to leave for Saudi Arabia. With a Ph.D. from AMU, in 1970 he left for Harvard to study for a Masters in comparative religion. Later, he joined the Muhammad Bin Saud University in Riyadh where he worked for 10 years. While he was there, he served as the organizer, *nazim-e-aala*, of JIH members and workers. Though his children are settled in the United States, he himself is presently based in Aligarh.

Dinner as a Mobilization Technology

As shown in the preceding pages, in the 1970s the JIH's transnational links with Saudi Arabia had become quite thick. By the mid-1980s, it had begun to work there as a quasi unit. Its circle of members in the Gulf countries functioned directly under the supervision of JIH headquarters in New Delhi. However, since the royal regimes in Saudi Arabia and Kuwait do not permit any political congregation, the JIH had to devise new methods to enable it to work there. Since in neither Kuwait nor Saudi Arabia is it allowed to work among native citizens, it concentrates mainly on Indians, Muslim as well as Hindu. Moreover, much like Vishwa Hindu Parishad in the West (Van der Veer 2002), in the Gulf countries it functions more as a cultural and social body rather than as a political organization.

On a government invitation, Saba Karim, the secretary of JIH, went to Kuwait in May 2002. From there, he also went to the United Arab Emirates and Saudi Arabia. JIH members in Kuwait and Saudi Arabia wanted to organize a meeting in his honour. Describing the modes of their functioning in the two countries, he says:

> Unlike India we do not have freedom to politically organize ourselves in Kuwait and Saudi Arabia. Even ulema or Imams, leave alone ordinary citizens, do not have freedom there. Only those who have certificates issued by the governments can deliver sermons in mosques. JIH members, therefore, hold meetings in the form of dinner parties. This is quite possible as they are rich enough to book a hall and arrange for dinner. Members congregate or disperse individually to escape the gaze of secret agents of the government. They do not walk together in public places as a group. At dinner we talk about the work of *tahreek* [namely JIH]. This is how we work there. The Saudi government does not bother us as we confine our activities to Indian nationals only.

As is evident from the above-mentioned observation, a curious paradox characterizes JIH's relationship with Gulf countries, particularly Saudi Arabia. Saudi Arabia's puritan, anti-Sufism Islam, based on strict *sharia* and backed by petroleum dollars, goes well with its own version of Islam. But its denial of political freedom to Islamists and its justification of a monarchy (as opposed to a caliphate) at home marks a crucial parting of ways within the Saudi regime. Karim elaborates it as follows:

> The Saudi Arabian government is Islamic in so far as it is based on *sharia*. Its intention, however, is to maintain monarchy. And Islam stands for Caliphate, not monarchy. ... The Bhartiya Janata Party here [in India] boasts of being democratic but in reality it is communal and fascist. It wants to bring fascism through democracy. Likewise, the Saudi regime wants to perpetuate monarchy through Islam.

In the wake of the first Gulf War when the Saudi government cracked down on anti-American Islamists, including *ulema*, and imprisoned hundreds of them, JIH's position vis-à-vis the Saudi government became starker. Denouncing the government, it observed: 'Rulers in the guise of protecting holy places [meaning mosques in Mecca and Medina], building mosques and distributing copies of the holy Quran have been serving the idol of the age [the USA] and are thus snakes in the sleeves of the Muslim *ummah*' (Muhammad 1992: 16, author's translation from Urdu). It concluded emphatically and rather harshly: 'Anti-Islamic policies of the Saudi government so far commonly garbed in religious language have now become as clear as daylight' (Muhammad 1992: 17).

Iranian Revolution

Following the victory of the Iranian revolution in 1979, optimism among many JIH members, particularly young SIMI members, was unusually heightened. As Asghar Rashid, a retired SIMI member, told me, 'they had almost gone mad'. They began to believe that their cherished dream of an Islamic state/system had become a reality and that it would also pave the way for an Islamic revolution in India. No one really knew or cared to think about how it could succeed in India, but there was an all-pervasive magical enthusiasm among Islamists. Their excitement knew no bounds. A deep sense of joy and hope filled the air. They had finally found the model for which they had been struggling and preaching for decades. It provided them with a living example that was now mobilized to achieve two objectives at once. It would arouse Muslims steeped in ritualistic Islam and corrupt Sufi (read Hinduistic) practices for a larger and true cause of Islamic revolution. It would also silence its critics for good, especially communists, who were its main adversary (Ali 1980).

Enthusiasm for the revolution was not just one sided. Islamists from Iran visited India to mobilize support for their nascent revolution.

Ali Hasan, then a young Islamist and now a top functionary in the present government in Tehran, was deputed to spread the revolution's message and win public opinion in its favour in India. He came into contact with SIMI in Aligarh and elsewhere. Surprised but impressed by the unbounded joy among its members, he asked it to organize a demonstration in support of the revolution. SIMI members marched in the streets of Delhi and other big towns and cities in celebration. With two Islamists from Iran, it held a demonstration of tens of thousands in Aligarh (Salfi n.d.).

With SIMI/JIH essentially a Sunni movement, this was the first demonstration in support of the Shiite revolution in India. No other Muslim group supported it. The late Maulana Abul Hasan Ali Nadwi, rector of the prestigious Lucknow-based Nadwa seminary, described its impact on India as 'tragic' and Ayatollah Khomeini's writings as 'militating against the fundamental Sunni beliefs' (Nadwi 1984: 13). The Deoband ulema went a step further and called Khomeini's beliefs blasphemous (Nomani 1984; Alqasmi n.d.). Moreover, they accused Maududi and Pakistan's Jamaat of supporting Khomeini's Islam and hence described them as 'brothers' (Alqasmi n.d.). The minority Shiite Indian community's initial response was also one of abject rejection. It regarded the revolution as un-Islamic because it negated Shias' fundamental belief in the hidden Imam Mahdi who alone was entitled to establish Islamic government, not Khomeini, the leader of the revolution, on his behalf. In Iran too, the traditional clerics opposed Ayatollah Khomeini, describing his concept of *vilayat-e-faqih*, rule of the clergy, as violating true Islam (Chehabi 1991).

For SIMI/JIH, the revolution in itself was a cause for celebration and emulation; it mattered little if it violated the core doctrinal beliefs of Shias or Sunnis or both. It saw a ray of hope for Islam's political power hitherto eclipsed under communism's global appeal. 'If one country established an Islamic system', happily noted one of its pamphlets celebrating the revolution, 'its impact would spread throughout the world and our country [India] would not be an exception' (Ali 1980: 64). More importantly, it seemed to offer a short cut to its ultimate goal of establishing a caliphate in India. 'That country [India] would become the best means of Islam's introduction, which we cannot achieve by years of efforts through *madrasa*s, books, propagation and advice. Our social protection [preservation of Muslim personal law] is greatly dependent on the establishment of the Islamic system' (Ali 1980: 64, author's translation from Urdu). Given such a warm reception, it was not difficult for the Iranian Hasan to mobilize Islamists in Aligarh. Shabab Jauhar and Kahood Rasmi became the most radical supporters of the revolution. Others soon followed them. According to a former SIMI member and a contemporary of Jauhar and Kahood at Aligarh, they were 'firebrand types' and believed 'revolution should come now, like Charu Majumdar's communist revolution at gunpoint'.[10] On Hasan's invitation, Jauhar went to Tehran to participate in a conference. He made at least three more trips to Iran and stayed there for months. Nazim Ilyas, another SIMI leader, visited Iran as well.

The celebration of the Iranian revolution should not be seen in isolation. Rather, it should be seen in conjunction with two other developments in South Asia. The assassination of Zulfiqar Ali Bhutto and the Islamization drive by the Zia-ul-Haq regime in Pakistan had given immense hope to Islamists in India. JIH members had come to believe that the establishment of *nizam-e-mustafa* in Pakistan was approaching. Once successful, it would also have a positive impact on India (Ali 1980). The Afghan jihad against the Russian invasion further strengthened their belief in an immediate revolution. They saw an Islamic revolution coming to Afghanistan as well. In an Urdu poem—'Funeral of a Martyr'—extolling the Afghan *mujahedeen* fighting against the Russians, Syed Urooj Ahmad Qadri, a top JIH leader who also served as its acting *amir* in the mid-1970s, wrote: 'The head of arrogance [Russians] would be smashed with the stones of your mountain land [Afghanistan]/In your mountain land the flag of truth [Islam] would surely fly high' (Qadri 1982: 6, author's translation).

Islam against Islam

The new network that had been set up between SIMI and Islamists in Iran was not the only influence of the Iranian revolution on the SIMI. The greatest impact was *methodological*, a new means by which to inaugurate the desired revolution. For the first time in modern history, it presented a new path of revolution—quick and by force. Unlike the Muslim Brotherhood of Egypt or Jamaat-e-Islami in Pakistan, which envisaged revolution through gradual processes of social transformation via channels such as schools, hospitals, universities, and through distributing literature and influencing public opinion (on Pakistan's Jamaat-e-Islami's method see Nasr 1994b), the Iranian revolution was sudden and forceful. In India, JIH's model was also gradualist; it intended to introduce change by moulding public opinion through *dawat*. Frustrated and disillusioned with JIH's failure to achieve any major breakthrough, some SIMI members abandoned the gradualist model to embrace the Iranian one.

As a result, SIMI split into two ideological streams—the moderate-gradualist and the radical, which supported revolution along Iranian lines. The split went beyond the movement's headquarters at Aligarh. It spread throughout India where, by 1981, SIMI had 461 members and 10,000 sympathizers (Kirmani 1982: 116).[11] While the official JIH leadership still supported the gradualist approach, the split had caused the loss of the Saudi Arabian regime's trust. The radical students considered Saudi Arabia as an enemy of the revolution because it was anti-Iran and a friend of the United States, 'the greatest Satan'. For them, its adherence to *sharia* was merely eyewash.[12] Moreover, it ruthlessly suppressed the Islamists at home who sought to overthrow the monarchy and implant the caliphate. Money earned from Saudi Arabia, they decreed, was *haram*.

This is illustrated by an interesting episode. Arshad Ayub, a SIMI member, was then in charge of the International Islamic Federation of Student Organizations (IIFSO), which Saudi Arabia had founded in 1969 to coordinate worldwide student organizations fighting for an Islamic system. While away from Aligarh during the holy month of fasting, *ramazan*, he asked Jauhar to take care of his house. With friends Jauhar moved in. To do *sehri* (an Islamic injunction during *ramazan* at night), he once opened Ayub's fridge to take out meat and remarked: 'Though it is *haram* because it is bought from money earned in Saudi Arabia, we would still eat it'. Such was the hostility of radicals towards Saudi Arabia.

In a classic *volte-face* a few years later, by which time lust for money had dowsed the radical fire within Jauhar, he went to Saudi Arabia. He worked there for several years and returned to become a lecturer at AMU. Now he has his own house and has also bought a Maruti car. 'Ideology barely stands', Rashid told me confidently, 'the lure of money'. But it was not just Jauhar who compromised; most SIMI members of his generation did. They have happily become part of the same un-Islamic system—in India and in other Muslim countries—that they ruthlessly criticized in the past.

As well as dowsing the flames of radicalism, money also contributed to the radicalization of SIMI. With the rise of right-wing Hindu communalism from the late 1980s, SIMI grew militant. In the mid-1990s, it declared Indian secularism to be idolatry and exhorted Muslims to wage jihad for the establishment of a caliphate (Ahmad 1997). Many people within JIH and some ex-SIMI members trace this militancy back to the impact of the Iranian revolution[13] and the Afghans' jihad against the Russians. Disagreeing with SIMI's call for a jihad, a very old JIH member told me that it was absolutely un-Islamic. According to him, SIMI's call is not jihad but *fasad fil arz*, mischief on earth, an Islamic legal term used to describe un-Islamic violence. In his view, the reasons for SIMI's militancy lie not with active militants in India but with passive, fully compromised and opportunist ex-SIMI members abroad. The ex-SIMI members abroad, he continued, pump money into India and incite the unemployed, emotional (*jazbaati*) youth to violence. I asked him why they would do it unless they thought it was for Islam's cause.

> What Islam? To spread *fasad fil arz* is not Islamic. These people want to gain a name and be leaders (*chaudhri*) from the backdoor. That is the reason. It is they who financed SIMI with foreign money and incited it towards extremism (*tashaddud*). They are doing business in the name of Islam. Unfortunately, people have traded Islam right from the beginning, except during the age of the four rightly guided caliphs.

Dual Impact

In the preceding pages, I described how JIH and SIMI developed links with Islamists in Saudi Arabia, the United States, and Iran, and the consequent migration of their members to those countries. I also showed how such transnational connections transformed their policy and thinking, and created conflict within the movement. The most notable change has been, as discussed, the radicalization of the JIH movement, especially of its student wing, SIMI. In the following pages, I want to show that transnationalism not just resulted in the solitary process of radicalization but also set in motion the simultaneous process of moderation.

In 1941, when Maududi founded Jamaat-e-Islami, he appealed to Muslims that if they were true they should not participate in any capacity in an un-Islamic system. He described a modern educational institution like AMU as a 'slaughterhouse' (*qatlgah*) of Islam (Maududi 1991: 45). Likewise, secularism, democracy, a British-style judiciary, and other modern institutions were all idols, *taghoot*; any form of participation therein was simply *haram* (Maududi 1987, 1999). His position on women was also extremely harsh: they must be covered from top to toe (Maududi 1953). Given this ideology, most people who joined Maududi's party resigned their government jobs. As evidence, I have mentioned the example of Yusuf, JIH's *amir*, who regarded his job in the Indian judiciary as *haram* and, therefore, resigned from it to become JIH's member. Until the late 1950s, JIH members rarely sent their children to AMU for study. When in 1947, a student influenced by Maududi's writings asked the first *amir* of JIH, Maulana Abul Lais Islahi Nadwi, if he could study in AMU, he replied: 'My heart is so disturbed by the demerits of the present education system that I do not have the courage to give you permission to study there' (quoted in

Siddiqi 2000: 69, author's translation from Urdu). In line with Maududi's ideology, in the first two general elections of independent India held in 1951 and 1956, JIH therefore asked Muslims in general and its members in particular not to commit sin by casting their votes in the elections. Electing people to parliament to legislate laws based on human reason as opposed to *sharia* was like worshipping idols (Maududi 1999; Nadwi 1951a). On the eve of the first parliamentary elections of independent India, the president of JIH said:

> A Muslim believes in the *sovereignty of Allah* that, among others, is the straight and foremost demand of his fundamental *kalimah* [an Arabic phrase uttered as a declaration to become a Muslim]. And it is an open matter that the entire hullabaloo about election is the spectacle (*tamaashaa*) of *sovereignty of man* whose relation, howsoever stretched, in no way can be linked with the sovereignty of Allah.
>
> (Nadwi 1951b: 63; italics added, author's translation from Urdu)

Then he strongly warned Muslims in the following words: 'If you go into details, you will realize that in whatever form you participate in elections, you are flouting the commandments and guidance of *sharia* at every step' (Nadwi 1951b: 63). Based on this logic, JIH boycotted the first two parliamentary elections. At the beginning of the 1960s, however, a fierce debate began within its top leadership about how long it could keep the party and movement aloof from elections. Should it not reconsider its position on secularism and democracy in the specific situation of India? A variety of factors pushed JIH to reconsider its position. The most important one, I think, was the fact that the Muslim masses not only rejected JIH's position but, as Krishna's (1967) study shows, they also enthusiastically participated in elections.

Towards Moderation

For 25 long years, JIH debated the issue of participation in elections. Finally, in 1985, its CAC decided that in India Muslims should not only participate in elections and accept secularism, but also guard against the onslaught on secularism by Hindu communal forces led by the BJP and the Rashtriya Swayamsewak Sangh (*Rudaad Majlis-e-Shoora* 1989). The debate on secularism and elections created a vertical division within JIH. The majority of its members stuck to the original position outlined by Maududi. A small minority called for a revision of old policy in the light of the changed situation in post-partition India. It eventually won against the majority view. Among the core leaders of the minority group were three members from Aligarh—Bedar, Kamal, and Saqlain—who had spent years in Saudi Arabia or the United States; the children of the first two are settled in the United States.

It would be misleading to say that they alone were responsible for the shift in JIH's ideology. More importantly, it is necessary to understand how the decision was made. Melucci (1996) argues that if movement leaders anticipate that a given decision is likely to spark dangerous internal conflicts, they try to buy as much time as possible before making it. Further, the decision mechanism is greatly depersonalized. In the case of JIH, we see both these factors at work. The decision to allow its members to participate in elections took more than 25 years. And when taken, not individual leaders but its executive body, the CAC, was *officially* held responsible. Unofficially, however, the three leaders see themselves as pioneers of change.

The details of how these three JIH leaders prevailed on the majority view is a rather complex story that I do not wish to tell here. Suffice it to note that they see themselves as harbingers of change. Their opponents too hold the same view. They accuse the trio of diverting the JIH from its original true line. They sarcastically call them 'electionists' and 'secularists'. Lamenting deviation from the original ideas of Maududi at the hands of these three leaders, a purist JIH member (and former Naxalite) told me:

> Yes, they are the ones who have betrayed Maulana Maududi and Islam. They say that those who are from *madrasa* do not understand the challenges of modern life. Islam needs to be interpreted in a new light. But I am not convinced. They are not serving Islam. As a matter of fact, they are cowards. The rejection of secularism and democracy, as Islam actually demands of us, means inviting the wrath of government. They are not prepared to do this. They do not want to go to jail or make sacrifices for Islam. How can they? Look at their houses! They have sprawling bungalows. They live in air-conditioned rooms. Mr ... also has a swimming pool. Their children are well settled. Having amassed wealth from Saudi Arabia and America, they want to preserve it. How can they speak for true Islam? That is why they say that we ought to accept secularism and democracy.

Conclusion

Before he became India's president, Zakir Hussain asked Husnain Syed, a member of JIH, if Maududi had ever said he was against Pakistan's creation. Syed's reply was revealing: 'He might have said it. However, Jamaat-e-Islami wants to establish Allah's kingdom on the entire earth. ... As Muslim, each country is ours, Allah's country is ours' (Syed 1997: 17). Syed's remarks, which were made in 1957, invoke transnationalism long before it became a buzzword. In this chapter, I have shown the need to study Islamist movements such as the JIH beyond the specifics of the nation-state and take into account their transnational dimensions. While arguing this case, I have made two points. First, I have shown why JIH's transnational links qualify it as a transnational social movement. In doing so, I have demonstrated the limitations and assumptions of social movement theories based as they are on the experiences of Western democracies. Further, I have argued why the theorization of social movements has excluded the dynamics of collective action in Muslim-majority societies, which are mostly undemocratic. A major reason for the exclusion has been the assumption that Muslim societies are not secular and lack 'modernity'; they therefore could at best have mutiny or rebellion but not the social movements that are the gift of modernity. I have, therefore, called for a broadening of theories to include the forms of collective action in poiities such as those of the Gulf and Iran that do not legitimize open mobilizations.

Second, I have demonstrated the fallacy of the alarmist thesis that holds that transnational ties between Islamist movements of two or more nation-states always and necessarily lead to their radicalization. While we must pay attention to the transnational dimensions of such movements, we should not fall prey to the grossly misleading views of Pipes, Lewis, and Huntington who claim that the outcome of transnational Islamist movements is their inevitable radicalization. Based on the ethnographic study of JIH and the SIMI, I have argued that their transnational interactions with Islamists in the Gulf countries, Iran, and the West did not simply spark their radicalization. While SIMI became radicalized, JIH underwent an immensely significant process of moderation as well. Moreover, there also ensued serious conflict within the movement as a result of which there was a fierce debate on what was true Islam. It continues to be important to study empirically the multidimensional outcomes of the transnationalism of specific Islamist movements before rushing into sweeping generalizations, which, like those of Pipes, Lewis, and Huntington, assert radicalization as their only outcome.

Acknowledgements

The author is thankful to Alisdair Rogers, editor of *Global Networks*, and two anonymous referees for their criticism and suggestions on this paper. The author would like to express his gratitude to Peter Van der Veer for his insightful comments on an earlier draft. The author is also thankful to Martin Van Bruinessen and Thomas Blom Hansen for their detailed criticism of several points in a previous version of the paper.

Bhaiya, Barak Kalir, Francio Guadeloupe, and Lotte Hoek have given useful suggestions. The author is thankful to them all. Finally, the author thanks the Netherlands Organization for Scientific Research for financially supporting his second fieldwork trip.

Notes

1. By Islamist, following Roy (1994) and Fuller (2003), I mean an activist who regards Islam as a complete system of life and believes in establishing an Islamic state as a foremost duty.
2. Their suspicion of me, I believe, was not entirely unfounded. The timing of my field work coincided with enquiries by government officials about JIH in general and SIMI in particular.
3. On some aspects of this conspiracy theory, see Ahmad (2004).
4. I do not want to be misunderstood as advocating a perennial difference between East and West as for instance, Chatterjee (1997) seems to suggest in a different context.
5. Maududi uses terms such as caliphate, Islamic government, Islamic revolution, Islamic system, and Allah's government interchangeably.
6. The names of all the informants, including this one, have been changed to ensure their anonymity.
7. The student wing of the Pakistani Jamaat was greatly influenced by the Muslim Brotherhood of Egypt. Said Ramazan, a Brotherhood member, had a tremendous impact on it. See Nasr (1994a).
8. For Jammat-e-Islami's network in the United States, see Mohammad-Arif's fascinating study (2002). It needs to be added that she deals more with the Jamaat-e-Islami of Pakistan than with that of India. See also, Kepel (1997). For Pakistani Jamaat's network and influence in United Kingdom, see Lewis (1994).
9. Hansen (2001) has shown beautifully how this mythical image that Indian Muslims have of Arab Muslims gets shockingly bulldozed during their daily interactions with them as immigrants in the Gulf.
10. The person quoted is a Muslim from West Bengal where under Charu Majumdar's leadership Naxalites, inspired by Mao Zedong, waged an armed struggle to bring about revolution in the late 1960s. In conversation with me, he would always compare Islamists of SIMI/JIH with the communists.
11. At that time, SIMI had two levels of membership. The fully committed and dedicated ones were called *ansars* and those below them were known as *members*.
12. An AMU, student of the puritan *ahl-e-hadis* sect told me that Saudi Arabia had the only Islamic government in the whole world. He dismissed Iran because Shias, to him, were not true Muslims.

13. After the Iranian revolution, Imtiaz Ahmed offered a thesis of 'unresponsiveness' in which he argued that Indian Muslims had remained 'totally untouched' by it (Ahmed 1980: 24). Based on a series of assumptions, the thesis lacked evidence. For instance, it did not even refer to the response of SIMI.

References

Ahmad, I. (1997) 'A new agenda for Muslim radicals' [Editorial page], *The Times of India*, New Delhi, 1 April.

Ahmad, I. (1998) *The Making of an Islamic Society in Post-independent India: A Study of the Jamaat-e-Islami Hind*, M.Phil dissertation, Jawaharlal Nehru University, New Delhi.

Ahmad, I. (1999) 'RSS versus the Jamaat', *World Focus*, 20(4), 16–19.

Ahmad, I. (2004) 'The Jewish hand: the response of the Jamaat-e-Islami Hind', in Van der Veer, P., and Munshi, S. (eds.) *Media, War and Terrorism*. London: Routledge Curzon, 137–54.

Ahmed, I. (1980) 'India: surprising isolation', *World Focus*, 1(5), 23–26.

Ali, S. (1980) *Islami Inquilab, mukhalif quwaten aur Musalman* [Islamic revolution, oppositional forces and Muslims]. Delhi: Markazi Maktaba Islami.

Alqasmi, S.A.S. (n.d.) *Do bhai: Abul Ala Maududi aur Imam Khomeini* [Two brothers: Abul Ala Maududi and Imam Khomeini]. Deoband: Shaikhul Islam Academy.

Altbach, P.G. (ed.) (1968) *Turmoil and Transition: Higher Education and Student Politics in India*. Bombay: Lalvani.

Altbach, P.G. (1966) 'The transformation of the Indian student movement', *Asian Survey*, 6, 448–60.

Aminzade, R., and Perry, E.J., Jr. (2001) 'The sacred, religious and secular in contentious politics: blurring boundaries', in Aminzade, R.A., Goldstone, J.A., McAdam, D., Perry, E.J., Jr., Sewell, W.H., Tarrow, S., and Tilly, C. (eds.) *Silence and Voice in the Study of Contentious Politics*. Cambridge: Cambridge University Press 155–78.

Bahadur, K. (1977) *The Jamaat-e-Islami of Pakistan*. Delhi: Chetna.

Bari, S.A. (2001) *Aazaad Hindustan me Muslim tanzeemen* [Muslim organizations in independent India]. New Delhi: Institute of Objective Studies.

Barker, C., Johnson, A., and Lavalette, M. (2001) 'Leadership matters: an introduction', in Barker, C., Johnson, A., and Lavalette, M. (eds.) *Leadership and Social Movement*. Manchester: Manchester University Press, 1–23.

Benítez-Rojo, A. (1996) *The Repeating Islands: The Caribbean and the Postmodern Perspectives* (2nd ed.). Durham: Duke University Press.

Binder, L. (1963) *Religion and Politics in Pakistan*. Berkeley: University of California Press.

Brass, P.R. (2003) *The Production of Hindu–Muslim Violence in Contemporary India*. Seattle/London: University of Washington Press.

Chatterjee, P. (1997) *Our Modernity* [Lecture no. 1]. Rotterdam: CEPHIS-CODESRIA.

Chehabi, H.E. (1991) 'Religion and politics in Iran: how theocratic is the Islamic republic', *Daedalus*, summer, 120, 69–91.

Dastoor-e-Jamaat-e-Islami (the constitution of the Jamaat-e-Islami) (n.d.) Rampur State UP: Maktaba Jamaat-e-Islami Hind.

Fuller, G.E. (2003) *The Future of Political Islam*. New York: Palgrave Macmillan.

Graff, V. (1990) 'Aligarh's long quest for "minority" status: AMU (amendment) Act, 1981', *Economic and Political Weekly*, 11, 1771–81.

Guidry, J.A., Kennedy, M.D., and Zald, M.N. (2000) 'Introduction', in Guidry, J.A., Kennedy, M.D., and Zald, M.N. (eds.) *Globalization and Social Movements: Culture, Power and the Transnational Public Sphere*. Ann Arbor, MI: Michigan University Press, 1–32.

Halliday, F. (1984) 'Labour migration in the Arab world', *Merip Report*, May, 3–10, 30.

Hansen, T.B. (2001) 'Bridging the Gulf: global horizons, mobility and local identity among Muslims in Mumbai', in Bates, C. (ed.) *Community, Empire and Migration: South Asians in Diaspora*. London: Palgrave, 261–85.

Hasan, M. (1979) *Nationalism and Communal Politics in India, 1916–1928*. New Delhi: Manohar.

Hindustan Times (2001) *Six Sedition Cases against SIMI Members*. www.hindustantimes.com/nonfram/290901/detcit06.asp.

Huntington, S.P. (1997) *The Clash of Civilizations and the Remaking of World Order*. London: Touchstone Books.

Islamic Voice (1998) *Fiqh Council Approves Genetic Engg. for Cures*'. www.islamicvoice.com/december.98/news.htm.

Jain, R.K. (1993) *Indian Communities Abroad*. New Delhi: Manohar.

Jalal, A. (1994) *The Sole Spokesman: Jinnah, the Muslim League and the Demand for Pakistan*. Cambridge: Cambridge University Press.

Jasper, J.M. (1997) *The Art of Moral Protest*. Chicago: Chicago University Press.

Jayaram, N. (1989) 'India', in Altbach, P.G. (ed.) *Student Political Activism: An International Reference Handbook*. New York: Greenwood Press, 91–101.

Kepel, G. (1997) *Allah in the West: Islamic Movements in America and Europe* (translated by Susan Milner). Cambridge: Polity Press.

Kirmani, Z. (1982) 'Student Islamic movement', *Dawat*, 14 April, 115–21.

Krishna, G. (1967) 'Electoral participation and political integration', *Economic and Political Weekly*, February, 179–90.

Kurzman, C. (2003) 'The poststructuralist consensus in social movement theory', in Goodwin, J., and Jasper, J.M. (eds.) *Rethinking Social Movements*. Lanham, MD: Rowman & Littlefield, 111–20.

Kurzman, C. (2004) 'Conclusion', in Wiktorowicz, Q. (ed.) *Islamic Activism: A Social Movement Theory Approach*. Bloomington: Indiana University Press, 289–303.

Lewis, B. (2003) *The Crisis of Islam*. London: Weidenfeld & Nicolson.

Lewis, P. (1994) *Islamic Britain: Religion, Politics and Identity among British Muslims*. London/New York: I.B. Tauris.

Lichterman, P. (1998) 'What do movements mean? The value of participant observation', *Qualitative Sociology*, 21, 401–18.

Madhavan, M.C. (1985) 'Indian immigrants: numbers, characteristics and economic impact', *Population and Development Review*, 11, 457–81.

Madni, S.A. (n.d.) *Jang-e-azadi me Jamiatul Ulma-e-Hind ki khidmaat* [Contributions of Jamiatul Ulma-e-Hind in the independence struggle]. New Delhi: Publicity Division of Jamiatul Ulma-e-Hind.

Marcus, G.E. (1995) 'Ethnography in/of the world system: the emergence of multi-sited ethnography', *Annual Review of Anthropology*, 24, 95–117.

Masud, M.K. (ed.) (2000) *Travellers in Faith: Studies of Tablighi Jamaat as a Transnational Islamic Movement for Faith Renewal*. Leiden: Brill.

Maududi, S.A.A. (1942) *Musalman aur maujudah seyasi kasmakash* [Muslims and the present political predicament], Vol. 3, Pathankot: Daftar Resala Tarjumanul Quran.

Maududi, S.A.A. (1953) *Purdah* [The veil]. New Delhi: Markazi Maktaba Islami.

Maududi, S.A.A. (1987) *Tahrik-e-azadi-e-Hind aur Muslamaan* [Indian independence struggle and Muslims] (edited and compiled by Khurshid Ahmad). Lahore: Islamic Publications.

Maududi, S.A.A. (1991) *Talimaat* [Education] (revised edn.). Delhi: Markazi Maktaba Islami.

Maududi, S.A.A. (1996) *Khutba-e-Madras* [The Madras address]. Delhi: Markazi Maktaba Islami.

Maududi, S.A.A. (1999) *Rasaael wo masaael* [Queries and responses], Vol. 1. New Delhi: Markazi Maktaba Islami.

Mejcher, H. (2004) 'King Faisal Ibn Abdul Aziz Al Saud in the arena of world politics: a glimpse from Washington, 1950 to 1971', *British Journal of Middle Eastern Studies*, 31, 5–23.

Melucci, A. (1996) *Challenging Codes: Collective Action in the Information Age*. Cambridge: Cambridge University Press.

Mohammad-Arif, A. (2002) *Salam America: South Asian Muslims in New York*. London: Anthem Press.

Muhammad, A. (1992) 'Saudi Arab me Ulema-e-Haq ki azeem jidd-o-jihed' [The great struggle of righteous ulema in Saudi Arab], *Rafiq-e-manzil*, July, 16–18.

Nadwi, A.H.A. (1984) 'Preface', in Nomani, M.M. (ed.) *Irani inquilab, Imam Khomeini aur Shiiat* [Iranian revolution, Imam Khomeini and Shiism], Lucknow: Al-Furqan Book Depot, 9–18.

Nadwi, A.L.I. (1951a) 'Esharaat' [Indications], *Zindgi*. January, 2–11.

Nadwi, A.L.I. (1951b) *Masla-e-intikhabaat aur musalmanan-e-hind* [The issue of elections and Indian Muslims]. Rampur: Maktaba Jamaat-e-Islami Hind.

Nasr, S.V.R. (1992) 'Students, Islam and politics: Islami Jamiat-e-Talba in Pakistan', *Middle East Journal*, 46, 59–76.

Nasr, S.V.R. (1994a) *The Vanguard of Islamic Revolution: the Jamaat-e-Islami of Pakistan*. Berkeley: University of California Press.

Nasr, S.V.R. (1994b) 'Maududi and the Jamaat-e-Islami: the origin, theory and practice of Islamic revivalism', in Rahnema, A. (ed.) *Pioneers of Islamic revival*. London: Zed Books, 98–124.

Nayyar, D. (1994) *Migration, Remittances and Capital Flows: The Indian Experiences*. Delhi: Oxford University Press.

Nomani, M.M. (1984) *Irani inquilab, Imam Khomeini aur Shiiat* [Iranian revolution, Imam Khomeini and Shiism]. Lucknow: Al-Furqan Book Depot.

Oommen, T.K. (1974) 'Student politics in India: the case of Delhi university', *Asian Survey*, 14, 777–94.

Oommen, T.K. (1995) *Alien Concepts and South Asian reality*. New Delhi: Sage.

Palmié, S. (2002) *Wizards and Scientists: Exploration in Afro-Cuban Modernity and Tradition*. Durham: Duke University Press.

Pipes, D. (2001) 'The danger within: militant Islam in America', *Commentary*, November, 19–24.

Qadri, M.S.A.U. (1982) 'Ek shaheed ka janaaza' [Funeral of a martyr], *Rafiq*, February–March, 6.

Roy, O. (1994) *The Failure of Political Islam* (translated by Carol Volk). London: I.B. Tauris.

Rudaad Majlis-e-Shoora, Jamaat-e-Islami Hind [Proceedings of Jamaat-e-Islami Hind's central advisory council] (1989). Delhi: Organizational department, Jamaat-e-Islami Hind.

Rudolph, L.I. et al. (1971) 'Student politics and national politics in India', *Economic and Political Weekly*, July, special number, 1655–68.

Salfi, A. (n.d.) *Aks-e-raah* [Shadow of the path]. New Delhi: Department of Organization, Student Islamic Movement of India.

Shah, G. (1991) *Social Movement in India: A review of Literature*. Delhi: Sage.

Siddiqi, M.N. (2000) *Islam, maashiaat aur adab: khutoot ke aaine me* [Islam, economics and literature: in the light of letters]. Aligarh: Educational Book House.

Sisson, R., and Wolpert, S. (eds.) (1988) *Congress and Indian Nationalism: The Pre-independence Phase*. Berkeley: University of California Press.

Smith, C.S. (1996) 'Correcting a curious neglect, or bringing religion back', in Smith, C.S. (ed.) *Disruptive Religion: The Force of Faith in Social Movement Activism*. New York: Routledge, 1–28.

Student Islamic Organization of India (1998) *SIO mannzil ba manzil*. New Delhi: Management Division, Student Islamic Organization of India.

Syed, H. (1997) *Mere teen mohseneen* [My three benefactors]. New Delhi: Milli Times International.

Tarrow, S. (1994) *Power in Movement*, Cambridge: Cambridge University Press.

Tarrow, S. (1999) *Power in Movement* (2nd ed.). Cambridge: Cambridge University Press.

Tarrow, S. (2003) 'Confessions of a recovering structuralist', *Mobilization*, 8(1), 135–41.

Tilly, C. (1984) 'Social movement and national politics', in Bright, C., and Harding, S (eds) *State Making and Social Movements*. Ann Arbor: University of Michigan Press, 297–317.

Tilly, C. (2002) *Stories, Identities and Political Change*. Lanham, MD: Rowman & Littlefield.

Van der Veer, P. (2002) 'Transnational religion: Hindu and Muslim movements', *Global Networks*, 2, 95–111.

Vertovec, S. (1999) 'Conceiving and researching transnationalism', *Ethnic and Racial Studies*, 22, 447–62.

Vishwa Y.K. (1973) *The Dynamics of Student Agitations*. Bombay: Somaya Publications.

Weiner, M. (1982) 'International migration and development: Indians in the Persian Gulf', *Population and Development Review*, 8, 1–36.

World Assembly of Muslim Youth (2004) *Our Aims*. www.wamy.co.uk.

12

Globalizing Hinduism

A 'Traditional' Guru and Modern Businessmen in Chennai

C.J. Fuller and John Harriss

> Affirming the Sanatana Dharma and Recording the History of a Billion-Strong Global Religion in Renaissance.[1]

> *The need for cultural revival in India is the need of the hour.* How are we to hand over our cultural values to our next generation when westernization is the current trend via the media, social and peer pressures [sic]. The Indian cultural forms will disappear from this nation if its constituent elements are not understood and imbibed by our next generation.[2]

The first of the two epigraphs mentioned at the beginning of this chapter is the masthead on the website of *Hinduism Today*, a magazine published in Hawaii since 1979, which enjoys a wide readership among overseas Hindus, especially in the United States. Using the standard modern phrase *sanatana dharma* or 'eternal religion' to refer to Hinduism, the epigraph is a striking example of how Hinduism may be proclaimed as a genuine global or world religion, flourishing as never before. The second epigraph comes from the website of a religious trust in Chennai (Madras) and it announces the *Vedic Heritage Teaching Programme (VHTP)*, which was designed in America but is also being promoted in India. The epigraph, which equates 'Indian' culture with the ostensibly Vedic Hindu religious tradition, expresses a profound anxiety that westernization may soon lead to its extinction.

Optimistic confidence about global Hinduism and pessimistic concern about Hindu Indian culture are obviously antithetical. Nevertheless, they belong to the same discourse of globalized Hinduism and highlight a crucial ambiguity that runs through it. This ambiguity is at the heart of our discussion, which focuses particularly on Swami Dayananda Saraswati, a Hindu holy man and patron of the *VHTP who* is popular among modern big businessmen in Chennai.[3]

The Chennai businessmen belong to the upper managerial-professional segment of the middle class. As Satish Deshpande comments, 'much of the celebratory rhetoric about globalization emanates from, and is aimed at, this group' (2003: 150). Indeed, we argue, there now exists a new, globalized upper-middle-class made up of 'non-resident Indians' or NRIs, together with prosperous Indians in India, mostly resident in major cities, whose work, education, and lifestyle link them closely to their relatives, colleagues, friends, and other associates in the NRI population. Many of these Indians also travel abroad frequently or have returned home after several years working overseas. The NRI category emerged in the early 1970s (Rajagopal 2001: 241–2); in America, and to a lesser extent in Britain and some other countries, NRIs have become one of the most prosperous, professionally successful, and best-educated of all ethnic minorities.

In statistical terms, the NRI population has made only a small difference to Hinduism's worldwide distribution because the overwhelming majority of Hindus still live in India. Financially and ideologically, however, the NRIs' impact has been far more decisive. The powerful Hindu nationalist organization known as the Vishwa Hindu Parishad (VHP) or World Hindu Council was founded in India in 1964, and the VHP of America was active by 1969 (Rajagopal 2001: 239). The rise of Hindu nationalism is a vital element in the contemporary development of overseas Hinduism and vice versa (Bénéï 1998), but it is not the whole story and in its earlier years, especially in America, the VHP was not a stridently political organization. Moreover, one key point is that the VHP's name—even to many Hindus who do not support the organization is a sign of a new truth: the emergence of a global diaspora whose Hinduism is a world religion on equal terms with Christianity or Islam. This idea is expressed on the masthead of *Hinduism Today's* website.

Easily accessible from *Hinduism Today's* website is a directory of 'saints, sages, swamis and satgurus', 'divine mothers', and Hindu religious organizations (ashrams, monasteries, teaching centres, etc.).[4] In this directory are many religious personages who live and work outside India or are based both in India and overseas, notably in the United States. Since Swami Vivekananda's famous visit to Chicago in 1893, travelling holy men have been a familiar phenomenon, but in the last two or three decades they have flourished as never before and they are key agents in the process of globalizing Hinduism. One of them is Swami Dayananda Saraswati.

Swami Dayananda Saraswati and His Activities

Swami Dayananda Saraswati (who is not to be confused with his namesake, the founder of the Arya Samaj) was born in 1930 in a village in Thanjavur District, Tamil Nadu.[5] He was his Smarta Brahman parents' second son and was named Natarajan; his father died when he was young, so he was mainly brought up by his mother. As a schoolboy, Natarajan reacted vigorously to the anti-Hindu and anti-Brahman Dravida Kazhagam movement, and in his own eyes, his experience as a young Brahman defending himself and his religion against overwhelming hostility had a formative influence on his life. After finishing school, the young Natarajan went to Madras to find work, like so many other rural Brahmans in the 1940s. He trained as a stenographer and taught himself English, worked for a Hindu magazine, which sought to combat the Dravidian movement's publications, served for a short time in the Indian Air Force, and finally became a typist in a large company.

In 1952, Natarajan went to hear Swami Chinmayananda lecturing at a *jnana-yajna* ('knowledge-sacrifice') session in Madras. Chinmayananda was the leading disciple of Swami Shivananda, founder of the Divine Life Society, and his lecture tours attracted large crowds across India in the 1950s. Chinmayananda's aim was apparently to 'convert Hindus to Hinduism', especially the 'faithless' educated class (McKean 1996: 178). Natarajan's life was transformed by Chinmayananda's teaching; he volunteered to work for him and started learning the Veda, and in 1953 he became the secretary of the newly founded Chinmaya Mission. He later gave up his typing job and also resisted his mother's attempts to find him a wife. In 1962, Chinmayananda suddenly initiated Natarajan as a sannyasi, an ascetic renouncer, a transformation that seemed natural to him but caused his mother and brothers great distress. Swami Dayananda was presumably given his new name at this time.

In 1963, Chinmayananda asked Dayananda to teach in Sandeepany Sadhanalaya, the Mission's centre in Bombay (now Mumbai). After about a year, however, Dayananda left Bombay and eventually arrived in Rishikesh, the famous North Indian pilgrimage centre at the head of the River Ganges. He stayed there for 3 years, concentrating on his religious studies and living in a hut that is now the site of his Rishikesh ashram. In 1964, Chinmayananda presided over the foundation of the VHP in Sandeepany Sadhanalaya, and in 1966 the

VHP held its first World Hindu Conference at the great Kumbha Mela festival in Allahabad, when Dayananda was reunited with Chinmayananda. Dayananda rejoined the Chinmaya Mission in 1967; he continued with Mission work and the *jnana-yajna* tours for 5 years, until he returned to teach in the Bombay centre in 1972.[6]

A few years later, Dayananda replaced Chinmayananda on a lecture tour to the United States, and after his third visit there, he was invited mainly by his American followers to teach a course on Hinduism in California. By 1982, Dayananda was working independently of the Chinmaya Mission and making repeated visits to America. In 1927, he began to teach in a new centre in Saylorsburg, Pennsylvania, founded by a combination of US and NRI devotees. In India, two centres for residential teaching were established—in Rishikesh (built in its modern form in the 1980s) and Coimbatore (1990), and throughout the country Dayananda and other swamis, who are his disciples, now give regular lectures and courses to both adults and children. In practice if not in name, Dayananda now heads an established Hindu mission, similar to the Chinmaya Mission or the Divine Life Society, which has its own teaching-centres-cum-ashrams in India and the United States, as well as other educational programmes; a growing cohort (more than 250 worldwide) of sannyasis and other former students who spread their guru's teachings, which are also reproduced in a steady output of publications; a large following of mainly middle-class supporters and disciples in both India and America, whose donations provide substantial financial support; and, last but not least, several promotional websites. In Chennai, the Sastraprakasika Trust supports and publicizes Dayananda's activities, and sells publications and tapes through its well-organized website. Separate websites are run by the centres in Rishikesh and Saylorsburg, and the Center for Traditional Vedanta set up in the United States under Dayananda's patronage.[7]

In every context, Dayananda is styled as a 'traditional teacher of Brahma Vidya or Advaita Vedanta', and his teaching centres are specifically said to be designed for the 'traditional teaching of Vedanta and Sanskrit'. The archaic name of the Saylorsburg and Coimbatore centres—Arsha Vidya Gurukulam—also pointedly emphasizes traditional teaching by a guru of the knowledge (*vidya*) deriving from the ancient sages (*rishi*). Seen in comparative perspective, however, Dayananda is a quintessentially modern guru, who teaches in English—although some of his fellow swamis do teach in Indian languages—and has a middle-class following in India and America, just like his own guru Chinmayananda (van der Veer 1994: 136–7).

In its essentials, Dayananda's teaching is also typical of contemporary Vedantic Hinduism or neo-Vedanta: it is monistic, being premised on the individual soul's identity with the Supreme Being, and it insists on the primacy of the Veda as the source of the 'eternal' *sanatana dharma* from which all religions later developed—not only Hinduism but other faiths such as Christianity and Islam as well. The Veda is also the foundation of Indian culture and society. Dayananda's apparent intention, however, is to distinguish himself from other Hindu holy men as above all else a traditional teacher, who is specifically committed to the value of Sanskrit. The Saylorsburg website, for instance, describes him as an 'outstanding teacher of the Brahma Vidya ... not a preacher giving sermons, nor is he a missionary trying to spread a particular belief. Also he is not a mystic promising subjective experiences'. Compared with the Shankaracharya of Kanchipuram, the most prominent and influential religious leaders in Tamil Nadu (Fuller 1999: 47–51)—or their rivals, the Shankaracharya of Sringeri—Dayananda can communicate with English-speaking, middle-class Indians much more directly, but like them, he is a Brahman renouncer who stands for tradition and orthodoxy. He thereby distances himself, too, from popular, non-Brahman religious cults in Tamil Nadu, like that of the goddess Parashakti and her 'god-man' Bangaru Adigalar of Melmaruvathur. Dayananda is also very different from eclectic god-men like the immensely popular, miracle-working Sathya Sai Baba or fashionable gurus like Sri Sri Ravi Shankar, who promotes his 'Art of living' from an American base but attracts a middle-class following in Chennai.[8]

In recent years, Dayananda has hardened his support for the VHP and the Hindu nationalist movement. Thus in 2002, when the controversy over Rama's temple in Ayodhya erupted again, Dayananda—then president of the Hindu Dharma Rakshana Samiti (Hindu Religion Protection Society)—was reported to have 'thundered at a public meeting' in Chennai that building the temple is a non-negotiable matter and Muslim leaders must 'yield to the majority' so that *dharma* can be reasserted in India.[9] Dayananda has also been persistently aggressive towards Christianity in his lectures, and he supported the Tamil Nadu government's controversial ordinance banning 'forcible' conversions, which was issued in 2002.[10] Dayananda has taken a leading role in the activities of the VHP of America, which sponsored the first Dharma Sansad, a meeting of Hindu religious leaders in the United States, at Saylorsburg in August 1998, and a year later he was one of four prominent swamis advertised as leaders of a 'whirlwind' pilgrimage from

Los Angeles to New York to promote Hindu *dharma* across the United States (although later reports imply that he did not actually take part).[11]

The activities pursued by Dayananda or given his patronage are extensive, and his disciples and followers in India and the United States—men and women, adults and children, domiciled Indians, NRIs, and white Americans—have diverse backgrounds, outlooks, and interests, even if they are all broadly middle class. About most of them, however, we lack detailed data, and this chapter instead focuses on the men, who count themselves as Dayananda's followers, running large or successful modern businesses in Chennai. A principal question to be explored is how and why there is apparently an elective affinity between Dayananda's teaching and the businessmen's socio-economic values and interests. To answer this question, we look at some aspects of the businessmen's religious beliefs and practices, and Dayananda's activities in Chennai, before examining the kind of Hinduism that he is promulgating.

Chennai Businessmen and Their Religion

Our evidence comes from interviews conducted in 2000 by John Harriss with 40 big businessmen in Chennai. This group included the chairmen or managing directors of Chennai-based firms listed in *The Economic Times*' rankings of the Top 500 Indian companies, as well as entrepreneurs in the city's rapidly developing software industry. Harriss's aim was to replicate Milton Singer's research, carried out in 1964 in Madras and described in his book, *When a Great Tradition Modernizes* (1972).[12]

Singer interviewed several men described as 'the industrial leaders of Madras' about their religious beliefs and practices, and he says that in general they conformed with the self-description given by one of them: 'a fellow who is not an orthodox Hindu but who believes in the essential tenets of Hinduism'. Singer characterized their religion as an 'industrial theodicy', in which beliefs and ethics were emphasized (Singer 1972: 342):

> In this sense, the effect of industry is to change the traditional conception of the essentials of Hinduism from an emphasis on correct ritual observances and family disciplines to an emphasis on philosophical principles, devotional faith and right conduct.

According to Singer, the 'main difference among the [Hindu industrialists] is between those who have been influenced by Gandhi's reinterpretation of the *Bhagavad Gita* and other scriptures'—mostly through the idea that modern work can be a moral duty and 'sacrifice'—'and those who are influenced by the more traditional gurus and teachers' (1972: 340), notably the Shankaracharyas of Kanchipuram and Sringeri. The businessmen, we are also told, viewed their success 'as a product of devotion to their calling and duty' and their 'careers as one path to salvation', so that their own and their companies' prosperity are 'expressions of divine will'; these opinions are endorsed by 'spiritual advisors' and 'pandits' (1972: 352–3). Among the businessmen, about half of whom were Brahmans (1972: 284), Singer felt that religion was regarded as a private matter, and he claimed that they 'compartmentalized', treating 'business and religion [as] different and separate spheres' (1972: 320). Singer derived some support for these arguments from an interview with Sri Chandrasekharendra Saraswati, the senior Shankaracharya of Kanchipuram, who became known as the Paramacharya (and died in 1994, aged 100). It was the Shankaracharya's view, for example, that 'formal and organized religion and "congregations" had waned, but that personal faith had increased'.[13]

Interviews at the turn of the twenty-first century with men in the same positions as those whom Singer met, including a good many from the same families, suggest a significantly different picture. Most strikingly, Singer never referred to experiences of the miraculous or the presence of 'god-men', although these are important to many contemporary businessmen. According to Singer, in the 1960s the industrial leaders' relationship with the Shankaracharyas was primarily about their philosophical teaching. In 2000, however, some businessmen told stories about miracles by the Paramacharya, as well as by 'god-men' such as Swami Rajagopala, who has an ashram in the Chennai suburb of Nanganallur and a considerable following among NRIs in the United States.

An example concerning the Paramacharya comes from a discussion with a prominent scientist, Govinda (pseudonym), who also runs a highly successful business. This man, like many others, has a picture of Chandrasekharendra on his desk. Govinda referred to a time when he was having a lot of trouble in his business from the then Chief Minister of Tamil Nadu over the Urban Land Ceiling Act. Govinda went to visit the Paramacharya, who said to him, 'What is this? You've come to me just for information? There is no problem'. Govinda returned to Chennai to be informed that the Chief Minister wanted to have breakfast with him, and he got the go-ahead for the project that he had long been seeking without success. On another occasion, he and his wife visited the Paramacharya with their youngest daughter who was then unmarried. At that time Govinda's wife was anxious about her marriage. The Paramacharya gave her a coconut. Govinda and his wife did not know why, but within 7 days the daughter's marriage was arranged. As far as Govinda is concerned, the Paramacharya was a living god (cf. Harriss 2003: 353–4).

In the case of Swami Rajagopala, a pamphlet produced by his American-based devotees recounts his story, which includes this account of the origin of the Shri Rajarajeshwari image now installed in his ashram's temple. Interestingly, the Paramacharya is involved in the miracle as well.

> 27 September 1957: 012 Thaiyappamudali Street, Madras. ... About 10 pm Sri Rajagopala Swami is offering oblations into the sacred fire. ... About midnight two devotees emerge from the worship room and report to the Swami. 'Come and see! There is something bright and shiny floating over the sacred fire!' The Swami goes in to take a look. Indeed, among the flames ... are floating a number of shiny gem-like stones. The Swami inserts a plate below them. As soon as they touch the plate they become heavy and the plate tilts to one side. ... The very next day, the gems which floated on fire are taken to the Sage of Kanchi, Sri Chandrasekharendra Saraswati. He who came to the aid of the Swami in the spiritual path just as a guru would, looks at these gems and in his divine sight, the biggest gem becomes as the Divine Mother Herself ... just as the sage pronounced. Within one year, the big gem transforms itself into the likeness of Sri Rajarajeshwari bearing conch, discus, sugarcane bow, and flower arrows.[14]

Miraculous occurrences in the god-man's life story, as well as during worship in the ashram's temple, are strongly associated with the reverence that people feel for Rajagopala. Among Chennai businessmen, there are devoted followers, too, of both Shirdi Sai Baba and Sathya Sai Baba, whose crucial associations with the miraculous are discussed by Lawrence Babb (1987, Part 3) and Deborah Swallow (1982), as well as in hagiographic accounts by devotees (e.g., Seshadri 1999). Moreover, contrary to Singer's suggestions about 'industrial theodicy', for many of the business leaders, in common with most middle-class people in Chennai, public ritual observance and support for temples have never ceased to be important. Thus, members of the Shri Vaishnava Brahman TVS family (the greatest of the Chennai business groups) have long given generous financial aid for renovating major temples, both Vaishnava and Shaiva, in Chennai, Madurai (the group's original home base), and elsewhere in Tamil Nadu. Singer's notes on his interviews show that he generally focused on his respondents' views on *dharma, karma*, and *moksha*, rather than on their religious practice and experience, so that the absence of data on the latter, as well as his idea of 'industrial theodicy', may have been products of his line of questioning.[15] Certainly, though, there are no significant references in Singer's book or notes to 'god-men', ritual observances, temple-building, or indeed the study of Vedanta—although there are quite a few references to the *Bhagavad Gita,* and relatedly to the idea of 'Do your Duty. Success depends on effort and the will of God'.

In comparison with Singer's account, our recent evidence shows more diverse, as well as more public, religiosity among businessmen in today's Chennai, where there is, in Maya Warrier's phrase (2003: 248), a 'dense religious supermarket' from which individuals pick and choose according to their personal preferences.[16] The trends apparent in the differences between Singer's observations and our own are also reflected in changes at the Kanchipuram monastery. The late Paramacharya, Chandrasekharendra, whom Singer met, was widely respected for his asceticism. In contrast, his successor, Jayendra Saraswati, who is currently the senior Shankaracharya, aspires to 'the imperial swami model', and the monastery has entered 'a more customer-centred phase, accompanied by its own mystification of the acharya, parcelling out his charisma when deemed appropriate'.[17] Today, therefore, the Shankaracharya of Kanchipuram—once the epitome of Brahmanical ascetic orthodoxy in Tamil Nadu—is actively promoting himself and the monastery, although by doing so he also attracts considerable criticism from more conservative Hindus.

We cannot discuss here the full diversity of the religious market in present-day Chennai. Swami Dayananda, however, is attractive to businessmen of a rather more philosophical bent, whose religious interests and activities are focused around him. These men explicitly describe Dayananda as a teacher, not a 'god-man' like Swami Rajagopal, and they are, in their own self-descriptions, 'followers of the Vedic Heritage', or perhaps more accurately of neo-Vedanta. They are also attracted to Dayananda because he seems able to apply his Vedantic learning to practical problems. Arvind Rajagopal describes his own reaction to Dayananda, whom he heard in Berkeley in the 1980s, in similar terms. He was[18]

> energetic and engaging: he inspired trust and confidence. One got the sense that here was someone pious and learned in the scriptures who was yet at ease in the modern world of affairs, and thus capable of providing practical advice relatively free of the frustrating do's and don'ts, prescriptions and proscriptions, that those in conventional households grow up with.

Dayananda's religious teaching also resonates with contemporary (especially United States) self-help and management ideas. Dayananda is sometimes invited to speak on business management, as he did at a function to launch a new software company in Chennai. At least two of the leading business houses fund the Sastraprakasika Trust, which propagates his teaching, and they and other businesses sponsor events such as the annual series of lectures on Successful Living that Dayananda gives in Kamaraj Hall, Chennai's largest auditorium. Two of Dayananda's disciples living in Chennai give regular courses on Vedantic philosophy, which also pick up on the theme of 'successful living'.

One of these courses was taught in 2000 on Sunday afternoons in a school hall in Adyar, south Chennai, a prosperous, upper-middle-class neighbourhood. The classes, conducted by Swami Paramarthananda on the *Bhagavad Gita* in English, though with occasional forays into Tamil, were always well attended by a diverse and decidedly middle-class audience of more than 200 people. Older people were strongly represented, but there were also a lot of young women and significant numbers of fairly young professionals of both sexes. The classes' stated aim was to show how the Vedanta helps us to develop a new vision of life—'the Vedanta is a painful, time-consuming reassessment of life'—and also helps us to be happy in spite of the situations in which we find ourselves. Paramarthananda worked steadily through the *Gita*, emphasizing its relevance to modern life and occasionally using very mundane examples to illustrate the notion of detachment. We should think, he said, not 'I need a cup of coffee', but 'A cup of coffee would be agreeable, although it's not important whether I have it or not'. He referred frequently to the virtues of self-control and moderation in everything and to how the *Gita* teaches us self-confidence: 'Never look down upon yourself. If you feel diffidence, think of yourself as part of God'. Another important idea that he stressed was that we should not be fatalistic: 'The Veda is anti-fatalist [and] it says "Always take charge of your life"'.

Two business leaders who are particularly devoted to Swami Dayananda are both men of about 40, who took MBAs at prestigious US universities after first studying engineering and accountancy (respectively) in local colleges in Chennai. Both are now enterprising and innovative chief executives of companies within their family business groups, responsible for introducing new methods of industrial organization and for branching out into the 'new economy' in the software industry. The two men travel widely and are, as we have witnessed, entirely comfortable in a Western environment. In short, both might be described as thoroughly 'modern' men who are quite at home in the globalizing world. But they are also very serious about their religion, and they and their wives are active in religious observance and scriptural study, which they prefer to do in English because, as one of them admitted, they find it difficult to follow complex ideas in Tamil. Both men have long-standing family connections with the Shankaracharya of Sringeri, but said that they derive their knowledge of the Vedas from Dayananda, who is regarded as particularly responsible for the religious revival, attributed to the 'Vedanta Movement', which they now see in Chennai. The businessmen are attracted by what they perceive to be the 'scientific' nature of Vedic teaching. One of them explained that, like mathematics, the Veda is based on a very few axioms, of which the most important is that 'God is infinite', and much is said to follow logically from this basic proposition. Both men have generally moderate though socially conservative views, and clearly they were also reassured by Dayananda's teaching about the legitimacy of their wealth. One was obviously uncomfortable with questions about caste and inequality in Indian society and sought to justify caste practices as being no different in substance from what occurs in other societies.

Dayananda himself is—or can be—a charismatic speaker, with a gift for comedy and metaphor. These qualities were apparent at a public meeting addressed by Dayananda in 2000, which was attended by several of the business leaders we are discussing. Dayananda spoke in English to a huge audience of men and women, young and old, on the theme of 'Hinduism—what it means and what it does not'. The meeting was organized by an association founded in 1999, the Citizen's Committee for Dharma Rakshana Sammelan, which has the aim of opposing religious conversion—perceived as an act of violence against Hinduism.[19]

In his lecture, Swami Dayananda spoke brilliantly and wittily in celebration of the knowledge contained within the Hindu tradition, often by making mocking comparisons with 'religions of the book'. He concluded this part of his address (to prolonged applause) with the words, 'I am happy that I am a Hindu, and that I am not afflicted by guilt'. Then he turned to the issue of conversion. He spoke about the launching of charities in remote, tribal areas to teach people there—who are 'non-Hindus' —that what they are doing is right and to support them in resisting the attentions of missionaries from other religions. 'Indians need no lessons in giving', he said, and Christians have no monopoly on compassion. Furthermore, 'Conversion is a violence. You [Christians] betrayed the trust we placed in you when you came and built your churches, when you started to convert. Conversion does violence to the person. I say, put a freeze on conversion'.[20] And he concluded with the words, 'Strength is being what you are. You are a nobody if you don't know that. It is in this sense that Hindus must be strong'.

Significantly, in his address Dayananda was continually switching between 'Hindus' and 'Indians', and in part of it he expressed unequivocal support for militant Hindu nationalism (cf. Harriss 2003: 357–9). As noted earlier, he has also supported banning 'forcible' conversions. We do not know how Dayananda's followers are responding to his advocacy. Yet it is noteworthy that the Sastraprakasika Trust in early 2002 chose to put on its website a press report which, without actually condoning the violence then being waged against Muslims in Gujarat, shifted the focus to the notion of a Muslim conspiracy behind the Godhra atrocity that started the killings. Moreover, although he, like others, clearly abhorred violence, one of the Chennai businessmen once told Harriss, 'You know, in my heart I am with the RSS'. In analysing Dayananda's appeal, however, the most important point here is his insistence that it is by being 'more truly' or 'more fully' themselves as Hindus—'Strength is being what you are'—that Indians can best tackle the problems of the modern world. The clear implication is that Indians do not become 'modern' by becoming more 'Western', but rather by becoming more thoroughly imbued with their own, primarily religious, Hindu cultural tradition. In other words, tradition *is* modernity, if you make it so. This is the potent idea that attracts some of the businessmen, and for many upper-middle-class people it is an interest in their own tradition and a commitment to their own religion that primarily account for sympathy with the RSS and Hindu nationalist ideology, not the other way round.

In his address, Dayananda briefly compared Hinduism with physics, but he generally says rather little about science and has insisted that the Vedanta must be distinguished from science because it is a means of knowledge independent of perception and inference.[21] Some businessmen in Chennai, however, including those with technical qualifications, understand Dayananda to be stating that the Vedantic tradition is scientific because it is primarily about the logical working out of some elementary principles, so that, like science, it is dynamic and always evolving. The religions of the book, on the other hand, seem static because they are so dependent upon a written canon and ancient custom. Hence, the Hindu tradition is perceived as more fully 'modern', for it is more scientific than the dogmatic traditions of Christianity or Islam. In fact, this idea has long been part of Hindu reformist thinking and its most vigorous advocate was the earlier Dayananda Saraswati, founder of the Arya Samaj. He insisted that the Veda was superior, as a scientific body of knowledge, to the Bible and Qur'an, and in one debate in 1877 with Christian and Muslim clerics he polemically forced his point home (Prakash 2000: 92–4). Very possibly, today's businessmen in Chennai are hearing in Dayananda's words ideas about science that have actually been current for more than a century. But what they are also hearing is his apparently pragmatic wisdom about the pressures of everyday life. Dayananda's messages about 'successful living', which were prominent in Paramarthananda's *Gita* classes as well, are clearly attractive to men who also read the rather similar mantras of leading business gurus, such as Tom Peters.[22] This similarity is not coincidental, as we shall see by considering some aspects of Dayananda's teaching in greater depth.

Dayananda's 'Traditional' Teaching

In many respects, as already noted, Dayananda teaches modern Vedantic Hinduism, which is monistic and emphasizes the authority of the Vedas and especially the Upanishads as the 'end of the Veda' (Vedanta)—although particular attention is also paid to the *Bhagavad Gita* (described by one Chennai businessman as the 'ABC of the Vedas'). Much of Dayananda's teaching has been published as edited transcripts of his lectures produced by his students. The publications can be divided into three main categories. First, there are the three tomes of the *Bhagavad Gita* 'home study course' (1,600 pages in total). Second, there are the longer books (100 pages or more) that are mostly translations and commentaries on specific texts, such as the *Gita* or *Sri Rudram*, although there is also an *Introduction to Vedanta* based on classes given in the United States. And third, there are short pamphlets containing transcripts of a few lectures on particular topics, or miscellaneous collections of homilies, prayers, or question-and-answer sessions. In addition, numerous tape-recorded cassettes of Dayananda's lectures are available, as well as a few audio-clips on the Sastraprakasika website.[23]

Another important publication is the *VHTP* compiled by Sunita and Sundar Ramaswamy, two of Dayananda's Indian disciples resident in the United States.[24] This ambitious programme, endorsed by Dayananda in his foreword, consists of teaching manuals and children's workbooks, as well as cassette tapes of scriptural texts, and is designed to teach Hinduism to children aged 6–15 over a 10-year period. In general, the *VHTP* is much better written than the other publications referred above.

One significant feature of many of the books and pamphlets, as well as the *VHTP*, is that they reproduce Sanskrit textual passages in both Devanagari script and standard scientific transliteration; Indian names and terms in the body of the English text are also systematically transliterated. Plainly, this scholarly concern for Sanskrit is partly intended to highlight the authentically traditional character of Dayananda's teaching. Yet despite the ostensible scholarship, the commentaries on scriptural texts are neither very profound nor often very clear.[25] On the other hand, this probably does not matter to Dayananda's followers because it is much more important that the crucial premise of monism—that all beings are ultimately inseparable from the one Supreme Being—is repeatedly restated through simple analogies, even if they are actually unclear or misleading.

Moreover, Dayananda's authenticity as a traditional teacher is demonstrated by his fluent discourses on scriptural texts, verses of which he can readily quote and recite verbatim from memory This in turn means that his 'pearls of wisdom' (to cite one of his pamphlet's titles) on a wide range of religious, moral, social, economic, and political questions are given credibility in his followers' eyes. Nonetheless, Dayananda's answers to these questions owe at least as much to popular Western, especially American, ideas as to the Vedanta, so that there are many implicit references to notions of individual self-help and the power of 'positive thinking'. In this respect, Dayananda's approach is not unusual; Vasudha Narayanan (1992: 171–2) mentions, for example, 'a supreme stress management program spiritual workshop' led by a swami in the Penn Hills temple in Pennsylvania, and one of the temple's youth camps whose theme was 'positive thinking and living'. Quite often, too, ideas that are primarily Christian in origin make an appearance. A patent example is the pamphlet on 'morning meditation prayers' for Dayananda's students in the United States, which is actually based not on any Hindu source but on a slightly modified version of the famous 'serenity prayer' that was adopted by Alcoholics Anonymous.[26]

More significant is the explication of key concepts. For instance, in an audio-clip Dayananda says that *moksha* means seeking freedom in life, without which everything seems meaningless. In a dialogue with a student, he explains that:[27]

> My concept of *moksha* is freedom from the sense of limitation and the sense of dependence for your security and happiness. It is not my concept—it is the Vedantic concept. ... [It means] freedom from the sense of inadequacy.

This might be equated with the definition given by S. Radhakrishnan, the most influential twentieth-century philosopher of Vedantic monism: '*Moksha* is spiritual realization. ... *Moksha* is self-emancipation, the fulfilment of the spirit in us in the heart of the eternal' (1971 [1927]: 58).

But Dayananda's interpretation more obviously reflects a less spiritual, more than this worldly idiom that echoes contemporary Western ideas about individual self-fulfilment, and in the dialogue just quoted, he insists that: 'The problem of sense of inadequacy is not a social problem but is an individual problem'.[28] Much of the same point was made, through a reference to *karma*, in Dayananda's Chennai address (Harriss 2003: 358–9). Furthermore, *moksha* for Dayananda is not a very remote and difficult goal, whereas in the orthodox Brahmanical tradition, in P.V. Kane's words, to know and become identified with the Godhead is the ultimate objective (1977: 1631):

> This can be achieved by one's own efforts, but [it] … is most difficult and requires the aspirant to give up egotism, selfishness and worldly attachments.

Compared with these demands, Dayananda's followers should surely have no more trouble pursuing his version of liberation than most people who try to overcome feelings of inadequacy by consulting a personal therapist, for, not coincidentally, *moksha* has been redefined as a psychological state that is fairly easy to attain, instead of a formidable objective that is achieved only through awesome austerities or super-abundant devotion.

Dayananda's outlook on this 'individual problem' appears to be at the heart of his appeal to Indian middle-class people and businessmen in particular. The epigraph on the title page of *Pearls of Wisdom* reads: 'There is no failure in life. There are only varieties of experience. We learn from experiences, not from failure'. In a repetitious (and uncharismatic) lecture on 'Indian philosophy and contemporary management' delivered in 1999 and sponsored by a leading company in Chennai, Dayananda sought to develop this argument about failure and derive it from the *Bhagavad Gita*. In the *Gita*, Krishna says that he manifests himself in human beings in the form of desires (which he does, though he qualifies this by referring to desires that are not inconsistent with righteousness [7.9]), and Dayananda claimed that this means that desire is a human privilege and a manifestation of divinity that actuates people to do things. In life, though, unfulfilled desires normally outnumber fulfilled ones, so that people feel a sense of failure and inadequacy. Krishna, however, teaches us to control desires (Actually, he tells us to renounce desires in order to obtain peace [2.55, 71], as is indeed confirmed in Dayananda's commentary)[29].

Krishna therefore gives us a 'programme for living', 'a plan for life', which ensures that if desires are kept under control, the process of trying to fulfil them—whether successfully or not—is enjoyable and we can learn from it. Hence, there are 'varieties of experience', not 'failures'. By the same token, working to try to achieve success is an enjoyable, educational experience, and controlling the human privilege of desires is managing the self; if everyone in a company does this, then the management needs only to communicate its needs to employees, because the latter actually manage themselves and enjoy their own work. Finally, Krishna teaches that when people enjoy the process of working, they are following their *dharma* and do not 'cut corners'—Dayananda's folksy translation of *adharma*.

Before his lecture—which converts religious teaching into a kind of toolkit for coping successfully with everyday life and work—Dayananda was introduced by a director of the company as a great Vedantic thinker and a great teacher of ordinary people on both theological and practical matters. Yet to interpret Krishna's address to Arjuna before the *Mahabharata* battle as a functionalist plan for good management is surely banal, and it is hard to believe that it really helped any businessmen in the audience to improve their companies' management, even if they were pleased to hear that their activities might have divine approval. On the other hand, to focus too specifically on the content of Dayananda's teaching on management is to miss the point, for his appeal primarily lies in his exemplary personage as a Brahman teacher who, in spite of his ascetic renunciation, nevertheless engages with the affairs of the modern world and presents them as if they were or could be made compatible with the Vedanta. Delivered by such a personage, a lecture about Krishna as a management guru is heard as proof that modern business and the Veda are mutually compatible, whereas a similar set of homilies about desire, failure, and so on would probably be ignored if they were uttered by someone of less stature.[30]

Business Success and Dayananda's Appeal in Chennai

Although Dayananda may address today's Chennai businessmen on failure and how to redefine it as experience, his attractiveness to them is probably significantly related to their self-confidence about themselves and their work, which they share with so many of the American NRIs who are also attracted to him. Admittedly, Singer's evidence suggests that the Chennai businessmen whom he studied in the mid-1960s displayed a similar self-confidence, although it is hard to believe that they were all as sure about divine will as he suggests, but, as we pointed out, Singer makes no reference to any modern gurus. Assuming this is not an oversight and that Singer's evidence is reliable (cf. Harriss 2003: 334–5), however, why should businessmen today be attracted to a guru like Dayananda, whereas their predecessors were content with the Shankaracharyas or their own understanding of Gandhian ideas?

One important part of the answer is that the economic, political, and religious situation has changed enormously. In the 1960s, Indian businessmen, even in major industrial companies and notwithstanding their foreign collaboration agreements, mainly operated within the highly regulated, heavily protected market of the Nehruvian planned economy. By the 1990s, following economic liberalization, the opening up of India's markets, and much more extensive international investment, trade, and collaboration, businessmen were operating in a far more competitive global economy. Many of them, like the Indian business press, are concerned to 'show what Indian business can do' in the globalizing economy, and most importantly, many believe that they can be successful. For the Chennai businessmen, if not for all Indians, the old question of whether Indians could actually do as well as foreigners in the modern world has been answered by the economic success achieved by some of them, both in India and abroad, especially in the United States.

Accompanying the changes in the Indian economy since the 1960s have been equally significant political changes, as Nehruvian socialist secularism and Congress hegemony have given way to religious nationalism and the BJP, together with a host of regional parties.[31] Within Tamil Nadu since the early 1990s—first during Jayalalitha's AIADMK regime (1991–1996), but afterwards under Karunanidhi's DMK (1996–2001) and the AIADMK again since 2001—there has been a wave of Hindu revivalism that is, to a significant extent, both cause and effect of the impact of Hindu nationalism on the state (Fuller 2003: 119–37). The Tamil Nadu government has become an active promoter of Brahmanical, Sanskritic Hinduism, especially in the temples, and its policy, combined with many people's growing prosperity, has led to an ever-rising number of spectacular temple renovation rituals (*kumbhabhisheka*), as well as considerable expenditure on extending old temples and building new ones. No figures exist to prove it, but at least in the major urban centres where middle-class affluence is concentrated the evidence suggests that increasing numbers of costly, elaborate rituals are also being held in both temples and homes. Similarly, the number of gurus and other Hindu religious personages who are active probably continues to grow, and all kinds of religious activities—from learned debates to new local festivals—are flourishing as never before. Dayananda, notwithstanding his devotees' special claims on his behalf, is actually only one of many holy men active in contemporary Hindu revivalism in Tamil Nadu.

In general terms, therefore, in Tamil Nadu as in much of India, the public sphere has been transformed during the last 10–15 years, so that it has become increasingly religious in tenor, and Hindus have become increasingly assertive about celebrating their religion publicly. They have also become more assertive about their own identity as Hindus in opposition to Muslims and Christians. These changes have taken place among Chennai businessmen, just like other Hindus, irrespective of how much support they extend to the Hindu nationalist movement. For the men studied by Singer, religion was a more private matter and more often left to wives and children (1972: 333) than it is for their successors today, who expressly disapprove of 'compartmentalizing' public business apart from private, home-based religion.

To return to Dayananda, like countless other holy men active in contemporary India, he seeks to explain how and why traditional Hinduism (as he portrays it) remains valid and important in the modern world because, properly understood, the Vedanta actually is modern. For many leading Hindus, at least since the late nineteenth century, denunciation of Western materialism and eulogy of Indian spirituality has been a central theme, but in Dayananda's teaching—apart from his criticisms of Christianity and Islam—any denunciation is mild. This is consistent with the fact that businessmen in Chennai—and presumably most of his other followers—display none of the anxious antipathy towards the West and its capitalist lifestyle found in many less-favoured sections of the Indian middle class. The reasons are of course obvious: unlike the majority of Indians who have no real experience of the West, many of the businessmen have studied, worked, and lived in Western countries, usually the United States; they often go there for business or pleasure as well, and they send their children there for education. These men now belong to a transnational Indian managerial-professional, upper-middle class, for whom the West—especially America—is simultaneously an icon of modernity and a familiar place where they are comfortable and successful. Dayananda's message is therefore not anti-Western, even though it insists on the value of Hinduism for Indians living in the West. As Rajagopal comments (2001: 247):

> Hindu spiritualism is seen as providing a necessary counterweight to the ills of a materialist society and, at the same time, as redeemable by the standards of that society itself.

A similar idea was voiced by one Chennai businessman:

> You don't find Indian businessmen running off to psychoanalysts like Americans, because they are able to find comfort in religion. Religion is a buffer against problems.

Furthermore, the Chennai businessmen do not display anxiety about a rapidly changing, highly competitive social world—and the need to validate their own prosperous position within it—that various scholars have seen as one important reason why Sathya Sai Baba and some other miracle-working religious virtuosi were so attractive to their predominantly urban middle-class followers, at least in the 1970s (Swallow 1982; Kakar 1983: Chapter 7; Babb 1987: Part 3; cf. Fuller 1992: 177–81). Maya Warrier (2003) criticizes this scholarship because in her study of the extremely popular female guru Mata Amritanandamayi of Kerala, and her middle-class devotees, she saw no evidence of anxiety among them. Our findings are the same as Warrier's. For the businessmen and their family members who are devotees today of Sathya Sai Baba (or Shirdi Sai Baba), or those (mentioned earlier) who like to stress the miraculous powers of the Paramacharya or Swami Rajagopala, social anxiety is also not a salient factor.

In general, though, however untroubled they may be about their own prosperity, Chennai businessmen can be defensive about social inequality. Moreover, they do not want to hear a message antagonistic to their class interests, and on economic and political inequality, Dayananda—like the overwhelming majority of other holy men—maintains a 'persistent and strategic silence' (McKean 1996: 268) in his lectures. Not only does he avoid inflammatory diatribes about Western materialism, Dayananda also preaches a socially conservative message that makes him, if only for negative reasons, congenial to businessmen. In addition, unlike the majority of contemporary Hindu holy men, Dayananda is a Brahman by birth, even though he does not make a lot of it. For almost all members of the Chennai upper middle class, however, irrespective of their caste background, Brahmans retain a cultural-cum-religious pre-eminence that enhances Dayananda's authority as a guru and traditional teacher.

The 'Cultural Vacuum' and 'Generic' Hinduism

However successful they may be, one important issue about which the Chennai businessmen freely admit to being worried is that they know less than they should about Hinduism, and that their children are likely to grow up knowing next to nothing about it. That is why, as this chapter's second epigraph emphasized, 'cultural revival' is 'the need of the hour' to prevent the extinction of the Vedic Hindu religious tradition. In his foreword to the *VHTP*, Dayananda explains that 'religious culture' used to be 'imbibed naturally from one's home and the cultural atmosphere of the immediate community Not any more. ... So the children have to be taught methodically the religious cultural forms and their meaning, in a class-room situation'. These worries are not of course entirely new among more westernized, middle-class Indians, but they have intensified in recent years.

In its advertisement for the *VHTP*, the Saylorsburg centre's website has a similar message to the Trust, but of course it is appealing directly to NRIs:

> [For the] second-generation Indian children ... the home is composed of a nuclear family wherein parental responsibilities are diverse. Western society, too, offers many alternative beliefs and ways of living. Given this situation, teaching the Vedic heritage to children emerges as an essential part of life in an immigrant Indian family or community.

The crucial point here is that the problem of religious cultural transmission is now seen as more or less identical in India and abroad. Thus, the *VHTP* is explicitly designed as a response to the dangers of 'the encroaching Westernization of India', as well as to the 'cultural vacuum' and 'increasing loss of cultural identity' faced by Indians outside India, to cite the white American's editorial note.

The *VHTP* is an ambitious project, which may in practice be overambitious. It comprises three large-format books for teachers—which cover mythology, theology, *dharma*, and the *Bhagavad Gita*—seven children's workbooks, one book on worship containing prayers and textual passages, and three cassette tapes on which the latter are recorded. Taken as a whole, the *VHTP propagates* the 'generic' neo-Vedantic Hinduism that Narayanan (1992) identifies as dominant among 'young urban professional Hindus' in America. Emphasized particularly are 'a symbolic or psychological explanation of religious phenomena, a syncretic approach to the deities and rituals, and [discussion] on the perceived connections between religion, western psychology, and stress management' (1992: 172–3). Paradigmatic, too, is the proposition that all rituals have inner, symbolic meanings that actually show that science and Hinduism are compatible (1992, 174; cf. Rajagopal 2001: 247). The reformulation of Hinduism in America can be seen as one part of its general transformation in the modern world, and there are also clear parallels with the modern history of other religions. Thus, in the nineteenth century, the earlier Dayananda Saraswati was insisting that science and Hinduism are compatible because the Veda is itself 'scientific'; very similar claims about scientific compatibility have often been made by modern Buddhists or Muslims. Nonetheless, in its particular combination of features, Narayanan's concept of 'generic' Hinduism does identify a distinctively NRI-American form of the religion.

Another characteristic feature of generic Hinduism is the 'controlled diet' of myths about the deities, so that single, 'true' storylines are highlighted, and alternative versions and meanings are eliminated, just as they are in the *Amar Chitra Katha* comic book versions of Hindu mythology so popular with children in India (Narayanan 1992: 169; cf. Hawley 1995). In the *VHTP* (like the comic books), sex, violence, and 'dysfunctional' behaviour in the deities' families are eliminated. Thus, for example, Daksha's sacrifice and Sati's death are recounted without any mention of Shiva's terrible, anguished rage, and when Krishna played his flute, we are told, 'all the *gopis* rushed to him leaving their household chores unfinished', which effectively washes away any eroticism in their moonlit dance with the god.[32]

On the other hand, for many if not most Hindus today, Krishna is a morally upright god, not an adulterous lover, in line with a more general trend to portray all Hindu deities as moral exemplars. In this respect, therefore, the *VHTP's* versions of myths are not exceptional. But it is also possible that converting Radha and the *gopis* into housewives portrays them as closer to an American Hindu wifely norm, and the expurgation of Hindu mythology may be reinforced by the impact of American family and gender ideology.[33] Thus, Prema Kurien explains that the 'idealized' traditional family 'is a central icon in the construction of an American Hinduism', although women, in their role as transmitters of tradition, can 'reinterpret the patriarchal images more in their favour and construct a model of gender that emphasizes the importance of male responsibilities' (1999: 650). Significantly, the *VHTP*, even in its exegesis of the *Laws of Manu*, emphasizes men's duties towards women and the equality of the sexes in its section on 'women in Vedic culture'.[34]

The *VHTP's* generic Hinduism, notwithstanding its simplifications, is mixed in with a preoccupation with Sanskrit accuracy, as already mentioned, as well as some fairly complicated discussion of Hindu philosophy. In Chennai, the *VHTP* is being used in some private schools popular with middle-class parents, notably the Arsha Vidya Mandir, founded in 2002 with the blessings of Dayananda and the Shankaracharya of Sringeri, and older Bala Vidya Mandir. Speaking in 2003, both schools' principals saw the programme as a valuable resource for overcoming the serious ignorance about Hindu religion and culture manifest in middle-class homes, but they also regarded it as hard to use, partly because its level of difficulty is so variable. One of the schools has therefore produced its own teachers' manual to supplement those supplied by the *VHTP*, both principals also send teachers to special training workshops, although one of them pessimistically commented that several years' training would actually be required before the *VHTP* could be used properly.

More detailed research would be needed to assess the pedagogical effectiveness of the *VHTP* in schools or at home. On the other hand, the programme certainly is a serious attempt to deal with the perceived problem of teaching traditional religious culture to middle-class and NRI children. Furthermore, even if the *VHTP* is not unique, its 'teach-yourself' cassette tapes are a rare example of using modern technology to reproduce the oral teaching of texts as found in religious schools (cf. Fuller 2001). This case of 'secondary orality'—oral transmission fostered by electronics, not by the absence of writing or printing—indirectly draws attention to the lack (as far as we can tell) of any Hindu websites for teaching scriptural texts, so that the *VHTP* displays a greater commitment to traditional Hindu religious teaching, as emphasized by Dayananda, than anything apparent on the World Wide Web.[35]

Taken as a whole, the *VHTP* exemplifies a mixture of Sanskrit perfectionism and simplified, generic Hinduism that closely mirrors the structure of Dayananda's own teaching, itself characterized by an often dissonant combination of authentic Sanskrit quotation and simplified or Americanized Vedanta. Nonetheless, in this combination lies Dayananda's special appeal as an exemplary, traditional, Brahman ascetic teacher who can speak about modern affairs and present them in the light of the Veda, which is truly modern, even though it is also ancient revelation. Such a combination is not entirely new, but in some significant respects it is a response to contemporary globalization.

Conclusion: Globalization and Hinduism

In his discussion of NRIs, Rajagopal argues that because Hindus are an ethnic minority in the United States, the meanings of 'Hindu' and 'Hinduism', and the characteristics of Hindu nationalism vary from those in India (2001: 263–70; cf. Kurien 2002: 114–16). In many respects, he is undoubtedly correct, but in the particular case under discussion it is more salient that the Chennai businessmen and their family members are attracted to a style of Hinduism that is also popular with NRIs. Thus, we contend, a distinctive characteristic of Dayananda's teaching is that it chimes with the perceived needs of a globalized, upper middle class of Hindus living both in India and overseas. This teaching celebrates the transformation of Hinduism into a universal, world religion that is going from strength to strength, but it is simultaneously predicated on the notion that westernized Indians now face the same problem as NRIs, especially in America, for they and their children are all endangered by a 'cultural vacuum' that may undermine the religion in spite of its global 'renaissance'. To bridge this gap between strength and potential weakness and to appeal to all his followers, Dayananda promulgates a generic Hinduism that in many respects is American made, combined with a sizeable quotient of Sanskrit scripture, the authentic core component of the eternal, Brahmanical Hindu tradition and, for Hindu nationalists, all Indian civilization as well.

Dayananda is engaged in a form of 'reintellectualization' of Hinduism, to borrow Dale Eickelman and Jon Anderson's term for a new way of presenting Islamic doctrine to a new public that includes large numbers of transnational migrants by using new media, most recently the Internet (cf. Anderson 1999). A key feature of this reintellectualization is that the thinkers responsible for it Dayananda in our Hindu case—'successfully join global and local communities of discourse and reach wider audiences than their predecessors' (Eickelman and Anderson 1999: 12). Obviously, there are major differences between Hinduism and Islam; in particular, whereas Hindus are overwhelmingly concentrated in India, the homeland of their religion, the new 'Muslim publics' discussed by Eickelman and Anderson bring together Muslims from many different nations, none of them dominant over all others, and in certain respects globalization encourages a 'de-centering' away from the Arabian peninsula (cf. Eickelman and Piscatori 1996: 137).

Yet new Hindu publics are emerging too, and one of them is formed by the globalized upper middle class to whom Dayananda appeals. Thus, when he mixes the language of self-help and English homilies imported from America with the words of Krishna and Sanskrit quotations, he is developing a new way of presenting Hinduism that chimes with what his business audience in Chennai wants to hear. To these businessmen and those close to them, Dayananda's version of Hinduism confirms not only that their confidence in their own success and position in the world is well placed, but also that their own and their children's ignorance of Hinduism is an outcome of westernization and globalization that can be overcome.

Notes

1. *Hinduism Today* website: www.hinduism-today.com.
2. Advertisement for *VHTP* on Sastraprakasika Trust website: http://www.dayananda.org/related-links.html
3. For encouraging and critical comments on an earlier draft of this paper, the authors thank Jackie Assayag, Véronique Bénéï, Henrike Donner, Haripriya Narasimhan, Arvind Rajagopal, and Chakravarti Ram-Prasad. For financial support for the research in Chennai, the authors thank the Economic and Social Research Council.
4. The directory is at: www.hinduismtoday.com/. It is part of the larger Directory of Hindu Resources Online.
5. The biographical sketch is based on *Swami Dayananda Saraswati: The Traditional Teacher of Brahma Vidya* (Chennai: T.T. Maps and Publications, n.d.), which was compiled by a devotee, Padma Narasimhan, and published in around 1990.
6. On the VHP's foundation and early years, and on Chinmayananda's pioneering work for the VHP of America, see Katju (2003: Chapter 2: 157–8).
7. These websites are: www.dayananda.org; www.arshavidya.org (Saylorsburg, through which the Rishikesh website can be quickly accessed); and www.vedantashala.org/ (Center for Traditional Vedanta).
8. Audio-clips of Ravi Shankar's platitudes can be heard on his website: www.artofliving.org.
9. *New Indian Express*, 25 March 2002, as reproduced on the Sastraprakasika website.
10. Dayananda, while claiming that the ordinance upholds basic human rights, insisted that the 'denigration of one's religion and the humiliation that accompanies the conversion experience are violations of the dignity assured to every human being'. This statement, made in March 2003, was accessed through the *Hinduism Today* website by searching for 'Dayananda'.
11. Reports posted on www.hinduism-today.com and (accessible through the search facility) the VHP of America website: www.vhp-america.org. No reports of Dharma Sansad meetings or pilgrimages after 1999 have been posted on these websites, consulted in summer 2003.
12. The research is described in detail in Harriss (2003).
13. This quotation comes from Singer's notes which are in his collected papers in the Regenstein Library, University of Chicago.
14. Quotation from the booklet *Sarvamangla Sri Rajarajeswari Ashram*, published by P.K. Seshan, Diamond Bar, California.
15. The relevant notes are in Box 129 of the Singer Papers in the Regenstein Library.

16. Jackie Assayag (personal communication) also comments on how our evidence suggests a kind of 'bricolage' of different elements of thought and practice in the religious market.
17. Quotations from Arvind Rajagopal (personal communication). The Kanchipuram monastery now has a website too: www.kamakoti.org.
18. Arvind Rajagopal (personal communication).
19. This committee is presumably linked to the Hindu Dharma Rakshana Samiti mentioned earlier.
20. Swami Dayananda's views on conversion are also set out in a pamphlet *Conversion is Violence*, published by Sruti Seva Trust, Arsha Vidya Gurukulam, Coimbatore.
21. See, for example, his pamphlet *Pearls of Wisdom* (pp. 4–5), published by Sri Gangadhareswar Trust, Swami Dayananda Ashram, Rishikesh.
22. Tom Peters is the author of *Thriving on Chaos: A Handbook for a Management Revolution* (1991), *Reinventing Work: The Brand You50* (1999), and over 70 other titles listed in 'best-selling' order on Amazon's website.
23. In August 2002, the website listed 23 books and pamphlets for sale (plus two video CDs) by Dayananda, although this is not a complete inventory of his publications; in its list of cassettes, it also listed 66 titles by Dayananda in English, plus about 150 more by three fellow teachers in English or Tamil.
24. Published by Sri Gangadhareswar Trust, Swami Dayananda Ashram, Rishikesh.
25. Many examples could be cited, but the following passage of commentary intended to elucidate monism is typical: 'All that is here is *Brahman*'. … So, too, every object like sun, moon, earth, space and time, is not separate from *Brahman*, even though each object has its own something to refer [sic] and it is that which is referred to by the words sun, moon, earth, space and time. … Between a word, *vacaka*, and its meaning, *vacya*, there is an invariable relationship. Even if you don't have a name for a form of clay, can you imagine the form without imagining the substance? This is what is the non-separate relationship between name and form [sic]. If all forms are *Brahman, Isvara*, then all names are of *Isvara*. And therefore, in one name which includes all names, I can see the *entire Jagat* [world] being non-separate from *Isvara*' (*Talks on Sri Rudram* [pp. 4–5], published by Sri Gangadhareswar Trust, Swami Dayananda Ashram, Rishikesh). The linguistic argument in this passage is specious, but even if it were not, the logic of the conclusion about Ishwara, the supreme God, would still be opaque.
26. *Morning Meditation Prayers*, published by Sri Gangadhareswar Trust, Swami Dayananda Ashram, Rishikesh. The modified serenity prayer is: 'O Lord, may I have the maturity to accept gracefully what I cannot change; may I have the will and effort to change what I can; and may I have the wisdom to know the difference between what I can and can not change'.

27. *Dialogues with Swami Dayananda* (p. 12), published by Sri Gangadhareswar Trust, Swami Dayananda Ashram, Rishikesh.
28. *Dialogues with Swami Dayananda* (p. 14).
29. *The Teaching of the Bhagavad Gita* (pp. 41–3), published by Vision Books, New Delhi; this book was edited by one of Dayananda's American students.
30. Deepak Chopra, a well-known Indian management guru, gave a talk in Syracuse, New York, in 2000. Haripriya Narasimhan (personal communication) informs us that an Indian friend who heard the talk told her that Chopra just said the same as their grandmothers, but coated in English jargon and Sanskrit tags. The same comment could be made about a lot of what Dayananda says, even though his style differs from Chopra's. See also Rajagopal's description of the 'avid crowd of engineers' who listened to an 'Upanishadic management consultant' at a Hindu nationalist organization's summer camp in the United States (2001: 261).
31. In the 2004 general election, a Congress-led coalition defeated the BJP and its allies. This was a significant reverse for the BJP, but the real winners were regional parties, rather than the Congress.
32. For these two stories, see *VHTP* (I, pp. 64–5, 82). In the *Amar Chitra Katha*, comic books, although sex is removed from the text, the pictures—as in the story of Mirabai and Krishna—can be romantic and erotic (Hawley 1995: 118–20), but this is not so for the rather crude pictures in the *VHTP's* children's workbooks.
33. Radha does not appear to have become a 'New Age' goddess of power and sex in America like Kali, who is now being 'Indianized' by NRI Hindus 'endeavouring to rein in what they perceive as excesses of feminist and New Age interpretations of the Goddess' (McDermott 2003: 285, 287–8). More generally, even though Dayananda has many white American devotees, his style of teaching is obviously antipathetic to New Age fantasies and no 'Indianization' process has ever been necessary.
34. See *VHTP* (2: 167–70).
35. The situation is curious, because recitations of the *Rudram* and other key Sanskrit texts are widely available on cassette tapes and compact disks. Although there are some Sanskrit prayers on the Internet, much more common are devotional hymns (*bhajan*). These can be found on sites accessible through Directory of Hindu Resources Online: www.hindu.org. It is an interesting contrast that one of the biggest Islamic websites—IslamiCity.com—Islam and the Global eCommunity—provides both high-quality recitation of the Qur'an and a simulation of its traditional oral teaching: www.islamicity.com (Qur'an button).

References

Anderson, J.W. (1999) 'The internet and Islam's new interpreters', in Eickelman, D.F., and Anderson, J.W. (eds.) *New Media in the Muslim World: The Emerging Public Sphere*. Bloomington: Indiana University Press, 41–56.

Babb, L.A. (1987) *Redemptive Encounters: Three Modern Styles in the Hindu Tradition*. Delhi: Oxford University Press.

Bénéï, V. (1998) 'Hinduism today: inventing a universal religion?' *South Asia Research*, 18, 117–24.

Deshpande, S. (2003) *Contemporary India: A Sociological View*. New Delhi: Viking Penguin.

Eickelman, D.F., and Anderson, J.W. (1999) 'Redefining Muslim publics', in Eickelman, D.F., and Anderson. J.W. (eds.) *New Media in the Muslim World: The Emerging Public Sphere*. Bloomington: Indiana University Press, 1–18.

Eickelman, D.F., and Piscatori, J. (1996) *Muslim Politics*. Princeton: Princeton University Press.

Fuller, C.J. (1992) *The Camphor Flame: Popular Hinduism and Society in India*. Princeton: Princeton University Press.

Fuller, C.J. (1999) 'The Brahmins and Brahminical values in modern Tamil Nadu', in Guha, R., and Parry, J.P. (eds.) *Institutions and Inequalities: Essays in Honour of Andre Beteille.* Delhi: Oxford University Press, 30–55.

Fuller, C.J. (2001) 'Orality, literacy and memorization: priestly education in contemporary South India', *Modern Asian Studies*, 35, 1–31.

Fuller, C.J. (2003) *The Renewal of the Priesthood: Modernity and Traditionalism in a South Indian temple*. Princeton: Princeton University Press.

Harriss, J. (2003) 'The great tradition globalizes: reflections on two studies of the "industrial leaders" of Madras', *Modern Asian Studies*, 37, 327–62.

Hawley, J.S. (1995) 'The saints subdued: domestic virtue and national integration *in Amar Chitra Katha*', in Babb, L.A., and Wadley, S.S. (eds.) *Media and the Transformation of Religion in South Asia*. Philadelphia: University of Pennsylvania Press, 107–34.

Kakar, S. (1983) *Shamans, Mystics and Doctors*. Boston, MA: Beacon Press.

Kane, P.V. (1977) *History of Dharmasastra*, Vol. 5, Part 2. Poona: Bhandarkar Oriental Research Institute.

Katju, M. (2003) *Vishva Hindu Parishad and Indian Politics*. New Delhi: Orient Longman.

Kurien, P. (1999) 'Gendered ethnicity: creating a Hindu identity in the United States', *American Behavioral Scientist*, 42, 648–70.

Kurien, P. (2002) '"We are better Hindus here": religion and ethnicity among Indian Americans', in Min, P.G., and Kim, J.H. (eds.) *Religions in Asian*

America: Building Faith Communities. Walnut Creek, CA: Altamira Press, 99–120.

McDermott, R.F. (2003) 'Kali's new frontiers: a Hindu Goddess on the Internet', in McDermott, R.F., and Kripal, J.F. (eds.) *Encountering Kali: In the Margins, at the Center, in the West*. Berkeley: University of California Press, 273–95.

McKean, L. (1996) *Divine Enterprise: Gurus and the Hindu Nationalist Movement*. Chicago: University of Chicago Press.

Narayanan, V. (1992) 'Creating the South Indian "Hindu" experience in the United States', in Williams, R.B. (ed.) *A Sacred Thread: Modern Transmission of Hindu Traditions in India and Abroad*. Chambersburg, PA: Anima Books, 147–76.

Prakash, G. (2000) *Another Reason: Science and the Imagination of Modern India*. Delhi: Oxford University Press.

Radhakrishnan, S. (1971 [1927]) *The Hindu View of Life*. London: Unwin Books.

Rajagopal, A. (2001) *Politics after Television: Religious Nationalism and the Reshaping of the Indian Public*. Cambridge: Cambridge University Press.

Seshadri (1999) *God in Our Midst: Poomvathar Sri Sathya Sai Baba*. Chennai: Amra Publishers.

Singer, M. (1972) *When a Great Tradition Modernizes*. London: Pall Mall Press.

Swallow, D.A. (1982) 'Ashes and powers: myth, rite and miracle in an Indian god-man's cult', *Modern Asian Studies*, 16, 123–58.

van der Veer, Peter (1994) *Religious Nationalism: Hindus and Muslims in India*. Berkeley: University of California Press.

Warrier, M. (2003) 'Processes of secularization in contemporary India: guru faith in the Mata Amritanandamayi Mission', *Modern Asian Studies*, 37, 213–53.

13

The Diasporic Imaginary and the Indian Diaspora*

Vijay Mishra

'All diasporas are unhappy, but every diaspora is unhappy in its own way' (Mishra 1996: 189). Diasporas refer to people who do not feel comfortable with their non-hyphenated identities as indicated on their passports. Diasporas are people who would want to explore the meaning of the hyphen, but perhaps not press the hyphen too far for fear that this would lead to massive communal schizophrenia. They are precariously lodged within an episteme of real or imagined displacements, self-imposed sense of exile; they are haunted by spectres, by ghosts arising from within that encourage irredentist or separatist movements. Diasporas are both celebrated (by late/post-modernity) and maligned (by early modernity). But we need to be a little cautious, a little wary of either position. Celebrating diasporas as the exemplary condition of late modernity—diasporas as highly democratic communities for whom domination and territoriality are not the preconditions of 'nationhood'—is a not uncommon refrain. In the late modern

*I wish to dedicate this paper to the late Boyd Anderson, with whom I shared many of my anxieties as a student in Weir House, Victoria University of Wellington 1964–1966. Boyd last contacted me from Nadi on his way to Berkeley in 1968. I had returned to Fiji and was teaching at a high school there. Little did Boyd realize when he rang me that my school was on another island, and I couldn't possibly reach him during his hours in transit. Years later I heard from Miles Fairburn, now Professor of History at the University of Canterbury, that Boyd had died young and in tragic circumstances.

I wish to thank Stephen Epstein for inviting me to VUW to deliver this lecture and for his editorial work on the published version.

celebratory argument on behalf of diasporas, diasporic communities are said to occupy a border zone where the most vibrant kinds of interactions take place and where ethnicity and nation are kept separate. In this argument, diasporas are fluid, ideal, social formations happy to live wherever there is an international airport and stand for a longer, much admired, historical process.

The tension between this position and the earlier modern reactionary reading is evident in the classic Hollywood film, *Casablanca* (1942). In it, as Catherine Portuges has pointed out, the opening sequence presents the spectator with 'polyglot crowds of hopeful refugees awaiting the miracle of an exit visa to a better world' (p. 50). Placed against Hollywood's own tendency to produce a cultural product that is homogeneous and unproblematically 'American', the 'irreducible particularity of their [the characters'] ethnic and regional voices' (p. 53) suggests that Michael Curtiz, the film's director and himself a Hungarian émigré, was introducing a discrepant diasporic narrative, a discordant, dialogic eruption, into the film as a statement about diasporic labour in the formation of Hollywood filmic practice and about alternative, unhappy, irreconcilable narratives embedded in voices that *Casablanca* dare not interrogate. After all, it is in *Casablanca* that Rick Blaine (Humphrey Bogart) when asked about his nationality replies, without any ironic intent, 'I'm a drunkard'.

The narrative of *Casablanca* posits escape to liberty as the universal ideal, even if the ideology is encased in a mushy romance. Ideology by virtue of its connection with the aesthetics of romance (which is how the film *Casablanca* has been popularly received) deflects a fundamental aspect of diaspora: its irreducible complexity at the level of lived social and political expression. The point, hidden from the film's diegesis, is that diasporas have a progressivist as well as a reactionary streak in them. Both forms of this 'streak' centre on the idea of one's 'homeland' as very real spaces from which alone a certain level of redemption is possible. Homeland is the *desh* (in Hindi) against which all the other lands are foreign or *videsh*. When not presented in this 'real' sense, homeland exists as an absence that acquires surplus meaning by the *fact* of diaspora so that Sikhs in Vancouver and Sri Lankan Tamils in Toronto clamour for a homeland (Khalistan, Tamil Eelam) or, in some quarters, Muslims seek a pan-Islamic utopia in the European heartland. It is not unusual for the two versions (the physical and the mental) to be collapsed into an ahistorical past going back to antiquity. We need to make an important qualification though. This reading of the homeland must be placed alongside another truth about diasporas: as a general rule—and the establishment of a Jewish homeland is the exception and not the rule—diasporas do not return to their homeland. Throughout the dark years of South African apartheid, few Indians (the Mahatma is the notable exception) returned to India. Neither have Fiji Indians returned, in spite of Fiji's current policy of institutionalized racism.

The intimations of theory are present in the outline of issues given above. Here I wish to reprise part of the argument, rework the archive, narrow the terms, and, above all, offer a theoretical framework for the study of diasporas. The task is not made any easier because diaspora is itself part of some other 'cover' field (perhaps postcolonial or multicultural studies) in a segmentation that is problematic. The placement of diaspora in this larger 'cover' field for many historians of diaspora is a recent theoretical issue because not too long ago the study of diaspora, and the definition of the term itself, was relatively straightforward. Both, analysis and definition, implied a grand narrative of the history of the Jewish people. To invoke diaspora presupposed a prior understanding of a linear narrative of dispersal and return of the original People of the Book. Depending upon one's point of view, this narrative could be rendered in epic terms or in terms of the uprooted, aimless wanderer in search of home. In the latter exegesis, Jewish history was represented through narratives of retribution and loss symbolized, at least in non-Jewish narratives, through the iconography of a wanderer or wayfarer whom even God had rejected. Although Charles Maturin never explicitly refers to the Jewish experience, most readers of his classic Gothic work *Melmoth the Wanderer* (1820) have sensed that Maturin here uses the Jewish experience as his unspeakable intertext. In the *Qur'an*, history is presented as a failure by the Jews to uphold a primal contract between man and God.

When we turn to descriptive predication, that is, definitions, 'diaspora' turns out to be a very culture-specific term. *The Oxford English Dictionary* (*OED*) refers quite explicitly to John vii, 35 ('the dispersion; ... the whole body of Jews living dispersed among the Gentiles after their Captivity') to make the connection clear. The *OED*, with its characteristic homage to the written word, locates the first use of the term in Deuteronomy xxviii, 25 where we find: 'thou shalt be a diaspora (or dispersion) in all kingdoms of the earth'. The recent opening up of the word to signify the lives of 'any group living in displacement' (Clifford 1994: 310) is a phenomenon that probably marks a postmodern move to dismantle a logocentric and linear view of human affairs that connected narratives and experiences to specific races and to origins: the model here was that of historical lexicography, of which the sublime example is the *OED* itself.[1]

The diasporic imaginary is a term I use to refer to any ethnic enclave in a nation-state that defines itself, consciously, unconsciously, or through self-evident or implied political coercion, as a group that lives in displacement.[2] I use the word 'imaginary' in both its original Lacanian sense (linked to the mirror stage of the ego and therefore characterized by a residual narcissism, resemblance, and homeomorphism[3]) and in its more flexible current usage, as found in the works of Slavoj ž ižek. ž ižek defines the imaginary as the state of 'identification with the image in which we appear likeable to ourselves, with the image representing "what we would like to be"' (1989: 105). ž ižek makes this point with reference to the question one asks the hysteric: not 'What is his object of desire?' but 'Where does he desire from?' (ž ižek 1989: 187). In a subsequent application of this theory to the nation itself, ž ižek connects the idea of what he calls the 'Nation Thing' to its citizens' imaginary identification with it. In this astute extension of the argument, the 'nation' (as the 'Thing' in Heideggerian parlance that 'presences' itself[4]) is accessible to a particular group of people of itself because it (the group) needs no particular verification of this 'Thing' called 'Nation' (1993: 210–12). For this group, the 'nation' simply *is* (beyond any kind of symbolization); it is more than just an imagined community, even if it is constructed out of fantasies about a particular way of life that may be enjoyed by a particular community or race. The 'way of life', which may be defined by any number of things: pub culture, sportsmanship (rugby in New Zealand is a classic case), capacity to live life fully, liberal values, non-negotiable connections with the land, or something totally nebulous, which has meaning only when declared as an absence ('Why can't they be like us?'), is seen to come under threat from the Other (multicultural community, diaspora), since the latter has ways of enjoying the Nation that do not necessarily mirror the forms of the nation's enjoyment of itself. Nor do these alternative forms of enjoyment correspond to how members of the dominant community would like the nation to be (as a reflection of their own selves). Racist phobia, ž ižek suggests, arises out of a proprietary sense of enjoyment of the 'Nation Thing' that is the exclusive property of a given group, community, or race. The politics of many right-wing parties (Jean-Marie Le Pen's National Front in France, Pauline Hanson's One Nation in Australia, Fijian nationalist parties) grew straight out of their racist phobia of (visible) minorities, both indigenous and diasporic (as in many settler nations), and diasporic (as in

Fiji). The current anti-Muslim nationalist rhetoric in large parts of the world (Western and non-Western) is another version of the phobia: what if these *hijab*-wearing women are really enjoying their diasporic lives amidst us, and constructing the nation 'Other-wise'?

But ž ižek is not speaking in the abstract about this 'Thing' called the nation. Drawing on Lacan's definitions of 'enjoyment', ž ižek attempts something rather different: he brings a corporeal element to definitions of the nation-state so that the nation is more than just a structure of feeling, an 'imagined' construct, without any foundation in the *real*. Here is ž ižek's crucial qualification made with an eye to definitions of the nation that have emerged in the wake of Benedict Anderson's influential work:

> To emphasize in a 'deconstructionist' mode that Nation is not a biological or transhistorical fact but a contingent discursive construction, an overdetermined result of textual practices, is thus misleading: such an emphasis overlooks the remainder of some *real*, nondiscursive kernel of enjoyment which must be present for the Nation qua discursive entity-effect to achieve its ontological consistency. (1993: 202)

If the enjoyment of the Nation Thing is the property of a specific community, then the Other is always seen as someone who wishes to 'steal [the nation's] enjoyment' (p. 203). But the fact remains that, in this imputation to the Other of a property that we possess (and 'we' here refers to those of us who own the foundational narrative of the nation), we repress the 'traumatic fact that *we never possessed what was allegedly stolen from us*' (p. 203). Enjoyment is therefore always of the 'imaginary', and we continue to impute to the Other what we ourselves wish to enjoy. In other words, the fantasies of our own enjoyment return to us once we have, negatively, imputed the same to the Other. In this respect, diaspora as Other has an important function to play in the construction of the fantasies of the nation-state as a Thing to be 'enjoyed'.

ž ižek, it must be said, constructs his argument with reference to the disintegration of the East European communist bloc as his test case. Here the argument is that the rise of nationalisms in Eastern Europe mirrors a democratic process that, in the West, has lost all its original vigour and excitement. These emergent nation-states as 'Other' give back to the West its original democratic message in the typically Lacanian form of the speaker getting back from the 'addressee his own message in its true, inverted form' (p. 208). In diasporas, then, the nation-state sees the loss of an ideal, the loss of its own organic connection to the Thing, which it had always taken for granted.

Diasporas signify a *Gesellschaft*, an alienated society without any 'organic laws', against the nation-state's own *Gemeinschaft* or 'traditional, organically linked community' (p. 211). The nation-state sees in diasporas reflections of its own past, its own earlier migration patterns, its own traumatic moments, and its memories of settlement. In the extended form of this argument, it is the absence of diasporic enjoyment of the Nation Thing in the dominant group itself (and which enjoyment is the presumption upon which the nation-state itself is based) that gives rise to the exclusion of diasporas from the national imaginary.[5] The theorization of this fact remains incomplete since the psychology that underlies the enjoyment, an enjoyment ultimately predicated upon melancholia and loss, is never fully understood. The effects of the enjoyment are, however, clear enough. It is the diasporic enjoyment of the Nation Thing absent among the 'proprietors' of the nation that gives rise to a range of responses, chief among them racist exclusion and cultural denigration, that in some sense attenuate, or even deflect, a psychology that underlies the (lost) enjoyment of the nation by the dominant community.[6]

It follows, then, that diasporas are embedded in nation-states that are already a 'Thing' created out of a specific kind of (lapsed) enjoyment of it. For the dominant citizenry, this 'enjoyment' is a matter of retrospect and exists in as much as it is owned and possessed by the dominant citizenry. For the latter, diasporas must have a homeland since only upon this presumption can the dominant group (or community or citizenry) define itself as a homogeneous entity.[7] Indeed, homeland as '[a] fantasy structure, [a] scenario, through which society perceives itself as a homogeneous entity' (Salecl 1994: 15)[8] is predicated on the construction of desire around a particularly traumatic event. The fantasy of the homeland is then linked, in the case of the diaspora, to that recollected trauma that stands for the sign of having been wrenched from one's mother (father) land. The sign of trauma may be the '[middle] passage' of slave trade or Indian indenture. The 'real' nature of the disruption is, however, not the point at issue here; what is clear is that the moment of 'rupture' is transformed into a trauma around an absence that, because it cannot be fully symbolized, becomes part of the fantasy itself. The Ukrainian famine for the Ukrainian diaspora, the Turkish massacres for Armenians[9] may be cited here, or the recent coups in Fiji may be seen as moments that trigger homeland fantasy by repeating the earlier traumatic moment for, after all, like Clorinda's cry in Tasso's epic *Gerusalemme Liberata*, when Tancred slashes at the tree which contains her spirit, it is the delayed act that compulsively repeats the original trauma: 'Why should you once again hurt this poor trunk, where I am pent by my hard destiny?' (2000, XIII: 42–43).

To think of diasporas in these terms, in terms of negation, in terms of discrepant or varied understanding of the enjoyment of the Nation Thing, also stipulates a consciousness of our own beings, and the necessity of intense self-reflection and finally recognition. If, for the dominant community, diasporas signify their own lapsed enjoyment of the Nation Thing, for diasporas to face up to their own ghosts, their own traumas, their own memories is a necessary ethical condition. To reformulate Derrida's 'Spectres of Marx', by which he meant the imperative of keeping the legacy of Marx visible even as we accept the imperative of globalization in a post-Soviet world order, what I believe is absolutely necessary for diasporas to do is to keep their own spectres of slavery and coolie life (and latterly graveyard shifts and work in sweatshops) firmly in place. There is, for the old Indian diaspora, a plantation history, a lived memory of the passage (*Chalo Jahaji*—'Fare forward, fellow voyagers'—is the title of a book by the leading historian of Fiji-Indian indenture, Brij Lal) that must be firmly kept in place. The reflection demands that we constantly revisit our trauma as part of our ethical relationship to the ghosts of diaspora. It also sends a clear signal that the idealist scenario endorsed by some diaspora theorists needs to be tempered by individual diaspora histories.

In the context of the degradations suffered by Sikh migrants in British Columbia, Sadhu Binning's observations in a poem with parallel Punjabi/English original texts act as an important reminder of another difficult, often unspoken, history so as to evoke precisely that ethical relationship to one's past:

we forget the strawberry flats we picked
stooping and crawling on our knees
we forget the crowded windowless trucks
in which like chickens we were taken there

we forget the stares that burned through our skins
the shattered moments
that came with the shattered windows
we forget the pain of not speaking
Punjabi with our children

multiplying one with twenty-five
our pockets feel heavier
changing our entire selves

and by the time we get off the plane
we are members of another class. (1994: 41–43)

To understand diasporas necessitates tampering with idealist notions of the exemplariness of diasporas in the modern world. Against a celebratory rhetoric (which would miss Binning's ironic reference to the value of the Canadian dollar in India), the necessity of understanding a diaspora's agony, its trauma, and its pain of adjustment (before people were unceremoniously ripped apart from their mother's wombs) with reference to other pasts and other narratives becomes decisive. And we need to accept that, contrary to idealist formulations about diasporas as symbolizing the future nation-state, diasporas are also bastions of reactionary thinking and fascist rememorations: some of the strongest support for racialized nation-states has come from diasporas; some of the most exclusionist rhetoric has come from them, too. Even as the hypermobility of postmodern capital makes borders porous and ideas get immediately disseminated via websites and search engines, diasporic subjects have shown a remarkably anti-modern capacity for ethnic absolutism. In part, this is because diasporas can now recreate their own fantasy structures of homeland even as they live elsewhere. The collapse of distance on the information highway of cyberspace and a collective sharing of knowledge about the homeland by diasporas (a sharing that was linked to the construction of nations as imagined communities in the first instance) may be addressed by examining the kind of work Amit S. Rai (1995) has done on the construction of Hindu identity. His research explores the new public sphere that the Indian diaspora now occupies as the diaspora itself becomes a conduit through which the conservative politics of the homeland may be presented as the desirable norm. In exploring six internet newsgroups (soc.culture.indian, alt.hindu, alt.islam, soc.culture.tamil, su.orig.india, and iNET), Rai finds that many postings construct India in purist terms, Hindu in nature and in which an anti-nationalist secularism appeases minorities. In their invocations of important Indian religious and cultural figures—Vivekananda, R.C. Dutt, and others—the subtext is a discourse of racial purity ('we must go to the root of the disease and cleanse the blood of all impurities', said Swami Vivekananda) and the sexual threat to Hindus posed by the Muslims in India. The double space occupied by the diaspora (hysteria for multiculturalism within the United States, and rabid racial absolutism for the homeland) is summarized by Rai as follows:

> Finally, this textual construction of the diaspora can at the same time enable these diasporics to be 'affirmative action' in the United States and be against 'reservations' in India, to lobby for a tolerant

pluralism in the West, and also support a narrow sectarianism in the East. (1995: 42)

Although Rai's conclusions may be suspected—the postings need not lead to the correlation he discovers—it should be clear that diasporas construct homelands very differently from the way in which homeland peoples construct themselves. For an Indian in the diaspora, for example, India is a very different kind of homeland than for the Indian national.

At the same time, and as we have suggested above, the nation-state needs diasporas to remind it of what the idea of homeland is. Diasporic discourse of the homeland thus represents a return of the repressed for the nation-state itself, its pre-symbolic (imaginary) narrative, in which the nation sees it own primitive past. Thus, historically both the Jewish and gypsy diasporas—two extreme instances of diaspora—have been treated by nation-states with particular disdain because they exemplify in varying degrees characteristics of a past that nation-states want to repudiate. For Franz Liszt, the gypsy diaspora was a 'crisis for Enlightenment definitions of civilization and nationalist definitions of culture' (Trumpener 1992: 860).[10] The Jews, equally a problem but with an extensive sense of history and civilization, carried all the characteristics of an ethnic community (*ethnie*) and thus represented both an earlier condition of the European nation-state and its mythical nemesis (Smith 1986: 22–30, 117). In late eighteenth-century France, and in Germany (unified only in 1871), the Jews posed, for the European, a problem for an understanding of how races entered the logic of modernity. As Jonathan M. Hess (2002: 4) has pointed out, between Christian Wilhelm Dohm's treatise on the improvement of the Jews (*On the Civic Improvement of the Jews: Ueber die bürgerliche Verbesserung der Juden*, 1781) and the unification of Germany, heated discussions on the 'moral, political and physical "regeneration" of the Jews' continued. David Michaelis (1717–1791) felt that the Jews were racially degenerate, by climate and physique quite incapable of standing up to the heroic German. To the French, hot on the heels of revolutionary fervour, the Jews were seen as 'the ultimate anti-citizen', a perfect case for a 'thought experiment' designed to test (Hess 2002: 5) 'revolutionary principles of the moral transformation of both individuals and the French nation as a whole'. Dohm had read the Jews totally negatively and seen their transformation into German enlightenment citizens as of utmost importance. It is not too difficult to read into this version of the modern citizen, as Zygmunt Bauman has done, a failure to tolerate difference (Hess 2002: 8), 'in the quest for uniformity and universalism', an attitude that Hess himself sees as a failure to understand the manner in which German Jewry negotiated (with considerable difficulty, given Christianity's claim to 'normative status in the modern world' and its supersession of Judaism) modernity from within by pointing out Judaism's own enlightened principles.[11]

If the gypsies were read as the absolute instance of a nomadic tribe, the profound historicity of the Jewish people gave their diaspora a privileged position in diasporic theory. Diasporic theory then uses the Jewish example as the ethnic model for purposes of analysis or, at least, as its point of departure. But Jewish diasporas were never totally exclusivist—'not isolation from Christians but insulation from Christianity' was their motto, as Max Weinreich put it—and met the nation-state halfway in its border zones. Jewish 'homelands', for instance, were constantly being re-created: in Babylon, in the Rhineland, in Spain, in Poland, and even in America with varying degrees of autonomy (Smith 1986: 117). Movement ceased to be from a centre (Israel/Palestine/Judaea) to a periphery and was across spaces of the 'border'. Against the evidence, Zionist politics interpreted the Jewish diaspora as forever linked to a centre and argued that every movement of displacement (from Spain to France, from Poland to America) carried within it the trauma of the original displacement (such as that from Judaea to Babylon). In retrospect, one can see how readily such logic would erase the idea of nation as 'palimpsestic text' and replace it with the idea of nation as a racially pure ethnic enclave. In a very significant manner, then, the model of the Jewish diaspora is now contaminated by the diasporization of the Palestinians in Israel and by the Zionist belief that a homeland can be artificially reconstructed without adequate regard to intervening history.[12]

The theoretical problematic posed here is not simply Zionist. In no less a work of art than George Eliot's *Daniel Deronda*, the 'Jew' enters the realist novel to take on world-historical questions of exile and what F.R. Leavis called the 'racial mission' (1962: 99).[13] Here what seems like a more powerful sexual desire on the part of Deronda for Gwendolen has to be repressed (and even denied) once Deronda is made aware of his race through Mordecai, Mirah's Zionist brother, and comes to feel 'he must glorify the possibilities of the Jew' (Eliot 1988: 405). In marrying Mirah and finally heading 'East' (Palestine), Daniel Deronda affirms his place in a larger history that transcends both emotion (love for Gwendolen) and nation (England as the immediate home) in favour of a new 'remaking', signalled by George Eliot in a chapter epigraph taken from Heine: 'Despite his enmity to art, Moses was a great artist ... he built pyramids of men, he sculpted obelisks of men, he took a poor peasant slave and made a people that would last for hundreds of years. He made Israel (*er Schuf Israel*)' (p. 637).

Years after George Eliot, we need to keep the Palestinian situation in mind in any theorization of diasporas, even as we use the typology of the Jewish diaspora to situate and critique the imaginary construction of a homeland as the central *mythomoteur* of diaspora histories.[14] The reason for this is that displaced Palestinians and their enforced mobility force us to distinguish between the Zionist project of Israel and the historically deterritorialized experiences of Jewish people generally. The latter point is made by Boyarin and Boyarin (1993). Echoing Max Weinreich, they reread the Jewish diaspora through a postcolonial discourse in which Jewishness is seen as a disruptive sign in the mosaic of history and an affirmation of a democratic ethos of equality that does not privilege any particular ethnic community in a nation.[15] Against the Zionist fictions of a heroic past and a distant land, the real history of diaspora is always contaminated by social processes and, in the end, by nationalist forces that govern diasporic subjects' lives. Indeed diasporas become more than just theoretical propositions once a morally bankrupt nation-state asks the question seen by Sartre as the nation's racist solution: 'What do we do with them now?' In the post-September 11 world order, that question is being asked about Muslims generally, diasporic or not. In that interrogative mood, diasporas too may be asked to declare whether they are 'for us or against us'. For me, Sartre's question remains what may be called the 'transcendental signified' against which we compose a diaspora theory. To forget this fear is to ignore one of the principal lessons of modern history.

A recent echo of such a question was heard in Fiji when, soon after the George Speight-led coup in May 2000, the indigenous Fijians very loudly asked precisely the question 'What do we do with them now?' of its own Indian diaspora. The idea of the lost homeland is triggered by the question in whatever form it is asked—or even when it is embedded in a statement such as Fijian Prime Minister Laisenia Qarase's 'Loss of political control and leadership is more than just an election result. It is a reflection of their [the indigenous Fijians'] worst nightmares' (*Time* 11 July 2005: 43). The question 'repeats' the trauma, it reinforces the imaginary and darkens (Boyarin and Boyarin 1993: 713) 'consciousness of a racial collective as one sharing space with others, devoid of exclusivist and dominating power'.

The generalist argument, however inelegantly presented above, acts as a template for a quite specific archive. To get my narrative right, to be able to say things about diasporas as exemplary as well as reactionary sites of late modernity, I want to speak about the 11 million strong Indian diaspora. Surprisingly, not much of a theoretical nature has been written about this diaspora. In the lead essay in the foundation issue of the journal *Diaspora*, William Safran (1991), for instance, devotes a mere 12 lines to the Indian diaspora and, given his brevity, oversimplifies the characteristics of this diaspora.[16] Admittedly, the Indian diaspora as we understand it is a comparatively recent phenomenon, although it may be argued that the modern Indian diaspora has a longer history that is in fact contiguous with an older wanderlust, the *ghummakar* tradition, which took the gypsies to the Middle East and to Europe, fellow Indians to Southeast Asia and Sri Lanka as missionaries and conquerors, and traders to the littoral trading community around the Arabian Sea. Rethinking the argument that 'it was poverty at home that pushed them [Indians] across the ocean [to Africa]', M.G. Vassanji writes in his recent novel *The In-Between World of Vikram Lall* (2004: 17) 'surely there's that wanderlust first, that itch in the sole, that hankering in the soul that puffs out the sails for journey into the totally unknown?' The Indian diaspora is, therefore, a complex social formation, in fact, an extraordinarily rich archive, which lends itself to theory and critical analysis.[17]

To explore the narrative of the Indian diaspora critically, we may want to read it as two relatively autonomous archives designated by the terms 'old' and 'new'. The old (that is, early modern, classic capitalist, or, more specifically, nineteenth-century indenture) and the new (that is, late modern or late capitalist) traverse two quite different kinds of topographies. The subjects of the old—'before the world was thoroughly consolidated as transnational' (Spivak 1996: 245)—occupy spaces in which they interact, by and large, with other colonized peoples with whom they have a complex relationship of power and privilege, as in Fiji, South Africa, Malaysia, Mauritius, Trinidad, Guyana, and Surinam; the subject of the new are people who have entered metropolitan centres of Empire or other white settler countries such as Australia, Canada, New Zealand, and the United States as part of a post-1960s pattern of global migration. The cultural dynamics of the latter are often examined within a multicultural theory. There are, of course, Indians, part-comprador, part-indenture, with long histories in many parts of Africa, notably East Africa, whose lifeworlds have been the subject of some very fine writing by the twice displaced Indian-Canadian writer M.G. Vassanji. As is clear from Vassanji's treatment of 'Shamsi' traders of Gujarat who migrated to East Africa, the binary of the 'old' and the 'new' offered here is not meant to isolate communities or to situate experiences within non-negotiable or exclusive frames. It should be self-evident that the 'old' has also become part of the 'new' through remigrations such as Fiji-Indians to Vancouver or Trinidadian-Indians to Toronto (one thinks of the transnational life of Ms. Neela Mahendra of Lilliput-Blefuscu, the unhappy South Pacific isles inhabited by the Indo-Lilly, in Salman Rushdie's novel *Fury*) and that the old has not been immune to a general electronic media culture that has tended to redefine subjectivities along the different lines of what Manuel Castells has called the 'net and the self'. I keep the distinction of the 'old' and the 'new' not because the binary has to be defended or that the binary is incontestable; it is made because Indian intellectuals of the diaspora (Appadurai, Radhakrishnan, and Bhabha, among many others) presume that the lives of the Indian NRIs (the 'new' diaspora of 'non-resident Indians') constitute the self-evidently legitimate archive with which to explore histories of diasporic subjectivities. They have also tended to presume that the 'new' presents itself as the dominant (and indeed the more exciting) site for purposes of diasporic comment.[18] The binary therefore has a strategic function: it recognizes an earlier phase of migration, the psychic imaginary of which involved a reading of India based on a journey that was complete, a journey that was final.[19]

The 'old' and the 'new' Indian diasporas (as I have called them) reflect the very different historical conditions that produced them.[20] The distinction between the old and the new becomes clearer when we note that the 'new' surfaces precisely at the moment of (post)modern ascendancy; it comes with globalization and hypermobility, it comes with modern means of communication already fully formed or in the making (airplanes, telephone, email, the internet, videocassettes, DVD, video-link, webcam) and it comes, since 2003, with the gift of dual citizenship from India: the Indian Citizenship Act 1955 has been amended to allow the Indian diaspora in the United Kingdom, the United States, Canada, Australia, Canada, Finland, Ireland, the Netherlands, and Italy to retain dual citizenship. In a thoroughly global world, the act of displacement now makes diasporic subjects travellers on the move, their homeland contained in the simulacral world of visual media where the 'net' constitutes the 'self' (Castells 1996), and quite unlike the earlier diaspora where imagination was triggered by the contents in gunny sacks: a Ganesha icon, a dog-eared copy of the *Ramayana* or the *Qur'an*, an old sari or other *deshi* outfit, a photograph of a pilgrimage, and so on.

Indeed, 'homeland' is now available in the confines of one's bedroom in Vancouver, Sacramento, or Perth as networking now takes over from the imaginary. Presented in this fashion, this is a great, positive yarn, about extremely flexible human beings. But even within the 'new' diaspora, this version is only part of the story. The Afghan refugees to Australia or the Fiji-Indians who are illegally ensconced in Vancouver are neither global nor (hyper)mobile. Their condition, unlike those of the upwardly mobile professionals in Silicon Valley, is not unlike those of people under indenture, for they had to work in sweat-shops during graveyard shifts or, as in the case of the illegal, cannot leave Vancouver, as they had no access to a passport. It is this complex diaspora story that I would want to tell with some of the privileges of the critical and self-reflexive native informant. But it is a story that is also a critique of an uneasy postmodern trend towards collapsing diasporic (and historical) differences.

An anecdote comes to mind here, an anecdote centred upon a question asked on my third journey to India in September 1994. The question was posed in Bombay, emblematic city, after Benjamin, of 'marginal types such as the collector, gambler, prostitute, and flâneur' (Patke 2000: 12). In this city of cynics and slum-dwelling cinema buffs, people's questions are not what they seem. So when the porter of the Bombay Radio Club (where once colonials came to listen to the BBC World Service over a chota peg) welcomed me with 'Where are you coming from?' I prepared myself for an ironic response. But I need not have worried: Indians do not have a sense of irony; the porter's question was no more than the Indian introduction, the Indian way of opening up a social space. I remembered an early V.S. Naipaul essay in which he recounts also being asked 'Where do you come from?' 'It is the Indian question ... [of] people who think in terms of the village, the district, the province, the community, the caste', he had added (1984: 43). I explained to the porter at the Radio Club my history, my origin in the sugar plantations of Fiji, the fact that, though a Brahmin (my surname would have given that away), I was basically working class, and had my forebears not left the Indo-Gangetic Plains in the nineteenth century, I would probably be illiterate and begging in Allahabad.

But it is only now, as I write down that encounter, that I realize the meaning of this very Indian question ('where are you coming from?') in the way in which Naipaul had understood it. Translated back into Hindi (*aap kahaan se aaye hai*), the question does not seek a full autobiography, but is instead only a means of 'locating' the addressee, because in India you are where you come from, and that may also mean the caste to which you belong, the family you married into, and the social and economic grouping willing to embrace you.

In Fiji—the first of my diasporic homes, but a lot more, my 'home-land'—'Where are you coming from?' (in the Fijian language) has a slightly different inflection, since it is rendered as 'Where are you staying?' (*o vaka tikotiko mai vei*). But 'staying' does not imply the here and now place of residence. It carries with it, as in the original meaning of the Hindi question, the more specific sense of ancestral village or, in Fijian, one's *koro*. One may live in another place for generations, but the answer given to '*o vaka tikotiko mai vei*' is always the name of one's *koro*. Fiji Indians too would answer this question by referring to their plantation village, that is, the plantation to which their forefathers came in the first instance.[21] After the 1987 coup, when Fiji Indian identity was not deemed to be self-evidently connected to Fiji, the indigenous Fijian shadowed the question (*o vaka tikotiko mai vei*) with the idea of the *vulagi*, the foreigner, whenever the addressee happened to be an Indian. The Fijian historian Asesela Ravuvu (1991: 58–60), in fact, is quite explicit: if a *vulagi* (here the Fiji Indian) 'does not comply to the host's (the *taukei's*, the Indigenous Fijian's) expectations, then he may very well leave before he is thrown out of the house'. Ask the question too often in any nation-state, and with the latter-day Fijian connotation, and you begin to produce the schizophrenic social and psychological formations of diasporas. A diasporic double consciousness comes to the fore once you link this question, finally, to the presumed ultimate solution of diasporas: 'What do we do with them now?' In Bombay, where inter-communal relationship remained tense when I arrived, this question had indeed been asked with reference to the Indian Muslim community. As a student of diaspora theory, I could see how easily a real or implied principle of exclusivism could 'diasporize' a community that had begun to be read ambivalently ever since the partition of India in 1947 created a Muslim homeland with a fanciful name (Pakistan, 'the land of the pure'). Where once 'Where are you coming from?' implied the beginning of inclusion into a community, now that query is shadowed by 'What do we do with them now?', which erupts into the social.

The question, with its shadow, is an 'interrogative dominant' in the cultural logic of diaspora because the diasporic imaginary is so crucially connected to the idea of a 'homing desire' (Brah 1996: 180), the idea that against one's *desh* ('home country') the present locality is *videsh* ('an other country'). Behind the use of *desh* stand ethnic doctrines based on exclusivism and purity and linked very often to a religiously based communal solidarity of the *ethnie* (Smith 1986). Behind it stands the denial that the homelands of diasporas are themselves contaminated, that they carry racial enclaves, with unassimilable minorities and other discrepant communities, and are not pure, unified spaces in the first place. Even in the Jewish case history that underpins readings of diaspora (by Safran, for instance), migration was largely from one in-between place to another and not from Palestine to a new land. Furthermore, historically Jewish homelands had been created wherever Jews had settled, in parts of the Middle East, in Poland, and elsewhere. Many Jews looked upon these enclaves as their homeland rather than to the Israel of the Book of Exodus. Their own diasporic episteme was located squarely in the realm of the hybrid, that is, in the domain of cross-cultural and contaminated social and cultural regimes. Though Jewish history also gives us the only successful instance of diaspora nationalism, a term that Ernest Gellner uses to define 'a third species of nationalism' beyond the enlightenment/democratic and eugenic (1983: 101–9), the lived experience of the Jews was not necessarily linked to a physical return to a homeland which, at any rate, is only possible with the return of the Messiah, as the members of the Neturei Karta maintain in Israel itself. It is thus the creation of its own political myths rather than the real possibilities of a return to a homeland that is the defining characteristic of diasporas. In a progressively multi-ethnic conception of the nation-state (in spite of the tragedy of the Balkan states and the break-up of the Soviet Union, which was a nation-state only through the politics of coercion), diasporic theory bears testimony to the fact that we live in a world 'where multi-ethnic and multi-communal states are the norm' (Hobsbawm 1992: 179).[22] The partition of India, the demands of the Tamil separatists in Sri Lanka, and the recent tragedy of racial cleansing in the Balkan states are very special, indeed aberrant, cases. The memorial (and fictive) reconstructions of the ancient Jewish homeland, of the Armenian golden age in the era of the early Gregorian church, of the free city-state of Ayodhya under the Hindu God Rama, or of the community of the faithful under Prophet Muhammad become the sublime signs of the ungraspable in the complex psychology of diasporas. Against this kind of discursive nostalgia (not uncommon among terrorist groups), the material history of diaspora leads us to deterritorialized peoples with a history and a future. This future, at least as an ideal, is the affirmation of the idea of the enlightenment/democratic nation-state currently threatened by racialized ethnic states.[23] For, as E.J. Hobsbawm (1992: 173) writes so lucidly, 'Wherever we live in an urbanized society, we encounter strangers: uprooted men and women who remind us of the fragility or the drying up of our own families' roots'.

The variable archives of diasporas notwithstanding the Jewish diaspora is the fundamental ethnic model for diaspora theory, and all serious study of diasporas will have to begin with it. But what we must now do is take away from that model its essentialist, regressive, and defiantly millenarian semantics and reread it through alternative models much more attuned to spatio-temporal issues and to a diaspora's own silenced discourses of disruption and discontinuity. In this argument, the Jewish experience is simultaneously history's conscience, its allegory of the democratic nation-state (Boyarin and Boyarin 1993), as well as a 'model of European transnationalism' (Boyarin 1996: 110). We place under erasure a narrative that requires, at every point, a theory of homeland as a centre that can either be reconstituted (as actually happened with the creation of Israel) or imaginatively offered as the point of origin. We need to replace it with a narrative of social interaction in the border zones of the nation-state. A people without a homeland is not an aberration, but an already prefigured cultural 'text' of late modernity. In other words, the positive side of diaspora (as seen in the lived 'internationalist' Jewish experience) is a democratic ethos of equality that does not privilege any particular ethnic community in a nation; its negative side (which is a consequence of its millenarian ethos of return to a homeland) is virulent racism and endemic nativism. This is not to say that Jews did not suffer in enlightened nation-states, nor should the argument be seen as a denial of the right to self-determination. What the argument does, however, is emphasize that the religious fossilization of the community (*vide* Smith) is not its permanent condition. What the community undergoes is a process of social semiosis whereby the tribe from a particular 'homeland' interacts with other cultures over a long period of time to produce diaspora. Against the fictions of a heroic past and a distant land, the real history of diasporas is always contaminated by the social processes that govern their lives. Indeed, the autochthonous pressures within diasporas, as discussed in the writing of Gellner, Smith, and Safran, are of concern to diasporic subjects only when a morally bankrupt nation-state asks the question 'What shall we do with them?' The unfortunate thing is that the question has been asked far too often (the Holocaust is the most obscene instance of the consequences of such a question) and continues to be asked even now.

As long as there is a fascist fringe willing to find racial scapegoats for the nation's own shortcomings and willing to chant 'Go home', the autochthonous pressures towards diasporic racial exclusivism, the pull of the imaginary, will remain strong. Addressing real diasporas does not mean that the discourses that have been part of diaspora mythology (homeland, ancient past, return, and so on) will disappear overnight. For after all, and as we have pointed out, diasporas remind nation-states in particular about their own pasts, about their own earlier migration patterns, about their traumatic moments, about their memories, their own repressed pain and wounds, and about their own prior and prioritized enjoyment of the nation. In the end, diasporas should not be thought of through the simplistic logic of the binary. We need to think about them as 'non-normative' communities, not necessarily locked into the binary of 'exile' (the condition of a declared stand against a homeland's policies and hence revered) and 'diaspora' (Barkan and Shelton's [1998: 4] 'chosen geography and exile'). We need to look at people's corporeal or even 'libidinal' investments in nations (as denizens or as outsiders); we need to read off a modernist 'transcendental homelessness' against lived experience, and we need to critically think through diasporas located in both white and non-white nation states. The theory of the diasporic imaginary outlined here attempts to address these issues and is, hopefully, a theory worthy of critical investment and reflection.

Notes

1. Jim Clifford is not alone in making diaspora a more fluid term to designate a late modern transnational formation that may be variously used to dismantle essentialist notions of social and national cohesion. A quick list of cultural theorists involved in critical diasporic politics would include Stuart Hall (black hybridity and diasporic empowerment), Paul Gilroy (diasporic flows and spaces), Homi Bhabha (diasporas as sites of a postcolonial counter aesthetic), Rey Chow (the Chinese diaspora and questions of translatability), Gayatri Spivak (subalternity and transnationality), Edward Said (exile as the intentional condition of being 'happy with the idea of unhappiness'), the Boyarin brothers (diasporic deterritorialization as the exemplary state of late modernity), William Safran (diasporas as part of narratives of centre and periphery), Arjun Appadurai (diasporic mobility and migration as the condition of the future nation-state), Ien Ang (the productivity of the multiple perspectives that come from the position of liminality), Jon Stratton (the Jewish experience as symptomatic of the ambivalent space occupied by diasporas between race and ethnicity), and Rajagopalan Radhakrishnan (the presencing of a double consciousness in an ethnic definition of diasporas). This sketchy summary doesn't take into account the massive studies of the construction of nation-states undertaken by E.P. Thompson, Ernest Gellner, Anthony Smith, Eric Hobsbawm, Partha Chatterjee, Benedict Anderson, and many others. Nor does the summary even skim the surface of studies of race, identity, and ethnicity with reference to visible diasporic minorities in nation-states. The extent to which an aesthetic version of postcolonial theory also began, essentially, as a theory of the diasporic experience of the 'border' hasn't been addressed seriously by scholars, although Arif Dirlik has implied as much.

2. See Clifford (1994: 310). Ien Ang (2001: 75) opts for a more neutral definition with reference to the Chinese diaspora(s): 'formations of people bound together, at least nominally, by a common ethnic identity despite their physical dispersal across the globe'.
3. See J. Laplanche and J.B. Pontalis (1980: 210) where they add, '(Lacan) holds that all imaginary behaviour and relationships are irremediably deceptive'. The imaginary functions as one of three terms (imaginary, symbolic, and real) and needs to be considered with reference to the other two. Here the real is a sort of substratum, the raw, primal state of the human organism (Lacan 1980: ix–x) and, I suggest, may be located in the realm of the corporeal, the body (where emotions are important), while the symbolic is the domain of culture where difference (linguistic, inter-subjective, and so on) are decisive. The trope of the imaginary is metonymy. I read diasporic subjectivities as metonymic representations, fragments of imaginary wholes, which remain forever partial and incapable of retrieving the full image that the metonym elides.
4. See Martin Heidegger, 'The Thing' (1975).
5. The Mauritian Indian case, on the face of it, presents itself as an exception to the rule, since the Indian diaspora has governed the island state since its independence on 12 March 1968. However, in as much as the prior, colonial, history of Mauritius created a cultural imaginary from which the Indians were largely excluded (a French-Creole cultural hegemony was prevalent), the Indian 'enjoyment' of the nation (as a new, creative *jouissance*) fits into the pattern I have outlined. An international conference of the Indian diaspora organized by the Mahatma Gandhi Institute/Human Service Trust, Mauritius (21–23 August 1993) was made up of delegates almost exclusively from India. The conference's excessively genuflective treatment of things Indian indicated a new way of enjoying the nation through a celebration of the nation's history of indenture past and its connections with homeland history.
6. I want to suggest that this psychology manifests itself in postmodern racism (or 'metaracism'), which often means that the demand for diverse cultural spaces and positions in a nation requires a politics of absolute difference as a means of organizing nations. In such a politics, diasporas then become victims of an epistemology of 'otherness' in which exclusion principles and practices are put in place because it is argued that this is what diasporas want. The shorthand rhetoric of the postmodern racist is the following: 'I am not a racist, indeed some of my best friends are South Asians, but they want to live their lives in that way, so why should I not support their right to be different?' This is the point at which a critical diaspora theory overlaps with a critical multiculturalism.
7. Of course, in any nation, communities that have had little difficulty in becoming part of the nation's grand narrative through assimilation cease to be diasporic in this sense.

8. I thank David McInerney for drawing my attention to Renata Salecl's work.
9. Marcella Polain, 'The Third Collision: The Armenian Genocide and After'. Paper presented to the Krishna Somers Foundation for the Study of Diasporas, Murdoch University, 13 August 2003.
10. The Third Reich killed 600,000 gypsies, almost one-third of the total population of European gypsies. In Romania, Slovakia, Germany, and Hungary, they still exist in the margins of mainstream cultural life. See Katie Trumpener (1992).
11. Jonathan M. Hess's study considers at length the links between modernity and the problematization of Jewish identity. There were those like Abraham Geiger (1810–1874) who read Jesus as a figure who 'bequeathed to modernity' modern characteristics—such as enlightenment and critical thinking—by virtue of his engagement with Judaism. As Hess cites (2002: 91), in an unpublished note (March 1770) Moses Mendelssohn wrote: 'And Jesus a Jew?—And what if, as I believe, he never wanted to give up Judaism?' Kant, of course, felt otherwise and denied that the 'pure religion of reason' (Christianity) had anything to do with Judaism. As Hess argues (2002), there was, in the end, something out of joint as modernity, in its attempt to create a universal subject, produced, from within its very principles of secular universalism, the language of anti-Semitism.
12. In 1914, the population of Palestine was around 690,000, of which fewer than 60,000 were Jews.
13. F.R. Leavis in his influential *The Great Tradition* writes about *Daniel Deronda* as two different books: one, the *Deronda* book, which is 'the bad half' (p. 94), and the other, 'the good part', which he calls the *Gwendolen Harleth* book (p. 100). To Leavis, George Eliot's Zionist inspiration results in an 'emotional flow' which leads to writing that is self-indulgent and, in the end, insincere. At the level of art, I think Leavis correctly suggests that the moral insight that could have come only though a forthright engagement with the Deronda-Gwendolen side of the plot gets attenuated because of the imperative of a 'racial mission' (a world-historical mission, after Lukács) that must insist upon the union, via a presumed love, of Deronda and Mirah, simply because the latter is a Jew and Gwendolen isn't.
14. I follow Edward W. Said, *The Question of Palestine* (1980). I thank my former Ph.D. student Maria Degabriele for drawing my attention to this work some years back.
15. The difference between Ashkenazi and Sephardim (or Mizrahim, 'Arab Jews') complicates a single narrative of Zionism. Further, the Holocaust or Shoah, 'the defining negative event of Jewish exilic existence' (Arad 2003: 5), as it gets rendered in contradictory Israeli state discourses, cautions us against constructing an unproblematic diasporic meta-narrative around the Jewish experience. In Gulie Arad's fascinating account, we read how the Shoah has shifted from conscious state-endorsed 'disremembrance'

(none other than the founding father of Israel, David Ben-Gurion, felt that Holocaust victims signified, in Gulie Arad's words, the futility of 'Jewish existence in exile') to a sign of 'Israel's collective identity'. But where once 'forgetting was essential to energize the task of creating a nation' (p. 11), the new emphasis on the Shoah as 'Israel's collective consciousness ... its political trope' (p. 16), largely in the wake of the 1973 Yom Kippur War, prevents Israel from creating a 'more inclusive counter-memory', and a less 'one-dimensional people' (p. 26). The point of Arad's persuasive argument is that diasporic memorializing (even of something as unpresentable and obscene as Auschwitz and Treblinka) 'is not sufficient for healing or for the prevention of future evil' (p. 26). This latter ethical imperative should never be lost in diaspora theory.

16. Although Safran concedes that the Indian diaspora is genuine in several respects (the characteristics imputed to this diaspora are, however, oversimplified: middlemen role, long history, integrationist, and particularist foci), he does not take up many of its self-evident features, such as homeland myth, insecurity, memory as trauma, and so on.
17. The South Asian ('Indian') diaspora is conservatively estimated at 11million: Europe 1.5 million (1.3 million in Great Britain), Africa 1.7 million (1.1 million in South Africa), Mauritius 600,000, Asia (excluding Sri Lanka) 2 million (1.2 million in Malaysia), Middle East 1.4 million (largely guest workers in the Gulf States), Latin America and the Caribbean 1 million (largely in Trinidad, Guyana, and Surinam), North America 2 million (1.2 million in the US), and the Pacific 800,000 (320,000 in Fiji). These figures, slightly modified, have been taken from Benedict Anderson (1994: 326–327, fn. 23). My figure of 11 million includes itinerant workers in the Middle East but not the Tamils of Sri Lanka, although it does include Sri Lankan Tamil migrants to the West. Anderson does not include the Tamils in Sri Lanka in his calculation either.
18. The experience of the 'new' and its vantage point as the determining condition of diaspora explains Salman Rushdie's uncomfortably naïve understanding of the Fijian coup of 2000 and the meaning of 'land' for indigenous peoples. In Rushdie's, one senses a dismissal of the necessity of historical research for the old Indian diaspora, which explains an error such as the following: 'most of Fiji's land, particularly on the main island of Viti Levu, is owned by Fijians but held by Indians on ninety-year leases' (2002: 301). In fact, only a very small percentage of this land (no more than 15 per cent) is held by Indians on lease. See also Salman Rushdie's novel *Fury* where the South Pacific island state of Lilliput-Blefuscu with its Indo-Lilly diaspora is modelled on Fiji.
19. Very generally—and with the proviso that these distinctions are, in historical terms, very provisional—we can speak of the Indian diasporas as the old diaspora of exclusivism (of plantation or classic capital or modernity) and the new diaspora of the border (of late modernity or

postmodernity). The old diaspora presents us with a case history that has been documented more or less from its moment of inception, as the Emigration Pass of each labourer contained detailed personal histories (caste, age, marital status, location, and so on). The late modern diaspora has been seen as a powerful source for postcolonial discourses of disarticulation (abandonment, displacement, dispersion, etc.) as well as a 'site' for the rearticulation of an intercultural formation through which global migration, the positioning of identities, and the nature of the bourgeois subject (have diasporas been instrumental in decentring the bourgeois subject in the first place?) may be interrogated. However, the homogenization of all Indian diasporas in terms of the politics of disarticulation/rearticulation and networking with reference to Britain, America or Canada has led to the fetishization of the new diaspora and an amnesiac disavowal of the old. Though less visible these days than the new in the story of modernity, the old Indian diaspora nevertheless constitutes a fascinating archive that can be placed relatively unproblematically alongside the 'normative' Jewish experience, because, in this instance too, a by and large semi-voluntary exodus of indentured workers began to read their own lives through the semantics of exile and dispersion.

20. The new occupies a desired space, the dreamworld of wealth and Western luxury, and is referred to in India as NRI (non-resident Indians). But in this space, a new form of racism (a metaracism) is on the ascendant and race and ethnicity get dragged into debates about multiculturalism. Writers and filmmakers of this diaspora, such as Salman Rushdie, Rohinton Mistry, M.G. Vassanji, Hanif Kureishi, Mira Nair, Deepa Mehta, Gurinder Chadha, Meera Syal, and Srinivas Krishna among others, raise theoretical questions about ethnicity and often speak of a diaspora whose overriding characteristic is mobility. Where the diaspora of exclusivism transplanted Indian icons of spirituality to the new land—finding a holy Ganges, an odd lingam, or other religious symbol in the new land—the diaspora of the border kept in touch with India, imported cultural artefacts that maintained the primal sanctity of the homeland intact. Diasporas of the border (so defined) in these Western democracies are visible presences—'we are seen, therefore we are', says the Chicano novelist John Rechy—whose corporealities carry marks of their hyphenated subjectivities (Castillo 1995, p. 113).

21. In Italian, the expression *mio paesano* (from *paese* a small town, village, or an entire country) suggests that the speaker is from the same nationality as the person who asks the question. Antonio Casella (Murdoch University Ph.D. student) informs me that the expression 'evokes a stronger, more localized sense of fellowship, identification and commonality with another person'.

22. Hobsbawm overstates the case. A number of Arab nation-states do not grant citizenship rights to foreigners, and some, like Saudi Arabia, do not

permit the construction of non-Islamic places of worship. Germany presents an interesting example since there German identity is 'defined not as affiliation to a state but to an ethnocultural nation' (Bammer 1998: 25). So Germans of ethnic descent living elsewhere are Germans (*das Volk*), while foreigners within Germany remain outsiders (*Volksfremde*).

23. See Lionnet (1998: 197–216) for a fascinating account of reactionary responses to migration in France and how even among liberals (as represented in French poster art) 'oppositional discourses are recuperated by the ideology of integration and citizenship, by a benign form of multiculturalism that insists on consensus and the celebration of differences with no room for the productive tensions caused by contestation and conflict' (p. 200).

References

Anderson, B. (1991) *Imagined Communities: Reflections on the Origin and Spread of Nationalism*. London: Verso.

Anderson, B. (1994) 'Exodus', *Critical Inquiry*, 20(2), 314–27.

Ang, I. (2001) *On Not Speaking Chinese*. London/New York: Routledge.

Appadurai, A. (1996) *Modernity at Large. Cultural Dimensions of Globalization*. Minneapolis: Minnesota University Press.

Arad, G.N. (2003) 'Israel and the Shoah: a tale of Multifarious taboos', *New German Critique*, 90, 5–26.

Bammer, A. (1998) 'The dilemma of the 'But': writing Germanness after the holocaust', in Barkan, E., and Shelton, M.D. (eds.) *Borders, Exiles, Diasporas*. Stanford, CA: Stanford University Press, 15–31.

Barkan, E., and Shelton, M.D. (1998) *Borders, Exiles, Diasporas*. Stanford, CA: Stanford University Press.

Bhabha, H. (1993) *The Location of Culture*. London: Routledge.

Binning, S. (1994) *No More Watno Dur*. Toronto: TSAR Publications.

Boyarin, D., and Boyarin, J. (1993) 'Diaspora: generation and the ground of Jewish identity', *Critical Inquiry*, 19(4), 693–725.

Boyarin, J. (1996) *Thinking in Jewish*. Chicago: University of Chicago Press.

Brah, A. (1996) *Cartographies of Diaspora*. London/New York: Routledge.

Castells, M. (1996) *The Rise of the Network Society*. Vol. 1 of *The Information Age: Economy, Society and Culture*. London: Blackwell.

Castillo, D. (1995) 'Interview with John Rechy', *Diacritics*, 25(1), 113–25.

Chatterjee, P. (1993) *Nationalist Thought and the Colonial World*. London: Zed Books.

Chow, R. (1993) *Writing Diaspora: Tactics of Intervention in Contemporary Cultural Studies*. Bloomington/Indianapolis: Indiana University Press.

Chow, R. (1998). *Ethics after Idealism: Theory-Culture-Ethnicity-Reading*. Bloomington/Indianapolis: Indiana University Press.

Clifford, J. (1994) 'Diasporas', *Cultural Anthropology*, 9(3), 302–38.

Derrida, J. (1994) *Specters of Marx* [Trans. Peggy Kamuf]. New York: Routledge.

Eliot, G. (1988) *Daniel Deronda*. Edited with an introduction by Graham Handley. Oxford: Oxford University Press.

Gellner, E. (1983) *Nations and Nationalism*. Oxford: Blackwell.

Gilroy, P. (1993) *The Black Atlantic: Modernity and Double Consciousness*. Cambridge, MA: Harvard University Press.

Hall, S. (2000) 'Conclusion: the multicultural question', in Hesse, B. (ed.) *Un/Settled Multiculturalisms*. London/New York: Zed Books, 209–41.

Heidegger, M. (1975) 'The Thing', in Heidegger, M. (ed.) *Poetry, Language, Thought* [Trans. Albert Hofstadter]. New York: Harper & Row, 165–86.

Hess, J.M. (2002) *Germans, Jews and the Claims of Modernity*. New Haven, CT/London: Yale University Press.

Hobsbawm, E.J. (1992) *Nations and Nationalism Since 1870*. Cambridge: Cambridge University Press.

Kant, I. (1992) 'An answer to the question: what is enlightenment?', in Waugh, P. (ed.) *Postmodernism: A Reader*. London: Edward Arnold, 89–95.

Lacan, J. (1980) *Écrits: A Selection*[Trans. Alan Sheridan]. London: Tavistock.

Lal, B.V. (2000) *Chalo Jahaji*: *On a Journey through Indenture in Fiji*. Canberra: Research School of Pacific and Asian Studies, Australian National University and Suva: Fiji Museum.

Laplanche, J., and Pontalis, J.B. (1980) *The Language of Psycho-analysis* [Intr. Daniel Lagache; Trans. Donald Nicholson-Smith]. London: The Hogarth Press.

Leavis, F.R. (1962) *The Great Tradition*. Harmondsworth: Penguin Books.

Lionnet, F. (1998) 'Immigration, poster art, and transgressive citizenship: France, 1968–1988', in Barkan, E., and Shelton, M.D. (eds.) *Borders, Exiles, Diasporas*. Stanford: Stanford University Press, 197–216.

Maturin, C.R. (1820) *Melmoth the Wanderer: A Tale*. Harmondsworth: Penguin Books.

Mishra, V. (1996) '(B)ordering Naipaul: indenture history and diasporic poetics', *Diaspora: A Journal of Transnational Studies*, 5(2), 189–37.

Naipaul, V.S. (1984) *The Overcrowded Barracoon*. New York: Vintage Books.

Patke, R.S. (2000) 'Benjamin's *Arcades Project* and the Postcolonial City'. *Diacritics*, 30(4), 3–14.

Portuges, C. (1998) 'Accenting L.A.: Central Europeans in diasporan Hollywood in the 1940s', in Barkan, E., and Shelton, M.D. (eds.) *Borders, Exiles, Diasporas*. Stanford, CA: Stanford University Press, 46–57.

Qur'an, The Holy (1917/1999) Translated by Maulana Muhammad Ali. Columbus, OH: The Ahmadiyyah Anjuman Isha'at Islam, Lahore, Inc.

Radhakrishnan, R. (2003) *Theory in an Uneven World*. Oxford: Blackwell.

Radhakrishnan, R.(1996) *Diasporic Meditations: Between Home and Location*. Minneapolis: University of Minnesota Press.

Rai, A.S. (1995) 'India on-line: electronic bulletin boards and the construction of a diasporic Hindu identity', *Diaspora*, 4(1), 31–57.

Ravuvu, A. (1991) *The Façade of Democracy: Fijian Struggles for Political Control 1830–1987*. Suva: Reader Publishing House.

Rushdie, S. (2001) *Fury*. London: Jonathan Cape.

Rushdie, S. (2002) *Step across this Line: Collected Nonfiction 1992–2002*. New York: Random House.

Safran, W. (1991) 'Diasporas in modern societies: myths of homeland and return', *Diaspora*, 1(1), 83–99.

Said, E.W. (1984) 'Reflections on exile', Granta, 13, 157–72.

Said, E.W.(1980) *The Question of Palestine*. New York: Vintage Books.

Said, E.W. (1979) *Orientalism*. New York: Vintage Books.

Salecl, R. (1994) *The Spoils of Freedom*. London: Routledge.

Sartre, J.P. (1974) *Between Existentialism and Marxism* [Trans. John Matthews]. London: New Left Books.

Smith, A.D. (1986) *The Ethnic Origins of Nations*. Oxford: Blackwell.

Spivak, G.C. (1996) 'Diasporas Old and New: women in the transnational world', *Textual Practice*, 10, 245–69.

Stratton, J. (2000) *Coming Out Jewish: Constructing Ambivalent Identities*. London: Routledge.

Tasso, T. 2000. *Gerusalemme Liberata* [Ed. and Trans. Anthony M. Esolen]. Baltimore, MD/London: Johns Hopkins University Press.

Trumpener, K. (1992) 'The time of the Gypsies: a "people without history" in the narratives of the West', *Critical Inquiry*, 18(4), 843–84.

Tulasidasa (1947) *Ramacaritamanasa* (*Ramayana*). Gorakhpur: Gita Press.

Vassanji, M.G. (2004) *The In-Between World of Vikram Lall*. Melbourne: Text Publishing.

ž ižek, S. (1989) *The Sublime Object of Ideology*. London: Verso.

ž ižek, S. (1993) *Tarrying with the Negative: Kant, Hegel and the Critique of Ideology*. Durham, NC: Duke University Press.

ž ižek, S. (1997) 'Multiculturalism, or, the cultural logic of multinational capitalism', *New Left Review*, 225, 28–51.

14

'Innocents Abroad' and 'Prohibited Immigrants'

Australians in India and Indians in Australia 1890–1910

Margaret Allen

In 1907, Eleanor Rivett, MA, a young modern woman and a graduate of Melbourne University, left Australia to become a missionary for the London Missionary Society in Calcutta. As she made her way from Colombo up to Calcutta, she stopped off in Madras and spent a day with Elsie Nicol, another Melbourne graduate. Nicol was running the YWCA hostel in Madras, where women students could stay while studying at Madras University. In following her vocation as a missionary in India, Eleanor was leaving behind her parents and her numerous siblings. But she and her brother David had made a vow that if he won the Rhodes scholarship he would spend some time with her in India. Later in 1907, she was able to take leave and explore the northern cities of India with David on his way to Oxford. They went to Benares, Lucknow, Kanpur, Agra, Delhi, and Bombay.[1] They were, she recalled, 'the innocents abroad', but it was 'a marvellous tour'.[2]

Eleanor Rivett was the first Australian to go to north India under the auspices of the London Missionary Society, and she would spend some 40 years there. But neither she nor Elsie Nicol was the first Australian to work as a missionary in India. As will be discussed later in this chapter, a number of Australian women and men went to India in that religious capacity. They felt drawn to travel far from their homes to take up the cause, as they saw it, of evangelizing the heathen of India. As they devoted themselves to their Christian work in India, many struggled with the long separation from home and family that such a step involved. For a number, such separations were eased somewhat when members of their family and friends visited them in India. Furthermore, missionaries were able to return home on furlough. Thus, the ships that serviced the routes between Australian ports and Colombo and other ports on the subcontinent would often carry a missionary or two. Such travellers felt called and definitely entitled to travel and to stay in India for long periods of time. They engaged in many activities there, such as establishing hospitals and running schools. For Australian women missionaries, the responsibilities as administrators, teachers, preachers, nurses, and doctors in the mission fields were broader than those they could have taken on in Australia. Some might claim that their religious vocation marked them off from those with a mere desire to travel and see the world, to make a career or simply experience foreign lands. But these women can also be understood in the same framework as those studied by Angela Woollacott in *To Try Her Fortune in London*. Observing that 'the industrialization of travel and [their] ... modern ambition for education, jobs, and careers promoted [these women's] mobility'. 'The Australian girl', she suggests, came to stand for 'modernity and independence'.[3]

Also on these ships might be another figure, whom I will describe, for the purposes of summary as 'an Indian'.[4] Usually a man, the Indian traveller might have lived in India, Australia, or another part of the Empire altogether. He could have been returning to Australia after a sojourn in India or a tourist seeking to enjoy the sights of Australia and other destinations. But, with the passage of the Immigration Restriction Act in the Commonwealth of Australia in 1901, such travel was limited and controlled. The Australian authorities categorized Indians, although British subjects, as 'natives of Asia', who had no automatic entitlement to travel freely between India and Australia. The Australians and the Indians had 'differential access to mobility'.[5] Although Indians were negotiating their own modernity, travelling around the world in pursuit of pleasure, greater opportunities, and personal transformation, Australian government policies increasingly categorized them as people whose movements should be strictly controlled. Australians tended to represent Indians as exotic and backward. As David Walker has pointed out, Australian accounts of travel in India tended to emphasize its 'antiquity and spiritual wealth'.[6] He found in Alfred Deakin's writing on India, that 'Ancient India was readily celebrated while modern India and Indians were routinely disparaged'.[7] In the discourse of modernity, Indians were represented as backward, fixed, and static. Woollacott has pointed out that: 'Western modernity must be viewed as having been created in a symbiotic relationship with its racially constructed others, and that racial hierarchies, including whiteness as a racial identity, have been integrally constitutive of modernity'.[8]

When the Reverend Theo B. Fischer of the Australian Churches of Christ, on a missionary tour to India in 1912, met some of the Indian lawyers at the High Court in Madras, he was clearly surprised to find that they were 'quite up in the politics of the world, acquainted with most English books of recent date, as well as standard works'.[9]

This chapter explores the differing experiences of Australian missionaries in India in the late nineteenth and early twentieth centuries and those of Indians who also sought to travel and improve their life chances in Australia. The newly federated Commonwealth of Australia was established, in part, 'to guard ... against the dangers of Asiatic immigration'.[10] The Australian government insisted upon the creation of a white nation, which meant that the movement of Indians seeking to travel to and from Australia was strictly controlled and often forbidden.

These developments can be viewed within the broader context of the British Empire, in which the movement of British Indians was increasingly being curtailed. As British subjects, Indians posed a challenge to the governments of the settler colonies. Their status as British subjects might have meant that they could travel and settle freely, but with the growth of colonial nationalism, governments sought to maintain the power and influence of white settlers.

Following the abolition of slavery, Indians had been transported around the Empire as indentured labourers and some had elected to stay on in the colonies at the end of their term of engagement.[11] Thus, there were Indian communities in South Africa, Malaya, Fiji, East Africa as well as in the Caribbean. By the late nineteenth century, Indians began to outnumber Europeans in the colony of Natal, which passed legislation to restrict their further immigration following the example of an American Act of 1896 (see Lake 2005). In 1897, the Natal government passed an act to 'prevent the importation of coolie labour from India'.[12] This used a language test to exclude those it classed as prohibited immigrants. New Zealand followed suit in 1899 and Australia in 1901.[13] Canada initially used a poll tax and shipping regulations to deter Indian immigration.[14]

The British government, while purporting to uphold the equality of British subjects across the Empire, colluded with colonial governments in their determination to discriminate against non-white British subjects. British officials suggested particular forms of words for colonial legislation that appeared not to discriminate against non-white

British subjects and the Empire's Japanese allies, while making it possible for colonial and later Dominion governments to prevent the entry of Asians to their countries, to prohibit their enfranchisement and their participation in particular trades and occupations.[15] The upholding of the rights of the British subject while denying them to British Indians and other non-white British subjects was, as Radhika Mongia notes, a good example of the 'rule of colonial difference'.[16] From time to time, the Viceroy and members of the Indian Civil Service contested this double standard and voiced criticism of particular pieces of legislation such as the Australian Immigration Restriction Act. In the official correspondence, there is evidence of resentment about Australian treatment of particular Indians and a refusal to accede to Australian requests to prevent Indians departing for Australia. Natal, Australia, and New Zealand had restricted immigration, and Canada was anxious to do so. Eventually, however, under the guise of wartime controls, the Government of India introduced a passport system in 1915, which controlled the movement of Indians, 'requiring passports from all Indians proceeding outside India'.[17]

Mongia has focused upon debates during 1906 to 1915, around 'Canadian demands that Indians emigrating to Canada should have passports',[18] while Radhika Singha has explored the development of passport policy of the Government of India from 1911 to 1923,[19] but a transnational approach allows for a broader address to such issues, bringing together policy developments across the British Empire, at least. Lake has shown the importance of looking further, to the United States, in examining the development of ideologies and techniques to restrict non-white immigration.

Indians resident in settler colonies often campaigned vigorously against racial discrimination. In South Africa, Mahatma Gandhi was a key figure in this resistance from the 1890s, and his experiences there were crucial to the later development of his political philosophy.[20] The treatment of Indians overseas was of continuing concern to the Indian nationalist movement in the early twentieth century. In 1901, Gandhi was instrumental in getting the Indian National Congress to pass a resolution on the rights of Indians in South Africa.[21] G.K. Gokhale and the Servants of India Society in Poona and H.S. Polak and the Indians Overseas Association, based in London, as well as numerous Indians across the Empire, kept these issues on the nationalist agenda.[22] The distinctions made between the white and non-white subjects of the Empire and, in particular, the denial of Dominion status to India continued to be condemned by Indian leaders in the interwar years.[23]

While Indians were campaigning for the protection of their rights as British subjects, Australians were able to move about freely and work and settle in all parts of the Empire, as Australian missionaries did in India. To discuss the missionary activity of Australians in India requires the examination of the work of a number of different Christian denominations, which before and well after federation were organized on a colonial and then on state basis. In 1882, the South Australian Baptist Missionary Society sent Ellen Arnold and Marie Gilbert to do *zenana* work in Faridpur, West Bengal, where they established the South Australian mission. A number of other Australians from the various colonies followed in their footsteps. Between 1882 and 1913, the Australian Baptist Mission Societies sent 54 women and 16 men to the field in Bengal.[24] The Reverend Silas Mead of Flinders Street Baptist Church in Adelaide was a strong promoter of the Baptist mission movement and has been dubbed the 'father of Australian Baptist missions'.[25] From 1892, his son Dr Cecil Mead and his wife, Alice, served as medical missionaries at Faridpur.

In the south of India, the Presbyterian Women's Missionary Association (PWMA) of New South Wales supported the Church of Scotland Zenana Mission with Mary MacLean, the first PWMA missionary to arrive in 1891. A few years later, the PWMA took over the mission at Sholingur, just north of Madras. Mary MacLean founded a school there and worked there for 20 years.[26]

Mission work in India was the goal for a number of dedicated young Australian women. In the early twentieth century, many students at Australia's fledgling universities supported the Missionary Settlement for University Women (MSUW) and its work with educated and higher caste women in India. The MSUW, which set up a settlement and then a hostel for women students in Bombay, had been established by women from Newnham, Girton, and Somerville Colleges in Oxford and Cambridge. Their identity as university women was central to the organization, which attracted strong interest from students in Australia, who heard about it from the networks of Empire. A Melbourne graduate, Susie Williams, came to know of the MSUW while she was a student at Newnham College, Oxford. She wrote home to her friends, also graduates from Melbourne University, and soon there were branches established at the universities in Melbourne, Sydney, and Adelaide.[27]

In 1903, Katie Fell, with her sister and their mother, Lady Helen Fell, stopped off in Bombay on their way back from a European tour. Katie had graduated with an Arts degree from Sydney University, where she had become involved in the Student Christian Movement. Inspired by its leader, John Mott, with his message about the evangelization of the world, she developed a particular interest in the MSUW. In London, its leaders had persuaded her to spend some time in Bombay, and she remained there for 6 months, the first Australian to be based there. Other Australian women later came to work at the settlement and the associated YWCA hostels in Madras and Calcutta. Elsie Nicol had come to India under the auspices of the MSUW and soon after was asked to run the YWCA hostel at Madras, on behalf of both organizations. There she came to love the young Indian women with whom she worked, one of whom, Nallemma Williams, a medical student from Ceylon, became a special friend and her bridesmaid, when she married in Madras, in 1909.[28] Nicol supported Nallemma Williams' selection as a delegate to the YWCA world conference in Paris in 1903. Australian supporters of the MSUW could follow the activities of the settlers, which were reported at length in various other missionary publications.

These women were accustomed to the idea of travel and service abroad in the missionary cause. India was an important site of Christian missionary endeavour and for Australian Christians, who sought to become missionaries, India was an important venue. In 1895, Charles Reeve, an experienced evangelist from Tasmania, established the Poona and Indian Village Mission (PIVM) in Poona.[29] He travelled regularly to England, Scotland, New Zealand, and Australia to recruit missionaries and to raise funds. A number of Australian men and women subsequently joined this mission, including Amy Parsons, a young Adelaide woman, who had initially gone to Faridpur in East Bengal in 1888 under the auspices of the South Australian Baptist Mission Society. In this, she followed the footsteps of Ellen Arnold and Marie Gilbert, who had been the first missionaries there in 1882.[30] But back in Adelaide on furlough in 1894, she was taken by Charles Reeve's message and joined the PIVM, where she served from many years. She continued to travel back and forth to Australia, only finally retiring to Australia in the late 1940s. Having spent virtually all her adult life in India, it is not surprising that she described India as 'The Land of My Adoption'.[31]

The PIVM and other missions depended on the railways and protection of the British Empire. They could count on the support of the British forces, should their preaching prove offensive to Indians, when, for example, they campaigned at holy sites on special religious occasions. From 1905, the PIVM missionaries started going to Hindu holy places at Pandharpur, near Poona, at the time of the *jutras*. When these missionaries were attacked in 1908, British authorities arrived to protect them and their mission. Twenty-six Indian men and boys were arrested, tried, found guilty, and sentenced variously to rigorous imprisonment and whipping.[32]

While Australian women missionaries sought to impart a Christian education to those in the settlements, many Indians in the late nineteenth century sought to enhance their education by travelling across the world to Europe and America. Although Hindus were concerned about travelling across 'the black waters', a steady stream of students made their way to British universities.[33] Moreover, Christian converts went to recruit more to the mission field. Others just wanted to see more of the world and to experience new places and see new people. Some Indian travellers published accounts of their travels.[34] One such was Hajee Mahomed, who made extensive tours around the world between 1886 and 1887 and again between 1893 and 1895. He was a man of Empire, Indian born, and in business in Cape Town. In the introduction to his book, he explained why he published an account of his travels: 'My principal object in publishing these pages is to give some idea, however faint and crude, to my countrymen, and particularly to my Mahomedan brethren, that beyond the narrow bounds of their home, there lies a world of joy and beauty'.[35]

On his second tour, he spent some time in Melbourne, Hobart, and Sydney, and was quite taken with the night life of Melbourne: 'On Saturday night, Melbourne, as is the case with large European cities, was gay and brilliant with illuminations and crowds of pleasure seekers going to theatres, concert and restaurants. I wandered about in amazement and wonder till a late hour'.[36] He enjoyed the sights in the Dandenongs and through his imperial connections was able to visit the Observatory. A Cape Town friend, settled in Melbourne, introduced him to the superintendent, Mr Ellery, who explained to him 'some of the wonders of the starry world'.[37] He then went north, where he enjoyed the beauty of Sydney, 'superior to Melbourne in its natural loveliness'.[38] In Hobart, he saw some business opportunities: 'I believe that if some enterprising countrymen of mine were to open a business in Indian cloth Japanese curiosities and Cutch [sic] and Delhi metal and art works, they are likely to do well'.[39] Generally, he found the colonists he met kind and polite. But he also noted the difficulties encountered by poor hawkers from Bengal, Kashmir, and the Sind: 'These traders appeared to be quite a harmless lot, working hard for their daily bread. They are perfectly innocent of English and do not know how very black they are painted by the jealousy and prejudice of writers in the Australian journals'.[40]

A number of Indian men had arrived in Australia from the mid-nineteenth century and often took work as hawkers or labourers.

Some arrived from elsewhere in the Empire. Otim Singh, for example, had worked as a 'supervisor in a large tobacco-plantation on Sumatra, on behalf of an English firm', where he, reportedly, had '200 coolies under his control'.[41] He returned to his home in the Punjab, where he purchased some land, but the call of distant lands caught him once more and he set sail for Batavia (Jakarta) to visit his brother, before arriving in Melbourne in 1890. He worked as an itinerant hawker in Victoria and later in South Australia, where he established a store and a prosperous business which he ran until his death in 1927.[42]

Otim Singh was one of many Indians living in Australia at the end of the nineteenth century when the Australian colonies began to legislate to restrict the entry of Indians and other 'Asiatics'. In New South Wales, for example, after an attempt to exclude Asians by name was 'reserved' by the Colonial Office, the Coloured Races Restriction and Regulation Bill, utilizing the 'Natal formula', was passed in 1897. Aliens, including Indians, had thenceforth to enter their names on an Aliens Register and around 90 Indians did so in Sydney between 1899 and 1902.[43] They were required to pay two shillings and six pence for this privilege. Acts to restrict Asian immigration were also passed in Western Australia, Tasmania, and Victoria.[44] At the time of federation, in 1901, one estimate calculated the number of Indians in Australia at 7637.[45] The Immigration Restriction Act of 1901, as noted earlier, classified Indians as 'natives of Asia' who could only enter Australia if they could pass a 'dictation test' in a European language, administered in such a manner as to exclude them. In the years following the passing of the Immigration Restriction Act, the number of Indians in Australia declined to around 3698 by 1911.[46]

Initially, after 1901, it became virtually impossible for any Indian to come to Australia, except some who had lived in Australia previously. It was possible for those already resident in Australia to gain a Domicile certificate and, after 1905, a Certificate of Exemption from the Dictation Test (CEDT). This operated like a passport, which allowed the holder to re-enter Australia within three years. It carried two photographs of the holder, a profile as well as full-face view and a handprint. It was possible for holders of such certificates to apply for extensions and some were able to stay away from Australia for 12 or more years before returning. But not all Indians who had resided in Australia were accorded the right to re-enter.

Marie de Lepervanche has argued that in the earliest years of federation, the definition of 'domicile' was very narrow, so that many who had lived for years in Australia were not granted a 'certificate of domicile'. Generally, those who had some capital in Australia were more likely to be allowed to return than those who had very little.[47] After 1903, it seems that 'applications for domicile were generally approved if evidence of good character and five years' residence was produced'.[48] In order to establish their worth, local police officers were required to make a check on the applicant for a Domicile certificate, or after 1905, a CEDT. Thus, in 1903, the Walgett police made enquiries about Burket Ali Khan, who applied for a certificate of domicile, as he wished to go to India for 'about three years or less, attending private business'. He had been in Australia since 1895 and was a storekeeper in partnership with Curam Bux, Nabob Khan, and Omar Khan at Comborah near Walgett. Although the police reported that Burket Ali Khan was 'not the owner of any land and his share in the business is not worth over £25', he was granted a certificate. The police report noted that they 'knew nothing against his character'.[49]

Thus, Indians who left Australia had to undergo quite rigorous scrutiny in order to be able to return to Australia. Their applications were accompanied by references, often from employers or people with whom they had done business, in which the referees acknowledged knowing the applicants for some time and testified to their good character. Often the police made a visit to the referees to get confirmation that the photograph on the application was that of the person for whom they had vouched.

Most Indians in Australia were men, and they found it difficult if not impossible to bring wives from India. In 1904, Hushnak Singh, a domestic servant of Narrabeen applied for 'a certificate of naturalization'. A Punjabi, he had been in Australia since 1898. He was, he wrote, 'a British subject' and formerly 'a trooper in 6th Bengal Lancer[s] Prince of Wales [Regiment]'. He planned to make a brief trip to India to marry and wanted the necessary documentation to enable him to bring his bride back to Australia. The Department of External Affairs informed him that naturalization was unnecessary as he was a British subject. His intended bride, however 'would be deemed a prohibited immigrant'. The Secretary Attlee Hunt advised, 'the Lady will have to pass the Education Test which may be imposed in any European language'.[50] It is not known what happened to Hushnak Singh and his bride, but it was very difficult for British Indians to bring their families to Australia.[51]

Until 1904, only Indians formerly resident in Australia and able to get a certificate of domicile were able to enter Australia. However, in 1905, following negotiations with the Government of India the regulations were relaxed and amended to allow for the visits and temporary stays of tourists, students, and *bona fide* merchants. The British authorities in India were required to issue passports, for visits to Australia, to those eligible under the revised regulations. The passport specifically devised for this purpose detailed the traveller's name and that of his father, given in both English and the vernacular. Information on this form also included the traveller's caste or clan, residence—detailing town or village and district or state—profession, age, and, for male travellers only, a description of distinctive marks. A full description of the purpose of the visit, its probable duration, the port of embarkation, and the names, ages, and relationships of members of the family accompanying the applicant were also to be given. This document and the accuracy of the information on it had to be vouched for and endorsed by a magistrate or political officer in India.[52]

Article 14 of the amended act worked to deter shippers from bringing prohibited immigrants to Australian ports. Huttenback notes: 'It required the master or owner of any vessel bringing a prohibited immigrant to the Commonwealth to return him whence he came at no cost to the state and to recompense the Government of Australia for any expenses incurred in the interim'. Shipping companies thus became extremely cautious in deciding whether to allow Indians to embark for Australia. In 1908, when Syed Iran Shah Sahid attempted to travel to Australia to bring back 'an aged relative who had settled there' he failed to secure a passage, although he had the required passport. He travelled four times to Colombo from Madras, but discovered that 'the steamer companies there refuse to book any natives of India to Australia unless they hold a pass from the Australian government allowing them to land'.[53] Similarly, Ghulam Jan, who planned to visit Australia 'to search for a brother who has not been heard of for many years' was also denied a passage by a shipping company at Colombo.[54] Further information had to be sent to the various shipping companies to explain the new arrangements for Indians with a legitimate passport allowing them to visit Australia.

Once Indian travellers landed in Australia, there was still a possibility of deportation. Ghulam Jan and the servant who had accompanied him ran into trouble shortly after their arrival in Australia in 1908. The West Australian police alleged that they were 'imposters', 'cadgers', and 'undesirables', and they were deported. This was despite the fact that a number of Ghulam Jan's 'countrymen and co-religionists' in Perth signed a memorial testifying that

> all can speak of the excellent character he has maintained during his sojourn in this city and the high esteem he is held in by all who have the

> pleasure of meeting him. We further wish to add that the Syed has been fortunate in his search, and found his brother in Port Hedland (W.A.) for which, and only purpose, he [The Syed] has visited this country.[55]

Indians had protested against the Australian policies since the late nineteenth century. In 1898, Indian traders in Melbourne had sent a memorial to the Government of India protesting against the Victorian colony's Immigration Restriction Bill and in the following year, 'Certain Sikhs resident in WA' sent a petition 'complaining of their disabilities under recent legislation in that colony'. Such protests continued after 1901. Merchants in an Indian business in Melbourne wrote to the press in 1902 in relation to the Immigration Restriction Act. They were seeking to get five Indians into the country to work in their business: 'the Act is operating very harshly upon us, and is likely to bring about results inimical to the interests of Australia and to the good feeling existing between fellow British subjects of two shades of colour'.[56] They warned of a boycott, or on the part of the Mohammedans, a 'jehad' just as they had done, they said, in regard to Natal when it introduced immigration restrictions. They advised that the National Congress of India 'have already taken the matter up, and may be expected to pass some resolution on the matter early in the coming year'.[57]

Indians across the Empire became more aware of Australian policies in 1905 when Mool Chand was deported. He was an Indian civil servant from Lahore who arrived in Perth on a visit in 1904. Having previously worked on the railways in India, in Uganda, and in the civil service of British North Borneo, he was an experienced man of Empire, able to travel around to take up work. When he was discovered working in a Perth business owned by a fellow countryman, Inder Singh, however, he was summarily deported. This led to a storm of protest from the Indian community in Western Australia and their supporters. Mool Chand instructed a Perth solicitor to institute action for damages for false imprisonment and illegal deportation against the Collector of Customs. He also stated his intentions to institute proceedings against Alfred Deakin, the Australian Prime Minister.[58]

When the Reverend Theo. Fischer of the Church of Christ was visiting missions in India, he was challenged about Australian policies: 'An official to whom we spoke in one place could not understand why Australia, which claimed to be a Christian country, would not admit him, for instance, to Australian shores'.[59]

Indian public opinion was often incensed by Australian immigration policies and Indians began to ask why, when they were being treated so badly by the Australian government, that Australian citizens could still enter India freely and take up jobs and establish businesses there. In late August 1905, three Indian doctors arrived in Perth. While they acknowledged that they had proper papers and did not have 'much difficulty' in landing in Australia, they were shocked to note that they were listed on their ship's papers as 'prohibited immigrants'.[60] They contrasted the cordial welcome they had received in England, with the efforts to debar them when they were merely making a short visit to Australia. Australian doctors visiting India, in contrast, were 'allowed every freedom'.[61] Furthermore, they would be 'free to come and go and given every help in the pursuit and investigations of their studies'. Certainly, Australian doctors visiting India were not required to carry special exemptions, nor were they on 'mustered up like sheep to pass an inspection' and subject to a penalty of £100 per head for their safe removal.[62]

While Australians—as white British subjects—enjoyed the freedom to travel and work and spread the Christian gospel in India, the White Australia Policy effectively debarred Indians from the enjoyment of reciprocal rights in Australia. The mobility of modernity was reserved for those deemed white.

Notes

1. The names for India cities in use in the period being discussed, i.e., Bombay, Madras, and Poona have been retained in this chapter.
2. Eleanor Rivett, *Memory Plays a Tune … Being Recollections of India 1907–1947* (Sydney: Author, 1965), 10.
3. Angela Woollacott, *To Try Her Fortune in London: Australian Women, Colonialism and Modernity* (Oxford: Oxford University Press, 2001), 8, 157.
4. I use this term in a broad and general manner to include Indian subjects of British rule and Indians living in the Princely States of India which were ruled indirectly by Britain. Of course after 1947, some of the people referred to in this paper may have been identified as Pakistanis. Australians often referred to Indians living in Australia as Afghans. It is possible that a couple of people referred to in this chapter as Indians, may have indeed been Afghans.
5. Radhika Viyas Mongia, 'Race, Nationality, Mobility: A History of the Passport', *After the Imperial Turn: Thinking With and Through the Nation*, ed. Antoinette Burton (Durham, NC/London: Duke University Press, 2003), 211.
6. David Walker, *Anxious Nation: Australia and the Rise of Asia 1850–1939* (St Lucia: University of Queensland Press, 1999), p 19.

7. Walker, *Anxious Nation*, 22. Alfred Deakin, a key figure in the moves towards federation and Prime Minister of Australia in the early twentieth century, wrote *Temple and Tomb in India* (Melbourne: Melville, Mullen and Slade, 1893) and *Irrigated India: An Australian View of India and Ceylon, Their Irrigation and Agriculture* (Melbourne: E.A. Petherick, 1893).
8. Angela Woollacott, 'White Colonialism and Sexual Modernity: Australian Women in the Early Twentieth Century Metropolis', *Gender, Sexuality and Colonial Modernities*, ed. Antoinette Burton (London: Routledge, 1999), 49.
9. T.B. Fischer, *A Month in India* (Melbourne: Austral Publishing Company, 1914), 111.
10. Myra Willard, *History of the White Australia Policy until 1920* (Melbourne: Melbourne University Press, 1923), 119.
11. See Kay Saunders (ed.), *Indentured Labour in the British Empire, 1834–1920* (London: Croom Helm, 1984).
12. Daniel Gorman, 'Wider and Wider Still?: Racial Politics, Intra-Imperial Immigration and the Absence of Imperial Citizenship in the British Empire'. *Journal of Colonialism and Colonial History* 3 (2002) (3): para 30. Available at http://muse.jhu.edu/journals/journal_of_colonialism_and_colonial_history/toc/cch3.3.html (accessed on 13 February 2003). See also Robert Huttenback, *Racism and Empire: White Settlers and Colored Immigrants in the British Self-Governing Colonies, 1830–1910* (Ithaca, NY/London: Cornell University Press, 1976), 139ff; Marilyn Lake, 'From Mississippi to Melbourne via Natal: the invention of the literacy test as a technology of racial exclusion', *Connected Worlds: History in Transnational Perspective,* eds. Ann Curthoys and Marilyn Lake (Canberra: Australian National University Press, 2005), 209–230.
13. Hugh Tinker, *Separate and Unequal: India and Indians in the British Commonwealth 1920–1950* (London: C. Hurst and Company, 1976), 22.
14. Mongia, 'Race, Nationality, Mobility'.
15. Marie de Lepervanche, *Indians in a White Australia: An Account of Race, Class, and Indian Immigration to Eastern Australia* (Sydney: Allen and Unwin, 1984), 56–71. There are extensive examples in National Archives (UK) Colonial Office papers CO 885/8 no. 158, CO 885/9, no. 168, CO 886/1 nos. 1–3, CO 886/2 no. 10, CO 886/3 no. 19, CO 886/4 no. 21. These files comprise correspondence and papers relative to the immigration of Asiatics into the Colonies and the treatments of Asiatics in the Dominions.
16. Mongia, 'Race, Nationality, Mobility'; see also Partha Chatterjee, *The Nation and Its Fragments: Colonial and Postcolonial Histories* (Princeton, NJ: Princeton University Press, 1993), 16–22.
17. Mongia, 'Race, Nationality, Mobility', 210.
18. Ibid., 196.

19. Radhika Singha, 'Exceptions to the Law, and Exceptional Laws: The Regulation of Mobility in Colonial India 1911–1923'(2005), unpublished paper presented to 20th International Congress of Historical Sciences, University of New South Wales, 7 July.
20. See Robert Huttenback, *Gandhi in South Africa: British Imperialism and the Indian Question, 1860–1914* (Ithaca, NY/London: Cornell University Press, 1971).
21. Tinker, *Separate and Unequal*, 23.
22. Ibid., 24; see also B. Chaturvedi collection in Indian National Archives (New Delhi).
23. Tinker, *Separate and Unequal*.
24. See Ros [sic] Gooden 'We Trust Them to Establish the Work': Significant Roles of Early Australian Baptist Women in Overseas Mission, 1864–1913', *This Gospel Shall be Preached: Essays on the Australian Contribution to World Mission*, ed. Mark Hutchinson and Geoff Treloar (Sydney: The Centre for the Study of Australian Christianity, 1998), 126–46; and Margaret Allen, '"White Already to Harvest": South Australian Women Missionaries in India', *Feminist Review* 65 (2000) (1): 92–107.
25. Rosalind Gooden, 'Silas Mead Baptist Missions Motivator', *Our Yesterdays* 2 (1994): 67–95.
26. Janet West, *Daughters of Freedom: A History of Women in the Australian Church* (Sutherland, NSW: Albatross, 1997), 207–8.
27. British Library Oriental and India Office Collection (OIOC) Mss Eur f 186/128 Missionary Society for University Women (MSUW) Annual Report 1900, p. 35.
28. OIOC MSS/Eur f 186/142 MSUW Quarterly Newsletter no. 40, January 1909, p. 7.
29. I am very grateful to Rachel Human (Kew, Victoria), Gillian Watch Whittall (Queensland) and Elisabeth Wilson (Hobart) for sharing information about Charles Reeve with me.
30. See Allen, "White Already to Harvest".
31. A. Parsons, 'Back to the Land of My Adoption', *White Already to Harvest* 25 (1920) (3): 59.
32. SIM Archives, North Carolina, USA. Poona and Inland Village Mission Records Box 5 Pandarharpur Station Diary 1908–1909 includes Report in *Bombay Guardian*, 10 October 1908.
33. Shompa Lahiri, *Indians in Britain: Anglo-India Encounters, Race and Identity 1880–1930* (London: Frank Cass, 2000), 5, 21–9.
34. Antoinette Burton, 'Making a Spectacle of Empire: Indian Travellers In Fin-de-Siècle London', *History Workshop Journal* 42 (1996): 128. See also *Pandita Rambai's American Encounter: The Peoples of the United*

States, translated and edited by Meera Kosambi (Bloomington, IN: Indiana University Press, 2003).

35. H.S.S. Mahomed, *Journal of My Tours around the World, 1886–1887 and 1893–1895* (Bombay: Duftur Ashkra Oil Engine Press, 1895), vii.
36. Ibid., 62.
37. Ibid., 64.
38. Ibid., 76.
39. Ibid., 66.
40. Ibid., 78.
41. H.T. Burgess, *Cyclopedia of South Australia*, Vol. 2 (Adelaide: Cyclopedia Company, 1909), 1019.
42. *Kangaroo Island Courier*, 10 December 1927, p. 2.
43. National Archives of Australia (NAA) Series SP 822/10 Aliens' Register (Sydney) 1898–1902.
44. de Lepervanche, *Indians in a White Australia*, 51–55.
45. Palfreeman, in de Lepervanche, *Indians in a White Australia*, 24.
46. de Lepervanche, *Indians in a White Australia*, 24.
47. Ibid., 57.
48. Ibid.
49. NAA Collector of Customs, Sydney Series SP 42/1 Correspondence Relating to Immigration Restriction and Passports 1898–1948 C1903/5965 re Burket Ali Khan.
50. NAA Department of External Affairs Series A1 Correspondence Files, 1904/2531 Hushnak Singh Naturalization.
51. Huttenback notes that while under the IRA 1901, an immigrant's wife and minor children could enter Australia, this section was suspended in March 1903 and deleted in the amended act of 1905. Huttenback, *Racism and Empire*, 308, note 72. De Lepervanche suggests that from 1906 Indian residents could bring their wives over for 6 months each year. Certainly from April 1919, resident Indians could bring their wives and minor children to live with them in Australia; see A.T. Yarwood, *Asian Migration to Australia: The Background to Exclusion 1896–1923* (Melbourne: Melbourne University Press, 1964), 135.
52. NAA Series A1 1925/27045 Admission of Indians, Cingalese [Sinhalese] and Burmese Merchants, students, and tourist travellers on passports.
53. Ibid. Acting Chief Secretary of Madras Government to Secretary Government of India 13 November 1908.
54. Ibid. Agent to Governor General, Baluchistan to Secretary to Governor General, Shimla 8 May 1908.
55. Indian National Archives (New Delhi), Foreign Department General A Proceedings, April 1909, numbers 36–38.

56. *Register,* Adelaide 22 December 1902, p. 3.
57. Ibid., 22 December 1902, p. 3; see also A.M. Zaidi, compiler, 1987–, *INC* [Indian National Congress]*: The Glorious Tradition 1885–1920*, vol. 1 (New Delhi: Indian Institute of Applied Political Research), 234–5.
58. NAA Department of External Affairs Series A1 Correspondence Files, 1908/11468 Deportation of Mool Chand 1905–8. In the event, Mool Chand did not pursue these actions.
59. Fischer, *A Month in India*, 111.
60. NAA Department of External Affairs Series A1 Correspondence Files, 1908/11468 Deportation of Mool Chand 1905–8, clipping from *Perth Herald*, 29 August 1905.
61. A number of Australian doctors worked in India at this time. Some were missionaries, while others were hired by the Indian authorities to work as 'plague doctors' giving inoculations and helping to overcome plague epidemics. Dr R. Hornabrook was one of the Australian doctors who worked in this capacity in India in 1902–1903. See Margaret Allen, 'Through Colonial Spectacles', *Journeying and Journalling: Creative and Critical Meditations on Travel Writing*, ed. Kate Douglas et al. (Adelaide: Wakefield Press, 2010), 133–48.
62. Allen, 'Through Colonial Spectacles'.

15

The Spatial, Social, and Political Incorporation of Asian Indian Immigrants in Dallas, Texas

Caroline B. Brettell

On 30 March 2002, Asian Indians in the Dallas–Fort Worth (DFW) metropolitan area assembled at the Richardson Civic Center at 6:30 p.m. for the 40th Anniversary Banquet of the India Association of North Texas (IANT). The theme, which was mentioned several times during the evening, was 'Merging for a Stronger America'. In addition to Indians, the mayors of several suburban towns (Plano, Frisco, Carrollton, Richardson) as well as the Mayor Pro-tem of Dallas were in attendance. Among other invited guests were a few fire and police chiefs from area communities, and Congressman Martin Frost.

In a room off the side of the main banquet hall, the entrance of which was flanked by two statues of Hindu goddesses, there were informative displays about Indian society and culture: about Bollywood, Indian history, Indian cuisine, and the demography of Indians in the United States and Texas. Behind the stage in the banquet hall was a screen framed by an Indian flag on one side and a US flag on the other side. Along one wall by the entrance were a couple of other displays, one depicting the Indian freedom fighters.

The evening opened with a lamp lighting ceremony; all the visiting dignitaries were invited to participate. The lighting of candles, a common occurrence at Indian events, is not only an act of purification but also, as the moderator for the evening explained, an expression of 'unity and oneness'. The national anthems of the United States and of India were then sung. Two speakers were introduced, one a local FBI agent who talked about safety and security in a post-9/11 world. He observed that the FBI could not function without being more inclusive and communicating with a cross-section of Americans, especially in an age of global terrorism. He ended his speech by saying that the FBI was looking for several hundred new recruits and that they needed a more diverse population, and he indicated that they would welcome Indian applicants. He even gave out the job website.

Congressman Martin Frost then spoke about his appearance at Thanksgiving Square (an ecumenical religious centre in downtown Dallas) in the fall of 2001 when the DFW Indian community presented him with a cheque for over $130,000 for the 9/11 fund. Indians, he said, are 'energetic and good Americans'. He praised not only the patriotism of the community, but also their values of family and hard work. He noted that the Indian immigrant population in the United States has the highest median household income of all immigrant groups and the highest level of education. This drew applause, as did Frost's offer of two summer internship positions in his Washington, DC, office to Asian Indian students. Like the FBI agent who had spoken before him, Frost was presented with a citation plaque and a cricket bat. Frost's speech was followed by a performance by the Darpan Dance Academy, who danced to a famous Indian freedom fighters song as well as to 'God Bless the USA' by Lee Greenwood. Their costumes incorporated the red, white, and blue of the American flag, and the orange, white, and green of the Indian flag.

The keynote speaker, Ambassador-at-large Dr Bhisma K. Agnihotri, then made his address. His job, he told the audience, is to represent NRIs (Non-Resident Indians) and PIOs (People of Indian Origin) to the Indian government. He began his speech by saying how moved he was by the dance performance because it recalled, through the freedom fighter song, the struggles that India had had in her history. He invoked the name of Gandhi. He talked about the fact that India was now working on dual citizenship, and he saw no problem with its passage in the Indian congress.[1] This would mean, he observed, that Indians could be 'good Americans and yet retain their ties to the homeland although they could not vote in India'. He encouraged them to think about investing in India. Indeed, he referred to another new law, whereby they could invest and take profits out of India in dollars. More than once he encouraged those present not only to 'run for congress' but also to retain 'Indian values'. He also spoke about conversations he had had with the second generation who wanted the Indian community in the United States to be united rather than divided. 'They are not interested in all the smaller associations', he said. Thus, while he acknowledged that more than 60 sub-organizations that the IANT represents were fine as places to socialize, the community needed to be unified when it mattered. He praised the DFW community for having established the India Association of North Texas so long ago, suggesting that they were far ahead of other Asian Indian communities in the United States where more differences were played out. He closed by calling on Indians to be part of the United States, not only to give to their communities, to participate, but also to be part of India.

The Mayor Pro-tem of the city of Dallas came to the stage to present the Ambassador-at-large the key to the city. He observed that while the United States was the first democracy in the world, India was the largest democracy in the world. He talked about how immigrants, including Indians, are part of the fabric of the city of Dallas, and he talked about the emphasis that this community in particular places on education. After introductions of several past presidents of the India Association, including the founder, dinner was served. Events such as this tell us a great deal about the incorporation of an immigrant population, as well as about the activities and institutions through which immigrants create community and express identity. The IANT was established in the 1960s and incorporated in 1976. It serves as an umbrella organization for the Asian Indian population in the DFW metropolitan area. It is one of many organizations (religious and secular) that have sprung up within an immigrant group that dates back to the early 1960s (when it was very small), but which has expanded rapidly since the 1980s and particularly in the 1990s.

In this chapter, I discuss the spatial, social, and political incorporation of Indian immigrants in DFW. Scholars such as historian Lawrence Fuchs (1990) have observed that, in the process of incorporation, immigrant groups found a range of organizations, including churches and other associations. They also set up media outlets for communication. They establish businesses that offer employment to co-ethnics, and finally they mobilize members of their group to engage in the political process. In short, they build a community. Here I focus on several aspects of this process of community building. Two questions relevant to broader concerns in the study of immigration guide my discussion. First, how does the process of incorporation proceed for immigrant populations who are increasingly settling in the suburbs rather than in the central cores of American cities? Second, what identities emerge in association with this process? Certainly, the symbolism and the discourse of the 40th anniversary dinner described at the outset of this chapter suggest that a bicultural and binational identity is a goal for Asian Indians in DFW. The data for this chapter are derive from the US census, in-depth interviews with 102 Indians (men and women), interviews with community leaders, as well as participant observation at community events, organizational meetings, and community celebrations.[2]

The Growth of the Indian Immigrant Population in DFW

In 1980, when Asian Indians were listed for the first time as a separate group in the US census, 387,223 were counted. By 1990, the number of Asian Indians in the United States had doubled to 815,447 and by 2000 the number of individuals in the United States self-identifying as being of Asian Indian ancestry had risen to 1.7 million. Asian Indians are now recognized to be one of the fastest growing minority populations in the United States, among the best educated, and with a median family income that is above that of non-Hispanic whites.

The growth of the Asian Indian population in the DFW metropolitan area has followed these national trends. A small number arrived in the early 1960s to work at the nuclear plant at Comanche Peak and in other scientific or technical fields at local universities or with local companies such as Texas Instruments and Collins Radio. They were generally step-migrants who had spent some time elsewhere in the United States, often as students. These were the pioneers who founded the IANT in 1962.

The population of foreign-born Asian Indians in DFW began to expand in the 1970s. In Dallas County, Asian Indians settled in Richardson, a near-in northern suburb of Dallas with, at least at the time, a very strong public school system. Table 1 presents the number of Asian Indians in the DFW SMSA/CMSA (Standard Metropolitan Statistics Areas/Consolidated Metropolitan Statistics Areas) between 1980 and 2000, for the four central counties of the DFW metropolitan area in 1990 and 2000, and for the two major cities in the same time period. The total population more than doubled between 1980 and 1990 and more than tripled between 1990 and 2000. Simultaneous with this rapid increase, the population began to move north from Richardson (Dallas County) to suburban Collin County, particularly to Plano and west towards Irving (still in Dallas County, but close to the border with Tarrant County). They also increased significantly in exurban Denton County.

Table 1

Asian Indians by County and Major Cities, DFW Metroplex 1980–2000

Region	*1980*	*1990*	*% Change 1980–1990*	*2000*	*% Change 1990–2000*
Collin County		703		5,753	718%
Dallas County		6,408		16,030	150%
Denton County		758		2,911	284%
Tarrant County		2,478		5,336	115%
Total		10,347		30,030	190%
City of Dallas		2,256		5,339	137%
City of Fort Worth		646		1,417	119%
DFW SMSA/PMSA	5,006	12,660	153%	42,852	238%

Source: US Censuses, 1980, 1990, 2000.

Note: In 1980, the total figure is for the entire SMSA. There are no figures at the county level for Asian Indians in particular. Rather Asians and Pacific Islanders are grouped together.

The growth of this community was simultaneous with the dramatic boom in the telecommunications industry in the area. By 2000, Dallas had more information sector jobs than all but two other US cities. To the north of the city of Dallas, companies such as Nortel, Alcatel, SBC, and Ericsson established their headquarters, joining TI and EDS. To the west of the city, along Highway 114 in North Irving, Texas, companies such as Nokia and Verizon opened offices, joining American Airlines, which owned Sabre throughout much of the decade of the 1990s. During this decade, many Asian Indians moved to the area on H1B temporary worker visas or on F1 student visas that were then converted to H1B visas. They took up employment in these high-tech industries, settling in the vicinity of their workplaces.

Another group of Asian Indians settled in South Irving and Arlington, the mid-cities (or near-in suburbs) sandwiched between Dallas and Fort Worth. Among them are those sometimes referred to by members of the first generation of Asian Indians in the area as the second-wave (family members, sometimes less well educated, who were sponsored under various family preference categories by earlier immigrants who have become naturalized citizens. Many of these second-wave immigrants have become small business owners in convenience stores, dry cleaners, motels or restaurants, or in small groceries and other specialty shops serving their own community. Among this group are individuals of Indian ancestry born and raised in Africa, the so-called 'twice migrants' (Bhachu 1985).

A third broad area of Indian settlement is in Mesquite, a near southeast suburban community in Dallas County. Many Indian Christians from the state of Kerala live there (although Keralites also live to the north and west of Dallas), and it is where the office of the Kerala Association is located. Table 2 provides the figures for Indian settlement in key suburban cities in DFW based on 2000 US census data. The growth of the population in Carrollton reflects a movement of this population towards the northwest and their settlement in the suburbs and exurbs that have grown up along Interstate 35 towards Denton–Lewisville and Flower Mound in particular. In general, the residential pattern of foreign-born Asian Indians in DFW forms a half circle of dispersed settlement, largely in the region's northern sector.

Table 2

Asian Indians in Key Cities in the DFW Metropolitan Area, 2000

City	*No.*	*% of Total for 10 Cities*
Dallas	5,339	22.1%
Fort Worth	1,417	5.8%
Richardson	1,684	7.0%
Garland	1,959	8.1%
Plano	3,524	14.6%
Carrollton	2,176	9.0%
Arlington	1,636	6.8%
Irving	4,295	17.8%
Grand Prairie	440	1.8%
Mesquite	1,648	6.8%
Total	24,118	

Source: US Census, 2000.

Clearly, the spatial incorporation of Asian Indians is largely suburban and reflects a more general trend noted by several researchers studying the settlement patterns of post-1980 immigrants to the United States (Mahler 1995; Li 1998; Alba et al. 1999, 2000; Singer 2003). Many of these immigrants are choosing the suburbs as their initial point of entry rather than settling in the inner city in ethnic enclaves as in previous eras of immigration. As Wood (1997: 70–1) has written: 'like other American frontiers in other generations, suburbs are now the geographical spaces in which Americans of all sorts of origins are creating America'. Indeed, demographer William Frey (2001) has recently referred to 'melting pot suburbs' to describe this new phenomenon.

It is legitimate to ask, given this dispersed pattern of spatial incorporation, how an immigrant population creates a sense of place: how is the locality dimension of an immigrant community constructed? Ray Oldenburg (1989: 16) has argued that places of conviviality and 'core settings of informal public life' must be created if communities are to thrive in the suburbanized cities of Western world. For Asian Indians in DFW, what are these places of informal interaction, and what role do these places play in the process of incorporation?

Spatial Incorporation: Localities of Informal Community

Asian Indians in DFW have established several localities of conviviality and informal community. One is Taj Mahal Imports, a grocery store located at the intersection of Beltline (running east-west) and Highway 75 (running north-south) in an old strip mall known as Richardson Heights. This mall is located at the centre of the half circle of settlement mentioned earlier and is a place where several other Indian entrepreneurs have opened businesses—including a travel agency, several restaurants, a few clothing stores, and a jewellery store. On Saturdays in particular, this shopping mall is a gathering place.[3] Not only do Indians come to do their weekly food shopping, but they also stop for conversation at the fast food (*chaat*) counter at the back of the store, or they pick up the latest business cards left by other Indian business owners. Young people who volunteer for various charitable service organizations such as ASHA or 'Art of Living' use the Taj as a meeting place where they can plan activities or sell tickets for upcoming events. In other words, a good deal of information sharing and mobilization occurs in the informal space provided by the Taj Mahal.

The Taj Mahal is also one of the keepers of the cultural calendar for Indians in DFW, an important dimension of community identified by Weibel-Orlando (1999) in her study of Native Americans in L.A. At the appropriate times of the year, the store sells ritual items important for the observation of particular festivals—candles for Diwali, the Indian New Year; coloured powders for Holi; *rakhi* (threads of dyed cotton or silk) for Raksha Bandhan; and statues of the elephant god Ganesh for Ganesh Chaturthi. Each year, in a side room at the store, the owner commissions a large *rangoli*, a traditional floor painting, as part of the Diwali festivities. People bring their children to the store to watch the development of the painting or to see the final product, which remains on display for several weeks. Notices of upcoming classical dance performances or concerts are posted at the store, and it is one of the places where tickets to the Anand Bazaar (a celebration of Indian Independence Day) and India Nite (a celebration of Republic Day) can be purchased.

These two events, both sponsored by the IANT, constitute other important localities for conviviality and informal community. The Anand Bazaar takes place each August on the weekend closest to August 15, the day in 1947 when India became independent. For several years, it has been held at Lone Star Park, the racetrack in the mid-cities area west of Dallas. Vendors of all kinds gather, some coming from as far away as Houston. Food, clothing, DVDs, and jewellery are sold. Several local businesses (restaurants, travel agencies, etc.) sponsor booths, and one year American Airlines had a booth advertising a new route to India via Zurich. There is usually a voter registration booth and in election years various candidates have had booths. Mortgage lenders, insurance agencies, and a host of non-profit organizations that want to reach out for community support also sponsor booths. Some of the religious and regional associations, as well as the Indo-American Chamber of Commerce, are also present. There are dance performances well into the night. Given the heat and the numbers (often upwards of 20,000), an outsider might imagine him- or herself actually to be in India.

India Nite takes place in late January, most recently in McFarlin Memorial Auditorium on the campus of Southern Methodist University. It begins at 4:30 in the afternoon and lasts until 8 or 8:30 p.m. It is at this time that the children who have been rehearsing all year in their dance classes have the opportunity to perform for the entire community. The evening begins with the youngest children and ends with the teenagers. More than 30 different groups perform both classical and more contemporary dances. In the latter case, the groups often choose well-known music from Bollywood films. The hall quickly fills up. One year, a group performed a dance where they waved both Indian and American flags. The theme of the dance was 'let us bow to the motherland', presumably both countries serving this purpose.

On India Nite, the gavel is passed from one president of the India Association to the next, and all the volunteers and sponsors are recognized at various points throughout the evening. This is, in other words, the occasion when community leaders are publicly presented. Indeed, special awards are given to acknowledge the contributions or achievements of specific individuals, including students who have excelled or business people who have supported major events. One year, Republican Congressman Pete Sessions was the invited guest, and it was announced that he had recently become a member of the Congressional Caucus on India and Indian Americans in Washington. Another year, Frank Pallone, a Democratic Congressman from New Jersey, and the founder of the Congressional Caucus, was also in attendance. Clearly, India Nite has become an instrument that situates the DFW Asian Indian community in relation to local and national power structures, and to both political parties.

While the programme is going on in the hall, in the foyer there is a good deal of 'meeting and greeting'. Indeed, audience members get up and down a good deal during the afternoon and evening, something that mystifies the managers of the SMU hall. It is not what they expect at a cultural performance. But, as one of the presidents of IANT said to me: 'When people get together at India Nite they forget that they are in the US. They act like Indians, which means they want to talk to one another, not just sit'.

The Richardson Heights shopping mall, with Taj Mahal Imports as its anchor store, and events such as the Anand Bazaar and India Nite, offers informal gathering places where communal public space is claimed by Asian Indians. It acts as centres for residentially dispersed immigrant population in a suburban metropolis. But Asian Indians have also constructed more formal gathering places that facilitate the process of social incorporation.

Social Incorporation: Building a Community Infrastructure

One measure of the social incorporation of immigrants is the organizations and associations they establish.[4] It is difficult to offer an exhaustive list of the associations that have emerged from and that serve the Indian population in the DFW area. Some are certainly more active than others, and there is no single place where they are all listed, nor is an up-to-date list maintained. Perhaps the best list is the 'Directory of Organizations' in *Bharati Magazine*, the monthly publication of IANT. In the fall of 2003, 81 different organizations were listed. The majority of these were religious (for example, the DFW Hindu Temple, the Jain Temple, the Sikh Temple, the Swaminaryan Church, the Marthomite and other Christian churches, and several mosques) or regional organizations (for example, the Kerala Association, the Bengali Association of Greater DFW, the Gujarati Association, the Telugu Association of North Texas, the Punjabi Cultural Society); but the list also includes an Indian Classical Musical Circle, the Indians Lions Club, various charity organizations, and some professional organizations such as the Visiting

Nurses Association or the India Institute of Technology Alumni Association. On the Ek Nazar website, a community bulletin board for Asian Indians in DFW,[5] close to 100 organizations are listed, although the number is fluid and changes annually. Here, too, organizations are categorized according to type (cultural/regional, devotional, professional, social, spiritual, sports) with a few listed under more than one category. Whatever the real number, clearly more than 80 ethnic organizations for an immigrant population that the census numbered at just under 43,000 in 2000 indicates a strong level of infrastructural activity and institutional integrity, another measure of community noted by Weibel-Orlando (1999).

Many of these organizations have similar structures—they all are run on a volunteer basis with a Board of Directors elected by the membership. They charge a nominal fee for membership ($20–$25 annually). Generally, they have a major banquet each year. The regional associations often have a summer picnic as well which brings people together from across the metropolitan area and sometimes from smaller towns in North Texas. The regional and religious organizations, as well as the India Association, have programmes for senior citizens who find it harder to connect in the United States than in India where there are neighbours and good public transportation. Many have programmes for children, including essay contexts, spelling bees, dance classes, language classes, and summer camps. As the President of the Punjabi Association put it, these activities are to halt 'radical Americanization. Children who attend these programmes and other events discover that their parents are not the only parents who want them to learn about their culture'. Some of these organizations also sponsor charitable events (blood drives, for example) and on occasion they raise funds for charitable programmes in India. Many of them have a regular publication and virtually all of them now have websites. Their missions are very similar: to promote the culture of the particular region and to provide 'fellowship'.

Not all members of the DFW Indian community are actively involved in these organizations. In a purposive sample of 102 Indians interviewed for a larger study of immigrant incorporation in the DFW metroplex, interviewees were asked about their participation in religious, school-based, professional, and ancestry-based organizations. Their responses, which were classified as high, moderate, or low levels of participation, are included in Table 3.

Table 3

Level of Participation in Associations (as percentages by age group)

	18–29 (N=13)	*30–49 (N=31)*	*50 or more (N=17)*	*% of Total Respondents*
MALES (N=61)				
Religious Organizations				
High	0%	16%	41%	20%
Medium	15%	13%	23%	16%
Low	69%	64%	23%	54%
None	15%	6%	12%	10%
Job Related Organizations				
High	0%	10%	6%	6%
Medium	0%	3%	3%	5%
Low	15%	29%	29%	25%
None	85%	58%	58%	64%
School Organizations				
High	15%	6%	6%	8%
Medium	0%	10%	0%	5%
Low	46%	35%	6%	29%
None	38%	48%	88%	57%
Ethnic Organizations				
High	0%	26%	35%	23%
Medium	0%	3%	12%	5%
Low	15%	22%	23%	21%
None	85%	48%	29%	51%
FEMALES (N=40)				
Religious Organizations				
High	9%	22%	45%	25%
Medium	18%	28%	9%	20%
Low	45%	33%	18%	32%
None	27%	17%	27%	22%
Job Related/Professional Organizations				
High	0%	5%	0%	2%
Medium	0%	0%	18%	5%
Low	9%	39%	18%	25%
None	91%	55%	64%	67%
School Organizations				
High	0%	5%	0%	2%
Medium	9%	5%	0%	5%
Low	18%	33%	9%	23%
None	73%	56%	91%	70%

Cont'd...

...Cont'd

Ethnic Organizations				
High	9%	22%	46%	25%
Medium	9%	11%	0%	7%
Low	35%	39%	27%	35%
None	46%	28%	27%	33%

The majority of those who described their level of participation in religious and ethnic based associations as 'low' are nevertheless aware of the two biggest community organizations: the Hindu Temple in Irving and the IANT. Indeed, many individuals who claimed not to be members of the IANT nevertheless acknowledged that they had attended the Anand Bazaar (mentioned earlier) at least once.

The differences according to age/stage of life course are striking. Young, unmarried men who are in the United States on H1B visas (as temporary skilled workers) claim that they make their friends at their places of work and do not need the socializing context of these organizations. Couples with children and those who are older and have been in the United States for some time are more actively involved in these organizations. When asked for reasons why they participate in religious organizations, 36 per cent of the men whose level of participation is high or medium cite habit or custom as the reason, while 18 per cent cited faith/obligation/duty. For women, the comparable figures are 38 per cent and 22 per cent. Sixteen per cent of the women mentioned that they participate because it gives them an opportunity to be involved in the community and to make social contacts. When asked about ethnic associations, 41 per cent of the men whose level of participation is high or medium said that they are involved for the social connections; 35 per cent said that they participate to give back to the community; and 18 per cent said that they participate to remain involved with their culture. One 40-year-old male respondent from Karnataka, speaking about the Kannada Association, described his involvement in the following way:

> This is my primary social group—people who come from the same region and speak my language. You want to get together with people of your same background because they share your culture. ... If you are of the same caste then you know a lot about people already and you can start with one another at a different place than if they are just strangers. You know what they eat, what they are like, it is easy to communicate. You can come to a city and not know anyone so you seek out these organizations to build up a group of friends whom you understand. In 2–3 months time through this organization we know 20–30 families very well. It makes you feel at home.

Women's responses were somewhat different. Thirty-eight per cent said that they participate to remain involved with their culture; 23 per cent said that they wish to give back to the community; and 15 per cent said that it is for their children. A 46-year-old Bengali woman encompassed several of these motives in her response. She not only noted the significance of these organizations for helping parents to teach their children about their culture but also admired their charity work. 'I feel like giving back to the community is important and I like to be part of such endeavors'.

Despite various levels of participation and the number of organizations to which individuals can belong, organizations are important in this particular community and, by comparison with other immigrant populations in DFW, the Asian Indians are very highly organized, perhaps a reflection of their high human capital.[6]

Media organizations constitute another important dimension of community infrastructure that facilitates the social incorporation of new immigrants. These include the more traditional radio organizations that have at some point in the construction of community institutions always been present among immigrant populations, as well as new Internet formats. The India Association produces a monthly magazine called *Bharati* that is mailed out to members. This magazine, supported by the advertisements of the many businesses in the area that serve the Asian Indian community, covers community news as well as Indian news. One of the leading Indian attorneys in the area contributes a regular column on aspects of immigration law, while local physicians write about various health issues. Among other articles that have appeared over the last two years are 'Five Job Mistakes Never to Make', 'Do Your Kids Feel Safe at School', 'Husbands and Wives and Retirement Traditions', 'Twenty Somethings Can Prepare For a Healthy Financial Future', 'Take Your Ticket to the Judge', and 'Low Down on Life Insurance'. In short, this is a publication that offers all kinds of tips that help individuals to negotiate US society successfully. But it equally informs immigrants about trends in India that would be of interest to them, with articles such as 'India Lifts Restraint on Land Investment' or 'Mumbai And Around'.[7]

The IANT also supports a radio programme on Saturday mornings that not only promotes various local businesses through advertising but also informs the community about various events. The largest amount of radio programming comes from Desi Masala radio, an organization originally founded in Houston that recently moved into the Dallas market and quickly set up 24/7 programming. In Dallas, Desi Masala has five paid staff members and about 20 volunteers who host various programmes. The function of the programming is to facilitate communication among Asian Indians. The reach, according to one staff member, is extensive:

> We have callers from India who send messages to people in Dallas and vice versa. This is possible because of our online features and we are one of the few Indian stations in the US to have it. Even Indians on the west coast comment on it and listen to us. We also have audiences in the Caribbean, people descended from very old emigrations to that part of the world. They have never been to India but this connects them to their past. We even have listeners in Australia. ... The listeners and this station are close. People tune in and they respond and they call in. They see it as a way to keep the community together and they show up when we do remotes because they know us. They record the songs we play. We are the only station really serving the community, and connecting them to home no matter how long they have been here. We keep the community informed and together.

This staff member went on to comment on what has become clearly a kind of brokerage role in the aftermath of 9/11. Mainstream media contacted them for comments on attacks on Muslims after that event as well as about any events going on in India. They invited an FBI agent to talk about security issues: 'The mainstream sees us as the representative of the community and the community sees us as the representative to the mainstream media'.

The programming is mostly music, and there is a lot to draw on because of the strength of the Asian Indian entertainment industry. Bollywood films are discussed. They offer a daily community calendar programme, during which they announce all the activities in the South Asian (including Pakistani) community around the area. They bring community people onto the radio in advance of major cultural events like the Anand Bazaar, or the celebration of Pakistani National Day, and they go on location on the day of particular events. They offer a weekly programme with an immigration lawyer who provides individuals with the opportunity to call in to ask about particular visas and the regulations regarding family sponsorship. Students often call to ask about how to change their visa status.

> Immigration is a big issue. It generates interest. Even after the show is over people call in to ask how they can get hold of the lawyer. It is good for him because he gets clients and he also helps the community and these are things they want to know about.

There is also a help line segment. On this programme, problems that people might have are addressed. For example, someone might be looking for employment after losing a job and will call in for help. Sometimes, employers will call in to say they have an opening. Some programmes deal with domestic abuse and connect people with counsellors. An individual who is having some kind of trouble with the law and does not know how to handle it will call asking for the name of a South Asian lawyer because they want to deal with someone who understands them.

According to a staff member, the topics they avoid are religion and politics, especially homeland politics:

> These are touchy subjects and we do not want to get people excited. We tried it early on and it was not a success. There are just different interpretations and different groups get upset and become one against the others—anything about India and Pakistan or Muslims and Hindus we try to avoid. But then we are also criticized by people who will say that there are serious things going on in India between Muslims and Hindus and we do not talk about it. We do carry a prayer direct from the Mosque on Friday afternoons because we have a large Muslim community of listeners but that is the extent of it. It is about 'pure' religion (a prayer), not about religious politics.

The audience for their programming is diverse and varies at different times of the day.

> People listen in the car from 7–9 a.m. on their way to work. Between 11 and 2 it is the older people. Many Indian immigrant families have brought their parents here. Then there are professionals who listen in their offices and people working at gas stations and in stores. Even truck drivers listen as they drive into the area from around the country: Young people right now are listening because they are interested in their culture. But perhaps we will have to change as the community grows.

Voluntary associations are important mechanisms of social incorporation because they facilitate social contacts. But social contacts and social incorporation are also facilitated by the ethnic media that provides a network of communication and information sharing vital for the construction of community.

Political Incorporation: Leadership, Naturalization, and Identity

In the context of the organizations, informational networks, and community activities described earlier, many members of the Asian Indian community in DFW begin to learn skills that are important for the process of political incorporation. These organizations, in other words, foster civic activity. Certainly, this message was transmitted powerfully at the 40th anniversary dinner of the India Association described at the beginning of this chapter. However, political incorporation is also measured at a more basic level as the process by which individuals engage with and benefit from the political system. A crucial step to engagement is naturalization. Being naturalized and active citizens allows immigrants to claim political space, assert their rights, and lobby for changes that are important to them.

Table 4 presents the data on immigration status for the 102 Indians interviewed for the broader study of new immigrants in the DFW area. Clearly, this is a population characterized by a high rate of naturalization. If one looks at these data by year of entry (Table 5), it is evident that the Indians move towards naturalization when the opportunity arises, taking advantage of the possibility to adjust their status at the appropriate time. They often first enter the United States as students (whether the pre-1980 cohort or more recent cohorts). Then, they move directly to lawful permanent residence (the pre-1980 cohort) or to a temporary work permit or some other temporary status, and from this status to the green card and eventually to naturalization. In a few cases, there are Indians—particularly nurses—who have entered with green cards and then become citizens. There also are some Indians who entered as dependents (generally wives of students or H1B workers) who became regularized when their husbands did.

Table 4

Immigration Status of Indians in DFW (at time of interview)

Current Immigration Status	*No.*	%
Naturalized Citizen*	47	46.1%
Lawful Permanent Resident (Green Card Holder)	26	25.5%
H-1B	15	14.7%
F-1	4	3.9%
H-4	4	3.9%
L-2	2	2.0%
EAD	2	2.0%
F-1 (OPT)	1	1.0%
E2	1	1.0%
Total	102	100.1%

*This includes one respondent born in the United States who returned to India as a baby and then returned to the United States as an adult.

What leads Asian Indian immigrants down this path to naturalization and hence to one of the most important rights of political incorporation, the right to vote? Interview respondents were asked twice about naturalization and citizenship. First, they were asked if they retained the citizenship of their country of origin and, if they responded 'yes', they were asked to explain why. Later in the interview, they were asked if they had naturalized and, if they responded 'yes', they were asked to explain why they had decided to do so. It is important to note that the probe was open-ended and coded later to capture common patterns in the responses.

Table 5

Current Immigration Status (at time of interview) of Asian Indians by Year of Entry

Current Immigration Status	*Year of Entry*				
	Pre 1980	*1980–1989*	*1990–1999*	*2000 or Later*	*Total*
H-1B	0	0	10	5	15
LPR	2	6	17	1	26
NATZ*	26	16	5	0	47
Other	0	0	2	12	14
Total	28	22	34	18	102

*NATZ includes those who said their Naturalization Application was pending. For 1990–1999, this category includes an individual who was born in the United States, returned to India as a baby, and then returned to the United States as an adult.

The responses to these questions are tabulated in Table 6. First and foremost, this population is guided by family decisions and by the realization that their future is in the United States, that the United States is where they are going to make their life and where their children were born and have grown up. Second, they are civic minded. This involves a concern for voting and showing a commitment to or pride in the United States Third, being able to travel and sponsoring a relative is clearly important. Taken together, these reasons account for more than 60 per cent of the responses. On the other hand, not being eligible for naturalization was the dominant reason (64 per cent) for not going through the naturalization process. Only a handful of persons actively choose not to pursue US citizenship and even fewer were waiting for the possibility of having dual citizenship or were planning to return to their country of origin.

Table 6

Reasons for Naturalizing/Not Naturalizing of Asian Indians in DFW

Reason for Naturalizing	*No.*	%
Family life in US/children US citizens	15	32.6%
To show commitment or pride in US	5	10.8%
To sponsor a relative	3	6.5%
To facilitate travel	3	6.5%
For Right to vote	3	6.5%
For legal rights/protection	2	4.3%
To qualify for government programs	2	4.3%
Because other family members naturalized	2	4.3%
To not worry about immigration status	1	2.2%
Combination of above reasons	2	4.3%
Other	1	2.2%
Refused to answer	1	2.2%
Missing data	6	13.0%
Subtotal	46	100%
Reason for Not Naturalizing	*No.*	%
Not yet eligible/or undocumented	36	64.2%
Choose not to	5	8.9%
No time/did not get around to it	2	3.6%
Plan to return to country of origin	2	3.6%
Waiting for dual citizenship	2	3.6%
Other	6	10.7%
Don't Know	1	1.8%
No Response	2	3.6%
Sub Total	56	100%
Total	102	

One respondent admitted that it was hard to go through with naturalization and that he and his wife did a lot of soul searching. Finally, they realized that their daughter could not be in India, that she would not fit in there, and that there would be fewer opportunities for her. Several other Indians mentioned this emotional turmoil. 'It is like giving up something. You feel like you are betraying your past', one female respondent reported. She went on to say that she and her husband finally made the decision after talking to an accountant about estate planning. 'It was going to be better for the kids and that is what motivated us. It gives you advantages and you feel more secure'. This respondent then added that the other reason that they naturalized is because 'the US is our adopted homeland and we want to contribute to the community'. But she added that this did not make her any less likely to do what she could for India as well. This sentiment was reinforced by another respondent: 'To me it is not unpatriotic to India to do it. You have to be true to where you live. You plant a seed somewhere else and the roots are the same; it just bears fruit in a new place'.

The sense of civic responsibility and participatory citizenship was perhaps best expressed by a 56-year-old male respondent who came in 1977: 'It is our responsibility to be part of the country and do something for the country. We are taking all the privileges and benefits, why not become a citizen. I did it with no hesitation and have even encouraged my children to go into the military'. Another respondent, a 49-year-old male who came in 1980, said that once he was married he and his wife decided they were going to settle in the United States: 'My sisters are both in this country. The job outlook was great. Citizenship would be a good thing to do for continued advancement in my employment and besides it would make travel a whole lot easier. Mentally we had decided to stay and I wanted to become an active member of society and that meant being able to vote'.

In their work on the Dominican Castillo family in New York City, Greta Gilbertson and Audrey Singer observe that few members of the family 'embrace US citizenship as a means to more active political or civic participation. When asked how they define a "good citizen" many emphasized that it was someone who was law abiding rather than someone who was politically or civically active' (2003: 46). By contrast, when asked about their major responsibility as residents or citizens of the United States, almost a third of the Indian respondents in DFW (31.4 per cent) said 'to be a good citizen, give back to the community', while a smaller proportion (27.5 per cent) said 'obey the law' as their first response, and an even smaller proportion (10.8 per cent) offered 'voting' or 'participation in elections' as their first response. Many of the Indian respondents made comments similar to a 49-year-old male from West Bengal who noted that volunteer work was not common in India except for what people do for their local temple. In the United States, he and his wife do a lot of volunteer work that they view as one of the best aspects of American culture: 'I have been coaching soccer for 15 years and love it'.

If political incorporation is about claiming the rights and exercising the responsibilities of citizenship, the data presented here suggest that the political incorporation of Asian Indians in DFW is high. This is not unexpected for an immigrant population with high human capital, as well as a population that comes from a country with a democratic tradition of which they are proud.

Incorporation and Identity

Isajiw (1997: 90) has argued that identity is one important dimension of social incorporation, together with structure and culture. He defines identity as a 'manner in which persons locate themselves psychologically in relation to one or more social systems, and the way they perceive others as locating them in relation to those systems'. Respondents in the DFW study were asked three questions about identity: 'What does it mean to be an American?' and 'What does it mean to be Indian?' followed by a third that asked about having a double identity ['Some people say you can be both American and Indian at the same time? Other people say that you have to choose between one and the other. What do you think?'].

The themes of opportunity, freedom, and personal space were particularly salient in the Asian Indian responses to the first question. A 61-year-old male respondent who arrived in the United States in 1964 started by saying, 'That is a hard question'. Then he continued, 'America is a country of opportunity. It is a place where children will have the most freedom. I have found this to be the case. America allows you to practice in your own way and to achieve community objectives'. A 30-year-old male, who arrived in 1994 and is naturalized, said:

> Lots of stuff. Freedom is big, freedom to be who you are, freedom to pursue happiness. That is a great thing enshrined in the constitution although sometimes it can lead to excess. But it is about allowing an individual to pursue whatever makes him happy no matter what his religion, sexual preferences, etc. You are allowed to be what you want to be within correct limits.

Some respondents answered by comparing America with India. India was often portrayed as a society where status is ascribed rather than achieved. 'In India we are all brought up like followers, to do things when somebody else asks and to do it well, but not to take a leadership role. In the US. I have learned how to be a leader and it means a lot to me'. Another respondent reinforced this perspective by observing that: 'In India things are shaped by custom and caste. There are fewer social restrictions here than in India. Even in work there is less independence there than it is here'. A third, after noting that the question was 'profound', said, 'Freedom to do what I want; to be successful on my own merits rather than through knowing someone, which is the way you achieve success in India'.

Several Indian respondents, also approaching the question within a reflective and comparative framework, commented on how much easier it is to live in the United States. Things happen more efficiently and more quickly. Life, in short, is more hassle-free. They expressed admiration for the hard work and volunteerism that characterizes Americans. However, others were critical of the lack of knowledge about the rest of the world that is common among Americans. Observed one 26-year-old female on an L2 visa: 'America is a great environment. It is more evolved. But at the same time people are provincial and not very adaptable. They like the familiar and do not care about the rest of the world. But they are also family oriented and try to balance work and family'. Some even contrasted the goodness of the people with a foreign policy (in a post-9/11 Iraqi War world) that is 'not so good'.

On the obverse question of what it means to be Indian, no matter what their background, respondents spoke about the preservation of their own culture (food, language, religion) or of a set of values that guide their lives. They talked about their deep cultural heritage, their strong family values, including the custom of living in joint family households. They often contrasted the individualism of Americans with the collectivism of Indians. Thus, one respondent offered, 'There is more self-sufficiency in the US and more warmth in India; families and groups of friends are "tighter" in India'. Another commented: 'In India the goal is to bring the whole society up; in the US you work for yourself and your children'. A third put it this way: 'Indians have heart. They enjoy simple pleasures. They take care of one another. It is different there. There is more neighborliness. What they do not have in monetary wealth they have in relationships and caring for others. They invest in relationships. These are the substitute for the absence of wealth'. This respondent went on to note that when he travelled back to India people dropped in, wanting to greet him and find things out. 'In fact everyone knows about everyone else in India. Here in America you make appointments to see people, there (in India) the doors are always open. There is a real affection for one another in India'.

On the question of having to choose or being both, the overwhelming majority of people thought that you can be both, that there is good and bad in each culture, and that you should take the best from both worlds. These immigrants did not see any conflict, although many Americans do not think it is possible to follow two or more different cultural traditions, to maintain identification and attachment to two separate nations, or to be fully engaged civically in several countries. Some respondents make the distinction between dual or multiple citizenship and dual nationality, the former referring to the political, social, and economic rights and obligations that a person enjoys or agrees to by virtue of having been born or having become a member of a particular state. Nationality is then defined in broader identificational and cultural terms. Another way of putting this is that they distinguish between the legal changes they experience as a result of becoming a citizen, but this does not mean that they change who they are. One Indian respondent, a 30-year-old male from Gujarat, expressed this compartmentalization in the following way:

> It depends on what you are talking about. If it is about culture, personality and character I think you can draw from both; if it is about a conflict between the US and my country I think I would be loyal to where I live; I am here using the resources here so I think I would have to be loyal to the US.

Another Indian respondent, a 48-year-old female from the state of Kerala who is a US citizen, was even more articulate on the subject:

> I feel a bit like an adopted child. I feel obliged to this country because I have been admitted here and it is such an open country. But in general the answer to this question is that it depends on what you are talking about. Are you talking about politics and bearing arms. In that case you would have to choose. If it is identity I can choose but you can look at me and see color and not give me a choice. This is a big country that allows you to be different. But Bombay also was a place that absorbed a lot of differences.

She concluded her response by noting that in some ways she acquired 'Indianness' here because it makes her distinctive.

Conclusion

In this chapter, I have discussed the spatial, social, and political incorporation of Asian Indian Immigrants in DFW, a suburban metropolis and an emerging gateway city of immigration (Singer 2004). Incorporation defines a process of inclusion, but one that can encompass the retention of one's own cultural identity simultaneously with the adoption of a new identity. As Isajiw (1997: 82) has argued, incorporation does 'not assume an end result of similitude. It allows for diversity to be an integral part of the whole [and] ... it avoids the pitfalls of zero-sumness'. Indians can reinforce their identity as Indians in the context of regional and religious organizations that celebrate cultural differences and cultural traditions. But they can claim equally their identity as Americans by using these organizations as vehicles for civic engagement. 'Merging for a Stronger America', the theme of the 40th anniversary dinner of the IANT, means to join the mainstream, but on one's own terms and with a powerful sense of the contributions one can make.

Organizations and media communication networks, both of which facilitate the process of social incorporation as well as the construction of new identities, are important to community development. The media (newspapers, radio, and, increasingly, cable television stations and the Internet) has long been identified as an ethnic support system for new immigrants. Radio programmes like those offered by Desi Masala link people together and foster conversation across the airwaves. While some shows promote cultural diversity, others educate new immigrants about life in the United States. Many of the local organizations that actually bring people together in shared physical spaces use the radio to inform the dispersed Indian population about their events and activities.

In addition to facilitating social incorporation, organizations and the media also foster political incorporation, but in distinct ways. The media informs while organizations serve as training grounds for community leaders. Bloemraad (2003: 365) emphasizes that it is these leaders who 'facilitate political and civic participation by representing and mobilizing the immigrant group'. Indeed, she suggests that an understanding of how leaders develop within an immigrant community is vital to an explanation of the process of political incorporation. What all these activities demonstrate is that Asian Indians in DFW are challenging the centrifugal forces of suburbanization with centripetal actions, creating localized formal and informal places and spaces where they can gather and where a sense of community and community leadership can be developed.

Notes

1. India's dual nationality law was pending at the time that the research for this project began but it has since been passed.
2. The data were collected under the auspices of a project titled 'Immigrants, Rights and Incorporation in a Suburban Metropolis' that has been supported by the National Science Foundation (BCS 003938). Other co-principal investigators involved with the project are James F. Hollifield, Dennis Cordell, and Manuel Garcia y Griego. Any opinions, findings, and conclusions or recommendations expressed in this paper are those of the author and do not necessarily reflect the views of the National Science Foundation.
3. See Brettell (2008a) for a more complete discussion of the Taj Mahal and other Indian enterprises in DFW. Such central places for residentially dispersed Indian immigrants have been described for other cities. One

might, for example, take note of the significance of the Jackson Heights area in the New York area (Lessinger 1995; Khandelwal 2002) or Devon Street for an equally residentially dispersed Indian population in Chicago (Rangaswamy 2000). In fact, Lessinger labels the Jackson Heights area of Queens a 'Little India':

In the absence of clearly defined Indian immigrant residential enclaves, this 'little India' offers a focus and a center to a population geographically dispersed throughout the greater metropolitan area by regularly concentrating large numbers of Indians in one place as shopkeepers, employees and customers (1995: 28).

For a discussion of the relevance of strip malls to the Vietnamese immigrant community in another area of dispersed settlement, Washington DC, see Wood (1997).

4. The study of the relationship between migration and voluntary associations was extensive when anthropologists first began to work in urban contexts, particularly in Africa (for example, Little 1965; Fallers 1967; Barnes and Peil 1977). Interest in this form of urban social organization waned, but more recently researchers are again turning their attention to such associations as mechanisms for incorporation (Schoeneberg 1985; Basch 1987; Jacobs et al. 2004).
5. See Brettell (2008b) for further discussion of Ek Nazar.
6. A more detailed discussion of these organizations is contained in a working paper (Caroline B. Brettell, 'Social Capital, Voluntary Organizations, and the Social Incorporation of Asian Indian Immigrants in the Dallas-Fort Worth Metroplex'). Certainly other studies of Asian Indians in other parts of the United States have also identified a high level of organizational activity (Leonard 1997; Rangaswamy 2000). In her analysis of community organizations among Native Americans in L.A., Weibel-Orlando (1999: 303–5) delineates categories of participation (core membership, selective membership, peripheral membership, non-associated) that might be equally applied to the case presented here.
7. There is no local newspaper, but in my research I found that many DFW Indians subscribe to one of two national newspapers, *India Abroad* (out of New York City) or the *India Tribune* (published in Chicago). For a discussion of *India Abroad* see Shukla (2003). Many also look at one of the national Indian newspapers on the Internet to keep informed about their home country.

References

Alba, R., Logan, J.R., and Stults, B.J. (2000) 'The changing neighborhood contexts of the immigrant metropolis', *Social Forces*, 79(2), 587–621.

Alba, R., Logan, J.R., Stults, B.J., Marzan, G., and Zhang, W. (1999) 'Immigrant groups and suburbs: a reexamination of suburbanization and spatial assimilation', *American Sociological Review*, 64, 446–60.

Barnes, S.T., and Peil, M. (1977) 'Voluntary association membership in five West African cities', *Urban Anthropology*, 6, 83–106.

Basch, L. (1987) 'The Vincentians and the Grenadians: the role of voluntary associations in immigrant adaptation to New York City', in Foner, N. (ed.) *New Immigrants in New York*. New York: Columbia University Press, 159–94.

Bhachu, P. (1985) *Twice Migrants: East African Sikh Settlers in Britain*. London: Tavistock.

Bloemraad, I. (2003) 'Institutions, ethnic leaders, and the political incorporation of immigrants: a comparison of Canada and the United States', in Reitz. J.G. (ed.) *Host Societies and the Reception of Immigrants*. La Jolla, CA: Center for Comparative Immigration Studies, University of California at San Diego, 361–401.

Brettell, C.B. (2008a) Meet Me at the Chat/Chaat Corner: The Cultural Embeddedness of Immigrant Entrepreneurs', in Barkan, E., Diner, H., and Kraut, A. (eds.) *From Arrival to Incorporation: Migrants to the US in a Global Era*. New York: New York University Press, 121–142. Brettell, C.B. (2008b) 'Immigrants in a Sunbelt Metropolis: the transformation of an urban place and the construction of community', in Hanley, L., Ruble, B., and Garland, A. (eds.) *Immigration and Integration in Urban Communities: Renegotiating the City*. Washington, DC: Woodrow Wilson Centre Press, 143–66.

Fallers, L. (1967) *Immigrants and Associations*. The Hague: Mouton.

Frey, W.H. (2001) *Melting Pot Suburbs: A Census 2000 Study of Suburban Diversity*. Washington, DC: The Brookings Institution, Center on Urban and Metropolitan Policy.

Fuchs, L.H. (1990) *The American Kaleidoscope: Race, Ethnicity and Civic Culture*. Hanover, NH: University Press of New England.

Gilbertson, G., and Singer, A. (2003) 'The emergence of protective citizenship in the USA: naturalization among Dominican immigrants in the post 1996 Welfare Reform Era', *Ethnic and Racial Studies*, 26, 25–51.

Isajiw, W.W. (1997) 'On the concept and theory of social incorporation', in Isajiw, W.W. (ed.) *Multiculturalism in North America and Europe*. Toronto: Canadian Scholars Press, 79–102.

Jacobs, D., Phalet, K., and Swyngedouw, M. (2004) 'Associational membership and political involvement among ethnic minority groups in Brussels', *Journal of Ethnic and Migration Studies*, 30, 543–59.

Khandelwal, M.S. (2002) *Becoming American, Being Indian: An Immigrant Community in New York City*. Ithaca, NY: Cornell University Press.

Leonard, K.I. (1997) *The South Asian Americans*. Westport, CT: Greenwood Press.

Lessinger, J. (1995) *From the Ganges to the Hudson: Indian Immigrants in New York City*. Boston, MA: Allyn & Bacon.

Li, W. (1998) 'Anatomy of a new ethnic settlement: the Chinese ethnoburb in Los Angeles', *Urban Studies*, 35, 479–501.

Little, K. (1965) *West African Urbanization: A Study of Voluntary Associations in Social Change*. London: Cambridge University Press.

Mahler, S.J. (1995) *American Dreaming: Immigrant Life on the Margins*. Princeton, NJ: Princeton University Press.

Oldenburg, R. (1989) *The Great Good Places*. New York: Paragon House.

Rangaswamy, P. (2000) *Namasté America: Indian Immigrants in an American Metropolis*. Philadelphia: University of Pennsylvania Press.

Schoeneberg, U. (1985) 'Participation in ethnic associations: the case of immigrants in West Germany', *International Migration Review*, 19(3), 416–37.

Shukla, S. (2003) *India Abroad: Diasporic Cultures of Postwar America and England*. Princeton: Princeton University Press.

Singer, A. (2003) *At Home in the Nation's Capital: Immigrant Trends in Metropolitan Washington*. Washington, DC: The Brookings Institution, Center on Urban and Metropolitan Policy.

Singer, A. (2004) *The Rise of the New Immigrant Gateways*. Washington, DC: The Brookings Institution, Center on Urban and Metropolitan Policy.

Weibel-Orlando, J. (1999) *Indian Country, L.A.: Maintaining Ethnic Community in Complex Society*. Urbana and Chicago: University of Illinois Press.

Wood, J. (1997) 'Vietnamese American place making in Northern Virginia', *The Geographical Review*, 87, 58–72.

16

Kolkata, Transnationalism, and the Diasporic Imaginary*

Pablo S. Bose

> I would like you to reach out and invest in a new India. Invest not just financially, but intellectually, socially, culturally and, above all, emotionally ... come engage with India.
>
> (NDTV.com 2007)

With these words Prime Minister Manmohan Singh welcomed participants to the Government of India's one of the first of the now annual celebrations of the Indian diaspora. Like many other national as well as regional governments and municipalities, the Indian state is today deeply involved in efforts to capitalize on the wealth and resources of its diasporas overseas. For many others—including scholars, international financial institutions, and social movements—the diasporic desire to participate in re-imagining and reshaping former homes remains a topic of keen interest. There are many reasons for such focus, especially the long-distance nationalism expressed within diasporic communities that has supported a variety of political causes from Ireland to Israel and from the Balkans to South Asia, among a myriad of other places.

In recent years, the attention paid to political connections has intensified and grown, with an especial emphasis on economic relationships. In part, this reflects ongoing struggles regarding global

*Elements of this paper were published in an earlier version as 'Dreaming of Diasporas: Urban Developments and Transnational Identities in Contemporary Kolkata', *Topia: Canadian Journal of Cultural Studies*, No. 17, Spring 2007, 111–30.

migration, as evidenced by debates concerning 'illegal immigration' on the one hand and 'brain drain' on the other hand. But it is also evidence of the sheer size and volume of diasporic capital in today's global economy. Remittances, money sent by workers back to their 'home' countries, grew in the last decade from US $66 billion in 2000 to over US $414 billion in 2009 (MPI 2011), with some observers estimating a further 35–250 per cent of these amounts are transferred through informal channels (Freund and Spatafora 2005: 1). For developing countries in particular, such figures represent a lucrative and mainly untapped source of funds. Attracting and utilizing diasporic capital—including investments, remittances, and property or business ownership—has become an increasingly important strategy for a number of national governments, especially in an era of declining foreign aid and unstable foreign investment.

Political and economic linkages, therefore, tend to dominate much of the research and literature on immigrant, diasporic, or expatriate communities and development in putative or ancestral homelands. This chapter argues, however, that a much broader reading of both capital and cultural flows related to diasporas is necessary to understand the implications of invitations to 'engage' with one's homeland. As Kapur (2005: 357 suggests:

> [it] is worth asking whether a less visible, quantifiable, and tangible form of remittances—namely social remittances and the flow of ideas—have a more critical impact than their pecuniary counterpart. The overseas experience must have some cognitive effect on migrants. At the same time, the communications revolution has led to an exponential growth of transnational telephone calls and email, as well as a sharp increase in international travel. As a result, not just elites but social groups at the lower end of the social spectrum are exposed to new information, not just new ways of making or selling things, but also new views of what is acceptable in terms of service standards, the role of the state, or the behaviour of politicians. The cumulative effect of millions of conversations—akin to filling a pond one drop at a time—is interesting to speculate upon.

It is the cumulative effect of conversations that is the focus of this chapter, in the context of the global Indian diaspora and development in the subcontinent. However, it is not the millions of conversations that flow between diasporas and homelands which are of primary concern here but rather certain dominant political and economic discourses that have helped to produce a monolithic vision of the Indian diaspora. Buttressed by government policy and reinforced through a range of cultural texts, this unitary view of the Indian diasporic experience—as primarily transnational, wealthy, successful, professional, and often narrow in its portrayal of gender, sexual, and religious identities—has been deployed for a variety of purposes both within India and its various diasporic communities. This chapter examines one such example, the use of the figure of the Non-Resident Indian (NRI), in the design and marketing of luxury condominiums on the fringes of the Indian metropolis of Kolkata. These new housing projects are built and marketed with a self-consciously global aesthetic in mind and are actively marketed to both overseas Indian communities and local elites as space in which one can embody a transnational, cosmopolitan, modern, and quintessentially urban lifestyle. Such projects have also emerged as a crucial element in the promotion of Kolkata as a 'global' city, one that can be an attractive destination for both foreign multinationals and successful diasporic sons and daughters overseas. While these new housing developments have engendered significant local criticism regarding their social and ecological impact, opposing their construction has been made especially difficult due to their symbolic importance as emblems of 'the new India' heralded by much of the dominant political and cultural discourse.

This chapter proceeds in three sections. The first begins by exploring the contested nature of diasporas and the distinctions between connections to place, nation, and home. In particular, I look at the construction of what I call 'the mythic Global Indian' through selected cultural texts and government policies. The second section provides an overview of urban development in Kolkata and the dominant representations of the city that have necessitated for some the desire to achieve (or reclaim) a global status. The final section examines how these two forces have been brought together—the idea of the global Indian diaspora on the one hand and the ongoing urban development in Kolkata's peri-urban fringes on the other hand—through the strategies of planning, design, and marketing luxury condominiums. In particular, I focus on some of the most prominent recently built housing projects and discuss in brief some of the advertising campaigns used to sell them.

Defining Diasporas and the Making of the 'Mythic Global Indian'

The label of diaspora has in recent years become an increasingly sought after—and contested—term. Communities that in the past might have referred to themselves as a cultural association, heritage group, philanthropic organization, or political action committee are increasingly self-identifying as an explicitly ethnic or national diaspora. Such groups are moreover being brought into larger intra-national and international conglomerations and diasporic structures, such as the global Chinese 'Huaren' (Ong 2003). National authorities such as the Government of India are also actively targeting wealthy diasporic individuals and organizations for fundraising and investment purposes and continue to promote the concept of a distinctly Indian 'overseas identity'. The diasporas have also become an increasing subject of study for development agencies as well as for academics within disciplines ranging from economics to anthropology to political science, and many others as well. Gilroy (2000: 23) suggests that:

> The idea of diaspora offers a ready alternative to the stern discipline of primordial kinship and rooted belonging. It rejects the popular image of natural nations spontaneously endowed with self-consciousness, tidily composed of uniform families: those interchangeable collections of ordered bodies that express and reproduce absolutely distinctive cultures as well as perfectly formed heterosexual pairings. As an alternative to the metaphysics of 'race', nation, and bounded culture coded into the body, diaspora is a concept that problematizes the cultural and historical mechanics of belonging. It disrupts the fundamental power of territory to determine identity by breaking the simple sequence of explanatory links between place, location, and consciousness. It destroys the naïve invocation of common memory as the basis of particularity in a similar fashion by drawing attention to the contingent political dynamics of commemoration.

Hall (1994: 396), moreover, offers a notion of diasporic experience as defined:

> [not] by essence and purity, but by the recognition of a necessary heterogeneity and diversity; by a conception of 'identity' that lives with and through, not despite, difference; by hybridity. Diaspora identities are those which are constantly producing and reproducing themselves anew, through transformation and difference.

But the 'diasporic turn' in the study of the so-called 'ethnic communities' has not been without challenge. Many critics complain that the idea is too often conflated with concepts such as transnationalism and more general processes of migration and population movement (Mishra 2004). Some argue that the concept of the diaspora must be recovered as a term that defines communities of hope living through exile and dreaming of home (Braziel and Mannur 2001). For writers like Gilroy, however, diaspora is a useful concept in opening up the question of identity beyond the particularities and atavisms of static, essentialized Selves, brought into clear definition by stark definition to the cultural practices and mores of ambiguous Others. Instead, diaspora can be a starting, rather than end-point, a node of intersection between physical, cultural, and economic spaces. Accordingly, the term has been used to describe a vast array of groups, from trading communities to labour migrants, from imperial functionaries to IT professionals seeking education or work abroad. In this chapter, I follow Gilroy and others such as Walsh (2004) who suggests that creating exclusionary boundaries around the term is both morally problematic and analytically unhelpful and that diaspora describes experiences of hybridity and culture that are not necessarily predicated on primordial ties to either land or blood. Ultimately, my use of diaspora is a way of illustrating the contested, shifting, and creative relationships between space, place, and power.[1]

These definitional debates over what constitutes a diaspora are, however, not readily apparent when one looks at the current imagining and mythologizing of the Indian diaspora—known by a variety of appellations including *desi*, NRI, Person of Indian Origin (PIO), and a host of others besides. Where once émigrés were viewed with suspicion and considerable resentment for 'abandoning' their former homelands, today large segments of the Indian diaspora are increasingly viewed by some through a heroic lens and are in this sense integral to the creation of a successful pan-Indian, 'global' identity. To understand how and why this shift has occurred, one needs to look carefully at the constitution of the global Indian diaspora itself. Who is and who is not counted as part of this group? What criteria define membership and exclusion?

The size of the Indian diaspora is variously estimated at anywhere between 18 and 40 million people worldwide (High Level Committee on the Indian Diaspora 2002). The wide discrepancy in figures has much to do with how one defines membership; the numbers include Indian citizens living outside of the country, those who have emigrated directly or recently from India, and those who have Indian or mixed-Indian heritage. Many of these groups do not necessarily claim membership in the Indian diaspora; for example, some of the descendents of indentured labourers in the Caribbean or trading classes who migrated to East Africa and were then forcibly expelled and resettled in North America. Some of these communities identify more with their more recent 'homes' than a primordial one. Being counted as part of the diaspora may not be a choice and may indeed have negative consequences.[2] There has also been a tendency to conflate 'Indian' with South Asian and include all those who hail from the region of the subcontinent as from the one nationality, whereas the region produces many diasporas, both national and sub-national. Prashad argues that:

> India is present today in the body of the Indians and others from the South Asian subcontinent, who now number 1.4 million in the United States. But these people are not all 'Indians'. Many are from Pakistan, Bangladesh, India, Sri Lanka, Bhutan, the Maldives, Africa, England, Canada, Fiji, or the Caribbean, and many are born and bred within the United States. The stain of ancestry and the hegemony of the word 'India' remains with us as we seek to make our own way through the morass of the contemporary world. (2000: 2)

It is difficult to know, therefore, who one is describing when one speaks of the Indian diaspora. For one thing, the claim that those from even the Indian parts of the subcontinent identify with India first and foremost is a tenuous one at best. Much of the literature on remittances and diaspora-influenced development has shown that many within overseas communities identify much more strongly with regional cultures, hometown associations, neighbourhood relationships, and familial bonds than with the nation-state (Levitt and de la Dehesa 2003; Ley 2004; Chami et al. 2005). In this sense, it is Gujarati, Punjabi, or Keralite identities—rather than an Indian one—that are predominant in the formation of the diasporic self. Locating such sub-national identities through instruments such as maps or censuses is, however, not easy, as any search for a Bengali diaspora demonstrates. Diasporas tend to be identified within host country census data by their association with nation-states (e.g., India, Mexico, Italy) or supra-national regions (e.g., Latin America, Eastern Europe). Any potential Bengali diaspora does not conform so neatly and discretely with such boundaries. The ethno-linguistic culture associated with parts of the eastern subcontinent straddles two major religions (Hinduism and Islam) and national borders (India and Bangladesh), not to mention distinctions based on caste, class, gender, and the rural-urban divide. Finding the *prabasi* (overseas) Bengali is therefore fraught with difficulties—perhaps a reason that it is an Indian rather than Bengali diasporic identity that is interpellated within the Kolkata example examined later in this chapter.

Nevertheless, Indian diasporas—variously defined—form significant minority populations not only in advanced industrialized countries such as the United States, United Kingdom, Canada, and Australia, but also in the Persian Gulf and throughout South East Asia, the Caribbean, Africa, and the South Pacific. Such a diverse presence may indeed suggest a truly 'global' reach for the Indian diaspora—situated in multiple locations, leaving from diverse trajectories, working in different occupations, and assuming a range of identities—yet I would argue that the dominant narrative of the diasporic Indian posits a specific and particular reading instead. This representation is of the 'successful' NRI/PIO, one founded on the notion of the Indian as the exemplar of the 'model minority'.

The overseas Indian who inhabits such an identity has often been characterized as 'hardworking, entrepreneurial, intelligent, and/or willing to be educated'; in other words, the antithesis of those 'troublesome' immigrants and minorities who have long been depicted as lazy, grasping, and needy (Prashad 2000: 3–6). This representation has lost much of its lustre in the post-9/11 era, as discourses of racialized securitization have to some degree overwhelmed the celebratory chords of globalization, and diasporic Indians often find themselves lumped into the category of 'threatening' dark-skinned Others. Yet it is hard to deny that significant sections of the Indian diaspora across the globe have indeed been highly successful and indeed prosperous in their new homes (Motwani et al. 1993). Indian IT engineers rank second in number only to Chinese immigrants in Silicon Valley and make up a sizable proportion of today's high-tech millionaires across the globe (Saxenian 1999). Some have estimated the combined gross assets of the Indian diaspora at around $300 billion (roughly equivalent to India's GDP), with a combined net worth of between $40 and $60 billion (High Level Committee on the Indian Diaspora 2002: 417). Nor have these successful émigrés been stingy with their good fortune; in recent years remittance flows to India outpaced China as the country receiving the largest volume of remittances in the world, totalling over $49 billion (MPI 2011). The Gujarati diaspora alone, which makes up less than 0.01 per cent of the population of the United States, is estimated to control over 5 per cent of that country's wealth (High Level Committee on the Indian Diaspora 2002: 169–77).

The apparent success of this group is also reflected in a wide variety of cultural texts, both within the subcontinent and many diasporic Indian communities. In films and literature, radio documentaries, television dramas and soap operas, news programmes, and on Internet blogs, the dominant narrative that emerges tends to privilege the migration and settlement experiences of affluent, highly educated, and highly skilled émigrés. At the same time, such representations tend to obscure the histories and contemporary experiences of numerous other groups who also left the subcontinent and identify with it. *India Today*, for example, a magazine with wide circulation both within India and abroad, featured special issues in 2003 and 2004 devoted to the diaspora and now include a 'Global Indian Report' in each publication. Their editorial made clear that they knew who the Indian diaspora were and why they should be celebrated:

> Last year, *India Today*, which shares a sense of adventure with these intrepid Indians, saluted their achievements in a special Global Indian issue. This year, we celebrate the second generation, or overseas-born Indians (OBIs), who may not call India their home but who are nevertheless more than the sum of the fragments of their parents' lives. Born in the two great migrations of the 1960s and 1980s to largely educated professionals, these navigators of the New and Old Worlds are slowly rising to great prominence in their homelands, often in areas their parents would not have dreamed possible. (*India Today* 2004: 3)

This statement is interesting not only for what it says but also for what it leaves out. There are, in this interpretation, only 'two great migrations' which have spawned the Indian diaspora. Such a reckoning leaves many out of the picture—descendents of indentured servants in the Caribbean, of traders in Africa, Sikh labourers who established themselves in farming and forestry sectors in North America, or the many millions who continue to labour today as taxi drivers, domestic workers, janitors, and in many other non-professional occupations in North America, Europe, and especially the Gulf States; in other words, all those others who have been part of successive waves of Indian emigration. These people have not disappeared, as the distribution of diasporic populations illustrates, but in terms of the myth of the global Indian diaspora, they may as well not exist.

If one were to look at Bollywood films and the glut of publications devoted to hybrid identities now popular within the subcontinent and abroad, it would seem that the only diasporic individuals deemed successful are IT workers and yuppies. Consider the categories within which *India Today* groups its OBIs: the politicians, the trailblazers, the professionals, the hybrids, and the entertainers. Those profiled include recording artists, advertising executives, doctors, software engineers, Hollywood actors, stock analysts, scriptwriters, venture capitalists, and US senators. This helps to give a narrow and monolithic impression of what constitutes the Indian diaspora, an impression that has become reinforced through successive regimes of government policy. As Desai (2004: 40–1) suggests in recent years:

> [the] deterritorialized nonresident Indians became imagined as crucial to the Indian economy and nation-state in filmic national narratives. Since then, the deterritorialized Indian has been imagined as internal and integral to the Indian nation-state. Consequently,

filmic representations, as well as state policies have shifted to reflect this discourse.

State policies that have echoed this cultural importance of the 'mythic Global Indian' include establishing a legislative committee to study the Indian diaspora across the globe, co-founding (with the Federation of Indian Chambers of Commerce) an annual celebration of overseas Indians, creating a Ministry of Overseas Indian Affairs in 2004, creating an Overseas Citizenship of India (OCI) programme (although this does not give holders passports, holding rights, or the ability to hold elected office), granting special visa privileges (through a PIO Card programme), allowing diasporic individuals special dispensation to own immovable property and invest in business ventures within India, and even allowing some NRIs (though not PIOs) to stand for election to the Indian parliament (Yelaja 2006). A former high-ranking civil servant who helped found the NRI division said of the initiatives of the Indian government towards its diaspora:

> Our destinies are interlinked. The overseas Indians are an excellent resource for us. If today India is shining, then the diaspora is shining too. We say to the diaspora that you have as much to gain from us as we do from you; it is a mutually beneficial relationship. (Sharma 2004)

In the following section, I shift the discussion from the nation-state and the diaspora to a local site, that of Kolkata. As stated previously, diaspora identities are more often linked to place than to nation-states; if so, how might Kolkata—often cited as a foundational touchstone of Bengali identity—be implicated in the dynamics discussed by this chapter?

Kolkata: Colonial City to Imperial Centre to Post-Industrial Wasteland?

A decade of neo-liberal urban development both within Kolkata and its periphery has steadily transformed the entire region's political and urban landscape. While the state of West Bengal as a whole is perhaps best known as a stronghold of leftist and revolutionary traditions and a fertile ground for land reforms and political decentralization, much of the post-Independence period has reified Kolkata's popular image as a city overwhelmed by poverty, pollution, population growth, and economic decline. But the state and the city have been undergoing remarkable changes in recent years. Globalization and the embrace of neo-liberal economic growth strategies both nationally and regionally have significantly altered the landscapes of Kolkata. 'International-style' housing complexes, industrial parks devoted to the informational technology and business process outsourcing sectors, foreign-funded environmental and infrastructure projects, and the construction of numerous luxury amenities for middle classes and elites hold the promise of reintegrating Kolkata into transnational circuits of economy and culture after decades of apparent stagnation.

Yet such apparent progress has come at a heavy price: a continuous cycle of evictions, expropriations, ecological degradation, and social protest speak to the weight of such costs. The future appears, therefore, as simultaneously bright, contested, and uncertain. In recent years, in particular the legitimacy of leftist governments at both state and municipal levels have been called into question, due in large parts to controversial plans that include embracing development of special economic zones, privatization of a range of services, and conversion of rural farmland into factories in places such as Nandigram and Singur. Yet while such controversies have received significant attention in both local and national public discourse, the ongoing struggles regarding urban change in Kolkata have received less attention. This chapter examines some of these dynamics with special attention to the environmental impacts of luxury housing construction within and on the edges of the city, the continued evictions of hawkers and pavement dwellers in the areas surrounding tourist attractions, and the displacements caused by environmental projects in the south and east of the city. At what cost is the once and future global city imagined and on which particular bodies are these burdens borne?

Kolkata has long extended its reach outside of its city limits, encompassing an amorphous and ever-changing 'hinterland' over which it exercises primacy. It is a primate city—once both nationally and internationally—and still exerts this dominance on a regional scale. Migrant labour has for centuries been attracted to the city from all across the subcontinent, especially the neighbouring provinces, to work in industries, agriculture, and as servants in and around the city. The city was an important point in the extension of nineteenth-century globalization and imperialism, through its prominent role in the British Empire; indeed, it was once described as the second city in the Raj, behind only London in receiving technological advancements such as city gas lights, or in its concentration of administrative and political power. It has also long been a crucial site of resistance and revolt, especially in the anti-colonial and nationalist struggles against the British. Even today its sphere of influence continues to be exercised over neighbouring Indian states as well as countries such as Bangladesh, Bhutan, and Nepal. It is the third largest urban agglomeration in India, following Mumbai and Delhi—the 2001 Indian Census gives the population of the city at well over 13 million. While India may still be a country of many villages, mega-cities such as Kolkata are increasingly the sites in which we see the concentration of many of the problems that confront the contemporary Indian nation as a whole. It is in these rapidly urbanizing cities with increasing population growth and concentration that one cannot avoid issues of mass unemployment, widespread illiteracy, the explosive growth of slums, snarling traffic congestion, loss of public and green spaces, alarming levels of water and air pollution, and a general deterioration of infrastructure and services.

Such problems contribute to the general sense of neglect and decline that has gripped Kolkata for decades, especially in the post-Independence period. In the early part of the twentieth century, it lost its position as national capital to Delhi, and by 1947 the province of Bengal—of which it was the centre—was divided in the partition that accompanied Britain's departure from the subcontinent. The eastern, mostly Muslim-populated wing of the province became East Pakistan, in what was a traumatic and violent process that was a lengthy and ongoing one. Kolkata's fate was an unenviable one; it experienced decline in both economic and political power, and its city services were overwhelmed by the enormous influx of refugees, somewhere between 3 and 6 million in the period following partition alone. Massive population transfers and violence accompanied partition but unlike North India, Bengal saw its effects happen more cyclically and at a lower level, with refugee flows continuing for close to 50 years, with spikes during various conflicts (such as the 1947 Partition and the 1971 civil war that created Bangladesh out of East Pakistan).

Calcutta[3] did not, of course, disappear from the political and economic landscape of India. West Bengal in the 1950s was still a leading industrial state in the country with established economic infrastructure and an extensive manufacturing industry (including automobiles, chemicals, and consumer goods), and its population at this time still maintained the highest per capita income levels in India. But as Delhi had replaced Kolkata as the political capital 40 years earlier, this period saw Mumbai begin to replace it as the economic capital. The 1960s saw considerable economic stagnation and capital flight from the city, a trend that continued through periods of profound political instability and turmoil. In 1977, an alliance of leftist parties took control of the state and ushered in an era of rural reforms and a measure of stability in West Bengal; for Kolkata, however, the following decades meant yet more capital flight west and north, the degradation of an ageing public infrastructure, a scramble for upper-middle-class housing construction, and an increase in corruption and inefficiency in municipal governance.

But the situation has changed considerably in the last two decades. After 1991, with the introduction of what is known as the liberalization era (following India's acceptance of neo-liberal economic reforms on the heels of an IMF assistance agreement), significant investment was focused on Kolkata, especially in the city's service sector as well as manufacturing in the industrial suburbs. This period has also seen an explosive growth of private and public-private partnerships as a way of redeveloping the city through new urban housing projects aimed at an emerging and global middle class. The state, in conjunction with municipal authorities, has also emphasized a cosmopolitan and business-friendly attitude among young entrepreneurs through educational and trading incentives, instituted long-term plans to ease traffic in Kolkata, drawing on Japanese assistance to construct flyovers in the city, and implemented user fees such as a water tax that is notably unpopular with the poorer segments of the population.

As a result of some of these changes and the new 'business-friendly' attitude of the Left Front before its recent electoral defeat, Kolkata has seen a rapid growth of financial and producer service sectors since the mid-1990s, including—as elsewhere in India—the proliferation of call centre firms servicing transnational corporations. The West Bengal Electronics Industry Development Corporation Ltd. has since the mid-1990s prioritized efforts to attract IT companies, initiatives that are paying off with the increasing location of outsourcing operations in Kolkata (WBIDC 2006). Recent arrivals include IBM, PricewaterhouseCoopers, Tata Consultancy Services, Cognizant, Wipro, and Satyam. The State government has declared IT a utility, thus disallowing strikes in it; it has set up a gem and jewellery park in Salt Lake and a toys park to attract investment in these sectors, and improved power and phone service across the state and especially Kolkata itself.

Perhaps most notoriously, the Government of West Bengal, along with the municipal government in Kolkata, initiated a series of urban 'renewal' and 'regeneration' measures in the last two decades. One of the best known was the euphemistically titled 'Operation Sunshine' in 1996, waged against hawkers and pavement dwellers, which included their forced removal and relocation to urban fringes in order to 'clean up the streets' of Kolkata. A later series of campaigns for the 'beautification of Calcutta' (2003–2005) similarly included multiple such evictions of slum and pavement dwellers.

All of these developments have not occurred without any challenge; whether forced evictions, ecological impacts, or economic ones. As previously noted, Kolkata and Bengal have long been sites of political ferment and agitation, from the nationalist to the Naxalite movement and many other struggles as well. The changes wrought on the landscape of Kolkata have indeed resulted in considerable organizing and opposition, whether against evictions, urban renewal, privatization, modernization, or a raft of other neo-liberal initiatives. Union movements, environmental groups, and populist struggles, among others, have all challenged these exclusionary visions of the future. But among many middle-class Bengalis and Kolkatans, there is today a great deal of confidence and optimism about the future. Some say approvingly that the 'city of joy' has become the 'city of flyovers' (Mukherjee 2004). A particular source of pride for many has been the surge in building construction in and around the city in recent years, especially in the number of 'international-style' luxury condominiums. In the final section of this paper, I turn to an examination of these housing complexes to see how the idea of the 'mythic Global Indian' and the idea of the 'global city' have taken concrete shape through recent transformations of urban space in Kolkata.

Kolkata and Diasporic Attachment

To think of Kolkata as a diaspora city requires, at first blush, considerable imagination. After all, the city has long faded from its former glory as imperial entrepot, political power, and cultural centre of the British Raj. Neither it nor the state of which it is the capital has the celebrated histories of migration and return of other Indian regions such as Punjab, Gujarat, or Kerala. Nor does it embody the cosmopolitan character of other post-colonial metropolises such as Mumbai, New Delhi, Hong Kong, Singapore, Manila, or Dubai, all with significant populations that have both emigrated and immigrated, and which also retain complex sets of diasporic relationships as points of departure, arrival, and circulation. When one talks of the new and emerging power of India, it is rarely the image of Kolkata that springs to mind. Much of the public discourse and scholarly research has focused on other places—the old staples of Mumbai and Delhi (Mehta 2004; Legg 2007) or perhaps newly fascinating ones such as Bangalore or Hyderabad (Ramachandraiah and Bawa 2000,; Srinivas 2002). Even an excellent recent collection of vibrant scholarship on urban spaces in South Asia reproduces such a focus, with chapters on Delhi, Mumbai, and Bangalore, and adding perspectives on less-studied cities such as

Shillong, Kathmandu, Karachi, and Colombo, yet Kolkata remains out of the picture (Anjaria and McFarlane 2011). The more recent work on Kolkata, while significant and groundbreaking in its own right (see especially Roy 2003; Chattopadhyay 2005), remains limited.

Does Kolkata function as such a territorial referent? Does it help to locate or anchor the émigré living overseas? After all, as noted previously, the diaspora from Kolkata and Bengal has neither the long history nor the sheer numbers of the Punjabi, Gujarati, or Keralite population abroad, not to mention all the many others who are putatively gathered within the folds of the 'global Indian'. And yet we can find traces of a Calcuttan diaspora—both intentional and unwitting—in both the past and the present. Torabully and Carter, in their wonderful and poetic study of migration, memory, belonging, and the construction of a diasporic identity among indentured labourers from India in the Caribbean, recount the stories of individuals going to Calcutta from rural villages for day labour and ending up thousands of miles away:

> The promised service was in Calcutta, not Mauritius ... Karoo was enticed to Calcutta with the promise of work on road repairs, and when the promised job did not materialize, was, like many others, inveigled into the emigration depot. (2002)

Many others have left more recently, following paths of employment, education, and empire. For some, such as the smaller Anglo-Indian, Chinese, and Jewish communities of Calcutta, the city has become less and less inviting (Blunt 2005). For others, especially the professional classes and intellectuals who have left Calcutta over the past 40 years, either for other parts of India and Asia or for Europe, North America, Australia, and other parts of the global North, the lure has most often been jobs and a better standard of living. Yet even for the latter, the city is remembered with ambivalence, with both its decay and its grandeur foremost in the minds of many. Certain of the city's streets, sounds, tastes, and smells continue to be recalled through nostalgia and sepia tones. Indeed, Suraiya suggests that:

> The emigrant experience is perfectly suited to a transplant of Calcutta. And since this can't be done with the real city, a mythical one has been invented to fit the need, an emotional precinct of love and squalor. Beyond the reach of urban blight and civic neglect, this portable city of the mind flourishes all the more as the real one declines. (2009)

But the reports of its demise seem to have been premature. Over the past 15 years, both the state of West Bengal and the city of Kolkata have been undergoing remarkable transformations. The Marxist government became 'business-friendly' and embraced a developmental model that mimics the Chinese experiments with capitalism and free market strategies. They opened up the city to foreign investment, with Kolkata in particular a hub for new IT and service sectors as well as food processing, horticulture, and agro-industries, simultaneously attempting to improve both urban and rural infrastructure. While the Marxists themselves were unceremoniously dumped from power in a recent state election[4] Kolkata is experiencing a renaissance of sorts, with multinational corporations returning to the city and a real-estate boom providing evidence of its supposed vitality and growth.

The peri-urban fringes to the east of the city have seen remarkable changes in particular during recent years. Many new industries have been located along the eastern edges of Kolkata, in or near publicly planned townships such as Rajarhat and Bidhannagar. There has also been a tremendous boom in new housing construction in these regions, primarily along the sides of or connected by the Eastern Metropolitan Bypass. The largest townships are designed to house up to half a million people, 78 per cent of whom planners hope will be middle- and upper-income earners (KMDA 2011). The housing complexes are surrounded by high-technology-oriented office buildings, convention centres, gated green spaces, schools, private hospitals, multiplex theatres, luxury hotels, golf courses, restaurants, and private roads.

Chakravorty (2005: 89) calls the developments along the city's eastern edges 'the most significant new spatial component of the reforms in Calcutta' and sees Bidhannagar and Rajarhat as emblematic of the new development strategy that has gripped Kolkata's urban planners. These 'international-style' luxury condominium complexes are designed and marketed towards an elite transnational diasporic subject—or for those who wish to live like them. Such assumed lifestyles and lifespaces are symbolic manifestations of the globalized future that has become a central aspiration for many urban planners, politicians, developers, and even social movements. For many critics, these are spaces meant primarily for high-tech professionals and government workers and are designed to facilitate Kolkata and West Bengal's active participation in the new information economy. If the new developments are indeed spatially segregated in such a fashion, what room then remains for the many millions of Calcuttans who do not fit into the rosy globalized future? What impacts are these new industries and building projects having on the local economy, ecology, and politics?

For the now-departed Marxist government and its New Economic Policy, the eastern fringes of Kolkata represented a particularly fruitful opportunity to aid in the transformation of the city. Unlike the famously noisy, polluted, and congested core of the old town, with its long history and masses of inhabitants, the eastern fringes held the possibility and the promise of the undiscovered country, a *tabula rasa* perfect for what Roy calls the 'territorial rewriting of the city's edges' (Roy 2003). It is here, therefore, that the most striking changes can be seen. Yet it is not only remarkable that the former wetlands on the peri-urban edges are now invaded not only by gleaming new office towers, theme parks, golf courses, and shopping malls, but also by the manner in which this transformation is occurring and its broader purpose. Kolkata's reshaping does not reprise the Marxist experiments with land and political reform in the countryside; instead, New Communism, argues Roy, manifests key elements of liberalization. In her view, this has meant locating the state itself as a site of market activity, positioning real estate development as a centrepiece of the city's productive economy, capitalizing on state assets such as public land, taking on the mantle of entrepreneurialism, and creating a distinct new geography, whose prime territory is the metropolitan region rather than the core city (Roy 2003).

But perhaps the most visible sign of the transformed and intensified process through which Kolkata and its periphery are being developed is in the nature of the agents of change. Unlike during previous eras, the current context has seen a veritable explosion of public-private partnerships doing the developing. No longer are state agencies and organizations taking the lead on their own. Instead, a complex matrix of institutional and informal linkages has taken their place. In some cases, these are partnerships between government agencies and private corporations, especially in order to build new housing complexes and luxury apartments. The Kolkata Metropolitan Development Authority has joined with private investors and corporations to build several apartment towers, townships, sports venues, IT logistics hubs in Bidhannagar and Rajarhat, and entertainment complexes (KMDA 2011). Along with the Kolkata Municipal Corporation, it has also launched joint ventures to develop highway improvement projects and to build hospitals, aquatic and adventure theme parks, high-tech and industrial parks, hydroelectric dams, the New Kolkata Township at Rajarhat, hotels, and port facilities. These are but a few of many examples of such partnerships that are helping to transform Kolkata.

In some cases, foreign government agencies and development banks are partnered with municipalities and state departments to undertake specific projects (KEIP 2011).[5] In yet other projects, diasporic capital—in the form of investments—are mobilized. The description of the following new development is witnessed in Rajarhat:

> It would be a slice of Americana on the fringes of the city. We would call it Rosedale Garden, an exclusive NRI (non-resident Indian) habitat in Action Area III of New Town, Rajarhat. It would offer NRIs the standard of living they are used to in the West. The complex would combine the best of both worlds, a blend of the conveniences of the West and the earthy charm of Bengal. It's not just about returning to one's roots, but also an urge, a commitment to make Bengal a better place.

A similar sentiment is echoed by an Indonesian group currently developing a township with the Kolkata Municipal Corporation:

> There are lots of rich Indians overseas. We intend also to sell to them. They will invest in this project and bring in the dollars. The NRIs want to buy a second home at home. (Ciputra Group of Indonesia 2006)

As we see in such statements, while produced through a process of neo-liberalization, the legitimation of the contemporary urban developmental vision in Kolkata is often tied to a particular notion of globalization or at least of global identity. Kolkata's position and success as an entrepreneurial city is in this sense dependent on its ability to materialize its connections to the networked global economy through the presence of transnational capital and transnational subjects—both where they live and where/how they work. As Chakravorty says of the transformation of Kolkata's eastern fringes, 'clearly the planners want this development to contain new (rather than relocated) industry of the type that is high-tech or global in nature' (2005:71). Similarly, if one looks at the ideal inhabitant of the newly reclaimed wetlands regions, images of a transnational subject—or those who can live such an imagined life-space—are invoked. South City Projects, the enormous complex referenced at the beginning of this chapter invites prospective buyers to 'live the way the world does' and 'promises a lifestyle of international standards' (South City Projects 2011). Bengal Silver Spring, another joint venture tells you that it is 'just the kind of place you would see in foreign glossies and regret you'd never get' and that living there will allow you to 'make a world of difference' (Silver Spring 2011). Vedic Village, a more explicitly 'Indian-themed' luxury condominium community, tells us that it 'is what reflects the best that Kolkata has to offer to an international audience—a veritable paradise on Earth!' (Vedic Village 2011).

These new developments are thus a potent symbol of many things. For those who dream of recovering Kolkata's former glory, the building of skyscrapers and luxury dwellings in the city's peripheral marshland signifies an ability to 'live like the world does'. For those who talk of becoming a 'world-class' city once again, the construction of dwellings for those who work in IT is perhaps only appropriate.

Conclusion

This chapter has suggested that the category of diaspora is a highly contested and rich terrain, utilized by multiple actors in shifting strategies and for various purposes. For some politicians and policymakers, the diaspora is seen as an untapped source of capital for development projects. To many developers, they are the ideal target group towards whom the design, construction, and marketing of luxury apartments is aimed. On the other hand, for those who might be displaced by the construction of said apartments, the diaspora might represent a foreign elite whose needs and desires supersede those of local, often marginalized populations.

The promises made by the advertising campaigns discussed earlier of course make no mention of such sacrifices or consequences. Instead, they offer those interested in living in these new developments the opportunity to live a global and transnational lifestyle. Are they effective? Interviews conducted with the promoters and developers of the projects suggest that between 25 and 75 per cent of the ownership in the condominium complexes is by overseas Indians; however, verifying such claims is difficult (Silver Spring 2004; South City Projects 2004; Vedic Village 2004). Many diasporic Bengalis purchase such properties through relatives within India and Kolkata, and registering foreign ownership—while officially mandated by state legislation—is rarely enforced (Palat 2003). On the other hand, marketing a building as being attractive to NRIs—perhaps already filled with NRI residents—has become a popular strategy for many promoters.

The central contention of this chapter then is that it is the *idea* rather than the *activities* of the diaspora that is crucial to our understanding of the processes and issues described earlier. As both the theoretical discussion and the case study suggest, there are many difficulties in mapping and measuring the precise scale and impact of diaspora-related development projects. Yet even if the evidence of diasporic development activities is difficult to track, the mythic power of the Indian diaspora remains a potent force for shaping identity and place. Regardless of how many diasporic Indians are actually purchasing properties in the new housing developments on the fringes of Kolkata, their symbolic importance and impact cannot be denied. Fundamentally, it is the *idea* of the diaspora—and a monolithic conceptualization at that—which is crucial for mobilizing key actors and constituting material transformations in the city.

Notes

1. That said, I recognize that there are many who are not comfortable with using terms such as 'transnational' interchangeably with 'diaspora'. In my view, however, an expansive definition is appropriate not on the basis of the lengthy etymologies and histories of the concepts but rather when one thinks of the practices and identities that these words may encompass. My use of diaspora synonymously with related concepts argues that such terms that transcend borders and predate nation-states are necessarily fluid and open to redefinition by nature.
2. Ong (2003) points out the case of ethnic Chinese communities in Indonesia, for example, who, while welcoming support from the global Chinese diaspora against attacks and scapegoating it faced from the Indonesian military and media during the East Asian financial crisis, did not necessarily consider themselves to be Chinese. Moreover, being identified in this fashion only contributed to accusations of disloyalty and national 'impurity' along ethnic/racial lines.
3. Although 'Calcutta' was renamed officially as 'Kolkata' in 2001, I have used both the names and its people 'Calcuttan' or 'Kolkatan' - in this chapter. Wherever Kolkata is discussed it refers to the present day city, and wherever Calcutta is discussed it refers to the past.
4. Owing primarily to a series of disastrous political miscalculations and, ironically, their pursuit of special economic zone initiatives that were displacing farmers with factories.
5. Examples include Japanese governmental aid in the construction of six Kolkata flyovers, the British Department of Foreign and International Development involvement in canal drainage in the peri-urban areas, and a joint Kolkata Municipal Corporation, Government of West Bengal, and Asian Development Bank initiative aimed at improving the metropolitan area's environment.

References

Anjaria, J.S., and McFarlane, C. (2011) 'Conceptualising the City in South Asia', in Anjaria, J.S., and McFarlane, C. (eds.) *Urban Navigations: Politics, Space and the City in South Asia*. London: Routledge, 1–22.

Blunt, A. (2005) *Domicile and diaspora: Anglo-Indian women and the spatial politics of home*. Malden, MA: Blackwell.

Braziel, J.E., and Mannur, A. (2003) 'Nation, migration, globalization: points of contention in diaspora studies', in Braziel, J.E., and Mannur, A. (eds.) *Theorizing Diaspora*. London: Blackwell, 1–22.

Chakravorty, S. (2005) 'From Colonial City to Globalising City? The Far-from-complete Spatial Transformation of Calcutta', in Marcuse, P., and Kempen, R.V. (eds.) *Globalising Cities: A New Spatial Order*. Oxford: Blackwell, 56–77.

Chami, R., Fullenkamp, C., and Jahjah, S. (2005) 'Are immigrant remittance flows a source of capital for development?', *IMF Staff Papers*, 52(1), 55–81.

Chattopadhyay, S.S. (2005) 'Capturing Kolkata', *Frontline*, 22(4), 2–15 July [homepage]. http://www.hinduonnet.com/fline/fl2214/stories/20050715003003500.htm (accessed on 14 July 2006).

Ciputra Group of Indonesia (2006) 'Kolkata West International City' [homepage]. http://www.ciputra.com/ (accessed on 3 July 2006).

Desai, J. (2004) *Beyond Bollywood: The Cultural Politics of South Asian Diasporic Film*. New York/London: Routledge.

Freund, C., and Spatafora, N. (2005) 'Remittances: transaction costs, determinants and informal flows', World Bank Policy Research Working Paper 3704, September.

Gilroy, P. (2000) *Against Race: Imagining Political Culture beyond the Color Line*. Cambridge: Belknap Press.

Hall, S. (1994) 'Cultural identity and diaspora', in Williams, P., and Chrisman, L. (eds.) *Colonial and Post-Colonial Theory*. New York: Columbia University Press, 392–403.

High Level Committee on the Indian Diaspora (2002) *Report of the High Level Committee on the Indian Diaspora*. http://indiandiaspora.nic.in/contents.htm (15 May 2006).

India Today (International Edition) (2004) 'The OBIs: a generation of overseas-born Indians that dares to dream'. Special Issue, January 19.

Kapur, D. (2005) 'Remittances: The New Development Mantra?' in Maimbo, S.M., and Ratha, D. (eds.) *Remittances: Development Impact and Future Prospects*. Washington, DC: The World Bank, 331–60.

Kolkata Environmental Improvement Project (KEIP) (2011) Homepage. http://www.keip.in/bl3/index.php (4 July 2011).

Kolkata Metropolitan Development Authority (KMDA) (2011) Homepage. www.kmdaonline.org (4 July 2011).

Legg, S. (2007) *Spaces of Colonialism: Delhi's Urban Governmentalities*. Oxford: Blackwell.

Levitt, P., and de la Dehesa, R. (2003) 'Transnational migration and the redefinition of the state: variations and explanations'. *International Migration Review*, 26(4), 587–611.

Ley, D. (2004) 'Transnational spaces and everyday lives', *Transactions of the Institute of British Geographers*, 29(2), 151–64.

Mehta, S. (2004) *Maximum City: Bombay Lost and Found*. New Delhi: Penguin Viking.

Mishra, D. (2004) 'Shuttling between identities: destiny of diasporic communities', in Sharma, K., Pal, A., and Chakrabarti, T. (eds.) *Interpreting Indian Diasporic Experience*. New Delhi: Creative Books, 171–76.

Motwani, J., Gosine, M., and Barot-Motwani, J. (eds.) (1993) *Global Indian Diaspora: Yesterday, Today and Tomorrow*. New York: Global Organization of People of Indian Origin.

MPI (2011) *Migration Policy Institute Data Hub: Migration Facts, Stats and Maps*. http://www.migrationinformation.org/datahub/remittances.cfm (18 June 2011).

Mukherjee, S. (2004) 'Fast forward on flyovers', *The Telegraph*, 27 August. http://www.telegraphindia.com/1040827/asp/calcutta/story_3678779.asp (15 May 2006).

NDTV.com (2007) 'Invest in New India: PM to diaspora', 7 January. http://www.ndtv.com/morenews/showmorestory.asp?category=National&slug=Invest+in+new+India%3A+PM+to+diaspora&id=99046 (18 January 2007).

Ong, A. (2003) 'Cyberpublics and diaspora politics among transnational Chinese', *Interventions*, 5(1), 82–100.

Palat, R. (2003) *A Complete Guide for the NRI (Non-Resident Indian)*. Mumbai: Jaico Books.

Prashad, V. (2000) *The Karma of Brown Folk*. Minneapolis: University of Minnesota Press.

Ramachandraiah, C., and Bawa, V.K. (2000) 'Hyderabad in the Changing Political Economy', *Journal of Contemporary Asia*, 30(4): 562–74.

Roy, A. (2003) *City Requiem, Calcutta: Gender and the Politics of Poverty*. Minneapolis: University of Minnesota Press.

Sarkar, A.N. (1990) 'The East Calcutta wetlands', in Chaudhuri, S. (ed.) *Calcutta the Living City: Volume II: The Present and the Future*. Delhi: Oxford University Press, 173–75.

Saxenian, A. (1999) *Silicon Valley's New Immigrant Entrepreneurs*. San Francisco, CA: Public Policy Institute of California.

Sharma, J.C. (2004) *Interview at the Ministry of External Affairs*, 18 March, New Delhi.

Silver Spring (2004) *Interview with Promoter* (Bengal Ahluwalia Projects), 27 April, Kolkata.

Silver Spring (2011) Homepage. http://www.thesilverspring.com/index.htm (3 July 2011).

South City Projects (2004) *Interview with Promoter*, 5 May, Kolkata.

South City Projects (2011) Homepage. http://www.southcityprojects.com/index.html (3 July 2011)

Srinivas, S. (2002) 'Cities of the Past and Cities of the Future: Theorizing the Indian Metropolis of Bangalore', in Eade, J., and Mele, C. (eds.) *Understanding the City: Contemporary and Future Perspective*. Oxford: Blackwell, 247–77.

Suraiya, J. (2009) 'Calcutta Chromosome'. *Outlook India*, 12 January 2009. http://www.outlookindia.com/printarticle.aspx?239452

Torabully, K., and Carter, M. (2002) *Coolitude: An Anthology of the Indian Labour Diaspora*. London: Anthem Press.

Vedic Village (2004) *Interview with Promoter*, 12 May, Kolkata.

Vedic Village (2011) Homepage. http://www.thevedicvillage.com (3 July 2011).

Walsh, R. (2003) 'Global Diasporas: Introduction', *Interventions,* 5(1): 1–11.

West Bengal Industrial Development Corporation (WBIDC) (2006) *Gateway to the East*. http://www.wbidc.com (17 May 2006).

Yelaja, P. (2006) 'New York to Nizamabad: Madhu Yaskhi is leading a double life as an Indian MP and a Manhattan lawyer', *Toronto Star*, 16 January, A4.

17

The Limits of Transnational Mobilization

Indian American Lobby Groups and the India-US Civil Nuclear Deal

Sangay Mishra

> This [the India-US Civil Nuclear Deal] is a defining moment for the 2 million Americans of Indian descent. We have been a model community in the US, yet we are still not accepted or respected in rural or middle America. With one stroke of the pen we can change all that.
>
> —Ramesk V. Kapur, Chairman, Indo-American Leadership Council.

The relationship between the attachments of immigrants to their home country and political participation in the country of settlement is highly debated. The conventional wisdom contends that a deeper attachment to one's home country acts as a barrier to participation in the United States. Engagement with the political issues of the country of origin is a reflection of disinterest or apathy towards American politics.

The new scholarship using a transnational perspective has questioned this conventional wisdom and points to the reality of dual attachment of immigrants in different realms of their social and political life and discusses the ways in which dual attachment shapes the political involvement of immigrants (Kyle 1999, 2000; Portes et al. 1999; Levitt 2001). Several studies have questioned the traditional assimilation model of political incorporation and argued that attachment to the country of origin or interest in its politics does not necessarily mean a lack of political involvement in the host country (Jones-Correa 1998; DeSipio 2003; Guarnizo et al. 2003; Lien et a1. 2004; Ramakrishnan 2005; Wong 2006).

This chapter looks at the contemporary transnational political engagement of the Asian Indian community in the United States to understand how involvement with issues of home country affects their political engagement in the United States. Analysing the lobbying efforts of Indian American groups in favour of the India-US Civil Nuclear Deal of 2006, this chapter argues that what appears be a purely nationalist framework pursued by Indian American groups—where representing the interest of India is at the heart of the lobbying campaign—is mediated by the group's need for recognition in the US political process: Such transnational involvement with the politics related to India is constantly shaped by their need for greater acceptance in the domestic realm of American politics.

The chapter further argues that the process of creating a space in US politics through lobbying on a foreign policy issue is laced with nationalism originating from the Indian state's strong nationalist platform to woo the Indian diasporic community. This platform is instrumental in shaping a very limited view of what issues pertaining to India should be pursued by the diasporic communities and what section of the diaspora is the natural representative of India's interest. This chapter concludes by looking at the limits of transnational political engagement in terms of who gets involved and argues that a limited elite participation is promoted by both sides—the diasporic politics emanating from India and the nature of political mobilization pursued by Indian American groups while lobbying for the nuclear deal. The analysis that follows is based on government documents, media reports, and the organizational documents from both India and the United States. This is supplemented with census data and participant observation of a yearly conference on the Indian diaspora organized by the Government of India and the Confederation of Indian Industries at New Delhi in January 2007.

Indian Immigrants in the United States

Even though the majority of Asian Indians are recent immigrants, the early history of immigrants from India can be traced to the late eighteenth century, when a small number of peasants from Punjab Province of British-ruled India started reaching the West Coast around 1898–1899 (Jensen 1988). The early immigrants from India, like other Asian immigrants, had to face severe discrimination, and they were not allowed to acquire US citizenship because of a racial prerequisite law that required a person to be white to become a US citizen.[1] The present phase of Asian Indian immigration started with the Immigration and Naturalization Act of 1965, which eliminated racial restrictions on immigration. This reform was influenced by the US Civil Rights Movement, which demanded racial equality, and was part of an effort by the United States to shore up its capability in scientific and military technology during the Cold War by opening the doors to skilled scientists and doctors from other countries.

There were two waves of post-1965 immigration of Indians to the United States. The first wave—under the special-skill provisions of the act—attracted a large number of doctors, engineers, and scientists who were highly educated and proficient English-speakers from urban backgrounds. The second wave, which took place mostly in the 1980s, consisted largely of relatives of the first-wave immigrants who were sponsored under the 'family-reunification' provision of the 1965 act (Mazumdar 1989; Prashad 2000). This group did not have the same levels of educational or professional training as the first group, and they generally settled in the lower rungs of the professional ladder. Since the 1990s, there has also been a large influx of software professionals from India arriving on H1B visas—to meet the demands of the information technology boom in the United States.

The Indian community has seen a sharp increase in recent years. According to the American Community Survey Report 2007, there are 2.7 million Asian Indians in the United States, of whom an overwhelming majority—73 per cent—are foreign born.[2] Among the foreign born, only 37.2 per cent came before 1990. The percentage of the foreign born who came between 1990 and 1999 and after 2000 were 39.3 and 23.5, respectively. Since a significant proportion is recent arrivals, the intensity of connection with the home country is stronger than that of other Asian groups (Mishra 2006).[3]

Due to the nature of immigration, the Indian American community has done well economically and professionally. This economic well-being is reflected in a median annual income of Asian Indians in the United States of $68,771, which is much higher than the median income of the total US population ($44,684). In addition, a significant number of upstart technology companies were founded by Indian immigrants alongside Taiwanese and mainland Chinese immigrants from 1990s onward (Saxenian 2002).

Even though the large number of successful professionals has generally defined the community's socio-economic profile, Indian Americans remain highly diverse. There are a significant number of poor and struggling people who generally do not become a part of the discussion about the community. About 9.7 per cent of the Indian American population is below the poverty line compared with a US national average of 13.1 per cent, and among the elderly—age 65 and older—11.4 per cent are below the poverty line compared with the US national average of 9.4 per cent.[4] Another less known fact about the Indian immigrant community is the presence of a significant number of undocumented immigrants. The estimates vary between 270,000 and 400,000.[5] According to the Department of Homeland Security, Indian immigrants rank sixth among undocumented immigrants from different countries.[6] Thus, the diversity within the population could not be more dramatic with a section that is constituted by successful professional entrepreneurs, on one hand, and those who survive below poverty line alongside undocumented immigrants, on the other hand. The discussion of internal diversity within the community becomes important for this analysis because the political discourse on the Indian American community—both in the United States and in India—centres only on the professional and entrepreneurial section of the community.

Nationalism and Elite Mobilization from India

The Indian immigrant community in the United States has always reflected political developments within India, and nationalism among the diasporic population is shaped by India's major political and ideological trends. The nationalism propagated by the Indian state among the diasporic population has ranged from a relatively benign advocacy of attachments to roots and investment in India to hard-core religious nationalism espousing the Hindu nation-state.

The Indian government's policy towards the diaspora in the post-independence period was characterized by many scholars as indifferent and disengaged (Gupta 1992; Lall 2001; Kerkhoff and Bal 2003). The migration of highly educated Indians to the United States was seen as a 'brain drain'. The discourse of brain drain-educated and professionally capable citizens leaving India for greener pastures in developed industrial countries in the West-acquired immense importance in that period. However, the policy of indifference and brain drain started to change in the 1980s and early 1990s, and a policy of active engagement with overseas communities slowly started to take shape.

Recent initiatives by the Indian government to move the diaspora to its list of policy priorities is, to a certain extent, rooted in changes in economic policy that India has been undertaking for the past several years. The large-scale transformation of the Indian economy based on principles of liberalization and opening to foreign investment accelerated the process of active engagement with the diaspora. This phase of economic restructuring in India is characterized, among other things, by an increasing emphasis on foreign capital investment. The Indian diaspora is considered important both for remittances and for its capability to invest capital in the Indian economy (Kapur 2003). Even though a significant part of remittance comes from Indian workers employed in the Persian Gulf countries, the economic profile of Indian immigrants settled in different advanced industrial countries—the United States, in particular—makes them the likely future investors in the Indian economy. The appointment of a High Level Committee (HLC) on the Indian diaspora in 2000—constituted by the Ministry of External Affairs to recommend a comprehensive policy towards the Indian diaspora—was the first time that the government seriously undertook the task of formulating a policy framework about its overseas population. The report highlights a particular segment of the diaspora that has acquired the most important position in all of the discussions about the diasporic population: the professionals of Indian origin living in the industrialized Western countries, particularly the United States, and their role in advancing the global technological revolution (Chaturvedi 2005):

> A section of financially powerful and politically well connected Indo-Americans have emerged during the last decade. They have effectively mobilized on issues ranging from the nuclear tests in 1998 to Kargil, playing a crucial role in generating a favorable climate of opinion in Congress and defeating anti-India legislation there, and lobbied effectively on other issues of concern to the Indian community. They have also demonstrated willingness to contribute financially to Inman causes, such as relief for the Orissa cyclone and the Latur and Gujarat earthquakes, higher technical education and innumerable charitable causes ... For the first time India has a constituency in the United States with real influence and status. The Inman community in United States constitutes an invaluable asset in strengthening India's relationship with the world's only superpower. Their receptiveness to India concerns will depend greatly on the quality of their interaction with the country of origin and their sensitivity to their concerns displayed in India. It is necessary for India to facilitate this interaction (HLC, 2002: xxi–xxii).[7]

The report recommended calling on Indian immigrants in the United States to work as India's ambassadors and to promote India's interests by using their economic and political clout. The report was also emphatic about the importance of financially successful Indian Americans in representing the interest of India and projected this section of the community as the ideal Indian immigrants to be courted and convinced to support India in its economic and political endeavours.

To facilitate greater connection with the diasporic community, the HLC report recommended many plans and policies to the government of

India. An independent Ministry of Overseas Indian Affairs at the central government level was created to deal with the issues related to diaspora. A yearly conference for the Indian diaspora was initiated by the government, and 9 January was marked as Pravasi Bharatiya Divas (Overseas Indian Day) as a symbolic gesture to celebrate the contributions of overseas Indians to India.[8] The change of policy on the question of dual citizenship also followed these initiatives, and the Citizenship Act of 1955—which stipulated that an Indian forfeits Indian citizenship when he or she acquires the citizenship of a foreign country—was changed. The government created a new category called Overseas Citizenship of India (*Compendium on Policies* 2007). Various policy initiatives to attract diaspora members to invest in India were announced.

Political parties in India have also shown greater enthusiasm in courting the diasporic population. All Indian parties have used the rhetoric of nationalism while engaging the diaspora, but there are significant differences among them. The Congress Party has generally emphasized the economic aspects of the diaspora's relationship to India and has used strong nationalist rhetoric to mobilize the overseas population for economic investment. Occasionally, it uses anti-Pakistan rhetoric in the context of representing the interests of India in international forums or in the United States. The Hindu nationalist Bharatiya Janata Party (BJP) has made serious attempts to mobilize overseas Hindus in support of its ideology of a Hindu nation, along with following the economic-investment framework to attract the diaspora.

Hindu nationalism or Hindutva—an ideology that propagates the establishment of India as a religious Hindu nation—has been systematically promoted among overseas Indians. There have been organized attempts in the United States to mobilize funds and other resources for the Hindutva cause. The ideology has tried to tap into the need of Hindu Indian immigrants for a cultural-religious identity in an American society defined primarily by racial identity (Rajagopal 2000). Although nationalism is a common theme in the attempt to attract diasporic communities to the country of origin, it is a particular kind of narrow religion-based nationalism that has been a part of the BJP's diasporic discourse.[9]

The political impetus emerging from India for the diaspora carries strong nationalist ideology and tends to focus on entrepreneurs and financially successful immigrants. The Pravasi Bharatiya conference held in New Delhi in 2007which I attended—saw most of the deliberations focusing on investment opportunities in India. Another important element of the 2007 conference was the spotlight on Indian Americans for lobbying with the US Congress in favour of the India-US Nuclear

Deal. The twofold aim of the Indian government to attract economic investment and have a diaspora that can represent India's interests has led to a framework in which economically successful immigrants become the model and occupy the centre of diasporic policy. This elite mobilization approach is reflected in various policy initiatives undertaken by the Indian government. It is particularly reflective in the political lobbying by Indian immigrants in the United States on the recent India-US Civil Nuclear Deal, the case to which I turn next.

The India-US Civil Nuclear Deal

The India-US Civil Nuclear Deal was aimed at carving out an exception for India from American laws limiting trade in nuclear technology with countries that have refused to sign the Nuclear Non-Proliferation Treaty (NPT) passed in 1970. The changing foreign policy imperatives of the United States after the Cold War and its geopolitical interests in Asia brought India and the United States closer, and the nuclear deal is an indicator of the Bush administration's willingness to go beyond the established policy of not having nuclear trade with countries that have not signed the NPT (Levi and Ferguson 2006).[10]

The India-US Civil Nuclear Deal is in essence a formal approval of India's status as a nuclear power. After the detonation of its first atomic bomb in 1974, India was considered to be following its nuclear ambitions outside the framework developed by the Western nuclear powers led by the United States. India never signed the NPT and continued its nuclear programme without American approval. This remained a source of contention between the two countries. The Bush administration announced a negotiated framework for cooperation with India on 18 July 2005, followed by an agreement on 2 March 2006. On the US side, the deal promised to help India become a partner with the United States in the realm of nuclear energy. This cooperation involved an agreement with India that establishes a legal framework for nuclear commerce.

The role of Indian immigrant groups came in the context of Congressional approval of the deal, which was required to change existing US law banning civil nuclear trade with India.[11] The approval of Congress became critical to move the deal forward, as there was a very real possibility that it would be buried in opposition by a strong non-proliferation lobby. A sizable group of Democrats along with Republicans were suspicious of this move by the Bush administration and saw the deal as equivalent to rewarding a state that, in the past, had defied the NPT. It was the resistance and uncertainty in Congress that made lobbying a critical prerequisite for the success of the deal. Indian

American organizations and enthusiastic supporters took it upon themselves to mobilize the community and its political resources to lobby for the bill's passage.[12]

Transnationalism and Immigrant Engagement with American Politics

The involvement of immigrant communities in the making of US foreign policy is hardly new. Cuban, Greek, and Jewish immigrant groups have been involved in this process because of their deep linkages to their countries of origin, as well as the possible impact of American foreign policy on their communities. However, involvement with foreign policy issues in America has often been seen through the prism of national loyalty and, as such, has been viewed as a sign of immigrant's greater loyalty to his or her country of origin. The treatment of Japanese Americans during internment was based on such an assumption, and the experience discouraged other groups from getting involved in the foreign policy arena. Paul Y. Watanabe (1999) argues that Asian Americans have sometime been perceived as tools—knowingly or unknowingly—of foreign entities and there is a view suggesting that Asian immigrant groups should stay away from foreign policy activism. For groups such as Cubans and Jews, where foreign policy activism is considered natural and often supported by the US government, questions of loyalty seldom arise (Watanabe 1999).

Transnational politics involving foreign policy activism on the part of an immigrant group has also been seen as a sign of lack of interest in domestic politics. A closer look at some of the foreign policy campaigns by immigrants suggests that they are also about acquiring a place and recognition in domestic politics. The issue of American foreign policy relating to the home country becomes a convenient rallying point for immigrant groups to get involved with the US political process and institutions. Anna Karpathakis's work on Greek immigrants in New York City argues on similar lines that concern with home-country issue led to engagements with the US political process (1999).

Indian immigrants with links and influence in Washington have periodically tried to intervene in foreign policy issues, finding moderate to low levels of influence on the policy outcomes.[13] One of the most significant campaigns by Indian American groups in this context was intervention in the proposed sale of Airborne Early Warning Surveillance Systems planes in 1987.[14] Groups such as the National Federation of Indian American Association (NFIA), the Indian American Forum for Political Education, and the Associations of Indians in America campaigned on this issue to stop the sale of the planes to Pakistan. The success of the Indian American groups' campaign can be measured by the fact that the groups were called before the Senate Foreign Relations Subcommittee to testify on the issue.

Jagat Motwani, testifying to the Senate Subcommittee on behalf of the NFIA in 1987, borrowed shrill nationalist rhetoric from India:

> I should add that a bomb in Pakistani hands is a source of concern, not only to India, but to other friendly countries around the world, including Israel, since it has been developed as an Islamic bomb. The events of the past 39 years attest to the fact that Pakistan has used US supplied military equipment against no other country except India, although the aid was given for use as defense against communist invasion. Once Pakistan has these sophisticated military weapons, it may not hesitate to use them against India. (Motwani 2003: 282–83)

The rhetoric was not only about parochial Indian nationalism, but it was also accompanied by a growing anxiety about creating space within the US political system for the Indian American community. Thomas Abraham, president of the NFIA, remarked about the testimony at the hearing, 'It is a historic moment for the Indian American community since we have been invited for the first time by the Senate Foreign Relations Subcommittee to present our views. It is recognition of our growing community in the US' (Motwani 2003: 284). Even though this campaign was limited to a foreign policy issue in Washington, the recognition by the US. Congress of Indian Americans as a legitimate voice on this issue was seen as a sign of the growing strength of the community.[15]

The India-US Civil Nuclear Deal came approximately 20 years after the 1987 campaign. The community has grown larger since the late 1980s, as has its eagerness to win a place in the political realm. The more sophisticated involvement of Indian American organizations with the Washington foreign policy establishment and lobbying world reflects the Indian American community's maintenance of a dual interest: the interest in issues related to India, as well as the urge to create a political space for the Indian American community in America. Over the years, Indian American organizations have been able to build linkages between these two interests.

Several Indian American groups played active roles in lobbying for the passage of the bill endorsing the India-US Civil Nuclear Deal. The issue galvanized community organizations as never before and brought groups with both Democratic and Republican leanings to the same platform. The United States-India Political Action Committee (USINPAC), the Indian American Security Leadership Council, the US

India Friendship Council, the US India Business Council, and other smaller groups and individuals worked together on this issue. At the end of April 2006, just before Congress was reconvened to start considering the Henry Hyde Act dealing with the nuclear deal, about 200 Indian American community leaders from across the country gathered in Washington to lobby their Senate and House members to approve the deal (Jones 2006).[16] Indian American leaders also had a strategy meeting with senior staff members at the White House, led by Karl Rove. The Indian American groups active on this issue were turning out to be important allies for the Bush administration, which was struggling to get the bill passed.

The importance of this issue for unifying disparate Indian American groups is reflected in the comment to the *Washington Times* made by an entrepreneur and activist:

> Our diaspora was always much more divided, but now we have the nuclear deal to unite us. ... I have been contacting my congressmen here in California, and I know many of my friends and colleagues are doing the same. This whole fight has brought out of the woodwork Indian-Americans who were never involved in politics at all. (Sands 2006)

The issue became a convenient rallying point for different Indian American groups, and it provided an opportunity for these groups to engage with the US political institutions on a specific issue.

A case in point is USINPAC, an organization that takes its inspiration from the American Israeli Political Action Committee as a model of ethnic lobbying. USINPAC has been organizing fundraisers for both Democratic and Republican politicians to mobilize bipartisan support for issues important to the Indian American community. The organization describes its strategic objective this way:

> To consolidate individual contributions by actively engaging with every politically active Indian American organization and individual via an effective platform and leverage the combined strength of contributor and community strength; to financially support candidates for public office, on bipartisan basis, who proactively address the concerns of Indian American community; to create a platform that enables entry of Indian Americans in the political process.[17]

By emphasizing the fundraising ability of the Indian American community, USINPAC has been developing a particular way to create political influence that relies on a small section of the community—the section that can make financial contributions. USINPAC used this strategy to mobilize support for the nuclear deal among lawmakers in Washington.

The nuclear deal also galvanized well-established, membership-based Indian American organizations such as the American Association of Physicians of Indian Origin (AAPI) and the Asian American Hotel Owners Association (AAHOA). The AAPI, representing about 41,000 doctors and 10,000 medical students of Indian origin, and the AAHOA, representing about 8300 members who own more than 20,000 small hotels and motels, contributed to the campaign and lobbied members of Congress from different areas. To express their support for the nuclear deal, these two organizations jointly held a luncheon in Washington, DC, that was addressed by Secretary of State Condoleezza Rice.[18]

The lobbying campaign on behalf of the India-US Civil Nuclear Deal was important for such groups not only because they wanted to support India's interest, but also because it was seen by Indian America as a test of the community's political maturity and acumen. 'This is the chance to show that the community has matured and can translate that into political effectiveness', said Sanjay Puri, chairman of USINPAC (McIntire 2006). The *Washington Times* echoed this sentiment:

> The political clout of one of the country's wealthiest and best-educated minorities is being put to the test as the Bush administration faces a tough fight in the Congress to pass a major civil nuclear power agreement with India, one the administration officials say could cement ties with an emerging world power and redraw the strategic map of Asia. (Sands 2006)

Smaller groups and individual initiatives also came together on this issue, motivated by the opportunity to strengthen the political influence of the Indian American community. Swadesh Chatterjee, one of the co-founders of the US India Friendship Council, put out a full-page advertisement in the *Washington Post* and raised $2.5 million to support the issue ('Nuclear Rallying Indians' 2006). Organizations involved in the campaign saw this as an issue through which they could reach out to members of Congress and the administration. Although the activism and lobbying on behalf of the nuclear deal is framed in terms of representing the interests of India, the mobilization patterns by Indian American groups suggests that this was an issue that brought a significant number of Indian American organizations together. Viewed through the traditional lens of political participation, this kind of engagement would be dismissed as a reflection of lack of interest in American politics. However, the political engagement of Indian American organizations involved dealing with domestic political institutions. This activism was not only instrumental in achieving a limited end, but it also became part of a broader, ongoing attempt to gain acceptance and recognition in American democracy.

Even though the lobbying efforts of Indian American groups is a significant step forward, political engagement through elite organizations carries serious limitations in terms of orienting and mobilizing the broader Indian American community for domestic political participation. Despite the apparent diversity among the groups, the lobbying campaign was spearheaded mostly by organizations that represent professional and entrepreneurial sections of the community. The emphasis on the fundraising capacity of the community to muster support from members of Congress was indicative of a participation model limited to the rich and professionally successful. There was little effort by these groups to reach out to the wider community on this issue. More important, the lobbying by Indian American groups did not reflect the debates that took place in India over the desirability of the nuclear deal. There was an intense debate in which powerful voices—leftist parties as well as the right-wing BJP and its allies—argued that the nuclear deal is equal to surrendering the sovereignty and foreign policy of India to the United States.[19] The leftist parties withdrew from the Congress-led United Progressive Alliance government on 8 July 2008 as a result of the unwillingness of the Congress Party to reconsider the deal. Indian American groups, however, followed the position adopted by the Indian government and only mobilized around the nationalist and militaristic position that the state put forward. Despite the opposition, the deal moved forward, and as a result, India is on its way to establishing nuclear trade with the United States and other countries. To better understand the tendencies of Indian American political mobilization, consider another important moment that affected the community significantly: the racial hate crimes and discrimination in the wake of 11 September 2001 attack on the World Trade Center. Most of the organizations active on the issue of the nuclear deal were largely absent in their response to the aftermath of the attacks on South Asian immigrants. But a different set of groups was very active. For instance, the South Asian Network in the Los Angeles area, with a few Muslim and Sikh organizations, played an important role in responding to post-9/11 hate crimes and the general atmosphere of fear among South Asian immigrants in the area. Similarly, in New York City, South Asian organizations such as Desis Rising and Moving, the Coney Island Avenue Project, the Council of People's Organization, the South Asian Youth Association, and small advocacy and service organizations were active on these issues. These groups intervened in individual cases as well as at the community level in mobilizing against hate crimes and stopping law-enforcement agencies from targeting particular communities. Organizations such as South Asian American Leaders of Tomorrow actively intervened on this issue in Washington and coordinated with other civil rights and ethnic groups at the national level to highlight cases of racial targeting.[20]

Looking at the nature of involvement in these two campaigns—post-9/11 hate crimes and the nuclear deal—it is very clear that the organizations active on the latter did not step forward on the former. The elite nature of the nuclear deal lobby is reflected in its approach of staying away from racial discrimination, an issue that affects the entire community. It is also reflected in the fact that these organizations were limited in the forms of political engagement they pursued. In contrast, the groups active after 9/11 did not get involved with the nuclear deal campaign because most of those organizations work on a multi-ethnic platform that includes immigrants from India, Pakistan, Bangladesh, and other South Asian countries. The nuclear deal was an issue that clearly represented the national interest of India as framed by the government of India. The South Asian organizations could not support a deal that enhanced India's military status vis-à-vis other South Asian countries in a subcontinent that has a history of hostility and conflict among different nations.

Conclusion

The Indian American groups involved in lobbying on the India-US Civil Nuclear Deal had two objectives underlying their campaign: to support the national ambitions of India and to use this as a unifying issue for the Indian American community to enhance its political effectiveness and influence as an American minority. Even though the nuclear deal was framed in nationalist language, the Indian American organizations did not act solely as representatives of India's interest because of the community's constant struggling with the question of recognition and acceptance in the United States. The entire campaign was framed in terms of the contribution of the Indian American community to American society. The lobbying campaign can be critiqued as a reflection of the community's distance from the issues of local or domestic politics. However, this would be a narrow reading based on an understanding of immigrant political participation and incorporation that gives primacy to certain forms of political participation and ignores the forms of political engagements related to the issues of the country of origin.

Furthermore, the nuclear lobbying campaign suggests that there are certain limitations and problems with this form of transnational political engagement, namely, elite mobilizations that take primacy over other kinds of participation that may involve broader outreach. Lobbying involves a limited section of the immigrant community—the well-educated professional and entrepreneur class and Indian American groups tend to project the fundraising capability of the community, displaying this as its primary political strength. Campaigns of this nature help to carve out political space for Indian Americans but carry the downside of failing to reach common Indian immigrants. A diasporic politics emanating from India that contributes to this elite form of political mobilization also promotes a narrow view of the immigrant population in which only successful entrepreneurs and professionals are accorded importance.

Notes

Epigraph: quoted in Jones 2006.

1. The racial naturalization laws were applied to all non-white immigrants. The issue ultimately reached the US Supreme Court in 1923 in the case of *Bhagat Singh Thind v. United States*, in which the court ruled that immigrants from India were not eligible for citizenship because they were not white. Ian Lopez (1996) discusses these cases carefully and links them to the construction of 'Whiteness' in legal discourse.
2. American Community Survey (2007). Available online at: http://www.census.gov/prod/2007pubs/acs-05.pdf (accessed on 6 August 2007).
3. The term 'Asian Indian'—a census category—and 'Indian immigrant' are being used interchangeably here. However, 'South Asian' is a separate category that includes immigrants from Pakistan, Bangladesh, and other South Asian countries.
4. US Bureau of the Census, *American Community Survey, 2007*. Available online at: http://www.census.gov/prod/2007pubs/acs-05.pdf (accessed on 6 August 2007).
5. Jeffrey S, Passel, 'Unauthorized Migrants: Numbers and Characteristics' [report], Pew Hispanic Center, Washington, DC (2005). Available online at: http://pewhispanic.org/files/reports/46.pdf (accessed on 12 August 2007); Department of Homeland Security, Office of Immigration Statistics, 'Estimates of the Unauthorized Immigrant Population Residing in the United States: January 2006', August 2007. Available online at: http://www.dhs.gov/xlibrary/assets/statistics/publications/ill_pe_2006.pdf (accessed on 10 August 2007).
6. Ibid.
7. 'Report of High Level Committee on Indian Diaspora', (HLC 2002, xxi–xxii) Available online at: http://indiandiaspora.nic.in/contents.htm (accessed on l0 August 2007).

8. Since 2003, the government of India, in collaboration with the Confederation of Indian Industries, has been organizing a yearly conference on this day for which thousands of diasporic Indians from all over the world travel to India. Over the past few years, the conference has acquired prominence in discussions of the Indian diaspora and has become an important platform from which the diasporic population is able to interact with representatives of government and business leaders. More and more, the conferences have become a place where investments in different sectors of the growing Indian economy are discussed and different states within India compete to attract capital from non-resident Indians and people of Indian origin.
9. The Hindu right-wing groups have been very active in the Indian diasporic community and particularly successful in establishing a network in the United States. They also have been mobilizing funds from the Indian immigrant community in the United States to support organizational work in India. The reports published by the watchdog group, Campaign to Stop Funding Hate, have chronicled the campaign by Hindutva groups to mobilize in the United States in the name of funding various relief projects in India but then used the funds for anti-Muslim campaigns in India: see the website at http://www.stopfundinghate.org.
10. There has been a vocal opposition to the India-US. Civil Nuclear Deal in India and in the United States. The opposition in India can be broadly divided. The first kind is from the main opposition party, the BJP, and its allies, who argue that India is compromising its nuclear programme by accepting American terms and conditions and by virtually accepting a ban on further nuclear tests. This view sees the deal as an act that limits India's sovereignty over matters related to its defence and foreign policy. The second kind is similar but comes from the left and states that, by aligning with the Untied States, India is abandoning its independent foreign policy and accepting hegemonic US policies. There is also a strong anti-nuclear lobby within the left that does not want India to pursue nuclear ambitions—civil or military—with or without American support.
11. As part of the deal, the Indian Government has reaffirmed its intent not to test nuclear weapons; promised to adhere to the highest international standards for controlling sensitive nuclear exports; and expressed its commitment to separate its civilian nuclear facilities from the military facilities, with only civilian facilities becoming eligible for US cooperation. India has also agreed to negotiate a system of permanent inspection for its civilian facilities with the International Atomic Energy Commission.
12. Other lobbying efforts were going on simultaneously to get a congressional majority to approve the deal. In addition to the mobilization by the Bush administration, the Indian government lobbied on Capitol Hill to get the required support for the deal. The Indian government hired the biggest Republican lobbying firm—Barbour Griffith and Rogers—to lobby on its behalf. US Corporations such as IP Morgan, Boeing, General Electric,

Dow Chemical, and Lockheed Martin also lobbied for the deal because it was expected to expand business opportunities (Kriplani 2007).

13. The history of transnational political involvement by Indian immigrants is as old as the history of the group in the United States. Early immigrants at the beginning of the twentieth century were deeply involved in the anti-colonial struggle against the British Empire for India's independence. The founding of the Ghadar Party by Indian immigrant, in the early 1900s and party's role in mobilizing public opinion in favour of India's independence is a classic example of transnational politics when the means of communication and extent of contact with the home country were far less developed than they are today (Jensen 1988).
14. The United States had proposed to sell the planes to Pakistan in the context cf its ongoing involvement in supporting *mujahedin* groups to fight against the Soviet military presence in Afghanistan. Pakistan was strong ally of the United States, and the planes were part of the US plan to monitor the Soviet-backed military movement near the Afghan border.
15. There were other smaller interventions by the Indian American community into foreign policy issues pertaining to India. Notable among them were the Brown Amendment, the sanction imposed by the United States on India after a nuclear explosion in 1998 and during the Kargil conflict between India and Pakistan.
16. The Henry J. Hyde United States-India Peaceful Atomic Energy Cooperation Act of 2006 describes the provisions of the India-US Civil Nuclear Deal.
17. See the website at http://www.usinpac.com.
18. 'Indian American Physicians and Hoteliers Lobby for N-Deal', 10 July 2006. Available online at: http://www.indiaenews.com/america/20060710/14274.htm (accessed on 15 September 2007).
19. Bidwai, 'India'.
20. These observations are based on 60 interviews conducted in New York City and Los Angeles with South Asian community members and activists between April 2006 and February 2007. The interviews focused on the issues of political participation both in the United States and the home country, racial discrimination, and transnationalism.

References

American Community Survey (2007) http://www.census.gov/prod/2007pubs/acs-05.pdf (accessed on 6 August 2007).

Chaturvedi, S. (2005) 'Diaspora in India's geopolitical vision: linkages, categories, and contestations', *Asian Affairs: An American Review*, 32(3), 141–68.

Compendium on Policies, Incentives and Investment Opportunities for Overseas Indians (2007). New Delhi: Ministry of Overseas Indian Affairs.

DeSipio, L. (2003) *Immigrant Politics at Home and Abroad: How Latino Immigrants Engage the Politics of their Home.* California: Tomas Rivera Policy Institute.

Guarnizo, L.E., Portes, A., and Haller, W. (2003) 'Assimilation and transnationalism: determinants of transnational political action among contemporary migrants', *American Journal of Sociology,* 108(6), 1211–48.

Gupta, A. (1992) 'The song of the non-aligned world: transnational identities and the reinscription of space in late capitalism', *Cultural Anthropology,* 7(1), 63–77.

High Level Committee (HLC) (2002) *Report of the High Level Committee on Indian Diaspora.* http://indiandiaspora.nic.in/contents.htm (accessed on 10 August 2007).

Jensen, J.M. (1988) *Passage from India: Asian Immigrants in North America.* New Heaven, CT: Yale University Press.

Jones, J. (2006) 'Indo-American lobby for nuclear deal', *Inside Bay Area,* July 10.

Jones-Correa, M. (1998) *Between Two Nations: The Political Predicament of Latinos in New York City.* Ithaca, NY: Cornell University Press.

Kapur, D. (2003) 'Indian diaspora as strategic asset', *Economic and Political Weekly,* February 1, 445–48.

Karpathakis, A. (1999) 'Home society politics and immigrant political incorporation: the case of Greek immigrants in New York City', *International Migration Review,* 33, 55–78.

Kerkhoff, S.K., and Bal, E. (2003) '"Eternal call of the Ganga": reconnecting with people of Indian origin in Surinam'. *Economic and Political Weekly,* September 20, 4008–21.

Kriplani, M. (2007) 'A new kind of Indian power', *Los Angeles Times,* January 20.

Kyle, D. (1999) 'The Otavalo trade diaspora: social capital and transnational entrepreneurship', *Ethnic and Racial Studies,* 22(2), 422–26.

Kyle, D. (2000) *Transnational Peasants: Migrations, Networks and Ethnicity in Andean Ecuador.* Baltimore, MA: Johns Hopkins Press.

Lall, M.C. (2001) *India's Missed Opportunity: India's Relationship with Non Resident Indians.* Aldershot: Ashgate.

Levi, M., and Ferguson, C.L. (2006) *US-India Nuclear Cooperation: A Strategy for Moving Forward.* New York: Council on Foreign Relations.

Levitt, P. (2001) *The Transnational Villagers.* Berkeley: University of California Press.

Lien, P. Te, Margaret, C., and Janelle, W. (2004) *The Politics of Asian Americans: Diversity and Community.* New York: Routledge.

Lopez, I. (1996) *White by Law: The Legal Construction of Race.* New York: New York University Press.

Mazumdar, S. (1989) 'Race and racism: South Asians in the United States', in Nomura, G. et al. (ed.) *Frontiers of Asian American Studies*. Washington: Washington State University Press, 25–38.

McIntire, M. (2006) 'Indian-Americans test their clout on atom pact', *New York Times*, June 5.

Mishra, S. (2006) 'Citizenship, political participation and transnationalism: South Asian immigrants in the US', paper presented at the Annual Meeting of the American Political Science Association, Philadelphia.

Motwani, J. (2003) *America and India: In a 'Give and Take' Relationship: Social-Psychology of Asian Indian Immigrants*. New York: Center for Asian, African and Caribbean Studies.

'Nuclear Rallying Indians' (2006), *Hindustan Times*, April 8.

Portes, A., Gurnizo, L., and Landolt, P. (1999) 'The study of transnationalism: pitfalls and promise of an emergent field', *Ethnic and Racial Studies*, 22(2), 217–37.

Prashad, V. (2000) *Karma of Brown Folk*. Minneapolis: University of Minnesota Press.

Rajagopal, A. (2000) 'Hindu nationalism in the US: changing configuration of political practice', *Ethnic and Racial Studies*, 23(3), 467–96.

Ramakrishnan, S.K. (2005) *Democracy in Immigrant America: Changing Demographics and Political Participation*. Stanford, CA: Stanford University Press.

Sands, D.R. (2006) 'Nuclear pact unifies Indian American: well-to-do minority "Galvanized" by opportunity for improved ties', *The Washington Times*, April 9.

Saxenian, A.L. (2002) *Local and Global Networks of Immigrant Professionals in Silicon Valley*. California: Public Policy Institute of California.

Stop Funding Hate. http://stopfundinghate.org/ (accessed on 18 July 2007).

United States-India Political Action Committee. http://www.usinpac.com/mission_objective.asp (accessed on 14 August 2007).

Watanabe, P. (1999) 'Asian American activism and US foreign policy', in Hu-Dehart, E. (ed.) *Across the Pacific: Asian Americans and Globalization*. Philadelphia, PA: Temple University Press.

Wong, J. (2006) *Democracy's Promise: Immigrants and American Civic Institutions*. Ann Arbor: University of Michigan Press.

Index